Canadian Edition

The
Gendered
Society

Michael S. Kimmel ┊ Jacqueline Holler

D1501870

OXFORD

UNIVERSITY PRESS

OXFORD
UNIVERSITY PRESS

8 Sampson Mews, Suite 204, Don Mills, Ontario M3C 0H5
www.oupcanada.com

Oxford University Press is a department of the University of Oxford.
It furthers the University's objective of excellence in research, scholarship,
and education by publishing worldwide in

Oxford   New York

Auckland   Cape Town   Dar es Salaam   Hong Kong   Karachi
Kuala Lumpur   Madrid   Melbourne   Mexico City   Nairobi
New Delhi   Shanghai   Taipei   Toronto

With offices in

Argentina   Austria   Brazil   Chile   Czech Republic   France   Greece
Guatemala   Hungary   Italy   Japan   Poland   Portugal   Singapore
South Korea   Switzerland   Thailand   Turkey   Ukraine   Vietnam

Oxford is a trade mark of Oxford University Press
in the UK and in certain other countries

Published in Canada by Oxford University Press

Library and Archives Canada Cataloguing in Publication
Kimmel, Michael S.
The gendered society / Michael S. Kimmel, and Jacqueline Holler.
— Canadian ed.

Includes index.

ISBN 978-0-19-543147-6

1. Sex role. 2. Sex differences (Psychology). 3. Gender identity.
4. Sex discrimination. 5. Equality. I. Holler, Jacqueline Zuzann, 1964– II. Title.

HQ1075.K55 2010   305.3   C2010-903819-3

Cover image: BLOOMimage

Oxford University Press is committed to our environment.
This book is printed on paper that contains a minimum of 50% post-consumer waste.

Printed and bound in the United States of America.
5 6 7 — 14 13 12

Contents

Preface

I write this preface after returning from a gender studies class in which my students discussed (among other things) a daily news item about the sexist lyrics to our national anthem, O Canada! Students were predictably divided, with some feeling that the words 'in all thy sons command' exclude women and others disagreeing. Some raised the issues of religion (whose God should 'keep our land'?) and colonialism (whose 'home and native land'?) and how effectively the anthem represents not just women, but the changing nature of Canadian society. As always, I came away from class with a sense of profound optimism about gender studies and the role it can play in creating respectful but challenging dialogue about important issues.

Creating this first Canadian edition of *The Gendered Society* has been a wonderful experience. Now in its third edition, the US edition has been adopted widely and translated into several languages. It has been an honour to adapt this text for Canadian readers.

For this edition, the book has been extensively rewritten and reorganized, guided by the suggestions of reviewers and my own sense of what might improve the book without fundamentally altering its nature. This version is substantially longer than the original, and I have made an attempt to Canadianize the work not just superficially—through replacing US examples with Canadian ones, for example—but by enhancing or downplaying themes according to their relevance in Canadian society. In addition, this Canadian edition contains new box features, images, chapter summaries, key-term definitions, and study/discussion questions. I hope that readers will find these new features appealing and useful.

Inevitably, though, this first Canadian edition is a work in progress. In order to maintain the features that have made *The Gendered Society* so appealing to so many, I have had to make some difficult choices. I look forward to hearing from readers what you like, what you find useful, and what you miss in this text.

Acknowledgements

I have long admired Michael Kimmel's work, and so my first acknowledgement should go to him. It has been a privilege to collaborate on this work. I have had the additional privilege of working with a wonderful editorial team at Oxford. Rebecca Ryoji deserves special thanks for her patient guidance. Jennifer Charlton and Nancy Reilly were also tremendously helpful in the early stages of the project, and it was a pleasure to work with Karri Yano during the copy editing process.

I am also fortunate enough to be surrounded by wonderful colleagues and graduate students. Among the latter is Alison Matte, who served as research assistant on this project. I would also thank Anita Shaw, Jeff Slack, Elizabeth Sharp, Charlene Myers,

Diandra Oliver, Victoria Harlos, Mercedes Dorrbercker, Ben Taylor, Agata Skorecka, and Dahne Harding. Being involved with their development as scholars has been tremendously inspiring for me. Similarly, I would like to thank the many undergraduate students who have engaged with me on the topics discussed in this text—and who make every course completely different from the one that preceded it. Teaching gender studies is always exhilarating precisely because we are all experts in gender—and I never come out of class without having learned something new.

Anonymous reviewers contributed innumerable helpful suggestions and criticisms to this project. I would like to thank Fiona Angus, Grant MacEwan College; Maryanne Fisher, Saint Mary's University; Claudia Malacrida, University of Lethbridge; Michelle Owen, University of Winnipeg; and Carrie Yodanis, University of British Columbia. Remaining shortcomings in this work are, of course, entirely my own.

My work, including but not limited to the writing of this book, has often tested the limits of my family's patience. To them, and particularly to my daughters Helga and Ursula, with whom I have some of my most interesting conversations about gender, I dedicate whatever is valuable in this text.

Credits

Grateful acknowledgement is made for permission to reprint the following:

Pages 54–6: Excerpt from *Sexing the Body: Gender Politics and the Construction of Sexuality* (New York: Basic Books, 2000), 253–5. Copyright © 2000 Anne Fausto-Sterling. Reprinted by permission of Basic Books, a member of the Perseus Books Group

Page 124: Excerpt from 'Hierarchies, Jobs, Bodies: A Theory of Gendered Organizations' by Joan Acker in *Gender & Society*, 4(2), 1990, p. 146. Copyright 1990 by Sage Publications Inc. Journals. Reproduced with permission of Sage Publications Inc. Journals in the format Textbook via Copyright Clearance Center.

Page 130: Excerpt from 'Doing Gender' by Candace West and Don Zimmerman in *Gender & Society*, 1(2), 1987, pp. 133–4. Copyright 1987 by Sage Publications Inc. Journals. Reproduced with permission of Sage Publications Inc. Journals in the format Textbook via Copyright Clearance Center.

Chapter 1

Introduction

Human Beings: An Engendered Species

Daily, we hear how men and women are different. We hear that we come from different planets. They say we have different brain chemistries, different brain organization, different hormones. They say our different anatomies lead to different destinies. They say we have different ways of knowing, listen to different moral voices, have different ways of speaking and hearing each other.

You'd think we were different species, like, say, lobsters and giraffes, or Martians and Venutians. In his best-selling book, pop psychologist John Gray informs us that not only do women and men communicate differently, but also they 'think, feel, perceive, react, respond, love, need, and appreciate differently'.[1] It's a miracle of cosmic proportions that we ever understand one another!

This **'interplanetary' theory** of complete and universal *gender difference* is also typically the way we explain another universal phenomenon: *gender inequality*. Gender is not simply a system of classification, by which biological males and biological females are sorted, separated, and socialized into equivalent sex roles. Gender also expresses the near-universal inequality between women and men. When we speak about gender we also speak about hierarchy, power, and inequality, not simply difference.

So the two tasks of any study of gender are to explain both difference and inequality or, to be alliterative, *difference* and *dominance*. Every general explanation of gender must address two central questions and their ancillary derivative questions.

First: *Why is it that virtually every single society differentiates people on the basis of gender?* Why are women and men perceived as different in every known society? What are the differences that are perceived? Why is gender at least one—if not the central—basis for the division of labour?

Second: *Why is it that virtually every known society is also based on* **male dominance**? Why do most societies divide social, political, and economic resources unequally between the genders? And why is it that men always get more? Why is a gendered division of labour also an unequal division of labour? Why are women's tasks and men's tasks valued differently?

It is clear, as we shall see, that there are dramatic differences among societies regarding the types of gender differences, the levels of gender inequality, and the amount of violence (implied or real) that are necessary to maintain both systems of difference and domination. But the basic facts remain: *Virtually every society known to us is founded upon assumptions of gender difference and the politics of gender inequality.*

On these axiomatic questions, two basic schools of thought prevail: **biological determinism** and **differential socialization**. We know them as 'nature' and 'nurture', and the question of which is dominant has been debated for a century in classrooms, at dinner parties, by political adversaries, and among friends and families. Are men and women different because they are 'hardwired' to be different, or are they different because they've been taught to be? Is biology destiny?

Most of the arguments about gender difference begin, as will this book, with biology (in Chapter 2). Women and men *are* biologically different, after all. Our reproductive anatomies are different, and so are our reproductive destinies. Our brain structures differ; our brain chemistries differ. Our musculature is different. Different levels of different hormones circulate through our different bodies. Surely, these add up to fundamental, intractable, and universal differences, and these differences provide the foundation for male domination, don't they?

The answer is an unequivocal maybe. Or, perhaps more accurately, yes and no. There are very few people who would suggest that there are no differences between males and females. What social scientists call **sex differences** refers precisely to that catalogue of anatomical, hormonal, chemical, and physical differences between women and men. But even here, as we shall see, there are enormous ranges of femaleness and maleness. Though our musculature differs, plenty of women are physically stronger than plenty of men. Though on average our chemistries are different, it's not an all-or-nothing proposition—women do have varying levels of androgens, and men have varying levels of estrogen in their systems. And though our brain structure may be differently lateralized, males and females both do tend to use both sides of their brain. And it's far from clear that these biological differences automatically and inevitably lead men to dominate women. Could we not imagine, as some writers already have, a culture in which women's biological abilities to bear and nurse children might be seen as the expression of such ineffable power—the ability to create life—that strong men wilt in impotent envy?

In fact, in order to underscore this issue, most social and behavioural scientists now use the term 'gender' in a different way than we use the term 'sex'. '**Sex**' refers to the biological apparatus, the male and the female—our chromosomal, chemical, anatomical organization. '**Gender**' refers to the meanings that are attached to those differences within a culture. 'Sex' is male and female; 'gender' is masculinity and femininity—what it means to be a man or a woman. Whereas biological sex varies little (though much more than we once thought, as discussed in Chapter 12), gender varies enormously. What it means to possess the anatomical configuration of male or female means very different things depending on where you are, who you are, and when you are living.

It fell to anthropologists to detail some of those differences in the meanings of masculinity and femininity. What they documented is that gender means different things to different people—that it varies cross-culturally. (We discuss and review the anthropological evidence in Chapter 4.) Some cultures, like that of mainstream North America, encourage men to be stoic and to prove their masculinity through strength and competition. Other cultures prescribe a more relaxed definition of masculinity, based on civic participation, emotional responsiveness, and the collective provision for the community's needs. And some cultures encourage women to be decisive and competitive, whereas others insist that women are naturally passive, helpless, and dependent. What it meant to be a man or a woman in seventeenth-century France and what it means among Aboriginal peoples in the Australian outback at the turn of the twenty-first century are so far apart that comparison is difficult, if not impossible. *The differences between two cultures are often greater than the differences between the two genders.* If the meanings of gender vary from culture to culture and vary within any one culture over historical time, then understanding gender must employ the tools of the social and behavioural sciences and history.

The other reigning school of thought that explains both gender difference and gender domination is *differential socialization*—the 'nurture' side of the equation. Men and women are different because we are taught to be different. From the moment of birth, males and females are treated differently. Gradually we acquire the traits, behaviours, and attitudes that our culture defines as 'masculine' or 'feminine'. We are not necessarily born different: We become different through this process of socialization.

Nor are we born biologically predisposed toward gender inequality. Domination is not a trait carried on the Y chromosome; it is the outcome of the different cultural valuing of men's and women's experiences. Thus, the adoption of masculinity and femininity implies the adoption of 'political' ideas that what women do is not as culturally important as what men do.

Developmental psychologists have also examined the ways in which the meanings of masculinity and femininity change over the course of a person's life. The issues confronting a man about proving himself and feeling successful will change, as will the social institutions in which he will attempt to enact those experiences. The meanings of femininity are subject to parallel changes, for example, among prepubescent girls, women in child-bearing years, and post-menopausal women, as they are different for women entering the labour market and those retiring from it.

Although we typically cast the debate in terms of *either* biological determinism *or* differential socialization—nature versus nurture—it may be useful to pause for a moment to observe what characteristics they have in common. Both schools of thought share two fundamental assumptions. First, both 'nature lovers' and 'nurturers' see women and men as markedly different from each other—truly, deeply, and irreversibly different. (Nurture does allow for some possibility of change, but it still argues that through the process of socialization males and females become dramatically different from each other.) And both schools of thought assume that the differences *between* women and men are far greater and more decisive (and worthy of analysis) than the differences that might be observed *among* men or *among* women. Thus, both 'nature lovers' and 'nurturers' subscribe to some version of the interplanetary theory of gender.

Second, both schools of thought assume that gender domination is the inevitable outcome of gender difference, that difference causes domination. To the biologists, it may be because pregnancy and lactation make women more vulnerable and in need of protection, or because male musculature makes men more adept hunters, or because testosterone makes them more aggressive with other men and with women, too. Or it may be that men have to dominate women in order to maximize their chances to pass on their genes. On the 'nurture' side, psychologists of 'gender roles' tell us that, among other things, men and women are taught to devalue women's experiences, perceptions, and abilities and to overvalue men's.

We argue in this book that both of these propositions are false. First, we hope to show that the differences between women and men are not nearly as great as are the differences among women or among men. Many perceived differences turn out to be differences based less on gender than on the social positions people occupy. Second, we argue that gender difference is the product of gender inequality, and not the other way around. In fact, gender difference is the chief outcome of gender inequality, because it is through the idea of difference that inequality is legitimated. As one sociologist recently put it, 'the very creation of difference is the foundation on which inequality rests'.[2]

Using what social scientists have come to call a 'social constructionism' approach—discussed further in Chapter 5—we make the case that neither gender difference nor gender inequality is inevitable in the nature of things nor, more specifically, in the nature of our bodies. Neither is difference—or domination—explainable solely by reference to differential socialization of boys and girls into sex roles typical of men and women.

When proponents of both nature and nurture positions assert that gender inequality is the inevitable outcome of gender difference, they take, perhaps inadvertently, a political position that assumes that inequality may be lessened or that its most negative effects may be ameliorated, but that it cannot be eliminated—precisely because it is based upon intractable differences. On the other hand, to assert, as we do, that the exaggerated gender differences that we see are not as great as they appear and that they are the result of inequality allows a far greater political latitude. By eliminating gender inequality, we will remove the foundation upon which the entire edifice of gender difference is built.

What will remain, we believe, is not some non-gendered androgynous gruel, in which differences between women and men are blended and everyone acts and thinks in exactly the same way. Quite the contrary. We believe that as gender inequality decreases, the differences among people—differences grounded in race, class, ethnicity, age, sexuality, *as well as* gender—will emerge in a context in which all of us can be appreciated for our individual uniqueness as well as our commonality.

Making Gender Visible For Both Women and Men

A dramatic transformation in thinking about gender has occurred over the past 30 years. In particular, three decades of pioneering work by feminist scholars, both in traditional disciplines and in women's studies, have made us aware of the centrality of gender in shaping social life. We now know that gender is one of the central organizing principles around which social life revolves. Until the 1970s, social scientists would have listed only class and race as the master statuses that define and proscribe social life. If you wanted to study gender in the 1960s in social science, for example, you would have found but one course designed to address your needs—Marriage and the Family. There were no courses on gender. But today, gender has joined race and class in our understanding of the foundations of an individual's identity. Gender, we now know, is one of the axes around which social life is organized and through which we understand our own experiences.

In the past 30 years, feminist scholars properly focused most of their attention on women—on what Catharine Stimpson has called the 'omissions, distortions, and trivializations' of women's experiences—and the spheres to which women have historically been consigned, like private life and the family.[3] Women's history sought to rescue from obscurity the lives of significant women who had been ignored or whose work had been minimized by traditional androcentric scholarship and to examine the everyday lives of women in the past—the efforts, for example, of laundresses, factory workers, pioneer homesteaders, or housewives to carve out lives of meaning and dignity in a world controlled by men. Whether the focus has been on the exemplary or the ordinary, though, feminist scholarship has made it clear that gender is a central axis in women's lives.

But when we think of the word 'gender', what gender comes to mind? It is not unusual to find, in courses on history of gender, psychology of gender, or sociology of gender, that the classroom is populated almost entirely by women. It's as if only women had gender and were therefore interested in studying it. Though more and more (brave) men are enrolling in women's studies classes, they remain a minority in courses dealing with gender.

It's our intention in this book to build upon the feminist approaches to gender by also making masculinity visible. We need to integrate men into our curriculum. Because it is men—or, rather masculinity—who are invisible.

'What?!' we can hear you saying. 'Did they just say "integrate men into our curriculum"? Men are invisible? Men aren't invisible. They're everywhere'.

And, of course, that's true. Men are ubiquitous in universities and professional schools and in the public sphere in general—not to mention in every subject in the university curriculum!

But when we study men, we study them as political leaders, military heroes, scientists, writers, artists. Men, themselves, are invisible *as men*. Rarely, if ever, do we see a course that examines the lives of men as men. What is the impact of gender on the lives of these famous men? How does masculinity play a part in the lives of great artists, writers, athletes, politicians, etc.? How does masculinity play out in the lives of 'ordinary' men—in factories and on farms, in union halls and large corporations? On this score, the traditional curriculum suddenly draws a big blank. Everywhere one turns there are courses about men, but virtually no information on masculinity.

Several years ago, this yawning gap inspired Michael Kimmel to undertake a cultural history of the idea of masculinity in the USA, to trace the development and shifts in what it has meant to be a man over the course of history.[4] What he found is that American men have been very articulate in describing what it means to be a man and in seeing whatever they have done as a way to prove their manhood, but that we hadn't known how to hear them.

Integrating gender into our courses is a way to fulfill the promise of women's studies— by understanding men as gendered as well. We continue to act as if gender applied only to women. Surely the time has come to make gender visible to men. As the Chinese proverb has it, the fish are the last to discover the ocean.

Race, class, and gender don't refer only to people who are marginalized by racial, class, or gender privilege, but to those who enjoy the privilege of invisibility. 'Whiteness' can (and must) be analyzed in terms of race just as can the experiences and identities of **racialized** people. When we talk about 'class', it doesn't only apply to lower or working classes. And masculinity is just as much about gender as femininity is. The very processes that confer **privilege** to one group and not another group are often invisible to those upon whom that privilege is conferred. What make us marginal or powerless are the processes we see. Invisibility is a privilege in another sense—as a luxury. Only white people in our society have the luxury not to think about race every minute of their lives. And only men have the luxury to pretend that gender does not matter.

Consider another example of how power is so often invisible to those who have it. You've probably noticed that Canadian e-mail addresses, like those of most people in the world, end with a country code (in our case, .ca). If you were writing to someone in South Africa, you'd put 'za' at the end or 'jp' for Japan or 'uk' for England (United Kingdom) or 'de' for Germany (Deutschland). But when you write to people in the United States, the e-mail address ends with 'edu' for an educational institution, 'org' for an organization, 'gov' for a federal government office, and 'com' or 'net' for commercial Internet providers. Why is it that the United States doesn't have a country code? From the point of view of the United States, a powerful and influential nation, all other countries are 'other' and thus need to be named, marked, noted. Once again, privilege is invisible.

There are consequences to this invisibility: Privilege, as well as gender, remains invisible. And it is hard to generate a politics of inclusion from invisibility. The **invisibility of privilege** means that many men, like many white people, become defensive and angry when confronted with the statistical realities or the human consequences of racism or sexism. Because privilege is invisible, those who have it may become defensive.

The continued invisibility of masculinity also means that the gendered standards that are held up as the norm appear to us to be gender-neutral. The illusion of gender neutrality has serious consequences for both women and men. It means that men can maintain the fiction that they are being measured by 'objective' standards; for women, it means that they are being judged by someone else's yardstick. At the turn of the twentieth century, the great sociologist Georg Simmel underscored this issue when he wrote:

> We measure the achievements and the commitments . . . of males and females in terms of specific norms and values; but these norms are not neutral, standing above the contrasts of the sexes; they have themselves a male character . . . The standards of art and the demands of patriotism, the general mores and the specific social ideas, the equity of practical judgments and the objectivity of theoretical knowledge . . .— all these categories are formally generically human, but are in fact masculine in terms of their actual historical formation. If we call ideas that claim absolute validity objectivity binding, then it is a fact that in the historical life of our species there operates the equation: objective male.[5]

Simmel's theoretical formulation echoes in our daily interactions. When a female professor makes a statement such as, 'Men are privileged in North American society', students might respond by saying, 'Of course, you'd say that. You're biased'. They'd see such a normative statement as revealing the inherent biases of gender, a case of special pleading. But when a man says it? An objective fact, transmitted by an objective professor: they'll probably take notes. Similarly, a white professor's statements on race privilege might be taken more seriously by students than the same comments made, say, by an Aboriginal colleague.

Such equations of 'objective=male' (or 'objective=white') have enormous practical consequences in every arena of our lives, from the elementary school classroom to professional and graduate schools and in every workplace we enter. As Simmel writes, 'Man's *position of power* does not only assure his relative superiority over the woman but it assures that his standards become generalized as generically human standards that are to govern the behaviour of men and women alike.'[6]

The Current Debate

North Americans are, at this moment, having a debate about masculinity—but we don't know it. For example, what gender comes to mind when you read about the following current North American problems: 'teen violence', 'gang violence', 'suburban violence', 'drug violence', 'violence in the schools'? And what gender comes to mind along with the words 'suicide bomber' or 'terrorist hijacker'?

Of course, you've imagined men. And not just any men—but younger men, in their teens and twenties, and relatively poorer men, from the working class or lower middle class. But how do our social commentators discuss these problems? Do they note that the problems of youth and violence are really problems of young *men* and violence? Do they ever mention that everywhere ethnic nationalism sets up shop, it is young men who are the shopkeepers? Do they ever mention masculinity at all?

No. Listen, for example, to the voice of one expert, asked to comment on the brutal 1998 murder of Matthew Shepard, a gay 21-year-old college student at the University of Wyoming. After being reminded that young men account for 80 per cent to 90 per cent of people arrested for 'gay-bashing' crimes, the reporter quoted a sociologist as saying that '[t]his youth variable tells us they are working out identity issues, making the transition away from home into adulthood'.[7] Aside from the offensiveness of linking brutal violence to 'working out identity issues', what about this '*youth* variable'? What had been a variable about age and gender was transformed into a variable about age. Gender simply disappeared. That is the sound of silence; what invisibility looks like.

Now, imagine that these were all women—all the ethnic nationalists, the militias, the gay-bashers. Would that not be *the* story, the *only* story? Would not a gender analysis be at the centre of every single story? Would we not hear from experts on female socialization, frustration, anger, PMS, and everything else under the sun? But the fact that these are men earns nary a word.

Take one final example. What if it had been young girls who opened fire on their classmates in Taber, Alberta; in Pearl, Mississippi; in Jonesboro, Arkansas; in Winnenden, Germany; or in Springfield, Oregon? And what if nearly all the children who died were boys? Do you think that the social outcry would demand that we investigate the 'inherent violence' of a particular culture? Or simply express dismay that young 'people' have too much access to guns? In these cases, no one seemed to mention that the young boys who actually committed those crimes were simply doing—albeit in dramatic form at a younger age—what American men have been taught to do for centuries when they are upset and angry. Men don't get mad; they get even. And very few mentions are made of the fact that the majority of victims of school shootings are female. (The gender of violence is explored in Chapter 12.)

We believe that until we make gender visible for both women and men we will not, as a culture, adequately know how to address these issues. That's not to say that all we have to do is address masculinity. These issues are complex, requiring analyses of the political economy of global economic integration, of the transformation of social classes, of urban poverty and hopelessness, of racism. But if we ignore masculinity—if we let it remain invisible—we will never completely understand society's problems, let alone resolve them.

Gender and Power: Hegemonic Masculinity and Emphasized Femininity

When we use the term 'gender', then, it is with the explicit intention of discussing both masculinity and femininity. But even these terms are inaccurate because they imply that there is one simple definition of masculinity and one definition of femininity. One of the important elements of a social-constructionist approach—especially if we intend to dislodge the notion that gender differences alone are decisive—is to explore the differences *among* men and *among* women, because, as it turns out, these are often more decisive than the differences between women and men.

Within any one society at any one moment, several meanings of masculinity and femininity co-exist. Simply put, not all North American men and women are the same. Our experiences are also structured by class, race, ethnicity, age, sexuality, region. Each of these axes modifies the others. Just because we make gender visible doesn't mean that we make these other organizing principles of social life invisible. Imagine, for example, an older, black, gay man in Toronto and a young, white, heterosexual farm boy in Manitoba. Wouldn't they have different definitions of masculinity? Or imagine a 22-year-old middle-class, Asian-Canadian, heterosexual woman in Vancouver and an elderly, poor, white, Scots-Canadian lesbian in Halifax. Wouldn't their ideas about what it means to be a woman be somewhat different?

If gender varies across cultures, over historical time, among men and women within any one culture, and over the life course, can we really speak of masculinity or femininity as though they were constant, universal essences, common to all women and to all men? If not, gender must be seen as an ever-changing fluid assemblage of meanings and behaviours. In that sense, we must speak of *masculinities* and *femininities* and thus recognize the different definitions of masculinity and femininity that we construct. By pluralizing the terms, we acknowledge that masculinity and femininity mean different things to different groups of people at different times.

At the same time, we can't forget that all masculinities and femininities are not created equal. North American men and women must also contend with a particular definition that is held up as the model against which we are expected to measure ourselves. We thus come to know what it means to be a man or a woman in our culture by setting our definitions in opposition to a set of 'others'—racial minorities, sexual minorities. For men, the classic 'other' is, of course, women. It feels imperative to most men that they make it clear—eternally, compulsively, decidedly—that they are unlike women. Robert McElvaine calls this the 'notawoman' definition of manhood, linking it both to competition among men and the deprecation of all things feminine.[8]

But one form of masculinity reigns supreme. For most men, this is the '**hegemonic**' definition—the one that is held up as the model for all. But hegemonic masculinity is not defined simply as a rejection of the feminine. Indeed, we might say that in contemporary North American society, the 'manly' man is defined both against the boy, the immature and powerless child, and the 'fag', the effeminate sexual 'other'. For R.W. Connell, **hegemonic masculinity** is 'constructed in relation to various subordinated masculinities as well as in relation to women'.[9] The sociologist Erving Goffman once described this hegemonic definition of masculinity like this:

> In an important sense there is only one complete unblushing male in America: a young, married, white, urban, northern, heterosexual, Protestant, father, of college education, fully employed, of good complexion, weight, and height, and a recent record in sports . . . Any male who fails to qualify in any one of these ways is likely to view himself—during moments at least—as unworthy, incomplete, and inferior.[10]

Goffman's definition makes it clear that like any ideal, the ideal of hegemonic masculinity is unattainable, based as it is on a version of virtually impossible competitive success. Even if a man manages to attain the status of Goffman's 'unblushing male', he cannot remain young, fit, and employed forever. Not surprisingly, most of our ideals of hegemonic masculinity are media images—like the Marlboro Man—who can remain fixed in their stoic and perfect performance of masculinity without ever growing old, getting weak, feeling doubt, or losing control of their emotions, families, or careers.

Given the power of hegemonic masculinity and the growth, in modern societies, of protest and counterculture identities, we should not be surprised that not everyone subscribes to the ideals of hegemonic masculinity. Indeed, particular resistant forms of masculinity, including queer, skinhead, punk, emo, and female/trans masculinities contest the power of the hegemonic stereotype while sometimes reinforcing many of its definitions of manhood, particularly the 'notawoman' definition. Hegemonic masculinity is thus an enormously powerful ideal despite, or because of, its unattainable and exaggerated quality.

There is no 'hegemonic' version of femininity, according to R.W. Connell, because hegemonic masculinity arose through competition among men within patriarchal societies. In a sense, this made masculinity more important, in many societies, than femininity. We've all heard the exhortation 'Be a man', but how many of us have ever used, or heard, the phrase 'Be a woman'? What would that even mean? In fact, in most societies the transition to womanhood is perceived as much more natural and simple than the comparable transition for men. Masculinity must be earned, femininity simply grown into.

This does not mean that women face no gendered expectations, or that their lot is somehow easier. Indeed, women too contend with an exaggerated ideal of femininity, which Connell calls '**emphasized femininity**'. Emphasized femininity is organized around (real or apparent) compliance with gender inequality and is 'oriented to accommodating the interests and desires of men'. One sees emphasized femininity in 'the display of sociability rather than technical competence, fragility in mating scenes, compliance with men's desire for titillation and ego-stroking in office relationships, acceptance of marriage and child care as a response to labour-market discrimination against women'.[11] Emphasized femininity exaggerates gender difference as a strategy of 'adaptation to men's power' stressing empathy and nurturance; 'real' womanhood is described as 'fascinating', and women are advised that they can wrap men around their fingers by knowing and playing by the 'rules'. In one research study, an eight-year-old boy captured this emphasized femininity eloquently in a poem he wrote:

> If I were a girl, I'd have to attract a guy wear makeup; sometimes. Wear the latest style of clothes and try to be likable. I probably wouldn't play any physical sports like football or soccer. I don't think I would enjoy myself around men in fear of rejection or under the pressure of attracting them.[12]

Gender Differences as 'Deceptive Distinctions'

The existence of multiple masculinities and femininities dramatically undercuts the idea that the gender differences we observe are due solely to differently gendered people occupying gender-neutral positions. Moreover, that these masculinities and femininities are arrayed along a hierarchy, and measured against one another, buttresses the argument that domination creates and exaggerates difference.

The interplanetary theory of gender assumes that, whether through biology or socialization, women act like women, no matter where they are, and that men act like men, no matter where they are. Psychologist Carol Tavris argues that such binary thinking leads to what philosophers call the 'law of the excluded middle', which, as she reminds us, 'is where most men and women fall in terms of their psychological qualities, beliefs, abilities, traits, and values'.[13] It turns out that many of the differences between women and men that we observe in our everyday lives are actually **deceptive distinctions**: not *gender* differences at all, but rather differences that are the result of being in different positions or in different arenas. It's not that gendered individuals occupy these ungendered positions, but rather that the *positions themselves* elicit the behaviours we see as gendered. The sociologist Cynthia Fuchs Epstein calls these 'deceptive distinctions' because, although they appear to be based on gender, they are actually based on something else.[14]

Take, for example, the well-known differences in communication patterns observed by Deborah Tannen in her best-selling book, *You Just Don't Understand*. Tannen argues that men employ the competitive language of hierarchy and domination to get ahead; women create webs of inclusion with softer, more embracing language that ensures that everyone feels okay. When couples communicate, women talk more, using language to create intimacy while their husbands speak less and use language instrumentally. To understand the opposite sex, Tannen argues, one must understand its 'genderlect'.[15]

But it turns out that men and women use language differently in different situations. The very same men who are silent at home may be very verbal at work, where they are in positions of dependency and powerlessness, and need to use conversation to maintain a relationship with their superiors; and their wives are just as capable of using language competitively to maximize their position in a corporate hierarchy. Education and class may also be a more important determinant of language use than gender. When he examined the recorded transcripts of women's and men's testimony in trials, anthropologist William O'Barr concluded that the witnesses' occupation was a more accurate predictor of their use of language than was gender. 'So-called women's language is neither characteristic of all women, nor limited only to women', O'Barr writes. If women use 'powerless' language, it may be due 'to the greater tendency of women to occupy relatively powerless social positions' in society.[16] Communication differences turn out to be 'deceptive distinctions' because rarely do we observe the communication patterns of dependent men and executive women.

We could take another example from the world of education, explored in Chapter 7. Aggregate differences in girls' and boys' scores on standardized math tests have led people to speculate that whereas males have a natural propensity for arithmetic figures, females have a 'fear of math'. Couple this with their 'fear of success' in the workplace, and you might find that women manage money less effectively—with less foresight, less calculation, less care. The popular writer Colette Dowling, author of the best-selling 1981 book *The Cinderella Complex* interviewed 65 women in their late 50s about money matters and found that only two had *any* investment plans for their retirements. Broke and bankrupt after several best-sellers and single again herself, Dowling argues that this relates to 'conflicts with dependency. Money savvy is connected with masculinity in our culture', she told an interviewer. 'That leaves women with the feeling that if they want to take care of themselves and are good at it, the quid pro quo is they'll never hook up with a relationship'. Because of ingrained femininity, women end up shooting themselves in the foot.[17]

But such assertions fly in the face of all available research, argues the financial expert Jane Bryant Quinn, herself the author of a bestseller about women and money. 'It *is* more socially acceptable for women not to manage their money', she told the same interviewer. 'But the Y chromosome is not a money management chromosome. In all the studies, if you control for earnings, age and experience, women are the same as men. At 23, out in the working world staring at a [retirement] plan, they are equally confused. But if those women quit working, they will know less and less about finance, while the man, who keeps working, will know more and more'.[18] So it is our *experience*, not our *gender*, that predicts how we'll handle our retirement investments.

What about those enormous gender differences that some observers have found in the workplace (the subject of Chapter 8)? Men, we hear, are competitive social climbers who seek advancement at every opportunity; women are co-operative team-builders who shun competition and may even suffer from a 'fear of success'. But the pioneering study by Rosabeth Moss Kanter, reported in *Men and Women of the Corporation*, indicated that gender mattered far less than opportunity. When women had the same opportunities, networks, mentors, and possibilities for advancement, they behaved just as the men did. Women were unsuccessful because they lacked opportunities, not because they feared success; when men lacked opportunities, they behaved in stereotypically 'feminine' ways.[19]

Finally, take our experiences in the family, examined in Chapter 6. Here, again, we assume that women are socialized to be nurturing and maternal, men to be strong and silent, relatively emotionally inexpressive arbiters of justice—that is, we assume that women do the work of 'mothering' because they are socialized to do so. And again, sociological research suggests that our behaviour in the family has somewhat less to do with gender socialization than with the family situations in which we find ourselves.

Research by sociologist Kathleen Gerson, for example, found that gender socialization was not very helpful in predicting women's family experiences. Only slightly more than half the women who were primarily interested in full-time motherhood were, in fact, full-time mothers; and only slightly more than half the women who were primarily interested in full-time careers had them. It turned out that marital stability, husbands' income, women's workplace experiences, and support networks were far more important than gender socialization in determining which women ended up full-time mothers and which did not.[20]

On the other side of the ledger, research by sociologist Barbara Risman found that despite a gender socialization that downplays emotional responsiveness and nurturing, most single fathers are perfectly capable of 'mothering'. Single fathers do not hire female workers to do the typically female tasks around the house: They do those tasks themselves. In fact, Risman found few differences between single fathers and mothers (single or married) when it came to what they did around the house, how they acted with their children, or even in their children's emotional and intellectual development. Men's parenting styles were virtually indistinguishable from women's, a finding that led Risman to argue that 'men can mother and that children are not necessarily better nurtured by women than by men.'[21]

These findings also shed a very different light on other research. For example, some recent researchers found significant differences in the amount of stress that women and men experience on an everyday basis. According to the researchers, women reported higher levels of stress and lower numbers of 'stress-free' days than did men. David Almeida and Ronald Kessler sensibly concluded that this was not a biologically based difference, a signal of women's inferiority in handling stress, but rather an indication that women had more stress in their lives, because they had to juggle more family and work issues than did men.[22]

Based on all this research, you might conclude, as does Risman, that 'if women and men were to experience identical structural conditions and role expectations, empirically observable gender differences would dissipate'.[23] Still, there *are* some differences between women and men, after all. But this research suggests that those differences are not as great, decisive, or impervious to social change as we once thought. It is the task of this book to explore both those areas where there appear to be gender differences but where there are, in fact, few or no differences, and also those areas where gender differences are significant and decisive.

The Meaning of Mean Differences

Few of the differences between women and men are 'hard-wired' into all males to the exclusion of all females, or vice versa. Although we can readily observe differences between women and men in rates of aggression, physical strength, math or verbal achievement, caring and nurturing, or emotional expressiveness, it is not true that all males and no females are aggressive, physically strong, and adept at math and science, and that all females and no males are caring and nurturing, verbally adept, or emotionally expressive. What we mean when we speak of gender differences are **mean differences**, differences in the average scores obtained by women and men.

These mean scores tell us something about the differences between the two groups, but they tell us nothing about the distributions themselves, the differences *among* men or *among* women. Sometimes these distributions can be enormous: There are large numbers of caring or emotionally expressive men and of aggressive and physically strong women. (See Figure 1.1.) In fact, in virtually all the research that has been done on the attributes associated with masculinity or femininity, the differences among women and among men are far greater than the mean differences *between* women and men. We tend to focus on the mean differences, but they may tell us far less than we think they do.

What we think they tell us, of course, is that women and men are different, from different planets. This is the 'interplanetary theory of gender difference'— that the observed mean differences between women and men are decisive and that they come from the fact that women and men are biologically so physically different.

For example, even the idea that we are from different planets—that our differences are deep and intractable—has a political dimension: To call the 'other' sex the

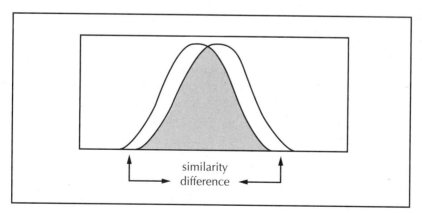

similarity
difference

Figure 1.1 Schematic rendering of the overlapping distributions of traits, attitudes, and behaviours by gender.

Although mean differences might obtain on many characteristics, these distributions suggest far greater similarity between women and men and far greater variability among men and among women.

'opposite' sex obscures the many ways we are alike. As the anthropologist Gayle Rubin points out:

> Men and women are, of course, different. But they are not as different as day and night, earth and sky, yin and yang, life and death. In fact from the standpoint of nature, men and women are closer to each other than either is to anything else—for instance mountains, kangaroos, or coconut palms . . . Far from being an expression of natural differences, exclusive gender identity is the suppression of natural similarities.[24]

The interplanetary theory of gender difference is important not because it's right—in fact, it is wrong far more often than it is right—but because, as a culture, we seem desperately to want it to be true. That is, the real sociological question about gender is not the sociology of gender differences—explaining the physiological origins of gender difference—but rather the sociology-of-knowledge question that explores why gender difference is so important to us, why we cling to the idea of gender difference so tenaciously, why we shell out millions of dollars for books that 'reveal' the deep differences between women and men but will probably never buy a book that says, 'Hey, we're all Earthlings!'

That, however, is the message of this book. Virtually all available research from the social and behavioural sciences suggests that women and men are not from Venus and Mars, but from planet Earth. We're not opposite sexes, but neighbouring sexes—we have far more in common with each other than we have differences.

Difference and Domination: Individuals in a Gendered Society

Whether we believe that gender difference is biologically determined or is a cultural formation, the interplanetary theory of gender difference assumes that gender is a property of individuals, that is, that gender is a component of one's identity. But this is only half the story. We believe that individual boys and girls become gendered—that is, we learn the 'appropriate' behaviours and traits that are associated with hegemonic masculinity and emphasized femininity—and then we each, individually, negotiate our own path in a way that feels right to us. In a sense, we each 'cut our own deal' with the dominant definitions of masculinity and femininity. That's why we are so keenly attuned to, and so vigorously resist, gender stereotypes—because we believe that they do not actually encompass our experiences.

But we do not cut our own deal by ourselves in gender-neutral institutions and arenas. The social institutions of our world—workplace, family, school, politics—are also gendered institutions, sites where the dominant definitions are reinforced and reproduced, and where 'deviants' are disciplined. We become gendered selves in a **gendered society**.

Speaking of a gendered society is not the same thing as pointing out that rocket ships and skyscrapers bear symbolic relationships to a certain part of the male anatomy. Sometimes function takes precedence over symbolic form. It is also only partially related to the way we use metaphors of gender to speak of other spheres of activity—the way, for example, each of the worlds of sports, sex, war, and work appropriates the language of the other spheres.

When we say that we live in a gendered society we imply that the organizations of our society have evolved in ways that reproduce both the differences between women and men and the domination of men over women. Institutionally, we can see how the structure of the workplace is organized around demonstrating and reproducing masculinity: The temporal organization and the spatial organization of work both depend upon the separation of spheres (distance between work and home and the fact that women are the primary child-care providers).

As it did with respect to the invisibility of gendered identity, assuming institutional gender-neutrality actually serves to maintain the gender politics of those institutions. And it underscores the way we often assume that if you allow individuals to express a wider range of gender behaviours, they'll be able to succeed in those gender-neutral institutions. So we assume that the best way to eliminate gender inequality in higher education or in the workplace is to promote sameness—i.e., we're unequal only because we're different.

This, however, creates a political and personal dilemma for women in gendered institutions. It's a no-win proposition for women when they enter the workplace, the military, politics, or sports—arenas that are already established to reproduce and sustain masculinity. To the extent that they become 'like men' in order to succeed, they are seen as having sacrificed their femininity. Yet to the extent to which they refuse to sacrifice their femininity, they are seen as different, and thus gender discrimination is legitimate as the sorting of different people into different slots.[25] Women who succeed are punished for abandoning their femininity—rejected as potential partners, labelled as 'dykes', left off the invitation lists. Thus gender inequality creates a double bind for women—a double bind that is based on the assumption of gender difference and the assumption of **institutional gender neutrality**.

Both difference and domination are produced and reproduced in our social interactions, in the institutions in which we live and work. Though the differences between us are not as great as we often assume, they become important in our expectations and observations. This book examines those differences—those that are real and important—and seeks to reveal those that are neither real nor important. We will explore the ways in which gender inequality provides the foundation for assumptions of gender difference. And, finally, we will endeavour to show the impact of gender on our lives—how we become gendered people living gendered lives in a gendered society.

Summary

Despite the persistence of the 'interplanetary theory' of gender difference, men and women are more similar than different. Gender difference exists, of course, but it is neither complete nor absolute. Still, virtually every human society is founded upon assumptions of gender differences, and most have also exhibited gender inequality in the form of male dominance. The frequency of both gender difference and gender inequality is often explained using arguments of biological determinism versus differential socialization, or 'nature versus nurture'.

While science provides evidence of significant biological differences between the sexes, definitions of gender differences vary greatly among cultures. This suggests that biological determinism ('nature') can't fully explain gender difference or domination. Developmental psychology provides ample evidence of differential socialization ('nurture'), suggesting that men and women are different because they are socialized to be different. While the differential socialization argument contests biological determinism, both arguments assume that men and women *are* dramatically different and that their differences produce gender inequality or domination. But men and women are not so dramatically different—and, what's more, this book argues that their differences *do not produce* inequality, but rather *are produced by* inequality.

To examine how inequality produces gender difference, we need to make gender visible in the way that feminist scholars have been doing it for the past 30 years. It's particularly important to stop acting as though only women have gender. We need to study masculinity to understand how some of our social norms are really 'masculine norms', based on the yardstick of 'universal' man. We also need to understand masculinity to really assess some of the most important issues we face, most notably violence.

When we study masculinity and femininity, though, we need to keep in mind that there is not just one form or 'essence' of manliness or womanliness that exists everywhere at all times. To be sure, each society holds up one version that is 'hegemonic'. R.W. Connell coined the term 'hegemonic masculinity' to describe the version of masculinity most celebrated in a culture at a given time. For Connell, the feminine counterpart is 'emphasized femininity', defined as a kind of exaggerated compliance with the desires of men and the system of gender inequality. So emphasized femininity and hegemonic masculinity are a kind of recipe for manliness and womanliness; though the recipe's ingredients vary from culture to culture, and change over time, the basic idea is that there *is* a recipe that men and women need to adhere to. Though not everyone in North American society—or any society—adheres to hegemonic masculinity, this gender ideology remains a force to be reckoned with in any society, organizing forms of masculinity in a continuum or hierarchy.

While we see hegemonic masculinity and emphasized femininity as powerful gender ideologies, it's important to recognize that many of the differences we attribute to being 'masculine' or 'feminine' may actually be 'deceptive distinctions', that is, the result of being in *different situations* rather than *of different genders*. Many so-called 'gender' differences—in language use, in financial habits, in family roles—may be the result of different experiences rather than gender differences per se. That is, when men are in 'female' situations, they act more 'like women'—and vice versa. This doesn't mean that gender differences don't exist, but it does mean that we need to use caution when we analyze gender difference.

Another reason we need to use caution when discussing gender differences is that we are generally taking about mean differences, differences between 'average' men and women. There are probably greater differences *among* men and women than *between* them, as Figure 1.1 suggests.

Finally, many of the gender differences we see around us are the result not of some intractable difference between the masculine and the feminine, but of individual people trying to make their lives in a gendered society. To understand gender differences, we therefore need to understand the way in which institutions and organizations are gendered—the way that they reproduce the differences between men and women and reinforce the idea of gender inequality. When we look at gendered institutions, as we do in the second part of this book, we can see how institutions, far from being gender-neutral, have been set up according to a set of gendered 'rules'. Thus even though we may not be from Mars or from Venus, when we engage with the institutions that constitute our social worlds, we come up against those rules—rules that make the 'gendered society'. In the pages that follow, we explore that gendered society through an examination of gender differences, an exploration of gender inequality and the way it creates difference, and an assessment of the impact of gender on our lives.

Questions for Critical Thinking

1. Can you think of examples of hegemonic masculinity or emphasized femininity in your own life or community?
2. How does the 'invisibility of privilege' operate? How might you experience privilege on the basis of gender, class, ethnicity, ability, sexuality? When you think of 'a Canadian citizen', what picture do you see?
3. Why do you think the 'interplanetary theory' of gender difference appeals so strongly to people?

Key Terms

biological determinism
deceptive distinctions
differential socialization
emphasized femininity
gender
gendered society
hegemonic
hegemonic masculinity
institutional gender neutrality
'interplanetary theory' of gender
   difference

invisibility of privilege
male dominance
mean differences
privilege
racialized
sex
sex difference
social constructionism

Part 1

Explanations of Gender

Chapter 2

Ordained by Nature

Biology Constructs the Sexes

> You may drive nature out with a pitchfork; she will nevertheless come back.
> —HORACE (65–8 BC)

> It is not human nature we should accuse but the despicable conventions that pervert it.
> —DENIS DIDEROT (1713–84)

What is human nature? That's an ancient and thorny question. It's no simpler to understand the 'nature' of men and women as gendered beings. Still, many people claim, with Sigmund Freud, that 'anatomy is destiny'. Though it's not clear that Freud ever intended that this statement be taken literally, many researchers believe that the differences in male and female anatomy provide the basis for observable differences between men and women. One recent researcher proclaimed his belief that 'the differences between the males and females of our species will ultimately be found in the cell arrangements and anatomy of the human brain'.[1] To biologists, the source of human behaviour lies neither in our stars nor in ourselves, as Caesar had suggested to Brutus— but rather in our cells.

Biological explanations hold a place of prominence in our explanations of both gender *difference* and gender *inequality*. First, biological explanations have the ring of 'true' science to them: Because they are based on 'objective scientific facts', the arguments of natural scientists are extraordinarily persuasive. Second, biological explanations seem to accord with our own observations: Women and men *seem* so different to us most of the time—so different, in fact, that we often appear to be from different planets.

There's also a certain conceptual tidiness to biological explanations, because the social arrangements between women and men (gender inequality) seem to stem directly and inevitably from the differences between us. Biological arguments can be used to argue that what *is* is what should be, that the social is natural.

This chapter will explore some of the biological evidence that is presented to demonstrate the natural, biologically based differences between the sexes and the ways in which social and political arrangements (inequality) directly flow from those differences. Biological differences can tell us much about the ways in which men and women behave. The search for such differences can also tell us a lot about our culture—about what we want so desperately to believe, and why we want to believe it.

Biological Differences, Then and Now

The search for the biological origins of the differences between women and men is not new. What is new, at least for the past few centuries, is that scientists have come to play the central role in exploring the natural differences between males and females.

Prior to the nineteenth century, most explanations of gender difference had been the province of theologians. God had created man and woman for different purposes, and those reproductive differences were decisive. These theological explanations continued to have meaning well into the nineteenth century when, for example, the American abolitionist preacher Reverend John Todd warned against women's suffrage, which would 'reverse the very laws of God'.[2]

But by the late eighteenth century, scientists were beginning to join the debate. After 1750, European anatomists—few of whom were women—published drawings of the male and female skeletons that exaggerated the pelvises of women and the crania of men, thus arguing for the sexes' 'natural' suitedness to their social roles.[3]

The debate intensified later in the nineteenth century under the influence of Darwin and the emerging science of evolutionary biology. In his path-breaking work *On the Origin of Species* (1859), Darwin posed several questions. How do certain species come to be the way they are? Why is there such astonishing variety among those species? Why do some species differ from others in some ways and remain similar in other ways? He answered these questions with the law of natural selection. Species adapt to their changing environments. Those species that adapt well to their environments are reproductively successful, that is, their adaptive characteristics are passed on to the next generation, whereas those species that are less adaptive do not pass on their characteristics. Within any one species, a similar process occurs, and those individuals who are best suited to their environment pass on their genes to the next generation. Species are always changing, always adapting.

Such an idea was heretical to those who believed that God had created all species, including human beings, intact and unchanging. And Darwin did believe that just as the species of the lower animal world evince intrinsic sex differences, so, too, do human beings. 'Woman seems to differ from man in mental disposition, chiefly in her greater tenderness and lesser selfishness', he wrote in *The Descent of Man*. Men's competitiveness, ambition, and selfishness 'seem to be his natural and unfortunate birthright. The chief distinction in the intellectual powers of the two sexes is shown by man's attaining to a higher eminence, in whatever he takes up, than can woman—whether requiring deep thought, reason, or imagination, or merely the uses of the senses and the hands'.[4]

No sooner had the biological differences between women and men been established as scientific fact than writers and critics declared all efforts to challenge social inequality and discrimination against women to be in violation of the 'laws of nature'. Many writers argued that women's efforts to enter the public sphere—to seek employment, to vote, to enter colleges—were misguided because they placed women's social and political aspirations over the purposes for which their bodies had been designed. Women were not to be *excluded* from voting, from the labour force, or from higher education as much as they were, as the Reverend Todd put it, 'to be exempted from certain things which men must endure'.[5] This position was best summed up by a participant in a debate about women's suffrage in Sacramento, California, in 1880:

I am opposed to woman's sufferage [*sic*] on account of the burden it will place upon her. Her delicate nature has already enough to drag it down. Her slender frame, naturally weakened by the constant strain attendant upon her nature is too often racked [*sic*] by diseases that are caused by a too severe tax upon her mind. The presence of passion, love, ambition, is all too potent for her enfeebled condition, and wrecked health and early death are all too common.[6]

Social scientists quickly jumped on the biological bandwagon—especially **social Darwinists**, who shortened the time span necessary for evolution from millennia to one or two generations and who causally extended Darwin's range from ornithology to human beings. In their effort to legitimize social science by allying it with natural law, social Darwinists applied Darwin's theory in ways its originator had never imagined, distorting his ideas about natural selection to claim decisive biological differences among races, nations, families, and, of course, between women and men. For example, the eminent French sociologist Gustav LeBon, who would later become famous for his theory of the collective mind and the irrationality of the crowd, believed that the differences between women and men (not to mention the differences between 'civilized' and 'savage' peoples) could be explained by their different brain structure. He wrote in 1879:

In the most intelligent races, as among the Parisians, there are a large number of women whose brains are closer in size to those of gorillas than to the most developed of male brains . . . All psychologists who have studied the intelligence of women . . . recognize today that they represent the most inferior forms of human evolution and that they are closer to children and savages than to an adult civilized man. They excel in fickleness, inconstancy, absence of thought and logic, and incapacity to reason. Without doubt, there exist some distinguished women, very superior to the average man, but they are as exceptional as the birth of any monstrosity, as, for example, of a gorilla with two heads . . .[7]

Much of the debate centred on whether or not women could be educated, especially in colleges and universities. One writer suggested that a woman 'of average brain' could attain the same standards as a man with an average brain 'only at the cost of her health, of her emotions, or of her morale'. Another prophesied that women would grow bigger and heavier brains and that their uteruses would shrink if they went to college. Perhaps the most famous social scientist to join this discussion was Edward C. Clarke, Harvard's eminent professor of education. In his best-selling book *Sex in Education: or, A Fair Chance for the Girls* (1873), Clarke argued that women should be exempted from higher education because of the tremendous demands made upon their bodies by reproduction.[8]

The implicit conservatism of such arguments was as evident at the beginning of the twentieth century as it is now. What's more, these arguments were often linked to regressive racist and classist views. 'How did woman first become subject to man as she is now all over the world?' asked James Long. 'By her nature, her sex, just as the negro is and always will be, to the end of time, inferior to the white race, and therefore, doomed to subjection; but happier than she would be in any other condition, just because it is the law of her nature'.[9] In Canada, 'woman's nature' was yoked to the mission of populating the nation with the 'right' sort of people. For Sophie Bevan, who wrote a letter to the (London) *Times* after a tour of North America, Canada would be lost to racial and class inferiors 'unless we can induce the right sort of British women to emigrate'; were such women to fail in their mission, she warned, 'we shall not have the Colonies peopled with our own race or speaking our own mother tongue.'[10]

Biological arguments thus became tied up not only with women's proper role, but with the hierarchical relationships among races and classes. The field of **eugenics** developed in the nineteenth century and spread its influence to Canada in the early twentieth century. Eugenics united feminists with social conservatives and progressives in the pursuit of biological improvement, often figured as the 'improvement of the race'. Admired Canadians like Emily Murphy and J.S. Woodsworth were fellow travellers of the movement. Adhered to by many, though discredited because of Nazi atrocities committed in its name, eugenics had significant influence in Canada, particularly in the West. British Columbia and Alberta enacted legislation permitting the involuntary sterilization of the 'mentally defective' (a blanket term that covered many forms of disability and mental illness). Ultimately, between 1929 and 1972, over 2,800 people were sterilized in this manner. Though Aboriginal people were only between 2 and 3 per cent of the population, they were 6 per cent of cases presented before the board that approved involuntary sterilization. Moreover, 70 per cent of Aboriginal people whose cases were presented to the board were ultimately sterilized, compared with approximately 47 per cent of cases involving Eastern and Western Europeans. Women, teenagers, and young adults were also overrepresented among those sterilized. Shockingly, eugenics legislation in the West was only repealed in the 1970s. In 1996, Leilani Muir won a judgment against the province of Alberta for wrongful sterilization, which was followed by a class-action suit brought by survivors of similar medical 'treatment'.[11]

The discrediting of such historical (if recent!) forms of **biological determinism** should make us cautious about the conclusions we draw from biology. Nonetheless, past misconceptions of scientists and misuses of scientific knowledge shouldn't cancel out the continuing importance and interest of research on biological difference. Today, serious biological arguments generally draw their evidence from three areas of research: (1) evolutionary theory, from sociobiology to 'evolutionary psychology'; (2) brain research; and (3) endocrinological research on sex hormones, before birth and again at puberty. The latter two areas of research are also used to describe the biologically based differences between heterosexuals and homosexuals, differences that are, as we shall see, often expressed in gendered terms.[12]

The Evolutionary Imperative: From Social Darwinism to Sociobiology and Evolutionary Psychology

Evolutionary biologists since Darwin have abandoned the more obviously political intentions of the **social Darwinists**, but the development of the new field of **sociobiology** in the 1970s revived evolutionary arguments. Edward Wilson, a professor of entomology at Harvard, helped to found this school of thought, which studies the biological basis of social behaviour in all animals, including human beings. All creatures, Wilson argued, 'obey' the 'biological principle', and all temperamental differences (personalities, cultures) derive from the biological development of creatures undergoing the pressure of evolutionary selection. The natural differences that result are the source of the social and political arrangements we observe today. Eventually, he confidently predicted, the social sciences and humanities would 'shrink to specialized branches of biology'.[13]

One of the major areas that sociobiologists have stressed is the differences in male and female sexuality, which they believe to be the natural outgrowth of centuries of evolutionary development. Evolutionary success requires that all members of a species consciously or unconsciously desire to pass on their genes. Thus males and females develop reproductive 'strategies' to ensure that our own genetic code passes on to the next generation. Sociobiologists thus suggest that the differences we observe between women and men today have come from centuries of advantageous evolutionary choices. As Wilson and fellow sociobiologist Richard Dawkins put it, '[F]emale exploitation begins here'. Culture has little to do with it, as Wilson argues, because 'the genes hold culture on a leash'.[14]

Take, for example, the size and the number of the reproductive cells themselves. Add to that the differential '**parental investment**' required to produce a healthy offspring, and—presto!—you have the differences between male and female sexual behaviour at a typical dorm party this weekend. 'He' produces billions of tiny sperm; 'she' produces one gigantic ovum. For the male, reproductive success depends upon his ability to fertilize a large number of eggs. Toward this end, he tries to fertilize as many eggs as he can. Thus males have a 'natural' propensity toward promiscuity. By contrast, females require only one successful mating before their egg can be fertilized, and therefore they tend to be extremely choosy about which male will be the lucky fellow. What's more, females must invest a far greater amount of energy in gestation and lactation and have a much higher reproductive 'cost', which their reproductive strategies would reflect. Females, therefore, tend to be monogamous, choosing the male who will make the best parent. From this theory, it's a simple matter to extrapolate in simplistic manners to the behaviour of modern men and women. This is particularly true when sociobiological research is digested by popular media. 'A woman seeks marriage to monopolize not a man's sexuality, but, rather, his political and economic resources, to ensure that her children (her genes) will be well provided for', writes journalist Anthony Layng. As sociobiologist Donald Symons puts it, women and men have different 'sexual psychologies' that drive women to be 'more choosy and more hesitant', while men are 'less discriminating, more aggressive, and have a greater taste for variety of partners'.[15]

Other evolutionary arguments examine different aspects of reproductive biology to spell out the differences between men and women and thereby explain the social inequality between them. For example, the separation of masculine and feminine spheres seems to have a basis far back in evolutionary time. Lionel Tiger and Robin Fox emphasize the social requirements for the evolutionary transition to a hunting-and-gathering society. First, the hunting band must have solidarity and co-operation, which require bonding among the hunters. Women's biology—especially their menstrual cycle—puts them at a significant disadvantage for such consistent co-operation, and the presence of women would disrupt the co-operation necessary among the men and insinuate competition and aggression. Women also are possessed of a 'maternal instinct'. Thus it would make sense for men to hunt and for women to remain back home raising the children. For Tiger, male bonding through the hunt produces the basis of human society, with effects that persist to this day.[16] Fair enough—but does that mean that separate spheres are 'in our genes'? Yes, writes Edward Wilson: 'In hunter-gatherer societies, men hunt and women stay at home. This strong bias persists in most agricultural and industrial societies, and, on that ground alone, appears to have a genetic origin . . . My own guess is that the genetic bias is intense enough to cause a substantial division of labour in the most free and most egalitarian of future societies'.[17]

Other evolutionary arguments have examined such behaviours as interspecies violence and aggression. As we shall see in Chapter 12, some sociobiologists have argued that rape is 'natural', a result of men's failed competition for mates. The breathless interpretive rush from male scorpion flies to human rapists is one example of sociobiology's biological determinism.

The newest incarnation of sociobiology is called '**evolutionary psychology**', which explains psychological traits, including differences between women and men, as evolutionary adaptations. One key insight of evolutionary psychology is simple: Our brains did evolve under vastly different conditions from those we live in today. Millions of years of evolution preceded what we think of as human history, and we are creatures produced by that dimly understood period. Comparisons with other primates, as well as theories on hominid evolution, can help us understand many behaviours, from language-use to play, from grandmothering to the choice of sexual partners. The key word here, however, is 'help'. Too often, however, evolutionary psychology falls into the reductionist patterns of sociobiology. Men are understood to be more aggressive, controlling, and managing—skills that were honed over millennia of evolution as hunters and fighters. After an equal amount of time raising children and performing domestic tasks, women are said to be more reactive, more emotional, 'programmed to be passive'.[18]

These differences lead us to completely different contemporary mating strategies as well. Psychologist David Buss surveyed more than 10,000 people from 37 different cultures around the world and found strikingly similar things about what women and men want in a mate. It can't be culturally specific if they all agree, can it? In every society, females placed a high premium on signs of economic prosperity, whereas men placed their highest premium on youth and beauty, whose signal traits were large breasts and ample hips—i.e., signs of fertility. Does it interest you that although these traits were important, the single trait most highly valued by *both* women and men was love and kindness?[19] This suggests that when we choose mates, we are acting on a complex set of impulses derived at least as much from our cultural influences as from the demands of our genes. The best evolutionary psychology acknowledges this while insisting that we understand the evolutionary roots of behaviour as motivating significant sex differences. For example, Margo Wilson and Martin Daly write about the evolutionary roots of a number of features of male dominance, most notably 'a sexually proprietary male psychology'. Instead of offering reductive statements about women's psychological adaptation and consequent passivity, Wilson and Daly offer an analysis that recognizes that men and women might have distinctly different and conflicting interests—a key concept in evolutionary psychology—with women nowhere nearly so monogamous as simplistic analyses might suggest.[20]

Indeed, studying women from an evolutionary perspective yields interesting questions that trouble the conventional narratives of monogamy on which sociobiology's view of women was built. Women are the only primate females who do not have specified periods of **estrus**. They are potentially sexually receptive at any time of their reproductive cycle, including when they are incapable of conception. Don't forget that in reality most women do not experience peaks of sexual desire during ovulation (which is what evolutionary biologists would predict, because women must ensure reproductive success) but actually just before and just after menstruation (when women are almost invariably infertile, though the ratio of female to male hormones is lowest). These findings can confound conventional theories. Referring to the inconsistency of data from studies on the cycling of female sexual desire, evolutionary psychologist David Buss and his co-authors lament research 'carried out without being explicitly informed by evolutionary theories of human mating'.[21] (Presumably, if researchers had known the theories, their data would have revealed that desire peaked with ovulation.) From this evidence of women's unruly and inconsistent desire, one might adduce that human females are uniquely equipped biologically—indeed, that it is their sexual strategy—to enjoy sex simply for its physical pleasure and not for its reproductive potential. And if the reproductive goal of the female is to ensure the survival of her offspring, then it would make sense for her to deceive as many males as possible into thinking that the offspring was theirs. That way, she could be sure that all of them would protect and provide for the baby because none of them could risk the possibility of his offspring's death and the obliteration of his genetic material. So might not women's evolutionary 'strategy' be promiscuity? [22]

One more bit of evidence is the difference between male and female orgasm. Whereas male orgasm is clearly linked to reproductive success, female orgasm seems to have been designed solely for pleasure; it serves no reproductive function at all. The human clitoris plays no part whatsoever in human reproduction but is solely oriented toward sexual pleasure. According to Elisabeth Lloyd, a philosopher of science at Indiana University, the capacity for female orgasm may be a holdover from parallel fetal development in the first eight or nine weeks of life. But the explanation for its persistence may be that orgasm is a reproductive strategy for promiscuous females. Sexual pleasure and orgasm may encourage females to mate frequently and with multiple partners until they have an orgasm. The males, on the other hand, couldn't be sure the offspring was *not* theirs, so they would struggle to protect and provide. Thus, female orgasm might be part of women's evolutionary strategy—and making sure females did *not* enjoy sex too much might be males' evolutionary response! [23]

This may not be so far-fetched. One recent study found that women reported that their partners increased their attentiveness and 'monopolization' behaviour—calling them often to check on their whereabouts, for example—just as they began to ovulate. But the women found that they fantasized far more about cheating on their partners at the same time. (They reported no increase whatever in sexual thoughts about their partners—so much for their evolutionary predisposition toward fidelity.) Although this suggests that the men had good reason to be more guarding and jealous, it also suggests that women 'instinctively want to have sex with as many men as possible to ensure the genetic quality of their offspring, whereas men want to ensure that their own genes get reproduced', according to a journalist reporting on the story. Equally selfish genes and equally a 'war between the sexes'—but one with a completely different interpretation.[24]

Another biological fact about women might make life even more confusing for males seeking to determine paternity. Barbara McClintock's research about women's menstrual cycles indicated that in close quarters, women's cycles tend to become increasingly synchronous; that is, over time, women's cycles will tend to converge with those of their neighbours and friends. (McClintock noticed this among her roommates and friends while an undergraduate at Harvard in the early 1970s.)[25] What's more, in cultures where artificial light is not used, all the women will tend to ovulate at the full moon and menstruate at the new moon. Although this might be an effective method of birth control in non-literate societies (to prevent pregnancy, you must refrain from sex when the moon approaches fullness), it also suggests that unless women were controlled, paternity could not be established definitively.

If males were as promiscuous as females they would end up rather exhausted and haggard from running around hunting and gathering for all those babies who might *or might not* be their own. How were they to know, after all? In order to ensure that they did not die from exhaustion, males might 'naturally' tend toward monogamy, extracting from women promises of fidelity before offering up a lifetime of support and protection to the potential offspring from those unions. Such males might invent ideals of female chastity, refuse to marry (sexually commit to) women who were not virgins, and develop ideologies of domesticity that would keep women tied to the household and children to prevent them from indulging in their 'natural' disposition toward promiscuity.

In fact, there is some persuasive evidence on this front. Because getting pregnant is often difficult (it takes the average couple three or four months of regular intercourse to become pregnant), being a faithful and consistent partner would be a far better reproductive strategy for a male. 'Mate guarding' would enable him to maximize his chances of impregnating the woman and minimize the opportunities for other potential sperm bearers.[26]

Do the arguments of evolutionary psychology and sociobiology make sense? Can we explain human behaviour by recourse to biology? Critics say no. Ultimately, these theories may tidily describe the intricate mating rituals of fruit flies or brown birds or *seem* applicable to an urban singles bar or the dating dynamics of high school and college students, but the neatness of their explanations may obscure the distinctions between human behaviours and those of other organisms. Anne Fausto-Sterling notes the tendency of many sociobiologists to reason backward from human categories, like rape, adultery, and slavery, to non-human organisms, thus obscuring the meanings and causes of these categories.[27]

Sociobiologists have been criticized for their inability to locate the genetic imperative for certain behaviours or for exaggerating the nature of genetic predisposition. Biologist Richard Lewontin, a passionate critic of sociobiology, argues that, 'no evidence at all is presented for a genetic basis of these characteristics [religion, warfare, co-operation] and the arguments for their establishment by natural selection cannot be tested, since such arguments postulate hypothetical situations in human prehistory that are uncheck-able'. And fellow evolutionary biologist Stephen Jay Gould denies that there is 'any direct evidence for genetic control of specific human social behaviour'. 'Genes don't cause behaviours', writes the neuroprimatologist Robert Sapolsky. 'Sometimes, they influence them'.[28]

Some sociobiological arguments seem to assume that only one interpretation is possible from the evidence. But there could be others. Psychologists Carol Tavris and Carole Wade, for example, ask why parents—women or men—would 'invest' so much time and energy in their children when they could be out having a good time. Although sociobiologists argue that we are 'hard-wired' for such altruistic behaviour, because our children are the repository of our genetic material, Tavris and Wade suggest that it may be simple economic calculation: In return for taking care of our offspring when they are young and dependent, we expect them to take care of us when we are old and dependent—a far more compact and tidy explanation—though perhaps just as simplistic.[29]

Sociobiological arguments have also been condemned for selective use of species when making comparisons between animal and human behaviours. Which species should we use as the standard of measurement? Among chimpanzees and gorillas, for example, females usually leave home and transfer to new tribes, leaving the males at home with their mothers; among baboons, macaques, and langurs, however, it's the males who leave home to seek their fortune elsewhere. So which sex has the wander-lust, the natural predisposition to leave home? Sociobiologists tend to favour male-dominant species to demonstrate the ubiquity of male dominance. But there are other species. For example, baboons seem to be female-dominant, with females determining the stability of the group and deciding which males are trustworthy enough to be their 'friends'. Then there is the female chimpanzee. She has sex with lots of different males, often up to 50 times a day during peak estrus. She flirts, seduces, and does everything she can to attract males—whom she then abandons and moves on to the next customer. Would we say that such evidence demonstrates that females are genetically pro-grammed toward promiscuity and males toward monogamy? Bonobos, our closest pri-mate relatives, are remarkably communal, generous, and egalitarian—and very sexy. And sociobiologists tend to ignore other behaviour among primates. For example, sex-ual contact with same-sex others is 'part of the normal sexual repertoire of all animals, expressed variously over the lifetime of an individual'.[30] In fact, same-sex sexual contact is ubiquitous in the animal kingdom—ranging from bighorn sheep and giraffes, both of which have what can be described only as gay orgies, to dolphins, whales, manatees, and Japanese macaques and bonobos, which bond through 'lesbian' sexual choices. But few posit a natural predisposition toward homosexuality. 'Simple-minded analogies between human behaviour and animal behaviour are risky at best, irresponsibly goofy at worst', writes neurobiologist Simon LeVay, himself author of some rather risky, at best, studies on gay brains (discussed later).[31]

Sociobiology has often been used to provide us with what Rudyard Kipling called a 'just-so story'—an account that uses some evidence to tell us how, for example, an elephant got its trunk, or a tiger its stripes. Just-so stories are children's fables, under-stood by the reader to be fictions, but convenient, pleasant, and, ultimately, useful fic-tions. Evolutionary psychology, though a relatively new field, has overcome some of the limitations of sociobiology, but remains committed toward relatively monocausal explanations. While critiquing, perhaps justly, the sometimes fuzzy understandings of pure cultural determinists, evolutionary psychologists can be as determinist as any. Does this mean that these fields have no value? Not at all. To be sure, human beings are not fruit flies. But we *are* the products of our biology and of millions of years of evolution. Nature undoubtedly plays a role, though few scientists would today claim that it produces anything stronger than a tendency that interacts with cultural influences to produce behaviour. As Richard Bribiescas states in his recent 'evolutionary history' of men, 'are men the product of nature or nurture? The answer is yes'.[32] Both nature and nurture form us. The difficulty comes in interpreting the evidence, which has too often been yoked to simplistic—and, frankly, sexist—biological determinism.

Testing the Gendered Brain: Sex Differences in Spatial and Verbal Skills

At the turn of the twentieth century, women were found to be scoring higher than men on comprehensive examinations at New York University. Because scientists 'knew' that women are not as smart as men, some other explanation had to be sought. 'After all, men are more intellectual than women, examination papers or no examination papers', commented the dean of the college, R. Turner. 'Women have better memories and study harder, that's all. In tasks requiring patience and industry women win out. But when a man is both patient and industrious he beats a woman any day'. (It is interesting to see that women's drive, ambition, and industriousness were used against them but that men were not faulted for impulsiveness, impatience, and laziness.) In the 1920s, when IQ tests were invented, women scored higher on those tests as well. So the experimenters changed the questions.[33]

This early debate over women's intellectual fitness has been replaced by a discussion of innate, sex-based aptitudes that remains a galvanizing force for debates about not just aptitude, but gender roles. For example, in 2005, then-President of Harvard University, Lawrence Summers, suggested in a speech that the underrepresentation of women in sciences, engineering, and mathematics (SEM) might be the result of men's innately greater representation at the highest levels of mathematical ability. The controversy that followed led to Summers' resignation from his position in early 2006; recently, however, conservative commentator Christine Hoff Sommers argued that persistent gender differences in *interests* (which she traces to innate tendencies) are the cause of women's underrepresentation in SEM.[34]

Sommers refrained from arguing that women were less skilled in mathematics. Test scores have continued, however, to show gender differences in relation to certain abilities, generally summarized as verbal, visuospatial, and quantitative. In a recent international literacy study, fourth-grade girls were found to outperform boys significantly in all 33 countries in which the study was conducted. Similar results were found for 15-year-olds in a 2002 Program for International Student Assessment (PISA) study. In Canada, 2003 PISA assessments of 15-year-olds revealed girls' significantly superior performance in reading; the gap has persisted in the 2006 measurement.[35] However, what are we to make of the fact that boys until very recently continued to outperform girls on the verbal component of the SAT, the standard university admissions test used in the USA? Clearly, what is meant by 'verbal' ability can vary.

Visuospatial abilities are, likewise, not one ability. Differences in these abilities begin to appear at about 4.5 years of age and persist into adulthood, though they are not always significant. Still, girls tend to outperform boys in all subjects, including math, until senior high school. Is this because puberty somehow impairs girls' visuospatial development, or is it because senior-high math introduces advanced geometry and calculus, which demand superior visuospatial skills? Both arguments have been advanced. Some of the greatest visuospatial gender differences emerge when young adults are asked to perform mental rotation tasks, which require a subject to imagine what a three-dimensional object looks like when rotated. Young men perform significantly better, on average, than young women. Why does this matter? It matters because these tasks, along with other visuospatial tasks, are central to success in science, math, and engineering—along, of course, with other skills, including the verbal skills at which girls apparently excel.

It is true that males widely outnumber females at the genius end of the mathematical spectrum. Indeed, it seems that there is simply greater variability in male test scores; men outnumber women at *both* ends of the spectrum. Even here, though, there are some intriguing suggestions of change. Twenty years ago, boys outnumbered girls 13:1 among those precocious 13-year-olds with SAT math scores over 700. Now there are only 2.8 boys for every girl in this group; still a distinct advantage for boys 'at the genius end', but a dramatic change from the situation in the late 1980s.[36]

But we are still left with the conclusion that, on average, boys are more mathematically capable and females more verbally capable. Is this accurate? Janet Hyde, a psychologist at the University of Wisconsin, has conducted a massive amount of research on this question. She reviewed 165 studies of verbal ability that included information on over 1.4 million people and included writing, vocabulary, and reading comprehension. She found no gender differences in verbal ability. But when she analyzed 100 studies of mathematical ability, representing the testing of nearly four million students, she did find some modest gender differences. In the general studies, females outperformed males in mathematics, except in those studies designed only for the most precocious individuals.[37] What Hyde and her colleagues—and virtually every single study ever undertaken—found is that there is a far greater range of differences *among* males and *among* females than there is *between* males and females. That is to say that the variance within the group far outweighs the variance between groups, despite the possible differences between the mean scores of the two groups.

We are left with a bewildering number of studies that seem to confirm the existence of some gender differences, but raise more questions than they answer. Do differences that emerge at the age of 4.5 years reflect 'nature' or 'nurture'? How might having greater parental encouragement toward spatially-oriented outdoors play (or indoors play, for example with Lego) affect boys' generally superior visuospatial abilities? What are we to make of the fact that differences seem to change in relatively short periods of time, as reflected both in SAT scores and, in Canada, in provincial skills assessments?[38]

Ultimately, the most convincing answers will be those that examine the interactions between brain structure and socio-cultural factors. Clearly, we need to assess gender differences in cognitive ability in a way that respects the complexity of these fields. In the words of one careful recent metastudy,

> Just as there are many related questions about sex differences in test scores and career choices, there are many variables that work together to present a level of complexity that is inherent in understanding complicated questions about the way people think and behave . . . There is no single factor by itself that has been shown to determine sex differences in science and math. Early experience, biological constraints, educational policy, and cultural context each have effects, and these effects add and interact in complex and sometimes unpredictable ways.[39]

That's not exactly a media sound bite; but the point is that the media sound bites misrepresent good research and over publicize the bad, encouraging us to simplistic perspectives on gender difference that often end up—surprise!—reinforcing old gender stereotypes.

'His' Brain and 'Her' Brain

As we've seen, discussions of gender difference in cognitive abilities have often explained them as the result of men's and women's different brains. Focusing on the brain to explain cognitive and other differences between women and men has a long history. In the eighteenth century, experts measured women's brains and men's brains and argued that, because women's brains were smaller and lighter, they were inferior. Of course, it later turned out that women's brains were not smaller and lighter relative to body size and weight and thus were not predictive of any cognitive differences. The late nineteenth century was the first heyday of brain research, as researchers explored that spongy and gelatinous three-pound blob in order to discover the differences between whites and blacks, Jews and non-Jews, immigrants and 'normal' or 'real' Americans, criminals and law-abiding citizens. For example, the great sociologist Emile Durkheim succumbed to such notions when he wrote, 'with the advance of civilization the brain of the two sexes has increasingly developed differently . . . [T]his progressive gap between the two may be due both to the considerable development of the male skull and to a cessation and even a regression in the growth of the female skull'. And another researcher argued that the brain of the average 'grown-up Negro partakes, as regards his intellectual faculties, of the nature of the child, the female, and the senile White'. But despite the fact that none of these hypothesized differences turned out to have any scientific merit, they all satisfied political and racist assumptions.[40]

Brain research remains a particularly fertile field of study, and scientists continue their search for differences between women and men in their brains. One writes that 'many of the differences in brain function between the sexes are innate, biologically determined, and relatively resistant to change through the influences of culture'. Popular books proclaim just how decisive these differences are. The male brain is 'not so easily distracted by superfluous information'; it is a 'tidier affair' than the female brain, which appears 'less able to separate emotion from reason'.[41] (Notice that these statements did not say—though they easily might have, based on the same evidence—that the female brain is capable of integrating *more* diverse sources of information and *better* able to synthesize feelings and thought.)

That brain research fits neatly into preconceived ideas about men's and women's roles is hardly a coincidence. In most cases, brain researchers (like many other researchers) find exactly what they are looking for, and what they are looking for are the brain-based differences that explain the observable behavioural differences between adult women and men. One or two historical examples should suffice. The 'science' of craniology was developed in the late nineteenth century to record and measure the effect of skull and brain differences among different groups. But the scientists could never agree on exactly which measures of the brain to use. They *knew* that men's brains had to be shown to be superior, but different tests yielded different results. For example, if one used the ratio of brain surface to body surface, then men's brains would 'win'; but if one used the ratio of brain weight to body weight, then women's brains would appear superior. No scientist could rely on such ambiguity: More decisive methods had to be found to demonstrate that men's brains are superior.[42]

Contemporary brain research has moved beyond craniology, and in recent years has been able to study images of living brains rather than merely dissecting dead ones. This has led to an explosion of more sophisticated research, much of which has focused on three areas: (1) the differences between right hemisphere and left hemisphere, (2) the ways in which males and females use different parts of their brains for similar functions, and (3) the differences in the tissue that connects those hemispheres.[43]

Some scientists have noticed that the right and left hemispheres of the brain seem to be associated with different cognitive functions and abilities. Right-hemisphere dominance is associated with visual and spatial abilities, such as the ability to conceive of objects in space. Left-hemisphere dominance is associated with more practical functions, such as language and reading. Norman Geschwind and Peter Behan, for example, observed that sex differences begin in the womb when the male fetus begins to secrete testosterone that washes over the brain, selectively attacking parts of the left hemisphere and slowing its development. Thus, according to Geschwind, males tend to develop 'superior right hemisphere talents, such as artistic, musical, or mathematical talent'. Geschwind believes that men's brains are more **lateralized**, with one half dominating over the other, whereas women's brains are less lateralized, with both parts interacting more than in men's.[44]

One minor problem with this research, though, is that scientists can't seem to agree on which it is 'better' to have and, not so coincidentally, which side of the brain dominates for which sex. In fact, they keep changing their minds about which hemisphere is superior and then, of course, assigning that superior one to men. Originally, it was the *left* hemisphere that was supposed to be the repository of reason and intellect, whereas the right hemisphere was the locus of mental illness, passion, and instinct. So males were thought to be overwhelmingly more left-brained than right-brained. By the 1970s, though, scientists had determined that the truth lay elsewhere and that the right hemisphere was the source of genius, talent, creativity, and inspiration, whereas the left hemisphere was the site of ordinary reasoning, calculation, and basic cognitive function. Suddenly males were hailed as singularly predisposed toward right-brainedness.

One neuroscientist, Ruth Bleier, reanalyzed Geschwind and Behan's data and found that in over 500 fetal brains from 10 to 44 weeks of gestation, the authors had found no significant sex differences—this despite the much-trumpeted testosterone bath.[45]

Perhaps it wasn't which half of the brain dominates, but rather the degree to which the brain was lateralized—that is, had a higher level of differentiation between the two hemispheres—that determined sex differences. Buffery and Gray found that female brains were more lateralized than male brains, which, they argued, interfered with spatial functioning and made women less capable at spatial tasks. That same year, neuroscientist Jerre Levy found that female brains were *less* lateralized than male brains, and so he argued that *less* lateralization interferes with spatial functioning. (There is virtually no current evidence for either of these positions, but that has not stopped most writers from believing Levy's argument.)[46] One recent experiment shows how the desperate drive to demonstrate difference actually leads scientists to misinterpret their own findings. In 1997, a French researcher, Jean Christophe Labarthe, tried to demonstrate sex differences in visual and spatial abilities. Two-year-old boys and girls were asked to build a tower and a bridge. For those of average birth weight or better (greater than 2,500 grams), there was no difference whatever in ability to build a tower, although 21 per cent of the boys and only 8 per cent of the girls could build a bridge. For children whose birth weight was less than 2,500 grams, though, there were no differences for either skill. From these skimpy data, Labarthe concludes that boys are *naturally* better at bridge-building than girls—instead of the far more convincing (if less mediagenic) finding that birth weight affects visual and spatial functioning![47]

Some research suggests that males use only half their brains while performing some verbal tasks, such as reading or rhyming, whereas females draw on both sides of their brains. A recent experiment reveals as much about our desire for difference as about difference itself. Researchers from the Indiana University School of Medicine measured brain activity of 10 men and 10 women as they listened to someone read a John Grisham thriller. A majority of the men showed exclusive activity on the left side of their brains, whereas the majority of the women showed activity on both sides of the brain. Although some might suggest that this provides evidence to women who complain that their husbands are only 'half-listening' to them, the study mentions little about what the minority of males or females were doing—especially when the total number was only 10 to begin with. Besides, what if they were listening instead to a Jane Austen novel? Might the males have 'needed' both sides of their brain to figure out a plot that was a bit less action-packed? Would the females have been better able to relax that side of their brain that has to process criminal intrigue and murder?[48]

But don't the differences in mathematical ability and reading comprehension provide evidence of different sides of the brain being more dominant among females and males? Although few would dispute that different sides of the brain account for different abilities, virtually all humans, both men and women, use both sides of their brains to reasonably good effect. If so, argues Levy, 'then males may be at a double disadvantage in their emotional life. They may be emotionally less sophisticated. And because of the difficulty they may have in communicating between their two hemispheres, they may have restricted verbal access to their emotional world'.[49]

If these tacks weren't convincing, perhaps both males and females use both halves of their brains but use them *differently*. In their popular book detailing these brain differences, Jo Durden-Smith and Diane deSimone suggest that in the female left hemisphere, language tends to serve as a vehicle for communication, whereas for males that hemisphere is a tool for more visual-spatial tasks, like analytical reasoning. Similarly, they argue, in the right hemisphere males assign more neural space to visual-spatial tasks, whereas females have more room left over for other types of non-verbal communication skills, such as emotional sensitivity and intuition.[50]

But what if it's not the differences between the hemispheres, or even that males and females use the same hemispheres differently? Perhaps it's the connections *between* the hemispheres. Some researchers have explored the bundle of fibres known as the corpus callosum (CC) that connects the two hemispheres and carries information between them. A sub-region of this connecting network, the splenium, was found by one researcher to be significantly larger and more bulbous in shape in females. This study of 14 brains at autopsy suggested that this size difference reflected less hemispheric lateralization in females than in males and that this affected visual and spatial functioning. But subsequent research failed to confirm this finding. One researcher found no differences in the size of the corpus callosum between males and females. What's more, in magnetic resonance imaging (MRI) tests on living men and women, no differences were found between women and men.[51]

But that doesn't stop some popular writers from dramatic and facile extrapolation. Here's Robert Pool, from his popular work, *Eve's Rib*: 'Women have better verbal skills than men on average; the splenium seems to be different in women and men, in shape if not in size; and the size of the splenium is related to verbal ability, at least in women'. *Time* magazine claimed that women's wider CCs were 'possibly the basis for women's intuition'. And the science editor at the *New York Times* claimed that women's big CCs discredited 'feminist ideologues' who linked girls' poor math performance to environmental factors. A recent popular book by psychologist Michael Gurian claims that only females with 'boys' brains' can grow up to be architects because girls' brains are organized to promote nurturing, love, and caring for children. Such a reductive statement is insulting not only to women—as if mathematical reasoning and spatial ability were somehow 'beyond' them—but to men, especially to fathers who seem to be fully capable of nurturing children.[52]

Here we see how enormously complicated research—the CC's function and structure are not perfectly understood, nor is the visual identification of a 'tubular' or 'bulbous' CC as straightforward as it might seem[53]—is boiled down through popular culture to become definitive 'proof' of gender stereotype.

One of the most recent brain-sex studies to make a splash is Louanne Brizendine's popular study *The Female Brain,* a bestseller already translated into many languages and sold around the world. Despite Brizendine's credentials, the old problem of the rush to interpretation persists. What's more, this book (not peer-reviewed) offered questionable data such as the canard that women used 20,000 words per day against men's 7,000. Withdrawn from subsequent editions, this erroneous claim nonetheless exemplifies the sloppiness that characterizes what Cordelia Fine calls 'our crude attempts to locate social pressures in the brain'.[54]

In fact, there seems to be little consistent evidence for significant brain differences between women and men. Even neuropsychologist Doreen Kimura understands that 'in the larger comparative context, the similarities between human males and females far outweigh the differences'. And Jonathan Beckwith, professor of microbiology and molecular genetics at Harvard Medical School, argues that 'there is absolutely no way at this point that they can make a connection between any differences in brain structure and any particular behaviour pattern or any particular aptitude'.[55]

If these arguments rest on flimsy evidence and flimsier interpretations, why do they persist? One brain researcher, Marcel Kinsbourne, suggests that it is 'because the study of sex differences is not like the rest of psychology. Under pressure from the gathering momentum of feminism, and perhaps in backlash to it, many investigators seem determined to discover that men and women 'really' are different. It seems that if sex differences do not exist, then they have to be invented'. We might laugh at Brizendine's assertion that the female brain is 'a high performance emotion machine', but this 'neurosexism', as Fine calls it, is no laughing matter. She points out that the **palliative system justification motive** allows us, whether we are advantaged or disadvantaged, to justify and rationalize existing social arrangements. So instead of feeling angry and stressed because a husband doesn't anticipate children's needs, a woman who subscribes to sexed-brain theory can resign herself to the limitations of hubby's 'male brain'. At their best, studies of the sexed brain offer intriguing food for thought; at their worst, as Fine warns, theories of brain sex offer 'a tidy justification for accepting the status quo with clear conscience'.[56]

Estrogen and Testosterone: Hormonal Bases for Gender Differences

Sex differentiation faces its most critical events at two different phases of life: (1) fetal development, when primary sex characteristics are determined by a combination of genetic inheritance and the biological development of the embryo that will become a boy or a girl; and (2) puberty, when the bodies of boys and girls are transformed by a flood of sex hormones that causes the development of all the secondary sex characteristics. Breast development for girls, lowering of voices for boys, the development of facial hair for boys, and the growth of pubic hair for both are among puberty's most obvious signs.

A significant amount of biological research has examined each of these two phases in an attempt to chart the hormonal bases for sex differentiation. Much of this research has focused on the links between sex hormones and aggression in adolescent boys and on the links between sex hormones and aggression in women and on problems of normal hormonal development and the outcomes for gender identity development. Summarizing his reading of this evidence, sociologist Steven Goldberg writes that because 'men and women differ in their hormonal systems' and 'every society demonstrates patriarchy, male dominance and male attainment', it is logical to conclude that 'the hormonal renders the social inevitable'.[57]

Earlier, we saw how Geschwind and Behan found that during fetal development it is the 'testosterone bath' secreted by slightly more than half of all fetuses that begins sex differentiation in utero. Geschwind and Behan found that this testosterone bath selectively attacks the left hemisphere, which is why males favour the right hemisphere. But the implication of fetal hormonal research is that the secretion of sex hormones has a decisive effect on the development of gender identity and on the expressions of masculinity and femininity. We've all heard the arguments about how testosterone, the male sex hormone, is not only the driving force in the development of masculinity in males, but also the biological basis of human aggression, which is why males are more prone to violence than women. We should remember that women and men have both testosterone *and* estrogen, although typically in dramatically different amounts. On average, men do have about 10 times the testosterone level that women have, but the level among men varies greatly, and some women have levels higher than some men. Testosterone levels also vary from culture to culture and from man to man. The contortions that can result from measuring different populations are exemplified by a finger-length study conducted at the University of Bath (UK) in 2004. (As further discussed below, relative ring-index finger length is thought to correlate with prenatal hormone exposure.) In the study, male 'hard' scientists had significantly higher levels of estrogen and lower testosterone levels than did male social scientists. Female social scientists were also found to have higher-than-average testosterone levels. Interesting research, but surely not proof, as one on-line news source trumpeted, that 'Male Scientists Not So Manly'![58]

This perception of testosterone as the 'masculinity hormone' pervades the media and less-careful research. In recent years, research has suggested some correlations between levels of testosterone and body mass, baldness, self-confidence, and even the ability and willingness to smile. Some wildly inflated claims about the effects of testosterone have led to both popular misconceptions and a variety of medical interventions to provide remedies. In one recent book, for example, psychologist James Dabbs proclaims that 'testosterone increases masculinity', which was translated by a journalist into the equation that 'lust is a chemical' as he looked forward to his 'biweekly encounter with a syringe full of manhood'. And, of course, today men can purchase testosterone patches or AndroGel™, a product that seems to promise masculinity in a tube.[59]

Although the claims made for testosterone are often ridiculous, ministering less to science and more to men's fears of declining potency, there are some experiments on the relationship between testosterone and aggression that appear convincing. Males have higher levels of testosterone and higher rates of aggressive behaviour than females do. What's more, if you increase the level of testosterone in a normal male, his level of aggression will increase. Castrate him—or at least a rodent proxy of him—and his aggressive behaviour will cease entirely. Though this might lead one to think that testosterone is the cause of the aggression, Stanford neurobiologist Robert Sapolsky warns against such leaps of logic. He explains that if you take a group of five male monkeys arranged in a dominance hierarchy from one to five, then you can pretty much predict how everyone will behave toward everyone else. (The top monkey's testosterone level will be higher than that of the monkeys below him, and levels will decrease down the line.) Number three, for example, will pick fights with numbers four and five, but will avoid and run away from number one and number two. If you give number three a massive infusion of testosterone, he will likely become more aggressive—but only toward number four and number five, with whom he has now become an absolute violent torment. He will still avoid number one and number two, demonstrating that the 'testosterone isn't causing aggression, it's exaggerating the aggression that's already there'.[60]

It turns out that testosterone has what scientists call a 'permissive effect' on aggression: It doesn't cause it, but it does facilitate and enable the aggression that is already there. What's more, testosterone is produced *by* aggression, so that the correlation between the two may, in fact, have the opposite direction than previously thought. In his thoughtful book, *Testosterone and Social Structure*, Theodore Kemper notes several studies in which testosterone levels were linked to men's experiences. In studies of tennis players, medical students, wrestlers, nautical competitors, parachutists, and officer candidates, winning and losing determined levels of testosterone, so that the levels of the winners rose dramatically, whereas those of the losers dropped or remained the same. Kemper suggests that testosterone levels vary depending upon men's experience of either dominance, 'elevated social rank that is achieved by overcoming others in a competitive confrontation', or eminence, where elevated rank 'is earned through socially valued and approved accomplishment'. Significantly, men's testosterone levels prior to either dominance or eminence could not predict the outcome; it was the experience of rising status due to success that led to the elevation of the testosterone level. (These same experiences lead to increases in women's testosterone levels as well.) [61]

Several recent studies have made the earlier facile correlation quite a bit more interesting. A Finnish study found no difference in testosterone levels between violent and non-violent men. But among the violent men, levels of testosterone did correlate with levels of hostility: The violent men with higher levels of testosterone were diagnosed with antisocial personality disorder. This supports the notion that testosterone has a permissive rather than causative effect on aggression, because it correlates with hostility *only* among the violent men. And a UCLA researcher found that men with *low* testosterone were more likely to be angry, irritable, and aggressive than men with normal or high levels of testosterone. Although Sapolsky's statement that 'testosterone is probably a vastly overrated hormone' may be an understatement, these last studies raise some troubling concerns, especially when compared with the questions about sexual orientation and hormone levels (discussed later).[62]

Some recent research approaches the relationship between testosterone and aggression from the other side. It turns out that marriage and fatherhood tend to depress the amount of testosterone in a man's body. In one study of 58 Boston-area men (nearly all of whom were Harvard graduate or professional students), unmarried men had higher levels than did married men, and that difference increased only slightly when the married man had a child. Those married men with children who spent a lot of time doing child care had even lower levels. Actually, the testosterone levels differed only slightly, and only in the evening; samples taken in the morning, when one had rested, showed no differences at all. Yet from these results, massive leaps of logic followed.

Because testosterone facilitates competition and aggression, fathers with children were opting out of this typically masculine activity. 'Maybe it's very adaptive for men to suppress irritability', commented Peter Ellison, one of the study's authors. 'Maybe the failure to do that places the child at risk'. Maybe. Or maybe Harvard graduate students have lower testosterone levels than other men in Boston. Or maybe by the end of the day, trying to balance work and family life, an involved father is simply depleted. (Stress reduces levels of testosterone.) From such tiny and inconsistent differences, one should leap to no conclusions whatever. This is particularly true given the huge variations in normal testosterone levels within individual men, among men in industrialized nations, and between men in industrialized nations and men in other parts of the world (whose average levels, for unknown reasons, are much lower). We simply don't know what a globally 'normal' level of testosterone might be and what causes the vast variations. We also don't know what an optimal level of testosterone might be, given the mixed effects of the hormone and its apparent potential to increase risks of certain illnesses.[63]

Despite this, some therapists prescribe testosterone for men as a sort of chemical tonic, designed to provide the same sort of pep and 'vim and vigour' that tonics and cure-alls promised at the turn of the twentieth century. Happy consumers swear by the results, and some therapists have even diagnosed a medically treatable malady (which should enable it to be covered by insurance) called 'andropause' or 'male menopause', treatable by hormone-replacement therapy for men. Health Canada's 2002 approval of Androgel™ was trumpeted as bringing relief to the 'one million Canadian men [who] have testosterone insufficiency', described as a 'medical condition linked to depressed mood and fatigue, reduced lean body mass and muscle strength, decreased bone density—which can lead to osteoporosis—lower interest in sex, and erectile dysfunction'. Despite the documented horrors of this widespread malady, few Canadians were able to either identify the medical condition (andropause) associated with low testosterone or the many symptoms associated with it. Fortunately, Solvay Pharma's educative efforts seem to have convinced physicians, at least if the claim that 46 per cent of polled physicians treat andropause can be believed.[64]

Meanwhile, body builders, athletes, and men seeking fat loss consume testosterone in the form of anabolic steroids. Testosterone in this form is a controlled substance, and its distribution or purchase without a prescription is illegal. Moreover, as most Canadians know, anabolic steroid use is banned in amateur sport. In 1988, one of Canada's greatest track athletes of all time, Ben Johnson, was stripped of his Olympic gold medal after testing positive for Stanazolol, a steroid taken orally. Such steroids remain widely available across Canada despite their illicit status.

Testosterone's effect on male sexual drive has been discussed almost as much as its effects on aggression and muscle mass. Clearly, testosterone has some effect: castrate a male guinea pig, and he stops mounting females. Administer testosterone, and he embraces his old role with enthusiasm. However, some intact male guinea pigs, in one classic experiment, showed much less interest in mating than others, despite similar levels of the manly hormone. And when the unenthusiastic breeders received more testosterone, they didn't get any sexier. So more testosterone doesn't necessarily equal more sex drive, as has been proved by experiments on men with normal testosterone levels. (There is, however, some evidence that testosterone increases sex drive in men with extremely low testosterone levels as the result of various traumas or disorders.)[65]

Despite its reputation as the manly hormone, testosterone is now seen as a panacea for women, particularly as regards their libido. Low testosterone levels have been linked to low libido in women, despite little understanding of what might constitute a 'normal' female libido. Some have also suggested that competition and aggression in women are linked to testosterone. Dr Patricia Schreiner-Engel, for example, has found higher testosterone levels in successful executive women than in homemakers, and has suggested that Queen Elizabeth I, England's sixteenth-century 'Virgin Queen', may have been a 'High-T' woman! Dr Barbara Sherwin of McGill University has also conducted research linking testosterone to increased libido in women. Though Dr Sherwin currently focuses on estrogen and its relationship to cognition, her research on the positive effects of testosterone supplementation has encouraged physicians to add a 'tiny dose' of testosterone to estrogen-based hormone replacement regimes for women, as the *New York Times* reported.[66]

Testosterone is a recent arrival on the women's health scene. The hormone most frequently associated with women is, of course, estrogen. (Interestingly, when the male and female sex hormones were named, male hormones, including testosterone, received the name 'androgens', roughly translatable as 'man-builder'. The female equivalent was termed estrogen or 'estrus-builder'.) Like men's testosterone levels, women's estrogen levels naturally fluctuate. Through a women's menstrual cycle, they rise and decline in relatively standard ways. This has led to interesting studies regarding estrogen's role in cognition and sexual desire throughout a woman's monthly cycle. By far the greatest interest in estrogen, however, has come from its precipitous decline in postmenopausal women. These women, by the middle of the twentieth century, were diagnosed as 'estrogen-deficient'. In the late twentieth century, North American women by the millions were prescribed 'estrogen replacement therapy' (ERT), which promised women an end to the symptoms of menopause along with protection from heart disease, improvement in mental clarity, and, not least, a more youthful appearance. 'Never before [had] a drug regimen been proposed on such a scale', writes Natalie Angier.[67] In 2002, the US National Institutes of Health prematurely halted a long-term trial of ERT because of alarming evidence that it significantly increased women's risk of heart disease, invasive breast cancers, stroke, and blood clots.[68] Since then, ERT has been prescribed more cautiously, but we still need to know more about estrogen and how it works. Are women over 50 really 'estrogen-deficient'? Why do women outside North America seem to need replacement therapy so much less than we do? Much attention is now being paid to the perimenopause, the period preceding the cessation of menstruation, which some researchers believe may begin as early as the age of 35. Once again, the culprit is estrogen. This time, it's not its decline that's the problem, but perhaps, an erratic and surging supply of the hormone.

Research on premenstrual syndrome (PMS) has provided yet another example of the way that hormones work—or are presumed to work—within the female body. During the days just before menstruation, some women seem to exhibit symptoms of dramatic and wildly unpredictable mood changes, outbursts of violence, anger, and fits of crying. Alec Coppen and Neil Kessel studied 465 women and observed that they were more irritable and depressed during the premenstrual phase than during midcycle. Such behaviours have led physicians to label these symptoms 'premenstrual syndrome'. PMS has been listed as a disease in the *Diagnostic and Statistical Manual of Mental Disorders (DSM-IV)* of the American Psychiatric Association, which guides physicians (and insurance companies) in treating illnesses. Despite the relative rarity of pathological PMS, the term has entered popular culture, so that any woman who is irritable on a given day is said to be 'PMSing'. PMS has even been used as a criminal defence strategy. Two British women, arguing that PMS is a form of temporary insanity, have used PMS as a successful defence in their trials for the murders of their male partners.

The politics of PMS parallels the politics of testosterone. 'If you had an investment in a bank, you wouldn't want the president of your bank making a loan under those raging hormonal influences at that particular period', one physician noted. 'There are just physical and psychological inhabitants that limit a female's potential'. Happily, PMS occurs for only a few days a month, whereas unpredictably high levels of testosterone in men may last all month. Perhaps these presumed bank investors might want to rethink their investment strategies. Or consider this observation by feminist writer Gloria Steinem:

> During those days immediately preceding her menstrual period (the PMS days), a woman's estrogen level drops to its lowest point in the monthly cycle. Thus, just before menstruation, women, at least hormonally, more closely resemble men than at any other point in their cycle![69]

Research on the 'sex hormones' makes it clear that they have important effects throughout our lives. But once again, these effects are too often oversimplified in ways that ignore the complexity of human behaviour, sexuality, and health itself. We need to understand mood, sexuality, and behaviour as complex admixtures of *many* influences, including the hormonal.

'As Nature Made Him'?

One of the most famous cases that purports to prove how biological sex is the sole foundation for gender identity concerned a Manitoba boy, Bruce Reimer. In 1966, Bruce and his identical twin Brian underwent cauterization circumcisions in a Winnipeg hospital. Brian's circumcision went smoothly, but Bruce's went terribly wrong, and his penis was nearly burned off. His distraught parents brought him to Johns Hopkins University Medical Center where, at the age of 21 months and under the aegis of Dr. John Money, he was surgically 'transformed' into a girl. Over the next decades, the newly named 'Brenda' was faced with several more aggressive (or abusive) surgical procedures, annual visits to Dr. Money's clinic, and massive doses of female sex hormones, while her parents struggled to conceal Bruce's story and raise Brenda as a girl. And not just 'a' girl—but a very frilly, feminine, and dainty girl at that. (Even though Brenda described herself as a tomboy as a child, Brenda's mother was determined that her 'daughter' be 'polite and quiet' and 'ladylike'.)

Despite their becoming poster children for Money's claims that gender identity is more malleable than originally thought and, indeed, that it can be changed, both twins grew up depressed and unhappy. Eventually, Brenda's situation was revealed to a sexologist, Dr. Milton Diamond at the University of Hawaii, a long-time foe of John Money's unorthodox ideas and practices. Under Diamond's supervision, Brenda reclaimed his male gender identity, renamed himself 'David', and became the man he said he felt he always was. 'Suddenly it all made sense why I felt the way I did', he told a journalist who eventually wrote a best-selling book about his life. 'I wasn't some sort of weirdo. I wasn't crazy'. David eventually married and adopted three children. His story, passionately told by journalist John Colapinto, became a book, *As Nature Made Him: The Boy Who Was Raised as a Girl*, and a TV documentary. Colapinto argues forcefully that David's case demonstrates that nature trumps nurture, that biology is destiny, and that meddling with Mother Nature is always disastrous. The case 'provides stark evidence that a person's brain predetermines sexual identity—not one's anatomy or social environment', was how a writer in the *Los Angeles Times* put it.[70]

But is the case that simple, that no matter how much tinkering one does, nature always trumps nurture? Any scientist should be wary of generalizing from a single case—especially a case with so many other factors that might have influenced the outcome. How would you feel about yourself, and your gender identity, if you were constantly being dragged to some hospital every few months throughout your early childhood, had your testicles removed while your damaged penis was left intact, had your genitals poked and prodded and surgically 'repaired', and if everyone paid what would no doubt feel like an inordinate amount of attention to your genitalia without ever telling you why? If your father became an alcoholic, your mother clinically depressed, your twin brother severely mentally ill? Drs Money and Diamond believed that a child without a complete penis could not possibly be a boy, and that a girl must be feminine—demur, restrained, and dressed in frilly clothes. Despite their apparent belief in gender malleability, they were rigid and doctrinaire. Were our gender roles more elastic, we wouldn't try so obsessively to coerce such behaviours from our children, who express far more variability than our norms about proper gender behaviour. Surely our gender identity is the result of a complex interaction of genetics, brain chemistry, hormones, and our immediate familial environment, nestled within a more general social and cultural milieu. No one cause of something so complex and variable as gender identity could possibly be extracted, especially from one such troubling case.[71]

Gay Brains, Gay Genes, or Gay Hormones?

One of the most interesting and controversial efforts by scientists who study the biological origins of behaviour has been the search for biological origins of sexual orientation. Recent research on brain structure and endocrinological research on hormones have suggested a distinctly homosexual 'essence', which will emerge regardless of the cultural conditions that shape its opportunities and experiences.

In recent decades, biological research has emerged as central in the demonstration of the fundamental and irreducible differences between homosexuals and heterosexuals.

And it should not surprise us that researchers have found what they hoped to find—that homosexual men's brains and hormone levels more closely resemble those of females than those of heterosexual males. Science, again, has attempted to prove that the stereotypes of gay men as 'effeminate' and lesbians as 'manly' are based not in cultural fears and prejudices, but in biological fact. For example, in the 1970s, the German researcher Gunter Dorner, director of the Institute for Experimental Endocrinology at Humboldt University in Berlin and his associates found that homosexual men possess a 'predominantly female-differentiated brain', which is caused by a 'deficiency' of androgen during the hypothalamic organizational phase in prenatal life and which may be activated to homosexual behaviour by normal or about-normal androgen levels in adulthood.[72]

More recently, Simon LeVay focused on the structure of the brain in an effort to uncover the etiology of homosexuality. Hoping that science can demonstrate 'the origins of sexual orientation at a cellular level', LeVay gives no credence to environmental determination of sexuality. 'If there are environmental influences, they operate very early in life, at the fetal or early-infancy stages, when the brain is still putting itself together', he argues. 'I'm very much skeptical of the idea that sexual orientation is a cultural thing'. LeVay noticed that, among primates, experimental lesions in the medial zone of the hypothalamus of monkeys did not impair sexual functioning but did suppress mounting attempts by the male monkeys on female monkeys. He also noticed that the size of this region of the brain is different in men and women. In his experiment, LeVay examined the brain tissues of 41 deceased people. Nineteen of these had died of AIDS and were identified as part of the risk group 'homosexual and bisexual men'; 16 other men were presumed to be heterosexual because there was no evidence to the contrary (6 had died of AIDS and the other 10 from other causes); and six were women who were presumed heterosexual (one had died of AIDS). These brains were treated and compared. Three of the four sections revealed no differences, but a fourth section, the anterior hypothalamus, a region about the size of a grain of sand, was found to be different among the groups. LeVay found that the size of this area among the presumably heterosexual men was approximately twice the size of that area for the women and the presumably gay men.[73]

But several problems in his experiments give us pause. LeVay and his colleagues failed to measure the cell number or density because 'of the difficulty in precisely defining the neurons belonging to INAH 3', the area of the brain involved. A number of the 'homosexual' men (5 of the 19) and of the women (2 of the 6) appeared to have areas of the brain as large as those of the presumed heterosexual men. And in three of the presumed heterosexual men, this area of the brain was actually very small. What's more, the sources of his data were widely varied. All the gay men in his sample died of AIDS, a disease known to affect the brain. (Reduced testosterone occurs among AIDS patients, and this alone may account for the different sizes.) And all the brains of the 'gay' men were preserved in a formaldehyde solution that was of a different strength than the solution in which the brains of the heterosexual men were preserved, because of the fears of HIV transmission, although there was no effort to control for the effect of the formaldehyde on the organs. It is possible that what LeVay may have been measuring was the combined effect of HIV infection and preservation in high densities of formaldehyde solution on post-mortem brain structure, rather than differences in brain structure between living heterosexuals and homosexuals. A recent effort to replicate LeVay's findings failed, and one researcher went further, suggesting that 'INAH-3 is not necessary for sexual behaviour in men, whether they chose men or women as their partners'.[74]

More recently, researchers have found that the brains of male transsexuals more closely resembled the brains of women than those of heterosexual, 'normal' men. Dutch scientists at the Netherlands Institute for Brain Research examined the hypothalamus sections of 42 men and women, 6 of whom were known to be transsexuals, and 9 of whom were gay men, whereas the rest were presumed to be heterosexual. Again they found that the hypothalamus in the transsexual men and women was smaller than those in the heterosexual or homosexual men. Although they were careful *not* to interpret their findings in terms of sexual orientation because the heterosexual and homosexual men's brains were similar, they did take their research to signal sex differences because the male transsexuals were men who felt themselves to be women. However, it may also be a result of transsexual surgery and the massive amounts of female hormones that the male transsexuals took, which might have had the effect of shrinking the hypothalamus, just as the surgery and hormones also resulted in other anatomical changes (loss of facial and body hair, breast growth, etc.).[75]

Another study suggests that gay men are different from heterosexual men and more like heterosexual women. A group of Swedish researchers exposed heterosexual men and women and gay men to chemicals derived from male and female sex hormones (extracted from sweat glands in the armpit for males and urine for females) and recorded which parts of the brain were most visibly stimulated on a PET scan. The brains of all three groups reacted similarly to various normal scents, like lavender or cedar: They recorded the information in the part of the brain that responds to olfactory sensations only. But when they were presented with testosterone, the part of the brain most closely associated with sexual activity (the hypothalamus) was triggered, but it remained quiescent among the heterosexual men; they responded only in the olfactory region. When presented with estrogen, by contrast, the females and gay men registered only in the olfactory area, whereas the heterosexual men responded strongly in the hypothalamus.[76] Although the response among journalists was a collective 'Eureka! The gay brain', the researchers themselves were far more circumspect about the meaning of the results. The different pattern of activity could be a cause of sexual orientation—or a consequence, Dr. Savic told a reporter. 'We cannot tell if the different pattern is cause or effect. The study does not give any answer to these crucial questions'.[77] For another thing, the research did not measure anything about lesbians, so we don't know what sorts of armpit scents would drive their hypothalamuses wild with desire.

More recently, two members of the same team performed new research that measured brain asymmetry using MRI imaging in a group of 90 heterosexual and homosexual men and women. The functional connection of subjects' brains was also measured, using PET scans that assessed blood flow during rest while breathing unscented air (no sexy hormones this time!). The researchers found that the brains of gay men resembled those of heterosexual women, while lesbian women's brains more closely resembled those of straight men. The researchers urged caution in interpreting their findings, stating that the study 'contributes to the ongoing discussion about sexual orientation by showing that homosexual men and women differed from the same-sex controls... in two mutually independent cerebral variables, which, in contrast to those studied previously, were not related to sexual attraction'. Once again, however, media commentators rushed to reductive conclusions. *Time* magazine led with an article called 'What the Gay Brain Looks Like', which quoted Dr Eric Vilain, a genetics professor at UCLA, as he mused on how gay men display only some 'feminized' brain traits, since they prefer younger partners (like heterosexual men) and engage willingly in casual sex (like heterosexual men), while women 'gravitate to older partners'. Further research, Dr Vilain suggested, would reveal that some parts of gay men's brains—the younger-partner area, presumably—remained masculinized.[78]

One recent study did examine lesbians' brain chemistry and found that the sounds emitted by the inner ears of lesbians fall in between the sounds emitted by the inner ears of men and heterosexual women, forming a sort of 'intermediate' zone between the two groups. (Lesbian emissions were stronger than men's but weaker than heterosexual women's.) Before we get carried away, though, we should mention that the research found no differences whatever between gay men and heterosexual men on such emissions.[79] 'You can't assume that because you find a structural difference in the brain that it was caused by genes', says researcher Marc Breedlove. 'You don't know how the difference got there.' Another adds that we 'are still unsure whether these signs are causes or effects'.[80] Maybe we should be more concerned about the sounds of bias and false difference that flow *into* our ears than the sounds that flow *out* of them. Again, the point is not that the brain plays no role in behaviour. However, the mad rush to identify the brain's control over every aspect of human behaviour—for example, a real or assumed preference for partners of a certain age—cheapens the value of basic research and, at its worst, provides support for tired stereotypes and questionable social policy.

Another attempt to show that sexual orientation has its basis in biology involves the so-called gay gene. For example, research on pairs of monozygotic twins (twins born from a single fertilized egg that splits in utero) suggests that identical twins have a statistically far higher likelihood of having similar sexualities (either both gay or both straight) than do dizygotic twins (twins born from two separate fertilized eggs). One genetic study involved 85 pairs of twins in the 1940s and 1950s. All 40 pairs of monozygotic twins studied shared the same sexual orientation; if one twin was heterosexual, the other was also; if one twin was homosexual, so, too, was the other twin. Such data were so perfect that subsequent scientists have doubted their validity.[81]

More recently, Elke Eckert and her colleagues found that in fifty-five pairs of twins, five had at least one gay member and that in a sixth pair, one twin was bisexual. Michael Bailey and Richard Pillard collected data on gay men who were twins, as well as on gay men who had adoptive brothers who lived in the same home before age two. The 161 respondents were drawn from responses to ads placed in gay periodicals and included 56 monozygotic twins, 54 dizygotic twins, and 57 adoptive brothers. Respondents were asked about their brothers' sexuality and were asked for permission to contact those brothers. About three quarters of the brothers participated in the study. Bailey and Pillard found that in 52 per cent of the monozygotic pairs, in 22 per cent of the dizygotic pairs, and in 11 per cent of the adoptive pairs, both brothers were homosexual or bisexual.[82]

Such findings were widely interpreted to mean that there is some biological foundation for men's sexual contact with other men. But several problems remain. The study was generated from self-identified homosexuals, not from a broad sample of twins.[83] What's more, there was no independent measure of the environment in which these boys grew up, so that what Bailey and Pillard might have measured is the predisposition of the environments to produce similar outcomes among twins. After all, biological predisposition should be more compelling than one-half. And the fact that fraternal twins of homosexual men were twice as likely as other biological brothers would mean that environmental factors *must* be present, because dizygotic twins share no more genetic material than other biological brothers. The increase in concordance could be just as convincingly explained by a continuum of similarity of treatment of brothers—from adoptive to biological to dizygotic to monozygotic—without any genetic component whatever.

Actually, what is most interesting in the twin studies is how little concordance there actually is. After all, having identical genetic material and the same family and environmental conditions should produce a greater concordance than, at best, half. There is, however, some evidence that homosexual orientations tend to occur more frequently in family constellations. Pillard and psychologist James Weinrich questioned 50 heterosexual and 51 homosexual men and their siblings. Only 4 per cent of the heterosexual men had brothers who were homosexual (the same percentage that had been found by Kinsey's studies in the 1940s), whereas about 22 per cent of the gay men had gay or bisexual brothers. 'This is rather strong evidence that male homosexuality clumps in families', said Weinrich, although there was no indication of the biological or genetic origin of this relationship. And the correlation, incidentally, did not hold true for women, as about the same percentage of the sisters of both groups said they had sisters who were lesbian. None said his or her parents were gay. This gender disparity might suggest that more than biology is at work here and that gender identity may have more to do with inequality than with genetics, but the research is nonetheless suggestive.[84]

Recently, sociologists Peter Bearman and Hannah Bruckner examined all the studies that purported that opposite-sex twins are more likely to be gay than twins who are of the same sex. They concluded that there are no hormonal connections whatever and that the level of sex stereotyping in early childhood socialization is a far better predictor of behavioural outcome than whether or not one has a twin of the opposite sex. Predicting sexual orientation from that evidence is sort of like predicting penis size from shoe size—there's not even a correlation, but if there were, it would be specious.[85]

The quest for a genetic link to homosexuality was predated by research on the relationship between hormones and homosexuality, which began almost as soon as 'sex hormones' were identified. At the turn of the twentieth century, many theorists held that homosexuals were 'inverts', creatures of one sex (their 'true' sex) trapped in the body of the other. Some argued that homosexuality was 'caused' by hormonal imbalances in utero that left males effeminate and therefore desiring men and left women masculine and therefore desiring women. In the 1970s, Dorner and his associates argued that low levels of testosterone during fetal development, a rather tepid hormonal bath, would predispose males toward homosexuality. If rats did not receive enough of their appropriate sex hormone during fetal development, 'then something would go wrong with the formation of the centres and with later sexual behaviour,' reported two journalists. 'Adult rats would behave in ways like members of the opposite sex. They would become, in a sense, "homosexual" '.[86]

Such research fit neatly with the era's anti-gay political agenda, suggesting as it did that male homosexuality in human beings was the result of insufficient prenatal masculine hormones or inadequate masculinity. Treatment of homosexuality—indeed, perhaps its cure—might be effected simply by injecting higher doses of testosterone into these men, whose recharged virility would transform them into heterosexuals with higher sex drives. When such an experiment was attempted, researchers found that the men's sex drive did indeed increase as a result of the testosterone injections. However, the object of their lusts did not change: They simply desired more sex with men! Hormone levels may affect sexual urges, and especially the intensity or frequency of sexual activity, but they are empirically and logically irrelevant to studies of sexual object choice.

Could prenatal stress account for a disposition toward homosexuality? In another series of studies, Dorner and his colleagues argued that more homosexual men are born during wartime than during peacetime. Their evidence for this claim was that a high proportion of the 865 men treated for venereal disease in six regions of the German Democratic Republic were born between 1941 and 1947. They theorized that because prenatal stress leads to a 'significant decrease in plasma testosterone levels' among rat fetuses, which also leads to increased bisexual or homosexual behaviours among the adult rats, why not among humans? Dorner theorized that war leads to stress, which leads to a lowering of androgens in the male fetuses, which encourages the development of a homosexual orientation. Based on this trajectory, Dorner concluded that the prevention of war 'may render a partial prevention of the development of sexual deviation'. (Well, perhaps—but only because wartime tends to place men together in foxholes without women, where they may engage in homosexual activity more frequently than during peacetime.)[87]

Even if these data were convincing, a purely endocrine account fails to satisfy. For example, one could just as easily construct a purely psychodynamic theory: In wartime, children tend to grow up more often without a father or to be separated from other members of the family. If homosexuality really occurs more frequently during wartime, it would be just as reasonable to take this as 'proof 'of certain psychodynamic theories of homosexuality, e.g., the lack of a father, a particularly close bond between mother and son.

Another just-so story? Perhaps. But, then, so are explanations about aggregate levels of testosterone during wartime. Although these arguments may not be convincing, they continue to exert significant influence over our commonsense explanations of gender difference.

The most interesting recent research on the relationship between prenatal hormones and sexual orientation has been carried out by University of California at Berkeley psychologist Marc Breedlove and his students. Breedlove is a far more careful researcher than most, and he is also far more cautious in the claims he makes. Breedlove measured the lengths of the index and ring fingers (second and fourth digits) and calculated the ratios between them for both heterosexual women and lesbians and for gay and heterosexual men. It's well known that for average women, the two fingers are usually the same length, whereas among average men, the index finger is more often significantly shorter than the fourth. This is assumed to be an effect of prenatal androgens on male fetuses. Breedlove found that the ratio between the two fingers was more 'masculine' among the lesbians than the heterosexual women; that is, that lesbians' index fingers were significantly shorter than their ring fingers. He found no differences between gay and straight men (both were equally 'masculine'), although another study did find significant differences between the two, with gay men's finger ratios being somewhat more 'masculine' than heterosexual men.[88]

Breedlove believed that the difference between lesbians and heterosexual women was due to the effect of increased prenatal androgens among the lesbians—thus rendering them more 'masculine'. Now this accords with traditional stereotypes that suggest that homosexuality is related to gender nonconformity. But one must be careful about overstating these stereotypes, because Breedlove found the exact opposite among men. Breedlove also found a relationship between birth order and sexual orientation for men. The greater the number of older brothers a man had, the higher the likelihood that he would be homosexual. In fact, subsequent researchers have suggested that each additional elder brother that a man has increases the likelihood that he will be gay by about 30 per cent. Breedlove hypothesized that this also was the result of prenatal androgenization of subsequent children. Although this might not appear controversial, it accords with other studies that find that gay men's levels of testosterone are significantly *higher* than those of heterosexual men. That is, gay men are more 'real men' than are straight men. (Other research that supports the argument that gay men are 'hypermasculine' includes studies that find that gay men's penis size is greater than that of straight men, despite the fact that gay men undergo puberty a bit earlier and are therefore slightly shorter than straight men; and that gay men report significantly higher amounts of sexual behaviour.) 'This calls into question all of our cultural assumptions that gay men are feminine', said Breedlove in an interview—a thought that some biological determinists and their political allies will not find especially comforting.[89]

This sort of research does give us pause. Brock University psychologist Anthony Bogaert did a similar study in which he found that there was no effect on sexual orientation by unrelated siblings in the same household (they had to be biological) but that older brothers who did not live with a person did influence the chances of that person's being gay. This seems to rule out socialization effects (older non-related brothers 'recruiting' the youngest through sexual coercion) or the outcome of seemingly harmless sexual play. Bogaert offers no speculation about why this might be the case or even about exactly what sorts of physiological mechanisms cause it. It might be nature's way of reducing the number of males competing for increasingly scarce (with large broods of males) females. If so, it not only signals some biological elements to the origins of sexual orientation, but also makes a strong case for the naturalness of homosexuality.[90] At least male homosexuality. No birth order phenomena have been posited as predictors of lesbianism.

Clearly, there is some evidence for biological factors in sexual orientation. Still, neither a gay brain, gay gene, nor gay hormone explanation fully satisfies, and we would be well advised to consider multiple factors, both biological and cultural, when we ponder what makes us gay—or what makes us straight.

Hormonal and Chromosomal Abnormalities: Research on the Intersexed

Much of the research on the biological basis of sex difference has been done by inference—that is, by examining cases of chromosomal abnormality or cases where hormones did not work 'properly,' thus giving a fetus too much of the 'wrong' hormone or too little of the 'right' one. These and other conditions result in some degree of sexual ambiguity, whether apparent at birth or evident only later in life. Once described as 'hermaphrodites', people affected by hormonal and chromosomal abnormalities are now described as **intersexed,** and account for as many as 1.7 per cent of all births.[91] In the twentieth century, it became possible to 'correct' the structural differences seen in intersexed children using both surgery and hormone therapy. By 1969, when Christopher Gordon and Ronald Dewhurst published *The Intersexual Disorders,* a uniform approach had developed. Thus ambiguous children were 'assigned' to the sex judged appropriate. Despite consensus on the need to correct the abnormalities of these children, they were seen as an appropriate research group—in some ways an ideal group—through which to study 'normal' sex differences. After all, if a baby girl's genitals were masculinized, perhaps she would exhibit other signs of masculinity, thus 'proving' that nature trumped nurture.

In some of the more celebrated research on fetal hormone development, Money and Ehrhardt reported on girls who had **androgenital syndrome** (AGS)—a preponderance of male hormones (androgens) in their systems at birth—and on another set of girls whose mothers had taken progestins during pregnancy. All 25 girls had masculine-appearing genitalia and had operations to 'correct' their genitals. The AGS girls also were given constant cortisone treatments to enable their adrenal glands to function properly. Money and Ehrhardt's findings were interesting. The girls and their mothers reported a higher frequency of tomboy behaviour in these girls. They enjoyed vigorous outdoor games and sports, preferred toy cars and guns to dolls, and attached more importance to career plans than to marriage. However, they showed no more aggression or fighting than other girls. Later research seemed to confirm the notion that 'prenatal androgen is one of the factors contributing to the development of temperamental differences between and within the sexes'.[92]

Appearances, however, can be deceiving. Medical researcher Anne Fausto-Sterling argues that several problems make Ehrhardt and her colleagues' research less convincing than it at first may seem. The research suffered from 'insufficient and inappropriate' controls: Cortisone is a powerful drug, and the AGS girls underwent calamitous surgery (including **clitoridectomy**), and there were no independent measures of the effects. Further, the 'method of data collection is inadequate' because it was based entirely on interviews with parents and children, with no impartial direct observation of these reported behaviours. Finally, 'the authors do not properly explore alternative explanations of their results', such as parental expectations and differential treatment of their very 'different' children.[93]

Androgenital syndrome is now more commonly described as **congenital adrenal hyperplasia** (CAH), an enzyme disorder that impairs normal hormonal development and produces, in (chromosomal) females, masculinization or ambiguous genitalia. CAH is one of the most common causes of intersexuality. Though CAH girls have the potential to bear children, their genitals may look more like those of boys than those of 'normal' girls. How else are they 'like boys'? Between 1968 and 2000, according to Fausto-Sterling, approximately one dozen studies 'looked for evidence of unusual masculinity in CAH girls'. Such evidence included activity and masculine play, mathematical ability, and, of course, sexual orientation toward women![94] Parents report that CAH girls really enjoy playing with boys' toys and show decidedly masculine affective styles. But does that mean that there is 'something in them that's innately male', as libertarian television celebrity and advocate of biological determinism John Stossel thinks?[95] Hardly. Methodological weaknesses and fragile results mark these studies. And though there is some evidence that girls with CAH have a visuospatial advantage, methodological issues make the evidence inconclusive. Finally, CAH girls seem to have no difficulty with their gender identity, according to multiple studies. In one recent study, though mothers reported that their CAH daughters exhibited 'masculinized' play, the girls themselves were happy and comfortable with their gender. The masculinized brains and genitals of CAH girls do not seem to correlate with masculine gender identity.[96]

Another set of experiments examined the other side of the equation—boys who received higher-than-average doses of prenatal estrogen from mothers who were treated with estrogen during their pregnancies. Irvin Green and his colleagues found that boys who received 'female' hormones in utero were less active and less athletic than other boys. However, all the boys' mothers were chronically and seriously ill during their infancy and childhood (which was not true for the control sample of 'normal' boys). Perhaps the boys had simply been admonished against loud and boisterous play in the house so as not to disturb their mothers and had simply *learned* to be content while playing quietly or reading.[97]

Another genetically male group of intersexuals are those affected by **androgen insensitivity syndrome** (AIS), a defect on the X chromosome that impairs androgen reception, preventing the fetus from responding to the famous 'testosterone bath' that converts it into an unambiguous boy. AIS children appear female at birth and are raised as girls. At puberty they develop characteristically feminine bodies, often with larger-than-normal breasts. AIS girls and women call into question many of the stereotypes about androgens and behaviour. In many cases, they find out about their condition only when they fail to menstruate—or, as in the case of Spanish hurdler María Martínez-Patiño, when they fail a sex test.[98] Are AIS girls more masculine than one might expect? Are they more likely to experience problems in gender identity? No. Indeed, as María writes, 'having had my womanliness tested—literally and figuratively—I suspect I have a surer sense of my femininity than many women'.

A famous case of genetically male but 'feminized' children comes from two relatively isolated villages in the Dominican Republic that seemed to produce a larger-than-expected set of genetically male hermaphrodites for at least three generations. These were babies born with internal male structures but with sex organs that resembled a clitoris more than they did a penis. Moreover, the testes had not descended at all, leaving what appeared to be a scrotum that resembled labia, as well as an apparently closed vaginal cavity. Their condition was the result of an extremely rare deficiency in a steroid, 5-alpha reductase. Eighteen of these babies were raised as girls and studied by a team of researchers from Cornell University.[99]

After these children had relatively uneventful childhoods, during which they played and acted like other little girls, their adolescence became somewhat more traumatic. They failed to develop breasts and noticed a mass of tissue in their groins that turned out to be testicles beginning a descent. At puberty, their bodies began to produce a significant amount of testosterone, which made their voices deepen, their muscles develop, and facial hair appear. Suddenly, these youngsters were no longer like the other girls! And so all but one of them switched and became males. One remained a female, determined to marry and have a sex change operation. (Another decided he was a male but continued to wear dresses and act as a female.) All the others were successful in making the transition; they became men, found typically masculine jobs (as woodchoppers, farmers, and miners), and married women.

Endocrinologist Julianne Imperato-McGinley and her Cornell colleagues interpreted these events as a demonstration of the effect of prenatal and pubertal sex hormones. They argued that a prenatal dose of testosterone had created 'male' brains, which had remained dormant within ambiguous and female-appearing physiological bodies. (This doesn't explain, however, how those supposedly masculine brains tolerated girls' play, since we are regularly told that gendered play is the result of brain-based aptitudes and interests.) At puberty, a second secretion of testosterone activated these genetically masculine brains, and the youngsters made the transition without too much psychological trauma.

They didn't, however, do it alone. The other villagers had made fun of them, calling them *guevadoces* ('eggs [testicles] at twelve') or *machihembra* ('first woman, then man'). But after they had made the move to become males, their neighbours were more encouraging and offered advice and gifts to ease the transition. Moreover, one might argue that these children had a less fixed relationship between early gender development and adolescent gender patterns precisely because of their ambiguous genital development. After three generations, they might have come to assume that a girl does not always develop into a woman. Anthropologist Gilbert Herdt argues that such 'gender polymorphic' cultures have the ability to deal with radical gender changes across the life cycle far more easily than do 'gender dimorphic' cultures, such as the United States, where we expect everyone to be either male or female for his or her entire life.[100] One might also ask what would have happened had these been little boys who, it turned out, had actually been female and were therefore invited to make a transition to being adult women. Who would choose to stay a girl if she could end up becoming a boy, especially in a culture in which the sexes are highly differentiated and males enjoy privileges that females do not? Would boys find a transition to becoming girls as easy?

Survey data suggest a somewhat different interpretation. Junior high school students in north Midwestern states (Michigan, Wisconsin, Minnesota, North and South Dakota) were asked what they would do if the next morning they awoke to find themselves transformed into the opposite sex. The girls thought about the question for a while, expressed modest disappointment, and then described the kinds of things they would do if they were suddenly transformed into boys. Become a doctor, fireman, policeman, or baseball player were typical answers. The boys, by contrast, took virtually no time before answering. 'Kill myself' was the most common answer when they contemplated the possibility of life as a girl.[101]

That may be a bit extreme. In fact, research on people with chromosomal and hormonal abnormalities suggests that while our biology has important effects, those effects are not easy to separate from the cultural contexts in which we grow into men and women. Indeed, the history of research and intervention on intersexuals suggests, rather, that we all need the same things: respect, fair and ethical treatment, and caution when entering the borderlands of biological sex.

The Politics of Biological Essentialism

Biological arguments for sex differences have historically tended to be politically conservative, suggesting that the social arrangements between women and men—including social, economic, and political discrimination based on sex—are actually the inevitable outcome of nature working in its mysterious ways. Political attempts to legislate changes in the gender order or efforts to gain civil rights for women or for gay men and lesbians have always been met with **biological essentialism**: Don't fool with Mother Nature! For example, sociologist Steven Goldberg, in his book *The Inevitability of Patriarchy*, argues that because male domination is ubiquitous, eternal, it simply has to be based on biological origins. There is simply too much coincidence for it to be social. Feminism, Goldberg argues, is therefore a war with nature:

> Women follow their own physiological imperatives . . . In this, and every other society [men] look to women for gentleness, kindness, and love, for refuge from a world of pain and force . . . In every society basic male motivation is the feeling that the women and children must be protected . . . [T]he feminist cannot have it both ways: If she wishes to sacrifice all this, all that she will get in return is the right to meet men on male terms. She will lose.[102]

Unequal social arrangements are, in the end, ordained by nature.[103]

But the evidence—occasionally impressive, often uneven—is far from convincing. If male domination is natural, based on biological imperatives, why, asks sociologist Cynthia Fuchs Epstein, must it be coercive, held in place by laws, traditions, customs, and the constant threat of violence for any woman who dares step out of line? Why would women want to enter male spheres, like colleges and universities, politics and the labour force, the professions, and the military, for which they are clearly biologically ill-suited?

Ironically, in the past decade, conservatives who argue that biological bases account for both sex differences and sexuality differences have been joined by some women and some gay men and lesbians, who have adopted an essentialism of their own. Some feminists, for example, argue that women should be pleased to claim 'the intuitive and emotional strengths given by their right-hemisphere, in opposition to the over-cognitive, left-hemisphere-dominated, masculine nature'.[104] Often a feminist essentialism uses women's experiences as mothers to describe the fundamental and irreducible differences between the sexes, rather than evolution, brain organization, or chemistry. Sociologist Alice Rossi argues that, because of their bodies, 'women have a head start in easier reading of an infant's facial expressions, smoothness of body motions, greater ease in handling a tiny creature with tactile gentleness'.[105]

Similarly, research on the biological bases of homosexuality suggests some unlikely new political allies and a dramatic shifting of positions. Gay-brain research may have generated little light on the etiology of sexual orientation, but it has certainly generated significant political heat. In a way, the promotion of gay essentialism is a political strategy to normalize gayness. 'It points out that gay people are made this way by nature', observes Robert Bray, the director of public information of the National Gay and Lesbian Task Force. 'It strikes at the heart of people who oppose gay rights and who think we don't deserve our rights because we're choosing to be the way we are.' Michael Bailey and Richard Pillard, the authors of the gay twin study, opined in a *New York Times* op-ed essay that a 'biological explanation is good news for homosexuals and their advocates'. 'If it turns out, indeed, that homosexuals are born that way, it could undercut the animosity gays have had to contend with for centuries', added a cover story in *Newsweek*. Such an understanding would 'reduce being gay to something like being left-handed, which is in fact all that it is', commented gay journalist and author Randy Shilts in the magazine. And Simon LeVay, whose research sparked the recent debate, hoped that homophobia would dissipate as the result of this research, because its basis in prejudice about the unnaturalness of homosexual acts would vanish. Gays would become 'just another minority', just another ethnic group, with an identity based on primordial characteristics.[106]

This political implication is not lost on conservatives, who are now taking up the social constructionist, 'nurture' theory of sexual orientation as firmly as they argue for intractable biologically based differences between women and men. Such thinking leads to the politically volatile though scientifically dubious 'conversion' movement that holds that, through intensive therapy, gay men and lesbians can become happy and 'healthy' heterosexuals.[107]

Conclusion

Biological research holds significant sway over our thinking about the two fundamental questions in the study of gender: the *differences* between women and men and the gendered *inequalities* that are evident in our social lives. But there are many problems with the research on biological bases for gender difference and more and greater problems with the extrapolation of those differences to the social world of gender inequality. Consider the problem of what we might call 'anthropomorphic hyperbole'. Simon LeVay writes that, 'Genes demand instant gratification'.[108] What are we to make of such an obviously false statement? Genes do not 'demand' anything. And which genes is he talking about anyway? Some genes simply control such seemingly unimportant and uninteresting things as eye colour or the capacity to differentiate between sweet and sour tastes. Others wait patiently for decades until they can instruct a man's hair to begin to fall out. Still others are so undemanding that they may wait patiently for several generations, until another recessive mate is found after multiple attempts at reproduction. Genes may play a role in the sexual decision-making of a species or even of individual members of any particular species; they do so only through an individual's interaction with his or her environment. They cannot possibly control any particular decision made by any particular individual at any particular time. With whom you decide to have sex this weekend—or even whether you *do* have sex—is not determined by your genes, but rather by you.

Another problem in biological research has been the casual assumption that causation always moves from physiology to psychology. Just because one finds a correlation between two variables doesn't permit one to speculate about the causal direction. As biologist Ruth Hubbard argues:

> If a society put half its children into short skirts and warns them not to move in ways that reveal their panties, while putting the other half into jeans and overalls and encouraging them to climb trees, play ball, and participate in other vigorous outdoor games; if later, during adolescence, the children who have been wearing trousers are urged to 'eat like growing boys' while the children in skirts are warned to watch their weight and not get fat; if the half in jeans runs around in sneakers or boots, while the half in skirts totters about on spike heels, then these two groups of people will be biologically as well as socially different.[109]

We know, then, what we *cannot* say about the biological bases for gender difference and gender inequality. But what *can* we say? We can say that biological differences provide the raw materials from which we begin to create our identities within culture, within society. 'Biological sexuality is the necessary precondition for human sexuality', writes historian Robert Padgug. 'But biological sexuality is only a precondition, a set of potentialities, which is never unmediated by human reality, and which becomes transformed in qualitatively new ways in human society'.[110]

We seem to want desperately to believe that the differences between women and men are significant and that those differences can be traced to biological origins. A cover story in *Newsweek* promised to explain 'Why Men and Women Think Differently', although the story revealed problems with every bit of evidence and concluded that 'the research will show that our identities as men and women are creations of both nature and nurture. And that no matter what nature deals us, it is we—our choices, our sense of identity, our experiences in life—who make ourselves what we are'.[111]

A better way to understand the influence of biology on our natures is through Anne Fausto-Sterling's simile that each of us is like a Russian nesting doll, with the smallest 'doll' representing our being at the cellular level, the next doll our organism, etc. The largest 'doll' is our own history as human beings. According to Fausto-Sterling, each one of these dolls is important and can be examined as significant, but each doll on its own is hollow: 'Only the complete assembly makes sense'.[112]

> The Russian doll:
> Is there some easy way to envision the double-sided process that connects the production of gendered knowledge about the body on the one surface to the materialization of gender within the body on the other? While no metaphor is perfect,

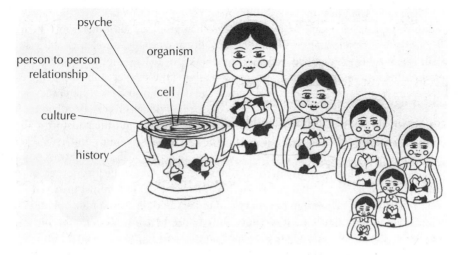

Figure 2.1 Anne Fausto-Sterling Unpacks Sex and Gender.

Drawing by Erica Warp for Anne Fausto-Sterling. From *Sexing the Body* by Anne Fausto-Sterling
© 2000. Published by Basic Books. Reprinted by permission of the author.

Russian nesting dolls have always fascinated me. As I take apart each outer doll, I wait expectantly to see if there is a smaller one within. As the dolls get tinier and tinier, I marvel at the delicacy of the craft that produces successively smaller dolls . . .

I find the Russian nesting doll useful for envisioning the various layers of human sexuality, from the cellular to the social and historical . . . Academics can take the system apart for display or to study one of the dolls in more detail. But each individual doll is hollow. Only the complete assembly makes sense. Unlike its wooden counterpart, the human nesting doll changes shape with time. Change can happen in any of the layers, but since the entire assembly has to fit together, altering one of the component dolls requires the interlinked system—from the cellular to the institution—to change.

While social and comparative historians write about the past to help us understand why we frame the present in particular ways (the outermost doll), analysts of popular culture, literary critics, and anthropologists tell us about our current culture (the second largest doll). They analyze our aggregate behaviours, think about how individuals and institutions interact, and chronicle social change. Other sociologists and psychologists think about individual relationships and individual development (the third largest doll), while some psychologists write about the mind or psyche (the fourth doll in). As the location (or as some would prefer, activity) that links events that occur outside the body to those that occur inside the organism (the second smallest doll), the mind plays an important and peculiar function. The brain is a key organ in the transfer of information from outside the body in and back again. And neuroscientists of many stripes try not only to understand how the brain works as an integrated organ but also how its individual cells function. Indeed, cells make the final, tiny doll found within the organism. In different organs, cells specialize for a variety of functions, They also work as systems, their history and immediate surroundings stimulating signals for particular genes—to contribute (or not) to cellular activities.

Using Russian nesting dolls as a framework suggests that history, culture, relationships, psyche, organism, and cell are each appropriate locations from which to study the formation and meanings of sexuality and gender. Developmental systems theory, whether applied to the assembled doll or to its subunits, provides the scaffolding for thought and experiment. Assembling the smaller dolls into a single large one requires the integration of knowledge derived from very different levels of biological and social organization. The cell, the individual, groups of individuals organized in families, peer groups, cultures, and nations and their histories all provide sources of knowledge about human sexuality. We cannot understand it well unless we consider all of these components. To accomplish such a task, scholars would do well to work in interdisciplinary groups. And while it is not reasonable, for example, to ask all biologists to become proficient in feminist theory, it *is* reasonable to ask each group of scholars to understand the limitations of knowledge obtained from a single discipline. Only non-hierarchical, multidisciplinary teams can devise more complete (or what Sandra Harding calls 'less false') knowledge about human sexuality.

How do we make sense of our totalities? How we do that, how we create identities out of our experiences, how we understand those experiences, and the choices we make—these are the province of social science, which tries to explore the remarkable diversity of human experience. Although biological studies can suggest to us the basic building blocks of experience and identity, it is within our cultures, our societies, and our families that those building blocks are assembled into the astonishingly diverse architecture that constitutes our lives.

Summary

Theories of 'essential' gender difference predate modern science, but have been mainly the province of scientists since the nineteenth century. Today, theories of biological sex difference focus on three areas of research: evolutionary theory, brain research, and endocrinology.

The influence of Darwinian evolutionary theory strengthened biological determinism through the theory that men and women had evolved for different functions and that this parallel evolution had produced gender roles, which were therefore 'natural'. Under the influence of social Darwinism, late nineteenth-century scientific arguments about the nature of men and women became both sexist and racist. By the early twentieth century, these perspectives were forged into the eugenics movement, which, along with social Darwinism, was discredited after the Second World War. In the 1970s, evolutionary theory spawned the new field of sociobiology, which studies the biological basis of social behaviour. The key insights of sociobiology relate to differences in male and female sexual strategies, which sociobiologists see as reflective of evolution. Sociobiologists stress the distinct imperatives of men and women; men seek to maximize reproductive opportunities, while women are more discriminating and cautious. Other sociobiologists have explained such phenomena as the division of labour (Wilson) and male bonding (Tiger).

More recently, evolutionary psychology has explained psychological traits, including differences between men and women, as the result of evolutionary adaptation. Mating strategies have been of particular interest to evolutionary pychologists, but the field has yielded insights in a wide variety of areas. Evolutionary psychology is better than sociobiology at accounting for the different and sometimes conflicting interests of men and women in mating; however, it has sometimes fallen into similar reductive reasoning.

Criticisms of evolutionary theory, particularly sociobiology, include its teleological tendency to reason backward from human behaviours and categories to animal models or 'causes'; the failure to locate genetic coding for specific behaviours; selective use of comparator species; and an exaggeration of the nature of genetic predisposition. Evolutionary theorists, whether sociobiologists or evolutionary psychologists, thus offer interesting but highly incomplete readings of human—gendered—nature.

Brain studies emerged from nineteenth-century social science and gender-related differences in testing in the twentieth century. Studies of the gendered brain developed into two related areas of study. The first examines sex differences in verbal and spatial skills. Persistent sex differences have been found in visuospatial ability, which seems to be stronger, on average, in males, and verbal ability, which seems to be stronger in girls. Moreover, there seems to be simply more variability among males. These findings may indicate the presence of brain-based sex differences, but many questions remain. Most notably, the visuospatial gap appears to be narrowing, at least in Canada, while the verbal gap remains strong. This suggests that these cognitive abilities, whatever their foundation in biology, are highly susceptible to cultural influence. The most careful recent research sees cognitive gender differences as the result of many factors.

The second, related, area of brain study focuses on the brain's structure and function, studying right-left hemisphere differences, use of different parts of the brain for similar functions, and differences in the tissue that connects the hemispheres. The male brain is generally viewed as more lateralized, with one side dominant over the other, than women's more 'integrated' brains. The discussion has sometimes been impaired by changing understandings of lateralization or the location of brain functions, and the implications of males' greater lateralization (if it exists) are not clear, although it has been presumed to explain males' visuospatial advantage. Other studies have focused on the use of parts of the brain, arguing that men and women use parts of the brain differently. Finally, the corpus callosum (CC) and its hindmost part, the splenium, have been seen as key to the structural differences between the male and female brains. In all of these areas, suggestive, though limited, findings have been transformed into media claims of 'male' and 'female' brains, reinforcing crude gender stereotypes.

Hormones, discovered and named in the twentieth century, are the focus of the third major area of sex-difference research. Testosterone, thought of as the 'masculinity hormone' in popular culture, has many effects, but its functions, normal levels, and effects are confusing and only now beginning to be well understood. While testosterone is clearly linked to aggression, it seems not to cause but to enable it. The hormone's relationship to libido is even less clear. This has not prevented outrageous claims and the creation of 'andropause', a so-called medical condition found among no-longer-young men who are suffering from a 'deficiency' of testosterone. Though women are now being encouraged to 'add a dash of testosterone' to their hormone regimens, the most important hormone for women is estrogen. Estrogen has been studied for its relationship to cognition and to sexual desire, but most of the interest in estrogen relates to menopause, when women naturally undergo a precipitous drop in hormone levels. In North America in the late twentieth century, millions of women underwent ERT to 'correct' this condition, at least until 2002 when the US National Institutes of Health cautioned women concerning the risk of hormone therapy. More recently, research has examined the 'perimenopause', another period of hormonal turbulence preceding the menopause itself. PMS, another effect of hormonal fluctuation, was 'discovered' in the 1980s and is now listed in the DSM-IV of the American Psychiatric Association. Women, like men, are thus now seen as greatly influenced (in mood, health, and behaviour) by their sex hormones. Hormones *are* important, but too often their effects are grossly oversimplified.

Research on the possible biological origins of homosexuality has focused on brain structure, a 'gay gene', and hormonal influences. Experiments have identified structural differences between the brains of homosexual men and those of 'straight' men, and between the brains of male transsexuals and non-transsexual heterosexual men. However, these studies have suffered from some methodological problems. One suggestive recent study measured brain asymmetry and found some significant differences between the brains of heterosexual and homosexual men and women. The search for a gay gene has deployed twin studies, which have yielded somewhat inconclusive proof, though there is some evidence, that male homosexuality tends to cluster in families and that having older brothers predisposes a boy to homosexuality—neither of which claims proves pure biological causation.

Some sex-difference research has studied the intersexed, people with hormonal or chromosomal abnormalities causing some degree of sexual ambiguity. The intersexed were once known as hermaphrodites, though this term has a more restrictive definition and has now fallen from use. Intersexuality (broadly defined) affects as many as 1.7 per cent of the population, and is expressed in a range of ways reflective of the different disorders that produce it. Since the 1960s, the intersexed have been subjected to dramatic interventions, often from infancy onward, to 'normalize' their sex and gender. They have also been seen as ideal subjects for the study of biological sex differences. Though there is some evidence that hormonal masculinization of girls in utero may make them more 'masculine' as children, these findings seem superficial and militate against girls' own apparent comfort with their gender identities. Intersexuals do not 'prove' that the essence of gender is biology.

Assertions of the biological bases for gender differences often have been linked to a conservative political agenda. However, this is changing, with both feminists and gay activists arguing determinist points of view and anti-gay conservatives becoming social constructionists, at least as regards sexual orientation. Often when we argue about these theories, we seem to be arguing about politics and the present; we want to believe that the differences between men and women are significant and can be traced to biology. And biology is important; but Anne Fausto-Sterling's metaphor of the Russian stacking dolls tells us that we are the sum of all our parts, of which our biology is only one.

Questions for Critical Thinking

1. What are the strengths of evolutionary explanations of gender difference and gender inequality? In your opinion, what can they explain (or help explain)? What behaviours and traits can they *not* explain?
2. Is women's underrepresentation in science, engineering, and math (SEM) careers the result of biological differences between men and women?
3. Do you believe (with Simon LeVay) that the discovery of a biological basis for homosexuality would increase acceptance of homosexuals?

Key Terms

androgen insensitivity syndrome
androgenital syndrome (AGS)
biological determinism
biological essentialism
clitoridectomy
congenital adrenal hyperplasia (CAH)
estrus
eugenics

evolutionary psychology
intersexed/intersexuals
lateralized
palliative system justification motive
parental investment
social Darwinism
sociobiology

Chapter 3

'So *That* Explains It'

Psychoanalytic and Developmental Perspectives on Gender

Upon no subject has there been so much dogmatic assertion based on so little scientific evidence, as upon male and female types of mind.

JOHN DEWEY, 'IS COEDUCATION INJURIOUS TO GIRLS?' (1911)

There's a famous cartoon of two babies, a boy and a girl, standing together. They're both holding open their diapers and peering down at their genitals. The caption reads, 'So *that* explains the difference in our salaries'. The cartoon adopts a popular idea about the theories of Sigmund Freud, the founder of **psychoanalysis**. As we saw at the beginning of the previous chapter, Freud claimed that 'anatomy is destiny'. He believed that the anatomical differences between males and females led them toward different personalities. However, he did not believe that such differences were biologically programmed into males and females at birth. On the contrary, Freud saw his work as challenging those who held that the body contained all the information it needed at birth to become an adult man or woman. He believed that the observed differences between women and men were traceable to our different experiences from infancy onward, especially in the ways we were treated in our families.

Gender identity, Freud maintained, was a crucial part of personality development—perhaps *the* most crucial part. Gender was acquired, moulded through interactions with family members and with the larger society. And it wasn't an easy acquisition; the route to appropriate gender identity was perilous and included the constant possibility of gender identity failure, which was manifested most clearly in sexual nonconformity, especially homosexuality. Of course, biology did play some role here: Freud and his followers believed that visible anatomical differences were decisive in the development of the child and especially that sexual energy, located in the body, propelled the child's experiences that determined gender identity. But the essence of psychological development was 'not based on any premise of inherent differences between the sexes, but solely on the different nature of their experiences'.[1] In a sense, Freud's ideas provide a bridge between biological or anatomical explanations of gender and theories of social construction. Throughout the twentieth century and into the twenty-first, scholars have continued to explore the psychological and developmental processes that produce gendered men and women.

Freud's Theory of Psychosocial Development

Freud proposed a stage theory of individual gender development, one in which each individual passes through a number of stages on his or her path to adult gender identity. These stages are set into motion by two factors: the composition or structure of the psyche and the realities of life.

Four elements comprise Freud's model of the psyche: **id**, **ego**, **super-ego**, and the **external world**. These elements together form the basic architecture of the self, and each has a decisive role to play in the formation of personality. The id represents our desire to satisfy our basic animal needs. Id is energy, drive, craving. Id 'knows' only that it wants gratification but has neither morality nor the means to acquire what it wants. Freud calls the id 'a cauldron filled with seething excitations'.[2] Unfortunately, the external world offers limited possibilities for instinctual gratification; the id's desires are constantly thwarted. How we cope with those frustrations determines personality development.

The ego, the rational, problem-solving portion of our personality, must discipline the id, tame it, and seek possible sources of gratification for it. Another part of the psyche, the super-ego, sees the limited possibilities for gratification offered by society as legitimate. Super-ego is the seat of morality, and it assists the ego in selecting effective strategies toward socially approved goals. Ego and super-ego are thus the brokers between the id and the external world. From these four elements, individuals fashion their psychological constitution: their drives for gratification, the limited possibilities offered by the world, the moralizing inner voice that tells us we do not deserve constant gratification, and the rational strategizer that tries to keep all these forces in balance. These different components of the self emerge gradually through a child's development.

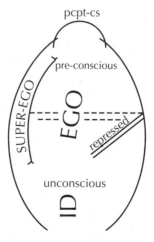

Figure 3.1
A recreation of Freud's own diagram of the organization of the human personality, as presented in a lecture in the 1930s. Note the relatively small size of the conscious part of the personality!

Prior to birth, Freud believed, all the infant's desires are gratified; in the womb we are sensuously content. But birth expels us from this enveloping Eden; hungry and alone, we can take nothing for granted. Now the infant transfers gratification to the mother's breast, seeking pleasure through ingesting food. This Freud calls the 'oral stage'. But just as the ego accommodates itself to this source of gratification, it's removed by weaning. In the next stage, the 'anal stage', gratification is achieved not by taking food in but through urination and defecation. But no sooner do we discover the joys of excretory creation that can compensate for the loss of the breast than we are toilet-trained, forced to repress that source of gratification until it is socially appropriate to do it, until, that is, it's convenient for grown-ups. Finally, after oral denial and anal repression, we reach what Freud calls the 'genital stage'. And here's where gender comes in.

Until now, both boys and girls experience roughly the same things. But at this stage our paths diverge sharply as we 'become' either masculine or feminine. This critical moment for the boy is called the '**Oedipal crisis**', after Sophocles' play *Oedipus, the King*. The resolution of the Oedipal crisis is vital—the boy learns to desire sex with women and to identify as a man. This is crucial in Freudian theory: *The boy achieves gender identity and sexual orientation at the same moment in time.* During the Oedipal stage, the boy desires sexual union with his mother, but he also realizes that he is in competition with his father for her affections. The little boy sexualizes his fear of the father, believing that if he were to compete sexually with his father, his father would castrate him. The boy's ego resolves this state of **castration anxiety** by transferring the boy's identification from mother to father, so that, symbolically, he can have sexual access to his mother. Thus the boy must break the identification with his mother, re-pudiate her, and identify with his father. This is a great shock—the mother has been the source of warmth and love and is the object of his desire; the father has been a more distant source of authoritarian power and is the source of the boy's terror. But by identifying with the father the little boy ceases being 'feminine' (identified with the mother) and becomes masculine, as he simultaneously becomes heterosexual, symbolically capable of sexual relations with mother-like substitutes. Almost literally, as the 1930s popular song put it, he will 'want a girl just like the girl that married dear old Dad'.

For girls, Freud believed, the path is complementary but not nearly as trau-matic. Girls retain their identification with the mother but must renounce their sexual desire for her in the phallic stage, developing what Swiss psychoanalyst Carl Jung named the **Electra complex**. Girls must acknowledge that they are incapable of sexual relations with the mother, because they lack the biological equipment that makes such relations possible. This is why Freud believed that women experience '**penis envy**'. The little girl understands that her only chance for sexual gratification is to retain her identification with the mother and to be sexually possessed by a man who can satisfy her so that she can have a baby, which will be her source of feminine gratification. In the process, she transfers the location of sexual gratification from the clitoris (an 'atrophied penis', in Freud's terms) to the vagina, i.e., she develops feminine, passive sexuality. Again, gender identity and sexual orientation go hand-in-hand. (Freud did acknowledge that his 'insight into these developmental processes in girls is unsatisfactory, incomplete, and vague'—given how it was really an effort to derive some complementary comparison with boys' development and was not a theory of girls' development itself.[3])

Three issues are worth noting in this account of gender identity and sexuality. First, *Freud dislocates gender and sexuality from the realm of biology.* There is nothing inevitable about males becoming masculine or females becoming feminine. Gender identity and sexuality are psychological achievements—difficult, precarious, and full of potential pitfalls. Gender and sexuality are accomplished within the family, Freud argues, not activated by internal biological clocks.

Second, *Freud links gender identity to sexual orientation,* making homosexuality a developmental *gender* issue rather than an issue of immorality, sin, or biological anomaly. Homosexuals are simply those who have either failed to renounce identification with the mother in favour of the father (gay men) or those who have failed to retain their ties of identification to the mother (lesbians). (This idea, of course, also served as the basis for therapeutic interventions designed to 'cure' homosexuals by encouraging gender-appropriate behaviours.)

Third, *Freud restates with new vigour traditional gender stereotypes* as if they were the badges of successful negotiation of this perilous journey. A boy must be the sexual initiator and scrupulously avoid all feminine behaviours, lest he be seen as having failed to identify with the father. A girl must become sexually passive, wait for a man to be attracted to her, so that she can be fulfilled as a woman. Femininity means fulfillment not as a lover, but as a mother.

It's important to remember that though Freud saw homosexuality as the failure of the child to adequately identify with the same-sex parent and therefore a problem of gender identity development, he did not believe in either the criminal persecution or psychiatric treatment of homosexuals. In fact, when Freud was contacted by a woman whose son was homosexual, he patiently explained why he did not think her son needed to be 'cured':

> Homosexuality is assuredly no advantage, but it is nothing to be ashamed of, no vice, no degradation; it cannot be classified as an illness; we consider it to be a variation of the sexual function . . . Many highly respectable individuals of ancient and modern times have been homosexuals, several of the greatest men among them . . . It is a great injustice to persecute homosexuality as a crime—and a cruelty too . . . What analysis can do for your son runs in a different line. If he is unhappy, neurotic, torn by conflicts, inhibited in his social life, analysis may bring him harmony, peace of mind, full efficiency, whether he remains homosexual or gets changed.[4]

It took another 40 years before the American Psychiatric Association declassified homosexuality as a mental illness, so Freud's opinion on this one wasn't as influential as some of the other aspects of his theory!

Still, many popular stereotypes about homosexuality continue to rely on Freudian theories of gender development. Many people believe that homosexuality is a form of gender nonconformity; that is, effeminate men and masculine women are seen in the popular mind as likely or 'latent' homosexuals, whereas masculine men's and feminine women's gender-conforming behaviour leads others to expect them to be heterosexual. In fact, we often believe we can 'read' someone's sexual orientation by observing his or her gender-stereotypic behaviour, as if really masculine men or really feminine women couldn't possibly be gay or lesbian.

Freud's theories have been subject to considerable debate and controversy. He based his theories about the sexuality of women on a very small sample of upper-middle-class women in Vienna, all of whom were suffering from psychological difficulties that brought them to treatment with him in the first place. Initially, Freud believed that many of his patients' psychological issues were the result of traumatic childhood sexual experiences, including incest. He published a paper asserting this claim, but retracted in the face of his colleagues' derision. Many people believe that Freud's theory of girls' development is profoundly flawed as a result, since it rested at least in part on the theory that when women told him of sexual experiences with their fathers, they were expressing their Oedipal (or Electran) desires rather than describing reality.[5]

Freud's theories of male development were based on even fewer clinical cases and on his own recollections of his childhood and his dreams. These are not the most reliable scientific methods, and his tendency to make sexuality the driving force of all individual development and all social and group processes may tell us more about his own life, and perhaps contemporary Vienna, than about other societies and cultures.

Although many today question Freud's theories on methodological, political, or theoretical grounds, there is no question that these theories have had a remarkable impact on contemporary studies and on popular assumptions about the relationship among gender identity, sexual behaviour, and sexual orientation.

Hollywood Goes Freudian: Transgenderism, Sexual Repression, and Murder

The degree to which Freudian ideas of psychosexual development, including the Oedipus complex and repression, became 'mainstream' can be judged from the many Hollywood films that address the topic. Freud probably wouldn't have agreed with the way in which gender and sexual development are portrayed in these films, however. One of the most common horror-film motifs of the past 40 years has been what Carol Glover calls 'the notion of a killer propelled by psychosexual fury, more particularly a male in gender distress'.

To list all of the movies—even the Hollywood ones—that draw from this notion would be impossible. Everyone agrees, however, on the first: Alfred Hitchcock's 1960 horror classic, *Psycho*, which established at least two genres, the psycho-thriller and the slasher film. *Psycho* features numerous elements now so iconic that they are reproduced and referenced throughout popular culture; among these, the 'shower scene' is probably most familiar.

As you probably already know, *Psycho* told the story of Norman Bates, a motel owner so dominated by and obsessed with his deceased mother that he has split his personality into two parts: one the arrested boy and the other the domineering, sexually repressive mother. When a lone woman (Janet Leigh as 'Marion') fleeing her home with embezzled funds stays at the Bates Motel, Norman becomes attracted to her. The 'Mother' part of his personality, which Norman 'channels' through donning his mother's clothes, must therefore, kill the object of his desire—hence the shower scene. However simplistic this view of the effects of 'inappropriate' parenting, it did strike a chord, leaving even Hitchcock, according to Glover, 'bewildered by the [film's] unprecedented success'.

Janet Leigh in the famous 'shower scene' from *Psycho* (1960).

In the years that followed, many films relied upon what was, at the time, the dominant mode of understanding gender identity and sexual development. In 1980, Brian de Palma released his own tribute to *Psycho, Dressed to Kill*. Starring Michael Caine as New York psychiatrist Dr Elliott, the film told the story of knife murders committed by the mysterious 'Bobbi', a transgendered (female-to-male) patient undergoing therapy with Dr Elliott. The ultimate revelation that Elliott *was* Bobbi was the shock ending to the drama. Helpfully, the film provides a culminating psychiatric evaluation; Dr Elliott, a psychiatrist explains, experienced gender confusion, but his 'masculine' personality rebelled against the idea of seeking reassignment. At the same time, his 'feminine' side (Bobbi) became jealous of and murdered women to whom Elliott was attracted. (Still following this?) Regardless of the cinematic merits of either *Dressed To Kill* or *Psycho*, they have been accused of cementing in the public mind simplistic and derogatory perceptions of non-gender-conforming people. As Barbara Creed suggests, 'while [such films] might present a critique of a culture fearful of changes in traditional sex roles, they also equate cross-dressing and transsexuality with monstrousness'.

Indeed, it might be argued that for many years, trans individuals were *most* commonly seen on screen in such 'monstrous' roles. In her 2009 doctoral dissertation, Joelle Ruby Ryan describes being in a conference hotel elevator with several male-bodied but female-attired individuals; when the elevator stopped for a male passenger, he grimaced and would not enter. Afterward, Ryan writes, 'internally I wondered: how do cultural codes that present gender-transgressive people as insane psychopaths, deviant killers, and monstrous, murdering machines function in the culture at large?'

Though Freudian understandings of sexual development have lost much of their influence, Freudian cinema studies remain potent. What's more, reductive interpretations of Freud's theories continue to inform Hollywood film. Slasher films continue to rely upon *Psycho*'s stereotypes. The 1983 film *Sleepaway Camp*,

Paramount/The Kobal Collection/Creamer, William

a B-grade slasher movie, has become a cult favourite for its 'shocker' ending featuring, you guessed it, the revelation that the murderer 'Angela' is actually a boy who was raised as a girl. Successful enough to have spawned numerous sequels, the film has generated legions of fans and controversy over its portrayal of the transgendered. While the *Sleepaway* franchise may not be high art, even critically acclaimed movies like 1999's *American Beauty* cannot resist the trope. In that movie, the protagonist Lester is murdered by a neighbour unable to come to terms with his own repressed homosexual desires.

These readings of gender and sexuality are interesting for what they suggest about our culture and the way it grapples with difference. But they also misrepresent the origins and nature of nonconforming gender and sexuality, and hide some troubling realities. Ruby lists more than 35 movies featuring transgendered killers between 1960 and 2005. Not until 1999's *Boys Don't Cry* did Hollywood represent more accurately the relationship of transgendered people with violence: that is, though there are no clear cases of transgendered killers on record, transgendered people are hundreds of times more likely than others to fall victim to murder.[6]

Sex Role Theories

Freud's theory that 'normal' gender identity and sexual preference were successfully acquired—or not—in childhood proved enormously influential. Freudian psychoanalytic theory spawned several different traditions in psychology. As we shall see in this section, some psychologists used various statistical tests to more precisely measure the differences between males and females at certain ages, forming the basis for **sex role theory**, which analyzes individuals' socialization into appropriate gender roles and identities.

In the early 1930s, just three decades after Freud developed his theories, Lewis Terman, a psychology professor at Stanford University, and his associate, Catherine Cox Miles, tried to codify masculinity and femininity into their component parts—traits, attitudes, and behaviours.[7]

Terman and Miles utilized a broad range of empirical measures to test gender identity and constructed a continuum from masculinity to femininity, along which any individual could be placed (according to answers on the Terman/Miles **M-F test**). As a result of inventories like the M-F test, gender identity came to be associated with a particular bundle of attitudes, traits, and behaviours that could be seen as indicators of successful gender acquisition. When embraced by social science in the 1940s, these inventories became the basis for sex-role theory.

The M-F test was perhaps the single most widely used means to determine successful acquisition of (or 'deviation from') gender identity and was used until the 1960s. (The final edition of *Sex and Personality* appeared in 1968.) As late as 1978, McGill researchers reported that it successfully differentiated male from female subjects when administered to students in Montreal—despite what we might see as the US-centric character of some of its questions (see below).[8] The test was quite wideranging, including Rorschach-like interpretations of ink blots, which were coded for gender appropriateness, as well as identification, sentence completion, and some empirical questions. Here is a small sample of the questions on the M-F test. (If you want to keep your own score on these few items—to make sure that your own gender identity is progressing 'normally'—you should score it the way that Terman and Miles suggested in 1936: If the response is 'masculine', give yourself a '+'; if feminine, score with a '−'. Interesting how these little value judgments creep into scientific research!)

Gendered Knowledge: In the following completion items there are right and wrong answers, and it was assumed that the more 'boyish' would know the right answer to questions 2, 3, and 5 and that the more girlish would know the answers to items 1 and 4. Girls who knew the answers to 2, 3, and 5 would be scored as more 'masculine'.

1. Things cooked in grease are: boiled (+), broiled (+), fried (−), roasted (+).
2. Most of our anthracite coal comes from: Alabama (−), Colorado (−), Ohio (−), Pennsylvania (+).
3. The 'Rough Riders' were led by: Funston (−), Pershing (−), Roosevelt (+), Sheridan (−).
4. Red goes best with: black (−), lavender (+), pink (+), purple (+).
5. The proportion of the globe covered by water is about: 1/8 (−), 1/4 (−), 1/2 (−), 3/4 (+).

Gendered Feelings: The test also included a variety of stimuli that was thought to provoke certain emotions. Respondents were to answer whether these things caused (a) a lot, (b) some, (c) little, or (d) none of the expected emotion. For example:

- Does: being called lazy; seeing boys make fun of old people; seeing someone cheat on an exam make you ANGRY?
- Does: being lost; deep water; graveyards at night; Negroes [this is actually on the list!] make you AFRAID?
- Does: a fly caught on sticky fly paper; a man who is cowardly and can't help it; a wounded deer make you feel PITY?
- Does: boys teasing girls; indulging in 'petting'; not brushing your teeth; being a Bolshevik make you feel that a person is WICKED?

[To score this section, give yourself a minus (−) for every answer in which you said the thing caused a lot of the emotion, except for the answer, 'being a Bolshevik', which was obviously serious enough for men to get very emotional about. On all others, including being afraid of 'Negroes', however, high levels of emotion were scored as feminine.]

Gendered Occupations, Appearances, Books: The test also included possible careers and their obvious sex-typing, such as librarian, auto racer, forest ranger, florist, soldier, and music teacher. There were lists of character traits (loud voices, men with beards, tall women) that those tested were asked to like or dislike, and a list of children's books (for example, *Robinson Crusoe, Rebecca of Sunnybrook Farm, Little Women, Biography of a Grizzly*) that they either liked, didn't like, or had not read.

Gendered People: There was a list of famous people whom one either liked, disliked, or did not know (Bismarck, Lenin, Florence Nightingale, Jane Addams). (Obviously, not having read a book or not knowing about a famous person could be seen as gender confirming or non-confirming.)

There were also questions about what you might like to draw if you were an artist (ships or flowers), what you might like to write about if you were a newspaper reporter (accidents or theatre), and where you might like to travel if you had plenty of money (hunt lions in Africa or study social customs; learn about various religions or see how criminals are treated). Finally, the test included some self-reporting about the respondent's own behaviours and attitudes. Such 'yes' or 'no' items (here listed with the scoring of a 'yes' answer) included:

- Do you rather dislike to take your bath? ($+$)
- Are you extremely careful about your manner of dress? ($-$)
- Do people ever say you talk too much? ($+$)
- Have you ever been punished unjustly? ($+$)
- Have you ever kept a diary? ($-$)

The research by Terman and Miles enabled a new generation of psychologists to construct a continuum between masculinity and femininity, along which any individual could be located, and thereby to chart the acquisition of gender identity by examining the traits, attitudes, and behaviours appropriate to each gender. If a boy or girl exhibited the appropriate traits and attitudes, parents could be reassured that their child was developing normally. If, however, the child scored too high on the 'inappropriate' side of the continuum, intervention strategies might be devised to facilitate the adoption of more appropriate behaviours. Artistic boys would be pushed toward rough-and-tumble play; tomboys would be forced into frilly dresses to read quietly instead of climbing a tree. Behind these interventions lay the spectre of the sissy, the homosexual male, who, Terman and Miles and other psychologists believed, had gender identity problems. As another psychologist, George W. Henry, wrote in 1937:

> In a large majority of . . . cases the tendencies to homosexuality as shown by attitude and behaviour can be observed in early childhood . . .To the extent that his interests, attitude and behaviour are out of harmony with his actual sex he is likely to meet with circumstances which will accentuate his deviation. Boys appear to be somewhat more vulnerable than girls and if they show undue feminine tendencies special care should be exercised to give them opportunity to develop masculine characteristics.[9]

By the 1950s, **social psychologists** were seeking to clarify the social requirements for both masculine and feminine sex roles. In their effort to understand the constellation of attitudes, traits, and behaviours that constitutes appropriate gender identity, these scholars elaborated and extended original classifications of the M-F scale offered by Terman and Miles. If masculinity and femininity could be understood as points on a continuum, a variety of abnormal behaviours could possibly be understood as examples of gender-inappropriate behaviour.[10] In the years after the Second World War for example, some psychologists hypothesized that the propensity toward fascism and Nazism stemmed from distorted assertions of gender identity. The authors of *The Authoritarian Personality* posited a typology of behaviours, based on the M-F scale, a scale that suggested that femininity and masculinity can describe both an internal psychological identification and an external behavioural manifestation. Their typology thus created four possible combinations instead of two:

Internal Psychological Organization

		Masculine	Feminine
External	Masculine	MM	MF
Behavioural			
Manifestation	Feminine	FM	FF

Two of the cells, upper left and lower right, would be considered 'gender appropriate'—males and females whose internal psychological identification matches their external behaviours. But those males whose scores placed them in the upper right cell—internally feminine, externally masculine—also scored highest on measures of racism, authoritarianism, and hypermasculinity. The authors proposed that such attitudes were the means for those who were insecure about their masculinity to cover up their insecurities—by more rigid adherence to the most traditional norms. This became known as the 'masculinity overcompensation thesis'.[11]

This notion became common wisdom in the 1950s. It resonated in popular advice about schoolyard bullies—that they are the *least* secure about their masculinity, which is why they have to try to prove it all the time. Interestingly, Sanford and his colleagues found that the men who scored in the lower left cell—externally feminine and internally masculine—were the most creative, artistic, and intelligent. It took a very secure man, indeed, to stray from the behavioural norms of masculinity!

A recent effort to revisit this thesis found that American men who felt that their masculinity was more 'threatened' would overcompensate. In 2005, Rob Willer conducted an experiment with 111 undergraduates at Cornell University. Using a questionnaire, he purported to be testing their gender identities, but instead randomly assigned them to either feminine or masculine groups. He then surveyed the participants through 'political' and 'car-buying' survey packets. Male participants who were told that they were 'feminine' were more likely to support the Iraq War, oppose gay marriages, and state their interest in purchasing an SUV—all of which had been identified with masculinity by students in an earlier survey. Interestingly, while male students' responses were altered by the (fake) gender identity 'diagnosis', female students were apparently unfazed by being told they were 'masculine'. While Willer himself has urged caution in interpreting the results, other studies have confirmed overcompensation. For example, one study published in 2007 found that young men who received bogus 'feminine identity' feedback were more likely to perceive effeminate (though not masculine) gay men with hostility, fear, and discomfort.[12]

Whereas Sanford and his colleagues had developed a typology of inner identities and external behaviours, Walter Miller and Guy Swanson saw a developmental sequence that accorded with Freudian theory. All children, both males and females, begin their lives as 'FF'—totally identified with and behaving like the mother. Boys then pass through the Oedipal stage, or 'FM', during which they continue to identify with the mother but begin to make a break from that identification, while they simultaneously acquire superficial masculine traits and behaviours. Finally, males arrive at 'MM', both internal identification and external behaviours that are gender appropriate. Thus authoritarianism, racism, sexism, and **homophobia** might now be seen as examples of psychological immaturity, a kind of arrested development. (The potential fourth stage, 'MF', was dropped from the study.)[13]

A second trajectory that coincided with these studies was sociological, based on the work of Harvard sociologist Talcott Parsons and others who sought to establish the societal necessity for masculinity and femininity. Writing in the wake of the Second World War Parsons became interested in human conflict and the effects of personality on social structures. He became interested in Freud's work and its applicability to social analysis. Parsons argued that society had two types of major functions, production and reproduction, and that these required two separate institutional systems, the occupational system and the kinship system, which, in turn, required two types of roles. **Instrumental roles** (occupational) demanded rationality, autonomy, and competitiveness; **expressive roles** (kinship) demanded tenderness and nurturing so that the next generation could be socialized. In this way, Parsons shifted the emphasis of sex-role identity development away from the 'need' of the infant to become either masculine or feminine to the need of society for individuals to fill specific slots. Fortunately, Parsons argued, we had two different types of people who were socialized to assume these two different roles.

Parsons suggested, however, that the allocation of roles to males and females did not always work smoothly. For example, in Western societies, the isolation of the nuclear family and the extended period of childhood meant that boys remained identified with the mother for a very long time. What's more, the separation of spheres meant that girls had their appropriate role model immediately before them, whereas boys did not have adequate role models. Thus, he argued, boys' break with the mother and their need to establish their individuality and masculinity often were accompanied by violent protest against femininity, and angry repudiation of the feminine became a way for the boy to purge himself of feminine identification. He 'revolts against identification with his mother in the name of masculinity', Parsons writes, equating goodness with femininity, so that becoming a 'bad boy' becomes a positive goal. This, Parsons suggests, has some negative consequences, including a '**cult of compulsive masculinity**':

> Western men are peculiarly susceptible to the appeal of an adolescent type of assertively masculine behaviour and attitudes which may take various forms. They have in common a tendency to revolt against the routine aspects of the primarily institutionalized masculine role of sober responsibility, meticulous respect for the rights of others, and tender affection towards women. Assertion through physical prowess, with an endemic tendency toward violence and hence the military ideal, is inherent in the complex and the most dangerous potentiality.[14]

For the girl, Parson theorized, the process is somewhat different. She has an easier time because she remains identified with the mother. Her rebellion and anger come from recognizing 'masculine superiority'—'the fact that her own security like that of other women is dependent on the favour—even 'whim'—of a man'. Suddenly she realizes that the qualities that she values are qualities that may handicap her. She may express the aggression that would invariably follow upon such frustration by rebelling against the feminine role altogether.

By the 1970s, sex role theory was, itself, facing significant critical scrutiny. Some thinkers found the binary model between roles, system needs, and males and females just a bit too facile and convenient, as well as politically conservative—as if changing roles meant disrupting the needs that *society* had. Others stressed the coercive nature of these roles: If they were natural and met readily evident needs, why did so many people rebel against them, and why did they need to be so rigorously enforced?

Two significant challenges came from social psychologists themselves. Sandra Bem and others explored the *content* of sex roles. The Bem Sex Role Inventory (BSRI) tested adult respondents on their perception of 60 different attributes, 20 of which were coded as 'feminine', 20 as 'masculine', and 20 more as 'fillers'. Although this replaced a continuum with categorical sex roles, Bem discovered that the most psychologically well-adjusted and intelligent people were those who fell in between the polar oppositions of masculinity and femininity. Bem's **gender schema theory** argued that we learn a gender identity, which becomes the basis for our individual views (schemas) of gender. As we grow and become adults, we evaluate our gender performances with regard to our **gender schemas**, which are also reinforced by society. This process, however, is not uniform. Individuals who completed the BSRI varied in the degree to which they subscribed to dichotomized views of gender roles and attributes. In her initial studies, Bem claimed that **androgyny**, 'the combined presence of socially valued, stereotypic, feminine and masculine characteristics', best described the healthily adjusted individual. What's more, Bem argued, given where most of us actually fall on the continuum, masculinity and femininity are hardly opposites.

Several empirical studies seemed to bear out the desirability of an androgynous personality constellation over a stereotypically feminine or masculine one. But subsequent studies failed to confirm the validity of these measures, and androgyny was discredited as a kind of wishy-washy non-personality, rather than the synthesis of the best of both worlds. Twenty years after her initial studies, Bem noted that the scale 'reproduces . . . the very gender polarization that it seeks to undercut'.[15] Gender schema theory nonetheless provides further understanding of how gender is learned by individuals, how society influences that learning, and how individuals can vary in their adherence to rigid gender norms.

Whereas proponents of androgyny challenged the content of sex role theory, Joseph Pleck challenged the form. In a series of articles that culminated in his book *The Myth of Masculinity*, Pleck advanced the idea that the problem was not that men were having a hard time fitting into a rational notion of masculinity but rather that the role itself was internally contradictory and inconsistent. Instead of simply accepting the American male sex role as a package, Pleck separated what he called the **'male sex role identity'** (MSRI) model into a discrete set of testable propositions. These included the following:

1. Sex role identity is operationally defined by measures of psychological sex typing, conceptualized in terms of psychological masculinity and/or femininity dimensions.
2. Sex role identity derives from identification-modelling and, to a lesser extent, reinforcement and cognitive learning of sex-typed traits, especially among males.

3. The development of appropriate sex role identity is a risky, failure-prone process, especially for males.
4. Homosexuality reflects a disturbance of sex role identity.
5. Appropriate sex role identity is necessary for good psychological adjustment because of an inner psychological need for it.
6. Hypermasculinity indicates insecurity in sex role identities.
7. Problems of sex role identity account for men's negative attitudes and behaviour toward women.
8. Problems of sex role identity account for boys' difficulties in school performance and adjustment.
9. Black males are particularly vulnerable to sex role identity problems.
10. Male adolescent initiation rites are a response to problems of sex role identity.
11. Historical changes in the character of work and the organization of the family have made it more difficult for men to develop and maintain their sex role identities.

When virtually all of these propositions turned out to be empirically false, Pleck argued that the male sex role itself was the source of strain, anxiety, and male problems.

Psychology was thus transformed from the vehicle that would help problematic men adapt to their rational sex role into the vehicle by which men had been fed a pack of lies about masculinity. The sex role system itself was the source of much of men's anxieties and pain. In its place, Pleck proposed the **male sex role strain** model (MSRS):

1. Sex roles are operationally defined by sex role stereotypes and norms.
2. Sex roles are contradictory and inconsistent.
3. The proportion of individuals who violate sex roles is high.
4. Violating sex roles leads to social condemnation.
5. Violating sex roles leads to negative psychological consequences.
6. Actual or imagined violation of sex roles leads individuals to over conform to them.
7. Violating sex roles has more severe consequences for males than females.
8. Certain characteristics prescribed by sex roles are psychologically dysfunctional.
9. Each gender experiences sex role strain in its work and family roles.
10. Historical changes cause sex role strain.

The net effect of this new model is to shift the understanding of problems from the men themselves to the roles that they are forced to play.[16] Subsequent research has explored the grappling with these contradictory role specifications by different groups of men and the problematic behaviours (such as sexual risk taking) that are expressions of men's efforts to reconcile contradictory role demands.[17]

But there remain problems with sex role theory that even these two ambitious efforts could not resolve. For one thing, when psychologists discussed the 'male' sex role or the 'female' sex role, they posited a single, monolithic entity, a 'role', into which all boys and all girls were placed. Through a process of socialization, boys acquired the male sex role, girls, the female one. But all males and all females are not alike. There are a variety of different 'masculinities' or 'femininities' depending on class, race, ethnicity, age, sexuality, religion, and region. If all boys or all girls were to receive the same socialization to the same sex role, differences in the construction of black masculinity, aboriginal femininity, rural masculinity, or middle-aged gay masculinity, would all be effaced. Sex role theory is unable to account for the differences *among* men or *among* women because it always begins from the normative prescriptions of sex *roles*, rather than the experiences of men and women themselves.

A second problem with sex role theory is that the separate roles into which males and females are sorted look similar and complementary to each other. When we say that boys become masculine and girls become feminine in roughly similar ways, we posit a false equivalence between the two. If we ignore the power differential between the two roles, then both privilege and oppression disappear. 'Men don't have power', writes pop therapist Warren Farrell, 'men and women have roles'.[18] Despite what men and women may *feel* about their situation, men as a group have power in our society over women as a group. In addition, some men—privileged by virtue of race, class, ethnicity, sexuality, etc.—have power over other men. Any adequate explanation of gender must account not only for gender difference but also for male domination. Theories of sex roles are inadequate to this task.[19]

This theoretical inadequacy stems from the sorting process in the first place. Sex role theorists see boys and girls sorted into those two separate categories. But what we know about being a man has everything to do with what it means to be a woman; and what we know about being a woman has everything to do with what it means to be a man. Constructions of gender are *relational*—we understand what it means to be a man or a woman in relation to the dominant models as well as to one another. And those who are marginalized by race, class, ethnicity, age, sexuality, and the like also measure their gender identities against those of the dominant group.

Finally, sex role theory assumes that only individuals are gendered, that gendered individuals occupy gender-neutral positions and inhabit gender-neutral institutions. But gender is more than an attribute of individuals; gender organizes and constitutes the field in which those individuals move. The institutions of our lives—families, workplaces, schools—are themselves gendered institutions, organized to reproduce the differences and the inequalities between women and men. If one wants to understand the lives of people in any situation, the French philosopher Jean-Paul Sartre once wrote, one 'must inquire first into the situation surrounding [them]'.[20]

Cognitive Development Theory

As theorists of sex roles attempted to clarify the manner in which individuals learn and fulfil their sex roles, some developmental psychologists sought to chart the sequences or stages of gender and sexual development in children. **Cognitive development theory** locates the trigger of gender development and gender identity formation slightly later in life than early childhood. Lawrence Kohlberg, a psychologist who taught at Harvard and the University of Chicago, developed this theory based on the Piagetian model of sequential cognitive development. Swiss psychologist Jean Piaget examined the developmental sequences in children's self-perception and their views of the world.

Children are active participants in their own socialization, Piaget argued, not simply the passive objects of social influence. But they learn in ways different from those of adults, according to their stage of development. Piaget applied this model to cognitive development, pointing out the sequences of tasks and mental processes appropriate to children of various ages.[21] Kohlberg argued that children learned gender roles according to their characteristic modes of cognition at different ages. Psychologists of this school thus argue that children are born more or less gender neutral; that is, no important biological differences between boys and girls at birth explain later gender differences. As they grow, children process new information through 'cognitive filters' that enable them to interpret information about gender.

One of the central developmental tasks of early childhood, Kohlberg argued, is to label oneself as either male or female. The point in time at which children learn 'I am a boy' or 'I am a girl' is a point after which self-identification seems fixed. The decision is *cognitive*, part of the pattern of mental growth in the organism. Early in life, children develop a gendered mental filter, after which new information from the social world is interpreted and acted upon in terms of its appropriateness to their gender identity. Even by age two, children have relatively stable and fixed understandings of themselves as gendered, and this categorization, Kohlberg argues, 'is basically a cognitive reality judgment rather than a product of social rewards, parental justifications, or sexual fantasies'. Things, persons, and activities are labelled, 'this is appropriate to who I am' or 'this is not appropriate to who I am'.[22]

According to this theory, children's early gender identities depend on concrete, physical cues like dress, hairstyle, and body size in their categorization of the world into two genders. Boys never wear dresses and have short hair; girls do wear dresses and have long hair. Many children believe that they can change their gender by getting haircuts or changing their clothing, because they believe gender identity is concrete and attached to physical attributes. Some children become upset if their parents engage in gender-inappropriate conduct (Daddy carries Mommy's purse, Mommy changes the tire). It is not until age five or six that most children have the cognitive machinery to recognize gender as an attribute of the person and not the result of the material props that we use to display gender. At that point, children begin to develop **gender constancy**, the idea that gender identity is permanent and unchanging, and cannot be changed simply because, for instance, one 'inappropriately' holds a purse.

By this view, the acquisition of a gender identity is a switching point in the child's life. After age six, the child sees the world in *gender* terms. The child cannot go back, because the process of acquiring gender identity is irreversible after age three or four. The child thus becomes capable of socializing him- or herself by subjecting behaviour to analysis on the basis of its gender appropriateness. Because so many aspects of behaviour depend on gender identity, the acquisition of an irreversible filter is necessary to human development, and to be expected in all societies.

Because there is no 'natural' relationship between gender identity and gender-role performances, the young child who 'knows' his or her gender possesses a label with very little content. However, the label is used to organize the new things that are experienced. This is done by observing who (in gender terms) leaves the house to go to work, who is in charge of the labour of the household, and who plays with cars or dolls (or at least who the child sees playing with these toys in the media). All of these activities are more or less gender-typed, mostly by who does them rather than by what is done. In addition, all children hear verbal exhortations of what boys do/don't do and what girls do/don't do. Children naturally tend to imitate models of behaviour, even if that imitation is not reinforced, and this includes the vast amount of gender-typical behaviour that is performed in front of them. Children swim in an ocean of gendered conduct, and it is terribly difficult to swim against the tide.[23]

Social learning of gender does not end in childhood. Acquisition of gender identity may begin early, but it continues throughout the life cycle. A child does not know most of the things that an adult knows or believes or likes or feels. Gender identity is more fluid than young children believe, and our gender socialization continues throughout our lives. And, equally important, we are active agents in our own socialization, not simply the passive receptors of cultural blueprints for appropriate gender behaviours.

Thus in a society there are always two factors that affect gendered behaviour: the demands of the social situation and one's prior experience of being a girl or a boy or a woman or a man. Cognitive learning theory provides information on how children learn to navigate the prescriptions of a gendered society, but it takes that society for granted. Other tools are needed to interrogate the context in which children are socialized.

Feminist and Other Challenges to Psychoanalysis and Developmental Psychology

As we have seen, Freud's key insights concerned the construction of gender identity and sexual orientation within the context of the family. This theory of psychosexual development offered a great challenge to assumptions of biological inevitability. Freud stressed the universality of sex differences but argued that such differences were produced— learned by children in interactions with their families and the larger society. He saw nothing inevitable about becoming either masculine or feminine, nor about becoming heterosexual. Sexual orientation and gender identity were achievements. Obviously, these theories had significant implications for feminism, which has also argued against the inevitability of society's arrangements regarding gender.

Many women have dismissed Freud's arguments because he argued that their development was the result of their coming to terms with the shame that would naturally follow from the realization that they did not have penises. Not only did his arguments place an absurd emphasis on a little flap of tissue, but also penis envy meant that women would always see themselves as inferior to men. What's more, Freud asserted that female development required the repudiation of the clitoris, the source of sexual agency and pleasure, for the more 'mature' sexuality of vaginal receptivity.

No sooner had Freud published his theories than his own women followers challenged the centrality of penis envy in girls' development. One of these followers was Melanie Klein, an Austrian-born psychoanalyst who worked, unlike Freud, largely with children. Klein developed **object-relations theory**, which examines the development of the self in interaction with others. In her studies of female development, she shifted emphasis away from penis envy toward girls' relationships with their mothers.

Indeed, she suggested, until the Oedipal crisis children of both sexes existed in a **primary feminine phase**, identified strongly with their mothers.

German psychoanalyst Karen Horney also contested Freud's views of female development. Her 1922 essay, 'On the Genesis of the Castration Complex in Women', suggested that a theory that posited one-half of the human race to be unsatisfied was itself theoretically problematic. Though Horney did not identify herself as a feminist, she pointed out that 'the actual social subordination of women' provided the context for women's development. Since then, women have patiently explained that it was men, not women, who saw the possession of a penis as such a big deal. After all, without one, how could women know what it felt like? As Horney put it:

> It is the male who experiences the penis as a valuable organ and he assumes that women also must feel that way about it. But a woman cannot really imagine the sexual pleasure of a penis—she can only appreciate the social advantages its possessor has.[24]

Perhaps women had a more political and social 'privilege envy' than any envy to do with the body.

In fact, Horney (and eventually Klein) argued, perhaps Freud had it backward. Perhaps women did not have penis envy as much as men had '**womb envy**'. Women, after all, can produce babies, apparently (at least in those cultures in which a rather uneventful moment nine months earlier is not remembered or not considered as significant) all by themselves! No matter what men do, they cannot create life. Austrian-American psychologist Bruno Bettelheim and several others suggested that the origins of women's subordination stemmed from men's fears of women's reproductive powers, and these researchers pointed to male initiation rituals that imitated birth as an indication of ritual appropriation masking significant envy.[25]

Another line of critique has been to reverse Freud's initial proposition. Instead of asking how and why women come to see themselves as inferior to men, why not ask how men come to see themselves as superior to women? Several feminist writers such as Nancy Chodorow, Lillian Rubin, Dorothy Dinnerstein, and Jessica Benjamin have posed that question.[26] Inspired by the object-relations school, these theorists pointed to the more deeply embedded masculine biases in Freud's formulation. Freud argued that the final achievement of gender development was individual autonomy—freedom from dependency on the mother and thus freedom from the need for group identification. Autonomy was achieved in the boy's renunciation of identification with his mother and subsequent identification with his father. However, in *The Reproduction of Mothering*, Chodorow argued that Freud inadvertently revealed the sources of men's sense of superiority and, thus, of male domination.[27]

What if, she argued, we were to suggest that the capacities for intimacy, connection, and community were healthy adult experiences? That would mean that the stage *before* the Oedipal crisis—when both boys and girls are deeply attached to their mother—was crucial. What happens is that boys lose that capacity for connection and intimacy in the break with the mother and the shift to the father, whereas girls retain that capacity. What's more, such a shift is so traumatic for boys—and yet so

necessary in our culture—that they must demonstrate constantly that they have successfully achieved it. Masculinity comes to be defined as the distance between the
boy and his mother, between himself and being seen as a 'mama's boy' or a sissy. So
he must spend a significant amount of time and energy demonstrating his successful
achievement of this distance, which he does by devaluing all things feminine—
including girls, his mother, femininity, and, of course, all emotions associated with
femininity. Male domination requires the masculine devaluation of the feminine. As
Chodorow puts it:

> A boy, in his attempt to gain an elusive masculine identification, often comes to de-
> fine his masculinity in largely negative terms, as that which is not feminine or in-
> volved with women. There is an internal and external aspect to this. Internally, the
> boy tries to reject his mother and deny his attachment to her and the strong depen-
> dency on her that he still feels. He also tries to deny the deep personal identification
> with her that has developed during his early years. He does this by repressing what-
> ever he takes to be feminine inside himself, and, importantly, by denigrating what-
> ever he considers to be feminine in the outside world.

Thus Freud provided a decidedly 'feminist' reading of male domination. He just
didn't know it, so fixated was he on the break with the mother as the crucial moment in
human development.[28]

Kohlberg's ideas have also come under critical scrutiny from feminist scholars.
Feminist critiques related not to Kohlberg's theories of gender acquisition discussed
above, but to his related work on moral reasoning and the stages of cognitive and
moral development. Kohlberg's stages proceeded from very concrete and practical
rules to the application of universal ethical principles. But when girls and boys were
evaluated, girls seemed 'arrested' at the third stage of moral development, a stage that
stresses mutual interpersonal expectations and relationships. (Kohlberg argued that
this difference followed logically from the more remote and abstracted nature of the
boy's relationship with his father, compared with the girl's more interdependent relationship with her mother.)

Carol Gilligan, one of Kohlberg's students, was not persuaded and believed the different types of moral reasoning ought not be hierarchically ranked. In her path-breaking book *In a Different Voice*, Gilligan suggested that such stages appear only when
men's lives are regarded as the norm. In her interviews with Harvard women undergraduates, Gilligan found very different criteria for moral decision-making. She heard
another moral voice besides the '**ethic of justice**'—that abstract, universal, ethical paradigm Kohlberg proposed as the final stage of moral development. There is also an
'**ethic of care**', stressing intimacy and connectedness, that seems to be followed more
often by women. From this, Gilligan suggested that the origins of aggression might be
different for women and men. For men, the ethic of justice demands the blind and indifferent application of sanctions; aggression stems from constraints on individual autonomy. Women, Gilligan writes, hear a different voice, wherein 'lies the truth of an
ethic of care, and the tie between the relationship and responsibility, and the origins of
aggression in the failure of connection'.[29]

Gilligan's work unleashed a broad controversy among feminist psychologists that has continued to ripple through the larger culture. Gilligan's work *seemed* to support arguments that women and men are fundamentally, irretrievably, and irreconcilably different. Other work building on that premise followed quickly, including works on cognition and epistemology and popular works that emphasized differences between women's and men's linguistic and mythical spheres.[30]

Ironically, groups that sought to exclude women from various arenas attempted to use Gilligan's arguments to legitimate discrimination. If women and men are so obviously different, their reasoning went, then excluding women from certain positions would not be discrimination, but rather really a way to honour and respect differences. Historically, men who argued against extending rights to women made exactly the same case that Gilligan made. Here, for example, is the nineteenth-century pessimist philosopher Arthur Schopenhauer, from his famous essay *On Women* (1851): 'It is because women's reasoning powers are weaker that they show more sympathy for the unfortunate than men, and consequently take a kindlier interest in them. On the other hand, women are inferior to men in matters of justice, honesty, and conscientiousness'.

More recently, two US military training institutes cited the differences between women and men as justifications for excluding women from their state-supported corps of cadets, and fire departments sought to exclude women from entering their ranks. Given that the legal code requires the indifferent application of the law and adherence to abstract principles, one might have also predicted a move to exclude women from serving as judges.[31]

Gilligan herself was more circumspect, deploring efforts to use her findings 'to rationalize oppression'. What she found is that 'educationally advantaged North American males have a strong tendency to focus on issues of justice when they describe an experience of moral conflict and choice; two thirds of the men in our studies exhibited a 'justice focus'. One third of the women we studied also showed a justice focus. But one third of the women focused on care, in contrast to only one of the 46 men'. Moreover, 'one third of both females and males articulate justice and care concerns with roughly equal frequency'. The psychological patterns Gilligan observed, she argued, are 'not based on any premise of inherent differences between the sexes, but solely on the different nature of their experiences'. To extrapolate from these data to claim that *men* and *women* differ on moral voices would be to distort her findings into stereotypes. She writes:

> The title of my book was deliberate; it reads, 'in a *different* voice', not 'in a *woman's* voice'. In my introduction, I explain that this voice is not identified by gender but by theme. Noting as an empirical observation the association of this voice with women, I caution the reader that 'this association is not absolute, and the contrasts between male and female voices are presented here to highlight a distinction between two modes of thought and to focus a problem of interpretation rather than to represent a generalization about either sex'. In tracing development, I 'point to the interplay of these voices within each sex and suggest that their convergence marks times of crisis and change'. No claims, I state, are made about the origins of these voices or their distribution in a wider population, across cultures or time (p. 2). Thus, the care perspective in my rendition is neither biologically determined nor unique to women. It

is, however, a moral perspective different from that currently embedded in psychological theories and measures, and it is a perspective that was defined by listening to both women and men describe their own experience.[32]

Gilligan's articulation of this 'different moral perspective' has been enormously influential within North America and around the world, not least in the field of legal studies. In a 1990 lecture at the Osgoode Hall Law School, Madam Justice Bertha Wilson, Canada's first female Supreme Court judge, cited Gilligan's research to argue that perhaps women judges and lawyers might 'succeed in infusing the law with an understanding of what it means to be fully human.'[33] Still, subsequent research has failed to replicate consistent binary gender differences in ethics; most researchers 'report no average differences in the kind of reasoning men and women use in evaluating moral dilemmas, whether it is care-based or justice-based.'[34] Moreover, many feminists, including legal scholar Catharine MacKinnon, have condemned the essentialism and danger inherent in Gilligan's work. Despite these criticisms, a generation of feminists has used Gilligan's work as a touchstone. Moreover, and most importantly, her insistence that the ethic of care not be considered a shabby second to justice-based reasoning has changed views of moral reasoning, regardless of thin evidence of consistent gender differences.

Feminist psychologists have raised important questions and exposed an androcentric bias in the psychological literature of gender identity and development. With men as the normative standard against which both men and women were evaluated, women always seemed to be coming up short. As Gilligan demonstrated, when psychologists began to shift their framework and to listen closely to the voices of women, new patterns of development emerged. This bias also had consequences in the lives of real people. For example, the *Diagnostic and Statistical Manual of Mental Disorders* (DSM), published by the American Psychiatric Association, is the diagnostic bible of mental illness professionals. For some time, the DSM has listed such mental illnesses as 'premenstrual dysphoric disorder' (PDD), its version of PMS, despite controversy over the existence, nature, causation and prevalence of the disorder. Psychologist Paula Caplan suggested that the DSM instead consider adding a new set of diagnoses, including 'Delusional Dominating Personality Disorder' (DDPD) to classify sexist behaviour as symptomatic of mental illness. And what about 'John Wayne syndrome' or 'macho personality disorder?' she asks. Her tongue-in-cheek quiz to identify DDPD (see Figure 3.2 on page 80) goes a long way toward exposing the gender biases in those ostensibly gender-neutral manuals.

Developmental Differences

So what are the real psychological differences between women and men? Developmental psychologists have pointed to some significant differences between males and females that emerge as we grow. Yet even these are mean differences; once again, there is more variation *among* men and *among* women than there is *between* women and men. When psychologists Eleanor Maccoby and Carol Jacklin surveyed over 1,600 empirical studies from 1966 to 1973, they found only four areas with significant and

DO YOU RECOGNIZE THIS MAN?*

A quiz you'll never see in *Cosmo* and *Redbook*

Men who meet at least six of the following criteria may have Delusional Dominating Personality Disorder! Warning: DDPD is pervasive, profound, and a maladaptive organization of the entire personality! (Check as many as apply.)

1. Is he . . .

❏ unable to establish and maintain meaningful interpersonal relationships?

❏ unable to identify and express a range of feelings in himself (typically accompanied by an inablility to identify accurately the feelings of other people)?

❏ unable to respond appropriately and empathically to the feelings and needs of close associates and intimates (often leading to the misinterpretation of signals from others)?

❏ unable to derive pleasure from doing things for others?

2. Does he . . .

❏ use power, silence, withdrawal, and/or avoidance rather than negotiation in the face of interpersonal conflict or diffculty?

❏ believe that women are responsible for the bad things that happen to him, while the good things are due to his own abllities, achievements, or efforts?

❏ inflate the importance and achievements of himself, males in general, or both?

❏ categorize spheres of functioning and sets of behavior rigidly according to sex (like believing housework is women's work)?

❏ use a gender-based double standard in interpreting or evaluating situations or behavior (considering a man who makes breakfast sometimes to be extraordinarily good, for example, but considering a woman who sometimes neglects to make breakfast deficient)?

❏ feel inordinately threatened by women who fail to disguise their intelligence?

❏ display any of the following delusions:

  • the delusion that men are entitled to the services of any woman with whom they are personally associated;

  • the delusion that women like to suffer and be orderd around;

  • the delusion that physical force is the best method of solving interpersonal problems;

  • the delusion that men's sexual and aggressive impulses are uncontrollable;

    the delusion that pornography and erotica are identical;

  • the delusion that women control most of the world's wealth and/or power but do little of the world's work;

  • the delusion that existing inequalities in the distribution of power and wealth are a product of the survival of the fittest and that, therefore, allocation of greater social and economic rewards to the already privileged are merited.

3. Does he have . . .

❏ a pathological need to affirm his social importance by displaying himself in the company of females who meet any three of these criteria:

  • are conventionally physically attractive; *or*

  • are younger;

  • are shorter;

  • weigh less;

  • appear to be lower on socioeconomic criteria; *or*

  • are more submissive . . . than he is?

❏ a distorted approach to sexuality, displaying itself in one or both of these ways:

  • a pathological need for flattery about his sexual performance and/or the size of his genitalia;

  • an infantile tendency to equate large breasts on women with their sexual attractiveness.

❏ emotionally uncontrolled resistance to reform efforts that are oriented toward gender equity?

The tendency to consider himself a "New Man" neither proves nor disproves that the subject fits within this diagnostic category.

Some women also fit many of these criteria, either because they wish to be as dominant as men or because they feel men should be dominant.

Freely adapted, with permission, from *They Say You're Crazy:*
How the World's Most Powerful Psychiatrists Decide Who's Normal (Addison-Wesley, 1995) by Paula J. Caplan.

Figure 3.2 Hypothetical Diagnostic Tool for Delusional Dominating Personality Disorder (DDPD) by Paula J. Caplan.

consistent sex differences: (1) verbal ability (advantage: girls); (2) visuospatial ability (advantage: boys); (3) mathematical ability (boys again!); (4) and levels of aggression (consistently higher among boys). They tested the validity of many other beliefs about sex and personality, and concluded that 'there are many popular beliefs about the psychological characteristics of the two sexes that have proved to have little or no basis in fact'.[35] More than 30 years later, when psychologist Janet Hyde reviewed 46 meta-analyses—studies that reviewed *all* the available studies on a certain topic—in a sort of 'meta-meta-analysis', she found that the size of the gender difference for 78 per cent of all the traits, attitudes, and behaviours measured by these studies was 'small or close to zero'. Hyde therefore advanced the '**gender similarities hypothesis**', claiming that 'males and females are similar on most, but not all, psychological variables'. [36]

Because only small actual differences are found between girls and boys, how do we account for the relative ineffectiveness of socialization activities (toys, play, television, schools) in shaping the behaviour of children in psychological experiments, and yet the continuing assignment to children and adults of roles on the basis of gender typing? Our answer can be only speculative. It appears that most psychological experiments offer boys and girls an opportunity to perform similar tasks without labelling the tasks as gender appropriate. In these contexts, males and females perform mostly alike. It would appear that the real power of gender typing resides less in the child than in the environments in which the child finds him- or herself. The social environment is the gendered society, filled with gendered messages and gendered activities. Even if the child possesses no fixed and permanent gender role, social arrangements will continually reinforce gender differences. In a gender-neutral experiment, social requirements are removed, and so the child does not behave in accord with a gender stereotype.

Perhaps it is not simply internalized beliefs that keep us in place as men or women, but also our interpersonal and social environments. Because there is considerable variation in what men and women actually do, maintaining gender-role differences may require the weight of social organization and constant reinforcement. Psychoanalysis provided a theory of how gender identity is acquired in early childhood. Theorists of sex roles and androgyny help us move beyond strictly psychological analyses of gender. Cognitive development theory explained the mechanisms by which children acquire stable understandings of gender and the processes of self-socialization that accompany gender constancy. Feminist psychoanalysts provide a much-needed corrective to the androcentric theories of Freud and push us to consider the effects of current gender arrangements on gendered development. But the inability of all of these theories to fully account for difference, power, relationality, cultural variation, and, above all, the institutional dimension of gender means that we will need to build other elements into the discussion. We turn next to anthropological discussions of gender.

Summary

Freud's theories of psychosocial development provide a bridge between anatomical explanations of gender and theories of social construction. Freud believed that, for boys, the Oedipal crisis required rejection of the mother and identification with the father;

for girls, the crisis involves the need to identify with the mother and abandon any thought of possessing her. Freud theorized that girls necessarily experienced 'penis envy' in this stage. The key insights of Freudian theory, for our purposes, are that Freud (a) dislocates gender and sexuality from biological inevitability; (b) links the acquisition of gender identity and sexual orientation; and (c) reinstates traditional gender stereotypes as the hallmark of healthy gender development. Still, Freud, unlike many of his contemporaries, did not view homosexuality as a moral failing or psychological disorder. Freud's theories have nonetheless been subject to severe criticism, not least because of the small clinical sample on which he based his cases and, perhaps most damningly, his retreat from evidence that his women patients were actually survivors of sexual traumas including incest. Despite these and many other criticisms, Freud's theories have had great impact.

Sex role theory took part of its impetus from Terman and Miles's studies of masculinity and femininity, published in 1936 as *Sex and Personality*, which relied upon the M-F test. By the 1950s, social psychologists were moving beyond the test to question the social requirements for male and female sex roles. The authors of *The Authoritarian Personality* theorized that males with feminine internal psychological identification overcompensated, thus yielding highest scores on measures of racism, hypermasculinity, and authoritarianism. Talcott Parsons and other sociologists examined the social utility of sex roles in production and reproduction, highlighting the unintended impact of gender roles on society and social organization. Sandra Bem and other social psychologists challenged the rigidity of sex role theory in the 1970s, further critiquing the 'health' of dichotomized gender roles. Bem found that individuals varied greatly in the rigidity of their gender schemas, and that the best-adjusted people were androgynous and did not polarize gender. Though androgyny was extensively critiqued, gender schema theory remains an intriguing explanation of how we learn gender. Joseph Pleck continued a social focus on gender identity and its social function. By testing and falsifying propositions identified with the male sex role, Pleck argued that the role itself was the problem, resulting in male sex role strain (MSRS). Thus sex roles were not necessarily adaptive or healthy, and might be inherently contradictory, inconsistent, and even psychologically damaging. Sex role theory thus developed significantly, but its problems remained. It (a) remains unable to account for varieties of masculinities and femininities and, more broadly, within-sex differences; (b) obscures the power difference between traditional men's 'roles' and women's 'roles' and cannot account for male domination; and (c) locates gendering in individuals, without giving enough attention to institutions.

Cognitive development theory, developed by Lawrence Kohlberg, argues that gender identity is developed in childhood, though somewhat more slowly than Freudian theory would have it. Kohlberg argued that children learn gender roles and identities according to age-related modes of reasoning. Children proceed by learning their own maleness or femaleness (by age two) and then interpreting gendered information from the outside world. At this age children may have both a fluid and an over-rigid understanding of gender, believing that they might change genders if they performed an action 'appropriate' to the opposite sex. By age six, children have acquired a stable and constant sense of gender and are capable of socializing themselves by analyzing behaviour on the basis of its appropriateness for males or females. Cognitive development theory offers insights into how children learn gender, but little information on how gender roles are developed in the first place.

Feminists and other critics have identified significant problems with Freudian and later theories of gender development. Freud's theory of penis envy in particular has been criticized, including by Freud's own women followers, psychoanalysts Melanie Klein and Karen Horney. They argued that girls were probably less envious of male anatomy than conscious of the power difference between men and women. Some advanced the theory of 'womb envy', while a later generation used Freud's theories to analyze the phenomenon of male dominance. Kohlberg's stages of moral reasoning have also been criticized, most significantly by Carol Gilligan, who introduced the idea that women tended to reason from an 'ethic of care', in contrast to men's more prevalent 'ethic of justice'. Gilligan's theories, though criticized, continue to be influential in a number of fields.

Finally, the real psychological differences between men and women may be more elusive than once thought. Maccoby and Jacklin's 1974 meta-analysis found only four areas of consistent difference; more recently, Janet Hyde's study also found few significant differences. She therefore advanced the 'gender similarity hypothesis', arguing that there are few actual psychological differences between the sexes. Though all of the theories examined have contributed to our understanding of gender differences in psychology, they fail to fully account for power, relationality, and institutional dimensions of gender. We therefore turn to sociological and anthropological explanations of gender in Chapter 4.

Questions for Critical Thinking

1. Some people believe that Freud's theories have been totally discredited and serve no further purpose. Would you agree? Which, if any, of his theories do you see as having merit? How have Freud's ideas remained active in popular culture and belief?

2. Why do you think sex role theory was so much more concerned with boys' successful acquisition of 'appropriate' gender identity? What about girls?

3. Looking at the M-F test and its questions decades after the questions were created, what do you think the text shows about the nature of gender identity? Are the features the test codes as 'masculine' or 'feminine' still seen as such today? How might culture, class, and ethnicity impact one's results on the test?

4. Have you ever seen 'overcompensation' in action? Do you agree with Bem's conclusion that the healthiest individuals are least likely to be hypermasculine or hyperfeminine? If so, why do you think this might be so?

5. Do you find cognitive development theory more convincing than Freud's theories of gender development? Where do the theories disagree or complement one another?

6. How would a 'care' perspective and a 'justice' approach evaluate a particular crime (choose any one you like). What are the strengths and weaknesses of these modes of moral reasoning? Can you think of Canadian issues that would benefit from analysis using an 'ethic of care'?

Key Terms

androgyny
castration anxiety
cognitive development theory
cult of compulsive masculinity
ego
Electra complex
ethic of care
ethic of justice
expressive roles
external world
gender constancy
gender schema
gender schema theory
gender similarities hypothesis
homophobia

id
instrumental roles
male sex role identity (MSRI)
male sex role strain (MSRS)
M-F test
object relations theory
Oedipal crisis
penis envy
primary feminine phase
psychoanalysis
sex role theory
social psychologists
super-ego
womb envy

Chapter 4

Spanning the World

Culture Constructs Gender Difference

Human nature is potentially aggressive and destructive and potentially orderly and constructive.

—ATTRIBUTED TO MARGARET MEAD

Biological models assume that biological sex determines gender, that innate biological differences lead to behavioural differences, which in turn lead to social arrangements. By this account, social inequalities are encoded into our physiological composition. Biological anomalies alone should account for variation. Psychological models of gender identity suggest that gender identity is the result of childhood development, which proceeds in more or less universal ways. But the evidence suggests otherwise. When children like the Dominican pseudo-hermaphrodites are raised as the other *gender* they can easily make the transition to the other *sex*. And how do we account for the dramatic differences in the definitions of masculinity and femininity around the world? And how come some societies have much wider ranges of gender inequality than others? On these questions, the biological record is mute and psychological theory often less than convincing.

Anthropological research on cultural variations in the development of gender definitions arose, in part, in response to casual biological determinism. The more we found out about other cultures, the more we learned about the diversity of cultural constructions of gender. Yet some themes do remain constant. Virtually all societies manifest some amount of difference between women and men, and virtually all cultures exhibit some form of male domination, despite variations in gender definition. So anthropologists have also tried to explore the link between the near-universals of gender difference and gender inequality. Some search for those few societies in which women hold positions of power; others examine those rituals, beliefs, customs, and practices that tend to increase inequality and those that tend to decrease it.

The Variations in Gender Definitions

When anthropologists began to explore the cultural landscape, one of the first things they found was far more variability in the definitions of masculinity and femininity than any biologist would have predicted. Men whose anatomy was identical seemed to exhibit dramatically different levels of aggression, violence, and, especially, aggression toward women. Women with similar brains, hormones, and ostensibly similar evolutionary imperatives have widely varying experiences of passivity, PMS, and spatial coordination.

One of the most celebrated anthropologists to explore these differences was Margaret Mead, whose research in the South Seas (Samoa, Polynesia, Indonesia) remains, despite some significant criticism, an example of engaged scholarship, clear writing, and important ideas. Mead was clear that sex differences are 'not something deeply biological', but rather are learned and, once learned, become part of the ideology that continues to perpetuate them. Here's how she put it:

> I have suggested that certain human traits have been socially specialized as the appropriate attitudes and behaviour of only one sex, while other human traits have been specialized for the opposite sex. This social specialization is then rationalized into a theory that the socially decreed behaviour is natural for one sex and unnatural for the other, and that the deviant is a deviant because of glandular defect, or developmental accident.[1]

In *Sex and Temperament in Three Primitive Societies* (1935), Mead explored the differences in those definitions, whereas in several other books, such as *Male and Female* (1949) and *Coming of Age in Samoa* (1928), she explored the processes by which males and females become the men and women their cultures prescribe. No matter what she seemed to be writing about, though, Mead always had one eye trained on the United States. In generating implicit comparisons between her own and other cultures, Mead challenged those Americans who believed that their culture's mores must be right and could not be changed. Her works, read throughout the world, provided ample fodder for a critique of modern industrialized societies and rigid traditional gender norms.[2]

In *Sex and Temperament*, Mead directly took on the claims of biological inevitability. By examining three very different cultures in New Guinea, she hoped to show the enormous cultural variation possible in definitions of masculinity and femininity. The first two cultures exhibited remarkable similarities between women and men. Masculinity and femininity were not the lines along which personality differences seemed to be organized. Women and men were not the 'opposite' sex. For example, all members of the Arapesh culture appeared gentle, passive, and emotionally warm. Males and females were equally 'happy, trustful, confident', and individualism was relatively absent. Men and women shared child rearing; both were 'maternal', and both discouraged aggressiveness among boys and girls. Both men and women were thought to be relatively equally sexual, though their sexual relationships tended to be 'domestic' and not 'romantic' or what we might call passionate. Although female infanticide and **polygamy** were not unknown, marriage was 'even and contented'. Indeed, Mead pronounced the political arrangements 'utopian'. Here's how she summed up Arapesh life:

> quiet and uneventful co-operation, singing in the cold dawn, and singing and laughter in the evening, men who sit happily playing to themselves on hand-drums, women holding suckling children to their breasts, young girls walking easily down the centre of the village, with the walk of those who are cherished by all about them.[3]

By contrast, Mead describes the Mundugamor, a tribe of headhunters and canni-bals, who also viewed women and men as similar but expected both sexes to be equally aggressive and violent. Women showed little 'maternal instinct'; they detested preg-nancy and nursing and could hardly wait to return to the serious business of work and war. 'Mundugamor women actively dislike child-bearing, and they dislike children', Mead writes. 'Children are carried in harsh opaque baskets that scratch their skins, later, high on their mother's shoulders, well away from the breast'. Among the Mundu-gamor, there was a violent rivalry between fathers and sons (there was more infanticide of boys than of girls), and all people experienced a fear that they were being wronged by others. Quite wealthy (partly as a result of their methods of population control), the Mundugamor were, as Mead concludes, 'violent, competitive, aggressively sexual, jeal-ous, ready to see and avenge insult, delighting in display, in action, in fighting'.[4]

Here, then, were two tribes who saw gender differences as virtually non-existent. The third culture Mead described was the Tchambuli, where, as in the United States, women and men were seen as extremely different. This was a culture in which **polygyny** was accepted. Here, one sex was composed primarily of nurturing and gossipy consumers who spent their days dressing up and going shopping. They wore curls and lots of jewellery, and Mead describes them as 'charming, graceful, coquettish'. These, incidentally, were the men, and they liked nothing better than to 'go off resplendent in feathers and shell ornaments to spend a delightful few days' shopping. The women were dominant, energetic, economic providers. It was they who fished, an activity upon which the entire culture depended, and it was they 'who have the real positions of power in the society'. Completely unadorned, they were efficient, business-like, con-trolled all the commerce and diplomacy of the culture, and were the initiators of sexual relations. Mead writes that '[w]hat the women will think, what the women will say, what the women will do lies at the back of each man's mind as he weaves his tenuous and uncertain web of insubstantial relations with other men'. By contrast, 'the women are a solid group, confused by no rivalries, brisk, patronizing, and jovial'.[5]

What Mead found, then, were two cultures in which women and men were seen as similar to each other and one culture in which women and men were seen as extremely different from each other—but exactly the opposite of the model familiar to us. Each culture, of course, believed that women and men were the way they were because their biological sex *determined* their personality. None of them believed that women and men were the outcome of economic scarcity, military success, or cultural arrangements.

Mead's findings were attacked almost immediately, first by ~~her ex-husband~~ Reo Fortune, who had shared her fieldwork, and then later by New Zealand anthropolo-gist Derek Freeman. The controversy over her theories continues to this day. She has been criticized for **cultural determinism**, for allowing herself to be duped by her informants, and for misrepresentation of the cultures she studied;[6] however, she made outstanding contributions to the field of anthropology and to feminist theories of gender construction. Her ideas, and the question of cultural variability, remain important topics of discussion. Mead urged her readers to 'admit men and women are capable of being moulded to a single pattern as easily as a diverse one'.[7] She dem-onstrated that women and men are *capable* of similar or different temperaments; she did not adequately explain *why* women and men turn out to be different or the same.

These questions remain: What are the determinants of women's and men's experiences? Why should male domination be nearly universal? These issues have been taken up by other anthropologists.

The Centrality of the Gender Division of Labour

In almost every society, labour is divided by gender (as well as age). Certain tasks are reserved for women, others for men. How do we explain this gender division of labour, if not by some biologically based imperatives?

One school of thought, **functionalism**, maintains that a sex-based division of labour was necessary for the preservation of the society. As society became increasingly complex, there arose a need for two kinds of labour: hunting and gathering. Functionalists differ as to whether this division of labour had any *moral* component, whether the work of one sex was more highly valued than the work of the other. But they agree that the sex-based division of labour was functionally necessary for these societies. Such models often assume that because the sex-based division of labour arose to meet certain social needs at one time, its preservation is an evolutionary imperative, or at least an arrangement that is not to be trifled with casually.

On the other hand, because the sex-based division of labour has a history, it is not biologically inevitable; societies have changed and will continue to change. And it's a very recent history at that. 'The sexual division of labour as we know it today probably developed quite recently in human evolution', writes anthropologist Adrienne Zihlman.[8] Moreover, this sex-based division of labour is far more varied than we might have assumed. In some cultures, women build the house; in others, they do the cooking. But in a few, it's the reverse. In most cultures women are responsible for child care. But not in all cultures, and women are certainly not doing it all. In some cultures, tasks are dramatically skewed and labour rigidly divided; others offer far more flexibility and fluidity. Today, a sex-based division of labour is functionally anachronistic, and the biological bases for specific social tasks being assigned to either men or women have long been eroded. In the place of such foundations, though, lie centuries of social customs and traditions that today contribute to our gender ideologies about what is appropriate for one sex and not the other. The gender-based division of labour has become a part of our culture, not a part of our physical constitutions.

In fact, our physical constitutions have become less determinative in the assignment of tasks and the choosing of careers. It may even be true that the less significance there is to real physical differences, the more emphasis we place on them ideologically. For example, men no longer need to have physical strength to be powerful and dominant. The most highly muscular men, in fact, appear in cultural sideshows of body-building competition, but they do no more physical labour than the average suburban husband. As for women, in most industrialized societies family planning and sexual autonomy have freed them from their 'biologically determined' restriction to child-bearing and child care.

Today, very few occupations exist for which only women or only men are strictly biologically suited. Ask yourselves: What occupations do you know of that *biologically* only women or only men could perform? Offhand, we can think of only three: for women, wet nurse and surrogate mother; for men, professional sperm donor. None of these is exactly a career of choice for most of us.

If a sex-based division of labour has outlived its social usefulness or its physical imperatives, it must be held in place by something else: the power of one sex over the other. Where did that power come from? How has it developed? How does it vary from culture to culture? What factors exaggerate it; what factors diminish it? These are among the questions that anthropologists have endeavoured to answer.

Theories of Gender Differentiation and Male Domination

Several theorists have tried to explain the sexual division of labour and gender inequality by reference to large, structural forces that transform societies' organizing principles. They've pointed to the impact of private property, the demands of war, and the importance of male bonding to hunting and gathering as possible explanations.

Private Property and the Materialism of Male Domination
In the late nineteenth century, Friedrich Engels applied ideas that he developed with his collaborator, Karl Marx, and assigned to private property the role of central agent in determining the division of labour by sex. In *The Origins of the Family, Private Property and the State*, Engels suggested that the three chief institutions of modern Western society—a capitalist economy, the nation-state, and the nuclear family—emerged at roughly the same historical moment—and all as a result of the development of private property. Prior to that, Engels asserts, families were organized on a communal basis, with group marriage, male-female equality, and a sexual division of labour without any moral or political rewards going to males or females. The birth of the capitalist economy created wealth that was mobile and transferable—unlike land, which stays in the same place. Capitalism meant private property, which required the establishment of clear lines of inheritance. This requirement led, in turn, to new problems of sexual fidelity. If a man were to pass his property on to his son, he had to be sure that his son was, indeed, *his*. How could he know this in the communal group marriage of precapitalist families?

Out of this need to transmit inheritance across generations of men the traditional nuclear family emerged, with monogamous marriage and the sexual control of women by men. And if inheritance were to be stable, these new patriarchs needed to have clear, binding laws, vigorously enforced, that would enable them to pass their legacies on to their sons without interference from others. This required a centralized political apparatus (the nation-state) to exercise sovereignty over local and regional powers that might challenge them.[9]

Some contemporary anthropologists continue in this tradition. American anthropologist Eleanor Leacock, for example, argues that prior to the rise of private property and social classes, women and men were regarded as autonomous individuals, who held different positions that were held in relatively equal esteem. 'When the range of decisions made by women is considered', she writes, 'women's autonomous and public role emerges. Their status was not as literal 'equals' of men . . . but as what they were—female persons, with their own rights, duties and responsibilities, which were complementary to and in no way secondary to those of men'. In her ethnographic work with Innu people on the Labrador peninsula, Leacock shows the dramatic transformation of women's former autonomy by the introduction of the fur trade. The introduction of a commercial economy turned powerful women into home-bound wives. Here again, gender inequality, introduced by economic shifts, resulted in increasing differences in the meanings of masculinity and femininity.[10]

Karen Sacks (now Karen Brodkin) examined four African cultures and found that the introduction of the market economy shifted basically egalitarian roles toward male dominance. As long as the culture was involved in producing goods for its own use, men and women were relatively equal. But the more involved the tribe became in a market exchange economy, the higher the level of gender inequality and the lower the position of women. Conversely, when women and men shared access to the productive elements of the society, the result was a higher level of sexual egalitarianism.[11]

Warfare, Bonding, and Inequality

Another school of anthropological thought traces the origins of male domination to the imperatives of warfare in primitive society. How does a culture create warriors who are fierce and strong? Anthropologist Marvin Harris has suggested two possibilities. The culture can provide different rewards for the warriors, based on their dexterity or skill. But this would limit the solidarity of the fighting force and sow seeds of dissent and enmity among the soldiers. More effective would be to reward virtually all men with the services of women, excluding only the most inadequate or cowardly men. Warrior societies tend to practise female infanticide, Harris observes, ensuring that the population of females remains significantly lower than that of males (and thus the males will be competing for the women). Warrior societies also tend to exclude women from the fighting force, because their presence would reduce the motivation of the soldiers and upset the sexual hierarchy. In this way, warfare leads to female subordination as well as **patrilineality**, because the culture will need a resident core of fathers and sons to carry out its military tasks. Males come to control the society's resources and, as a justification for this, develop patriarchal religion as an ideology that legitimates their domination over women.[12]

Two other groups of scholars use different variables to explain the differences between women and men. **Descent theorists**, like Lionel Tiger and Robin Fox, stress the invariance of the mother-child bond. Men, in contrast, lack the tie that mothers have with their children, because for most of human history they could never be certain of biological paternity. How, then, can they achieve that connection to the next generation, the connection to history and society? They form it with other men in the hunting group. This is why, Tiger and Fox argue, women must be excluded from the hunt. In all societies, men must somehow be bound socially to the next generation, to which they are not inextricably, biologically connected. Male solidarity, or what Tiger called 'male bonding', and monogamy are the direct result of men's needs to connect with social life.[13] **Alliance theorists** like Claude Levi-Strauss are less concerned with the need to connect males to the next generation than they are with the ways that relationships among men come to organize social life. Levi-Strauss argues that men turn women into sex objects whose exchange (as wives) cements the alliances among men. Both descent and alliance theorists treat these themes as invariant and natural, rather than as the outcomes of historical relationships that vary dramatically not only over time but also across cultures.[14]

Determinants of Women's Status

Virtually every society of which we have knowledge claims some differentiation between women and men, and virtually every society exhibits patterns of gendered inequality and male domination. Yet the variety within these universals is still astounding. Gender differences and gender inequality may be more or less pronounced. It is not simply the case that the higher the degree of gender differentiation, the greater the gender inequality, although this is generally the pattern. One could, conceivably, imagine four such possibilities—high or low levels of gender differentiation coupled with either high or low levels of gender inequality.

What, then, are the factors that seem to determine women's status in society? Under what conditions is women's status improved, and under what conditions is it minimized? Economic, political, and social variables tend to produce different cultural configurations. For example, one large-scale survey of different cultures found that the more a society needs physical strength and highly developed motor skills, the larger will be the differences in socialization between males and females. It also seems to be the case that the larger the family group, the larger the differences between women and men. In part this is because the isolation of the nuclear family means that males and females will need to take the others' roles on occasion, so that strict separation is rarely enforced.[15]

One of the key determinants of women's status has been the division of labour around child care. Women's role in reproduction has historically limited their social and economic participation. Although no society assigns all child care functions to men, the more that men participate in child care and the freer women are from child rearing responsibility, the higher women's status tends to be. There are many ways to free women from sole responsibility. In non-Western societies, several customs evolved, including employing child nurses who care for several children at once, sharing child care with husbands or with neighbours, and assigning the role of child care to tribal elders, whose economic activity has been curtailed by age.[16]

Relationships between children and their parents have also been seen as keys to women's status. Sociologist Scott Coltrane found that the closer the relationship between father and son, the higher the status of women is likely to be. Coltrane found that in cultures where fathers are relatively uninvolved, boys define themselves *in opposition* to their mothers and other women and therefore are prone to exhibit traits of **hypermasculinity**, to fear and denigrate women as a way to display masculinity. The more mothers and fathers share child rearing, the less men belittle women. Margaret Mead also emphasized the centrality of fatherhood. Most cultures take women's role in child rearing as a given, whereas men must learn to become nurturers. There is much at stake, but nothing inevitable: 'every known human society rests firmly on the learned nurturing behaviour of men'.[17]

That men must learn to be nurturers raises the question of masculinity in general. What it means to be a man varies enormously from one culture to another, and these definitions have a great deal to do with the amount of time and energy fathers spend with their children. Such issues are not simply incidental for women's lives either; it turns out that the more time men spend with their children, the less gender inequality is present in that culture. Conversely, the freer women are from child care—the more that child care is parcelled out elsewhere and the more that women control their fertility— the higher will be their status. Coltrane also found that women's status depends upon their control over property, especially after marriage. A woman's status is invariably higher when she retains control over her property after marriage.

Interestingly, recent research on male bonding, so necessary to those theories that stress warfare or the necessity of attaching males to the social order, also seems to bear this out. Sociologist and geographer Daphne Spain argues that the same cultures in which men developed the most elaborate sex-segregated rituals were those cultures in which women's status was lowest. Spain mapped a number of cultures spatially and found that the greater the distance the men's hut was from the centre of the village, the more time the men spent at their hut. And the more culturally important the men's rituals were, the lower women's status. 'Societies with men's huts are those in which women have the least power', she writes. If you spend your time away from your hut, off at the men's hut with the other men, you'll have precious little time, and even less inclination, to spend with your family and to share in child rearing![18]

Similarly, anthropologist Thomas Gregor found that all forms of spatial segregation between males and females are associated with gender inequality. The Mehinaku of central Brazil, for example, have well-institutionalized men's huts where the tribal secrets are kept and ritual instruments are played and stored. Women are prohibited from entering. As one tribesman told Gregor, '[t]his house is only for men. Women may not see anything in here. If a woman comes in, then all the men take her into the woods and she is raped'.[19]

These two variables—the father's involvement in child rearing (often measured by spatial segregation) and women's control of property after marriage—emerge as among the central determinants of women's status and gender inequality. It is no wonder that they are also determinants of violence against women, because the lower women's status in a society, the higher the likelihood of rape and violence against women. In one of the most wide-ranging comparative studies of women's status, Peggy Reeves Sanday found several important correlates of women's status. Contact was one. **Sex segregation** was highly associated with women's lower status, as if separation were 'necessary for the development of sexual inequality and male dominance'. (By contrast, a study of a sexually egalitarian society found no ideology of the desirability of sex segregation.) Of course, women's economic power, that crucial determinant, is 'the result of a sexual division of labour in which women achieve self-sufficiency and establish an independent control sphere'. In addition, in cultures that viewed the environment as relatively friendly, women's status was significantly higher; cultures that saw the environment as hostile were more likely to develop patterns of male domination.[20]

Finally, Sanday found that women had the highest levels of equality, and thus the least frequency of rape, when both genders contributed about the same amounts to the food supply. When women contributed equally, men tended to be more involved in child care. Ironically, when women contributed a lot, their status was also low. So women's status tended to be lower when they contributed either very little or a great deal and more equal when their contribution was about equal.

We can now summarize the findings of cross-cultural research on female status and male dominance.

1. Male dominance is lower when men and women work together, with little sexual division of labour. Sex segregation of work is the strongest predictor of women's status.
2. Male dominance is more pronounced when men control political and ideological resources that are necessary to achieve the goals of the culture and when men control all property.
3. Male dominance is 'exacerbated under colonization'—both capitalist penetration of the countryside and industrialization generally lower women's status. Male dominance is also associated with demographic imbalances between the sexes: The higher the percentage of marriageable men to marriageable women, the lower is women's status.
4. Environmental stresses tend to exaggerate male domination.[21]

Rituals of Gender

One of the ways anthropologists have explored the cultural construction of gender is by examining specific gender rituals. Their work suggests that the origins of these rituals lie in non-biological places. Because questions of reproduction and child-rearing loom so large in the determination of gender inequality, it makes sense that a lot of these rituals are concerned with reproduction. And because spatial segregation seems to be highly associated with gender difference and gender inequality, **ritual segregation**—either in space or time—may have also been a focus of attention. For example, the initiation of young males has been of particular concern, in part because of the relative disappearance of such formal cultural rituals in modern industrialized nations. Initiation rituals provide a sense of identity and group membership to the men who participate in them.

Many cultures, especially settled agricultural and pastoral societies, include **circumcision,** the excision of the foreskin of a boy's penis, in a ritual incorporating a male into the society. The age at which this ritual is performed varies; one survey of 21 cultures that practise circumcision found that four perform it in infancy, 10 when the boy is about 10 years old (before puberty), six perform it at puberty, and one waits until late adolescence.

Why would so many cultures determine that membership in the world of adult men requires genital alteration? Theories, of course, abound. In the Jewish Bible, circumcision is a visible sign of the bond between God and man, a symbol of man's obedience to God's law. (In Genesis 17:10–11, 14, God commands Abraham to circumcise Isaac as a covenant.) But circumcision also seems to have been seen as a way of acquiring a trophy. Successful warriors would cut off their foes' foreskins to symbolize their victory and to permanently disfigure and humiliate the vanquished foe. (In I Samuel

18:25, King Saul demands that David slay 100 enemies and bring back their foreskins as a bride-price. David, a bit overeager, brings back 200.)

In other cultures, ethnographers suggest, circumcision creates a visible scar that binds men to one another and serves as a rite of passage to adult masculinity. Whiting, Kluckhohn, and Anthony argue that it symbolically serves to sever a boy's emotional ties to his mother, and therefore to ensure appropriate masculine identification. Other writers point out that cultures that emphasize circumcision of young males tend to be those where both gender differentiation and gender inequality are greatest. Circumcision simultaneously cements the bonds between father (and his generation) and son (and his generation), links the males together, and excludes women, visibly and demonstrably. Circumcision, then, tends to be associated with male domination, as do other forms of male genital mutilation. In a very few cultures, for example, the penis is ritually bled by cutting. Such cultures still believe in bleeding as a cure for illness—in this case, illness brought about by sexual contact with women, who are believed to be impure and infectious. And we know of four cultures that practise hemicastration, the removal of one testicle. In one culture, people believe it prevents the birth of twins.[22]

Female 'circumcision,' more generally known as **female genital mutilation** (**FGM**) or **female genital cutting** (**FGC**), is also practised in many cultures, most of them in Africa. The World Health Organization recognizes four 'types' of FGC/FGM, from the removal of the hood of the clitoris (analogous to male circumcision) all the way to **infibulation**, which involves the removal of most of the external genital tissue and the sewing together of the remaining tissue with only a very small opening left to allow for urination. It is interesting that FGC/FGM is often performed

△ Introcision

■ Infibulation (with clitoridectomy)

▲ Clitoridectomy

■ Excision (including removal of labia/majora)

▲ 1 Malinke
2 Vai
3 Bambara
4 Nupe
5 Yoruba
6 Igbo

Map 4.1 Female genital alterations.
From *Sexual Practices* by Edgar Gregersen.

by adult women, and it takes place in societies that also practise male circumcision. The goals of such genital alteration range from improving the appearance and hygiene of the genitals to preventing female promiscuity. It is estimated by the World Health Organization that 130 million girls and women have undergone some form of FGC/FGM.[23]

Female 'Circumcision'

Here is a description of FGC/FGM from one who underwent it, a Sudanese woman now working as a teacher in the Middle East:

I will never forget the day of my circumcision, which took place 40 years ago. I was six years old. One morning during my school summer vacation, my mother told me that I had to go with her to her sister's house and then to visit a sick relative in Halfayat El Mulook [in the northern part of Khartoum, Sudan]. We did go to my aunt's house, and from there all of us went straight to [a] red brick house [I had never seen].

While my mother was knocking, I tried to pronounce the name that was on the door. Soon enough I realized that it was Haija Alamin's house. She was the midwife [who performed circumcisions on girls in my neighbourhood]. I was petrified and tried to break loose. But I was captured and subdued by my mother and two aunts. They began to tell me that the midwife was going to purify me.

The midwife was the cruellest person I had seen . . . [She] ordered her young maid to go buy razors from the Yemeni grocer next door. I still remember her when she came back with the razors, which were enveloped in purple wrappings with a crocodile drawing on it.

The women ordered me to lie down on a bed [made of ropes] that had a little hole in the middle. They held me tight while the midwife started to cut my flesh without anesthetics. I screamed till I lost my voice. The midwife was saying to me 'Do you want me to be taken into police custody?' After the job was done I could not eat, drink, or even pass urine for three days. I remember one of my uncles who discovered what they did to me threatened to press charges against his sisters. They were afraid of him and they decided to bring me back to the midwife. In her sternest voice she ordered me to squat on the floor and urinate. It seemed like the most difficult thing to do at that point, but I did it. I urinated for a long time and was shivering with pain.

It took a very long time [before] I was back to normal. I understand the motives of my mother, that she wanted me to be clean, but I suffered a lot.[24]

It is interesting that both cultures that circumcise men and those that practise FGM/FGC tend to be those where men's status is highest. The purpose of the ritual reveals some of this difference. For men, the ritual is a marking that simultaneously shows that all men are biologically *and culturally* alike—and that they are different from women.

Thus it can be seen as reinforcing male dominance. This cannot, however, explain the prevalence of male circumcision in twentieth-century North America. Historically, there was some evidence that male circumcision was medically beneficial, because it reduced the possibilities of penile infection by removing the foreskin, a place where bacteria could congregate. (This is no longer the case; rates of penile infection or urethral cancer show no significant differences between those men who have and have not been circumcised.) Circumcision was also viewed as preventing excessive masturbation. Thus, in twentieth-century North America, infant circumcision became a routine part of hospital birth. Until 35 years ago, most boy babies in Canada were routinely circumcised. Today, more than 90 per cent of newborn male Canadians are left intact.[25] Among advanced industrial societies, only the United States continues widespread routine infant circumcision, and even there the practice is being abandoned.

For women, genital alteration has never been justified by medical benefits; indeed FGC/FGM is medically dangerous, both at the time of the cutting, when many girls succumb to infections, and, in many cases, during childbirth. Moreover, FGC/FGM directly impedes adequate sexual functioning and is designed to curtail sexual pleasure. FGC/FGM seems to be associated with men's control over women's sexuality.

Control over women's sexuality is an important part of many reproductive and sexual rituals, according to Jeffrey and Karen Paige in their book *The Politics of Reproductive Ritual*. Paige and Paige offer a materialist interpretation of these rituals, locating the origins of male circumcision, **couvade**, and **purdah** in the culture's relationship with its immediate material environment. Take couvade, for example. This is a ritual that men observe when their wives are having babies. Generally, the men observe the same food taboos as their wives, restrict their ordinary activities, and even seclude themselves during their wives' delivery and postpartum period. What could possibly be the point of this? Some might think it is anthropologically 'cute', as the men often even imitate the symptoms of pregnancy, in apparent sympathy for their wives. But Paige and Paige see it differently. They argue that couvade is significant in cultures where there are no legal mechanisms to keep the couple together or to assure paternity. Couvade is a way for men to fully claim paternity, to know that the baby is theirs. It is also a vehicle by which the men can control women's sexuality by appropriating control over paternity.[26]

Paige and Paige also examine the politics of purdah, the Islamic requirement that women conceal themselves at all times. Ostensibly, this requirement is to protect women's chastity and men's honour—women must be completely covered because they 'are so sexy, so tempting, so incapable of controlling their emotions and sexuality, the men say, that they are a danger to the social order.' It is as if by concealing women, men can harness women's sexuality. But this is only half the story. It also suggests that *men* are so susceptible to temptation, so incapable of resistance, such easy prey, that they are likely to fall into temptation at any time. In order to protect women from *men's* sexual rapaciousness, men must control women and take away the source of the temptation.[27]

Currently, political campaigns are being waged to prohibit FGC/FGM as a violation of women's human rights. In Kenya, some women have developed alternative rituals to enable girls to come of age without any forms of genital mutilation. For example,

'Cutting Through Words' is one ritual that provides a celebration of adulthood that honours the girl and her family. 'We need to tread carefully since female genital mutilation is deeply rooted into the culture', says Priscilla Nangurai, headmistress of a church-sponsored girls' boarding school who has been one of the advocates of change. 'We can end it through education, advocacy, and religion'.[28]

However, some defenders of FGC/FGM suggest that such campaigns are motivated by Western values. They insist that afterward women are revered and respected as members of the culture, and that there are 'acceptable' forms of FGC that are ignored by Western commentators.[29] (So far, there are no widespread political campaigns against male circumcision, though some individuals have recently begun to rethink the ritual as a form of genital mutilation, and a few men are even undergoing a surgical procedure designed to replace the lost foreskin.)[30] Others counter that the right to control one's own body is a fundamental human right and that cultures that practise such behaviours must conform to universal standards. To a great degree, these debates have diminished as African women take leadership roles in the elimination of FGC/FGM. One particularly influential group is known as the Tostan movement. In 1991, the NGO Tostan ('breakthrough' in Wolof) was formed to spark basic education and community development in Senegal. After 1997, women who had been through Tostan's education program began a campaign to end FGC/FGM through village-by-village voluntary abandonment of the practice. Since then, thousands of villages in Senegal and some in other African countries have abandoned FGC/FGM and child marriage.[31]

Beauty Contests

Gender inequality means that women and men have different access to the sorts of resources that would enable them to succeed in the dating and marriage market. Men have greater access to money and material goods; in the absence of such resources, women most often use their physical attractiveness as a currency. In the 1970s, an

Frans Lemmens/Getty Images

Wodaabe beauty contestant.

activist used to stage male beauty contests in which men would parade around in bathing suits and formal attire to be judged by a panel of female judges, so they could experience objectification first-hand. One culture, however, does this routinely. Among the Wodaabe of Mali, each year the men dress up in ceremonial garb, paint their faces and lips, and parade in front of the women, who choose which man they will sleep with. As documented in Werner Herzog's fascinating film *Herdsmen of the Sun*, the Wodaabe prize height, white teeth, and white eyes, and so the men try desperately to set off their teeth (by staining their lips black for contrast), stand on tiptoes, and open their eyes as wide as possible. The women cluster together and observe, mock, and judge them, and then each chooses her partner for the evening. Bert Parks is not the emcee.

How Many Genders are There?

The discussion of gender difference often assumes that differences are based on some biological realities that sort physical creatures into their appropriate categories. Thus we assume that because there are two biological sexes (male and female—or so we assume, as we'll discuss in Chapter 11), there must only be two genders (men and women). But some research challenges such bipolar assumptions. Some societies recognize more than two genders—sometimes three or four. Research on indigenous and traditional cultures is particularly fascinating and provocative. The Navajo (*Diné*), for example, appear to have had three genders—one for masculine men, one for feminine women, and another, called the **nadle**. *Nadles* might be either clearly male or genitally ambiguous, and performed tasks assigned to both women and men; they were typically treated as women and addressed using feminine kinship terms. But let's not jump to conclusions: Being treated as a woman was not a demotion in Navajo society, where women historically have had high status and are accorded special rights and privileges, including sexual freedom, control over property, and authority to mediate disputes. *Nadles* were considered lucky or beneficial for a community and were granted high status.[32]

The *nadle* is an example of what anthropologists call **berdaches**, a group also found in Southeast Asia and the South Pacific. (The term is considered offensive by First Nations and other Aboriginal people, who increasingly use the term '**Two-Spirited**'.) *Berdaches* are members of one biological sex who adopt the gender identity of the other sex, although such a practice is far more common for males than for females. In his path-breaking study *The Spirit and the Flesh*, anthropologist Walter Williams explored the world of the *berdache* in detail. These were men who dressed, worked, and generally acted as women—though everyone knew that they were biologically male. Among the Crow in North America, the *berdaches* were simply males who did not want to become warriors.[33]

Consider how we treat males who dress and act like women. In general, they are outcasts; acting like a *berdache* in mainstream North American culture is not recommended if you value your health and your life. Among the indigenous cultures of the Great Plains, though, the *berdaches* were revered as possessed of special powers, enjoyed high social and economic status, and frequently controlled ritual life. Anthropologist Sabine Lang documented the wide range of cross-gender activities engaged in by *berdaches* in North American indigenous cultures.[34]

Though there are far fewer documented instances of *female* biological sex and third gender, there are examples from around the world.[35] Among the Nahane of northern BC and the Yukon, a husband and wife might decide that they had too many daughters and too few sons to hunt for them when they got old. They would choose one of their daughters to live like a man. When she was about five years old, the dried ovaries of a bear were tied to her belt, and she was treated as if she were a boy from then on. As an adult, she would most likely have lesbian sexual relations.[36] In Albania, a family without sons might designate a daughter as a '**sworn virgin**'. Such a daughter would adopt a masculine identity and behaviour, for the rest of her life living like a man and enjoying the privileges of maleness, except sexual relations—they promised lifelong chastity— and the dubious honour of being a target for blood feuds. Though most remaining sworn virgins are elderly, they testify to a life of social acceptance and even prestige.[37]

These stories should caution us against regarding third genders as analogous to modern transgendered or homosexual people; indeed, the term 'Two-Spirited' recognizes the distinct rootedness of this category in indigenous cultures. Third-gender people followed many different paths to their identities. Some were designated at birth, some chose a new identity in adulthood, some responded to family needs for a differently-gendered member. But third-gender people were not 'expressing their identity' in

Number of tribes from which the trait has been reported

Figure 4.1 Components of the woman-man (male-bodied *berdache*) role.

From *Men as Women, Women as Men: Changing Gender in Native American Cultures* by Sabine Lang, translated by John L. Vantine, University of Texas Press, Copyright © 1998.

the ways characteristic of modern societies. Indeed, the variability of the phenomenon of third genders shows that culture, rather than the expression of individual gender-bending tendencies, is the central actor here.

The Mohave (*Aha macave*) of the western United States seemed to have four genders and permitted both women and men to cross genders to carefully demarcated roles. A boy who showed preferences for feminine clothing or toys would undergo a different initiation at puberty and become an **alyha**. He would then adopt a female name, paint his face as a woman, perform female roles, and marry a man. When they married, the *alyha* would cut his upper thigh every month to signify 'her' menstrual period, and he would learn how to simulate pregnancy and childbirth. Martin and Voorhies suggest how this was accomplished:

> Labour pains, induced by drinking a severely constipating drug, culminate in the birth of a fictitious stillborn child. Stillborn Mohave infants are customarily buried by the mother, so that an alyha's failure to return to 'her' home with a living infant is explained in a culturally acceptable manner.[38]

If a Mohave female wanted to cross genders, she would undergo an initiation ceremony to become a **hwame**. *Hwame* lived men's lives—hunting, farming, and the like—and assumed paternal responsibility for children, though they were prohibited from assuming positions of political leadership. Neither *hwame* nor *alyha* was considered deviant.

Biologically male third genders are relatively widespread. In southern Mexico's Zapotec communities, **muxes** are biological men who dress as women and fulfil characteristically female roles—today, often as hairdressers or wedding planners.[39] In India, **hijras**, generally biologically male or intersex, were once seen as members of a caste and continue to form a community. They perform female gender roles and, though often socially marginal, also have a religious function. In 2009, both Pakistan and India recognized them as members of a distinct gender.[40] In the Middle East, we find a group of Omani males called '**xanith**' who are biologically males, but whose social identity is female. If they want to be seen as males, they are permitted to do so, and they then may engage in heterosexual sex. Some 'become' women, even going as far as marrying men. And still others move back and forth between these positions throughout their lives, suggesting a fluidity of gender identity that would be unthinkable to those who believe in biological determinism. Certainly, the key challenge to biological determinism that emerges from study of third (and fourth) genders is many cultures' refusal to see gender and biological sex as inextricably linked.

Sexual Diversity

Studies of gender diversity are complemented by studies of sexual variation. Taken together, they provide powerful arguments about the cultural construction of both gender and sexuality. Anthropologists have explored remarkable sexual diversity and thus have suggested that biological arguments about the naturalness of some activities and arrangements may be dramatically overstated. Take homosexuality. Not only is homosexual activity ubiquitous in the animal kingdom, but also it is extraordinarily common in human cultures. What varies is not the presence or absence of homosexuality—those are pretty much a constant—but the ways in which homosexuals are treated in those cultures. We've already seen that many cultures honour and respect those who transgress gender definitions and adopt the gender of the other sex. Some of these might be considered 'homosexual', if your definition of 'homosexual' has to do only with the biological sex of your sex partner.

Even by that definition, though, we find astonishing variation in the ways in which homosexuals are regarded. In 1948, anthropologist Clyde Kluckhohn surveyed North American aboriginal groups and found homosexuality accepted by 120 of them and rejected by 54. Some cultures (Lango in East Africa, Koniag in Alaska, and Tanala in Madagascar) allow homosexual marriages between men. Some cultures have clearly defined homosexual roles for men and women, with clearly defined expectations.[41]

In a remarkable ethnography, Gilbert Herdt described the sexual rituals of the Sambia, a mountain people who live in Papua New Guinea. The Sambia practise ritualized homosexuality as a way to initiate young boys into full adult manhood. Young boys ritually daily fellate the older boys and men so that the younger boys can receive the vital life fluid (semen) from the older men and thus become men. 'A boy must be initiated and [orally] inseminated, otherwise the girl betrothed to him will outgrow him and run away to another man', was the way one Sambia elder put it. 'If a boy doesn't eat semen, he remains small and weak'. When they reach puberty, these boys are then fellated by a new crop of younger boys. Throughout this initiation, the boys scrupulously avoid girls and have no knowledge of heterosexuality until they are married. Neither the boys nor the older men think of themselves as engaging in homosexual behaviour: The older men are married to women, and the younger men fully expect to be. There is no adult homosexuality among the Sambia. But these young boys must become, as Herdt puts it, 'reluctant warriors'. How else are the boys to receive the vital life force that will enable them to be real men and warriors?[42]

Nearby, also in Melanesia, are the Keraki, who engage in a related practice. There, the boys are sodomized by older men, because the Keraki believe that without the older men's semen, the boys will not grow to be men. This ritual practice occurs until the boys enter puberty and secondary sex characteristics appear—facial hair, dropped voice—at which point the ritual has accomplished its task. When an anthropologist asked Keraki men if they had been sodomized, many responded by saying, 'Why, yes! Otherwise how should I have grown?' Other ritualized homosexual practices have been reported from other cultures.[43] Interestingly, such ritual practices, as among the Sambia and Keraki, are more evident in cultures in which sex segregation is high and women's status is low. This conforms to other ethnographic evidence that suggests that elaborate rituals of male bonding have the effect of excluding women from ritual life and thus correlate with women's lower status. Sex segregation is almost always associated with lower status for women.[44]

Some cultures take permissiveness regarding homosexuality to a remarkable level. Among the Aranda of Australia, Siwans of northern Africa, and Keraki of New Guinea, every male is homosexual during adolescence and bisexual after marriage. The purpose of this is to divert adolescent sex away from young girls and prevent teenage pregnancy and therefore to keep the birth rate down in cultures that have very scarce resources. The well-studied Yanomamo have an institutionalized form of male homosexuality as well as female infanticide. This warrior culture fears population explosion and the depletion of resources to females.[45]

The Etero and the Marind-anim, both in New Guinea, prefer homosexuality to heterosexuality, even though they maintain heterosexual marriages. How, you might ask, do they solve the problem of reproduction? The Etero place a taboo on heterosexual sex for most of the year but prohibit gay sex when the moon is full (and thus when all the women are ovulating). For the Marind-anim, even that much sexual contact with the opposite sex is undesirable. Their birth rate is so low that this warrior culture organizes raids every year, during which it kidnaps the babies of other cultures, raising them to be happy, healthy—and, of course, homosexual—Marind-anim.[46]

One Melanesian society, called 'East Bay' in William Davenport's ethnographic study, practises 'institutionalized male bisexuality' in the forms of sexual relations among boys and between boys and men. Nearly every male has extensive homosexual sexual contact at some point in (or even throughout) his life, though all are also heterosexual and married to women. (None is exclusively homosexual.) Women and men are seen as relatively equal in terms of sexual drive, and there are no taboos against contact with women.[47]

Sexual Customs as Gender Diversity

Sexual customs display a dizzying diversity, implying that sexual behaviour is anything but organized around reproduction alone. Where, when, how, and with whom we have sex varies enormously from culture to culture. Ernestine Friedel, for example, observed dramatic differences in sexual customs between two neighbouring tribes in New Guinea. One, a highland tribe, believes that intercourse makes men weaker and that women are naturally prone to tempt men, threatening them with their powerful sexuality. They also find menstrual blood terrifying. These sexual ideologies pit women against men, and many men would rather remain bachelors than risk contact with women. As a result, population remains relatively low, which this culture needs because it has no new land or resources to bring under cultivation. Not far away, however, is a very different culture. Here, both men and women enjoy sex and sex play. Men worry about whether women are sexually satisfied, and they get along relatively well. They have higher birth rates, which is manageable because they live in a relatively abundant and uncultivated region, where they can use all the hands they can get to farm their fields and defend themselves.[48]

Sex researchers have explored the remarkable cultural diversity of sexual behaviours and in so doing have exposed the ethnocentrism of those arguments that stress the inevitability and naturalness of our own behaviours. Though most of these studies might be less than absolutely reliable, they indicate great cultural variation in what is considered 'normal'.

For example, some cultures never have sex outside. Others believe that having sex indoors would contaminate the food supply (usually in the same hut). What about rates of sexual contact? According to some studies, the Zande have sex two or three times a night and then once again upon awakening. Chaga men have about 10 orgasms a night, and Thonga men try to have sex with as many as three or four of their wives each night. But few beat the Marquesa: Although it's not uncommon for a Marquesan man to have

30 or more orgasms a night, it is normal to have at least 10. Older married men are exempted: They have only about three or four a night. By contrast, the Yapese have sex only once a month or so. During this encounter, the man sits with his back against the side of the hut and his legs straight out. The woman straddles him, and he inserts his penis into her vagina a little bit and then proceeds to stimulate her for several hours while she has dozens of orgasms.[49]

Whereas for us kissing is a virtually universal initiation of sexual contact—'first base', as it were—other cultures find it disgusting because of the possibility of exchanging saliva. 'Putting your lips together?' say the Thonga or the Siriono. 'But that's where you put food!' Some cultures practise almost no foreplay at all, but instead go directly to intercourse; others prescribe several hours of touching and caressing, in which intercourse is a necessary but sad end to the proceedings. Some cultures include oral sex in their lovemaking; others have never even considered it. Alfred Kinsey found that 70 per cent of the American men he surveyed in 1948 had had sex only in the missionary position and that 85 per cent had an orgasm within two minutes of penetration. In his survey of 131 aboriginal cultures, Clyde Kluckholn found the missionary position preferred in only 17.[50]

In our culture, it is men who are supposed to be the sexual initiators and women who are supposed to be sexually resistant. We've all heard stories about men giving women aphrodisiacs to make them more sexually uninhibited. The latest is Rohypnol, the 'date rape drug', which men apparently put into unsuspecting women's drinks to make them more 'compliant' or at least unconscious (which, in these men's minds, may amount to the same thing). How different are the Trobriand Islanders, where women are seen as sexually insatiable and take the initiative. Or the Tukano-Kubeo in Brazil. Here, women are the sexual aggressors and may even avoid getting pregnant or abort a pregnancy because pregnancy would mean forgoing sex. Women, not men, commit adultery, but women justify it by saying that it was 'only sex'. Tukano-Kubeo men secretly give the women anaphrodisiacs to cool them down.[51]

These are but a few examples. When questioned about their practices people in these cultures give the same answers we would. 'It's normal', they'll say. And they've developed the same kind of self-justifying arguments that we have. The Bambara (of Mali), for example, believe that having sex during the day would produce albino children, whereas the Masai believe daytime sex can be fatal. So members of these cultures have sex only at night, and apparently, there are no albinos born and no fatalities during sex. In India, the Chenchu, by contrast, believe that sex at night will lead to the birth of blind babies. So they have sex only during the day and thus avoid having blind children. The Yurok (*Oohl*) of California believed that practising cunnilingus would keep the salmon from running. No oral sex, no shortage of salmon. Such sexual variety suggests that the biological imperative toward reproduction can take many forms but that none is more 'natural' than any other.

Anthropology as History

Anthropological research has helped to expose the faulty logic of those who argue that the universality of gender difference or of male domination is somehow natural and inevitable. By exploring the variety of cultural definitions of masculinity and femininity and by examining cultural configurations that either magnify or diminish gender inequality, cross-cultural research has taken us beyond apparent biological imperatives. In another sense, anthropological research on our human ancestors has also provided a historical retort to biological inevitability. Take, for example, the arguments we saw earlier that male domination was a natural development in the shift to hunting-and-gathering societies. Remember the story: Men's superior physical strength led them naturally toward hunting, whereas weaker women stayed home and busied themselves with gardening and child rearing. Tidy and neat—but also, it appears, historically wrong.

It turns out that such stories actually read history backward, from the present to the past, seeking the historical origins of the patterns we find today. But recent research suggests that meat made up a rather small portion of the early human diet, which meant that all that celebrated hunting didn't count for much at all. And those weapons men invented, the great technological breakthrough that enabled cultures to develop—placing cultural development squarely on the backs of men? Turns out that the great technological leap was more likely slings that women with babies developed so they could carry both baby and food. It may even be true that the erect posture of human beings derives not from the demands of hunting, but rather from the shift from foraging for food to gathering and storing it. Although celebrants of 'masculinist' evolution credited the demands of the hunt for creating the necessity of social (male) bonding for the survival of the community, surely it is the bond between mother and infant that literally and materially ensures survival. Painting a more accurate anthropological picture would require that we acknowledge that females were not simply passive and dependent bearers of children, but rather were active participants in the technological and economic side of life.[52]

Another way to look at this is suggested by Helen Fisher. She notes startling similarities between contemporary American culture and early human cultures. The elements we have inherited as the biologically natural system—nuclear families, marriages with one partner for life, the dramatic separation of home and workplace—all seem to be relatively recent cultural inventions that accompany settled agricultural societies. On the other hand, divorce and remarriage, institutionalized child care, and women and men working equally both at home and away are more typical of the hunting-and-gathering societies that preceded ours—and lasted for millions of years. It may be, Fisher suggests, that after a brief evolutionary rest stop in settled agricultural domains (during which time male domination, warfare, and monotheism all developed), we are returning to our 'true' human evolutionary origins. 'As we head back to the future', she suggests, 'there's every reason to believe the sexes will enjoy the kind of equality that is a function of our birthright'.[53]

If this sounds a bit too mythical, there is a school of feminist anthropology that goes much further. Most anthropologists agree with Michelle Rosaldo, who concluded that 'human cultural and social forms have always been male dominated', or with Bonnie Nardi, who finds 'no evidence of truly egalitarian societies. In no societies do women participate on an equal footing with men in activities accorded the highest prestige'.[54] But one school of feminist anthropologists sees such universality as 'an ethnological delusion', and this school argues that there have been, and are, societies in which women and men have been, and are, equal. What's more, there also may have been societies in which women were the dominant sex. Based on archaeological excavations in Crete and elsewhere, Marija Gimbutas and Riane Eisler and others have argued that neolithic societies were goddess-worshipping, gender-equal, virtual Gardens of Eden, in which women and men may have occupied separate spheres but were equal and mutually respectful. Symbolized, Eisler writes, by the chalice—the symbol of shared plenty—these ancient peoples evidenced a 'partnership' model of human interaction.[55]

Then, the story goes, the barbarians invaded, instituting male domination, introducing a single omnipotent male God, and unleashing 'the lethal power of the blade'— a violent and hierarchical world drenched in the blood of war and murder. We've been living under such a brutal dominator model—'in which male dominance, male violence, and a generally hierarchic and authoritarian social structure was the norm'— ever since. In such a world, 'having violently deprived the Goddess and the female half of humanity of all power, gods and men of war ruled', Eisler writes, and 'peace and harmony would be found only in the myths and legends of a long lost past'.[56]

Another just-so story? Probably. One should always be skeptical of arguments that point to a dimly lit historical past for our models of future social transformation, because they so often rely on selective evidence and often make for retrogressive politics. And one should be equally uneasy with sweeping categorizations of 'female' peace-loving cultures being swept aside by brutally violent 'male' ones. After all, the contemporary world, for all its murderous, rapacious, and bloodthirsty domination, is *far* less violent than hunter-gatherer societies. Ethnographic data suggest that only about 10 per cent of such societies rarely engage in war; most cultures are engaged in conflict either continuously or more than once a year. The !Kung bushmen celebrated by Eisler as the 'harmless people' have a murder rate higher than that of Detroit or Washington, DC. 'The sad archeological evidence', writes Frances Fukuyama, 'indicates that systematic mass killings of men, women, and children occurred in neolithic times. There was no age of innocence'.[57]

On the other hand, why would we want to believe that male domination is somehow natural and inevitable? Some of Eisler's arguments are on firm evolutionary footing: It is likely, for example, that descent was originally traced through **matrilinearity**. This would make descent far more certain in cultures that did not understand the relationship between sexual intercourse and birth nine months later. And one can believe the credible evidence that women played a greater role in early human societies, without assuming one momentous calamity of invasion when that Edenic world was forever lost.

There is even some evidence of cultures that, although not fully female-dominated, evince women's power in all public and private arenas. Maria Lepowsky's impressive ethnography of the Vanatinai, a matrilineal, decentralized culture in New Guinea, found no evidence of male domination—no men's huts, no special ceremonial cults. Boys as well as girls care for their younger siblings. Men do child care. And both women and men exercise sexual freedom. Women have, Lepowsky writes, 'equal opportunities of access to the symbolic capital of prestige derived from success in exchange'. Though Lepowsky found some evidence that exclusively male activities held more prestige than women's, she argues that both women's and men's economic participation give everyone possibilities of prestige and honour.[58]

Peggy Sanday's fascinating study of the matrilineal Minangkabau of western Sumatra, one of the largest ethnic groups in Indonesia, is a case in point. Instead of looking for a mirror-image world, in which women wield power as men do, Sanday finds instead a culture in which women's ways of governing parallel men's ways and at times even supplant men's ways. Here, women are self-confident and independent of their husbands, and although men hold many of the formal political offices, women 'rule without governing'. They 'facilitate social bonding outside the machinations of political power', which enables 'the men's job of adjudicating disputes according to the rules of *adat* [customs] and consensus decision-making'.[59]

Women's status varies widely, depending on many cultural factors. And that alone makes it clear that male domination is not inevitable.

The Values of Cross-Cultural Research

If anthropologists have demonstrated anything, it is the rich diversity in human cultural arrangements and the disparate definitions of gender and sexuality that we have produced within our cultures. Several theories explain the historical origins of these patterns and suggest ways we can modify or abandon some historically coercive or exploitative practices without doing damage to our evolutionary legacy. **Cultural relativism** also suggests that, in this enormous cultural variety and historical evolution of custom and culture, we may shed those customs we no longer need, even if once they served some societal purpose. 'Assertions of past inferiority for women should therefore be irrelevant to present and future developments', writes Eleanor Leacock.[60] Still, questions linger. Given such diversity of sexuality and gender, why is male dominance so universal? If it's not inevitable, how do we explain its persistence? Here, the answers may be a bit closer to home, in the institutions that help constitute the gendered society.

Summary

Anthropological research on gender-related cultural variation arose in part in response to biological determinism. Despite dramatic cultural variations, however, some themes remain constant. Virtually all cultures observe sex differences and exhibit some form of male dominance. Anthropologists therefore try to explore links between gender difference and gender inequality; to examine societies in which women hold power; and to examine rituals, beliefs, and customs that either increase or decrease inequality.

One of the most celebrated anthropologists to explore cross-cultural variation in gender was the twentieth-century American anthropologist Margaret Mead. In several influential works, she examined differences in definitions of masculinity and femininity and the processes by which males and females became 'normal' men and women within their cultural contexts. She believed that men and women were capable of being moulded into a variety of different definitions. Though her findings were critiqued almost immediately and remain controversial, she stimulated great interest in (and much further research on) the cultural construction of gender.

Other anthropologists have examined the determinants of gender differences and gender inequality. One of the most important topics examined has been the gendered division of labour, which is virtually universal although the tasks assigned to men and women vary from culture to culture. Functionalists view the sex-based division of labour as the result of necessity, and tend to believe that it contains elements of inevitability. In modern industrialized societies, however, the division of labour is anachronistic, held in place where it still exists by other factors, particularly the greater power of men. We are therefore thrown back upon gender inequality.

For well over 100 years, theorists have attempted to explain gender inequality by reference to larger societal forces. Engels attempted to link male dominance to the emergence of private property and early capitalist accumulation, which he thought enhanced men's need to control women's sexuality in order to ensure paternity. Contemporary anthropologists have continued to examine the impact of accumulation and other economic factors upon gender relations.

Another group of scholars traces male domination to warfare and hunting. Marvin Harris argues that warrior societies develop patrilinearity, male dominance and, for purposes of legitimation, patriarchal religion. Descent theorists like Lionel Tiger and Robin Fox emphasize that men's uncertain paternity drives them to form bonds with other men in the hunting/warfare group (rather than with women and children). Alliance theorists like Claude Levi-Strauss focus instead on the defining of acceptable marriage partners, which leads to a system in which men exchange women to cement alliances amongst them, a practice that diminishes women's status as a prerequisite for social cohesion.

The determinants of women's generally lower status have been examined by a number of scholars. The consensus among them is that there are four non-exclusive contributors to male dominance: sex segregation of work; men's control of property; historical factors like capitalism, colonization, and demographic changes; and environmental stresses.

Anthropologists have explored cultural constructions of gender through examining specific gender rituals. Though they vary dramatically, some, like genital alteration, are quite widespread. Male circumcision and FGM/FGC are widespread practices in a number of cultures and can have a variety of meanings and purposes. In general, however, both are associated with cultures in which men are dominant. Jeffrey and Karen Paige suggest that many widely differing reproductive rituals have in common their rootedness in anxieties about paternity and female sexuality.

Another avenue for exploring the cultural construction of gender has been research on so-called third and fourth genders, individuals of one biological sex who perform gender roles normally associated with the other sex. Some societies recognize multiple genders and do not view gender as inextricably linked to biological sex. Much research has focused on the *berdache*, a third gender found in many indigenous American cultures. In general, *berdaches* historically enjoyed high social status. First Nations and other aboriginal cultures now prefer the term 'Two-Spirited' when referring to this phenomenon. Other research has examined third genders in other cultures. There are few commonalities among third genders, except that it seems to be (or to have been in the past) much more common for biologically male individuals to be assigned 'female' gender than the opposite. Third genders challenge biological determinism but should not be read as equivalent to modern transgendered identities.

Studies of sexual diversity have further complicated our view of what is normal or biologically determined. Homosexuality is present in virtually every human culture, yet viewed very differently. Sexual customs vary dramatically too; frequency of intercourse and orgasm, acceptability of sexual practices, and views of male and female sexual appetites are all areas of significant variability, indicating that biological imperatives are an unreliable or at least incomplete guide to human sexuality.

Anthropological theory has gone far beyond the man-the-hunter theory in recent years. Most anthropologists now concede that traditional narratives of early human history ignored or underestimated the contributions made by women to survival, success, and technological innovation. While most feminist anthropologists argue that human societies have always privileged men, others have argued for the current, historical, or prehistoric existence of egalitarian (or even matriarchal!) societies. While there is little evidence for any prehistoric or historic **matriarchy**, there is widespread evidence of variability in the degree and nature of male dominance, suggesting that there is nothing inevitable about women's and men's status in any given society.

Anthropological research has demonstrated rich diversity in human cultures and arrangements regarding gender. Many scholars have attempted to account for this diversity and for the variation in women's status throughout the world. No completely compelling theory of male dominance has been suggested; a sociological perspective thus adds a critical dimension to anthropological, biological, and psychological explanations of the gendered society.

Questions for Critical Thinking

1. Of the four critical determinants of women's status—sex segregation of work, men's control of property, historical factors, and environmental stresses—which do you think is most important? Is any one of these explanations unconvincing?
2. What do *you* believe caused male domination in so many human societies?
3. Can you think of any rituals of gender that emphasize reproduction or sexuality in your own society or culture? Do the rituals you can think of have anything to do with the control of women's sexuality or anxiety over paternity?
4. What does the presence of third genders in a given society indicate about that society's views of gender?
5. In your opinion, what would constitute evidence *for* or *against* theories that neolithic societies were more egalitarian than the historical societies that followed?

Key Terms

alyha
berdache
alliance theorists
circumcision
couvade
cultural determinism
cultural relativism
descent theorists
female genital mutilation/female
    genital cutting (FGM/FGC)
functionalism
hijras
hwame
hypermasculinity

infibulation
matriarchy
matrilineality
muxes
nadle
patrilineality
polygamy
polygyny
purdah
ritual segregation
sex segregation
sworn virgin
Two-Spirited
xanith

Chapter 5

The Social Construction of Gender Relations

Sociological and Feminist Perspectives

> Society is a masked ball, where everyone hides his real character, and reveals it by hiding.
>
> —RALPH WALDO EMERSON, 'WORSHIP' (1860)

> My self . . . is a dramatic ensemble.
>
> —PAUL KLEE

In one of its most thoughtful definitions, **sociology** was described by C. Wright Mills as the intersection of biography and history, its goal to locate an individual in both time and space and understand the contexts in which a person constructs his or her identity. Sociology's bedrock assumption, upon which its analyses of structures and **institutions** rest, is that individuals shape their lives within both historical and social contexts. We do not do so simply because we are biologically programmed to act in certain ways, nor because we have inevitable human tasks to solve as we age. Rather, we respond to the world we encounter, shaping, modifying, and creating our identities through those encounters with other people and within social institutions.

Thus sociology takes as its starting points many of the themes raised in earlier chapters. Sociological perspectives on gender assume the variability of gendered identities that anthropological research has explored, the biological 'imperatives' toward gender identity and differentiation (though sociology locates the source of these imperatives less in our bodies and more in our environments), and the psychological imperatives toward both autonomy and connection that modern society requires of individuals in the modern world. To a sociologist, both our biographies (identities) and histories (evolving social structures) are gendered.

Like other social sciences (and like feminist theory, as we shall see below), sociology begins with a critique of biological determinism. Instead of observing our experiences as the expressions of inborn, interplanetary differences, the social sciences examine the variations among men and among women, as well as the differences between them. The social sciences thus begin with the explicitly social origin of our patterns of development.

Our lives depend on social interaction. Literally, it seems. In the thirteenth century, Frederick II, emperor of the Holy Roman Empire, decided to perform an experiment to see if he could discover the 'natural language of man'. What language would we speak if no one taught us language? He selected some newborn babies for what has been called, with good reason, 'the forbidden experiment'. The babies were given basic care, but speech, songs, and lullabies—the stuff of normal parent-child interaction—were strictly prohibited. All the babies died. And you've probably heard those stories of 'feral children'—babies who were abandoned and raised by animals, became suspicious of people, and could not be socialized to live in society after age six or so. In many of the stories, the children died young, as did many of the 'isolates', those little children who were locked away in closets and basements by sadistic or insane parents. Those who did manage to survive were profoundly damaged.[1]

Isolated Children

Some children have been isolated from almost all human contact by abusive care-givers. One of the best-documented cases of an isolated child was 'Isabelle', who was born to an unmarried, deaf-mute teenager. The mother's parents were so afraid of scandal that they kept both mother and daughter locked away in a darkened room, where they had no contact with the outside world. In 1938, when she was six years old, Isabelle escaped from her confinement. She was unable to speak except to make croaking sounds, she was extremely fearful of strangers, and she reacted to stimuli with the instinct of a wild animal. Gradually she became used to being around people, but she expressed no curiosity about them; it was as if she did not see herself as one of them. But doctors and social scientists began a long period of systematic training. Within a year she was able to speak in complete sentences, and soon she was able to attend school with other children. By the age of 14, she was in the sixth grade, happy and well-adjusted. She managed to overcome her lack of early childhood socialization, but only through exceptional effort.

Studies of other isolated children reveal that some can recover, with effort and specialized care, but that others suffer permanent damage. It is unclear exactly why, but no doubt some contributing factors are the duration of the isolation, the child's age when the isolation began, the presence of some human contacts (like Isabelle's mother), other abuse accompanying the isolation, and the child's intelligence. The 1994 film *Nell* starred Jodie Foster as a near-isolate who gradually learns language and social interaction well enough to fall in love with her doctor (played by Liam Neeson).

Such stories suggest that biology alone—that is, our anatomical composition—doesn't determine our development as we might have thought. We need to interact, to be socialized, to be part of society. It is that interaction, not our bodies, that makes us who we are.

Often, the first time we hear that gender is socially constructed, we take it to mean that we are, as individuals, not responsible for what we do. '"Society" made me like this', we might say. 'It's not my fault'. This is a device that we use to deflect individual accountability and responsibility. It is a misreading of the sociological mandate. When we say that gender identity is socially constructed, what we *do* mean is that our identities are a fluid assemblage of the meanings and behaviours that we construct from the values, images, and prescriptions we find in the world around us. Our gendered identities are both voluntary—we choose to become who we are—and coerced—we are pressured, forced, sanctioned, and often physically beaten into submission to some rules. We neither make up the rules as we go along, nor do we fit casually and without struggle into pre-assigned roles.

For some of us, becoming adult men and women in our society is a smooth and almost effortless drifting into behaviours and attitudes that feel as familiar to us as our skin. And for others of us, becoming masculine or feminine is an interminable torture, a nightmare in which we must brutally suppress some parts of ourselves to please others—or, simply, to survive. For most of us, though, the experience falls somewhere in between: There are parts we love and wouldn't part with, and other parts where we feel we've been forced to exaggerate one side at the expense of others. It's the task of the sociological perspective to specify the ways in which our own experiences, our interactions with others, and the institutions combine to shape our sense of who we are. Biology provides the raw materials, whereas society and history provide the context, the instruction manual that we follow to construct our identities.

A Social Constructionist Perspective

In the first chapter, we identified four elements of a social constructionist perspective on gender. Definitions of masculinity and femininity vary, first, *from culture to culture*, and, second, *in any one culture over historical time*. Thus social constructionists rely on the work of anthropologists and historians to identify the commonalities and the differences in the meanings of masculinity and femininity from one culture to another and to describe how those differences change over time.

Third, gender definitions also vary *over the course of a person's life*. The issues confronting women when they are younger—in both the workplace and intimate relationships, for example—will often be very different from the issues they face at menopause or retirement. And our behaviours and attitudes change too. For example, men often report a 'softening' when they become grandfathers, developing greater interest in caregiving and nurturing than when they became fathers.

Finally, as discussed previously, definitions of masculinity and femininity will vary *within any one culture at any one time*—by race, class, ethnicity, age, sexuality, education, region of the country, etc.

Social constructionism thus adds specific dimensions to the exploration of gender. What constructionism contributes are the elements that the social psychology of sex roles cannot explain adequately: difference, power, and the institutional dimensions of gender. To explain difference, social constructionism offers an analysis of the plurality of gender definitions; to explain power, it emphasizes the ways in which some definitions become normative through the struggles of different groups for power—including the power to define. Finally, to explain the institutional dimension, social constructionism moves beyond socialization of gendered individuals who occupy gender-neutral sites to the study of the interplay between gendered individuals and gendered institutions.

Beyond Sex Role Theory

As we saw in Chapter 3, social psychologists located the process of acquisition of gender identity in the developmental patterns of individuals in their families and in early childhood interaction. Specifically, sex role theorists explored the ways in which individuals come to be gendered and the ways in which they negotiate their ways toward some sense of internal consistency and coherence, despite contradictory role definitions. Sociologists have identified six significant problems with sex role theory—problems that require its modification.

First, *the use of the idea of role has the curious effect of actually minimizing the importance of gender.* Role theory uses drama as a metaphor—we learn our roles through socialization and then perform them for others. But to speak of a gender role makes it sound almost too theatrical and thus too easily changeable. Gender, as Helena Lopata and Barrie Thorne write, 'is not a role in the same sense that being a teacher, sister, or friend is a role. Gender, like race or age, is deeper, less changeable, and infuses the more specific roles one plays; thus, a female teacher differs from a male teacher in important sociological respects (e.g., she is likely to receive less pay, status, and credibility)'. *To make gender a role like any other role is to diminish its power in structuring our lives.*[2]

Second, *sex role theory posits singular normative definitions of masculinity and femininity.* If the meanings of masculinity and femininity vary across cultures, over historical time, among men within any one culture, and over the life course, we cannot speak of masculinity or femininity as though each were a constant, singular, universal essence. Is there really only *one* male sex role and only one female sex role?

By positing this false universalism, sex role theory assumes what needs to be explained—how the normative definition is established and reproduced—and explains away all the differences among men and among women. Yet differences—race, class, ethnicity, sexuality, age, region—all inform, shape, and modify our definitions of gender. Sex role theory cannot fully accommodate these differences. A more satisfying investigation must take into account these different definitions of masculinity and femininity constructed and expressed by different groups of men and women. Thus social constructionists speak of *masculinities* and *femininities.*

What's more, sociologists see the differences among masculinities or femininities in a manner opposite to that of sex role theorists. The latter, if they can accommodate differences at all, see these differences as aberrations, as failure to conform to the normal sex role. In early studies of sex roles, social psychologists argued that, for example, black men or women or gay men or lesbians evidenced either 'too much' or 'too little' adherence to their appropriate sex role. In that way, homosexuals or people of colour were seen as expressing sex role problems.

Social constructionists, on the other hand, believe that the differences among definitions of masculinity or femininity are themselves the outcome of the ways in which those groups interact with their environments. Thus we cannot understand the differences in masculinity or femininity based on race or ethnicity without first looking at the ways in which institutional and interpersonal racial inequality structures the ways in which members of those groups actively construct their identities.

This leads to a third arena in which sociologists challenge sex role theory. Gender is not only plural, it is also relational. But *sex role theory posits two separate spheres, as if sex role differentiation were more a matter of sorting a herd of cattle into two appropriate pens for branding.* Boys get herded into the masculine corral, girls the feminine. Such a static model also suggests that the two corrals have virtually nothing to do with one another. 'The result of using the role framework is an abstract view of the *differences* between the sexes and their situations, not a concrete one of the *relations* between them.'[3] But what surveys indicate is that men construct their ideas of what it means to be men *in constant reference* to definitions of femininity. What it means to be a man is to be 'notawoman', as Robert McElvaine claims; indeed, social psychologists have emphasized that although different groups of men may disagree about other traits and their significance in gender definitions, the 'antifemininity' component of masculinity is perhaps the dominant and universal characteristic.

Fourth, *sex role theory ignores the fact that because gender is plural and relational, it is also situational.* What it means to be a man or a woman varies in different contexts. Those different institutional contexts demand and produce different forms of masculinity and femininity. 'Boys may be boys', cleverly comments feminist legal theorist Deborah Rhode, 'but they express that identity differently in fraternity parties than in job interviews with a female manager'.[4] Gender is thus not a property of individuals, some 'thing' one has, but rather a specific set of behaviours that is produced in specific social situations. And thus gender changes as the situation changes.

Sex role theory cannot adequately account for either the differences among women and men or their different definitions of masculinity and femininity in different situations without implicitly assuming some theory of deviance. Nor can it express the relational character of those definitions. In addition, sex role theory cannot fully account for the power relationships between women and men and among different groups of women and different groups of men. Thus the fifth and perhaps most significant problem in sex role theory is *that it depoliticizes gender, making gender a set of individual attributes and not an aspect of social structure.* 'The notion of "role" focuses attention more on individuals than on social structure, and implies that "the female role" and "the male role" are complementary (i.e., separate or different but equal)', write sociologists Judith Stacey and Barrie Thorne. 'The terms are depoliticizing; they strip experience from its historical and political context and neglect questions of power and conflict'.[5]

But how can one speak of gender without speaking of power? As pointed out in the book's introduction, a pluralistic and relational theory of gender cannot pretend that all masculinities and femininities are created equal. North American men and women must also contend with a singular vision of both masculinity and femininity, specific definitions that are held up as models against which we all measure ourselves. As we saw, R.W. Connell calls these the 'hegemonic' definition of masculinity and the 'emphasized' version of femininity. Both are normative constructions, the ones against which others are measured and, almost invariably, found wanting. The hegemonic definition is a 'particular variety of masculinity to which others—among them young and effeminate as well as homosexual men—are subordinated.'[6] We thus come to know what it means to be a man or a woman by setting our definitions in opposition to a set of 'others'—racial minorities, sexual minorities, etc. One of the most fruitful areas of research in sociology today is trying to specify exactly how these hegemonic versions are established and how different groups negotiate their ways through problematized definitions.

Sex role theory's inability to explore the relationship between gender and power leads to the sixth and final problem—*sex role theory is inadequate in comprehending the dynamics of change.* Movements for social change, like feminism or gay liberation, become movements to expand role definitions and to change role expectations. Their goal is to expand role options for individual women and men, whose lives are constrained by stereotypes. But social and political movements are not about only expanding the opportunities for individuals to break free of the constraints of inhibiting sex roles, to allow their 'true' selves to emerge; they are also about the redistribution of power in society. They demand the reallocation of resources and an end to forms of inequality that are embedded in social institutions as well as sex role stereotypes. Only a perspective that begins with an analysis of power can adequately understand those social movements. A social constructionist approach seeks to be more concrete, specifying tension and conflict not between individuals and expectations, but rather between and among groups of people within social institutions. Thus social constructionism is inevitably about power.

What's wrong with sex role theory can, finally, be understood by analogy. Why is it, do you suppose, no reputable scholars today use the terms 'race roles' or 'class roles' to describe the observable aggregate differences between members of different races or different classes? Are such 'race roles' specific behavioural and attitudinal characteristics that are socialized into all members of different races? Hardly. Not only would such a term flatten all the distinctions and differences among members of the same race, but also it would ignore the ways in which the behaviours of different races—to the extent that they might be seen as different in the first place—are the products of racial inequality and oppression and not the external expression of some inner essence.

The positions of women and ethnic minorities have much in common, as sociologist Helen Hacker pointed out in her groundbreaking article 'Women as a Minority Group', which was written more than a half-century ago. Hacker argued that systematic structural inequality produces a 'culture of self-hatred' among the target group. And yet we do not speak of 'race roles'. Such an idea would be absurd, because (1) the differences within each race are far greater than the differences between races; (2) what it means to be white or black is always constructed in relationship to the other; (3) those definitions make no sense outside the context of the racially based power that white people, as a group, maintain over people of colour, as a group. Movements for racial equality are about more than expanding role options for people of colour.

Ultimately, to use role theory to explain race or gender is to blame the victim. If our gendered behaviours 'stem from fundamental personality differences, socialized early in life', suggests psychologist David Tresemer, then responsibility must lie at our own feet. This is what R. Stephen Warner and his colleagues call the 'Sambo theory of oppression'. '[T]he victims internalize the maladaptive set of values of the oppressive system. Thus behaviour that appears incompetent, deferential, and self-degrading is assumed to reflect the crippled capabilities of the personality.[7] In this worldview, social change must be left to the future, when a more egalitarian form of childhood socialization can produce children better able to function according to hegemonic standards. Social change comes about when the oppressed learn better the ways of their oppressors. If they refuse, and no progress is made—well, whose fault is that?

A Note About Power

One of the central themes of this book is that gender is about difference and also about inequality, about power. At the level of gender relations, gender is about the power that men as a group have over women as a group, and it is also about the power that some men have over other men (or that some women have over other women). It is impossible to explain gender without adequately understanding power—not because power is the consequence of gender difference, but rather because power is what produces those gender differences in the first place.

To say that gender is a power relation—the power of men over women and the power of some men or women over other men or women—is among the more controversial arguments of the social constructionist perspective. In fact, the question of power is among the most controversial elements in all explanations of gender. Yet it is central; all theories of gender must explain both difference and domination. Whereas other theories explain male domination as the result of sex differences, social constructionism explains differences as the result of domination.

Yet a discussion about power invariably makes those with gender, race, sexual, or class privilege uncomfortable or defensive. When challenged by the idea that the gender order means that men have power over women, men often respond with astonishment. 'What do you mean, men have all the power? What are you talking about? I have no power at all. I'm completely powerless. My wife bosses me around, my children boss me around, my boss bosses me around. I have no power at all!' Most men, it seems, do not feel powerful.

Here, in a sense, is where feminism has failed to resonate for many men. Much of feminist theory of gender-based power derived from a symmetry between the structure of gender relations and women's individual experiences. Women, as a group, were not *in* power. That much was evident to anyone who cared to observe a corporate board, a university board of trustees, or a legislative body at any level anywhere in the world. Nor, individually, did women *feel* powerful. In fact, they felt constrained by gender inequality into stereotypic activities that prevented them from feeling comfortable, safe, and competent. So women were neither in power, nor did they feel powerful.

That symmetry breaks down when we try to apply it to men. Because, although men as a group may be *in* power, most individual men are not 'in power', and they do not feel powerful. Men often feel themselves to be equally constrained by a system of stereotypic conventions that leaves them unable to live the lives to which they believe they are entitled. The feeling of powerlessness is one reason why so many men believe that they are the victims of reverse discrimination.

Like gender, power is not the property of individuals—a possession that one has or does not have—but rather a property of group life, of social life. Power *is*. It can neither be willed away nor ignored. Here is how the philosopher Hannah Arendt put it:

> Power corresponds to the human ability not just to act but to act in concert. Power is never the property of an individual; it belongs to a group and remains in existence only so long as the group keeps together. When we say of somebody that he is 'in power' we actually refer to his being empowered by a certain number of people to act in their name. The moment the group, from which the power originated to begin with . . . disappears, 'his power' also vanishes.[8]

To a sociologist, power is not an attitude or a possession; it's not really a 'thing' at all. It cannot be 'given up' like an ideology that's been outgrown. Power creates as well as destroys. It is deeply woven into the fabric of our lives—it is the warp of our interactions and the weft of our institutions. And it is so deeply woven into our lives that it is most invisible to those who are most empowered.

In addition to its focus on power, sociology adds three crucial dimensions to the study of gender: (1) the life-course perspective, (2) a macrolevel institutional analysis, and (3) a microlevel interactionist approach.

Gender Through the Life Course

We've suggested that role theory is ill-equipped to account for the significant differences among different groups of women or men—differences of class, race, ethnicity, sexuality, and so on. Gender identities and expressions vary far more than the prescriptive roles to which we are presumably assigned. Nor can role theory fully embrace the changes in gender identity over the course of our lives. Sex role theory overemphasizes the developmental decisiveness of early childhood as the moment that gender socialization happens. Developmental psychologists have provided compelling evidence concerning the acquisition of gender identity in early childhood. Through socialization, especially in families and schools, the basic elements of gender identity are established, the foundation laid for future elaboration and expression.

But the story doesn't stop there. At its least convincing, some developmental psychology proposes that once one acquires gender identity it is fixed, permanent by age five or six. Sociologists embraced some of that idea, although they often pushed the age limit up to that tumultuous period called 'adolescence'. Surely, though, gender identity was fixed indelibly by puberty, which is marked, after all, by all the physical changes that mark the full-fledged assumption of adult masculinity and femininity.

Sociologists used to think that the three primary institutions of socialization were the family, school, and church; the three primary bearers of their socializing message were parents, teachers, and religious figures (priests, ministers, rabbis, imams, and the like). This model has proved inaccurate for two reasons. First, it assumes that socialization is a smooth process that is accomplished by the end of childhood, when family, school, and church have receded in significance in a person's life. Second, it views the socialization process from the point of view of the socializer, not the socialized. That is, from the point of view of the child, the chief agents of socialization—parents, teachers, and religious figures—translate as grown-ups, grown-ups, and grown-ups.

Kids know better. They also know that a primary agent of their socialization is their peer group—the other boys and girls, and later men and women—with whom they interact. They also know that the images and messages that daily surround them in the media are constantly giving them messages about what men and women are supposed to look and act like. Media and peer groups are, today, part of the pentagram of socializing institutions.

Media and peer groups, however, do not recede after early childhood; indeed, one might say they pick up where family, church, and school leave off. Some of the messages from peer groups and media reinforce what we've learned; other messages directly contradict those earlier messages. And it's up to us to sort it out.

Gender socialization continues throughout the life course. The process is neither smooth nor finite—it's bumpy and uneven and continues all our lives. What masculinity or femininity might mean to us in our 20s will change dramatically by our 40s or our 60s. And although a small part of that explanation has to do with biological stages of development—puberty, reproductive years, menopause, aging—these stages vary so significantly from culture to culture that sociologists search for the meaning of such biological shifts in the ways in which changing bodies interact with their social context.

Take, for example, a well-known 'factoid' about the differences between male and female sexuality. We hear, for example, that males reach their sexual 'peak' at age 18 or so but that women arrive there somewhat later, perhaps in their early to mid-30s. This biological mismatch in hitting our sexual stride is often attributed to different maturational trajectories or different evolutionary strategies. He reaches his sexual peak when he is capable of producing the greatest number of high-quality sperm, while she reaches her sexual peak at the age where her greatest number of fertile ovulatory cycles occur and before age-related risks begin to affect her ability to bear healthy offspring.[9] But can we explain this divergence solely in terms of different rates of maturation, hormones, and bodies? Probably not. This divergence in sexualities is far more easily and convincingly explained by putting male and female sexuality in context and by questioning some of the assumptions that researchers make. What would increasing evidence of a female sexual peak at 40 (when fertility and hormone levels begin to decline precipitously) do to the idea of the evolutionary function of women's sexual desire? What about evidence that the prevalence of sexual dysfunction in women actually declines with advancing age?[10] Clearly, when dealing with human sexuality, we need to consider not just hormonal and evolutionary factors, but more importantly the social context in which women and men shape and express their sexuality.

Or consider that staple of daytime self-help talk shows: the **mid-life crisis**. In the 1970s, two best-selling books, *Seasons of a Man's Life* (D.J. Levinson, Darrow, Klein, M.H. Levinson, and McKee, 1978) and *Passages* (Sheehy, 1976) popularized the belief that middle-aged men (and to a lesser extent, women) go through a developmental 'crisis' characterized by a pressure to make wholesale changes in their work, relationships, and leisure. Thirty years later, the mid-life crisis remains a popular concept, the subject of pop psychology books and websites offering advice to people who struggle with the symptoms of the 'crisis': depression, angst, irrational behaviour, and strong urges to seek out new partners.

Careful research clearly demonstrates that this so-called crisis is not typical. Disconfirming research became available shortly after the concept was introduced (Costa and McCrae, 1978; Valliant, 1978), and more recent research finds no empirical support for mid-life crisis as a universal experience for either men or women. Mid-life *does* present a series of developmental challenges, and some middle-aged people do respond in ways that fit the stereotype—red sports car and all! However, people go through challenges and crises in every life stage. The triggers are usually changes in work, health, or relationships rather than a mere accumulation of birthdays.[11]

In the largest study to date on mid-life, Elaine Wethington demonstrated that the mid-life crisis is far from inevitable. Yet more than 25 per cent of those over age 35 surveyed (all residing in the United States) *believed* that they have had such a crisis. Upon further investigation, about half of these reports reflected only a time of stressful life events, not a sustained period of loss of balance and searching.[12]

Belief in mid-life crisis may partially hinge on what's called '**confirmation bias**', whereby a single case or a few cases of the expected behaviour confirm the belief, especially when the behaviour is attention-getting or widely reported. Less obvious disconfirming behaviour is easier to ignore. In other words, if we happen to know a man who spent the year after his forty-fifth birthday getting a divorce, dating a 22-year-old, buying a sports car, and taking up skydiving, we might believe in the mid-life crisis, even though we know a dozen other middle-aged men who have done none of these things.

On the other hand, the mid-life crisis may be so compelling because it feels right; in this sense, it may simply ring true to many middle-aged people trying to find **narrative coherence** in their lives and the world around them.[13] After all, there is increasing evidence that human happiness—in North America and globally—follows a 'U-shaped' pattern. That is, happiness is high in early life, declines to its lowest levels somewhere around the early 40s, and then climbs to high levels again as we age.[14] What's clear, however, is that mid-life changes cannot be simply reduced to the expression of an unchanging gender identity (or a changing biology). These complex changes need an equally complex analysis.

Clearly, gender is a lifelong project, and the life course itself is gendered. For example, as people age in the contemporary West, men receive less stigmatization than do women. It's not uncommon for a man to date or marry a woman 20 years younger, but rare—and labelled bizarre—when an older woman dates or marries a younger man. In the media, much older men are commonly paired as romantic leads with much younger women. But women are almost never paired romantically with younger men in the movies (unless the women are around 23 and the 'younger man' is 15, as in *Private Lessons, Tadpole,* and *Summer of '42*). In 2004's *Alexander*, Angelina Jolie, then 29, played the mother of Colin Farrell, precisely one year younger. Though much is changing in this regard, it is still newsworthy when a film portrays the relationship between a 50-year-old woman and a man in his 20s, as does Stephen Frears's film *Chéri* (2009).

As the meaning of age varies by gender, so, too, does the experience of aging. The meanings of masculinity and femininity that we take into adulthood and beyond resonate in different ways as we age. For example, men and women face retirement differently. Men in retirement often end up with a more attenuated friendship and support network, fewer friends, and greater sense of isolation—which in turn might lead to earlier death because loneliness and isolation are risk factors for aging people. Women are far more likely to have maintained close contact with children, with workplace colleagues, and with friends and head into retirement with their larger friendship and support network intact. Buttressed by that support, women will be less isolated and lonely and therefore likely to live longer. Could this different expression of different gender ideologies partly explain the difference in women's and men's life expectancies? Not entirely, to be sure. But it probably pushes a bit.

As the reference to difference in life expectancy shows, gender is just as salient at the end of our lives as it was during them. Because women live longer than men, the elderly (particularly the very elderly) are more likely to be female. According to StatsCan data, in 2005 70 per cent of Canadians over 90 were women, as were 52 per cent of those 65 to 69.

But why do women live longer? To be sure, some part of the explanation is surely physical: Physicians have long speculated that women have stronger constitutions and more immunity to disease. They are less likely to fall victim to heart disease, because testosterone increases the level of 'bad' cholesterol (low-density lipoprotein), whereas estrogen increases the level of 'good' cholesterol (high-density lipoprotein). British researcher David Goldspink (2005) found that men's hearts weaken much more rapidly as they age: Between the ages of 18 and 70, their hearts lose one quarter of their power, but healthy 70-year-old women have hearts nearly as strong as those of 20-year-olds (but don't worry, regular cardiovascular exercise can slow or stop the decline). But surely part of the reason has to do with the ways that gender structures our sustaining networks of friends and kin.

However, the lifespan gap is decreasing. The gap between Canadian men and women has narrowed from 5.4 years in 1999 to 5.2 years in 2000 and 4.8 years in 2004.[15] (If nothing else, this is further proof that one cannot attribute this gender difference to biology alone.) What sociological reasons might account for this change? Some have suggested that as gender inequality lessens and more women work outside the home, it's to be expected that the gap will decrease. The problem with this explanation is that the life expectancy gap is decreasing everywhere, in both gender-polarized and egalitarian countries: 5.80 years in Norway and 5.70 years in Sri Lanka, 7.95 years in France and 4.31 years in Mongolia. In fact, it seems to be decreasing more rapidly in gender-polarized countries: 2.51 years in Ethiopia, 1.81 years in Pakistan; and in seven countries, including Bangladesh, Malawi, Namibia, and Afghanistan, men are living longer than women.

Sociologists explain this by pointing out that rich and poor countries are diverging far more than women and men are in those countries. In poor countries, both sexes are increasingly susceptible to poor nutrition or health care, HIV, or violence and war, while women are particularly vulnerable to increased maternal mortality. In wealthy countries, better health care and nutrition mean that both women and men are living longer. By 2040, women in Western nations will live to be about 100, and men will live to be 99.[16] The social effects of an aging population are many, and may include important implications for gender. The strength of sociology's life course approach is that it permits us to understand that gender is not simply a role, but a complex interplay among biology, identity, and environment that changes through an individual's lifespan in ways that affect not only the individual, but his or her society.

Gender as an Institution

The earlier argument that power is the property of a group, not an individual, is related to the argument that gender is as much a property of institutions as it is part of our individual identities. One of the more significant sociological points of departure from sex role theory concerns the institutional level of analysis. As we've seen, sex role theory holds that gender is a property of individuals—that gendered people acquire their gender identity and move outward, into society, to populate gender-neutral institutions. To a sociologist, however, those institutions are themselves gendered. Institutions create gendered normative standards, express a gendered institutional logic, and are major factors in the reproduction of gender inequality. The gendered identity of individuals shapes those gendered institutions, and the gendered institutions express and reproduce the inequalities that compose gender identity.

To illustrate this, let us undertake a short thought experiment. To start with, let's assume that (1) men are more violent than women (whether biologically derived or socialized, this is easily measurable by rates of violent crime); that (2) men occupy virtually all the positions of political power in the world (again, easily measurable by looking at all political institutions); and that (3) there is a significant risk of violence and war at any moment.

Now, imagine that when you awaken tomorrow morning each of those power positions in all those political institutions—every president and prime minister, every mayor and governor, every state, federal, or local official, every member of every parliament or congress around the world—was filled by a woman. Do you think the world would be any safer from the risk of violence and war? Do you think you'd sleep better that night?

Biological determinists and psychologists of sex roles would probably answer yes. Whether from fundamental biological differences in levels of testosterone, brain chemistries, or evolutionary imperatives, a biological perspective would probably conclude that because females are less violent and aggressive than men, the world would be safer. (It is ironic, then, that the same people who believe these biological differences are also among the least likely to support female candidates for political office.) And those who observe that different socialization produces women who are more likely to avoid hierarchy and competition and to search instead for peaceful solutions by another gendered value system would also breathe a collective sigh of relief.

'But', some of you say, 'what about the women who have already *been* heads of state? What about Golda Meir, Indira Gandhi, and Margaret Thatcher? They're not exactly poster girls for the ethic of care, are they?'

Indeed, not. And part of the reason why they were so unladylike in political office is that the office itself demands a certain type of behaviour, independent of the gender of the person who holds it. As we'll see in Chapter 8, one woman, or one member of a visible minority, can do little to transform an institution. Often it seems that no matter who occupies positions, he—or she—can do little to transform them.

This observation is the beginning of a sociological perspective—the recognition that the institutions themselves express a logic—a dynamic—that reproduces gender relations between women and men and the gender order of hierarchy and power. Men *and* women have to express certain traits to occupy a political office, and their failure to do so will make the officeholder seem ineffective and incompetent. When then-Justice Minister Kim Campbell was photographed bare-shouldered behind legal robes, many people believed that she was somehow diminished—and had diminished her office. Similarly, former MP Belinda Stronach was often subjected to gendered slurs ('dog', 'bitch') and sexist media comments about her attractiveness during her time in office.[17] Of course, men are not immune to this sort of criticism. A man too concerned about his appearance may appear weak, duplicitous, or of suspect masculinity, as Reform Party founder Preston Manning found out when he became leader of the opposition in the House of Commons and undertook what came to be called his 'Eastern makeover'.

To argue that institutions are gendered is *only* the other half of the story. It's as simplistic to argue that the individuals who occupy those positions are genderless as it is to argue that the positions they occupy are gender-neutral. Gendered individuals occupy places within gendered institutions. And thus it is quite likely that if all the positions were filled with the gender that has been raised to avoid conflict instead of the gender that is accustomed to drawing lines in the sand, the gendered mandates of those institutions would be affected, modified, and moderately transformed. In short, if *all* those positions were filled with women, we might sleep more peacefully at night—at least a *little* bit more peacefully.

To say, then, that gender is socially constructed requires that we locate individual identity within a historically and socially specific and equally gendered place and time and that we situate the individual within the complex matrix of our lives, our bodies, and our social and cultural environments. A sociological perspective examines the ways in which gendered individuals interact with other gendered individuals in gendered institutions. As such, sociology examines the interplay of those two forces—identities and structures—through the prisms of socially created difference and domination.

Gender revolves around these themes—identity, interaction, institution—in the production of gender difference and the reproduction of gender inequality. These themes are quite complex, and the relationships between and among them are also complicated. These are the processes and experiences that form core elements of our personalities, our interactions with others, and the institutions that shape our lives. These experiences are shaped by our societies, and we return the favour, helping to reshape our societies. We are gendered people living in gendered societies.

A social constructionist perspective, however, goes one step further than even this. Not only do gendered individuals negotiate their identities within gendered institutions, but also those institutions produce the very differences we assume are the properties of individuals. Thus 'the extent to which women and men do different tasks, play widely disparate concrete social roles, strongly influences the extent to which the two sexes develop and/or are expected to manifest widely disparate personal behaviours and characteristics'. Different structured experiences produce the gender differences that we often attribute to people.[18]

Let's illustrate this phenomenon first with a mundane example and then with a more analytically complex one. At the most mundane level, think about public washrooms. In a clever essay on the 'arrangement between the sexes', the late sociologist Erving Goffman playfully suggested the ways in which these public institutions produce the very gender differences they are supposed to reflect. Though men and women are 'somewhat similar in the question of waste products and their elimination', Goffman observes, in public, men and women use sex-segregated washrooms, clearly marked 'gentlemen' and 'ladies'. These rooms have very different spatial arrangements, such as urinals for men and more elaborate 'vanity tables' and other grooming facilities for women. We think of these as justifiably 'separate but equal'.

But in the privacy of our own homes, we use the same bathrooms and feel no need for separate space. What is more, virtually no private homes have urinals for men, and few have separate and private vanity tables for women. (And, of course, in some cultures, these functions are performed publicly, with no privacy at all.) If these needs are biologically based, Goffman asks, why are they so different in public and in private?

> The *functioning* of sex differentiated organs is involved, but there is nothing in this functioning that biologically recommends segregation; *that* arrangement is a totally cultural matter . . . Toilet segregation is presented as a natural consequence of the difference between the sex-classes when in fact it is a means of honouring, if not producing, this difference.[19]

In other words, by using separate facilities, we 'become' the gentlemen and ladies who are supposed to use those separate facilities. And that means we are not just gentlemen who stand up or ladies who powder their noses; washrooms imply much more about who the 'standard' human being is. Until recently, most washrooms had very few accommodations for the disabled; in North America, almost no washrooms contain accommodations (for example, smaller fixtures) for children. Men's washrooms seldom contain diaper changing tables, as many frustrated fathers can attest; this both reflects and creates an assumption that the 'average' man does not need to change diapers. Public washrooms thus reinforce a whole set of assumptions about gender, size, ability, and social function.

At the less mundane, but certainly no less important, level, take the example of the workplace. In her now-classic work, *Men and Women of the Corporation*, Rosabeth Moss Kanter demonstrated that the differences in men's and women's behaviours in organizations had far less to do with men's and women's characteristics as individuals than it had to do with the structure of the organization. Organizational positions 'carry characteristic images of the kinds of people that should occupy them', she argued, and those who occupied them, whether women or men, exhibited those necessary behaviours. Though the criteria for evaluation of job performance, promotion, and effectiveness seem to be gender-neutral, they are, in fact, deeply gendered. 'While organizations were being defined as sex-neutral machines', she writes, 'masculine principles were dominating their authority structures'. Once again, masculinity—the norm—was invisible.[20]

In a series of insightful essays, sociologist Joan Acker has expanded on Kanter's early insights and specified the interplay of structure and gender. It's through our experiences in the workplace, Acker maintains, that the differences between women and men are reproduced and through which the inequality between women and men is legitimated. Institutions are like factories, and what they produce is gender difference.

Institutions accomplish the creation of gender difference and the reproduction of the gender order, Acker argues, through several 'gendered processes'. These gendered processes mean that 'advantage and disadvantage, exploitation and control, action and emotion, meaning and identity, are patterned through and in terms of a distinction between male and female, masculine and feminine'. She observes five of these processes:

1. the production of **gender divisions**—the ways in which 'ordinary organizational practices produce the gender patterning of jobs, wages, and hierarchies, power and subordination'. In the very organization of work, gender divisions are produced and reinforced, and hierarchies are maintained—often despite the intentions of well-meaning managers and supervisors.
2. the construction of symbols and images 'that explain, express, reinforce, or sometimes oppose those divisions'. **Gender images**, such as advertisements, reproduce the gendering of positions so that the image of a successful manager or business executive is almost always an image of a well-dressed, powerful man.
3. the interactions between individuals—women and men, women and women, men and men, in all the forms and patterns that express dominance and submission. For example, conversations between supervisors and subordinates typically involve power dynamics, such as interruptions, sentence completion, and setting the topic for conversation, which, given the gendered positions within the organization, will reproduce observable conversational gender differences.
4. the internal mental work of individuals 'as they consciously construct their understandings of the organization's gendered structure of work and opportunity and the demands for gender-appropriate behaviours and attitudes'. This might include patterns of dress, speech, and general presentation of self.
5. the ongoing logic of organizations themselves—how the seemingly gender-neutral theories of organizational dynamics, bureaucracy, and organizational criteria for evaluation and advancement are actually very gendered criteria masquerading as 'objective' and gender-neutral.[21]

As we've seen, sex role theory assumed that gendered individuals enter gender-neutral sites, thus maintaining the invisibility of gender-as-hierarchy and specifically the invisible masculine organizational logic. On the other hand, many organizational theories assume that genderless 'workers' occupy those gender-neutral sites. The problem is that such employees are assumed to be able to devote themselves single-mindedly to their jobs, have no children or family responsibilities, and may even have familial supports for such single-minded workplace devotion. Thus the genderless job-holder turns out to be gendered as a (stereotypical) man. Once again, the invisibility of masculinity as the unexamined norm turns out to reproduce the power differences between women and men, because women are more likely to have the responsibilities that, according to the logic above, make them less committed employees.

One or two more examples should suffice. Many doctors complete college by age 21 or 22, medical school by age 25 to 27, and then endure three more years of internship and residency, during which time they are occasionally on call for long stretches of time, sometimes even two or three days straight. They thus complete their residencies by their late twenties or early thirties. Such a program is designed for a male doctor—one for whom the birth of children will not disrupt these time demands, and one who may even have someone at home taking care of the children while he sleeps at the hospital. No wonder women—today the majority of Canadian medical students—began to complain that they were not able to balance pregnancy and motherhood with their medical training.

According to *Maclean's* magazine, 'soon the entire health care system will be dominated by female physicians', which causes concern, particularly because women 'have been shown in the past to work fewer hours than their male counterparts'. Another article discussed the plight of a pregnant Toronto woman who had gone through three doctors in the past few years—'and every one of them was a woman who'd left for her children'.[22] Discussions have often emphasized that women just don't want to work as much or as hard as male physicians traditionally have; some have darkly grumbled about the cost of training physicians who end up leaving the field after a relatively short career.

These discussions have rarely mentioned the fact that the medical profession, like other high-pressure fields, has always relied upon a highly gendered division of labour—not just within hospitals but within the homes of its physicians. Male doctors have traditionally worked more hours than their female counterparts do, but most were still able to have families. Why? Because they had 'doctor's wives'—that is, their wives played an essential support role. In the classic model, a young woman supported her partner (often financially) while he attended school, and then stayed home to manage the family and household (and, sometimes, the accounts). Thus some semblance of a 'normal' life could be combined with the demands of the job. For various reasons, this model of family is not one most women doctors can access. So it's not just about women's lack of commitment to the profession, or about personal choices. It's about how family and workplace are gendered, and how medical practice was designed on the basis of gendered assumptions.

Similarly, lawyers just out of law school who take jobs with large corporate law firms are expected to bill up to 50 to 60 hours per week—a process that probably requires working 80 to 90 hours per week. Assuming at least six hours of sleep per night, a one-hour round-trip commute, and one half-day of rest, these young lawyers are going to have a total of about 17 hours per week to eat, cook, clean their house, talk with and/or make love with their spouse (or date if they're single), and spend time with their children. Without that half-day off on the weekend, they have about one hour per day for everything else. Failure to submit to this regime places a lawyer on a 'mommy track' or a 'daddy track', which means that everyone will think well of that lawyer for being such an involved parent but that he or she is certain never to be promoted to partner, to join all the rest of the lawyers who made such sacrifices for their careers.

Or, finally, take academic tenure. In a typical academic career, a scholar completes a Ph.D. about five to six years after the MA, or roughly by the early thirties. Then he or she begins a career as an assistant professor and has six more years to earn tenure and promotion. This is usually the most intense academic work period of a scholar's life—he or she works night and day to publish enough scholarly research, prepare and teach courses, and serve on the many committees that govern and manage universities. The thirties are also the most likely child-bearing years for professional women. The academic tenure clock is thus timed to a *man's* rhythms—and not just any man, but one who has a wife or other family supports to relieve him of family obligations as he works to establish his credentials. Remember the adage 'publish or perish'? Often, to academics struggling to make tenure, it feels as though publishing requires that family life perish. Small wonder that according to 2001 StatsCan data, 49.6 per cent of all academic women aged 35 to 39 had no children under the age of 12 at home, which made them significantly less likely to have children even than women lawyers and women physicians.[23]

In 1988's *Working Girl,* Melanie Griffith's suit was a virtual replica of Harrison Ford's.

Observing the institutional dimension also offers the possibility to observe adjustment and readjustment within institutions as they are challenged. Sometimes, their boundaries prove more permeable than originally expected. For example, what happens when the boundaries between work and home become permeable, when women leave the home and enter the gendered workplace? Judith Gerson and Kathy Peiss suggest that boundaries '*within* the workplace (e.g., occupational segregation) and interactional micro level boundaries assume increased significance in defining the subordinate position of women'. Thus occupational segregation can reproduce gender difference *and* gender inequality by assigning women to secondary statuses within organizations. For those women who enter non-traditional positions, though, micro level boundary maintenance would come into play—'the persistence of informal group behaviour among men (e.g., after-work socializing, the uses of male humour, modes of corporate attire)—act to define insiders and outsiders, thus maintaining gender-based distinctions'.[24] How women attempted to breach these boundaries can be seen in the heavily padded shoulders of the 1980s 'power suit'. In its female version, the power suit attempted to mimic a typically masculine torso profile and thus make the wearer look more 'corporate'.

Embedded in organizational structures that are gendered, subject to gendered organizational processes, and evaluated by gendered criteria, then, the differences between women and men appear to be the differences solely between gendered individuals. When gender boundaries seem permeable, other dynamics and processes can reproduce the gender order. When women do not meet these criteria (or, perhaps more accurately, when the criteria do not meet women's specific needs), we see a gender-segregated workforce and wage, hiring, and promotional disparities as the 'natural' outcomes of already-present differences between women and men. It is in this way that those differences are generated and the inequalities between women and men are legitimated and reproduced.

One should, of course, note that it is through these same processes that the 'differences' between working-class and professional men, between the disabled and the able-bodied, between Aboriginals and non-Aboriginals, between whites and visible minorities, between immigrants and non-immigrants, and between heterosexuals and homosexuals are also produced and that the inequalities based on class or race or sexuality are legitimated and reproduced. Making gender visible in these organizational processes ought not to blind us to the complex interactions with other patterns of difference and principles of inequality. Just as a male pattern becomes the unexamined norm, so, too, does a white, able-bodied, heterosexual, and middle-class pattern become the unexamined norm against which others' experiences and performances are evaluated.

The idea of **organizational gender neutrality**, then, is the vehicle by which the gender order is reproduced. 'The theory and practice of gender neutrality', writes Acker, 'covers up, obscures, the underlying gender structure, allowing practices that perpetuate it to continue even as efforts to reduce gender inequality are also under way'.[25] Organizations reflect and produce gender differences; gendered institutions also reproduce the gender order by which men are privileged over women and by which some men are privileged over other men.

'Doing Gender': The Interactionist Approach

There remains one more element in the sociological explanation of gender. According to sex role theory, we acquire our gender identity through socialization, and afterward we are socialized to behave in masculine or feminine ways. It is thus the task of society to make sure that the men act in the masculine manner and that the women act in the feminine manner. Our identity is fixed, permanent, and—now—inherent in our personalities. We can no more cease being men or women than we can cease being human.

In an important contribution to the social constructionist perspective, sociologists Candace West and Don Zimmerman argued that gender is less a component of identity—fixed, static—that we take with us into our interactions, than it is the product *of* those interactions. They argued that 'a person's gender is not simply an aspect of what one is, but, more fundamentally, it is something that one *does*, and does recurrently, in interaction with others'. We are constantly 'doing' gender, performing the activities and exhibiting the traits that are prescribed for us.[26]

If our sex role identity is inherent, West and Zimmerman might ask, in what does it inhere? What are the criteria by which we sort people into those sex roles to begin with? Typically, our answer returns us to biology and, more specifically, to the primary sex characteristics that we believe determine which gender one will become. Biological sex—externally manifested genitalia—becomes socialized gender role. Those with male genitalia are classified in one way; those with female genitalia are classified in another way. These two sexes become different genders, which are assumed to have different personalities and require different institutional and social arrangements to accommodate their natural—and now socially acquired—differences.

Most of the time we carry around these types of common-sense understandings. We see **primary sex characteristics** (those present at birth) as far more decisive than **secondary sex characteristics** (those that develop at puberty) for the assignment of gender role identity. But how do we know? When we see someone on the street, it is his or her *secondary* sex characteristics that we observe—breast development, facial hair, musculature. Even more than that, it is the behavioural presentation of self—how someone dresses, moves, talks—that signals to us whether that someone is a man or a woman. It would be a strange world, indeed, if we had constantly to ask to see people's genitals to make sure they were who they appeared to be!

gross. pig

One method that sociologists developed to interrogate this assumption has been to imagine that primary and secondary sex characteristics did not match. As we have seen, in many cases, intersexed infants—whose primary sex characteristics cannot be easily discerned visually—have their genitals surgically reconstructed. Intersexuality pushes us to reconsider the genitals as the defining feature of biological sex. Gender, as William Reiner, a urologist and psychiatrist who treats intersex children, says, 'has far more to do with other important structures than external genitals'.[27]

Perhaps, but the genitals remain the common sense 'location' of biological sex. In a brilliantly disconcerting study, *Gender: An Ethnomethodological Approach*, Suzanne Kessler and Wendy McKenna proposed two images in which primary and secondary sex characteristics did not match (see Figures 5.1 and 5.2). Which one is the 'man', and

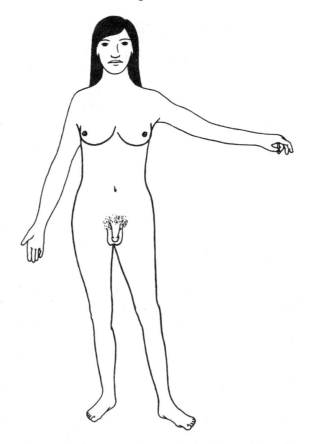

Figure 5.1 Figure with penis, breasts, hips, no body hair, and long hair.

From *Gender: An Ethnomethodological Approach* by Kessler and Mckenna. Copyright © 1985 by University of Chicago Press. Reprinted by permission of John Wiley & Sons, Inc.

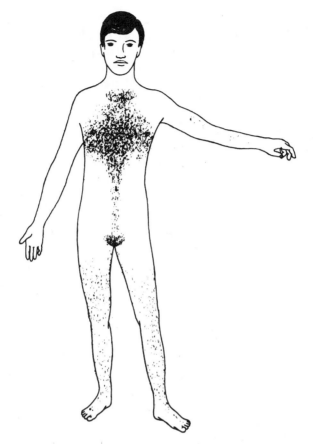

Figure 5.2 Figure with vulva, no breasts, no hips, body hair, and short hair.

From *Gender: An Ethnomethodological Approach* by Kessler and Mckenna. Copyright © 1985 by University of Chicago Press. Reprinted by permission of John Wiley & Sons, Inc.

which is the 'woman'? How can you tell? If you base your decision on primary sex characteristics—the genitals—you would have to conclude that many of the people with whom you interact in daily life might be hiding their 'true' selves. But, if you base your decision on what you see 'above the waist', which is more visible in daily life, you would have to conclude that many people may actually be a different sex from that which they appear to be.

Looking at those images, one might be tempted to dismiss this as the stuff of fantasy. After all, in real life, people's genitals match their secondary sex characteristics, and we are always easily able to tell the difference, right? Well, maybe not always. In the popular 1992 film *The Crying Game* it was revealed, to both the audience and the film's protagonist simultaneously, that Dil, the woman lead was in love with, was actually a man. North American audiences were profoundly shocked, so much that this became *the* story of the film, obscuring its considerable political content. Such confusion is often the basis for comedy. Knowing whether someone is male or female is far more important to the observer than it often is to the observed, as fans of the television program *Saturday Night Live* will recall with the ambiguous character, 'Pat'. People who interacted with Pat were constantly trying to trick him/her into revealing what he/she 'really' was, while Pat nonchalantly answered their questions and eluded every rhetorical trap.

Of course, these are all media creations, and in real life, 'passing' is far more difficult and far less common. But one reason we enjoy such ambiguous characters is because gender certainty is so important to us. Without it, we feel as if we have lost our social bearings in the world and are threatened with a kind of 'gender vertigo', in which the dualistic conceptions that we believe are the foundations of our social reality turn out to be more fluid than we believed or hoped.[28] It's as though our notions of gender are anchored in quicksand. One sociologist reported how she became disturbed by the sexual ambiguity of a computer salesperson:

> The person who answered my questions was truly a salesperson. I could not categorize him/her as a woman or a man. What did I look for? (1) Facial hair: She/he was smooth skinned, but some men have little or no facial hair. (This varies by race, Native Americans and Blacks often have none.) (2) Breasts: She/he was wearing a loose shirt that hung from his/her shoulders. And, as many women who suffered through a 1950s adolescence know to their shame, women are often flat-chested. (3) Shoulders: His/hers were small and round for a man, broad for a woman. (4) Hands: Long and slender fingers, knuckles a bit large for a woman, small for a man. (5) Voice: Middle range, unexpressive for a woman, not at all the exaggerated tones some gay males affect. (6) His/her treatment of me: Gave off no signs that would let me know if I were of the same or different sex as this person. There were not even any signs that he/she knew his/her sex would be difficult to categorize and I wondered about this even as I did my best to hide these questions so I would not embarrass him/her while we talked of computer paper. I left still not knowing the sex of my salesperson, and was disturbed by that unanswered question (child of my culture that I am).[29]

Transvestites and cross-dressers reveal the artifice of gender. Gender is a performance, a form of drag, by which, through the successful manipulation of props, signs, symbols, behaviours, and emotions, we attempt to convince others of our successful acquisition of masculinity or femininity. Cross-dressers know better, or rather, know different: As 'social constructionists', they know that successfully being a man or a woman simply means convincing others that you are what you appear to be. Just ask RuPaul who seems to float almost effortlessly between the two, and who says, 'We are born naked. The rest is drag'. Or ask Alison Laing, a husband and a father, who spends about 80 per cent of his time dressed in women's clothes and 20 per cent dressed as a man. 'We don't have to live in gender boxes', he says.[30]

Most of us find the walls of those boxes enormously comforting. We learn gender performance early in childhood, and it remains with us virtually all our lives. When our gender identities are threatened, we will often retreat to displays of exaggerated masculinity or exaggerated femininity. And when our sense of others' gender identity is disrupted or dislodged, we can become anxious, even violent. 'We're so invested in being men or women that if you fall outside that easy definition of what a man or woman is,

(l) WireImage/Getty Images; (r) © Mitchell Gerber/CORBIS

Gender as performance: Two genders of RuPaul

a lot of people see you as some kind of monster', commented Susan Stryker, who is a male-to-female transsexual. Many transgendered people are murdered or attacked every year.[31]

The fascinating case of 'Agnes' reported by Harold Garfinkel also demonstrates these themes. Agnes was first encountered in the late 1950s by a psychiatrist, Robert Stoller, and by Garfinkel, a sociologist. Though Agnes appeared in every way to be a very feminine woman, she also had a penis, which she regarded as a biological mistake. Agnes 'knew' she was a woman and acted (and demanded to be treated) as a woman. 'I have always been a girl', she proclaimed to her interviewers, and she regarded her early childhood socialization as a relentless trauma of being forced to participate in activities for boys, like sports. Because genitals were not 'the essential signs of her femininity', Agnes instead referred to her prominent breasts and her lifelong sense that she was, in fact, female. 'Her self-described feminine feelings, behaviour, choices of companions, and the like were never portrayed as matters of decision or choice but were treated as *given* as a natural fact', writes Garfinkel.[32]

Understanding how we do gender, then, requires that we make visible the performative elements of identity and also the audience for those performances. It also opens up unimaginable possibilities for social change; as Suzanne Kessler points out in her study of intersexuals:

> If authenticity for gender rests not in a discoverable nature but in someone else's proclamation, then the power to proclaim something else is available. If physicians recognized that implicit in their management of gender is the notion that finally, and always, people construct gender as well as the social systems that are grounded in gender-based concepts, the possibilities for real societal transformations would be unlimited.[33]

Kessler's gender utopianism does raise an important issue in the sociological perspective. In saying that we 'do' gender, we are saying that gender is not only something that is done to us. We create and re-create our own gendered identities within the contexts of our interactions with others and within the institutions we inhabit.

Constructing Gender: Feminist Views and Movements

Almost 300 pages into her famous book *The Second Sex*, Simone de Beauvoir issued a statement that became the cornerstone of **second-wave feminism**'s view of gender: 'One is not born, but rather becomes, a woman.'[34] Writing from the perspective of a curious philosopher, Beauvoir systematically analyzed the evidence for the biological character of gender before turning to its historical and psychological construction. She argued persuasively that men had defined themselves in opposition to women, creating in Woman a mysterious, dangerous, and misunderstood Other.

These powerful insights made *The Second Sex* one of the key texts of the twentieth-century feminist movement, but they were not wholly original to Beauvoir. Indeed, Mary Wollstonecraft argued in the late eighteenth century that the 'defects' of women were caused not by their nature but by the 'deforming' influences of society.[35] So feminist thought has a long relationship with social constructionism.

Still, during the nineteenth century, **first-wave feminists** tended to avoid dramatic statements about social construction. In twenty-first century Canada, it's difficult to imagine the world feminists confronted in the 1800s: a world of frank colonial exploitation in which race-based slavery existed; in which women and children (and men) were routinely and viciously exploited in employment; in which women in many countries enjoyed virtually no legal protection from abuse, property rights within marriage, or parental rights. The issues taken on by feminists in 1800s Europe and America were many, from the well-known battle for women's suffrage and the abolition of slavery to campaigns involving temperance, marital property, and men's sexual privilege.

While most feminists accepted the 'natural' differences between men and women, they turned those distinctions over, arguing, for example, that women's heightened moral sense made them ideal candidates for activities in the public sphere. And even feminists who resisted the idea of women's suffrage and accepted innate sex difference believed that many of the limitations placed upon women were the result not of weak female nature, but of the manner in which women were raised, educated, treated, and excluded from many societal benefits and institutions.

The first-wave feminist movement steadily gained momentum from the 1850s until the end of the First World War, eventually coming to focus on the vote as the means to advance the status of women and, more generally, social progress. In the wake of the war, as nation after nation granted women suffrage, the feminist movement began to fragment until, by the Second World War, many people believed that feminism was a thing of the past. Indeed, much of what women had fought for had been achieved. What was left?

The answer to that question came from several places. Probably the first work to make a significant contribution to the discussion was Beauvoir's *Second Sex*, discussed above. Published in French in 1949, the book was translated (however weakly) into

English only four years later, and continues to be translated into other languages. In North America, another important work that found a massive popular audience was Betty Friedan's *The Feminine Mystique*. First published in 1963, Friedan's book was based on surveys of her college graduating class, which revealed that despite living lives of relative privilege and apparent success, suburban women were deeply uneasy with their lives and identities. Friedan argued that women were provided with a role that required them to define themselves entirely in terms of others (husbands and children), leading to a deep malaise which she called 'the problem with no name'. Though the work has been criticized in the years since its publication, it struck a chord with readers; by the end of 1964, the book had sold 1.3 million copies, becoming the non-fiction bestseller of the year.[36]

By the late 1960s, driven by the political ferment and critical social movements of the time, women were not only reading Friedan and Beauvoir but meeting with others and organizing meetings and protests. Feminism had once again become a social movement as well as a philosophy. In Canada, women's groups demanded that the government respond to their concerns. As a result, Prime Minister Lester B. Pearson created a Royal Commission on the Status of Women, which conducted hearings throughout the nation in 1968, receiving hundreds of briefs on everything from pensions to the Indian Act and family law. The commission made 167 recommendations, many of which were implemented in the 1970s.

Like first-wave feminists, the feminists of the late 1960s and early 1970s attempted to increase women's legal rights and combat continuing inequalities between the sexes. But the new feminists differed from their predecessors in their willingness and ability to discuss, analyze, and protest power imbalances in personal and intimate relations. **Consciousness-raising**, which brought women together in small groups to discuss every aspect of their lives, allowed women to perceive that experiences and thoughts they had felt to be theirs alone were indeed the result of gender construction, shared widely with other women.

Proclaiming that 'the personal is political', second-wave feminists protested beauty pageants, created shelters for survivors of domestic and sexual abuse, and constantly pushed their society to recognize the interlocking of gender and power in everyday life, including in 'universal' language. Though they were often seen as dangerous radicals in the 1970s, second-wave feminists catalyzed many changes in society, from the overhauling of criminal and family law to the use of the title 'Ms' to describe women. Much of what they fought for we now take for granted.

Of course, a movement of such size inevitably became both diverse and fractious. As a movement for social justice, moreover, feminism was constantly pushed to criticize its own assumptions, practices, and exclusions. To a great degree, while critiquing the marginalization of women, second-wave feminism struggled with intra-movement issues on the basis of class, ethnicity, and sexual orientation. As a result, various streams or schools of feminism emerged during the second wave; they are not so much discrete bodies of thought as areas of emphasis, however, and feminist theory today draws from all of these areas.

The most 'mainstream' form of second-wave feminism, which was highly successful in achieving legal reforms, is generally known as **liberal feminism**. Focusing on the reform of society to make it as gender-neutral as possible, liberal feminists emphasize safe legal abortion, an end to legal discrimination, shared parenting and housework, and political and workplace equality.

Marxist and socialist feminisms are critical of this stance, arguing instead that economy, not merely a lack of legal and customary equality, was at the heart of women's previous oppression as a 'sex-class'. For socialist feminists, economy, law, and culture all play a role in the subordination of women, as do racial and class discrimination.

Radical feminism, meanwhile, argues that patriarchy, and particularly its control over women's sexuality, is the root of women's second-class status. Rather than simply changing women's legal rights in the workplace, women need to combat patriarchal violence in the form of rape, domestic abuse, and warfare.

Lesbian feminism took this one step farther, claiming in the 1970s that hetero-sexuality itself oppressed women, and that lesbianism—or even complete separation from the world of men—could be a liberating political option. Feminists in a school sometimes known as **difference feminism** have also tended to focus on separation from men. Basing their theory on psychoanalytic and psychological theories of gender difference, particularly the work of Carol Gilligan (see Chapter 4), they argue for a woman-centred culture that would value women's difference instead of seeing it as evidence of inferiority.

While **multiracial and ethnic feminisms** partake of all of these theoretical orientations, they have emphasized the racial dimensions of gender inequality and criticized the racism found even within feminist movements themselves. Many multiracial feminists have also critiqued liberal feminism for its embrace of individualism, which some see as a Western construct often imposed on non-Western and non-white 'Others'.

By the 1980s, second-wave feminism had become a large, international, and diverse movement. This was amply demonstrated by the global conferences on the status of women convened by the United Nations in Mexico City (1975), Copenhagen (1980), Nairobi (1985), and Beijing (1995), where it became clear that women's issues differed widely on the basis of location—not just national location, but also ethnic and class status.

Though the peak of feminist activism was probably sometime in the early 1980s, feminism has continued to be a vibrant social movement and an important theoretical orientation. Scholars who study gender in many academic disciplines have been profoundly influenced by feminist theories and methodologies, which of course also inform research in women's, gender, and sexuality studies. **Post-colonial** and **post-modern feminisms**, both of which emerged during the 1990s, continue to be important in academic inquiry and, particularly in the case of post-colonial feminism, within social movements. At the same time, **third-wave feminism** has emerged within popular culture, contesting some of the beliefs of second-wave feminists and celebrating ethnic diversity, complex identity, individual agency, and self-expression (whether in sexuality, in dress, or in art). With an important on-line presence, third-wave feminism is arguably the version most familiar to contemporary youth.

Feminism has contributed immeasurably to our understanding of the social construction of gender. Feminism has also embraced the idea that gender cannot be analyzed independently of other modes of domination and determinants of social relations. Feminist consensus today recognizes **intersectionality**, 'the relationship among multiple dimensions and modalities of social relations and subject forma-tions', as the best way of understanding gender. Thus one cannot, according to most feminists, analyze the category 'women' without recognizing that the category 'women' is complicated by issues of ethnicity, class, culture, sexuality, ability, etc. In-deed, these complications may mean that talking about 'women' may be meaningless in a given situation. According to Leslie McCall, this may be 'the most important theoretical contribution that women's studies, in conjunction with relation fields, has made so far'.[37] Aside from this important theoretical contribution, feminist *activism* has also, quite obviously, changed Canadian (and other) societies over the course of the past 40 years.

Toward an Explanation of the Social Construction of Gender Relations

We have argued that gender is socially constructed: that it is neither the expression of biology or simply a role. Then how *shall* we think about gender? The elements of a defi-nition seem clear enough. We'll explore three related levels: (1) identity, (2) interaction, and (3) institution—and, of course, the interactions among them, in order to explain the related phenomena: gender difference and gender inequality.

First, *we understand that gender as an identity is not a 'thing' that one possesses, but rather a set of activities that one does.* When we do gender, we do it in front of other people; it is validated and legitimated by the evaluations of others. Gender is less a property of the individual than it is a product of our interactions with others. West and Zimmerman call gender a 'managed property', which is 'contrived with respect to the fact that others will judge and respond to us in particular ways'. Women and men are distinct social groups, constituted in 'concrete, historically changing—and generally unequal—social relationships'. What the great British historian E.P. Thompson once wrote about class applies equally to gender. Gender 'is a relationship, not a thing'—and like all relationships, we are active in their construction. We do not simply inherit a male or female sex role, but we actively—interactively—constantly define and redefine what it means to be men or women in our daily encounters with one another. Gender is something one *does*, not something one *has*.[38]

Second, *we understand that we do gender in every interaction, in every situation, in every institution in which we find ourselves.* Gender is a situated accomplishment, as much an aspect of interaction as it is of identity. As James Messerschmidt puts it, 'gen-der is a situated accomplishment in which we produce forms of behaviour seen by oth-ers in the same immediate situation as masculine or feminine'. Gender is what we bring to these interactions and what is produced in them as well.[39]

Third, *we do gender not in a genderless vacuum but, rather, in a gendered world, in gendered institutions.* Our social world is built on systemic, structural inequality based on gender; social life reproduces both gender difference and gender inequality. We need to think of masculinity and femininity 'not as a single object with its own history, but as being constantly constructed within the history of an evolving social structure'. As Katherine Pyke defines it, gender is:

> an emergent property of situated interaction rather than a role or attribute. Deeply held and typically non-conscious beliefs about men's and women's essential natures shape how gender is accomplished in everyday interactions. Because those beliefs are moulded by existing macrostructural power relations, the culturally appropriate ways of producing gender favour men's interests over those of women. In this manner, gendered power relations are reproduced.[40]

In short, social constructionism is able to explain both what is really different between women and men and what is not really different but only seems to be, as well as the ways in which gender difference is the product of—and not the cause of—gender inequality. We are gendered people living gendered lives in a gendered society—but we do actually live on the same planet. (In fact, it may be that only on this planet would such differences make a difference.)

In the remainder of this book, we'll look at some of the institutions that create gender difference and reproduce gender inequality—families, schools, workplaces—and observe some of the ways in which those differences and that inequality are expressed through our interactions with one another—in love, sex, friendship, and violence.

Summary

Beginning from a critique of biological determinism, the social sciences (including sociology) and feminist theory view human behaviour as largely socially constructed. As the experiences of social isolates suggest, even basic human behaviour is determined by interaction with others. The belief that we are the product of interactions rather than of our biology is referred to as social constructionism.

As discussed in Chapter 1, the four elements of a social contructionist perspective are that gender varies from culture to culture, in any one culture over historical time, over the course of a person's life, and within any one culture at any one time. Social constructionism thus offers the ability to explain variations within gender, and thus adds an analysis of difference, power, and gender's institutional dimensions.

In contrast, sex role theory is more limited in its ability to explain these phenomena. Social constructionists identify six related problems with sex role theory, which minimizes the importance of gender; posits singular definitions of masculinity and femininity; ignores the relational dimension of gender; negates the situational quality of gendered interactions; depoliticizes gender by making it an individual, not societal, attribute; and, finally, cannot account for the dynamics of change. Indeed, sex role theory almost implies that the roles people play are the result of fundamental personality differences socialized early in life *rather* than the result of power-laden social relations themselves. In some senses, then, sex role theory 'blames the victim'.

This book, in contrast, argues that gender is fundamentally about differences *and* power. Gender is not just a role, but a powered relationship between men and women that also operates among groups of men and women. This doesn't mean that all men are powerful, or that all women are powerless; it means that men *as a group*, in most places in the world, are more powerful than women as a group. Power is not just an individual possession, but a property of group and social life. It is deeply woven into our lives, our interactions, and our institutions. For sociologists and feminists, power is a central part of gender analysis. Sociology also adds three essential components to the study of gender. First is a *life-course approach*, which acknowledges how much gender varies through the course of any individual's life. Childhood, early adulthood, middle age, and senior years bring tremendous transformations in experiences of and perspectives on gender. For social constructionists, these changes are the result not of biological processes of maturation and aging but of the *meanings* societies ascribe to these processes and the changing institutions in which an individual finds him- or herself.

The second critical contribution of sociology to the study of gender is a *macrolevel institutional analysis*. Sociologists consider institutions of the utmost importance to the constitution of any society and its individual members. Institutions, like individuals, are gendered. They create normative gendered standards, express gendered logic, and are major factors in the reproduction of gender inequality. Scholars have studied many social institutions— from paid employment to public washrooms—and have uncovered compelling evidence that institutions are not 'gender-neutral' sites, but places that reinforce gender difference and reproduce the gendered social order.

Finally, sociology contributes a *microlevel interactionist approach* that sees gender not as a fixed character or set of traits that we acquire through role socialization, but as something that emerges and changes through various social interactions. Gender, in this view, is something that we perform differently in various situations in our lives. Gender is not something we 'have', but something we 'do'.

These views are shared not only by sociologists but by feminist theorists and activists. Feminists have long argued that women were not essentially different from men as had been claimed, but were instead socialized differently. Though first-wave feminists were less likely to advance this claim, second- and third-wave feminists became strong proponents of social constructionism. Feminists of all 'waves' contributed a cogent analysis of gendered power, and organized activism to confront male privilege. This activism has had a massive effect on society, to such an extent that many feminist claims of the past are now regarded as 'standard operating procedure', from women's voting rights to reformed sexual assault laws. Still, as feminism became a massive social movement in the 1970s, it became increasingly diverse and fractious, with many different 'schools' or approaches with diverse perspectives on power and social construction of gender. Despite these differences, in Canada and around the world, feminism has catalyzed dramatic changes and contributed to our knowledge and awareness of the social construction of gender. Among the most important theoretical contributions of recent feminism, intersectionality stands out as a recognition that gender analysis is complicated by other features of social relations, for example racism.

This chapter has argued that gender is neither an expression of biology nor a role. Instead, we argue, gender difference and gender inequality emerge at three levels: identity, interaction, and institution. At the level of identity, gender is not a possession, but a set of activities that one performs for others. At the second level, interaction, we perform gender in accordance with our situations. We bring gender to our interactions and produce gender through those interactions at the same time. Finally, we do gender in gendered institutions, within evolving social structures built on structurally unequal gender relations. Our differences are not just within us, and this book argues that they are smaller than we often think. But we are gendered people, and more importantly, we have gendered interactions within a gendered society.

Questions for Critical Thinking

1. Considering the four elements of a social constructionist perspective—that definitions of gender vary from culture to culture, in any one culture over time, over the course of an individual's life, and within any one culture at any one time—can you identify examples of each variation from your own knowledge or experience?
2. Given that power is situational, can you imagine examples of how someone might be powerful in one situation and yet relatively powerless in another?
3. Thinking about a particular social interaction, can you explain how gender is a thing that one *does* and not a thing that one *has*? Do you agree with this assessment of how gender identity works?
4. Consider any particular social institution you can think of—or perhaps one with which you are personally familiar. How does that institution (a) create normative gendered standards; (b) express a gendered logic; and (c) reproduce gender inequality?
5. How do you believe feminist theory or activism has affected your life? Do you believe that feminism has continued relevance in either examining or challenging the construction of gender? How would the concept of intersectionality affect a gendered analysis of your life or your community?

Key Terms

confirmation bias
consciousness-raising
difference feminism
first-wave feminism
gender divisions
gender image
institution
intersectionality
lesbian feminism
liberal feminism
Marxist and socialist feminisms
mid-life crisis

multiracial/ethnic feminisms
narrative coherence
organizational gender neutrality
post-colonial feminism
post-modern feminism
primary sex characteristics
radical feminism
second-wave feminism
secondary sex characteristics
social constructionism
sociology
third-wave feminism

Part 2

Gendered Identities, Gendered Institutions

Chapter 6

The Gendered Family

Gender at the Heart of the Home

Nobody has ever before asked the nuclear family to live all by itself in a box the way we do. With no relatives, no support, we've put it in an impossible situation.

—MARGARET MEAD

I don't like nostalgia unless it's mine.

—LOU REED

In the 1980s and 1990s, many North Americans believed that the family was 'in crisis'—falling apart because of high rates of divorce, teen pregnancies, single parenthood, 'latchkey children', and gay men and lesbians demanding the right to marry and have or adopt children. While Canada never had an equivalent of the 1980s American 'Moral Majority', Canadians have been concerned about the apparently uncertain fate of the family in the modern world. As an example, REAL Women of Canada was founded in 1983 to counter the perspective of federally funded 'anti-family, anti-life' feminist groups represented by Status of Women Canada.[1] To REAL Women and other social conservatives in North America, the 'traditional' nuclear family of the 1950s, of *Leave It to Beaver* and other sitcoms of the period—defined by one of its defenders as 'a legal lifelong sexually exclusive, heterosexual monogamous marriage, based on affection and companionship, in which there is a sharp division of labour with the female as full time housewife and the male as primary provider and ultimate authority'— was fast disappearing under the double-barrelled assault of a permissive society and a welfare state. In the USA, scores of punitive policy initiatives have been proposed or implemented to shore up this 'besieged' institution, including laws that would restrict divorce, repress women's right to choose abortion, reiterate a heterosexual norm in family life, and recast marriage from a legal contract to a sacred 'covenant'.[2]

All of the hysterical commentary on family decline was right on one thing: The North American family *is* changing. But if the family feels like one of the most fragile of social institutions, it is also perhaps among the most resilient. It's never been ossified into a static form, except in some mythic constructions that the family has 'always' looked like this or that. Discussions of the 'traditional' family often ignore the many changes in this basic institution over the course of human history. What we call 'traditional' may in fact be a very recent construction. Canadian families have changed dramatically over the course of our history, and the family form continues to adapt to changing circumstances.

If the nuclear family is not exactly in crisis, then what is all the noise about? Some part of the family values debate rests on what we might call 'misplaced nostalgia'—a romanticized notion that the family form of the 1950s is a timeless trope that all family forms ought to emulate. In the 1960s, anthropologist Raymond Birdwhistell labelled this 'the sentimental model' when he described the way people in rural Kentucky talked about or 'remembered' their families—which, as he pointed out, bore little resemblance to the families in which they actually lived. Often our descriptions of the family conform more to this mythic model than to our actual experiences.

Much of the family values debate is a displaced quarrel with feminism, which is often wrongly blamed for or wrongly credited with what may be the single greatest transformation of North American society in the twentieth century—the entry of women into the workplace. This process long antedates second-wave feminism, although the attack on the 'feminine mystique' launched by the women's movement in the 1960s gave working women a political peg upon which to hang their aspirations and longings.

Finally, much of the debate about the crisis of the family is based on a misreading of history. Although we think of the family as the 'private' sphere, a warm respite from the cold competitive world of the economic and political life, the family has never been a world apart. The modern family was built upon a wide foundation of economic and political supports; it is today sustained by an infrastructure that includes public funding for roads, schools, and home-buying and the legal arrangements of marriage and divorce. The workplace and family are deeply interconnected; the 'family wage' organizes family life as well as economic life, expressing an idealized view of what the family is and should be. This public component of the private sphere is often invisible in current debates about the family, in part because it is so deeply ingrained in our historical development.

A Brief History of the Canadian (and North American) Family

Though this discussion will focus primarily upon Canada after colonization, any history of the Canadian family must begin with **Aboriginal** peoples. Access to pre-contact history is difficult, given the paucity of sources, but it's clear that Aboriginal families were different in many ways from the 'ideal' family structures imagined by colonizing Europeans (and imposed upon Aboriginal people with damaging consequences).

Before Europeans colonized Canada, First Nations and Inuit people lived in family structures based on diverse traditions and practices. **Nuclear families** were important everywhere, as they were to Europeans. But overlapping with nuclear and **extended family** structures were **clan** structures that also provided a concept of 'family ties', as can be seen through common prohibitions on marrying someone from one's own clan.[3]

Aboriginal families shared an emphasis on extended family and clan in their definition of kinship. In part because of the importance of such extended kin, pre-contact

Aboriginal families cannot be described as patriarchal. Though the 'sexual contract' varied widely among Aboriginal groups, and some granted men greater status, many Aboriginal groups were relatively egalitarian or, more accurately, practiced **gender complementarity**. That is, a division of labour assigned different tasks to men and women, but male privilege either did not exist or was limited by other forms of customary power. Though not all Aboriginal groups were matrilineal or **matrilocal**, matrilineality was common. Among some groups, particularly the Iroquoian nations, the customary power of women as mothers extended to significant control over both material resources and political structures. For this reason, some Aboriginal women today argue that 'equality' is a meaningless goal for them, since they once enjoyed a different but celebrated role much more attractive than simple equality to men.[4]

In early colonial Canada, New France's missionaries attempted to inculcate Christian family life, including male domination and female obedience, in First Nations people. Their successes were limited not only by the relatively few Aboriginal groups with whom they worked, but also by resistance, particularly on the part of women.[5] However, not all Aboriginal people resisted Christian teachings; some women (and men) adopted the new religion and adapted its 'spiritual toolkit' to meet their needs and perhaps, to reassert a traditional balance of gendered power. [6]

Other groups of Europeans were much less interested in reforming Aboriginal families than they were in joining them. For European fur traders, the knowledge and kin ties of First Nations wives were sometimes literally a lifeline and always critical to success.[7] The children of fur traders and their wives (whether officially married or 'country wives') became the founders of the Métis people, one of Canada's three recognized Aboriginal groups and a distinct culture of great significance to the nation's history.

The Métis family, however, did not become the Canadian norm. As European colonization spread, more European women arrived, and settlers began to create agrarian (and to a much smaller extent, urban) households based on marriages between European men and women. These households were unlike the nuclear families we now think of as traditional. Agrarian households, like Aboriginal ones, were productive entities in which everyone worked to ensure family survival. Women enjoyed customary control over household matters and performed valued and essential tasks. Still, European settler families were based in a tradition that granted greater prestige and status to men; these families were not, therefore, egalitarian. Men defined manhood through their status as landowners, heads of household, and participants in community and political life. Women owed men respect and deference.

Still, it's worth noting some of the ways in which these settler families differed from what we now think of as the norm. There was far less differentiation between 'his' and 'her' spheres: Women and men both worked in and around their homes; women produced many of the things needed for the family; and everyone worked to a rhythm of family time, not industrial time. Some of this rhythm is captured by a diary entry written by Mary Smith of Cape Breton in 1891, when she was 79:

> A verry dry high easterly wind. The first tub Butter full 22 lbs. The little mare very sick. The boys hear helping doctor her. Flora washed her weeks washing. I washed breakfast dishes then cleared the kitchen cupboard and washed all the things that

was in it and after that the men moved it out of the clothes room into the kitchen. I washed dinner dishes and then had a rest and Sarah moved everything out of the dining room took up the carpet and swept and dusted and I washed the windows. The two girls washed up the floor and Sarah got tea ready and after tea she churned. Flora picked the geese and then put them down in the calf pasture; the children and G.P. finished picking stone a little while after dinner and then the men fixed the fence to keep the geese in. Sarah cleaned up the milk house all ready to wash the shelf and the floor and Flora and the girls finished it up.[8]

Men's work and women's work were separate, but occurred within the same spaces and times, complementing one another, in US historian Laurel Thatcher Ulrich's famous metaphor, like the 'warp and weft' of a piece of gingham. Men's work and women's work were distinct and separate, like the contrasting colours within the cloth, but they were woven together.[9] Children worked alongside the men and women, growing into their distinct gendered duties as they grew into adulthood.

In pre-industrial Canada, just as women and men were involved in the worlds of work, fathers and mothers were both involved in child rearing. Though mothers undoubtedly did the lion's share, fathers took over more responsibility as children grew, particularly as sons began to learn the skills and behaviours that would be required of them as men. Women, however, were charged by custom with infant care and the rearing of young children. Given the high fertility and infant mortality of the time, the lives of women were disproportionately dedicated to birthing, caring for, and, sadly, burying children. Both men and women had a relatively low average lifespan.

This family structure was changed in Canada, as elsewhere, by the linked processes of industrialization and urbanization, which began (however tentatively) in the first decades of the nineteenth century and spread throughout the nation by 1900. By about 1850, throughout the industrializing world, a gap between work and home was growing, both in reality and in ideology, to create the **separation of spheres**. Family life 'was wrenched apart from the world of work', and the workplace and the home clearly demarcated as *his* and *hers*. In 1849, Alfred Lord Tennyson expressed this separation of spheres in a poem, 'The Princess':

> Man for the field and woman for the hearth: Man for the sword and for the needle she: Man with the head and woman with the heart: Man to command and woman to obey; All else confusion.[10]

Men experienced this separation in two ways. First, for most men, work shifted from home and farm to mill and factory, shop, and office; 'work' now became synonymous with paid labour, which would have implications for both men and women. As farm mechanization spread, the agricultural workforce shrank and men moved to where work was. Men now marched to a different beat as the day's rhythm shifted to the incessant pounding of industry. Second, men's share of the work around the home was gradually industrialized and eliminated as such tasks as fuel gathering, leather working, and grain processing shifted to the external world. This further 'liberated' men to exit their homes and leave the rearing of both sons and daughters to their wives.

If men were liberated, women's position was as exalted in popular literature as it was potentially imprisoning in reality. In popular literature, from pulpits and in high art, women's (unpaid) labour was reconceptualized, not as 'work' at all, but rather as a God-given mission. Although some home-based work was gradually eliminated, such as spinning and weaving, much of women's sphere remained intact; women still cooked meals and baked bread, even if their husbands no longer grew and milled the grain or butchered the meat they cooked. 'Domestic' labour was now increasingly known as 'housework' and associated with women.

As men's and women's spheres separated, care was taken to delineate that the relationship between the sexes should remain hierarchical. As Catharine Beecher and Harriet Beecher Stowe wrote in their celebrated book, *The American Woman's Home* (1869):

> When the family is instituted by marriage, it is man who is head and chief magistrate by the force of his physical power and requirement of the chief responsibility; not less is he so according to the Christian law, by which, when differences arise, the husband has the deciding control, and the wife is to obey.[11]

Many historians of Europe and North America argue that this new ideology actually represented a historical decline in women's status. But men's 'liberation' from the home was also partly illusory, because they were also in exile from it. As early as the 1820s and 1830s, US critics were complaining that men spent too little time at home. 'Paternal neglect at the present time is one of the most abundant sources of domestic sorrow', wrote the Reverend John S.C. Abbott in *Parents Magazine* in 1842. The father, 'eager in the pursuit of business, toils early and late, and finds no time to fulfill . . . duties to his children'. Theodore Dwight attempted to persuade men to resume their responsibilities at home in *The Father's Book* (1834), one of the USA's first advice books for men.[12]

The family had now become the 'haven in a heartless world' that the great French writer Alexis de Tocqueville observed when he visited the United States in the early 1830s. 'Shorn of its productive functions, the family now specialized in child rearing and emotional solace, providing a much needed sanctuary in a world organized around the impersonal principles of the market'.[13]

Of course, the ideology and reality of the separate spheres were largely white and middle class, but they were imposed on others as the norm. Everywhere, working-class and non-white women continued to work outside the home, while the men shared housework and child care more readily out of economic necessity if not because of ideological commitment. Cast 'primarily as workers rather than as members of family groups, [minority] women laboured to maintain, sustain, stabilize, and reproduce their families while working in both the public (productive) and private (reproductive) spheres'.[14] In Canada, during the 1800s and well into the twentieth century, many families were sustained not by a male '**breadwinner**', but by the pooled earnings of men, women, and children. Until the late nineteenth century (and in Quebec, the twentieth century), the earnings of all family members belonged legally to the family's male head. At a time when the average man consumed more alcohol than men do today, the allocation of family income to excessive drinking fuelled the **temperance movement**, which united feminists and religious reformers.[15] The picture of family found in separate-spheres ideology was reproduced in the experience of few Canadians (or Americans, for that matter).

As the family changed and became associated with women, its economic and social importance also declined, its integration into the community attenuated. As if to compensate for this shift, the nuclear family's symbolic importance increased. Events that had been casually organized were routinized as family events; community celebrations became household celebrations. US historian John Gillis writes:

> When men had worked at home, mealtimes had seldom been private, or even very regular. Holidays had revolved around community festivals and visiting rather than home-cooked meals and private family celebrations. Leisurely dinner hours, Sunday family time, and nuclear family togetherness on holidays such as Christmas were invented during the mid-nineteenth century.[16]

By the turn of the twentieth century, North American commentators were fretting about the crisis of the family. In the USA, the divorce rate had been steadily climbing since soldiers returned from the Civil War. 'In 50 years, there will be no such thing as marriage', predicted the esteemed Harvard psychologist John Watson at the dawn of the new century.[17] Canada saw no such increase in divorce before 1900, as is discussed below; but Canadian Christian commentators, too, worried about the dissolution of the ideal Christian family and the decline of masculine family leadership (as they would 100 years later).[18] And as large-scale immigration flooded North America with non-British immigrants, white concerns about '**race suicide**' and sexual contact between white women and non-white men spread, particularly in provinces, like British Columbia, that experienced significant Asiatic immigration.

At about the time when these crises seemed acute, Canadian Aboriginal people's family lives became the target of reformist zeal. From the passage of the Indian Act (1867) to the end of the nineteenth century, reports consistently advocated the education of Aboriginal children, and both residential and day schools were established in various locations across the country. By 1920, amendments to the act had made school attendance mandatory. The goal of schooling was frankly assimilationist. In the words of Duncan Campbell Scott, the 'whole object' was 'to continue until there is not a single Indian in Canada that has not been absorbed into the body politic, and there is no Indian question, and no Indian department'.[19] Because Aboriginal parents were viewed as an obstacle to the acculturation of their offspring, separating children—even extremely young children—from their parents for up to ten months at a time was seen as appropriate and desirable. By 1931, there were 80 church-run **residential schools** in operation throughout Canada.

As is now notorious, the residential school experience was devastating for the entire Aboriginal community. In addition to enduring painful separations from their parents and communities, children in these schools generally received substandard education, were poorly nourished, and were subjected to aggressive forced acculturation. The most damaging aspect of life in the residential schools, however, was undoubtedly the abuse that many students suffered. Students were beaten and tortured for 'infractions' including speaking their native languages, and many were sexually abused by the clergy who taught in the schools, by lay staff members, and even by other students. In 2007 the federal government implemented financial compensation for survivors of these traumas, but the effects of 'residential school syndrome', as it is now known, linger in Aboriginal communities.

The crisis produced in the Aboriginal family by assimilationist legislation was severe indeed; but commentators through the twentieth century were more concerned with what they perceived as a general decline of the family. Indeed, the separation of spheres provided the foundation for a virtual perpetual crisis of the family throughout the twentieth century. Some of this crisis was presumed to result from women's abandonment of their 'proper sphere' just as its nature was being codified.

Indeed, from the 1850s on, North American women had been demanding more rights—to property, to education, to employment, and to protection from marital abuse. In the 1870s, some Canadian women began to lobby for the vote. By the 1890s, women were being granted municipal voting rights; women's suffrage at the national level became law in 1918. (The right to vote, however, was denied to women who were part of a group excluded from the vote, such as Chinese-Canadians and Aboriginal people.) Women's new ability to vote (and, increasingly, to attend higher education and earn their own money) exemplified the era of the so-called '**New Woman**', the independent modern woman who did not need to depend upon a man. Not everyone approved.

Between the First and Second World Wars, women's efforts to leave the home—to go to college, enter the labour force, join unions, attend professional schools—and manage their fertility were met with significant resistance, and men's interest in home waxed and waned. Nonetheless, women continued to enter employment outside the home, even during the Great Depression, when many felt that employed women were 'stealing men's jobs'. In Toronto in 1931, one of every four wage-earners was a woman, and many Canadian women found themselves the sole breadwinners for their families.[20] Economic realities, if not ideological commitment, drove many women to work, even as the ideal of the Canadian family remained the nuclear family with a male breadwinner at its head.

The Second World War disrupted this pattern further, as women entered the labour force in dramatic numbers, driven by the wartime shortage of male labour and federal incentives such as the full tax exemption for working wives regardless of income.[21] But the post-war economic boom, fuelled by massive government expenditures in highway and school construction and veterans' bills (for example, the 1942 Veterans' Land Act) that made land and home ownership a reality for an increasing number of families, also stabilized this aberrant family form: the nuclear family of June and Ward Cleaver and their children Wally and the Beaver.[22]

The post-war era brought a dramatic increase in marriage rates and a sharp decline in the ages of first marriage. Whereas today's marriage rates and marriage ages are in keeping with averages for the twentieth century, the era 1945–1960 stands out as dramatically different, as 'young men and women . . . reacting against the hardships and separations of depression and war . . . married unusually early.'[23] In the USA in 1946, the marriage rate hit an all-time high of 14.2 per 1000 (compared to 9.6 in 1867). A similar pattern emerged in post-war Canada, where traditionally higher ages at first marriage dropped significantly. By 1950, about half of women aged 20 to 24 were married. (In 2002, by comparison, only about 11 per cent of similarly aged women were married. Even in 1871, only 38 per cent of Canadian women in this age group had entered matrimony.)[24]

Thus, despite some distinctions between Canada and the USA, we can see that across North America a distinct 1950s pattern of family life emerged. This model—characterized by high rates of marriage (and young age at marriage), high fertility, and low and stable rates of divorce—'was the product of a convergence of an unusual series of historical, demographic and economic circumstances unlikely to return again', in the words of two leading family historians.[25] Though many people continue to view the 1950s nuclear family as an ideal, we should not pretend that it is timeless or 'traditional'.

Yet as soon as this new family form emerged, it was declared to be natural—that is, both biologically inevitable and morally appropriate. The effort to reinforce it became a constant hum in our ears. 'The effort to reinforce traditional norms seemed almost frantic', writes historian William Chafe, 'as though in reality something very different was taking place'. In academia, the structural-functionalist school of social science gave this new family model legitimacy, arguing that the isolated **suburban** nuclear family, with distinct separation of spheres, served the needs of both children and society. The family system required both expressive (female) and instrumental (male) components to function appropriately, wrote sociologist Talcott Parsons, and this could be accomplished only in a family in which the housewife mother maintained the home for her breadwinner husband who worked outside it. Here's how another American sociologist described this domestic paradise in 1955:

> Father helps mother with the dishes. He sets the table. He makes formula for the baby. Mother can supplement the income of the family by working outside. Nevertheless, the American male, by definition, *must* 'provide' for his family. He is *responsible* for the support of his wife and children. His primary area of performance is the occupational role, in which his status fundamentally inheres; and his *primary* function in the family is to supply an 'income', to be the 'breadwinner'. There is simply something wrong with the American adult male who doesn't have a 'job'.
>
> American women, on the other hand, tend to hold jobs *before* they are married and to quit when 'the day' comes; or to continue in jobs of a lower status than their husbands. And not only is the mother the focus of emotional support for the American middle-class child, but much more exclusively so than in most societies . . . The cult of the warm, giving 'Mom' stands in contrast to the 'capable', 'competent', 'go-getting' male. The more expressive type of male, as a matter of fact, is regarded as 'effeminate', and has too much fat on the inner side of his thigh.[26]

A generation of middle-class men tried to toe the line of bland conformity as suburban breadwinners; here was the corporate clone of countless satires, the 'man in the grey flannel suit'. And a generation of women cooked and cleaned, dusted and mopped, washed and ironed, toiling to meet ever-increasing standards of cleanliness and the 'unconscious and therefore potent' rules governing how houses and children should be managed.

For many parents and children of the baby boom, this family form worked well. Middle-class North Americans took family vacations, hung out together in family rooms, and purchased family-sized packages of prepared foods—when they weren't practising gourmet French cooking. They walked together to the local library or movie theatre. Some husbands doted on their wife-companions, and together they built lives more stable, comfortable, child-centred, and companionable—divorce being a last resort—than anything their own parents had ever envisioned.

But the veneer of domestic bliss only partially concealed an increasing restlessness on the part of both husbands and wives (not to mention their children, for whom the 1960s would provide many creative [and not so creative] outlets for their discontent). Many women and men felt frustrated and unhappy with this supposedly 'natural' family form. Some fathers felt alienated from their families, and especially from their children. Full-time housewifery and motherhood were 'something new and historically unprecedented', and wives, labouring under the 'senseless tyranny of spotless shirts and immaculate floors', swallowed their growing resentment as the world passed them by. In his 1957 panorama of American culture, *America as a Civilization*, historian Max Lerner discussed the 'ordeal' of the modern woman, arguing that 'the unhappy wife has become a characteristic culture type'.[27]

Such unhappiness also fuelled an increasingly politicized anger. Women had won significant and unprecedented rights in the early twentieth century, and yet their lives seemed to run on as they always had. As Doris Anderson wrote in a *Chatelaine* editorial in October 1958, 'We have had the vote for a good long 40 years', and yet,

> We seem to be stuck at an awkward halfway point. We're constantly being praised for advances that were made by women almost two generations ago. It's true that we have some of the most elaborate kitchens, the sleekest figures, and the best clothes in the world But it's incredible that we are not serving our country as effectively as other women do where the right to vote is as new and remarkable as a push-button stove.[28]

North American women's discontent boiled over in 1963, when Betty Friedan's feminist call to arms, *The Feminine Mystique*, rang like a tocsin across those neatly manicured suburban lawns and campus quadrangles. Calling the suburban home a 'comfortable concentration camp', she declared that real life lay outside worrying about dishpan hands and diaper rash. And men, especially young men, saw new possibilities outside the responsible role of the suburban breadwinner: beatniks, playboys, and juvenile delinquents presented three alternatives. The era's popular music exposed the ironies of the 'well-respected men' and their wives, gulping vast quantities of 'mother's little helper'.[29]

In fact, no sooner was it fully established and acknowledged than this 'traditional' family began to crack under the enormous weight put on it. The family was supposed to be the sole source of comfort and pleasure in an increasingly cold, bureaucratic world; the marital union was the single most important and sustaining bond of intimacy and friendship that a person could have. Gone were the more 'traditional' supports of community networks, civic participation, and extended kinship ties—now the family was supposed to provide for all psychological and emotional needs. It was almost too much to bear: The 'traditional' family was an anachronism from the moment of its birth.

State of the Canadian Family

Much of the talk of 'crisis' is really about nostalgia for a short-lived family form that was less well adapted to modern society than its proponents thought. Does this mean that we shouldn't worry about the family? Of course not. The family is still critical to the health of our society, and we need to pay attention to problems that impact people's ability to build and sustain healthy families. Since the early 1980s, many families have indeed been in trouble, partly because of changes in public policy that have produced growing social inequality.

In 1970, 15 per cent of all US children under age 18 were living in families defined as 'poor'; today that number is closer to 25 per cent.[30] Canada's rate of **child poverty** may look good compared to that of the USA, but we have the second-worst rate among industrialized nations. (The rate is highest in British Columbia, one of the wealthiest provinces.) As of 2008, despite admonitions from the United Nations, Canada's child poverty rate remains stuck at 11.3 per cent (23 per cent according to the *Vital Signs* report): however, there have been some recent policy changes, including federal child benefits and tax credits, that have had beneficial effects. Poverty rates for children of single mothers and Aboriginal children are significantly higher than the average.[31]

Indeed, Aboriginal families are worse off, on average, on most indicators. In June 2009, the National Collaborating Centre for Aboriginal Health at the University of Northern British Columbia released the study it produced with UNICEF Canada for UNICEF's State of the World's Children 2009 report. *Aboriginal Children's Health: Leaving No Child Behind* is a damning comment on the state of children's health in a nation recognized as one of the best places in the world in which to live. Canada is ranked third in the world on the Human Development Index; but when the index is applied to Aboriginal people only? The ranking slips to 68.

The report contains further information of Aboriginal children's health that should deeply concern every Canadian. For example, the on-reserve First Nations child mortality rate is up to seven times the general Canadian rate. Aboriginal teens become pregnant at seven times the Canadian rate. Aboriginal children are also at greatly increased risk of tuberculosis, diabetes, suicide, substance abuse, fetal alcohol syndrome, living in poverty and substandard housing, poor nutrition, and being unimmunized.[32]

These poorer prospects for Aboriginal children are a reflection of the generally poorer conditions in which Canada's First Nations, Inuit, and Métis people live. Though the Aboriginal population of Canada is growing dramatically (in part because of changes in reporting, but also because of actual growth), many Aboriginal individuals and communities suffer from endemic poverty and intractable social problems. None of these problems can be divorced from the broader context of colonialism and its interventions into Aboriginal life. For Aboriginal people, improving the health and well-being of their communities is synonymous with redressing the broader effects of colonialism and re-establishing control of their identities, communities, and affairs:

> Aboriginal families are nested in communities and nations which have seen their lands alienated, their laws dismissed as 'customs' and their beliefs ridiculed. Families have been at the centre of a struggle between colonial governments bent on absorbing

'Indians' into Euro-Canadian society and parents, Elders, and leaders, who have been equally determined to maintain their identities as peoples with unique and continuing responsibilities in the world. The current challenges that Aboriginal families face are rooted in that history of struggle. The future trajectory of Aboriginal family life will be determined in large part by the success of Aboriginal collectives in establishing their place as peoples and nations within Canada.

In recognizing the challenges faced by the Aboriginal family, we must recognize the damaging effects of family-related policies: the residential school experiment; the 'sixties scoop' that saw massive child apprehensions by the child welfare system and the redefinition of Aboriginal women as 'bad mothers'; Section 12(1)b of the **Indian Act**, which disenfranchised many women and children; and many other interventions. However, we should guard against regarding the Aboriginal family as somehow dysfunctional or irreparably damaged. In fact, Marlene Brant Castellano writes, there are tremendously hopeful signs of renewal within Aboriginal communities, suggesting an emergence 'from the shadow of colonization that has marred perceptions and distorted relationships for generations.'[33]

Child poverty and the challenges facing Aboriginal families aside, the *shape* of Canadian families is also changing. For example, Canadian families have steadily become smaller since 1971. The average family then contained 3.7 persons; by 2006 it contained 3. During the same period, lone-parent families have gone from 9.45 per cent to 15.7 per cent of all families. Of families raising children, 25 per cent are now headed by a lone adult; and these families tend to have more children than families headed by two adults. The two-parent family ideal has never been a reality for everyone, but such families seem to be becoming less and less common. According to 2006 census data, legally married couples with children now make up only about a third of all Canadian families, compared to well over half in 1981.[34]

As the latter statistic makes clear, we're marrying less. Though there was a small increase in marriages around the year 2000, the Canadian marriage rate has steadily declined to a record low, by 2003, of 4.7 marriages per 1000, less than half the 1940s rate of 10.9. In 2006, for the first time (according to Census data), more than half of the adult population of Canada was unmarried. Canada's declining marriage rate is echoed in other nations such as the United Kingdom and Australia, which have rates similar to ours.[35] (Interestingly, however, Canada's marriage rate is significantly lower than that of the US, where the 1998 rate of 8.3 per 1,000 was the lowest in 40 years.) Those of us who do marry are doing it later and later. The average age at marriage for both men and women is now over 30 years, after a long post-war period in which the pattern of early marriage did not change significantly.

At the same time, **common-law marriage** has increased dramatically. The number of common-law unions has increased dramatically since 1981, when the federal government began keeping statistics on the phenomenon. According to the 2001 census, about 14 per cent of all unions were common-law. This number conceals significant regional variations; in Quebec, for example, more than 30 per cent of families are based on common-law unions. By 2001, 13 per cent of all children aged 0 to 14 lived in families headed by common-law couples.

Table 6.1. Changing Canadian couples, 2001 to 2006

Couples in census families	2001		2006	
	Number	Percentage	Number	Percentage
All couples	7,059,830	100.0	7,482,775	100.0
Opposite-sex couples	7,025,630	99.5	7,437,430	99.4
Married	5,901,425	83.6	6,098,445	81.5
Common-law	1,124,200	15.9	1,338,980	17.9
Same-sex couples	34,200	0.5	45,345	0.6
Married	. . .	. . .	7,465	0.1
Common-law	34,200	0.5	37,885	0.5

. . . not applicable
Note:
1. Same-sex married couples were not enumerated in 2001.
Sources: Statistics Canada, censuses of population, 2001 and 2006.

If marriage rates are down and rates of common-law union up, families also seem more fragile than in the past. By 2003, nearly 40 per cent of marriages could be expected to end in divorce before they reached their thirtieth anniversary. Small wonder that REAL Women of Canada claims that the family is enduring 'perilous times'.[36] The growth and acceptance of divorce represent a significant historical change in Canadian society.

Between 1857 and 1968, Canada's divorce laws changed very little, and there were few divorces by modern standards. In 1900, there were only 11 divorces granted in the entire country (though divorces increased dramatically thereafter, especially after the First World War). The greatest increases, however, followed the liberalization of the **Divorce Act** in 1968. Rates more than doubled from 54.8 (per 100,000 people) in that year to 124.2 the year after. Thereafter, throughout the 1970s and well into the 1980s, the divorce rate continued to climb to a peak of 362.3 in 1987. Since then, rates have declined. Our current rate is 221 per 100,000 population, a fairly high rate, but still significantly lower than the US rate and less than half of the Russian Federation's rate.[37]

Table 6.2. Crude divorce rates. 1968—2005. Divorces per thousand people

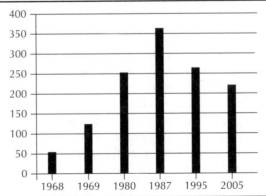

Sources: Statistics Canada, *Report on the Demographic Situation in Canada 1998–1999;* Anne-Marie Lambert, *Divorce: Facts, Causes, and Consequences.*

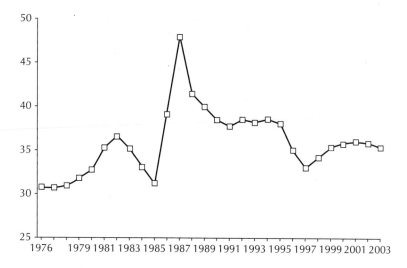

Figure 6.1 Number of divorces expected in Canada per hundred married couples between 1976 and 2003.

'Divorces expected' reflects a likelihood (based on divorce rates) for a couple to be divorced before their twenty-fifth anniversary. Since 2001, the likelihood of divorces for Canadian couples appears to be declining. Note the peak year of 1987. (A new Divorce Act came into effect in 1985.)

Source: Divorces, expected, Canada, 1976-2003, http://www4.hrsdc.gc.ca/.3ndic.1t.4r@-eng.jsp?iid=76, Human Resources and Skills Development Canada, 2003. Reproduced with the permission of the Minister of Public Works and Government Services Canada, 2010.

So what's happening to the North American family? Is it falling apart? Another way to look at the state of the family is suggested by an article in *Newsweek* that asserted that 'the American family does not exist'. Rather, the article suggested, 'we are creating many American families, of diverse styles and shapes . . . We have fathers working while mothers keep house; fathers and mothers working away from home; single parents; second marriages . . . childless couples; unmarried couples with and without children; gay and lesbian parents'.[38] The same is even more true in Canada, where our families represent diverse cultural traditions as well as a broad spectrum of legally recognized patterns: couples in same-sex marriages and their children; heterosexual couples living in common-law relationships with their biological offspring; and married heterosexuals living in 'blended' stepfamilies are all representative of broad trends within the changing Canadian family.

As the family has changed, so, too, have our ideas about it. American family sociologist Scott Coltrane writes that 'support for separate spheres and the automatic dominance of men has weakened dramatically in the past few decades, though a substantial minority of Americans still clings to the so-called traditional view'. Canadians have changed their views even more than have our neighbours to the south. In 1975, when Reginald Bibby began the nationwide surveys that have become known as the Project Canada Survey Series, we were quite a conservative lot, and in Bibby's word, 'bigotry was alive and well'.

More than a third of us, for instance, believed that a woman shouldn't work outside the home if her husband was capable of supporting her. Half of us believed that black people and white people should not marry. Three quarters of us believed homosexuality was aberrant—and abhorrent.

Today, in contrast, 40 per cent of Canadians believe there is no ideal family model. The vast majority of Canadians—94 per cent—approve of interracial marriage, and more than two thirds approve of same-sex marriage. Our opinions on a vast range of subjects have changed to embrace the ideas of multiculturalism, diversity, and relativism, which we increasingly see as part of our national identity. Bibby links our changing views to a number of social changes, in particular official multiculturalism, the baby boomer generation, and the 'XX factor', the increasing influence of women in public life. (On most measures in the survey, women have been consistently less conservative than men.) Interestingly, however, while Canadians are accepting of diversity, most still aspire to the 'traditional' family model themselves—testament to the enduring power of nostalgia.[39]

Ambivalence and disagreement about ideal family forms persist all over the world, but attitudes are changing. In the 1997 Global Study of Family Values conducted by the Gallup Organization, fewer than half of those questioned agreed that the 'traditional' male breadwinner/female housewife model is desirable: United States (48 per cent), Chile (49 per cent), France (46 per cent), and Japan (46 per cent). In only one country, Hungary, did a majority agree (66 per cent); in several countries less than one-third of the population supported this family structure, including Spain (27 per cent), India (28 per cent), Germany (28 per cent), and Taiwan (26 per cent).

The 'traditional' family, a normative ideal when it was invented, has never been the reality for all families. And it is even less so today. (In fact, what is the only census family structure declining in numbers in Canada? Married couples with children under the age of 24.) The 'traditional' family (comprising a breadwinner dad, a stay-at-home mom, and their children) represents the last outpost of traditional gender relations. Families have been and remain gendered institutions; they reproduce gender differences and gender inequalities among adults and children alike. Families raise children as gendered actors and remind parents to perform appropriate gender behaviours. It is no wonder, then, that each specific aspect of family life—marriage, child rearing, housework, divorce—continue to express the differences and the inequalities of gender, even as both gender and the family undergo dramatic changes.

Gendered Marriage

Frank Sinatra's 1955 film and Oscar-nominated song 'Tender Trap' captured the gendered view of marriage that many people hold to this day. It runs something like this. A woman devises some clever scheme to 'trap' a man. When she's successful, her friends all celebrate the upcoming nuptials with delighted anticipation at a bridal shower. Women celebrate their weddings—they have finally 'landed' a man. Their future is secure. By contrast, men 'mourn' their upcoming nuptials. They've been trapped, and the future that stretches out before them is now heavy with responsibilities laid upon them by the 'ball and chain', the smiling warden of their personal prison. The stag party, traditionally held the night before the wedding, exudes a mournful, elegiac quality underneath its raucous exterior as the groom goes out with his male friends for his 'last night of freedom', a night that often consists of smoking fat cigars, getting rip-roaring drunk, and watching porn movies and/or hiring lap dancers or prostitutes.

If you believed this cultural definition of marriage—something she wants and he has to be coerced or tricked into—you would think that marriage benefitted women, that it was 'their' domain. (It's the exact opposite of how we think about sex: as 'his' domain. Sex is something that she 'has' and he 'wants', and he is willing to do pretty much anything, including promising eternal love and fidelity, in order to get it.) Yet according to much social science research, you would be mistaken—as you would also be mistaken about that view of sex. In the early 1970s, sociologist Jessie Bernard identified two distinct marriages, 'his' and 'hers'. And, she argued, 'his is better than hers'. Marriage benefits *men*. All psychological measures of indices of happiness and depression suggest that married men are much happier than unmarried men, whereas unmarried women are somewhat happier than married women. (The greatest difference is between married and unmarried men.) A greater proportion of men than women eventually marries; husbands report being more satisfied than wives with their marriages; husbands live longer and enjoy better health benefits than unmarried men, as well as better health than women (married or unmarried); and fewer men than women try to get out of marriage by initiating divorce. After divorce, men remarry much more quickly than women, and widowers die sooner than widows after the death of a spouse. Married men earn more than single men. And single men are less likely to be employed, tend to have lower incomes than married men, and are more prone to crime and drug use.[40]

All this suggests that marriage is a better deal for men than it is for women. And how could it be otherwise? Given the traditional division of labour in the family (she works, he doesn't) and the non-traditional division of labour outside the family (he works, and she probably does, too), the husband who works outside the home receives the emotional and social and sexual services that he needs to feel comfortable in the world. His wife, who (probably) works as well, also works at home providing all those creature comforts—and receives precious few of them in return. As *New York Times* writer Natalie Angier summed up this research, 'marriage is pretty good for the goose much of the time, but golden for the gander practically all of the time'.[41]

To be sure, marriage also benefits women and is therefore positive for both men and women. According to sociologist Linda Waite, married people have more sex more often than unmarried people and enjoy it more. Married people have longer life expectancies and fewer health problems, lower levels of risky behaviour, suicide, depression, and other psychological problems. And married people save more.

Some of these benefits are explained by other factors that have little, if anything, to do with the matrimonial state. For example, married men's higher incomes seem to come from the unequal politics of housework (the wife's doing the housework frees the married man to work longer hours), and the fact that married couples save more has more to do with women in the labour force than it does with being married. And the fact that the benefits of marriage fall far more readily toward men would suggest that marriage increases, not diminishes, gender inequality. Women and men are unequal going into their marriages, and marriage only exacerbates this inequality by benefitting men more than women.[42]

And yet both men and women are happy with their marriages. In 1995, according to Bibby's survey, 95 per cent of married Canadian men reported that they were happily married. Women were only slightly less satisfied, at 89 per cent. And married Canadians are much more likely than unmarried ones to report general satisfaction with their lives.[43]

What's more, while marriage may benefit him more than it does her, there is one area that remains women's domain: not marriage itself, perhaps, but certainly the wedding. For women far more than men, the wedding itself remains virtually a goal in itself: a day important enough to plan for months, and a day that routinely costs more than a young couple might need for a down payment on a first home. For example, in a 2009 poll of 1,344 readers of Canada's *Wedding Bells* magazine, brides-to-be reported that they were spending an average of $19,274 on 'the big day'. Despite the current economic downturn, planned spending has actually increased. And planning the wedding requires not just money but time. The average reader surveyed in 2006 spent more than ten months planning and arranging her wedding.

There is no other ritual in contemporary Canada that we celebrate with the fervour (and dollars) granted to the white wedding. And the wedding expresses a traditional gendered logic out of sync with the rest of our lives. *Wedding Bells* readers reported that 48 per cent of their fiancés had requested permission from their fathers to marry them; 69 per cent plan to take their fiancés' names after marriage. The romance of traditional marriage, it would seem, is alive and well—on the wedding day, at least.[44]

Both women and men remain interested in getting—and staying—married. For women in particular, but arguably for both sexes, marriage remains an important part of a successful life plan. In recent years, however, some of the subjective measures of marital happiness have declined for both women and men. Can the family continue to absorb the shock, as these forces buffet an institution that is at once so enduring and so fragile?

Gendered Parents, Gendering Children

One cause of the decline in marital happiness is, surprisingly, children. Couples who remain childless report higher levels of marital satisfaction than do those with children. They're better educated and more likely to live in cities, and the wives are more committed to their careers. For those who have children, marital happiness sinks with the arrival of the first baby, plunges even further when the first child reaches school age, and drops further when the child reaches the teenage years. Husbands begin to feel better about their marriages once their children turn 18, but wives don't feel better about their marriages until after the children leave home, according to Mary Bebin, a sociologist at Arizona State University. In Canada, older couples are generally more satisfied with their marriages, especially if both partners are retired.[45] Yet having and raising children are two of the major purposes of the family, its raison d'être. If one of the chief purposes of the family is to maintain both gender inequality and gender difference between the parents, then its other chief purpose is to ensure that those gendered identities are imparted to the next generation. It is in the family that the seeds of gender difference are planted, that we first understand that being a man or a woman, a boy or a girl, has different, and unequal, meanings.

Gender socialization begins at birth and continues throughout our lives. How do parents influence gender differences in their children? Parents possess a set of gender-specific ideas of what their children need; that is, they were themselves socialized to some belief in what girls and boys of various ages are like. Through education and text-books, the popular press, child-rearing manuals, 'old wives' tales', admonitions from friends and relatives, reports from other parents, and adages (such as 'What are little girls made of? Sugar and spice and everything nice' and 'What are little boys made of? Snips and snails and puppy dogs' tails'), they have developed not only the construct 'child', but also constructs 'boy child' and 'girl child', and they attach different expecta-tions to them.

Parents also have hopes and desires for what kinds of adults their children will be and what types of roles they will play (however vaguely defined) and ideas about what adult 'personality' characteristics are most valuable for effectively playing those roles. In addition, parents observe what they perceive as 'typical behaviour' of girls and boys of their own child's age. Throughout childhood, gender difference and gender inequal-ity are created and reinforced through play, the media, and the schools.

Gender typing begins even before the child is born. Prior to the widespread use of ultrasound and amniocentesis (a medical technique that can be used to detect genetic defects as well as the gender of the fetus), parents spent hours speculating about the sex of the as-yet unborn child, often making guesses based upon the amount of kicking and other intrauterine behaviour. Relatives and friends contributed opinions on whether the baby was 'high' or 'low' and made such comments as, 'With that much activity, it must be a boy!' In those cases in which prenatal scanning is not used and in those countries where these medical developments are not available, parents still spend time speculating about the sex of their child.

Announcing the child's birth announces its gender—typically a card that says, 'It's a Boy!' or 'It's a Girl!' on the front. Before you know anything else about the baby, you know its sex. Only when you open the card do you know the child's name, other vital characteristics, and, often, who the parents are! The amused remarks of visitors during the first days echo the same gendered sentiments. Although some people may feel that gender stereotyping is inappropriate, in a majority of cases boys are still greeted with such comments as 'What a brawny little guy', and girls are more likely to elicit such comments as 'She's beautiful; she's so petite!' or 'It won't be too long before she's a mother, too'.

During infancy, expectations about how each gender ought to be treated lead to different behaviours by parents and other adults. One fairly obvious difference in the treatment of infants is environmental. The colours, motifs, and accessories placed in an infant's bedroom are in many cases gendered, as are the clothes in which the newborn is dressed. While the effects of this on infant development are difficult to assess, the shaping of the environment makes it clear that the gender of the child is important to the parents—so much so that a parent who has erroneously anticipated a child of one sex will complain, 'But now I have to repaint the nursery!'

Studies of differential infant treatment have yielded a large body of research that we can only briefly summarize. Scholars disagree on how differently parents treat their infants, and on the nature and cause of the differences that do emerge; this suggests that we should treat these data with caution. Nonetheless, some of the distinctions that do emerge in infancy are interesting. During the first six months of children's life, several studies have found, mothers tend to look at and talk to girl infants more than to boy infants, and mothers tend to respond to girls' crying more immediately than they do to boys'. In fact, these behaviours tend to be greater for girls over the first two years of life. Boys, on the other hand, receive more touching, holding, rocking, and kissing than do girls in the first few months, but the situation is reversed by age six months. By one year, female infants are allowed and encouraged to spend significantly more time than males in touching and staying in close proximity to their mothers. The girls are encouraged to move away at later ages, but never as much as boys are.

Parents' interest in building autonomy or independence seems to explain this difference. As a result of gender stereotypes, parents believe that boys rather than girls should be independent, and parents encourage boys to explore and master their world. Many mothers start to wean their sons from physical contact with themselves at an earlier age. Nonetheless, parents' early treatment of their infant is usually not a deliberate effort to teach the child a 'proper' gender role, but rather reflects the fact that the parents themselves accept the general societal roles for men and women. Though no longer universal, it is still the case that often sons are treated as though they are 'naturally' sturdy and active; they are played with more roughly and are greeted with smiles and other indications of pleasure when they respond appropriately. And girls are still thought to be more delicate and gentle, and sweetness and co-operation are likely to elicit parental approval.

Other adults reinforce these different parental behaviours. Researchers have found that people interact with infants based more on their assumptions about what is appropriate for the gender than on the characteristics of the child itself. For example, subjects in one experiment consistently gave gender-specific toys (dolls for girls, hammers for boys) to infants who, they were told, were either girls or boys. They described the babies, whose sex they did not know, with highly gendered adjectives—'strong' and 'big' for boys and 'soft' and 'pretty' for girls. (Obviously, in this kind of experiment, the subjects were as likely to be right as they were to be wrong, and so they were describing the infants more in terms of information received *about* them than any direct observation of them.) One experiment showed a videotape of a nine-month-old's reaction to a jack-in-the-box, a doll, a teddy bear, and a buzzer. Half the observers were told the child was a boy; the other half were told it was a girl. When asked about the child's expressions of anger, fear, and pleasure, the observers saw different emotions when the child played with the jack-in-the box. The child's reaction was agitated, and then the child cried. Those who thought the child was a boy thought 'he' was angry; those who thought the child was a girl thought 'she' was afraid.[46]

As the child moves from the infant to the toddler stage, somewhere around age two, research shows that gender-typing increases. Parents exhibit differential tolerance for behaviours and emotions. Boys' aggression, competition, and anger are more readily tolerated than when exhibited by girls. Girls, on the other hand, are permitted to show fear more than are boys—and of course we all know the traditional proscription against tears evidenced in the statement 'Big boys don't cry'. Boys' independence, aggression, and suppression of emotion are rewarded, and failure to comply brings increasing disapproval. Girls are encouraged to express emotions and control aggression, and they are given more opportunities to be dependent; crying is tolerated longer than among boys. Boys are encouraged to separate from their mothers and from the world of women. While even a teenager may proudly claim to be 'daddy's little girl', to be a 'mama's boy' is stigmatized.

In general, parents are more restrictive with their daughters and create more limits on their acceptable behaviour from a very early age. But when it comes to explicitly *gendered* behaviours, parents tend to be more tolerant of non-conforming behaviour on the part of girls than on the part of boys—and fathers tend to be generally less tolerant of such behaviour, regardless of the sex of the child, than are mothers. These findings are summarized as indicating that '[f]athers tend to police [non-gender conformity] more than mothers, and everyone polices boys more than girls'.[47]

The toys children play with are designed to be sold as girls' toys or boys' toys. Girls are given dolls and doll houses; boys get trucks and building blocks and are told that they are 'sissies' if they want to play with girls' toys. These labels come originally from adults, because it has been noted that, at age two-and-a-half, many boys prefer dolls and doll houses; they are urged away from them because parents consider them to be girls' toys. Even at preschool age, boys report that their fathers believe that playing with girls' toys is 'bad'.

Parental responses to play are quickly absorbed by children, who shortly thereafter display quite different toy and game preferences. Advertisements, salespeople, and other agents of socialization all reinforce these cues from parents, and children pick up cues all around themselves. These toys are also seen as embodying certain emotional traits that are consistent with men or women. Psychologist Bernice Lott argues that toys for girls encourage dependency on others, whereas toys for boys stress independence and problem solving.[48]

From a very early age, physical appearance is tied to social definitions of masculinity and femininity. Girls are rewarded for their looks and for appearing attractive, whereas boys are more frequently rewarded for physical performance. These differences continue well into adolescence. Girls are taught to capitalize on good looks, cuteness, and coyness and learn to look in mirrors and seek reflections of themselves from others. Boys, in contrast, discover that athletic ability and performance are what count for males.

The earliest interaction with other children is an arena where children express and utilize the gender expectations that they have picked up from parents and the world around them. Researchers have found that after only one year in school, children tend to discriminate in their choices of playmates, choosing those of their own sex and excluding those of the opposite sex.

Most experimental research suggests that boys and girls begin very early to develop two gender cultures that are dramatically different. Though they do not begin their lives in sex-segregated play worlds, children increasingly play with members of their own sex. In these sex-segregated play worlds, boys learn the prototypes of behaviours that will be expected of them as men, including those behaviours that characterize the sexual expectations of adult men. At the same time, girls learn prototypes of the behaviours that will be expected of them as women, also including sexual expectations. Boys' play is more rough-and-tumble and competitive, designed to permit some boys to win and others to lose. Boys attempt to influence the direction of the play with direct demands; girls use more subtle and indirect methods to try to influence each other. Boys play to achieve dominance; girls play to make sure everyone has a good time. Even where children's toys seem similar, language used to describe those figures delineates gendered expectations. The standard 11-inch human figure made for girls (think Barbie) is a 'doll', but one made for boys is called an 'action figure' (think GI Joe).[49]

In their play worlds, boys and girls accomplish their gender identities in different ways. Girls are often 'banned' from some sports and allowed to play others only under simpler rules (e.g., touch or flag football). Even when they play the same sports, boys and girls do not play them together. When asked why they didn't, they replied, almost amused, with statements like 'Don't you know, boys don't play with girls', as if the adults were strange not to already know that.

In general, boys tend to acquire masculinity as much by avoiding anything feminine as by imitating men directly. By contrast, girls' activities and identities seem to be more directly modelled on imitation than on repudiation or avoidance of masculinity. On the surface, this observation echoes Freud's idea that for boys, separation from the mother entails a lifelong repudiation of femininity as the mechanism by which the boy establishes his autonomy; for girls, the project is to root one's identity in identification with the mother, thereby reinforcing the concreteness of the identification. But this may be a result of the materials from which children construct their gender identities rather than the result of some innate drive. For example, think about the kinds of images boys and girls see in comic books and television shows. Think about the kinds of role playing that boys and girls do. Boys will role-play mythic heroes, whereas girls often role-play mothers, nurses, and teachers—not to mention supermodels. That is, boys learn that their future vistas are limitless, playing at identities that defy conventional limits; girls learn that their future worlds are bounded by concrete social constraints or, increasingly, defined by their appearance. Though this has changed significantly in recent years, it has changed far more for girls than for boys.

From Barbie to Bratz

That toys are gendered is hardly news. A stroll through your neighbourhood Toys 'R' Us would suggest that there is a clearly demarcated gender division of toyland, a pink zone and a blue zone as clear as the parted Red Sea. Boys' toys have remained remarkably constant—militarized or sports themed toys, games, and action figures (please don't call them 'dolls'!). Girls' toys have always anticipated traditional women's roles—dressing up as nurses, choreographing elaborate tea parties, and, of course, playing with dolls resembling babies, who seem to be differentiated only by the verisimilitude of their bodily functions (some 'wet', others nursed, and others seem to have colic).

Fifty years ago, Barbie changed all that: She was a near-grown-up, with massive breasts and feet that were shaped permanently in a high-heel pose. She did things— was a cheerleader, drove a car, and loved to shop. Not that Barbie was a proto-feminist icon; she still constructed herself entirely through accessorizing and taught girls what it means to self-objectify. But she embodied a different form of femininity than simply anticipating the role of mother.

In 2001 a new girl, or rather several girls arrived on the scene: Bratz, the most popular dolls in the world, owned by hundreds of millions of girls worldwide and racking up $2 billion in sales a year. By the last quarter of 2006, Bratz had surpassed Barbie's US market share, becoming 'the clear No. 1 fashion doll in the USA'. At first blush, Bratz seem less sexualized—their heads, not their breasts, are oversized. What's more, they're much more multicultural than the perennial über-blond Barbie. Are they a progressive improvement?

In some ways, of course, Bratz and Barbie are more alike than different. Both are fashion-obsessed—Bratz are billed as having 'a passion for fashion'—and apparently in need of outfits for virtually every occasion. Both are manufac-tured under dubious labour conditions. And both promote a particular body image that con-

My Scene doll 'Chelsea'

Bloomberg via Getty images

forms much more to Connell's emphasized femininity than to a desire for health. Barbie in her original incarnation had huge breasts, a tiny waist, and small hips. Though she's been made over with smaller, more realistic breasts and bigger hips, her body remains a rare combination of thinness and voluptuousness. As mentioned above, Bratz have smaller breasts, but they still aren't especially athletic, and they're very thin. What causes most consternation among parents, though, is the Bratz face: a tiny nose, lips that make Angelina Jolie's look thin, and massive, heavy-lidded eyes that cover almost a third of the face. These features are completed by a generous spackling of makeup that makes the Bratz dolls look 'like pole dancers on their way to work at a gentleman's club'.

So Bratz are like Barbies in promoting an unrealistic image of feminine beauty. But they're also different. They're sassy, and they seem to talk back. Bratz go out to bars and discos (portable bar not included)—on their own!

Thus Bratz represent a hypersexualized, post-feminist vision of femininity in which **'grrrl power'** has been translated into being as sexually predatory as and drinking as much as guys. Just when girls are achieving more than they've been able to throughout much of history, they're reminded that looking and acting like an oversexed Valley Girl are still the model of femininity to strive for. 'Even at her most Malibu', one mother writes, 'Barbie wasn't nearly as sexualized as these dolls are'.

Not to be outdone, Barbie has reimagined herself as 'MyScene' Barbie and comes in versions like 'Juicy Bling', whose clubbing outfit includes a microminiskirt that will make most parents shudder. And Barbie continues to strike back; in late 2008, Mattel won a massive legal victory against Bratz. MGA industries was ordered to stop making the pop-ular dolls, whose designer was working for Mattel when he made the drawings on which Bratz were based.[50] So while parents debate which doll is a worse influence on young girls, Mattel and MGA fight over the spoils.

Early gender distinctions are far from absolute, but the direction of change has tended to go in only one way. Some girls are 'tomboys' and may be allowed to play in informal neighbourhood games when extra players are needed. But it is only in recent years that formal organized sports leagues, such as in soccer and softball, have been opened to girls. For boys, opportunities to play at girls' games are rare; the label 'sissy' is more negative than the label 'tomboy'. Girls have more 'boy toys' than boys have 'girl toys'. There is a series of 'boy things' that is all right for girls to do, but, by and large, there is no transfer the other way.

This asymmetry in crossing over to the other gender's play style also indicates how masculinity is far more rigid a role construction than is femininity and how that rigidity is also part of the coercive mechanisms of gender role socialization. Gender is not simply the expression of what is 'right' and 'appropriate'; rather, our cultural definitions of what is right and appropriate are derived from the ways in which adults see things and, in part, depend upon who it is that makes up the rules in the first place. Children's play both expresses and anticipates the inequality that informs gender relations in adulthood.[51]

Boys and girls both understand the inequality between women and men and understand, too, that their less-than-equal status gives girls a bit more latitude in the types of cross-sex (gender-inappropriate) behaviour they may exhibit. Though this is changing, girls think they'd be better off as boys, and many of them declare that they would rather be boys than girls. By contrast, boys tend to see being girls as a fate worse than death. 'If I were a girl', one third-grader said, 'everybody would be better than me, because boys are better than girls'.

Statements like this make us wince because they reveal how deeply connected are gender difference and gender inequality and how the former serves as the justification for the latter. This little boy, like millions of other little boys, has come to understand that his status in the world depends upon his ability to distance himself from femininity. By exaggerating gender difference, he both assures and reassures himself of his higher status. It is largely through the routine daily events of family life that children learn what it means to be boys or girls, and it is through those same events that gender inequality is reproduced between grown-up women and men. Children's interactions 'are not preparation for life', sociologist Barrie Thorne concludes. 'They are life itself'.[52]

The Gendered Politics of Housework and Child Care

We are living through a historic, fundamental transformation of family life. Perhaps the greatest single shock the family has had to absorb has been the large-scale entry of women into the workplace. This is, perhaps, the most profound and dramatic social change in recent North American society, rippling outward to transform every other social institution. That women now work outside the home as a matter of course, of economic necessity, and of ambition has dramatically altered the life of the modern family. Some would like to turn back the clock to the rather unusual and short-lived family form that emerged in the 1950s and reassert it as the norm. Such a vision is unlikely to be embraced by most men, let alone most women, who today work outside the home because they want to and because they have to—and because it's good for them, good for their husbands, and good for their children.

Working mothers report higher levels of self-esteem and are less depressed than full-time housewives. Yet they also report lower levels of marital satisfaction than do their husbands, who are happier than the husbands of traditional housewives. Why would this be so? In part, because women's workload actually increases at home, whereas the men benefit by having almost the same amount of work done for them at home and having their standard of living buttressed by an additional income.[53]

So women today are working more but enjoying family life less. Consistently, and in every industrial country, women report higher levels of stress than do men.[54] Perhaps one reason women are so tired and unhappy is that they remain responsible for what sociologist Arlie Hochschild has called 'the **second shift**', the housework and child care that every family must do to function properly. The movement of women from the home to the workplace has not been accompanied by a comparable movement of men back into the home. The transformation promised by women's entry into the labour force is a 'stalled revolution', a revolution that depends, now, on changes in men's attitudes and behaviours.

In 1970, a young feminist writer described what she saw as 'the politics of housework'. In the spirit of the feminist slogan 'the personal is political', Pat Mainardi argued that the separation of spheres that defined the traditional family and made housework 'women's work' was a reflection of male domination, not the expression of some feminine biological predisposition toward laundry or dishwashing. Women did housework and child care because they *had* to, she argued, not because they *wanted* to or because of some genetic master plan. And men didn't do housework because they could get out of it.[55]

Few people actually *like* doing housework. 'A woman's work is never done, and happy she whose strength holds out to the end of the [sun's] rays', wrote Martha Moore Ballard in her diary in 1795. Nearly a century later, Mary Hallock Foote wrote: 'I am daily dropped in little pieces and passed around and devoured and expected to be whole again next day and all days and I am never *alone* for a single minute'. And in 1881, Helen Campbell wrote that spring housecleaning was 'a terror to every one, and above all to gentlemen, who resent it from beginning to end'. Perhaps Emily Dickinson said it best (using the passive voice). "'House' is being 'cleaned,'" she wrote. 'I prefer pestilence'. (Of course, she wasn't the one cleaning it; Bridget and her other servants simply disturbed her peace.)[56]

Dozens of studies have assessed the changing patterns of housework, child care, and the different amounts of investments in family life. Who does what? How do people decide? Are men doing more now than they used to? Can they be encouraged/asked/cajoled/forced to do more? One statistic about family involvement is revealing of a larger pattern. Most studies, as you will see, suggest how little men's participation in family life has changed. In one respect, though, it has changed dramatically and completely. Thirty years ago, virtually no fathers were present at the births of their children; today, more than 90 per cent are present in the delivery room. If men *want* to change their involvement in the family, there is evidence that they are capable of doing so quickly and relatively easily.[57]

When it comes to other areas of family involvement, though, like housework, the evidence reveals little change. Virtually all researchers have come to the same conclusion: Men's participation in family work has been 'surprisingly resistant to change'. One study of 489 married couples found that men share household responsibility 'only occasionally'. Another found that after marriage, the amount of time a woman spends doing housework increases by 17 per cent, whereas a man's *decreases* by about 33 per cent. (That's because he used to do things like cook and clean for himself, but now he doesn't think he has to.) And still another found the fraction of men who fully share housework to be about one-fifth. (But the one-fifth who do share housework were the husbands in the happiest couples in the study.) The percentage of housework that men do compared with women decreases as men grow older; this may, in part, be because the changes in men's household participation occurred relatively recently, and older men grew up expecting to do little to none.[58]

More recent studies have found men's participation in housework increasing, but gradually. For example, Canada's General Social Survey of 2005 found that men had increased their housework hours from an average of 2.1 per day in 1986 to 2.5 in 2001. Women, on the other hand, had decreased theirs from 4.8 in 1986 to 4.2. Some have suggested that it's logical that women work more hours at home on average, since their average paid-employment hours are fewer, and since women tend to decrease their unpaid work as their paid work increases. But the 2005 GSS found that while women decreased their housework hours to 4.3 per day, they increased their paid work to 4.4 hours. Men's and women's total workdays, nonetheless, look similar at 8.8 hours and 8.7 hours respectively.[59] This suggests that on average, men and women are doing about as much work. So why do women feel otherwise, and why do women report more stress than do men, according to StatsCan data?

First, these data may be complicated by everything that the averages conceal—for example, the existence of women who work full time and then 'come home and do the second full-time job', in the words of one woman. Moreover, certain types of work, such as eldercare, planning and organizing family life, and 'emotion work', might go unreported.[60]

Thinking of work in terms of hours spent is undoubtedly valuable, allowing interesting comparisons not only between the sexes but among nations and ethnic groups. But thinking about housework only in these terms may also obscure some of the gendered character of work in the home. For example, if one person spends two hours mowing the lawn while the other spends two hours preparing dinner, cleaning the living room, and planning a shopping trip while simultaneously getting the children bathed and through their homework, one may feel considerably more stressed (and unfairly burdened) than the other, even though their hours worked are identical. Women's greater tendency to multitask may thus be a factor in their greater stress. As Meg Luxton points out, some of the increase in men's domestic labour may reflect taking over aspects of this multitasking, as when, for example, a father 'watches the children' while his wife prepares dinner. In this case, his hours of unpaid labour may increase without diminishing hers (though she may be pleased with the arrangement).[61]

Women may also be held responsible for the home in ways that men are not. Men tend to see their participation in housework *in relation* to their wives' housework; women tend to see their work as necessary for family maintenance. Though one seldom hears men referring to 'babysitting' their own children these days, men still use terms like 'pitch in' or 'help out' to describe the time they spend in housework—as if the work was their wives' to do. 'When men do the dishes it's called helping', Anna Quindlen, op-ed writer for the *New York Times*, observed wryly. 'When women do dishes, that's called life'. And it may not even be all that helpful. According to the Center for Work-Life Policy, 40 per cent of professional wives felt that their husbands actually create *more* work around the house than they perform.[62] Bearing responsibility for allocating tasks and planning family life is in itself work, though it may go unrecognized even while it elevates women's stress levels.

Another problem with the numbers results from self-reporting. Although men report that they currently do between one-fifth and one-fourth of all domestic labour, there is some evidence that asking people how much housework they do leads to rather large inaccuracies, because people often report how much they think they ought to be doing, not how much they actually do. Both women and men over report the amount of housework they do—according to one study, men over report by about 150 per cent, more than double the over reporting by women (68 per cent). Interestingly, more-privileged husbands with egalitarian gender attitudes tend to over report at a higher rate than more traditional husbands, who probably believe that they should not be doing so much housework. Less-privileged 'stay-at-home moms' are more likely to over report their housework than more-privileged working mothers because only such inflated hours could justify their staying at home. The over reporting by men was so significant that the researchers doubt 'that husbands have increased their supply of domestic labour to the household in the past 25 years'.[63]

Other survey methodologies have yielded results suggesting that men's participation in housework has increased somewhat over the past quarter-century, though probably not as much as men themselves might claim. When American couples were asked to keep accurate records of how much time they spent doing which household tasks, men still put in significantly less than their wives. The most recent study using time diaries found that men were doing 16 hours of housework per week—up from 12 hours in 1965. (This is 400 per cent of the amount of housework that Japanese men do, but only 66 per cent of the housework that Swedish men do.) Men's increased participation has not been a steady progressive rise; rather, it increased from 1965 to 1985 and has levelled off since.[64]

In fact, the major finding of these recent studies is not that men are doing more housework but rather that less housework is being done—by anyone. In 1965, American women did 40 hours a week; now they do 27, so the amount of total time that men and women spend doing housework has decreased from 52 hours to 43 hours per week. And marriage tends to exacerbate the differences between women and men. It turns out that men reduce their housework when they form a couple and increase it when they leave; women increase their time spent in housework when they form a couple and reduce it when they leave.[65]

Housework turns out to fluctuate a lot by timing, season, and marital status, and among different groups of men. Not all men are doing more housework; or, rather, some men are doing more of it than others. Men's changing experience of family life depends on age, race, class, and level of education. Younger men, for example, are doing far more around the house than their fathers did—though their wives still do a lot more. A poll of women younger than 30 in *Ladies Home Journal* in May 1997 found that 76 per cent said they do most of the laundry; 73 per cent do most of the cooking; 70 per cent do most of the housecleaning; 67 per cent do most of the grocery shopping; and 56 per cent pay most of the bills. In Canada, the numbers are similar: 77 per cent of women prepare meals on an average day, compared with 29 per cent of the men, and 54 per cent of the women clean up after meals, compared with 15 per cent of the men.[66]

Though we tend to think that sharing housework is the product of ideological commitments—progressive, liberal, well-educated, middle-class families with more egalitarian attitudes—the data suggest a more complicated picture that has less to do with ideological concerns. In every single subcategory (meal preparation, dishes, cleaning, shopping, washing, outdoor work, auto repair and maintenance, and bill paying), for example, black American men do significantly more housework than their white counterparts. In more than one-fourth of all black families, men do more than 40 per cent of the housework, i.e., men's 'share' of housework comes closer to an equal share. In white families, only 16 per cent of the men do that much. And blue-collar fathers, regardless of race—municipal and service workers, policemen, firefighters, maintenance workers—are twice as likely (42 per cent) as those in professional, managerial, or technical jobs (20 per cent) to care for their children while their wives work. This difference comes less from ideological commitments and more from 'informal flex time', a split-shift arrangement with one's spouse, which is negotiated by about one-fourth of all workers in the United States and by one-third of all workers with children under age five.[67]

The presence of children increases the gender gap, and children learn the gender expectations that their parents teach them. One 1991 study found that daughters of women working full-time did more than 10 hours a week of housework; sons did less than three hours a week. Men seem to maintain the contradictory ideas that they want to shield and protect their wives from life's unpleasantness, although they steadfastly refuse to perform a task as degrading as washing out the toilet. According to demographer Martha Farnsworthe Riche, 'The great lesson of the past 15 to 20 years is that men don't care if the house is clean and neat, by and large'. Or, as one wife noted, wearily, 'I do my half, I do half of [my husband's] half, and the rest doesn't get done'.[68]

But when it comes to being fathers, men are evidently willing to do more. A poll in *Newsweek* magazine found that 55 per cent of fathers say that being a parent is more important to them than it was to their fathers, and 70 per cent say they spend more time with their children than their fathers spent with them. A 1995 survey sponsored by the USA's Families and Work Institute found that 21 per cent of the 460 men surveyed said that they would prefer to be home caring for their families if they had enough money to live comfortably. (This is actually a fairly low percentage because the amount these men believed they needed in order to live comfortably was over $200,000.)[69]

And they've had some support in becoming more active fathers. Dr. Benjamin Spock's multidecade best-selling book *Babies and Child Care* noted (and perhaps even encouraged) the shift in thinking about fathers' involvement. In the first edition, Dr. Spock suggested that men could be somewhat involved in child care:

> Some fathers have been brought up to think that the care of babies and children is the mother's job entirely. This is the wrong idea. You can be a warm father and a real

man at the same time . . . Of course I don't mean that the father has to give just as many bottles or change just as many diapers as the mother. But it's fine for him to do these things occasionally. He might make the formula on Sunday.

In the 1998 edition, however, Dr. Spock records the shifts his work has helped to bring about:

> Men, especially the husbands of women with outside jobs, have been participating increasingly in all aspects of home and child care. There is no reason why fathers shouldn't be able to do these jobs as well as mothers . . . But the benefit may be lost if this work is done as a favour to the wife, since that implies that raising the child is not really the father's work but that he's merely being extraordinarily generous.[70]

Despite what some women might think, Canadian men are ahead of their US and UK counterparts in their participation in child care. One major policy shift that has enabled this shift was the extension of parental benefits to men through the Employment Insurance (EI) program. As the program has grown, so has men's participation. In 2000, only 3 per cent of Canadian men took paid parental leaves. By 2006, that rate had jumped to 20 per cent. The majority of fathers now take some time off at or around the births of their children. Fathers also now take significantly more time off work for personal and family reasons; in 1997, the average man used 1.8 days this way, while fathers in 2006 missed, on average, 6.3 days of work. (This is more than claimed by women, whose time off work has remained relatively stable in the same period.) But we have some distance to go before men and women take equal responsibility for their children's day-to-day lives. Former US Congresswoman Pat Schroeder used to tell a revealing story from her own life. Just after her first election, her husband explained to a journalist from *Redbook* that, in the future, it would be he who would be taking the children to the pediatrician. When she read the interview, Schroeder immediately telephoned her husband and said, 'For $500, what is the name of the children's pediatrician?' He responded, somewhat sheepishly, that what he had meant was that he would be *willing* to take the children, if she asked him to.[71]

This anecdote is telling in another way. Men consistently report that they would *like* to spend more time with their children and families, *if they only could.* Many men say they want to do more, but demands of work continue to get in their way. Others fear being seen by their colleagues and bosses as less committed to their careers and fear being placed on a 'daddy track' from which there will be no advancement. According to a recent US study, conducted by sociologist David Maume, when children are sick, women are still overwhelmingly more likely to be the ones who stay home from work to care from them. Highly successful women were less likely than other women to stay home with children, while highly successful men were more likely to stay home. This suggests that the ideology of workplace commitment may be less forgiving of women than of men. Though such variations exist, women remain disproportionately the ones who sacrifice work for family in this particular way.[72]

Men often say that they want to be involved fathers and to spend more quality time with their children. But rarely are they willing to make sacrifices in order to do it. The payoffs, however, when they do, can turn out to be great. Men who do more housework are also better fathers. And men who have closer relationships with their children report greater marital satisfaction and better health. They feel less stress (if you can believe that!) and less pressure to be successful, powerful, and competitive. They also live longer, causing the normally staid British financial magazine *The Economist* to quip, 'Change a nappy, by God, and put years on your life'. 'When males take full responsibility for child care', sociologist Barbara Risman points out, 'they develop intimate and affectionate relationships with their children'. Nurturing their children is good for men's health. And, of course, while men's child care doesn't necessarily include doing the dishes, increased family involvement by men benefits women, freeing them from the obligations of the second shift. And that enhances gender equality: Recall that anthropologists found consistently that women's economic and political status is highest in those cultures in which men do more domestic work.[73]

Increasing men's participation in housework and child care will require a combination of micro-level and macro-level supports. Individually, men have to *want* to do more, and they will also need support from their wives and from their male friends, co-workers, and colleagues. They'll need to know *how* to do it, as well, learning the set of skills that, taken together and performed regularly, constitutes nurturing and caring— cooking, cleaning, laundry. 'Unless fathers do a greater share of the work at home, mothers will remain disadvantaged in working outside the home. Mothers can't win unless fathers change, too'.[74]

That women continue to perform the lion's share of the second shift puts enormous strains on marriage. Balancing work and family pulls working women in different directions, and either way they move, they are bound to feel guilty and frustrated. One high-level executive who recently quit her job confessed that she 'had as much going my way as any working mother could have. And I was absolutely flat-out. All I managed to do were the kids and my job. I could have continued to do this indefinitely, but I would have been a shell of myself'.[75]

The 'Constructed Problems' of Contemporary Family Life

Obviously, a woman or a man who feels like a 'shell of myself' cannot provide a strong foundation on which to build a family, with a vibrant marriage and healthy children who are nourished physically and emotionally. Yet, increasingly, that's how parents feel, and their relationships with each other and with their children suffer as a result. Without a concerted national policy to assist working women and men to balance work and family obligations, we continue to put enormous strains on two sets of bonds, between husbands and wives and between parents and children, and virtually guarantee that the 'crisis' of the family will continue. And we will also continue to face a series of 'constructed problems'—problems that stem from the strain felt by individual families as they negotiate the increased pressures of sustaining dual-career couples, dividing housework and child care in the absence of help from the outside, and grappling with the contradictions between gender ideologies and a changing society. These problems are also the result of gender inequality—both its persistence and efforts to remedy it. Only when we develop a sustained effort—both individually and politically—to reduce gender inequality in the home, the workplace, and the nation will these constructed problems begin to ease.

Daycare

Despite the lingering feeling among many Canadians that parents (usually mothers) should care for young children in the home, this is no longer practical. As is discussed in Chapter 8, the vast majority of women with young and school-aged children now work outside the home at least some of the time. That means, for most children, the need for some form of daycare.

That women's entry into the workforce would necessitate more daycare has been recognized since 1970, when the first national child care program was proposed. In 1984, when Brian Mulroney's Conservative government came to power, it promised a program—but never delivered. Liberals were critical, but by the time they took power in 1993, deficits provided the rationale for scrapping the plan. Quebec moved forward independently in the late 1990s, creating a heavily subsidized (and heavily subscribed) provincial plan. In the 2004 election campaign, the Liberals promised to resuscitate the idea of national daycare, offering $5 billion to fund 250,000 spaces by 2009. Before the proposal was implemented, the Liberal government fell.

The new Conservative government under Stephen Harper, elected in 2006, brought in a plan called 'Choice in Child Care'. Designed to placate conservative critics who view daycare funding as unfair to 'traditional' families, the plan offered all parents of children under six a monthly $100 payment to be used as each family saw fit. Canadian children thus continue to be 'served' by a patchwork of care, much of it unregulated and some of it substandard. According to Jody Dallaire of the Child Care Advocacy Association of Canada, 'the federal government has simply failed to meet the child care needs of Canadian families'. As a result, our existing child care arrangements, Rianne Mahon writes, 'work to reinforce class differences between families while at the same time contributing to the maintenance of unequal gender relations within them'.[76]

In 2002–2003, more than half of Canadian children aged six months to five years were in some form of childcare (compared to 42 per cent eight years earlier). We continue to argue over the 'problem' of daycare; that is, is it harmful to children? In the past 30 years, some striking claims have been made for both the benefits and the harms of daycare. 'Having a nanny read you a story isn't the same as having your mother do so', writes William R. Mattox, a senior writer for the conservative Family Research Council. 'A mother's worth cannot be reduced to the cost of what a paid substitute might command. To suggest that it can is like saying that the value of a woman making love to her husband is equal to the going rate for prostitutes in the area'.[77]

Despite such dramatic claims, the most common conclusion from the research on the impact of daycare on children's development has been that there are no negative psychological, intellectual, developmental, or emotional consequences to being in daycare. In fact, there is some evidence that quality child care has positive effects on children's curiosity, ability to share, ability to create friendships, and preparation for school. For some children, particularly those of low socio-economic status, lifelong literacy skills may be enhanced by quality child care. What's more, a 1996 US National Institutes of Health study found that children's attachment to their mothers is not affected by whether or not they are in daycare, what age they enter, or how many hours they spend there.[78]

On the other hand, there may be good reasons to worry about daycare. Recently, some studies have linked time spent in daycare to poorer outcomes for children. As reported in 2003, a long-term study conducted by the NIH's National Institute of Child Health and Human Development found links between assertive, disobedient, and aggressive behaviours and children's amount of time in care between the ages of birth and 4.5 years. (Importantly, though, the study found that the most important predictor of a child's behaviour was the mother's sensitivity to the child's emotions, regardless of hours spent in care.) More recently, a study found that as the number of Quebec children in daycare increased from 1994 to 2002, so did children's anxiety and depression. In fact, the authors claim, '[f]or almost every measure, we find that the increased use of child care was associated with a decrease in their well-being relative to other children'. And for some children in relatively low-quality daycare settings, stress (as measured by cortisol levels) is a constant companion, perhaps leading to anxiety and depression.[79] Some conservative commentators might feel that such research proves how wrong it is to put children in care. A more cautious approach to this research suggests that we need to be concerned about the *quality* of care that children are receiving.

So there really is a 'problem' with day care: There's not enough of it, it's not affordable, and the government and our employers don't seem to care very much about our children. But that is not the 'problem' that we are asked to worry about. Instead, we keep thinking about it in terms of whether or not women—not parents—should be placing their children in daycare in the first place. The 'problem' of day care turns out to be a debate about whether or not women should be working outside the home. And this means we're asking the wrong question. For one thing, it poses a class-based contradiction, because we encourage poor women to leave the home and go to work and ask middle-class women to leave the workplace and return home. Since the late 1990s, most provinces have enacted reforms to social assistance, cutting benefits and making fewer people eligible. The most extensive reforms were in Ontario, where benefits were cut to encourage recipients to enter paid employment. Only seniors and the disabled were exempted. After 1998, single mothers had to demonstrate that they were attempting to find work or retrain in order to continue to receive benefits. Similar efforts to encourage mothers of young children to find employment have been made in British Columbia. 'It is difficult to argue that poor mothers should find jobs but that middle class mothers should stay home', writes family researcher Andrew Cherlin.[80]

Nor is there any reason why they should, because there is little evidence that mothers' working outside the home adversely affects children. In fact, most of the evidence indicates that both direct and indirect benefits accrue to children of working mothers. Such children tend to have expanded role models, more egalitarian gender role attitudes, and more positive attitudes toward women and women's employment. Daughters of employed women are more likely to be employed, and in jobs similar to those of their mothers, than are daughters of non-employed women. Moreover, adolescent children of working mothers assume more responsibility around the home, which increases their self-esteem.[81]

While the debate about the effects of daycare continues, children continue to enter care. Whatever our political commitments and beliefs, we cannot await the outcome of this long-term debate to ensure the health and development of the many Canadian children currently in daycare. A comparison with other industrial nations is instructive here. Throughout the European Union, for example, child care is available, affordable, and expedient. Parents still balance career and family, albeit uncertainly— but they do it with far more social support than North American parents do. In Canada in 2006, there were only enough regulated child care spaces for one out of every six children needing space. In neither Europe nor North America do women show any inclination to leave the labour force, but rather they seem to be demanding that the work world accommodate their family needs—and not the other way around. But this would demand that we stop seeing child care as an issue for individual women and start seeing it as a societal issue of importance to all of us. As Joan Peters argues, women can work outside the home successfully 'only if men take half the responsibility for child care'. Again, the 'solution' turns out to be social and political. Both nationally and in each family, the solution turns out to be greater gender equality—not women working less outside the home, but rather men working more inside and for it.[82]

Teenage Pregnancy

In the USA, teenaged pregnancy remains a hot-button issue, which was proved recently by response to the movie *Juno* (2007), the so-called 'Gloucester Pregnancy Pact', and the pregnancy of Bristol Palin, daughter of the 2008 vice-presidential candidate Sarah Palin. Bristol's speedy conversion from teen mother into abstinence advocate is ample evidence of the continuing stigmatization of pregnant adolescents. Yet despite widespread disapproval of teenage pregnancy, the United States currently has the highest rate of births to teenage mothers of all industrial nations—double that of the next-highest country, the United Kingdom (which includes all of Ireland in its tabulation). And after many years in which the US adolescent pregnancy rate dropped, it has in the past three years begun to increase again. Canada's rate, in comparison, is less than half the USA's rate, and dropping.[83]

Calling adolescent pregnancy a problem may in itself be problematic. Interestingly, the same people who complain about women's *delaying* child-bearing (while they wallow in unbridled sexual consumerism) are also among the loudest critics of teen pregnancy. Is it a problem of a sort of 'Goldilocks' mentality—you should have children when you are not too young and not too old, but rather 'just right' in terms of age? Actually, it often seems that the problem of teenage motherhood is a mask for what is really bothering its critics—apparently uncontrolled female sexuality. Some concern stems from a disguised critique of feminism, which enables women to explore a healthy and safer sexuality. In the USA, efforts to stop teen motherhood have included increasing restrictions on access to birth control and even birth control *information* and restrictions on abortion, including parental consent and waiting periods.

On these questions, the research is unanimous: Restricting access to information about birth control, access to birth control, and access to abortion has no bearing on rates of sexual activity. In fact, virtually all studies of the effect of sex education indicate a *decrease* in rates of sexual activity, greater sexual selectivity, and higher rates of safer sex practices. Young people will continue to become sexually active in their midteens, whether or not they have access to birth control or information about it. In fact, restricting access is the surest way to encourage unwanted pregnancy.

Attempting to 'solve' teen pregnancy through restricting sexual expression and information is also a way to blame women for men's irresponsibility. Politically, we are saying to young women that if they are going to dance (become sexually active), they will have to pay the piper (bear the consequences of unwanted pregnancies). But if, as we also know, it takes two to tango, perhaps the solution to the crisis of young motherhood lies in both increasing the abilities of these young women to become responsible (adequate health care, birth control information, and access to birth control) and in fostering a more responsible young manhood. In fact, casting the crisis as 'babies having babies' masks another serious problem—young girls' sexual victimization by men. Many of the fathers of babies born to teenage mothers are *not* themselves teenagers, but rather are adult men whose predatory sexual behaviour goes unnoticed when the problem is cast in this way. Indeed, according to research conducted by sociologist Mike Males, younger girls are more likely than older teens to have partners much older than they are.[84]

Though the stigmatizing of adolescent mothers and pregnant teenagers is damaging and wrongheaded, there are probably reasons to feel good about Canada's declining rate of teenage pregnancy. While pregnancy is not a 'problem' for all adolescents, young age at pregnancy is associated with poorer outcomes for mother and child and greater risks of abuse. The effects on mothers' education and economic status are generally deleterious. (Bear in mind that adolescent mothers, more often than not, are single mothers and therefore part of a vulnerable group quite aside from their age.) Adolescent pregnancy rates are thus considered an important health and social indicator. Canada's declining rate of teenage pregnancies—a rate that includes abortions, live births, and miscarriages—is a sign that young women have 'increasing opportunities and capacity to control their sexual and reproductive health'.[85] That kind of control, and not repressive regulations or social stigma, builds healthy young women and healthier families.

'Fatherlessness' and Lone Parenting

The question of men's responsibility also surfaces in the debates about fatherlessness. A 2005 article laments the 'tsunami' of US-style 'radical fatherlessness' striking black families in Toronto, linking it to the wave of shootings then terrorizing that city. In recent years, many North American commentators have noticed that fathers are not around, having left their children either through divorce or cavalier indifference. Recent works such as David Blankenhorn's *Fatherless America* or David Popenoe's *Life Without Father* have blamed absent fathers for causing myriad social problems, ranging from juvenile delinquency to crime and violence to unemployment. 'In families where the father is absent, the mother faces an impossible task: She cannot raise a boy into a man. He must bond with a man as he grows up', writes psychologist Frank Pittman. It is a mistake to believe that 'a mother is able to show a male child how to be a man'. 'Boys raised by traditionally masculine fathers generally do not commit crimes', adds Blankenhorn. 'Fatherless boys commit crimes'. In a home without a father, Robert Bly writes somewhat more poetically, 'the demons have full permission to rage'. This has consequences for both the fathers and the boys, creating in one moment two sets of unattached and unconstrained males roaming around the streets. 'Every society must be wary of the unattached male', family researcher David Popenoe reminds us, 'for he is universally the cause of numerous social ills'.[86]

It is true that more children of both sexes are being raised in lone-parent homes and that the 'single parent' doing that child raising is more often than not a woman. Causes of the increase include long-term growth in divorce rates (more than three-fifths of lone mothers have been married). Canada's rates of single motherhood, however, lag behind those of the USA. Whereas just over one-tenth (11 per cent) of US children were being raised by unmarried mothers in 1970, nearly one-fourth (24 per cent) were being raised that way as of 1996, and more than one-quarter (26 per cent) of all births were to single women. In Canada, by contrast, while the number of lone-parent families has increased, lone-parent families are still only about 12.4 per cent of census families. Canada's rate of single motherhood is significantly lower than that of the USA. In both countries, the number of lone fathers has increased more rapidly than the rate for mothers, in part because of a turn away from awarding sole custody to mothers. Lone-father families in both countries now account for about 20 per cent of all lone-parent families—without much appreciable decrease in the 'raging demons' referred to above.[87]

Lone-parent families are, not surprisingly, at risk of poverty. According to Statistics Canada data, the 550,000 woman-headed lone-parent families in Canada in 2004 had an average after-tax income of $27,700. Despite the fact that almost 70 per cent of lone mothers worked, 38 per cent of female-headed lone-parent families fell below the low-income cut off line (LICO). Lone-parent families headed by men were better off; only 13 per cent of them fell below the LICO. (But compared to two-parent families, of whom only 7 per cent fell below the LICO, lone fathers were also disadvantaged.) So insofar as 'fatherlessness' leaves families financially vulnerable, it is indeed a crisis and a major contributor to making women and children the new face of poverty.

It's also true that the other side of the 'feminization of poverty' coin is the 'masculinization of irresponsibility'—the refusal of fathers to provide economically for their children. What is less certain, however, is the impact of fathers on the myriad social problems with which their absence seems to be correlated. Involvement by non-resident fathers does provide some benefits to children and consistently predicts higher academic achievement—which argues for maintaining fathers' connection to their children. And although fatherlessness may be correlated with high crime rates, that does not mean that fatherlessness *caused* the criminality. In fact, it might just be the other way around. To be sure, high crime rates and fatherlessness are indeed correlated. But it turns out that they are *both* products of a larger and more overwhelming problem: poverty.[88]

The US National Academy of Sciences reports that the single best predictor of violent crime is not fatherlessness but rather 'personal and neighbourhood income'. And, it turns out, fatherlessness also varies with income; the higher the income bracket, the more likely that the father is home—which suggests that the crisis of fatherlessness is actually a crisis of poverty. In his impressive ethnographic research on street gangs in Los Angeles, Martin Sanchez-Jankowski found 'as many gang members from homes where the nuclear family was intact as there were from families where the father was absent' and 'as many members who claimed close relationships with their families as those who denied them'. Clearly something other than the mere presence or absence of a father is at work here.[89]

The confusion of correlation and causation also reveals a deeper confusion of consequence and cause. Fatherlessness may be a consequence of those larger, deeper, more structural forces that drive fathers from the home and keep them away—such as unemployment or increased workplace demands to maintain a standard of living. Pundits often attempt to transform the problem of fatherlessness into another excuse to blame feminism, and specifically women working outside the home. They yearn for a traditional nuclear family, with traditional gender inequality. For example, David Popenoe writes nostalgically about the family form of the 1950s—'heterosexual, monogamous, life-long marriage in which there is a sharp division of labour, with the female as the full-time housewife and the male as primary provider and ultimate authority'—without pausing to underscore that such a family form was also dramatically unequal when viewed from a gender perspective. Such a vision substitutes form for content, apparently under the impression that if only the family conformed to a specific form, then the content of family life would dramatically improve.[90]

This emphasis on form over content is most evident in the prescriptions about fatherlessness. You would think, naturally, that the solution is for fathers to be truly and deeply involved in family life, to share child care, if not housework, and to become a passionate presence in the lives of their children. You'd be wrong. Blankenhorn and others who lament fatherlessness do not issue a clarion call for a new fatherhood, based on emotional receptivity and responsiveness, compassion and patience, care and nurture (which are, after all, the *human* qualities one needs to be a good father in the first place). Instead Blankenhorn rails against him:

> He is nurturing. He expresses his emotions. He is a healer, a companion, a colleague. He is a deeply involved parent. He changes diapers, gets up at 2 a.m. to feed the baby, goes beyond 'helping out' in order to share equally in the work, joys, and responsibilities of domestic life.

How utterly 'selfish' of him. Obviously, this sensitive New Age father does all this because he 'reflects the puerile desire for human omnipotentiality in the form of genderless parenthood, a direct repudiation of fatherhood as a gendered social role for men'. Let's assume for the moment that this sentence is actually sensible. It means that the *real* father is neither nurturing nor expressive; he is neither a partner nor a friend to his wife, and he sleeps through most of the baby's infantile helplessness, oblivious to the needs of his wife and child. Men are fathers, but they don't have to actually *do* any real parenting. The father 'protects his family, provides for its material needs, devotes himself to the education of his children, and represents his family's interests in the larger world'—all valuable behaviours, to be sure. But they are things that do not require that he ever set foot in his child's room.[91]

Divorce, Child Custody, and Children

'Forget about climate change', writes Kate Fraher:

> Forty years ago the social equivalent of it hit Canada. It was not a tsunami, something that crashes to the shore and destroys everything in sight all at once, but rather more like the slow and graduate creep of rising temperatures or tides. The problem? Canada's divorce rate multiplied five times from the end of the 1960s to the mid-1980s.[92]

Divorce may be a social problem—but not exactly for the reasons that many political commentators claim it is: High divorce rates are not shattering the family. Looked at historically, high rates of divorce are merely accomplishing by conscious action what higher mortality rates had accomplished in an earlier period. As historian Lawrence Stone put it, 'the median duration of marriage today is almost exactly the same as it was 100 years ago. Divorce, in short, now acts as a functional substitute for death: both are means of terminating marriage at a premature stage'. (Of course, he adds, the psychological effects are not the same.)[93]

Nor does the number of divorces necessarily indicate a loss of faith in marriage. In fact, writes sociologist Constance Ahrons, author of *The Good Divorce*, Americans 'like marriage so much that many of us will do it two, three, or more times'. In the USA, remarriages now comprise about half of all marriages every year. Canadians are more circumspect, at least in their intentions. Since the 1990s, divorced Canadians seem less interested in remarriage, with more than 60 per cent of them (and more women than men) claiming that they do not want to marry again. Still, about 70 per cent of divorced men and 58 per cent of divorced women (excluding those in Quebec) remarry.[94]

The 'problem' with divorce is more accurately linked to the constructed problem of fatherlessness and the real problem of gender inequality. Divorce reform was promoted, after all, by women who, at the turn of the last century, sought to provide legal recourse to those who wanted to escape marriages that were desperately unhappy and others that were brutally, even violently oppressive. The option of divorce loosened the marital knot to keep it from choking women. Like birth control and abortion, both of which have also generated heated debates, divorce undermined men's power over women and reduced gender inequality in the family.

Although liberalized divorce laws may have reduced gender inequality within marriage, they seem neither to have reduced it entirely nor to have reduced it after the marriage is dissolved. Just as there are 'his' and 'her' marriages, there are also 'his' and 'her' divorces because divorce affects wives and husbands differently. Divorce exaggerates gender differences in the marriage, exacerbating gender inequality. In the mid-1980s, US family researcher Leonore Weitzman calculated that following divorce, the woman's income drops a precipitous 73 per cent, whereas her ex-husband's income increases 42 per cent. In recent years, these data have been revised as overly dramatic, but no research suggests that the economic and social statuses of women and men after divorce are equivalent, and researchers still agree that women's resources decline more than men's. As sociologist Paul Amato writes, 'the greater the inequality between men and women in a given society, the more detrimental the impact of divorce on women'. This trend, observable for the past 30 years, is still with us, according to a study published in 2009 by University of Toronto researcher Tahany Gadalla; according to that study, the most dramatic effects on women's incomes are observable in the year after divorce, but effects continue for several years thereafter. In a number of nations, including Canada, the USA, Germany, Sweden, the United Kingdom, and the Netherlands, the same pattern holds; women experience a sharp short-term drop in income after divorce, while men experience a modest increase in income.[95]

Aside from effects on income, divorce has other important effects. Over half of all divorces in Canada involve couples with children still at home. When parents cannot agree on arrangements for the care of their children, the courts step in to adjudicate custody. While historically men have been advantaged in cases of marital dissolution, by the end of the nineteenth century courts were increasingly influenced by the so-called 'tender years' principle. According to this idea, the interests of children (particularly young children) were best served by placing them in their mother's custody, at least until puberty or just before (when they were thought to need their same-sex role model). This model was replaced in the 1980s (i.e., in the Divorce Act of 1985) by the gender-neutral principle of the best interests of the child, which dictated that only the best interests of a particular child should influence a custody decision. The best interests of the child were presumed to include regular visitation by the non-custodial parent, which led to the incorporation of the friendly parent principle. This encouraged the awarding of custody to the parent most likely to permit the other access.[96]

While the principles of Canadian child custody are gender-neutral, in practice women tend to be more likely to receive custody than are fathers. This has led to a large fathers' rights movement throughout North America and to the identification of 'Parental Alienation Syndrome', an alleged phenomenon resulting from the attempts of mothers to poison their children's minds against their fathers. Some of the wilder claims of fathers' rights activists have no doubt discredited allegations of gender bias in the courts, and women's continued greater responsibility for child-rearing surely plays a role in judges' more frequently awarding custody to mothers.[97]

Father's rights groups claim that, invariably, joint custody is preferable for children. And it does seem that, all things being equal, joint physical and legal custody ought to be the norm in custody decisions. Here, of course, 'all things being equal' means that there is no discernible danger to the child of sexual or physical abuse; that the parents can manage to contain their own post-divorce conflict and prevent the children from becoming pawns in a parental power struggle; and that the parents agree to equally support the children financially and emotionally. Such arrangements may be more difficult for parents than for children, who often report 'a sense of being loved by both parents', as well as 'feeling strongly attached to two psychological parents, in contrast to feeling close to just one primary parent'. Contrary to some popular opinion, joint custody 'does not create uncertainty or confusion' and seems to benefit children, who say they are more satisfied with the arrangement than those in single-custody homes and that they consider having two homes advantageous.[98]

We know, too, that joint custody will benefit men, who will, by maintaining a legal connection to their children, be far more likely to continue to share financial responsibilities for their development. What's more, joint custody may relieve the deep sense of loss, disengagement, and depression often experienced by men who are cut loose from continued involvement with their families. On the other hand, mandated joint legal custody may not be so good for women. Feminist legal theorist Martha Fineman argues that mandated joint legal custody may appear to be gender-neutral but that gender 'neutrality' in one arena in a system of overall gender inequality may actually perpetuate gender discrimination. As Fineman writes:

> What may have started out as a system which, focusing on the child's need for care, gave women a preference *solely* because they had usually been the child's primary caretaker, is evolving into a system which, by devaluing the content or necessity of such care, gives men more than an equal chance to gain the custody of their children after divorce if they choose to have it, because biologically equal parents are considered as equal in expressive regards. Non-nurturing factors assume importance which often favours men.[99]

Perhaps the most judicious system of child custody will be one that recognizes the difference in 'inputs' between parents in the actual experiences of the children—time spent in child care, level of parental involvement in child development—while at the same time presuming that both parents are capable of and interested in (absent any evidence to the contrary) continued committed and involved relationships with their children. Fathers' 'rights' after divorce will come more readily if the fathers have recognized their responsibilities during the marriage.[100]

Greater involvement of fathers may also help thwart the tendency of many men to disappear from their children's lives after divorce. Many divorced fathers 'lose almost all contact with their children over time', writes David Popenoe. Whether this is because the father is bereft to be kept from regular contact with his children or because after the marital bond is severed he experiences a euphoria of 'freedom' and considers himself to have escaped from a conflict-ridden family situation, it appears that many men 'see parenting and marriage as part of the same bargain—a package deal', write sociologists Frank Furstenberg and Andrew Cherlin. 'It is as if they stop being fathers as soon as the marriage is over'. In one US study of 11- to 16-year-old children living with their mothers, almost half had not seen their fathers in the previous 12 months. Nearly half of all divorced fathers in the United States pay no child support; in Europe the comparable number is about one quarter.[101]

Non-custodial mothers, however, though stigmatized, rarely lose contact with their children after divorce, maintaining family connections over employment possibilities and new relationships. In addition, divorced men exhibit increased symptoms of psychological and emotional distress. Divorce seems to affect women more adversely in material and financial terms and men more adversely in emotional and psychological terms.[102]

What predicts continued involvement of parents in their children's lives after a divorce is the quality of the relationship between the ex-spouses prior to the divorce. And ironically, it also appears that it is the men who were more involved with their children prior to the divorce who are most likely to disappear after it, whereas those men who were relatively uninvolved prior to divorce tended to become more active with their children afterward. In part, as the University of British Columbia's Edward Kruk observes, this counterintuitive difference stems from the less-involved fathers also being more 'traditional' in their outlooks, which would increase their sense of commitment to family life even after divorce; whereas more 'liberal' men were more likely to see themselves as 'free' from family responsibilities.[103]

Paternal withdrawal, it turns out, actually affects the father-daughter relationship most significantly. This may surprise those who believe that the father-son bond is the most fragile and most hard-hit by post-divorce fatherlessness, but it illustrates how frequently daughters are ignored in that literature and how both boys and girls benefit from paternal responsibility and continued presence in their children's lives.[104]

Discussion of parenting after divorce leads naturally to one of the most contentious themes in the study of divorce: its effects on children. In a widely publicized study of 61 families in an affluent California suburb, psychologist Judith Wallerstein found that a significant number of children 'suffer long-term, perhaps permanent detrimental effects from divorce', whereas other children repress these effects, only to have them emerge years later. Ten years and even 25 years after divorce, those problems had not disappeared. 'When people decide to divorce, it has a short-term and long-term traumatic effect upon the children that makes their subsequent life journey more difficult', she writes. A lousy marriage, she concludes, beats a good divorce.[105]

Although such dire warnings as Wallerstein's have claimed countless magazine covers and public discussion, there is far less social science in her work than at first meets the eye. Wallerstein had no control group. What's more, about one-third of the original children of the families she studied were not interviewed for this survey—are they the ones who adjusted successfully and moved on with their lives? We cannot know. And finally, and most damning, the original participants in the study were recruited through a promise of free therapy for divorcing couples who were having a difficult time of it. What Wallerstein *really* found, then, was that the children of psychologically impaired divorcing parents have some difficulties themselves down the road.[106]

Still, no one doubts that divorce is difficult for children or that all things being equal, being raised by two parents (of whatever sex) is probably better than being raised by one. For starters, with two parents, each is less likely to be tired and overworked. Single-parent families are also more likely to be poor. When stepparents are added to the mix, certain risks increase (e.g., for girls especially, sexual abuse). The debate really concerns what we mean by 'all else being equal'. If we compare, for example, the educational achievement scores, sense of well-being, or levels of psychological and emotional adjustment of children who are raised in undivorced two-parent families with those of children raised in single-parent, post-divorce families, we find that those children in single-parent families manifest lower levels of well-being, self-esteem, educational attainment, and adjustment than those in two-parent homes.

But such comparisons are misdirected, because they compare two types of families—divorced and intact—as if they were equivalent. Divorce is not a remedy for marriage; it is a remedy for a *bad* marriage. And when researchers compare the outcomes for children being raised in a post-divorce family with the outcomes for children being raised in an intact—*but unhappy*—family, the evidence is clear. The consequences of divorce on children depend on the level of marital conflict prior to the divorce.

Perhaps the most level-headed researcher to weigh in on these issues is Andrew Cherlin, a sociologist and demographer at Johns Hopkins University. His research found that the line of causation ran exactly counter to Wallerstein's clinical assertions. 'We found that children whose parents would later divorce *already* showed more emotional problems at age 7 than children from families that would stay together', he writes. The University of Alberta's Lisa Strohschein concurs. Her longitudinal research indicates that 'the family dynamics that increase the likelihood of later divorce first act to increase the mental health problems of dependent children'. Another British study tracking 17,000 families also found that children's problems long antedate divorce and that problems among young children can, in fact, be a good predictor of eventual divorce. Other longitudinal research has found that children in families that eventually divorce manifest problems long before the actual divorce. The authors argue that many of the consequences attributed to divorce may, in fact, derive from the marital conflict and family stress that precede a divorce, rather than from the divorce itself. Blaming the problems of children on their parents' divorce 'is a bit like stating that cancer is caused by chemotherapy', argues the president of the Family and Divorce Mediation Council of Greater New York. 'Neither divorce nor chemotherapy is a step people hope to have to take in their lives, but each may be the healthiest option in a given situation'. [107]

Most research on divorce actually finds that after the short-term trauma of divorce, most children adjust well. Most children recover from the stress of divorce and show few adverse signs a few years later if they have adequate psychological supports and economic resources. One study found that children in divorced families did, indeed, feel lonely, bored, and rejected more often than those in intact families—but that children in families led by unhappily married couples felt the highest levels of neglect and humiliation. [108]

The most systematic research on these issues has been undertaken by family sociologists Paul Amato and Alan Booth and their colleagues. Divorce, Amato and Booth conclude, 'is beneficial for children when it removes them from a high-conflict marriage'. But, like marriage, divorce ought not be entered into casually or without thought, because the consequences can be deleterious 'when it removes them from a low-conflict marriage'. [109]

The solution that some propose to the problem of divorce is, of course, simple: make divorce harder to obtain. In the USA, three states have instituted 'covenant marriages', which, unlike the contractual legal marriage, demand that couples take literally and seriously the provision of ''til death do us part'. Such measures have not been taken in Canada. But William Gairdner, author of *The Trouble with Canada* and himself divorced, has argued that tougher divorce laws are needed to keep people from 'taking the easy way out'. Yet most family researchers agree that such a triumph of form over content—making divorce harder to get without changing the content of the marriage—would 'exacerbate the bitterness and conflict that are associated with the *worst* outcomes of divorce for kids'.[110]

Divorce is a serious undertaking and not to be undertaken casually. But it is a 'necessary "safety-valve" for children (and parents) in high conflict households'. Divorce might better be seen as a social indicator that something is wrong not with one-half of all marriages, taken individually, but rather with the institution of marriage, that the foundation upon which marriage rests cannot sustain and support one-half of all the marriages that take place—without some serious efforts on the part of policy-makers. US Family therapist Betty Carter pointed out that if any other social institution were failing so many of the people who entered it, we would demand that the institution change to fit people's new needs, not the other way around.[111]

Families Formed by Same-Sex Unions

Another recent constructed problem is that of gay and lesbian families. But the problems of gay families—marriage, child rearing—are actually less about families and more about the legal status of homosexuals. In North America, the rights of gay men and lesbians to form families (with all of their attendant rights and responsibilities) became a major issue in the 1990s and in the first few years of the new century. Canada and the USA have diverged sharply in this area, as in many other areas of family life.

In Canada, the road to legal same-sex marriage began in 1999, when the Supreme Court ruled that those in same-sex partnerships must be extended the same rights as those in heterosexual partnerships. In response, the House of Commons passed a bill stating that marriage was limited to the union of a man and a woman. Nonetheless, by 2003, both Ontario and British Columbia courts had ruled that banning same-sex marriage was unconstitutional. (Alberta, by contrast, vowed to use the notwithstanding clause to block gay marriage should it be decreed). Gay couples began getting marriage licences in Ontario, and then-Prime Minister Jean Chretien announced that he would introduce legislation to legalize same-sex marriage. On July 20, 2005, Bill C-38 received royal assent, defining civil marriage in Canada as 'the lawful union of two persons to the exclusion of all others'. This permitted partners of the same sex to wed, making Canada the fourth nation in the world to legalize same-sex marriage. Though there was outrage among many Canadians, along with vows to make the issue an election hot potato, there has been little attempt to dislodge it, particularly after a 2006 Angus Reid poll showed that most Canadians were in favour of keeping the legal change.[112]

In the USA, in comparison, acceptance of same-sex marriage has not been as rapid, though lobbying efforts have been strong. As in Canada, lobbying for same-sex marriage rights emerged in the 1990s as the logical outcome of gay-rights activism from the 1960s on. In response, a number of states rushed through legislation enshrining a heterosexual definition of marriage. This rear-guard action was crowned by President Bill Clinton's September 1996 signing of the Defense of Marriage Act, which defined marriage as male-female in character and defended the right of states to refuse recognition to same-sex marriages conducted in other jurisdictions. Both the USA's strong evangelical Protestant tradition and a kind of generalized 'moral panic' played a role in ensuring that marriage would remain a matter between a man and a woman.

Still, lobbying and legal challenges continued, and in 2004, both Massachusetts and the city of San Francisco implemented same-sex marriage. By 2008, five other states had either legalized gay marriage or made a commitment to do so. One of those states, California, underwent two rapid shifts in policy within the course of a year. First, in May 2008, the California Supreme Court overruled the ban on same-sex marriages, leading to the implementation of such marriages the following month. However, opponents of same-sex marriage were successful in getting a constitutional amendment known as Proposition 8 onto the ballot in the November 2008 general election. The proposition was passed by a slim majority, and upheld by the court in May 2009. California thus has a ban on gay marriage, but also recognizes as legal the marriages of some 18,000 same-sex couples who married during the six-month period when they had the right to marry!

Same-sex marriage, then, is more contentious a topic in the USA than it was in Canada, where it is now accepted by a large majority, as Bibby's surveys (described above) suggest. There are some signs that acceptance in the USA is growing. Speaking to a campus crowd in July 2009, Bill Clinton reversed his earlier position, stating that he is 'basically in support' of same-sex marriage. Nonetheless, Americans seem even more opposed to same-sex marriage than they were in 2007; a recent Gallup poll found that 57 per cent remain opposed, 40 per cent in favour, with much greater support among younger people and self-identified liberals.[113]

Why, given such opposition, do gay and lesbian couples seek legal recognition of their relationships? One reason is because so many benefits accrue to married couples—benefits that heterosexual couples often take for granted. These benefits include the right to inherit from a spouse who dies without a will; the right to consult with doctors and make crucial medical decisions if the partner is incapacitated; the right to make decisions about a deceased spouse's body; the right of residency of a foreign spouse; the right to social benefits; the right to include a spouse on one's health plan; the right to visit a spouse in a government institution like a prison or hospital; and the right to immunity from having to testify against one's spouse in a legal proceeding. Aside from these pragmatic considerations, marriage is more than a legal right, more than a relationship. It is an institution, the bedrock institution of our ideal of the family. Without the right to marry, it is codified into law that gay relationships are less valuable, less important, than heterosexual ones.

For gay people as for straight ones, marriage is also about children and the desire to found a family unit that goes beyond the couple and their lifetimes. Legal recognition of their unions aids same-sex couples in adopting children both within North America and globally, and permits non-biological parents to be registered as the parents of the children they love. This, in turn, allows gay parents the same rights to visitation and custody that heterosexual parents have and prevents them from being legally barred from their children's lives by a vindictive ex-partner. Legal recognition also helps prevent the stigmatization of gay people as unfit parents who are inherently dangerous to children.[114]

In the late 1960s, one woman lamented her position, not as a lesbian, but rather as a non-parent:

> One of my mother's big disappointments was the fact that there would be no grandchildren. I love both of my parents a great deal, and I would do almost anything for their happiness, but I couldn't do that. I think I was saddened too, when . . . I knew that I wasn't ever going to have children. And I would like to have some . . . for myself.[115]

Just as heterosexual women once felt they were forced to choose between having a career and having a family, many gay men and lesbians feel forced to choose between acknowledging their sexuality and having a family. And just as women today are unwilling to make that choice, wanting to 'have it all', so, too, are gays and lesbians, who have decided that their homosexuality ought not to disqualify them as good parents.[116]

None of the fears of gay parenting has materialized. Despite REAL Women of Canada's claim that '[s]ame-sex parenting is harmful to children', there is no evidence that gay fathers or lesbian mothers exert any special negative influence on child development or that they sexually abuse their children. In fact, the few studies that have been conducted show that 'the outcomes for children in these families tend to be better than average'. Much of the research on gay parenting has involved lesbians. A 2003 study commissioned by the federal government found no evidence that lesbian-led families produced poorer outcomes; indeed, of 100-plus studies reviewed by Concordia University researcher John Hastings, more found superior outcomes for children of lesbian parents than found weaker outcomes.

Research on lesbian mothers suggests that their children, both boys and girls, have patterns of gender identity development similar to those of children of heterosexual parents at comparable ages and display no differences in intelligence or adjustment. Some differences emerge, including findings that fathers 'smack' children more than do lesbian co-mothers, and that lesbian co-mothers show more interaction with children than do fathers. These may have some implications for research on parenting by gay male couples, but such research is in its infancy. At this point, 'quality of mothering', rather than sexual orientation, is the crucial determinant of children's development.[117] As the 15-year-old daughter of a lesbian mother put it:

> I think I am more open-minded than if I had straight parents. Sometimes kids at school make a big deal out of being gay. They say it's stupid and stuff like that. But they don't really know, because they aren't around it. I don't say anything to them, but I know they are wrong. I get kind of mad, because they don't know what they are talking about.

This statement echoed a recent New Jersey court decision, which found that children in gay and lesbian families

> emerge better equipped to search out their own standards of right and wrong, better able to perceive that the majority is not always correct in its moral judgments, and

better able to understand the importance of conforming their beliefs to the requirements of reason and tested knowledge, not the constraints of currently popular sentiments or prejudice.

Such sentiments, as family sociologist Judith Stacey points out, might well 'serve as
child-rearing ideals for a democracy'.[118]

A recent meta-analysis of social science studies of gay and lesbian parenting suggests that children of these parents are more accepting of homosexuality and may be
more likely to indicate a willingness to consider homosexual relationships themselves, although they are no more likely to identify themselves as 'gay' than are
children of heterosexual parents. More interestingly, however, are the *gender* consequences, as opposed to the sexual ones: Daughters of lesbian and gay parents are
more assertive, confident, and ambitious, and sons are less conforming to traditional
notions of masculine aggression and domination and more fluid in their gender
identities.[119]

Although some opposition to gay marriage has come from within the gay and
lesbian community itself, where some have expressed fears that the desire for
marriage is a repudiation of a more radical vision of gay liberation, the case for gay
marriage and family finds increasing support both inside and outside the gay
community.

The Family of the Future

Perhaps the most consistent finding to emerge from the literature on divorce, custody,
and sexual orientation is that the form of the family—intact, divorced, single-parent,
lesbian, or gay—matters far less for children and adults than its content. This is the key
issue, and we distract ourselves from developing policies and personal relationships
built to nurture and sustain children because we are so preoccupied with the size and
shape of the package. A home filled with love, respect, and support, where parents
spend both quality time and quantity time with their children and with each other, is
the strongest predictor of future physical, emotional, and psychological health of both
the children and their parents. A home free from violence should be the birthright of
every child (but isn't, as discussed in Chapter 12). Family sociologist Arlene Skolnick
writes that the most reliable studies 'find that family structure—the number of parents
in the home or the fact of divorce—is not in itself the critical factor in children's well-
being. In both intact and other families, what children need most is a warm, concerned
relationship with at least one parent'.[120]

For example, a recent longitudinal study followed 126 Harvard undergraduates
since their student days in the 1950s. Thirty-five years later, 116 of them were re-
evaluated. Of these, 25 per cent who had rated their parents as loving and caring had
developed major illnesses, whereas 87 per cent of those who had rated their parents as
uncaring had experienced at least one serious health problem. (The researchers
controlled for other potential causes, such as family history of illness, parental death or
divorce, smoking habits, and marital experiences.) Men who had a low perception of

the parental care and love that they received as children had a far greater risk of becoming ill in midlife.[121]

It was in the nineteenth century that the ideology of the separation of spheres was invented and imposed, 'imprisoning' women in the home and 'exiling' men from it. In the latter half of the twentieth century, the structural foundations of that ideology eroded, and it came under increasing ideological attack. Our prediction is that the twenty-first century will witness a 'reintegration of spheres', in which home and work will become increasingly similar, and men and women will be more active participants in both spheres. We should 'insist on a closer integration between people's professional lives and their domestic lives', writes social critic Christopher Lasch. 'Instead of acquiescing in the family's subordination to the workplace, [we] should seek to remodel the workplace around the needs of the family . . . ' And on the home front, an increasing number of people are 'telecommuting' to work, travelling from bedroom to home office, and using computers, fax machines, modems, and telephone lines to conduct paid work, while they cook for their children and clean the house during breaks.[122]

The most dramatic shift in family life in the twenty-first century will surely be the changing roles of men, just as the most dramatic demographic shift in the workplace in the twentieth century was the entry of women. Family sociologist Scott Coltrane predicts that as wives are employed longer hours, identify more with their jobs, and provide a larger share of family income, men will do increasing amounts of housework. What's more, he argues, as 'fathers become more involved in baby care, they will begin to take more responsibility for routine child care, and a significant minority will move beyond the role of household helper'. In the workplace, men will increasingly identify as fathers, just as within the home, women have increasingly identified as workers.[123]

When men and women fully share housework and the raising of children, gender inequality in the family will gradually decrease, and the gender stereotypes and gender differences that were presumed to be the source of that inequality will also gradually begin to dissolve. After all, as we learn from anthropologists, those societies in which men take a larger role in child care are those in which women's status tends to be highest. Plus, a society in which women and men share parenting will be a society in which they are also equally active in the labour force. A change in the private sphere will bring about dramatic changes in the public sphere.

Think, for a moment, about the implications of shared parenting and housework, about the full impact of the reintegration of spheres. A child who experiences love and nurturing from his or her father and mother will come to see that nurturing is something that *adults* do, not something that women do and that men may or may not do, depending on whether there's a good game on the television. So all children, both boys and girls, will expect to be nurturing when they become adults. Similarly, a child will also see that working is something that *adults* do, not something that men do and that women may or may not do, depending on whether their husband 'allows' it or whether they're raising children. In this sense, shared parenting might be a crucial step in 'degendering' the two most highly gendered experiences we have, the two experiences that Freud himself identified as the most crucial elements of healthy adult life: love and work.

Robert Frost wrote these oft-quoted lines:

Home is the place where, when you go there
they have to take you in.

Our families are places in which we are both constrained by duty and obligation and inspired by love, respect, and honour. Love, we've found, can abide in traditional families, in single-parent families, and in gay and lesbian families. It can sustain children in intact families or after divorce. What matters is the content of the family, not its form. Love can abide, nourish, and sustain—wherever it lives, and in whatever form.

Summary

The emergence of the 'family values' debate in the 1990s highlighted the changing family. But the family has always changed. Moreover, far from being the 'haven in a heartless world', the family has always been part of society, linked to other social institutions and supported, in modern times, by significant state supports.

The Canadian family has changed dramatically over the past 500 years. With industrialization (circa 1850) came the emergence of the notion of separate spheres for men and women. The new family model claimed that men should be breadwinners and women 'homemakers', in a domestic sphere newly construed as non-productive.

Soon thereafter, however, women began to push for rights and possibilities outside their allotted domestic sphere. By the beginning of the twentieth century, women were becoming assimilated into employment (including breadwinning), education, and political rights. As the twentieth century progressed, most people still supported the ideological construct of the male breadwinner and the female homemaker, resisting changes in women's roles.

The Second World War ended, both government policy and a wave of nostalgia pushed women back into the home. Men and women embraced this nostalgia, marrying and having children early, and divorcing little. The 1950s family model they created was almost immediately enshrined as the most 'natural' and healthiest form possible. However, by the late 1950s, women's discontent was evident, and in the 1960s it boiled over into a bona fide social movement against confinement in domesticity. This change, along with many others, placed strain on the post-war nuclear family model, which had become an anachronism almost as soon as it was created.

The current Canadian family undoubtedly faces stresses. Canada's rate of child poverty continues to be unacceptably high, and Canada's Aboriginal families face tremendous challenges, not least poverty and the continuing legacy of residential schools. Canadian families are also changing in other ways: families are smaller, couples are less likely to be married, and divorce is more common than it was for most of Canadian history. Our ideas about family have also changed. Canadians are highly accepting of diversity in family structures, even while they aspire to a 'traditional' family model in their own lives. In this, Canadians are on the vanguard of a global trend.

Marriage remains important to many of us, and its cultural script remains highly gendered. We still think of it as something women want and men try to avoid. Marriage is gendered, but research shows that it's actually better for men than for women, as measured by health and happiness indicators. The gendered division of labour within marriage may be largely responsible for this. Though women may bear an unequal burden in this division of labour, marriage remains an important part of the female 'success plan', and women remain disproportionately interested in weddings.

Marital happiness is negatively affected by child-rearing. Child-rearing, like marriage itself, remains highly gendered. We still gender-type infants, arranging their environments and clothing to conform with our expectations for their gender. Most research suggests that we treat them slightly differently, particularly in terms of encouraging autonomy and exploration in males and closeness in females. We also attribute gendered emotions and motivations to infant behaviour.

Gender-typing increases as children enter the toddler stage. Though girlhood and to some extent boyhood have changed in the 50 years since Mattel's Barbie made her debut, the gendered cultures of childhood are very much alive. And boys continue to see femininity as lower in status than masculinity.

The gendered cultures of childhood are an anachronism given the major transformations of the past 50 years, and particularly given the large-scale entrance of women into the workplace. That change has transformed the family. On the other hand, there are signs that the transformation of the family is incomplete. Women everywhere report greater stress than do men, in part because of the 'double shift', which requires women to both work outside the home and retain responsibility for the domestic sphere. For women's second shift to change dramatically, men must learn and be supported to do child care and housework, and to share full responsibility for all aspects of family life.

Many of the 'constructed problems' of family life arise from public policy and from the struggle between gender ideologies and a changing society. Daycare is an excellent example. While more than half of Canadian children regularly access daycare, we continue to argue about whether daycare is harmful to children. Daycare is not a 'women's problem', or a luxury, but an increasingly necessary support for the Canadian family.

A similar constructed problem is teenage pregnancy. It remains a major issue in the USA, but in Canada has diminished dramatically (except among Aboriginal teens). Often ignored in all of this is the responsibility of men, particularly the adult men who are most often the partners of pregnant teens. A sounder approach avoids stigmatizing teen mothers while helping young women build the fullest control possible over their reproductive health and sexual choices.

The question of 'fatherlessness' arises regularly with regard to crime and social dislocation. While more children are being reared in lone-parent families, particularly those headed by women, Canada has a significantly lower rate of lone parenthood than does the USA. Moreover, poverty, not the simple presence or absence of a father in the home, is the most likely explanation for the participation of lone-parented youth in crime.

The discussion of fatherlessness is clearly related to changes in divorce and child custody over the past 30 or 40 years. Since divorce was liberalized in Canada in the late 1960s, the divorce rate has increased dramatically (though it has begun to decline again). Like marriage, divorce remains gendered. The majority of Canadian divorces also involve minor children. Since the 1980s, Canadian courts have been encouraged to consider the child's best interests in making child custody decisions; mothers are more likely to receive custody than fathers. This has led to the growth of a fathers' rights movement that argues against alleged gender bias in the courtroom.

The effects of divorce upon children have been studied, particularly in the USA, since the dramatic increase in the divorce rate some 40 years ago. One of the major findings to emerge from newer studies is that children in families that will later divorce show mental health problems even before the divorce; marital conflict, not divorce itself, may be responsible for these problems. Ultimately, though, divorce is less a problem in itself than an indicator of strains on the institution of marriage and our expectations of it.

Families formed by same-sex unions have been the focus of much discussion, some of it hysterical, over the past 20 years. Canada legalized same-sex marriage in 2005. Most Canadians are accepting of this change. In the USA, in contrast, changes to heterosexual marriage have been polarizing. For those seeking same-sex marriage, marriage conveys both practical benefits and the opportunity to participate in the institution we consider the bedrock of society. Studies have shown that outcomes for children of these families are at least as good as for children of heterosexual couples.

The overwhelming consensus of research on the family is that the form of the family matters much less than its content. Much more important than the number or sex of one's parents is a home filled with love, respect, and support; adequately sustained by material resources; and free of violence and abuse.

Questions for Critical Thinking

1. Why, in your opinion, has the 1950s nuclear family become frozen in our minds as the 'ideal' and 'traditional' family?
2. Why does child-rearing lead to such a decline in marital happiness, in your opinion?
3. Why do you think men have been more eager to embrace child care than to take on housework?
4. How 'gendered' do you think contemporary child-rearing practices are? In your experience, can you think of examples of differential treatment of girls and boys?
5. Thinking about marriage as a gendered institution, do you think that same-sex marriage will change the nature of that institution?

Key Terms

Aboriginal
breadwinner
child poverty
clan
common-law marriage
Divorce Act
extended family
gender complementarity
grrrl power
Indian Act

LICO
matrilocal
New Woman
nuclear families
race suicide
residential schools
second shift
separation of spheres
suburban
temperance movement

Chapter 7

The Gendered Classroom

Formal Education and the Hidden Curriculum

The Higher Education of Women is one of the great world battle-cries for freedom; for right against might. It is the cry of the oppressed slave. It is the assertion of absolute equality.

—HENRY FOWLE DURANT, PRESIDENT, WELLESLEY COLLEGE,
'THE SPIRIT OF THE COLLEGE' (1877)

'Math class is tough' were the first four words Barbie ever spoke. When Mattel introduced Teen Talk Barbie in 1992, a new group of her nearly 800 million owners heard more than a teenager's complaint—even if that teenager was the buxom blond bombshell whose feet were designed to fit into high heels. That group heard the way gender inequality and gender differences are reproduced.[1]

The interplanetary theory of gender tells us that boys and girls are fundamentally and categorically different, that boys excel in science and math, play violently in the playground, and shout out in class; that girls, on the other hand, sit quietly, speak softly, play gingerly, and excel in French and in literature. At the same time, of course, we sit in the same classroom, read the same books, listen to the same teachers, and are supposedly graded by the same criteria.

But are we having the same experience in those classes? Not exactly. Our gendering experiences begin even before we get to school. By the time we enter our first classroom, we are learning more than our ABCs, more than spelling, math, and science, more than physics and literature. We learn—and teach one another—what it means to be men and women. And we see it all around us in our schools—who teaches us, what they teach us, how they teach us, and how the schools are organized as institutions. Both in the official curriculum—textbooks and the like—and in the parallel '**hidden curriculum**' of our informal interactions with both teachers and other students, we become gendered. This is reinforced in the parallel curriculum presented by the mass media. And the message that students get—from both the content and the form of education—is that women and men are different and unequal, that the inequality comes from those differences, and that, therefore, such inequality is justified. Consider, though, the opposite position—that the differences we observe are the *products*, not the cause, of gender inequality. As law professor Deborah Rhode writes, 'What schools teach and tolerate reinforces inequalities that persist well beyond childhood'.[2]

Traditional Education: Learning to be a Man

Most of us are aware that formal education has historically been limited by sex and class (and in many cases in the modern world, by race). In the eighteenth century, education was largely reserved for upper-class boys and men. Women were viewed as insufficiently rational by 'enlightened' thinkers, while those rooted in the Christian tradition used other justifications for the exclusion of female students from anything but rudimentary education. In the eighteenth century as throughout history, some girls and women, particularly religious women and those of elite status, became highly educated; but the idea of being educated was powerfully linked to the idea of being masculine.

This was also true in Canada's colonial history. In New France, education was in the hands of the Catholic Church. Nuns and friars provided education to girls and boys in towns and, to some extent, rural areas. However, most children received only a basic education; 'learning', for them, meant the less formal process of vocational learning within the home or, in some cases, in apprenticeship. Higher education was confined mainly to those entering the clergy or professions, who were often educated in the colony's Jesuit colleges. After the British takeover, Canada's system imitated that of England. Canada's first university outside Quebec, King's College, was established at Windsor, Nova Scotia in 1789; from then until Confederation, Canada's universities would be staffed by Britons and would emulate traditions and trends from the mother country.

Throughout the nineteenth century, formal education expanded significantly, particularly because Canada's rulers saw education as the best way to assimilate Canada's diverse society into something resembling a nation. By the 1820s, there was significant support for state education, though there was also resistance, particularly from the Catholic Church in Quebec. After the rebellion of 1837–38, education was seen as even more valuable in moulding 'freely obedient subjects'—and in correcting the 'gender imbalance' in Quebecois society, according to Arthur Buller's report on education in the region:

> The difference in the character of the two sexes is really remarkable. The women are the men of Lower Canada. They are the active, bustling, business portion of the *habitans* [*sic*]; and this results from the much better education which they get gratuitously, or at a very cheap rate, from the nunneries which are dispersed over the province.

By Confederation, governments were giving financial support to Catholic and 'public' schools, though this support was small by twenty-first-century standards. By the end of the nineteenth century, most parents were enrolling their children in school, even before almost all of the provinces passed legislation making school attendance mandatory. (Only Quebec held out until 1943, as a result of parental, church, and employer opposition.)

The presence of girls within this system was uncontroversial, but there was disagreement concerning what girls should be learning. Egerton Ryerson, one of the most influential figures in nineteenth-century Canadian schooling, felt that girls should be educated for their 'proper sphere' and not for paid employment. Girls were discouraged from pursuing the 'difficult' courses required, for example, for university admission. So while 'universal' education was a commonly held goal, some forms of exclusion remained part of the system. As we discussed in the previous chapter, Aboriginal students were to go to separate schools where most received a substandard education; in addition, the treatment received at the school has marred Aboriginal communities' relations with formal education to this day. And black-white segregation within nineteenth-century schools was tolerated even though it was against the law.[3]

Canada's education system, both at the primary and higher levels, expanded dramatically precisely during the phase when education was most linked, throughout the British Empire, to notions of '**imperial manhood**'. According to these ideas, education played a major role in creating the ideal British subject. Boys all over the empire learned about the triumphs of British civilization, were instructed in manly Christian morality, and developed healthy bodies and character through playing British sports. *Tom Brown's Schooldays*, published in 1857, was the apogee of this 'new educational ethos', presenting Rugby school as a microcosm of the well-ordered British society. Sports and education thus became ever more linked with ideas about what it meant to be masculine—not to mention British. In the form of 'muscular Christianity', these ideas spread throughout North America.[4]

We've seen earlier how during this same period, the ideology of the separate spheres saw men and women as fulfilling completely different destinies. Not surprisingly, in the nineteenth century many argued that 'manly' education was not suited for women. Opponents of women's equality argued that higher education for women would result in 'monstrous brains and puny bodies' with 'flowing thought and constipated bowels', because it would violate the 'plan' women's bodies held for them. Many of the Victorian opponents of women's education believed that women could not withstand and would not wish to subject themselves to the rigours of higher education, while others deplored the possibility that educated women would seek employment outside the home. The University of Toronto had to be compelled by law to permit women to attend classes, and the male medical students welcomed their female colleagues by filling their seats with filth. Nonetheless, the first degree granted to a woman in the British Empire went to a Canadian, Grace Annie Lockhart, who received her B.Sc. from Mount Allison in 1875.[5]

While some worried about higher education for women, others worried that the presence of women in universities would 'emasculate' and 'water down' the university curriculum and degender both men and women. In his influential treatise on adolescence, the great psychologist G. Stanley Hall warned against coeducation because it 'harms girls by assimilating them to boys' ways and work and robbing them of their sense of feminine character', whereas it harms boys 'by feminizing them when they need to be working off their brute animal element'. By making boys and girls more alike, he warned, coeducation would 'dilute' the mysterious attraction of the opposite sex—that is, coeducation would cause homosexuality. (Of course, Hall could not yet have previewed Alfred Kinsey's studies of human sexuality, which found that most homosexual experimentation among males occurred precisely in those single-sex—institutions—all-male schools, summer camps, Boy Scouts, the military, and prisons—that Hall believed would be palliatives against homosexuality.)

Of course, there were also strong supporters of women's education in both Canada and the USA, such as the founders and first presidents of historically women's colleges, like Henry Durant (Wellesley) and the 'Methodist millionaires' who supported the extension of women's education in nineteenth-century Ontario. Many supporters of women's education were essentially conservative in their view of education, but Durant went as far as to argue that the real meaning of women's education was revolt—'against the slavery in which women are held by the customs of society—the broken health, the aimless lives, the subordinate position, the helpless dependence, the dishonesties and shams of so-called education'.[6]

By 1900, about 10 per cent of Canadian university undergraduates were women. By 1920, the proportion had increased to about 25 per cent. Women were 'stuck' at this rate until the 1960s, when rates began to increase dramatically. By 1980–1981, the majority of students enrolled in university were women, a trend that has continued to the present.[7] An education that 150 years ago was a training in manhood has opened to women. The classrooms that women struggled so hard to enter, however, did not accommodate them completely willingly. Women entered gendered classrooms, and our classrooms continue to be gendered in ways both predictable and surprising.

The Gendered Classroom

Today, Canada's schools enrol about five million students, with close to one million students in post-secondary education.[8] (As detailed in the previous chapter, the majority of Canada's preschool-aged children are also in care, but there is no early childhood education system in place as of yet.)

Canada's education system, relative to systems in much of the world, is gender-neutral. Yet the formal educational gendering process begins the moment we enter the classroom and continues throughout our educational lives. Take an environmental example: in preschools and kindergarten classes, we often find the heavy blocks, trucks, airplanes, and carpentry tools in one area and the dolls and homemaking equipment in another area. Although they may be officially 'open' to anyone for play, the areas are often sex-segregated by invisible but real boundaries.

In the elementary school years, informal play during out-of-school hours involves different sports, different rules, and different playground activities, but the rule of segregation is the same. Boys and girls learn—and teach each other—what are the appropriate behaviours and experiences for boys and girls and make sure that everyone acts according to plan.

What's less visible are the ways the teachers and curriculum overtly and subtly reinforce not only gender difference, but also the inequalities that go along with and even produce that difference. The classroom setting reproduces gender inequality. 'From elementary school through higher education, female students receive less active instruction, both in the quantity and in the quality of teacher time and attention', note education professors David Sadker and the late Myra Sadker, summarizing the research in their important book, *Failing at Fairness*. (The study was published in 1995, but the 2009 revised edition finds the situation the same.) Many teachers perceive boys as being active, capable of expressing anger, quarrelsome, punitive, alibi-building, and exhibitionistic, and they perceive girls as being affectionate, obedient, responsive, and tenacious. When boys 'put girls down', as they often do at that age, teachers (female usually) often say and do nothing to correct them, thus encouraging the boys' notion of superiority. Many teachers assume that girls are likely to 'love' reading and 'hate' mathematics and sciences, and they expect the opposite of boys. This shortchanges both sexes.[9]

Teachers call on boys more often and spend more time with them. They ask boys more challenging questions than they do girls and wait longer for boys to answer. They urge boys to try harder, constantly telling boys that they can 'do it'. One study found that in all 10 of the college classrooms observed, boys were more active, regardless of the gender of the teacher, though a female teacher increased girls' participation significantly. Another study from the UK found that boys received more attention than did girls, including receiving more reprimands (with a small group of boys the focus of most reprimands); boys also were asked and answered more questions. However, girls asked more questions of the teacher and requested more help. The report sponsored by the American Association of University Women summarized these studies when it concluded that whether 'one is looking at preschool classrooms or university lecture halls . . . research spanning the past 20 years consistently reveals that males receive more teacher attention than do females'. Part of the reason for this is that boys demand more attention, and part of the reason is that teachers also treat boys and girls differently. When the Sadkers were researching their book, they asked teachers why they paid more attention to the boys. The teachers told them things like: 'Because boys need it more' and 'Boys have trouble reading, writing, doing math. They can't even sit still'.[10]

Journalist Peggy Orenstein observed another junior high school class, where boys 'yelled out or snapped the fingers of their raised hands when they wanted to speak, [while the] girls seemed to recede from class proceedings'. As one girl told her, 'Boys never care if they're wrong'.

As these examples suggest, teachers and others often rely on what Leanne Dalley-Trim calls 'common-sense' understandings of masculinity in their work with boys. Instead of seeing abusive behaviours as intolerable and avoidable, for example, teachers dismiss them as what boys do. Based on her research in Australia, Dalley-Trim argues that when teachers accept certain behaviours as 'just boys being boys', they risk supporting simplistic ideas about masculinity that harm boys and girls alike. Teachers may also stereotype girls while taking the opposite approach to their misbehaviour. Diane Reay's study of girls in a largely working-class London (UK) classroom reported that teachers were far less tolerant of girls' misbehaviour, describing misbehaving seven-year-olds as 'little cows', 'real bitches', and 'too mature'. In the gendered classroom, both sexes are stereotyped.[11]

Interactions with teachers and other students are one important part of the gendered classroom, but they are not the only influence upon children. Early in the school years, children learn to read, and to rely upon the textbooks prescribed by their teachers. Canadian research shows that teachers use textbooks for up to 90 per cent of classroom time, and that the structure of these textbooks significantly influences the decisions that teachers make. So textbooks matter. (As we shall see in a later chapter, students also observe the content of other media-television, films, or cartoons.) Do these materials counter sex typing, or do they reinforce it? Textbooks can be one way in which the school-based curriculum reinforces gender stereotypes and makes stereotypes feel as though they were based on something 'natural'.

Until recently, studies of children's books and anthologies have consistently reported traditional sex differences and pro-male biases. Females have been vastly underrepresented, and often absent, in pictures, in titles, and as main characters. In addition, female characters have usually been cast in insignificant or secondary roles. Their activities have been limited to loving, watching, or helping, whereas males have engaged in adventuring and solving problems. Women have not been given jobs or professions; motherhood has been presented as a full-time, lifetime job. The son in the family has worn trousers, and the daughter has worn a skirt; he has been active, she has been passive. In biographies, women have often been portrayed as dependent. For example, Marie Curie has been depicted as a helpmate to her husband, rather than as the brilliant scientist and Nobel Prize winner that she was.

In 1972, Leonore Weitzman and her colleagues surveyed winners of the Caldecott Medal for the best children's books published in the USA from 1967 to 1971. Since then, the research has been updated twice, most recently in 1987, and the researchers now find that though females are more visible in the books, their portrayal still reveals gender biases. In 1975, the US Department of Health, Education, and Welfare surveyed 134 texts and readers from 16 different publishers, looking at the pictures, stories, and language used to describe male and female characters. 'Boy-centred' stories outnumbered 'girl-centred' stories by a 5:2 ratio; there were three times as many adult male characters as adult female characters; six times as many biographies of men as of women; and four times as many male fairy tales as female. Recalling her American history classes, one scholar recently remembered a strange biological anomaly—'a nation with only founding fathers'. Though recent surveys suggest that history texts are improving, children's illustrated books and teacher-training texts continue to demonstrate substantial gender bias. One recent Alberta study shows that teachers are often unaware of the ideological content of children's literature and may therefore adopt books uncritically. And in some cases, school boards, such as the one in Surrey, BC, have attempted to ban library books that present same-sex parents as 'normal'. [12]

One shouldn't underestimate the changes of the past 40 years. In children's books today, girls and women are far more likely than before to be depicted as the main character and far less likely to be depicted as passive, without ambition or career goals. In fact, the major change in all media images—books, television, and movies—has been that women are no longer cast as domestic helpmates or workplace subordinates. But gender stereotypes still prevail. There has been no comparable change in the depiction of men or boys in children's books, no movement of men toward more nurturing and caring behaviours. As in real life, women in our storybooks have left home and gone off to work, but men still have enormous trouble coming back home.

Gender Divergence in Adolescence: Girls

The combination of exclusion from the curriculum, gender stereotypes in the media, and the often-invisible discrimination in the classroom itself results in a divergence between girls and boys by adolescence. In elementary school, girls have somewhat higher **self-esteem** and higher achievement levels than boys; in junior high, though girls' achievement continues, their self-esteem plummets. (Boys' self-esteem also declines, though less precipitously.) While Dove Canada, Girl Guides, the YWCA, and Big Brothers Big Sisters launch campaigns to increase girls' self-esteem, no single organization can change one tremendous shock to the system. In early adolescence, girls find out that they are more valued for their appearance than for their talents. In this period in their lives, girls begin to understand the nature of emphasized femininity—that their socially valued role is to be attractive to men.

Some scholars have found that in early adolescence, girls and boys enter a period of **gender intensification** in which they view gender roles as more rigid than they did before adolescence. More and more, girls view their appearance as the measure of their worth. One Irish study found that physical appearance was 'the single best predictor of global self-worth' for adolescent girls in mixed-sex schools.[13]

One young girl, Ashley Reiter, a winner of the US Westinghouse Talent Competition for her project of mathematical modelling, remembered the day she won her first math contest, which coincided with the day she got her first pair of contact lenses. When she showed up at school the next day, triumphant about her victory, '[e]veryone talked about how pretty I looked', she recalled. 'Nobody said a word about the math competition'. Is it any wonder that, in one survey, adolescent girls were about half as likely as boys to cite their talents as 'the thing I like most about myself', but about twice as likely as the boys to cite some aspect of their appearance? Or, as feminist literary critic Carolyn Heilbrun puts it, that girls sacrifice 'truth on the altar of niceness'.[14]

Declining self-esteem is not, however, universal or inevitable. One longitudinal study of US girls between 9 and 14 found the typical decline in white girls but not in black girls. The researchers proposed that cultural differences in attitudes toward physical appearance and body size may be the reason for black girls' relative resilience. Another study conducted in Manitoba found that sports participation may increase self-esteem (though not necessarily for girls with a very 'feminine' gender role orientation).[15] In other words, if girls live in a culture that values girls as more than just decoration and that values bodies that are not stick-thin, they might be better off. As it stands, many girls experience their adolescence as a time of self-loathing and insecurity. Eating disorders, such as anorexia and bulimia, are significant problems from junior high school through college, and the evidence is that their frequency is increasing—and at increasingly younger ages.

The classroom 'chilly climate' for girls also takes place within the sexually 'hostile environment' of many schools. Adolescent girls are sexual targets everywhere in our culture, and schools are no exception. In some cases, students attract the sexual attention of teachers. In BC, for example, of 37 teachers disciplined by the BC College of Teachers between 1998 and 2003, 24 were involved in inappropriate sexual relationships. Between 1989 and 1996, Ontario had more than 100 cases of the same. Though these data have not been broken down by sex, comparative studies from the USA show that the vast majority (96 per cent) of perpetrators are male, while about 76 per cent of victims are female. (Nonetheless, such relationships seem to concern officials more when they involve homosexuality or a male victim.)[16]

Teachers, however, are less identified as persecutors than are peers. In 1980, the USA's first survey of **sexual harassment** in schools found the problem widespread. Canada has been no different. In the early 1990s, June Larkin and Pat Staton authored a report for the Ontario Ministry of Education that found frequent harassment in the province's schools. Larkin and Staton's report contained shocking verification of what girls already knew: that, for example, the practice of boys' 'rating' girls on physical attractiveness using numbers was common, even in elementary schools. And much of the behaviour described as harassment went far beyond this. In the 1990s, June Larkin conducted a study of students from four Canadian high schools representing urban, rural, and small-town settings and diverse populations. Many of the students considered the behaviours they experienced as 'just guys being guys', reserving the term sexual harassment for physical assaults like rape. And yet students described incidents of sexual harassment, sometimes combined with racism, that in extreme cases spilled over into threats of violence:

> It was in my science class, and we had this teacher who was totally against women and everything about them . . . He called his own wife a bitch, things that were unbelievable. In that class we learned everything he felt about women and towards women . . . like I learned nothing about science that year.
>
> . . . there was one guy in my first class . . . he'll go, 'When are you going to sleep with me?' . . . He'll go 'I hear black women are good in bed'.
>
> I was talking to a guy . . . who sits behind me . . . He said a sentence and ended up calling me 'a bonehead'. I then said, 'You're the one who's a boner'. He said, 'You'd better shut up before I stick my dick up your ass so hard you won't be able to breathe'.

Larkin concludes, not surprisingly, that because of the hidden curriculum of sexual harassment, 'life for many female students is often a grim battle against a hostile and threatening school environment'. Both the Toronto School Board and the Canadian Centre for Addiction and Mental Health have recently collected statistics showing how common the experience of sexual harassment (and even sexual assault) is within Canadian schools. At the rarest end of this threatening continuum, sexual violence and school shootings (as discussed in Chapter 12) both disproportionately target girls. As bullying of girls by *female* peers also shows signs of increasing, girls become even more vulnerable.[17]

In the USA, **Title IX**, which prohibits discrimination in schools, has given students and their parents a way to battle sexual harassment in schools. In 1991, 19-year-old Katy Lyle was awarded $15,000 to settle a lawsuit she brought against her Duluth, Minnesota, school district, because school officials failed to remove explicit graffiti about her from the walls of the boys' bathrooms, even after her parents complained several times. That same year, the US Supreme Court unanimously sided with a young girl, Christine Franklin, in her case against the Gwinnett County, Georgia, school board, and awarded her $6 million in damages resulting from a violation of Title IX.

And yet sexual harassment continues in the USA as in Canada. According to a study commissioned by the American Association of University Women, nearly four-fifths of girls (78 per cent) and over two-thirds of boys (68 per cent) have been subjected to harassment. In both cases, it's almost invariably boys who are the perpetrators. In the infamous case of the Spur Posse, a group of relatively affluent young boys in southern California simply took these messages a little further than most. In 1993, a large group of young women and girls—one as young as 10!—came forward to claim that members of the Spur Posse had sexually assaulted and raped them. Members of the group of boys apparently competed with one another to see who could have sex with the most girls.

When some of these young women accused the boys of assault and rape, many residents of their affluent suburb were shocked. The boys' mothers, particularly, were horrified when they heard that their 15-year-old sons had had sex with 44 or 50 girls. A few expressed outrage. But the boys' fathers seemed to glow with pride. 'That's my boy', declared the dads in chorus. 'Nothing my boy did was anything any red-blooded American boy wouldn't do at his age', gloated one father. 'My dad used to brag to his friends', one Posse member confessed on a TV talk show. And we wonder where the kids get it from?[18]

What About the Boys?

Given the divergent patterns of adolescence, you might think that the systematic demolition of girls' self-esteem, the denigration of their abilities, and the demotion of their status would yield positive effects for boys, that boys would rise as the girls declined. But that isn't what happens. In fact, from early childhood on, boys, on average, seem to learn more slowly and face more risks of learning and behavioural challenges. One recent UK study finds five-year-old girls dramatically outperforming boys on most measures of early learning. In the elementary grades, boys are about four times more likely to be sent to child psychologists and far more likely to be diagnosed with dyslexia and attention deficit disorder (ADD) than are girls. Beginning in elementary school and continuing throughout their schooling, boys receive poorer report cards; they are far more likely to repeat a grade. Nine times more boys than girls are diagnosed as 'hyperactive'; boys represent 58 per cent of those in special education classes, 71 per cent of the learning disabled, and 80 per cent of the emotionally disturbed. Nearly three-fourths of all school suspensions are of boys. By adolescence, boys are more likely to drop out, flunk out, and act out in class. Their self-esteem also drops during adolescence—not, admittedly, as much as girls' self-esteem, but it does drop.[19]

These data are often used to suggest that boys, not girls, are the new victims of significant gender discrimination in schools. After all, what happens to boys in schools? They have to sit quietly, raise their hands, be obedient—all of which does extraordinary violence to their 'natural', testosterone-inspired, rambunctious playfulness. 'Schools for the most part are run by women for girls. To take a high spirited second or third grade boy and expect him to behave like a girl in school is asking too much', comments Christina Hoff Sommers, author of *The War Against Boys*. The effect of education is 'pathologizing boyhood'. 'On average, boys are physically more restless and more impulsive (than girls)', comments school consultant Michael Thompson.

'We need to acknowledge boys' physical needs, and meet them'. While we've been paying all this attention to girls' experiences—raising their self-esteem, enabling them to take science and math, deploring and preventing harassment and bullying—we've ignored the boys. 'What about the boys?' asks the backlash chorus.[20]

Make no mistake: Boys' needs do merit our serious attention, and many parents are clearly concerned not just about national indicators but about their own sons. Recently, Leonard Sax published his *Boys Adrift* to massive popular acclaim. This study promises to decode the 'epidemic' of underachievement among boys and young men, and some of Sax's arguments and data are compelling (despite the self-help tone of the book and its 'Five Factors'). Sax argues that boys are in trouble, and their trouble is caused by a combination of inappropriate teaching methods, video-game use, the over prescription of drugs like Ritalin, devaluation of masculinity, and environmental endocrine disruptors. The book has been successful enough to permit Sax to quit medical practice in favour of full-time advocacy and speaking tours.[21]

Sax makes some excellent points about the over diagnosis of ADHD, effects of environmental toxins on children, and the harms of the gaming obsessions now so common among young men. However, his desire to prove that boys' *biological* needs are being neglected by society leads him perilously close to simplistic biological determinism. For example, he claims that boys universally tend to draw action rather than people, using a limited and monochrome palette, and that teachers discourage and diminish boys by asking them to use more colour and draw people. It's difficult to understand how this drawing style is an expression of some inherent sex tendency given the long-term achievements of men in fields like, for example, figure painting. (The tradition of Western painting, as any visit to the Louvre will tell you, has long been dominated by men—and they used colours and drew faces!) Do boys paint black cars because of their biology, or because of boy culture? (And what did they draw before cars came along?)

As we've seen, there is little evidence that boys' aggression is biologically based. Rather, we understand that the negative consequences of boys' aggression are largely the social by-product of exaggerating otherwise healthy and pleasurable boisterous and rambunctious play. (And girls too are quite capable of being boisterous and rambunctious.) Why do boys exaggerate their play in this way? So that they may better fit in with other boys. As boys grow and learn the expectations of adults and their peer culture, they over conform to the expectations of their peers. Some people think that concerns about boys' aggression are all about 'controlling' boys' naturally exuberant and physical play because of hysterical fear. Sax, for example, marshals examples of foolish exaggerations of 'zero tolerance' policies on guns, which he refers to as 'zero intelligence'—cases in which students were sent home for brandishing a two-dimensional 'gun', or for bringing a miniature GI Joe weapon to school. But there are many boys and girls who can testify to the less innocuous practices of boys' aggression. Instead of uncritically celebrating 'boy culture', we might inquire instead into the experience when boys cease being themselves and begin to posture and parade an exaggerated masculinity before the evaluative eyes of other boys.[22]

We might inquire into the experience of the majority of boys (according to the AAUW study cited above) who are harassed in school, generally but not exclusively by other boys, and generally through the assertion of sexual dominance ('suck my dick!'). Another frequent and pervasive form of sexual harassment of boys in school is the policing of heterosexuality and normative masculinity. Most commonly, this occurs through abusive imputations of homosexuality ('sissy', or more commonly today, even in elementary schools, 'faggot!'). For **LGBTQ** students, these comments (and the acts of violence that sometimes accompany them) dramatically limit feelings of safety. According to a 2008 survey by Egale Canada, 75 per cent of LGBTQ students feel unsafe at school, and half of straight students agree that their schools are unsafe for LGBTQ people. For all students, the daily reiteration of 'faggot', 'dyke', and 'that's so gay' reinforce the messages that abuse and domination are OK, that heterosexuality is the norm, and that non-heterosexuals are fair game.[23]

Accusations of homosexuality provide a way to police heterosexuality, but as every student reading this knows, they are also a way to police gender and punish those, gay or straight, who don't conform to stereotypical gender norms. Here is Dave, explaining how he 'knows' if a guy is gay: 'if they show any sign of weakness or compassion, then other people jump to conclusions and bring them down. So really it's a survival of the fittest. It's not very good to be sensitive. If you have no feeling or compassion or anything like that, you will survive'. Or listen to the words of famous American gender theorist Eminem. When asked in 2001 why he was always rapping about 'faggots', Eminem replied that calling someone a 'faggot' is not a slur on his sexuality, but rather on his gender. 'The lowest degrading thing that you can say to a man . . . is to call him a faggot and try to take away his manhood. Call him a sissy. Call him a punk. "Faggot" to me doesn't mean gay people. "Faggot" just means taking away your manhood'.[24]

Perhaps the central mechanism that maintains gender inequality in schools is the way boys see success in terms of gender conformity. High schools have become far more than academic testing grounds; they're the central terrain on which gender identity is tested and demonstrated. And unlike the standardized tests for reading and arithmetic, the tests of adequate and appropriate gender performance are administered and graded by your peers, by grading criteria known only to them.

In one study of middle and high school students in Midwestern US towns, 88 per cent reported having observed bullying, and 77 per cent reported being a victim of bullying at some point during their school years. Another national survey of 15,686 students in grades six to ten published in the *Journal of the American Medical Association* (JAMA) found that 29.9 per cent reported frequent involvement with bullying—13 per cent as bully, 10.9 per cent as victim, and 6 per cent as both. One-quarter of kids in primary school, grades four to six, admitted to bullying another student with some regularity in the three months before the survey. And yet another survey found that during one two-week period at two Los Angeles middle schools, nearly half the 192 kids interviewed reported being bullied at least once. More than that said they had seen others targeted.[25]

Most of the kids who are targeted cope; they're resilient enough or have enough emotional resources to survive reasonably intact. Many try valiantly, and often vainly, to fit in, to conform to these impossible standards that others set for them. Some carry psychological or even physical scars for the rest of their lives. Some withdraw, become depressed, alienated, or despondent. Some self-medicate with drugs or alcohol. (And a few boys explode. There have been well over 50 school shootings in North America since 1980, some of which have been linked to bullying.)[26]

But bullying harms kids profoundly. If we considered the moment when one boy becomes 'the fag' and the other an abuser, we might find a psychological 'disconnect', equivalent to that observed by Carol Gilligan with young girls. Gilligan and her associates described the way that assertive, confident, and proud young girls 'lose their voices' when they hit adolescence. It is the first full-fledged confrontation with gender inequality that produces the growing gender gap in adolescence.

Gender inequality means that just at the moment when girls lose their voice, boys *find* one—but it is the inauthentic voice of hegemonic masculinity: of bravado, of constant posturing, of foolish risk taking and gratuitous violence. According to psychologist William Pollack, boys learn that they are supposed to be in power and thus begin to act like it. 'Although girls' voices have been disempowered, boys' voices are strident and full of bravado', he observes. 'But their voices are disconnected from their genuine feelings'. Thus, he argues, the way we bring boys up leads them to put on a 'mask of masculinity', a posture, a front. They 'ruffle in a manly pose', as the poet William Butler Yeats put it, 'for all their timid heart'.[27]

Boys' bravado may dampen their achievements. In one recent study, sociologist Shelley Correll compared thousands of eighth-graders in similar academic tracks and with identical grades and test scores. Boys were much more likely—remember, their scores and grades were identical—to say, 'I have always done well in math' and 'Mathematics is one of my best subjects' than were the girls. The boys were no better than the girls—they just thought they were.[28]

This difference, and not some putative discrimination against boys, is the reason why girls' mean test scores in math and science are now, on average, approaching those of boys. While girls tend to devalue their abilities and study more, too many boys who overvalue their abilities remain in difficult math and science courses longer than they should; they pull the boys' mean scores down. A parallel process is at work in the humanities and social sciences. Girls' mean test scores in English and foreign languages, for example, also outpace boys' scores. But this is not because of 'reverse discrimination', but rather because the boys bump up against the norms of masculinity. Boys regard English as a 'feminine' subject. The research by Shelley Correll, for example, found those same boys who had inflated their abilities in math suddenly rated themselves as worse than their female classmates in English and languages.[29]

Pioneering research in Australia by Wayne Martino and his colleagues found that boys are uninterested in English because of what an interest might say about their (inauthentic) masculine pose. 'Reading is lame, sitting down and looking at words is pathetic', commented one boy. 'Most guys who like English are faggots' (that word again!), commented another. The traditional liberal arts curriculum is seen as feminizing; as Catharine Stimpson recently put it sarcastically, 'real men don't speak French'.[30]

It is not the school experience that 'feminizes' boys, but rather the ideology of traditional masculinity that keeps boys from wanting to succeed. 'The work you do here is girls' work', one boy commented to a researcher. 'It's not real work'. Added another, '[w]hen I go to my class and they [other boys] bunk off, they will say to me I'm a goody

goody'. Such comments echo the consistent findings of social scientists since James Coleman's path-breaking 1961 study that identified the 'hidden curriculum' among adolescents in which good-looking and athletic boys were consistently more highly rated by their peers than were good students.[31]

What is the hidden curriculum for boys? Simply, hegemonic masculinity. Boys learn that to 'succeed' in school is to be a 'bad lad', in Leanne Dalley-Trim's phrase. They learn that real men don't value academic achievement, or as one forthcoming student in one of Jacqueline's classes put it, that 'in high school, doing honours chemistry or something is for wusses'. They learn that sexual harassment (of girls and of each other) is a handy way to establish domination. And they learn, above all, to disguise their own vulnerability. To be sure, we should not confuse exuberance with disruptive behaviour; but viewing disruptive behaviour as boy's biological imperative, rather than as their performance of a masculine stereotype, won't help us either.[32]

Challenging stereotypes, decreasing tolerance for school violence, and decreasing bullying enable both boys and girls to feel safer at school. Those who would simply throw up their hands in resignation and sigh that 'boys will be boys' would have you believe that nothing can or should be done to make those classrooms safer. Indeed, those four words, 'boys will be boys', may be the most depressing words in educational policy circles today.[33]

The classroom is not immune to the strong influences emanating from popular culture, which celebrates a particularly limited form of masculinity (as we shall see in Chapter 9). But to create a healthier school experience for adolescents of both sexes, what is needed is not a return to simplistic notions of gender difference, but a commitment to addressing the ways in which gender cultures and gender ideologies themselves produce such radical gender divergence in adolescence—to the detriment of both sexes.

Where are the Men? The Post-Secondary 'Crisis'

As recently as 10 years ago, discussions of gender and post-secondary education were most likely to discuss the 'chilly classroom climate' for female students or equity among male and female faculty members.[34] Today, a new concern has arisen. Women's participation in post-secondary education continues its upward trajectory, which we can see as a trend that began well over a century ago when women fought to gain access to university classrooms. Across North America—and in most of the high-income countries belonging to the Organization for Economic Co-operation and Development—women now constitute the majority of students on college campuses.

Women now outnumber men in the social and behavioural sciences by about three to one, and they've made inroads into such traditionally male bastions as engineering, where they now make up about 20 per cent of all students, and biology and business, where the genders are virtually on par. In 2004, for the first time, most graduating Canadian medical students were women. The growth in female participation in post-secondary education has caused some hysterical comment. One reporter, obviously a terrible statistics student, tells us that if present trends continue, 'the graduation line in 2068 will be all females'.[35]

But the numbers cited by critics conceal some interesting variations. First, enrolments are in general going up. In 1990, only 28 per cent of young Canadian adults aged 20 to 24 were enrolled in some form of post-secondary education (PSE: for example, university, college, or trades training). By 2006, that rate had increased to 40 per cent. However, in both Canada and the USA, women's enrolments are increasing much more quickly than those of men. In 2006, 44 per cent of Canadian women were enrolled in PSE, versus 36 per cent of their male counterparts. In the USA, the 'female majority' means that women now face tougher admission competition in private institutions, which are permitted to discriminate on the basis of sex to maintain gender balance.

Second, the female 'majority' is only at the undergraduate level. Men in the US still obtain most of the doctorates and professional degrees. And finally, men still outnumber women at the top schools. Of the eight traditional 'Ivy League' universities in the USA, six have male majorities. And that doesn't even begin to approach the gender disparities at the top technical universities. Nor does anyone seem driven to distraction about the gender disparities in nursing, social work, or education, traditionally far lower-paid occupations than those professions where men still predominate (engineering and computer sciences).

Those who suggest that feminist-inspired reforms have been to the detriment of boys seem to believe that gender relations are a zero-sum game and that if girls and women gain, boys and men lose. In fact, however, the reasons for the gender gap in postsecondary education may not be as simple as women's gains at the expenses of men. According to Michael Hoy, an economist at Guelph University, the gender imbalance in university exists because women can expect a higher '**educational premium**' than can men. That is, because women traditionally have had poor access to well-paid jobs unless they have advanced education, they are more willing to enrol in PSE. Or as one of Jacqueline's students put it, 'guys can get good jobs in the bush without it, so why go to school?'

The danger, of course, is that as Canada's economy shifts and resource-extraction-based jobs diminish, many men may find themselves without the qualifications for other kinds of work. And we probably should pay attention to signs that some young men may be 'dropping out'; for example, the number of young men who spend more than seven hours a week playing video games. But women have not 'taken' men's places at university. In fact, affordability, accessibility, and class are the real issues, and they're pretty gender-neutral. This is not to say that we shouldn't worry about young men's apparently opting out of PSE; but we need to go beyond the simplistic understandings that dominate media coverage.[36]

The 'battle of the sexes' is not a zero-sum game-whether it is played out in our schools, our workplaces, or our bedrooms. Both women *and* men, girls *and* boys will benefit from real gender equality in education. 'Every step in the advancement of woman has benefited our own sex no less than it has elevated her', was how an editorial in the Amherst College (Massachusetts) campus newspaper, *The Amherst Student*, put it when the school first debated co-education at the turn of the twentieth century.[37]

The School as Gendered Workplace

Just as historically women and girls were excluded from the classroom as students, so too were women excluded from the profession of teaching. In the eighteenth and nineteenth centuries, teaching had been seen as a respectable profession for a man. But the mid- to late-nineteenth-century gender ideology of the 'separation of spheres' meant that women were pushed out of other arenas of work, and they soon began to see elementary education as a way they could fulfill both their career aspirations and their domestic functions of maternal nurturance.

This coincided conveniently with the expansion of public elementary school education. Remember that nineteenth-century budgets for education and social services were minuscule compared to ours. Public education was therefore expanding dramatically at a time when it was woefully underfunded. The solution, according to Alvin Finkel,

> . . . was to hire young women as the teaching force and pay them miserable salaries on the grounds that they would supposedly soon marry and leave teaching to be supported financially by their husbands. In contrast, men were employed at relatively decent wages for the positions of superintendents, inspectors, principals, and headmasters. As in the health field, there was a gender hierarchy for the workforce that left women in a subordinate position to men.[38]

As a result, elementary education became 'feminized'. This meant that the occupational prestige and salaries of teachers dropped, discouraging men from entering the field and ensuring that it would become even more populated by women. Teaching was 'women's work'. (Or more correctly, 'spinster's work', since women who married were expected to leave the teaching workforce; 'marriage bans' were common throughout North America until the 1940s.)[39] But school administration has remained largely a masculine arena. Thus the school came to resemble every other social institution in North American society.

The frightful consequences of a female teaching force were much debated at the start of the twentieth century. Some warned of the 'invasion' of women teachers as if it were the 'Invasion of the Boy Snatchers'. One of the founders of American psychology, J. McKeen Cattell, worried about this 'vast horde of female teachers' to whom boys were exposed. In a foreshadowing of Leonard Sax's argument, commentators argued that this had serious consequences. A boy taught by a woman, one admiral believed, would 'render violence to nature', causing 'a feminized manhood, emotional, illogical, non-combative'. Another worried that 'the boy in America is not being brought up to punch another boy's head or to stand having his own punched in a healthy and proper manner'.[40]

Throughout the twentieth century, women still held most of the primary education positions and virtually all positions in pre-kindergarten and special education. Only during the Depression, when opportunities for men contracted severely, did Canadian men enter normal school (teachers' college) in substantial numbers. In 1994, 72.5 per cent of all US public and private school teachers were women, and 60 per cent of women teachers were in the elementary grades. At about the same time in Canada, about 60 per cent of teachers were women. That number had increased to 69 per cent by 2005.

Male teachers, both in Canada and the USA, tend to cluster in secondary education, and are much more likely to enter administration. (In Canada, only 16 per cent of school principals are women.) In addition, the percentage of teachers who are male is dropping in North America and Europe, prompting one Ontario report to call for vigorous attempts to attract men to the profession. Ontario is not alone; one Irish article claims that the decline in male teachers is 'robbing boys of their role models'. Often, according to Wayne Martino and Michael Kehler of the University of Western Ontario, the call for male teachers is driven by a 'recuperative masculinity politics'. That is, the media have created a '**moral panic**' based on the idea of rampant fatherlessness and a lack of appropriate role models, which they blame for social ills. The manly male teacher, therefore, needs to ride in and save boyhood from feminization. The idea rests on, and celebrates, the value of traditional hegemonic masculinity and interplanetary gender difference.[41]

But despite these impassioned calls, men are not flooding the classrooms of North America (or anywhere else, for that matter). Men are dissuaded from entering teaching by stereotypes about men in female-dominated professions and, some say, because they are afraid of allegations of sexual misconduct. But the major reason why men don't flood into teaching is related to the pay. As we'll see in Chapter 8, sex composition of the labour force is related to its salary structure. It is virtually axiomatic that the greater the proportion of women in the field, the lower the salary.

This has several implications. The first relates to female teachers; within the educational field, women continue to earn less money than men doing the same jobs. Some of this is explained by qualifications, but one careful study removed that kind of variable and found that 'salary discrimination against female teachers exists in all high school sectors'. At every level of the educational system, men continue to out earn their female colleagues.

The second implication of the teaching salary structure relates to men. While they may often be better paid than their female colleagues, it should be noted that salaries in teaching are low compared to salaries in male-dominated professions and trades. This is particularly true in the USA, where a study in the 1990s found that median earnings of male teachers were 18 per cent below the median earnings of male professionals, and even below the median earnings of men with Bachelor's degrees, though many teachers had Master's degrees. (The study yielded inconclusive results for female teachers, because women 'still earn substantially less in the marketplace than men'.) And the situation has been getting worse, according to Statistics Canada data and analysis; between 1981 and 2001 real wages declined 'in female-dominated disciplines, such as health and education', while real wages in areas such as engineering, mathematics, and computer science increased.[42]

Should we then be surprised that the number of men in these female-dominated fields declined along with wages? While it is recognized that teaching salaries aren't attractive to men, too often media coverage slips into arguing that men can't enter teaching because of their 'breadwinner role' (more on that in the next chapter) rather than recognizing that both male and female teachers are underpaid relative to other professions, and that teaching, like operating heavy equipment or doing an energy audit, is hard work—even if most of the people who do it are women.

The heroic male teacher, Hollywood style

For more than 50 years, the movies have been grappling with the role of the teacher in inspiring, mentoring, and saving at-risk students. The first of these films was 1955's *Blackboard Jungle*, with its rock-and-roll soundtrack and its edgy tale of a white teacher confronting unruly and cynical black youth.

Twelve years later, the actor who played one of those cynical youths got his chance to be the teacher-hero. 1967's *To Sir, With Love* starred Sidney Poitier as the idealistic American (and black) teacher saddled with a room full of working-class, mainly white, hard-bitten London teenagers. The movie, which also spawned a hit song, was a huge success, and put a new kind of hero on the map: the 'teacher-saviour', in the words of William Ayers.

According to Ayers, the teacher-saviour is the teacher who recognizes that schools are in the business of saving students. While his colleagues, 'the slugs', aren't up to the challenge, the teacher-saviour is marked not necessarily by his overwhelming success but by his refusal to give up on students. This teacher just won't abandon the kids, no matter what, and therefore wins their grudging respect and transforms lives.[43]

Twenty years after *Sir*, Edward James Olmos starred in yet another successful teacher movie, *Stand and Deliver* (1989). In this film, based on a true story (they usually are), Olmos played a high-school mathematics teacher confronted with—you guessed it—a hard-bitten, unruly, largely Latino class of underachievers, this time in East Los Angeles. He never gives up on his students, not even when they are accused of cheating on a major exam. In the end, the students perform brilliantly on a repeat math exam, succeeding academically, exonerating themselves, and validating their teacher's pedagogy and courage.

The saviour-teacher is not always found in the inner-city classroom, however. In the same year that *Stand and Deliver* was released, Robin Williams starred in his own teacher movie, *Dead Poets' Society.* In this film, the teacher faces not an unruly mob but a pack of prep-school conformists. The result, however, is the same; Williams teaches these academically solid, privileged boys how to live life consciously and fully.

You may have noticed something about this list of movies. If the male teacher is a minority in the classroom, he's a dominant figure on the big screen. Indeed, it's pretty hard to find a female teacher to place in the company of these icons (and the others we haven't even mentioned). Drew Barrymore's Ms Pomeroy from 2001's *Donnie Darko* is a nuanced character, but she is hardly the focus of the movie (and is counterbalanced by a highly stereotypical portrayal of an uptight, aging female teacher). Female teachers are usually a support to storylines rather than their focus and are often stereotyped as obstacles to the main characters rather than as mentors or role models.

One exception from the 1990s can be found in *Dangerous Minds*, a 1995 release loosely based on the true story of a Marine who became a teacher of—that's right—a group of hard-bitten inner-city children. Though it's hard to imagine a more feminine actor than Michelle Pfeiffer, it's interesting to see how her image transforms through the movie, as she takes on some of the masculine characteristics of the typical saviour teacher. By the film's end, she is much tougher, right down to her black leather jacket.

The male teacher-hero is often an outsider. If he's white, perhaps he is a loner coming from some failure in the past. He may also be constructed as the white saviour of otherwise helpless people of colour, a tendency seen in 1974's *Conrack* (and, though with a female lead, *Dangerous Minds*). If he's from an ethnic minority, he's battling the odds, showing that with moral rectitude, education, and guts, anyone can succeed. Whether he's white or of colour, to succeed in his difficult task, he has to fight: *for* his students (usually against unfeeling administrators) and even *against* his students, as in *Blackboard Jungle, To Sir, with Love* and *Stand and Deliver.* In short, he has to teach his students through example (and through his own brutal trials) what it means to be a man.

Our obsession with teacher-heroes, or antiheroes, isn't all bad. Teachers are important role models to many children, and for children with troubled families, a teacher can be a hero and a lifeline. But we should ask ourselves why these heroic teachers are so often male, and why so many of the ideas associated with hegemonic masculinity are repeated in these films.

Sometimes these pop-culture stereotypes can even colour our views of real teachers. For example, a recent survey of New Zealand school principals found that they wanted more male teachers (only 18 per cent of Kiwi teachers are male); but they didn't want just *any* men. While rugby-playing 'real men' were sought as appropriate 'role models' and 'father figures', effeminate men were distrusted. In one case, a principal described passing over male candidates with 'limp handshakes' in favour of 'strong' female candidates. (You can probably see where the principal in question was going with this: As Martino and Kehler argue, homophobia is often part of the discussion of the need for male teachers.)

In the wake of this study, one interesting thing happened; one teacher's college put up a billboard recruiting male students with an image of a man knitting and the slogan 'Real Men Teach (and Knit)'. Rather than trying to prove how macho male teachers could be, perhaps by showing one jumping out of a plane or pumping iron, this particular training institute decided to take on limiting stereotypes of masculinity. So even if Hollywood and some principals don't always know it, boys and men are changing, and our view of the male teacher should too. So watch the big screen— you may see a knitting teacher-hero there sometime soon.[44]

If the number of male teachers has declined at the elementary and secondary levels, the number of women teaching at the post-secondary level has increased. In 1999, women were 29.2 per cent of full-time university professors; by 2005 this had increased to 35.5 per cent. The percentage of women teaching full-time at college was even greater. The same increase has occurred in the USA. The division of labour that saw women dominate primary education while men shared primary education and dominated higher education is now changing. Increasingly, *all* teaching is becoming a women's profession.

The implications of women's greater presence in post-secondary teaching are not necessarily that gender equity is even close to having been achieved. As the statistics above indicate, women are less and less represented the higher up the educational ladder one climbs. In the USA, more than two-thirds of women teach at two- and four-year colleges; men are equally divided between research universities and all other institutions. And the 'uneven distribution of the sexes within academia', noted by sociologist Martin Trow in

1975, continues. Men continue to dominate in sciences, where teaching loads are lower and the number of research and teaching assistants is highest. For example, women make up 45 per cent of all lecturers, 35 per cent of all assistant professors, 25 per cent of all associate professors, and about 10 per cent of all professors in the sciences and engineering. By contrast, women dominate in the semi-professions (nursing, social work, education) and those fields that require significant classroom contact, like languages.[45]

Women also dominate the ranks of the most populous arena of post-secondary teaching—untenured lecturers and instructors. Part-time instructors, victims of both an educational glut and covert gender discrimination, currently teach up to one-half of all university classes, yet they are paid by the course or hired on yearly contracts. In Canada in 1999, only about 15 per cent of university professors were non-permanent; by 2005, the proportion had more than doubled, to almost a third. In the USA, well over half of such 'flexible workers' are women. Only about one-third of untenured women are on the tenure track in the USA. In Canada, while 88 per cent of male faculty members are either tenured or on the tenure track, only 65 per cent of women are either tenured or in positions that could get them **tenure**. And if women are underrepresented on the tenure track, they are a tiny percentage of senior-level university administrators.[46]

One reason for this disparity, of course, is that just like in all other workplaces, the efforts to balance work and family fall disproportionately on women's shoulders. At all ranks, and in all types of educational institutions, female professors and teachers with children spend much more time on family life (child care, care for aging parents and relatives, housework) than do their male counterparts.[47] Balancing work and family remains an obstacle to women's advancement in education—just as it does in every other workplace.

The classroom, then, remains gendered. This is true whether it's a kindergarten class or a fourth-year university seminar. Changes have occurred; for example, more and more women are making it to the rank of full professor, where they have been greatly underrepresented. Moreover, the dual pay scales that once existed for male and female teachers are no more. But the overall feminization of the profession may have damaging consequences: not the feminization of male students, but declining status and wages for the vocation. Statistics Canada's finding that salaries for all educators rose more slowly than the average worker's compensation over recent years is an indication of what may await.

The Gender of Education Today

One might think that, after so many years of educational reform, and especially with much attention to the differences between girls and boys, things would be getting better. Simple enumeration of equality may not be the answer. One teacher told journalist Peggy Orenstein that after learning that teachers paid more attention to boys than to girls, she explained to the class that henceforth she was going to call on both sexes exactly equally and that to make sure she did, she would hold the attendance roster in her hand. What happened next surprised her. 'After two days the boys blew up', she told Orenstein. 'They started complaining and saying that I was calling on the girls more than them. I showed them it wasn't true and they had to back down. I kept on doing it, but for the boys, equality was hard to get used to; they perceived it as a big loss'.[48]

Jacqueline remembers a similar revelation in her undergraduate education in the late 1980s. In an English course in which students were discussing Chaucer, the professor separated the men and women. Each group would discuss The Miller's Tale while the other group listened silently. The women went first, and stood silently while the men discussed the tale and its ribald humour. However, when it was the women's turn, the male students repeatedly interrupted the discussion. The professor looked on smiling; of course, he had suspected that would happen, and there's nothing a teacher likes better than when a lesson goes according to plan!

Seriously, however, equality is virtually always seen as a loss by the privileged group. If a teacher gives exactly equal time to heterosexuality and to homosexuality, to people of colour and to white people, to women and to men, he or she is invariably going to be criticized as being biased in favour of the 'minority' group (even when, as in the case of women, that group is a majority). To some degree, this has happened with education. As girls' achievements have grown, a system originally designed for boys is now seen as 'girl-friendly' and 'boy-hostile'. The nature of the system is invoked to explain increasingly sex-differentiated student achievement. (Interestingly, there wasn't much of a debate about that when girls' achievements lagged.) At the same time, we have surveyed the very real problems faced by students in the gendered classroom, and these problems need addressing.

So what is the answer? A return to single-sex schools? Many educators think so. There are now hundreds of single-sex schools in the USA (49 of them public), with 'a handful of pioneers' in Canada. Many school districts are experimenting with single-sex schools or single-sex classrooms. In the USA, there have been notable experiments with single-sex schools for black boys and girls. In a sense, such schools propose a 'racial' or 'gender' remedy for a problem of 'class'—because *children*, both boys and girls, would no doubt thrive in schools with lot of resources, small classes, and fabulously trained teachers. Kenneth Clark, the pioneering African-American educator, was unmoved by the call for single-sex classrooms for black kids. 'I can't believe that we're actually regressing like this. Why are we still talking about segregating and stigmatizing black males?' he asked. (He should know: His research provided the empirical argument against 'separate but equal' schools in the US Supreme Court's landmark *Brown v Board of Education* civil rights decision in 1954.)[49]

Still, such schools have produced results in academic achievement, pride, school completion, and behavioural change that should be respected. For boys at high risk of dropout and gang involvement, for example, strict discipline, exposure to male mentors who think that learning is cool, encouragement, and high expectations combine to produce powerful results. Small wonder that the principal of Brooklyn's Excellence Charter School calls what he's doing 'the new civil rights movement'.[50]

As to the educational outcomes of single-sex schooling, the research is inconclusive.[51] Much of the earliest research on single-sex schools failed to isolate all of the variables in its quest to prove that single-sex was better. For example, single-sex schools are, for the most part, *private* schools, with all of the advantages that implies. They also tend to offer a more structured and formal environment with rigorous expectations; that, rather than the same-sex environment, might produce changes in achievement and behaviour. Still, there are suggestive signs that girls learn better in same-sex classrooms, that they are more willing to enter 'non-traditional' subjects, and, interestingly, that they score better on particular self-esteem indicators. Most recently, a study conducted at the

University of California found that graduates of girls' schools scored higher on the Standard Admissions Test (SAT) and had greater confidence in math and computing. For boys the results regarding achievement are less consistent.[52]

In the 1990s, much of the discussion about single-sex schooling was about overcoming the disabilities of a gendered society. So girls, the argument went, would be served by schools that gave them confidence to explore non-traditional areas and to see their bodies in terms of mastery instead of sexiness. In some ways, those sentiments are still alive. Leonard Sax (yes, that's right, the author of *Boys Adrift* and also a powerful advocate of single-sex schooling) says that in single-sex schools, boys can overcome gender stereotypes; 'the jocks and the geeks can become one and the same'. Surely overcoming the boundaries created by normative masculinity is a good thing.[53]

But today, many single-sex schools seem increasingly to buy into rigid gender norms. It's difficult not to feel concerned about some of the stereotyping associated with the promotion of one-sex environments. Sax claims that of the 360 single-sex schools in the USA today, about 300 are founded on 'neuroscience'. That is, they subscribe to a particular interpretation of the difference between male and female brains. That produces such bases for curriculum as the ideas that girls are scared of snakes; that boys can't hear, smell, or see as well; that boys need to be moving to learn; that a girl, on the other hand, needs to 'share something from her own life that relates to the content in class' in order to learn; and so on.[54]

The proposals for single-sex schools seem often to be based on such facile, and incorrect, assessments of some biologically based different educational 'needs' or learning styles. Listen to a statement from the National Association for Single Sex Public Education:

> Girls and boys differ fundamentally in the learning *style* they feel most comfortable with. Girls tend to look on the teacher as an ally. Given a little encouragement, they will welcome the teacher's help. A girl-friendly classroom is a safe, comfortable, welcoming place. Forget hard plastic chairs: put in a sofa and some comfortable beanbags . . . The teacher should never yell or shout at a girl. Avoid confrontation. Avoid the word 'why' . . . Girls will naturally break up in groups of three and four to work on problems. Let them. Minimize assignments that require working alone. (www.singlesexschools.org)

Most female readers of this statement will be offended by the condescending message. 'Avoid the word "why"?' Wouldn't that pretty much defeat the purpose of education? And what does it assume is a sound pedagogical philosophy for boys? Answer: Make the classroom dangerous and inhospitable, seat students on uncomfortable chairs, yell at them, confront them, and always ask why. To put it as charitably as possible, perhaps such organizations believe they have the best interests of children at heart. They base their claims, though, on the flimsiest of empirical evidence and the wildest of stereotypical assertions. Every day, real boys and girls prove such insulting stereotypes wrong.

What's more, isn't it the role of schools, and education in general, to take us *out* of our comfort zones? To expose us to new experiences and expectations, and thus to make us something more than what we were when we came in? One of the most compelling aspects of the new single-sex schools is the way they call forth the best from students through what are, for many children, novel social experiences and expectations: formality, decorum, civility, respect, punctuality, responsibility.

But when it comes to gender, single-sex schools increasingly retreat into hackneyed stereotype. The findings of the only systematic study of a pilot program for single-sex schools in California reported rather depressing results. Traditional gender stereotypes remained in full effect; in fact, such schools actually perpetuated stereotypes that girls are good and boys are bad, which should prompt some reconsideration from those who want to 'rescue' boys from meddling feminists. In the end, after three years, five of the six school districts closed their single-sex academies.[55]

Let's just accept these ideas of radical difference for a moment, for the sake of argument. It may well be true, as University of Saskatchewan professor Trevor Gambell suggests, that boys don't want to read books with female protagonists. But shouldn't that be a reason to encourage them to do so rather than a reason to redefine the curriculum so that boys never have to identify with a girl? And it may be true that many girls are more likely to relate class materials to their own lives. But shouldn't that be a reason to find ways to show them the beauty of pure abstraction?[56]

John Dewey, perhaps the USA's greatest theorist of education and a fierce supporter of women's equal rights, was infuriated at the contempt for women suggested by such ideas. Dewey scoffed at 'female botany,' 'female algebra,' and for all I know a 'female multiplication table,' he wrote in 1911. 'Upon no subject has there been so much dogmatic assertion based on so little scientific evidence, as upon male and female types of mind'.

Though Dewey himself stereotyped the sexes, his discussion of the benefits of coeducation is revealing, because he thought that education should not just reproduce who we are but change it for the better. Coeducation, Dewey argued, is beneficial to women, opening up opportunities previously unattainable. Girls, he suggested, become less manipulative and acquire 'greater self-reliance and a desire to win approval by deserving it instead of by 'working' others. Their narrowness of judgment, depending on the enforced narrowness of outlook, is overcome; their ultra-feminine weaknesses are toned up'. What's more, Dewey claimed, coeducation is beneficial to men. 'Boys learn gentleness, unselfishness, courtesy; their natural vigour finds helpful channels of expression instead of wasting itself in lawless boisterousness', he wrote.[57]

Truly transformative education, instead of encouraging only one sex to ask why, encourages that question constantly, of all its students, and of its own practices and pedagogy. In coming years, educators may continue to use single-sex schooling to combat the social woes of a society and peer culture that put incredible, and gendered, pressures on both girls and boys. But as with the family, the form of education is probably much less important than its content. One can only hope that our schools (whether single-sex or coeducational) focus on content; and that they retreat from the kind of thinking that would retrench the most ridiculous (and damaging) of gender stereotypes.

Summary

School is the second primary socializing institution in the traditional sociological schema. We enter education as gendered beings, already exposed to gender difference and gender inequality through families, peers, religions, and media. The classroom reproduces these differences and the inequality that often goes with them.

Education was traditionally limited by sex and class, and in the modern world, has been limited by race. Until the nineteenth century, most Canadian children received very little education, and education was conducted under church auspices. By the late nineteenth century, formal education had expanded significantly, and primary education became mandatory in most provinces. Education was conceived of in gendered terms, particularly for boys who were to learn 'manliness'. In addition to being gendered, education was often segregated by race. At the same time, women were pressing to enter post-secondary education, from which they had been excluded. By 1900, about ten per cent of university students were women; not until the 1960s did women's participation rates increase dramatically. By the 1980s, female students had become the majority.

Today Canada's millions of students are schooled in an officially gender-neutral system. But unofficial gendering is still a large part of the classroom. Environments and play considered appropriate for one sex by teachers, parents, and peers may not be allowed to the other sex. The classroom also reproduces inequality in terms of the amount and nature of attention that students receive from teachers. Too often, teachers (like the rest of us) rely on 'common-sense' understandings of masculinity and reinforce stereotypes. Textbooks and children's storybooks also may reproduce stereotypical views of gender.

As students enter the secondary-school classroom, they encounter gender intensification both in their own thinking and in the environments around them. For girls, this often takes the form of steeply declining self-esteem. The classroom can be a chilly climate for high-school girls, and this is compounded by sexually hostile environments in many schools. Sexual harassment is a common problem for secondary-school girls.

Boys do not escape unscathed. Their self-esteem declines too, though not as precipitously as girls'. Boys are, however, much more prone to a number of problems, and demonstrate less academic success on average. While some argue that this is the result of a feminine education system geared to girls, a more plausible explanation sees cultural influences as the cause. Boys are the most frequent harassers of both boys and girls; but boys are harassed too. Homophobia and the aggressive reinforcement of hegemonic masculinity are the hallmarks of this kind of abuse. Boys (and men) have accounted for virtually every school shooting. Sometimes, boy shooters may be bullied outsiders. While most boys don't react this way, bullying clearly damages boys. Indeed, in adolescence many boys disconnect from their true selves in favour of an exaggerated masculinity that views core human values, and education, as signs of weakness. The problem, then, is not feminization of boys, but an exaggerated masculinization that equips them poorly for the world outside the gendered classroom.

At the post-secondary level, the female majority among students has commentators concerned. But men still outnumber women at the doctoral level and in professional degrees. Men are less likely to attend PSE than are women, probably because they perceive greater earning possibilities without advanced training. In the long run, this may be a poor strategy, given the long-term decline in well-paid resource-sector jobs.

Women also outnumber men in the teaching profession. The presence of women in teaching dates to the nineteenth-century expansion of education, when a cheap workforce was needed. In elementary and secondary schools, women became, and remain, a large and growing majority. This has prompted calls for the recruitment of more male teachers. Some have called this a moral panic, as media blame the lack of male teachers for a variety of social ills. Popular movies reinforce the idea that the saviour-teacher is almost always a male who can save his students from the worst social problems that today's youth face. The panic over male teachers also reinforces stereotyped notions of masculinity and gender difference. Men are less and less likely to be present in the classroom, though, largely because of teaching salaries. These salaries are lower than in male-dominated professions, and have been decreasing relative to those professions for over 20 years.

At the post-secondary level, the number of women instructors has increased dramatically, but women are still much more likely to be found in certain disciplinary areas and in non-permanent positions. The 'mommy track' accounts for some of this discrepancy.

As girls' achievements have grown within education, there is increasing concern about a decline in boys' relative performance. Single-sex education has arisen to address these concerns. There are some benefits, particularly social ones, to such education; the research on educational benefits, however, remains inconclusive. A particular concern with the recent explosion of such schools is that most base their curriculum on stereotypical and unsupported ideas about gender difference. In so doing, they may reinforce damaging stereotypes and limit students' growth. In the end, the key to education is not its form but its content; and truly transformative education will mean not retrenching, but changing, the rules of the gendered classroom.

Questions for Critical Thinking

1. Was there a 'hidden curriculum' in your elementary or high school(s)? What was it? Did it change from elementary to high school? Can you remember a point at which gender began to mean more to you and your peers?
2. Are you in favour of single-sex schooling? What are its advantages and disadvantages?
3. Do you think it important for the teaching force to contain both men and women? Why or why not?
4. Who plays a bigger part in the classroom for students: the teacher or peers?
5. Comparing the role of the family and the classroom in shaping children's gendered identities and attitudes, which do you think exerts greater influence?

Key Terms

chilly climate
educational premium
gender intensification
hidden curriculum
hostile environment
imperial manhood

LGBTQ
moral panic
self-esteem
sexual harassment
tenure
Title IX

Chapter 8

Separate and Unequal

The Gendered World of Work

We must make haste, for when we home are come,

We find again our Work but just begun;

So many things for our Attendance call,

Had we ten Hands, we could employ them all . . .

Yet without fail, soon as Daylight doth spring,

We in the Field again our work begin.

—MARY COLLIER, *THE WOMAN'S LABOUR* (1739)

Freud once wrote that the two great tasks for all human beings are 'to work and to love'. And it is certainly true that people have always worked—to satisfy their basic material needs for food, clothing, and shelter, to provide for children and loved ones, to participate in community life, as well as to satisfy more culturally and historically specific desires to leave a mark on the world and to move up the social ladder. So it shouldn't surprise us that virtually every society has developed a division of labour, a way of dividing the tasks that must be done in order for the society as a whole to survive. And because gender, as we have seen, is a system of both classification and identity and a structure of power relations, it shouldn't surprise us that virtually every society has a *gendered* division of labour. There are very few tasks, in very few societies, that are not allocated by gender. This doesn't necessarily imply that the tasks assigned to one gender are less or more significant to the life of the community than the tasks assigned to the other. One might use a variety of criteria to assign tasks, and one might determine the relative values of each in a variety of ways. Valuing women's work over men's work, or vice versa, is not inevitable; it is an artefact of cultural relationships.

All this hardly comes as a surprise. But what might surprise contemporary North American readers is that the gendered division of labour that many have called 'traditional', the separation of the world into two distinct spheres—the public sphere of work, business, politics, and culture and the private sphere of the home, domestic life, and child care—is a relatively new phenomenon. As we saw in Chapter 6, the doctrine of separate spheres was not firmly established until the nineteenth century, and even then it was honoured as much in the breach as in its fulfillment.

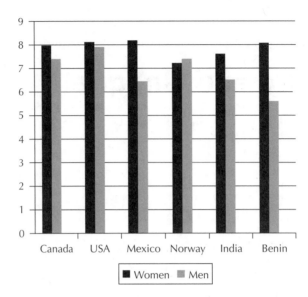

Figure 8.1 Hours worked per day, by gender, in selected nations.

In almost every nation, women work more hours each day than do men.

Source: United Nations, *Human Development Report, 2007/2008* (New York: United Nations Development Programme, 2007).

And what also might surprise us is that this universal gendered division of labour tells us virtually nothing about the relative values given to the work women and men do. And, interestingly, it turns out that in societies in which women's work is less valued—that is, in more traditional societies in which women's legal status is lower—women do *more* work than the men do, up to 35 per cent more in terms of time.

The Changing Gender Composition of the Labour Force

Perhaps the most significant change in the relationship of gender and work is the enormous shift in the gender composition of the labour force. In the twentieth century, the percentage of both women and men entering the labour force increased, but women's rate of increase far outpaced men's. In fact, while men's long-term rates have either stagnated or in some cases declined, the longitudinal trend for women is one of consistent increased participation. The percentage of women working rose from 16.2 per cent in 1911 to more than 62 per cent by 2008. Marriage and children slowed that entry, but the trajectory is still the same. While only 20 per cent of women workers in 1941 were married, by 1971 66 per cent were. And where few married women with children worked outside the home for much of the twentieth century, by 2003 more than 80 per cent of women in the 25–54 age group were working, despite the fact that these are also the years when women are most likely to have children at home. In recent years, women with children at home have been one of the fastest-growing groups in the labour force.

As of 2002, the participation rates for women with young and school-aged children stood at 71 and 82 per cent respectively. This dramatic increase in labour force participation has been true for all races and ethnicities, and in both Canada and the USA.[1]

Women's entry into the labour force has taken place at every level, from low-paid clerical and sales work through all the major professions. 'The increasing representation of women among the ranks of managers in organizations', writes sociologist Jerry Jacobs, 'is perhaps the most dramatic shift in the sex composition of an occupation since clerical work became a female dominated field in the late 19th century'.[2]

We've come a long way, indeed, from the mid-nineteenth century, when a young Mary Taylor wrote to her friend Charlotte Brontë that 'there are no means for a woman to live in England, but by teaching, sewing, or washing. The last is the best, the best paid, the least unhealthy and the most free'. These changes have rippled through the rest of society, gradually changing the relationship of the family to the workplace. Gone forever is the male breadwinner who supports a family on his income alone. Today, the norm is the dual-earner couple.[3]

The Persistence of Gender Ideologies

Such statements acknowledge that whereas the realities of home and workplace have changed, our ideas about them have lagged far behind. Many North Americans still believe in the 'traditional' **male breadwinner/female housewife model** even if our own lives no longer reflect it. Our adherence to gender ideologies that no longer fit the world we live in has dramatic consequences for women and men, both at work and at home.

Since the early nineteenth century, the workplace has been seen as a masculine arena, where men could test and prove their manhood against other men in the dog-eat-dog marketplace. Working enabled men to confirm their manhood as breadwinners and family providers. The workplace was a site of 'homosocial reproduction'—a place where men created themselves as men. As psychiatrist Willard Gaylin writes:

> nothing is more important to a man's pride, self-respect, status, and manhood than work. Nothing. Sexual impotence, like sudden loss of ambulation or physical strength, may shatter his self-confidence. But . . . pride is built on work and achievement, and the success that accrues from that work. Yet today men often seem confused and contradictory in their attitudes about work.[4]

Gaylin captures a contradiction at the heart of men's relationship to the workplace: On the one hand, it is the most significant place where men prove manhood and confirm identity, but on the other hand, proving oneself in the workplace can be lonely, insecure, and incompletely fulfilling. 'I have never met a man—among my patients or friends', Gaylin writes, 'who in his heart of hearts considers himself a success'.[5]

Yet why would men be unhappy in an arena whose homosociality they struggle so hard to maintain? Part of the reason relates to the workplace as a testing ground of masculinity. Here's one example. Though most married couples are now dual-earner couples, when the wife out earns the husband all sorts of assumptions might bubble up to the surface: His masculinity may no longer be tied to being the only worker, but rather it may be tied to making the most money to support the family. If he makes less than his wife does, both partners may engage in **deviance neutralization**, understating her income or exaggerating his contribution to preserve the idea of the male breadwin- ner. Both members of a couple may regard her work as more flexible no matter what she does. For example, psychologist Francine Deutsch found that a couple made up of a male physician and a female professor believed that academic work was more flexible, meaning that she should be the one to make accommodations for the sake of the cou- ple's children. A couple made up of a female physician and a male professor? Surpris- ingly (or not), both members of this couple regarded medical practice as more flexible than academic work.[6]

Still, gender ideologies about breadwinning are currently in much flux: A *News- week* poll found 25 per cent of respondents thought it unacceptable for a wife to earn more than her husband, but 35 per cent of men said they'd quit their jobs or reduce their hours if their wives earned more money. And though traditional gender stereo- types would have us believe that women would be content to marry less attractive but financially stable men (whereas men would be happier marrying very attractive women, without regard to finances), 50 per cent of American women now say that earning po- tential is 'not at all important' in their mate choice.[7]

If earning power relative to women is a fraught topic for men, another reason for male dissatisfaction has to do with the nature of the workplace. Given the demands of corporate or factory life, men rarely, if ever, experience any ability to discuss their inner lives, their feelings, their needs. The workplace becomes a treadmill, a place to fit in, not to stand out. Men often feel that they are supposed to be tough, aggressive, competitive— the 'king of the hill', the boss, their 'own man', on 'top of the heap'. Asked why he worked so hard, one man told an interviewer:

> I don't know . . . I really hate to be a failure. I always wanted to be on top of whatever I was doing. It depends on the particular picture but I like to be on top, either chair- man of the committee or president of an association or whatever.[8]

Most men, of course, are neither at the top of the hierarchy nor likely to get there. Raised to believe that there are no limits, they bump constantly into those limits and have no one to blame except themselves. And because men conflate masculinity with workplace success, they remain unaware that the work they are doing is also producing and reproducing gender dynamics; they see it as just 'work'.[9] Men, as the saying goes, are 'unsexed by failure': They cease to be seen as *real* men.

In the all-male workplaces of the twentieth century, women's role was often to 'lubri- cate' the male-male interactions. Many women performed what sociologist Arlie Hoch- schild calls 'emotion work', making sure that the masculine workplace was well-oiled and functioning smoothly. So, for example, women performed jobs like stewardess, office manager, cocktail waitress, and cheerleader to make sure the male-male interactions went smoothly—and remained unmistakably heterosexual.[10]

This view of women's work as 'auxiliary' was widely shared. The traditional idea was that women worked either because they *had* to—because they were single, working class, and/or the sole economic support for their children or themselves—or because they wanted to earn the extra pocket money ('play money') that they, as middle-class consumers, wanted for their trifles. This often made women's work seem somehow illegitimate, even to women themselves. After all, if real men proved themselves in the workplace, real women were supposed to be at home caring for their families. In fact, 90 per cent of Canadian women still say that it is 'definitely' or 'probably' preferable for a parent to stay home to raise young children. The same number of full-time women workers say that they would like to work part-time to spend more time with their families. But such a position belies women's actual experience and the complexity of the 'choices' involved in balancing work and family life. Women work, the political columnist Katha Pollitt writes, 'because we enjoy our jobs, our salaries, the prospect of a more interesting and secure future than we would have with rusted skills, less seniority, less experience'.[11]

The combination of the persistence of traditional gender ideologies and changes in economic and social realities makes today's workplace a particularly contentious arena for working out gender issues. On the one hand, women continue to face gender discrimination: They are paid less, promoted less, and assigned to specific jobs despite their qualifications and motivations, and they are sometimes made to feel unwelcome, like intruders in an all-male preserve. On the other hand, men say they are bewildered and angered by the changes in workplace policy that make them feel like they are 'walking on eggshells', fearful of making any kind of remark to a woman lest they be hauled into court for sexual harassment.

The Persistence of Gender Discrimination in the Workplace

For many years, the chief obstacle facing women who sought to enter the labour force was sex discrimination. Discrimination occurs when we treat people who are similar in different ways, or sometimes, when we treat people who are different in similar ways. For example, to exclude one race or gender from housing, educational opportunities, or employment would be a form of discrimination. On the other hand, people with certain physical disabilities are seen as legally *different* and thus deserving of antidiscrimination protection. Treating them 'the same' as able-bodied people—failing to provide wheelchair-accessible facilities, for example—is therefore also a form of discrimination.

In gender discrimination in the workplace, employers have historically referred to a variety of characteristics about women in order to exclude them, e.g., women don't really want to work; they don't need the money; they have different aptitudes and interests. It was assumed that women either couldn't do a job or that, if they could, they would neither want to nor need to do it. What these arguments share is a belief that the differences between women and men are decisive and that these differences are the source of women's and men's different experiences. Such arguments have also provided the rationale for race discrimination in employment and education. Today, there are no legal grounds for racial discrimination.

This is not completely true, however, when it comes to gender. Discrimination on the basis of gender is permissible, but only under the most exceptional of circumstances.

The basis for the discrimination may not rely on any stereotypic ideas about the differences between women and men, and the discrimination must be based on a '**bona fide occupational requirement**' (BFOR).

Consider, for example, the case of a nine-year-old girl who applies to work as a lifeguard at the beach. Denying her the job would not be a case of either gender or age discrimination because one would equally deny the job to a nine-year-old boy, and because age is a BFOR for the performance of the job.

While few jobs preclude workers of any identifiable group, job requirements may have the effect of discrimination. For instance, up until the 1970s, the RCMP (and many other Canadian police forces) had height and weight requirements for would-be cadets. These requirements made it very difficult for women and members of certain ethnic groups to enter the force in large numbers. What's more, these requirements bore little relation to the evolving character of policing. While the 6'2", 225-pound Mountie in red serge might have been an awe-inspiring sight, much of modern policing is considerably more complex than looking imposing. Thus height and weight requirements have been replaced by the more holistic Physical Abilities Requirement Evaluation (PARE), which measures a candidate's ability to perform a number of tasks related to apprehending a suspect, which is a bona fide and critical part of the job of policing.[12]

Few people today would uphold traditional exclusionary requirements of height and weight. But legal decisions also consider whether job-related tests like the PARE might themselves be discriminatory. A landmark decision of this kind was handed down by the Supreme Court of Canada in 1999, in a case brought by Tawney Meiorin, a BC firefighter. Meiorin had performed her job satisfactorily for several years when a new firefighters' fitness test was introduced. She failed one component of the test, and was therefore dismissed. She argued that the test was discriminatory (because of women's generally lower aerobic capacity) and invalid as a measure of a BFOR. The Supreme Court agreed, arguing that '[n]o credible evidence showed that the prescribed aerobic capacity was necessary for either men or women to perform the work of a forest firefighter safely and efficiently', and implementing a more stringent set of guidelines (often known as the **Meiorin test**) for employers to consider in establishing job-related requirements.[13]

Most legal cases of workplace discrimination have involved women bringing suit to enter formerly all-male workplaces. One interesting recent case, however, explored the other side of the coin. The Hooters restaurant chain was sued by several US men who sought employment as waiters in restaurants. Historically, Hooters hired only 'voluptuous' women to work as their 'scantily clad' bartenders and food servers. The male plaintiffs, and their lawyers, argued that such a policy violates equal employment statutes. Hooters countered that its restaurants provide 'vicarious sexual recreation' and that 'female sexuality is a bona fide occupation', citing other all-female occupations like Playboy Bunnies and the Rockettes. Hooters waitresses 'serve Buffalo wings with a side order of sex appeal', was the way one newspaper columnist put it. Company spokesman Mike McNeil claimed that Hooters doesn't sell food; it sells sex appeal—and 'to have female sex appeal, you have to be female'. The US Equal Employment Opportunity Commission (EEOC) quietly dropped its own investigation, saying it had better cases to pursue. Eventually, the case was settled out of court, with Hooters paying $3.75 million to the men and their attorneys and adding a few men to its staffs as bartenders—but not as waiters.[14]

Sex Segregation

Outright gender discrimination is extremely difficult to justify. But far more subtle and pervasive mechanisms maintain gender inequality. Perhaps the most ubiquitous of these is **sex segregation**, which, writes sociologist Barbara Reskin, 'refers to women's and men's concentration in different occupations, industries, jobs, and levels in workplace hierarchies'.

Segregation can be either 'horizontal' or 'vertical'. **Vertical segregation** refers to segregation associated with differences of education, experience, and skill within the same field. So in law, for example, there are legal secretaries, clerks, paralegal professionals, lawyers, and judges, among other workers, and the genders are represented differentially in these hierarchically ranked occupations. **Horizontal segregation** refers to segregation within occupations in different fields that are roughly similar in terms of educational and skill requirements, for example truck driving and secretarial work, or engineering and teaching. Thus sex segregation becomes, itself, a 'sexual division of paid labour in which men and women do different tasks, or the same tasks under different names or at different times and places'. Different occupations are seen as more appropriate for one gender or the other, and thus women and men are guided, pushed, or occasionally shoved into specific positions.[15]

In fact, sex segregation in the workplace is so pervasive that it appears to be the natural order of things, the simple expression of women's and men's natural predispositions. Though almost equal numbers of women and men go off to work every morning, we do not go together to the same place, nor do we have the same jobs even when we do work in the same spaces. In 2003, 70 per cent of women workers were employed in teaching, nursing and related health professions, clerical, or sales and service. Men remain a majority in managerial positions, well-paid trades and construction jobs, and careers related to sciences, engineering, and mathematics.

Though women have been broadening their areas of employment, women's paid work remains less diverse than that of men. And yet women have colonized men's arenas far more then the reverse; in part this is because once again, 'his' is recognized as better than 'hers'. We give more value (and pay) to occupations we associate with stereotypically 'masculine' characteristics such as strength, competition, and assertiveness than to occupations associated with 'female' traits such as co-operation and nurturing. Because of this, men may be reluctant to enter female-dominated fields that offer poorer pay and the stigma of being 'unmasculine'.[16]

Sex segregation starts early and continues throughout our work lives. And it has significant consequences for incomes and experiences. Job segregation by sex is the single largest cause of the pay gap between the sexes. According to StatsCan data from 1996, the situation in Canada was similar. Women outnumbered men in all of the 10 lowest paid occupations in Canada, while men dramatically outnumbered women in all of the 10 highest

Recruitment poster from the Oregon Center for Nursing

paid occupations (though women have made significant inroads in some of them, such as general and family medical practice). In both the highest and the lowest paid occupations, men were paid more, on average, than women. And despite all these changes, in 2001 sales and secretarial positions remained the most common occupations for women.[17]

Explanations of sex segregation often rely on the qualities of male and female job seekers. Because of differential socialization, women and men are likely to seek different kinds of jobs for different reasons. The girl who plays with dolls grows up to be a nurse, the boy who plays with trucks a construction worker. However, socialization *alone* is not sufficient as an explanation. 'Socialization cannot explain why a sex-segregated labour market emerged, why each sex is allocated to particular types of occupations, and why the sex typing of occupations changes in particular ways over time'. Instead, we need to think of sex segregation as the outcome of several factors—'the differential socialization of young men and women, sex-typed tracking in the educational system, and sex-linked social control at the workplace, at the hiring stage and beyond'.[18]

Socialization alone is also unable to explain why construction may pay better than nursing. Professions that are male dominated tend to have higher wages; professions that are female dominated tend to have lower wages. And though one might be tempted to explain this by the characteristics of the job, it turns out that the gender composition of the position is actually a better predictor. One of the easiest ways to see the impact of sex segregation on wages is to watch what happens when a particular occupation begins to change its gender composition. For example, clerical work was once considered a highly skilled occupation, in which a virtually all-male labour force was paid reasonably well. (One is reminded, of course, of the exception to this rule, the innocent and virtuous Bob Cratchit in Charles Dickens's *A Christmas Carol*.) In the early part of the twentieth century, in both Britain and North America, though, the gender distribution began to change, and by the middle of the century, most clerical workers were female. As a result, clerical work was re-evaluated as less demanding of skill and less valuable to an organization; thus workers' wages fell. As sociologist Samuel Cohn notes, this is a result, not a cause, of the changing gender composition of the workforce.[19]

Veterinary medicine, also, was long a male-dominated field. In the late 1960s, only about 5 per cent of American veterinary students were women. Today that number is closer to 80 per cent, and the number of female veterinarians has more than doubled since 1991, whereas the number of male veterinarians has declined by 15 per cent. In both the USA and Canada, women are either the majority of veterinarians or poised to become so. And vet incomes have followed the changing gender composition. In the 1970s, when males dominated the field, veterinarians' incomes were right behind those of physicians; today, veterinarians earn approximately half of what physicians do. 'Vets are people with medical degrees without the medical income', commented one veterinary epidemiologist. And women vets earn less than male ones.[20]

The exact opposite process took place with computer programmers. In the 1940s, women were hired as keypunch operators, the precursors to computer programmers, because the job seemed to resemble clerical work. In fact, however, computer programming 'demanded complex skills in abstract logic, mathematics, electrical circuitry and machinery, all of which', sociologist Katharine Donato observed, 'women used to perform in their work' without much problem. However, after programming was recognized as 'intellectually demanding', it became attractive to men, who began to enter the field and thus drove wages up considerably.[21]

As William Bielby and James Baron write, 'men's jobs are rewarded according to their standing within the hierarchy of men's work, and women's jobs are rewarded according to their standing within the hierarchy of women's work. The legitimacy of this system is easy to sustain in a segregated workplace'. Stated simply, 'women's occupations pay less at least partly *because* women do them'.[22]

A US lawsuit against Wal-Mart, the world's largest chain of retail stores, illustrates the problem of sex segregation. Although 72 per cent of Wal-Mart's hourly sales employees were women, they represented less than 33 per cent of the company's managers (compared with 56 per cent at competitors), according to the lawsuit filed on behalf of nearly three-quarters of a million women. A decision in the case is expected late in 2009. A lawsuit against Home Depot in the 1990s, alleging similar sex segregation, was settled out of court for $65 million (plus $22.5 million in lawyers' fees).[23]

In general, legal remedies for sex segregation have yielded mixed results. Perhaps the most widely cited case in sex segregation was the 1980s case of EEOC v. Sears, a case brought by the US Equal Employment Opportunity Commission against the giant chain of retail stores. The EEOC had found that Sears had routinely shuttled women and men into different sales positions, resulting in massive wage disparities between the two. Women were pushed into over-the-counter retail positions, where commissions tended to be low and where workers received straight salary. Men, on the other hand, tended to concentrate in sales of high-end consumer goods, such as refrigerators and televisions, which offered high commissions.

Sears argued that this sex-based division of retail sales resulted from individual choice on the part of its male and female labour forces. Differential socialization, Sears suggested, led women and men to pursue different career paths; women were interested in positions that offered them more flexibility, and were more relationship-centred and less competitive. The EEOC, by contrast, argued that although Sears did not intend to discriminate, such outcomes were the result of gender-based discrimination. The US Supreme Court upheld Sears's acquittal on sex discrimination charges, in part because the Court said that no single individual woman had stepped forward and declared that she had sought to enter high-commission sales or had been refused because of these stereotypes.[24] But the case drew attention to the phenomenon of segregation and the ways in which our notions of men's work and women's work contribute to the differential earnings of the sexes.

Precarious Employment

Another way in which the sexes are segregated is in the very *nature* of their employment relationships. We have already seen how women and men cluster in different types of position. When most of us think about these positions, however, we overlook the fact that positions in retail, for example, may be considerably different from typically 'masculine' jobs in the nature of the employment contract. Typically female jobs in retail or child care very often can be categorized as **precarious employment**.

When most of us think of 'having a job', we think about having a contract with one employer for whom we work on a regular basis through the year. We may assume that our job will pay a reasonable, legally-conforming hourly wage, and that we will be entitled to some basic job security (for example, layoff notice). We may expect that we will receive some form of employment benefits, including contribution to Employment Insurance (EI) and the Canada Pension Plan (CPP). We may also expect that 'employment' means that we will have some kind of ability to support a family, purchase a home, and live in the way that most Canadians deem normative. When we think of employment in this way, we are thinking about a 'standard employment relationship', which some scholars see as linked to the notion of breadwinning and the 'family wage'.

The idea of precarious work, in some ways, depends on the notion of the family wage. Regardless of the importance of women's (and sometimes children's) employment to family sustenance, their employment has always been seen as adjunct and marginal to male earnings. This has allowed employers to hire women on terms that would be unacceptable to most men, because female work was 'just for **pin money**'.

So in contrast to the standard employment relationship, precarious employment is characterized by uncertainty (you might be laid off at any time); lack of control over working conditions (absence of a union or collective agreement); lack of regulatory protection (for example, through Labour Relations Boards or similar governmental oversight); and low income (sometimes not even determined on an hourly basis).[25]

Since 1970, precarious employment has been one of the fastest-growing areas of work, to the point where today, over one-third of Canadian jobs are judged to fall into this category. Since the recent economic downturn, job loss has come mainly in the area of full-time jobs, while job creation has been overwhelmingly in part-time and temporary positions. In Canada and globally, precarious work seems to be the wave of the future.

Much of the growth in women's labour-force participation since 1970 has come from their entry into this kind of work, which can include self-employment, temporary work, the holding of multiple jobs, and part-time or on-call labour. According to the Ontario Federation of Labour, 40 per cent of women, compared with about 29 per cent of men, are working in precarious employment. Women are 60 per cent of part-time temporary and 75 per cent of part-time permanent employees, for example. Racialized, immigrant, and young men are also overrepresented in this form of work.[26]

> Consider the underpaid retail sales clerk who is forced to scrounge up hours on a weekly basis because there are no full-time jobs available. Or the long-haul truck driver, forced to become an owner-operator (technically self-employed) and then compete with other drivers for work. What about the home care worker, who is hired as a temporary worker and does not know for certain if work will still be available month after month? Or the warehouse worker, who is working for low pay and faces a perpetual probationary period because they were hired through an employment agency?[27]

One might also add, consider the nanny allowed to enter Canada on a 'temporary' visa, unlike other workers who can enter as landed immigrants. She, like agricultural workers and other 'contingent' employees, may find herself protected very minimally, if at all, by the labour standards in place to govern standard employment relationships.[28]

Our tolerance of precarious employment relies on gendered (and racialized) ideas, like the idea that women are working not to support families but to earn 'extra' money—or the idea that foreign women working as domestic workers may be poorly paid, but are still 'better off' than in their own countries and therefore do not merit the protections granted to Canadians doing similar work. The existence of such employment also relies on gender inequality in that women may choose to enter such employment because they find it flexible enough not to conflict with their family responsibilities. However, precarious employment contributes to the vulnerability of women (and other affected groups) to economic downturns or changes in personal circumstances. It makes women more likely, for example, to slip into poverty upon divorce. And most obviously, women's overrepresentation in precarious employment contributes to the gender wage gap.

Income Discrimination—The Wage Gap

At both the aggregate level and the individual level—whether we average all incomes or look at specific individuals' wages for the jobs they do—women earn less than men. This wage difference is called the '**wage gap**'.

In both Canada and the USA, the wage gap shrank dramatically between 1981 and 1996. In the former year, Canadian women's median earnings were 62.5 per cent of those of men; by 1996, that figure had increased to 73.5 per cent. By 2000, if differences in hours worked were taken into account, female earnings were somewhere around 80 per cent of those of men. Much of this change was caused not by massive increases in women's wages, but rather by two developments: first, the decline in men's wages caused by the loss of jobs in the high-wage skilled manufacturing sector of the economy, and second, the entry of some women into high-paid male-concentrated fields.[29]

The major declines in the last 20 years of the twentieth century have lulled some into believing that the wage gap is disappearing on its own. However, there are troubling signs that this might not be true. Since 2000, the wage gap has remained stagnant after a period of dramatic change. Looking at young workers (20 to 25) is a way of assessing the wage gap, since their labour market experience and job tenure tend to be equal regardless of sex (the gendered effects of child-bearing and child rearing, most notably, tend not to affect this group). Yet in 2005, young women employed full-time earned only 85 per cent of the earnings of their male counterparts. Why did the gap stagnate? Principally, it seems, because young men's earnings rose sharply after a period of stagnation. The Alberta oil boom gave back what plant closures in the 1980s and 1990s had taken away. When we talk about a closing wage gap, then, we are often talking about what happens to men's wages rather than real growth in women's.[30]

So the wage gap persists, and is complicated by age, ethnicity, ability, and level of education. For example, education greatly increases earnings for both men and women. Nonetheless, in 2006, young men employed full-time earned about $10,000 more than their female counterparts, whether they were university-educated or lacking high-school graduation. (For example, median earnings for young women without a high-school diploma hovered just above $20,000, while young men in the same educational category earned about $31,000.) The gap increases with age.

There are three main causes for the wage gap: women's unequal responsibility for child-bearing and child rearing, discrimination, and sex segregation. We can see the functioning of the first in typical life cycles. Women and men enter the labour force at more comparable starting salaries. But as women continue their careers, they tend to accumulate fewer years of full-time work experience and shorter job tenures, largely as a result of their family responsibilities. This has a calamitous effect on women's wages and fuels the growing gap across the life span. In fact, women who drop out of the labour force have lower real wages when they come back to work than they had when they left. Two sociologists recently calculated that each child costs a woman 7 per cent in wages. The result is that women aged 50 to 54 earn only 72 per cent as much as men. [31]

But the wage gap is not simply the result of women's disproportionate responsibility for family care. Discrimination and sex segregation are also important. In every field, women tend to be concentrated at the bottom of the pay scale. They face discrimination in hiring, and particularly in promotion (as further discussed below). Across all industries, women make up nearly 50 per cent of the workers but much fewer of the managers. Numbers of Canadian women managers registered 40 per cent growth between 1981 and 2001, according to StatCan, but women are still only about a third of the manager group (and tend to cluster at lower levels of management). This means that within any occupational category, women are less likely than men to get the promotions to management that bring higher salaries. And women cluster at the bottom of the pay scale even within high-prestige, highly paid occupations such as medicine. Sociologist Judith Lorber described the reason why female physicians earn less than male physicians. 'The fault may not lie in their psyches or female roles, but in

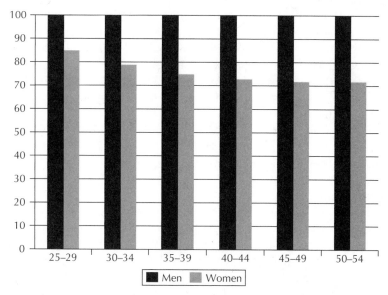

Figure 8.2 The wage gap by age group, 2006 (full-time, full-year employees).

Source: Statistics Canada, *Earnings and Income of Canadians over the Past Quarter Century, 2006 Census* (Ottawa: Ministry of Industry, 2008).

the system of professional patronage and sponsorship which tracked them out of their prestigious specialties and 'inner fraternities' of American medical institutions by not recommending them for the better internships, residencies, and hospital staff positions, and by not referring patients', she writes.[32]

Finally, sex segregation itself explains the wage gap. As already discussed, it seems that 'women's work' is simply not valued as highly as the work we assign to men. Simply knowing that work is done by women, or is somehow 'feminine' work, still means that it will be seen as meriting less money than so-called 'men's work'. Is this changing? A 2008 study of 260 Ontario undergraduates suggests not. In that study, though participants rated male- and female-typed jobs similarly in terms of qualification, skills, and working conditions, they still assigned lower salaries to jobs within 'female' domains. The wage gap, it would seem, is more resilient than once thought.[33]

How have women coped with this income inequality? In the 1860s, one woman came up with a rather novel solution:

> I was almost at the end of my rope. I had no money and a woman's wages were not enough to keep me alive. I looked around and saw men getting more money, and more work, and more money for the same kind of work. I decided to become a man. It was simple. I just put on men's clothing and applied for a man's job. I got good money for those times, so I stuck to it.[34]

Novel, yes, but not exactly practical for an entire gender! So women have pressed for equal wages—in their unions, professional associations, and in every arena in which they have worked. But women face a double bind in their efforts to achieve workplace equality. On the one hand, traditional gender ideologies push them away from those occupations that pay well and toward lower-paying sectors of the economy. On the other hand, when they enter higher-paying fields, they face obstacles, as we shall see below. As women have entered previously male-dominated workplaces, supported by public legislation that prohibits discrimination, its more subtle manifestations continue, as detailed below.

Challenges to Workplace Integration

Glass ceilings (and cellars?)

One consequence of sex segregation is discrimination against women in promotion. Women face the twin barriers of the '**glass ceiling**' and the '**sticky floor**', which combine to keep them stuck at the bottom and unable to reach the top. The sticky floor keeps women trapped in low-wage positions, with little opportunity for upward mobility. The glass ceiling consists of 'those artificial barriers, based on attitudinal or organizational bias, that prevent qualified individuals from advancing upward within their organization into management level positions.'[35]

In 1995, the US government's Glass Ceiling Commission found that the glass ceiling continued 'to deny untold numbers of qualified people the opportunity to compete for and hold executive level positions in the private sector.'[36] Most significantly, the glass ceiling keeps women from being promoted equally with men. Women hold less than 10 per cent of all corporate board seats in the USA. Between 95 per cent and 97 per cent of all senior managers are men, and almost all of them are white. (Indeed, the glass ceiling's effects are multiplied when race is brought into the equation.)

Business Week surveyed 3,664 business school graduates in 1990 and found that a woman with an MBA from one of the top US business schools earned an average of $54,749 in her first year after graduation, whereas a man from a similar program earned $61,400. This gap—12 per cent—actually widened as these business graduates progressed. A 1993 study of the Stanford University Business School class of 1982 found that only 10 years after graduation, 16 per cent of the male graduates were CEOs, chairmen, or presidents of companies, compared with only 2 per cent of the female graduates.

Again, these different trajectories have virtually nothing to do with the ambitions or aspirations of the men and women who occupy these positions. For two years, an economist followed five female and five male trainees in a large Swedish multinational corporation (with 6,000 employees). All came from similar backgrounds, had similar education, and had similar goals and ambitions. All 10 aspired to top management positions. After their training, they all still were similar. At the end of the two years, all the men and none of the women had entered the top management group.

The glass ceiling occurs under a variety of circumstances. Corporate management may be either unable or unwilling to establish policies and practices that are effective mechanisms to promote workplace diversity. The company may not have adequate job evaluation criteria that allow for comparable-worth criteria, or it may rely on traditional gender stereotypes in evaluation. Limited family-friendly work-place policies will also inhibit women's ability to rise.

Perhaps the most important element that reinforces the glass ceiling is the informal or even unconscious effort by men to restore or retain the all-male atmosphere of the corporate hierarchy. When hiring and promoting, we tend to prefer those like us. If most of those in a position to hire are male, white, and able-bodied, they may—consciously or unconsciously—choose candidates with whom they're comfortable. Such candidates are likely to be male, white, and able-bodied. 'What's important is comfort, chemistry, rela-tionships and collaborations', one manager explained. 'That's what makes a shop work. When we find minorities and women who think like we do, we snatch them up'. One British study of female MBAs, for example, found that by far the 'most significant' and 'most resistant' barrier to women's advancement was the ' "men's club" network'.[37]

Sometimes the culture clash between women and the old boys' club is overt. In 2008, the first female senior executives at Bell ExpressVu filed a lawsuit and a human rights com-plaint alleging gender discrimination based on a 'macho corporate culture' at Bell. In 2005, they claimed, they were forced to participate in an 'over the top' martial-arts themed retreat. Soon afterward, both women were fired. But often, because the glass ceiling is about 'culture' rather than overt discrimination, it is difficult to perceive even for those facing it. (It was called glass, after all, because of its invisibility.) In the words of Moya Green, CEO of Canada Post, 'I can say I didn't feel the so-called glass ceiling until I got close enough to see it'. And sometimes the ceiling is even internal. One recent American study found that women un-derestimate their leadership abilities, while men overestimate theirs.[38]

Some companies have already instituted policies designed to enable women to break through the glass ceiling in hiring, promotion, and retention. These companies tend to be among the more forward-looking companies. For example, in 1992, Reebok International initiated a diversity program in hiring practices by developing effective college recruitment policies and internships for women and minorities. In two years, the company tripled its minority employment to 15 per cent of its US workforce and increased the number of women to more than 50 per cent. The Bank of Montreal tar-geted promotion, and between 1991 and 1993 the bank increased the percentage of women at the executive level from 29 per cent to 54 per cent. The bank also initiated a program that specified targets for promoting and retaining women and minorities and developed a series of gender-awareness workshops for senior management.

Despite broad consensus that the glass ceiling exists, writer Warren Farrell argues that *men* are the true victims of sex discrimination in the workplace. Men, Farrell ar-gues, are the victims of the '**glass cellar**'—stuck in the most hazardous and dangerous occupations. In fact, Farrell argues, of the 250 occupations ranked by the *Jobs Related Almanac*, the 25 worst jobs (such as truck driver, roofer, boilermaker, construction worker, welder, and football player) were almost all male. In Canada, men are 30 times more likely to die on the job than are women. The most dangerous industries (in ranked order) are mining, quarrying, and oil drilling; logging and forestry; and fishing and trapping—all heavily male-dominated.[39]

So Farrell has a point: Many of the jobs that men take *are* hazardous—and made more so by an ideology of masculinity that demands that men remain stoic and uncomplaining in the face of danger. Thus on dangerous construction sites or off-shore oil rigs, men frequently shun safety precautions, such as safety helmets, as unsuitable for 'real' men. So are men, not women, the ones being discriminated against? Such a conclusion flies in the face of both evidence and reason. First, most of the dangerous industries offer high pay—certainly much higher pay than the jobs that are almost exclusively female. These occupations can hardly be regarded as a 'cellar' when it comes to compensation. Second, the jobs that are the most exclusively male are also those whose workers have fought most fiercely against the entry of women in the first place. For example, the nation's fire departments have been especially resistant to women joining their 'fraternal order', allowing them to enter only under court order and often admitting women with a significant amount of harassment. It would be odd to propose that men's domination of fire-fighting is the result of discrimination against men or to blame women for not entering those occupations from which they have been excluded by men's resistance. Indeed, when individuals enter 'non-traditional' segregated workplaces, they often face significant challenges.

When the Ceiling is an Escalator: Differential Experiences with Tokenism

Often, when a few men or women enter workplaces dominated by the other gender, the form integration takes is **tokenism**. Tokens are people who are admitted into an organization but who are recognizably different from the large majority of the members of the organization. But tokens are more than simply the members of a numerical minority: Tokens are accepted not *despite* their minority status but rather *because* of it. They are actively discouraged from recruiting others like themselves and become eager to fit in and become part of the organizational mainstream. Typically, tokens may even become more strongly wedded to organizational norms than do members of the numerical majority.

According to Rosabeth Moss Kanter, whose pioneering work, *Men and Women of the Corporation*, first analyzed the problem, tokenism widens the contrasts between groups rather than narrowing them, as the contrasts between the token and the majority are exaggerated to become the sole difference. Tokens, Kanter writes, are thus 'often treated as representative of their category, as symbols rather than as individuals'.[40] The token is always in the spotlight—everyone notices him or her, but only because he or she is different. Tokens are rarely seen as similar to others in the group. Thus tokens have a double experience of visibility—they are *hyper*visible as members of their 'category', but they are completely *invisible* as individuals.

Think about a situation where you were virtually the only 'something' in a group. It could be that you were the only man or woman, the only white person or person of colour, the only gay or straight person in a group. How did you feel when someone would turn to you and say, 'So, how do Aboriginal people feel about this issue?' or 'What do women say about this?' At that moment you cease to be an individual and are seen only as a representative of the group. Chances are you responded by saying something like, 'I don't know. I'm not all women or all Aboriginal people. You'd have to take a survey'. If you can imagine that experience of hypervisibility and invisibility all the time in your workplace, you'll begin to have an idea of what tokenism feels like.

Simultaneous hypervisibility and invisibility have serious consequences. 'The token does not have to work hard to have her presence noticed, but she does have to work hard to have her achievements noticed', Kanter writes. The token is often forced to choose between the two—' 'trying to limit visibility—and being overlooked—or taking advantage of the publicity—and being labelled a "troublemaker"'. This can take an enormous emotional and psychological toll:

> Tokenism is stressful; the burdens carried by tokens in the management of social relations take a toll in psychological stress, even if the token succeeds in work performance. Unsatisfactory social relationships, miserable self-imagery, frustrations from contradictory demands, inhibition of self-expression, feelings of inadequacy and self-hatred, all have been suggested as consequences of tokenism.[41]

Kanter argues that her theory of tokenism holds regardless of whether the tokens are male or female. But men's and women's experiences as tokens are often very different. Subsequent research has suggested dramatically different experiences when women are the tokens in a largely male work world and when men are the tokens in a largely female occupation.[42]

Based on what we have said about workplace segregation and the persistence of gender ideologies, one would expect that men entering jobs dominated by women would face discrimination similar to that faced by women entering male-dominated workplaces. In fact, studies suggest that the opposite is true. Men entering mostly female occupations don't bump up against a glass ceiling; instead, they ride on what sociologist Christine Williams calls the '**glass escalator**'. That is, 'the effects of sexism can outweigh the effects of tokenism when men enter non-traditional occupations', leading to the preferential hiring and promotion of these 'non-traditional' workers. Williams conducted interviews with 76 men and 23 women in four fields—nursing, librarianship, elementary education, and social work. She found that men experienced *positive* discrimination when entering those fields; several people noted a clear preference for hiring men. And men were promoted to managerial positions more rapidly and frequently, thus making men overrepresented in the managerial ranks. Men who do women's work, it appears, may earn less than men who work in predominantly male occupations, but they earn more and are promoted faster than women in the same occupation.[43]

Men did experience some negative effects, especially in their dealings with the public. For example, male nurses faced a common stereotype that they were gay. Male librarians faced images of themselves as 'wimpy' and asexual; male social workers were seen as 'feminine' or 'passive'. One male librarian found that he had difficulty establishing enough credibility so that the public would accept him as the children's 'storyteller'. Ironically, though, Williams found that these negative stereotypes of men doing 'women's work' actually added to the glass escalator effect 'by pressuring men to move *out* of the most female-identified areas, and *up* to those regarded as more legitimate and prestigious for men'.[44]

Williams concluded that men 'take their gender privilege with them when they enter predominantly female occupations: this translates as an advantage in spite of their numerical rarity'. Men, it seems, win either way. When women are tokens, men retain their numerical superiority and are able to maintain their gender privilege by restricting a woman's entry, promotion, and experiences in the workplace. When men are tokens, they are welcomed into the profession and use their gender privilege to rise quickly in the hierarchy. 'Regardless of the problems that might exist', writes Alfred Kadushin, 'it is clear and undeniable that there is a considerable advantage in being a member of the male minority in any female profession.'[45]

Sexual Harassment

Sexual harassment exists in various arenas—for example, schools, as discussed in Chapter 6—but in the workplace, it has been a common challenge to processes of employment integration. Sexual harassment was first identified as a form of sex discrimination in the mid-1970s. As women identified the problem, they began to litigate. In Canada, the landmark case, *Bell v. Ladas* (1980), involved two women who alleged that their boss, the owner of the Flaming Steer Steak House in Niagara Falls, Ontario, had sexually harassed them and had eventually fired them when they refused to accede to his sexual advances. Though both complaints were dismissed, the case provided Canada with a definition of sexual harassment and clarified that, as sex discrimination, it was prohibited. (Sexual harassment itself was not prohibited at that time.) In 1989, sexual harassment was further defined in *Janzen v. Platy*. This was the first time that sexual harassment had made it to the Supreme Court of Canada, which reinforced the idea that sexual harassment was sex discrimination and defined such harassment as 'unwelcome conduct of a sexual nature that detrimentally affects the work environment or leads to adverse job-related consequences for the victim of the harassment'.[46]

In the USA, sexual harassment was defined through litigation in 1976, several years before Canada's first case. Feminist lawyer Catharine MacKinnon argued that sexual harassment is a violation of Title VII of the 1964 Civil Rights Act, which makes it 'an unlawful employment practice for an employer . . . to discriminate against any individual with respect to his compensation, terms, conditions, or privileges of employment, because of such individual's race, colour, religion, sex, or national origin'. Sexual harassment, MacKinnon argued, violates this law because it discriminates against women on the basis of their sex, and what's more, sexual harassment creates a hostile environment for working women.[47]

Sexual Harassment Hollywood-style

As discussed below, the galvanizing media moment for sexual harassment in North America was surely the 1991 Clarence Thomas hearings in which Anita Hill gave gripping and personal testimony about her harassment at the hands of the would-be US Supreme Court Justice. But this was not the first time sexual harassment had entered the public eye. The 1980 Hollywood film *9 to 5*, starring Jane Fonda, Lily Tomlin, and Dolly Parton, features a sexist boss who treats his employees abysmally and who sexually harasses the Dolly Parton character in

Warner Brothers/The Kobal Collection/Foreman, Richard

such a manner as to destroy her credibility within the workplace. Through an insane set of plot twists, the three women end up kidnapping their boss and holding him captive while they implement a stunning array of workplace reforms that boost company productivity. The top-grossing comedy of 1980, *9 to 5* dealt with sexual harassment substantially, introducing it to audiences unfamiliar with the concept in an unthreatening manner that nonetheless recognized the seriousness of the issue.

The next major film to deal with sexual harassment, 1994's *Disclosure*, took a dramatic and very different approach, not least because its central character is a heterosexual man harassed by a woman. In the film, Michael Douglas plays a software executive who finds out that his new boss is a woman with whom he has previously conducted an affair; she attempts to reinitiate the affair and, when rebuffed, accuses him of sexual harassment (a kind of quid pro quo harassment in itself). While the film draws attention to the possibility of men's being sex-

Warner Bros/Baltimore/Constant/The Kobal Collection/Hamill, Brian

Two faces of sexual harassment? Charlize Theron in *North Country* (above) and Demi Moore as sexual harasser in *Disclosure* (top).

ually harassed, the situation depicted in the film is atypical, to say the least. But then that's precisely what one would expect of a sexual-harassment film that somehow managed to merit the label 'hot-button date movie of the year'!

A more realistic portrayal of sexual harassment had to wait for the twenty-first century. The 2005 film *North Country*, starring Charlize Theron, recounted the true story of Lois Jenson, a mineworker in Eveleth, Minnesota, and her battles with a particularly vicious form of hostile environment harassment. Like the few other women mineworkers, Jenson, a single mother and daughter of a mineworker, was repeatedly threatened, humiliated, groped, stalked, and assaulted until she and 20 other women miners went to court in 1984 and eventually won a landmark sexual discrimination lawsuit—the first class-action sexual harassment case in US history. 'It really was about getting a better paying job with benefits. I didn't go there to bring up issues. I just wanted to make a decent life for my family', Jenson said in an interview. Unlike *Disclosure*, the film presents sexual harassment unglamorized: not a 'hot' thriller-style confrontation between two high-powered executives, but a grinding battle over power in the workplace.

Despite important litigation during the 1980s, it was not until the 1990s that the extent of the problem and its effects on women in the workplace began to be fully recognized in North America. In October of 1991, Anita Hill declared that she had been sexually harassed by Clarence Thomas when she worked for him at the EEOC, and suddenly millions sat transfixed before their television sets as Thomas's confirmation hearings to the US Supreme Court took a dramatically different turn. Hill alleged that she had been subjected to unwanted sexual advances, vile pornographic attempts at humour, and constant descriptions of Thomas's sexual prowess—even after she had made it clear that she was not interested in dating her boss.

After the hearings, thousands of North American women came forward to describe what they had earlier kept as shameful personal secrets. An Angus Reid poll of October 1991 found that more than a third of Canadian women who had worked outside the home reported that they had experienced sexual harassment on the job, while over 90 per cent of women who responded to a 'women in trades' survey reported being harassed. A 1993 StatsCan survey on violence against women found that 87 per cent of women reported having experienced some form of sexual harassment. Suddenly women had a name for what had been happening to them for decades in the workplace. By 1997, most North Americans had come to believe that Anita Hill had been telling the truth.[48]

Since that time, sexual harassment has become a major issue in North America. The EEOC handles about 5000 complaints of sexual harassment per year. And it's not just lawyers and other professionals. In fact, the number of cases filed with the EEOC more than doubled between 1990 and 1995, from about 7,500 in 1990 to about 15,500 in 1995 and again in 1996—and the majority of those cases were from women in blue-collar jobs. Women were far more likely to experience sexual harassment in traditionally male-only jobs like mining, construction, transportation, or manufacturing than they were in professional and white-collar jobs. Clearly, when women try to 'cross over' into male-dominated jobs, they are seen as invaders, and sexual harassment is a way to keep them out. In some cases, as in firefighting and emergency services, complaints of sexual harassment have become a virtual epidemic.[49]

Sexual harassment takes many forms, from sexual assault to mocking innuendo. Typically, it takes one of two forms. Legally speaking, Canadian law does not distinguish between them in the manner of US law, but the distinctions between the two are useful for thinking about what sexual harassment really is. In the most obvious form, know as **quid pro quo sexual harassment**, a trade of sexual contact is offered for a reward or the avoidance of punishment: 'sleep with me and you'll get promoted' or 'don't sleep with me and you'll get fired'. Thus, for example, did US Senator Robert Packwood end his congressional career—after nearly a dozen former female staffers accused him of unwanted kissing, fondling, attempts at sexual contact, and inappropriate remarks during his ~~otherwise distinguished~~ 27-year career. → coddling

The (arguably more common) second form is more difficult to define. It is generally understood as the creation of a '**hostile environment**', one in which women (or others) feel compromised, threatened, or unsafe. One well-known example involves the Richmond, BC fire department. Between 2000 and 2006, several female firefighters alleged their sexual harassment at the hands of male co-workers. For example, one firefighter claimed that she had faced 'a culture of systemic discrimination and harassment', including the display of hardcore pornography, the placing of a condom with a sexual slur on it in her locker, human feces in her boots, and tampering with her equipment. The slew of complaints included revelations that police had investigated the department over allegations of sexual abuse of minors at fire halls in the late 1970s—allegations supported in sworn affidavits by retired firefighters. Small wonder that Vince Ready, an arbitrator called in to mediate the complaints, referred in his report to the department's 'juvenile and hostile' workplace culture.[50]

Whether sexual harassment is manifest as quid pro quo or hostile environment, it is rarely simply about sexual attraction between employees. Of course co-workers can become sexually attracted to one another; but when sexual attention becomes persistent or unwanted and one party suffers, the issue is power, not sexual attraction. And in fact, few cases of sexual harassment have origins in sexual attraction. Sexual harassment is, in fact, just the opposite of attraction: repulsion. It is about making workers feel unwelcome in the workplace, about reminding them that they do not belong because the workplace is men's space. As legal scholar Deborah Rhode writes, it is a 'strategy of dominance and exclusion—a way of keeping women in their places and out of men's'.[51]

Indeed, as we have seen, sexual harassment need not involve any pretence of sexual attraction whatsoever, nor need it be directed at women. It can also take the form experienced by an 'older' Ohio firefighter who sued his department after complaining that mud-soiled adult diapers and pornographic materials depicting older men having homosexual sex had been placed in his gear. Here, the worker didn't belong—not because of sex, but because of age. What's more, one of the alleged harassers was female. Though most harassers remain male, this case shows us that sexual harassment is fundamentally about power, not sex.[52]

As this case shows, men too can be harmed by sexual harassment from others. In March 1998, the US Supreme Court ruled that men can be the victims of sexual harassment by other men, even when all the men involved are heterosexual (for example, when a straight man persistently attacks another straight man's heterosexuality or masculinity). Between 1990 and 2008, the number of sexual harassment complaints to the EEOC by men has doubled from 8 to 16 per cent. In Canada since 2005, men have filed 34 sexual harassment complaints with the Canadian Human Rights Commission. Men—particularly in Canada—are thus a small minority of complainants, but these numbers suggest that men are no longer willing to put up with being demeaned at work, or what used to be considered just 'good fun between guys'.[53]

This is the context in which we must consider the question of sexual harassment, its gendered political economy, so to speak. Sexual harassment in the workplace is a distorted effort to put women back in their place, to remind them that they are not equal to men in the workplace, that they are, still, after all their gains, just women, even if they are in the workplace. As proof of this, consider that a recent US longitudinal study found that female managers are 137 per cent more likely to experience harassment than other female workers. Such harassment, according to the author of the study, is a way to 'strip them of their organizational power'. Heather McLaughlin, a sociologist at the University of Minnesota and the study's primary investigator, argues that 'Male co-workers, clients, and supervisors seem to be using harassment as an equalizer'. [54]

And it works. Harassed women report increased stress, irritability, eating and sleeping disorders, and absenteeism. A recent Ontario study found that women lose jobs or quit them to escape harassment, but still experienced unsatisfactory resolutions, deterioration of family relationships, loss of self-confidence, and increased substance use. At the societal level, sexual harassment stymies women's equality. And it is costly. Both private and public sectors lose millions because of absenteeism, reduced productivity, and high turnover of female employees.[55]

Until recently, the workplace has been a male space, a homosocial preserve. But that world has vanished forever. It is now virtually impossible for workers to go through their entire working lives without having female colleagues, co-workers, or bosses; what's more, many men have always suffered from the 'masculine testing ground' of workplace culture and are no longer willing to tolerate abuse. The integration of women into all-male workplaces may have sparked a great deal of sexual harassment, but in fighting against that harassment, women have improved the workplace for everyone.

Remedies for Workplace Inequality

Despite all the arguments about gender difference that presume that men and women are from different planets, the fact is that comparable percentages of women and men are in the workplace and for the same reasons. Yet the workplace remains a decidedly unequal arena, plagued by persistent sex segregation, wage inequality, sex discrimination, and sexual harassment. These inequalities exaggerate and even create the differences we think we observe. How can the workplace become a more equal arena, a place in which women *and* men can earn a living to support themselves and their families and experience the satisfaction of efficacy and competence?

One arena of change is the application of existing law. In 1951, the United Nations' International Labour Organization passed Convention 100, which required signatories to 'promote and . . . ensure the application to all workers of the principle of equal remuneration for men and women workers for work of equal value'. While most countries have ratified the convention, few have attempted to implement it. Those that have had to grapple with two concepts under the rubric of **pay equity**: equal pay for equal work and equal pay for work of equal value. While the first is now non-controversial, the second has been far more difficult to grapple with. And yet the second concept is the most important, because, as we have seen, wage inequality emerges not from paying men and women differently for doing exactly the same tasks, but from sex segregation. Sex segregation takes very similar skills and tasks and hives them off into 'his' and 'her' versions, allocating them 'his' and 'her' pay along the way. So to implement true pay equity, we must wrangle with the messy concept of work's value.

In the USA, the 1963 Pay Equity Act prohibits employers from paying different wages to men and women who are doing the same or essentially the same work, while Title VII of the 1964 Civil Rights Act guarantees the absence of discrimination based on race, sex, or national origin. To date, 30 states have undertaken some form of pay equity reform, and about $527 million has been disbursed by 20 state governments to correct wage discrimination, but much more needs to be done. In Canada, pay equity laws have been passed by the federal and some provincial governments. In Quebec and Ontario, some public-sector women workers have received hundreds of millions of dollars in pay equity settlements.[56]

There have been similar developments in the private sector. In the 1990s, workers at Bell Canada launched a request for salary adjustments based on sex segregation. As late as 2002, 69 per cent of female workers were concentrated in areas called 'clerical', while just over half of male employees were in the category of 'skilled craft and trade workers'. Because of differential valuation of gendered jobs very similar in function and training requirements, women were heavily overrepresented at the bottom of the pay scale, leading to 'a pink/blue collar, female/male divide'. In 2002, after a decade of wrangling, Bell reached a settlement with workers worth $178 million.[57]

In order to establish pay equity, one has to establish comparable worth. This requires a systematic review of jobs, ordering them on criteria of complexity and skills required so that they can be compared and thus wages allocated on a more gender-equal basis. Not surprisingly, this has proved difficult and controversial. Pay equity schemes have therefore taken a very long time, and have emphasized responding to complaints. The federal government's impatience with pay equity was expressed in the 2009 Public Sector Equitable Compensation Act (Bill C-10), which seeks to add consideration of 'qualifications and market forces' and refers cases previously heard by the Canadian Human Rights Commission to the Public Service Labour Relations Board. While the outcome remains unclear at this point, pay equity remains a controversial concept, despite its importance to wage equality.[58]

Workplace equality also requires interventionist strategies in hiring and promotion. Although in recent years the trend has been for the United States to abandon affirmative action policies, such policies were enormously effective in levelling the playing field. When Barbara Babcock, an assistant attorney general in the Carter administration, was asked how she felt about getting her position because she was a woman, she replied, 'It's better than not getting your job because you're a woman'. But there are other ways to intervene in hiring and promotion that do not raise the spectres of 'affirmative action' or 'quotas'. Today, most **employment equity** policies emphasize creating attractive workplaces for diverse employees and creating the broadest possible candidate pool from which to draw the most qualified candidate.[59]

In both Canada and the USA, discrimination on the grounds of pregnancy is prohibited, and employers may neither fire a woman for becoming pregnant nor fail to accommodate her pregnancy. However, once children are born, the issue becomes murkier. First, breastfeeding, universally recommended by the World Health Organization and pediatricians for healthy infant development, is protected in Canada but not necessarily in the USA. In August 2009, the Ohio Supreme Court affirmed the right of Totes/Isotoner to fire an employee for taking breaks to pump breast milk for her five-month-old infant. The court ruled that 'Breastfeeding discrimination does not constitute gender discrimination.'[60]

If breastfeeding can make a woman a bad employee, the continuing demands of child care can at best put her on the '**mommy track**'—a subtle way that workplace gender inequality is reproduced. The 'mommy track' refers to the ways in which workplace discrimination transmutes itself into discrimination against those workers who happen to take time off to get pregnant, bear children, and raise them. Though as we have seen, it is illegal to discriminate against women because of pregnancy, women are often forced off the 'fast track' (focused on career and promotion) onto the mommy track because of what appear to be the demands of the positions they occupy. Young attorneys, for example, must bill a certain number of hours per week; failing to do so will result in their being denied partnerships. A woman thus faces a double bind: To the extent that she is a good mother, she cannot rise in the corporate world; to the extent that she rises in the corporate world, she is seen as a bad mother. And as we have seen, no matter her choices, being a woman with a family will have a significant effect on her employment and earnings through the lifespan.[61]

This being the case, the most obvious set of remedies to workplace inequality falls under the general heading of '**family-friendly workplace policies**'—that collection of reforms, including on-site child care, flexible working hours, and parental leave, that allows parents some flexibility in balancing work and family life. *The National Report on Work and Family* reported in December 1997 that these were among the most significant criteria in helping companies to retain qualified and well-trained personnel. Several different kinds of policy reforms have been proposed to make the workplace more 'family friendly'—to enable working men and women to effect that balancing act. These reforms generally revolve around three issues: on-site child care, flexible working hours, and parental leave.

Canada's workplaces are ahead of those of the USA in some respects, principally because of the federal government's EI-funded parental benefit plan, which offers substantial parental leaves that can be accessed by parents of either sex. (The USA is one of the few nations with no legal requirement for paid maternity leave—or paternity leave.) But much remains to be done. Nonetheless, even the highest-pressure sectors are perceiving the importance of family-friendly policies to 'retaining the high-performing employees we rely on to serve the needs of our clients', in the words of Karen Wensley of Ernst & Young. The global accounting powerhouse won a 2009 award for its progressive policies on leave and flexible hours, and has vowed to stay the course despite tough economic times.[62]

In the end, workplace equality will require significant ideological and structural change—both in the way we work and in the way we live. We still retain outmoded ideas about what motivates us to work and what skills we bring when we get to work. John Gray's *Mars and Venus in the Workplace* rehashed his stereotypes about how men and women approach situations differently. According to Gray, in the workplace men 'retreat to a cave' when they have a problem to work out by themselves, whereas women 'demonstrate sharing, co-operation, and collaboration'. Except that such interplanetary styles depend at least as much on the problem to be solved as on the gender of the person solving it! To make men feel more comfortable, Gray recommends that we take photos of male workers alongside their achievements and ask about their favourite football teams—ideas that Lucy Kellaway, a writer for the *Financial Times*, found 'ill conceived, outdated, and bizarre'.[63]

Structural change is as important as replacing tired clichés. As sociologists Ronnie Steinberg and A. Cook write:

> Equal employment requires more than guaranteeing the right to equal access, the right to equal opportunity for promotion, or the right to equal pay for equal, or even comparable worth. Additionally, it warrants a broader policy orientation encompassing social welfare laws that assume equality within the family; widespread use of alternative work arrangements that accommodate the complexities of family life within two-earner families; and a rejuvenated union movement, with female leadership more active at work sites in defending the rights of women workers. Social welfare laws, family policy, and government services must create incentives toward a more equal division of responsibilities for family and household tasks between men and women. Increasing child care facilities, as well as maintaining programs to care for the elderly, would help alleviate some of the more pressing demands made on adults in families . . . This also means that tax policy, social security laws, and pension programs must be amended to make government incentives to family life consistent with a family structure in which husbands and wives are equal partners.[64]

Another sociologist, Karen Oppenheim Mason, writes that gender inequality in the workplace is likely to remain 'unless major revisions occur in our ideology of gender and the division of labour between the sexes'. Ultimately', she concludes, 'job segregation is just a part of the generally separate (and unequal) lives that women and men in our society lead, and, unless the overall separateness is ended, the separateness within the occupational system is unlikely to end either'.[65]

But reform will be worth it. Workplace equality will enable both women *and* men to experience more fulfilling lives—both in the workplace and outside of it.

Conclusion: Toward a Balance of Work and Family

Despite enormous and persistent gender inequality in the workplace, women are there to stay. Women work for the same reasons that men work—to support themselves and their families, to experience the sense of accomplishment, efficacy, and competence that comes from succeeding in the workplace. Both men and women work because they want to and because they have to. Indeed, women's entry into paid employment is a long-term trend that may soon culminate in a female-majority workforce. In the recent economic downturn, more than two-thirds of Canadian jobs lost were jobs filled by men, while in the USA 82 per cent of job losses have affected men. This has caused writers to speak of a 'he-cession' or 'man-cession'. Many of the jobs lost were in well-paid areas like finance, manufacturing, and construction. Ironically, the poorer-paid, female-dominated occupations have proved much more resilient. Many women have found themselves breadwinners, albeit sometimes badly paid ones! [66]

The struggle to balance work and family is even more acute in such situations. 'Our jobs don't make room for family obligations', writes Stephanie Coontz. 'To correct this imbalance, we need to reorganize work to make it more compatible with family life'. That is to say, we will never find that balance if all we do is tinker with our family relationships, better organize our time, outsource family work, juggle, or opt out. It will be possible only when the workplace changes as well. [67]

Summary

While every society has developed a gendered division of labour, the public-private divide so familiar to North Americans was a creation of the nineteenth (or even more the twentieth) century. Still, the most enduring legacy of that same period is the enormous shift in the composition of the paid labour force; while in 1900 only a minority of women were in the labour force, by 2000 the majority were. Even mothers of young children are now likely to be employed.

But gender ideologies persist in the area of employment as elsewhere. In particular, the male breadwinner/female housewife model still influences everything from how we evaluate a man's masculinity to the 'validity' of a woman's paid employment.

Sex discrimination has been the greatest obstacle to the integration of women into paid employment. While very few jobs can be said to actually require one sex or the other, many jobs have had requirements that have deliberately or unconsciously excluded women, such as height requirements. As a result, more stringent requirements now require that to be legal, discrimination must be the result of a bona fide occupational requirement (BFOR) related to the demands of a job. In the USA, Hooters restaurant was able to argue that female sexuality was a BFOR for its servers.

More subtle than sex discrimination, sex segregation concentrates men and women in different occupations. Vertical segregation concentrates women and men in different categories within the same field, while horizontal segregation concentrates them in roughly similar categories within different fields. Sex segregation is so pervasive that we hardly notice it. It matters because we allocate value and pay differentially, and preferentially to task we associate with men and masculinity. Socialization is not sufficient to explain sex segregation; nor is the explanation of socialization able to explain why segregation produces a wage gap.

While the wage gap has closed considerably over the past 25 years, it remains significant. Moreover, since 2000, the gap has remained stable. Its causes are child-bearing/child rearing, discrimination, and sex segregation, all of which interact in complicated ways.

Given the importance of discrimination and segregation to the wage gap, workplace integration is surely a key remedy. Yet there are significant challenges to such integration. The first is a form of gender discrimination that emerges within integrated workplaces. Women find their mobility within organizations limited by the sticky floor and glass ceiling. The glass ceiling consists of many practices and biases, usually informal or even unconscious, that limit women's access to promotion. Despite consensus on the existence and damaging effects of the glass ceiling, however, some commentators feel that men are really the ones trapped in a glass cellar of dangerous and dirty work. While there is no doubt that men are disproportionately clustered in the most dangerous occupations, this is not simply the result of discrimination in a way comparable to the glass ceiling effect.

As workplaces are integrated, women (and minorities) within previously male-dominated workplaces are often treated as tokens—representatives of their 'group' who are both invisible (as individuals) and hypervisible (as members of a minority group within the organization). Tokenism can be stressful for individuals, and fails to truly integrate a workplace. Interestingly, men in female-dominated workplaces, it has been argued, do not experience classic tokenism; instead, they are more likely to be placed onto a glass escalator, to be preferred in hiring and promotion.

Another common response to workplace integration has been sexual harassment. Since the 1970s, in both Canada and the USA, sexual harassment has been legally defined and prosecuted. In the 1990s, largely as a result of attention paid to the Anita Hill-Clarence Thomas hearings, many women came forward to share experiences of harassment in their workplaces. Two forms of harassment were legally distinguished in the USA: quid pro quo and hostile environment. Neither form is fundamentally about sexual attraction; instead, both aim at asserting power. Not surprisingly, therefore, sexual harassment can involve men as victims, and can also involve perpetrators who are not sexually oriented toward their victims.

Remedies for workplace inequality include pay equity, interventionist hiring and promotion strategies, and family-friendly workplace policies that are the opposite of the 'mommy track'. Today, the emphasis is less upon workplace policies as 'women's issues' and more on the creation of better workplaces for men and women. In this way, the long struggle of women for justice within paid employment can be seen to be a benefit to all workers.

Questions for Critical Thinking

1. What do you believe are the causes and implications of the long-term trend to greater workforce participation by women?
2. Can you think of fields or workplaces in your community in which there are examples of horizontal and/or vertical segregation? What about your university or post-secondary institution?

3. Does the glass cellar exist? Why are men overrepresented in dirty, dangerous jobs? Will this always be the case?
4. Does sexual harassment law make it impossible to begin a sexual relationship with a co-worker? Where is the line between sexual attraction and sexual harassment?
5. Which needs to change more to produce work-family balance: work or family?

Key Terms

bona fide occupational requirement (BFOR)

deviance neutralization

employment equity

family-friendly workplace policies

glass ceiling

glass cellar

glass escalator

horizontal segregation

hostile environment sexual harassment

male breadwinner/female housewife model

Meiorin test

mommy track

pay equity

pin money

precarious employment

quid pro quo sexual harassment

sex segregation

sexual harassment

sticky floor

tokenism

vertical segregation

wage gap

Chapter 9

The Gendered Media

Difference and Domination Glamourized

> Mass media schools the young in the values of patriarchal masculinity. On mass media screens today, whether television or movies, mainstream work is usually portrayed as irrelevant, money is god, and the outlaw guy who breaks the rules prevails.
>
> —BELL HOOKS, *WE REAL COOL: BLACK MEN AND MASCULINITY*

To say that the media are a gendered institution, as bell hooks suggests above, is to say simply that they are an institution, like all other institutions (schools, churches, families, corporations, or states, for example), that (1) reflects existing gender differences and gender inequalities, (2) constructs those very gender differences, and (3) reproduces gender inequality by making those differences seem 'natural' and not socially produced in the first place.

Media *reflect* existing gender differences and inequalities by targeting different groups of consumers with different messages that assume prior existing differences. Often, women and men don't use or consume the same media—there are women's magazines and men's magazines, chick flicks and action movies, chick lit and lad lit, pornography and romance novels, soap operas and crime procedurals, guy video games and girl video games, blogs and 'zines—and, of course, advertising that is intricately connected to each of these different formats. There are also multiple medias based on race, class, ethnicity, and age (think of the complex rating system that says what age level is appropriate for some media content). Each of these genres *constructs* gender by offering us models of what manhood or womanhood might be.

The gendered media are part of a gigantic cultural apparatus that *reproduces* gender inequality by making it appear that such inequality is the natural result of existing gender differences. First, the media create the differences; then the media tell us that the inequality is the natural result of those differences.

The Media as Socializing Institution

That the media are a primary institution of socialization is an essential starting point in our analysis. And such a perspective takes us far beyond the traditional sociological canon. If you were to pick up an introductory sociology textbook from, say, the 1950s or even the 1970s, you would find that there were three major institutions tasked with the socialization of children: family, religion, and education. Their purpose was the gradual and complete inculcation of a society's values, leading to an acceptance of the legitimacy of established norms and a belief in the institutional apparatuses designed to maintain social cohesion and stability. And you would read that the agents—people—charged with those socializing tasks were, naturally, parents (family), teachers (education), and religious figures (clergy).

All well and good, and, of course, largely true. But to a child, the earlier list above—parents, teachers, and clergy—sounds more like 'grown-ups, grown-ups, and grown-ups'. And any child could tell you that the primary agents of socialization are also their friends, their peers, and the images of themselves they see represented in the media. We must now revise all those old textbooks to include the *five* primary institutions of socialization: family, schools, and religious institutions, to be sure—and also peer groups and the media.

But it's not that simple. The media are quite unlike other social institutions in some ways. *First*, the media are not based on personal interaction (think of school, religion, and family) and direct communication; as is obvious, they are mediated communication, and until recently, their influence seemed to go in one direction only. Thus many of the debates about the effects of the media present the media as the sole actor in the drama—and the consumer, namely us, as passive consumers, as sponges who uncritically soak up all the messages we're fed.

To the social scientist, of course, nothing could be further from the truth. Not the media, but rather the interaction of consumers and media, remains the constitutive force in gender relations. We are not blank slates upon which these institutions imprint a uniform cultural code. Were that true, how could we explain the massive diversity we observe around us? In every arena—some more, some less, of course—we are active agents of our own socialization, active participants in this process. We bring our selves—our identities, our differences—to our encounters with various media; and we can take from them a large variety of messages. We need to also consider the way we act on the media, the way we consume it, actively, creatively, and often even rebelliously. Increasingly, we have the ability to 'talk back' to media in ways that complicate the producer-consumer relationship.

The media are also not one thing. As the plural title ('media') suggests, this institution comprises many, many forms of communication, types of ownership, ideological stances, and goals. So a *second* distinction between the media and other primary socializing institutions is that, in some ways, the media are considerably more complex. While complex and contradictory in their messages, schools have a curriculum, religions have core texts and institutions, and families their own ideological foundation. The media, in contrast, are comparatively multivarious and lawless.

When we talk about what 'the media' do, we need to be careful to specify which medium we're talking about. In his classic 1964 study *Understanding Media*, the great Canadian philosopher Marshall McLuhan, father of media studies, famously claimed that 'the medium is the message'. What he meant by this is that the medium of communication inevitably affects the user and the nature of the messages received. He urged us to think not only about what we usually think of as the message (content), but how the medium (form or technology) affects us. Taking this lesson to heart, we can't talk about a message received from television as though it's the same as information received in a conversation with a friend or from print or from an Internet blog or text message. In each case, the nature of the medium is a critical part of what we need to consider.

We also need to consider that even each medium contains within it an immense number of variations. So when we talk about the message that 'the movies' carry about gender, we are obviously engaged in gross oversimplification. Are we talking about Canadian movies? American movies? American indie movies? Hollywood movies? Movies directed by Steven Spielberg, or movies directed by Ingmar Bergman? Good media studies, therefore, are very particular in their analyses and careful in their claims.

The question is never whether or not the media do such and such, but rather *how* the media and their consumers interact to create the varying meanings that derive from our interactions with those media. We need to think differently about the media, to treat them as another central institution in our lives, not some outside influence that tells us what to do. The media are a primary institution of socialization. And like all the institutions whose mission is our socialization, the media are deeply gendered. The media are so saturated with images of gender—from normative depictions of appropriate or inappropriate behaviours to images that capture our aspirations and imaginations—that it is sometimes barely noticeable. Sometimes, in fact, that seems to be the chief function of many media—to entertain us by presenting various images of men and women and enabling us to identify with, aspire to, or laugh at them. The ability of media representations to captivate, entertain, shock, and inspire us should not blind us to their role in our socialization as gendered beings.

'His' and 'Hers' Media: Separate and Unequal

Let's look first at gender differences—both in media use and in media content. What we use, what we watch, what we consume—for many years, these have been clearly marked by gender so that we'll know what to choose. Even today, there are his and her magazines, books, TV shows, radio shows, satellite radio, movies, video games. He has *Maxim* and *FHM* and *Sports Illustrated* and *Playboy* and *Penthouse*; she has *Chatelaine, Elle, Flare, Canadian House and Home, Vogue, Glamour, Modern Bride*, and *Cosmopolitan*. He has Spike TV and dozens of sports-related channels; she has the W Network, Oxygen, and Lifetime. He has action flicks and horror movies, 007 and Freddy; she has chick flicks like *Bridget Jones's Diary* and *Pride and Prejudice*. He has *CSI* and *Law and Order* and other crime procedurals; she has *Desperate Housewives* and *Days of Our Lives*. He has on-line pornography and poker; she has on-line shopping, craft blogs, and e-mail contact with family and friends. He has Eminem, 50 Cent, and Nickelback; she has Ani diFranco, Nelly Furtado, and 'grrl power' music. He has GI Joe; she has Barbie and Bratz. Right?

Well, yes and no. By now maybe many of the male readers of this book are nodding their heads in agreement. 'Yeah, that's true, that's the stuff I watch and I would never watch or listen to what *she* likes. Yuck'. And maybe many women are saying, 'Huh? I like some of the so-called "his" media! And I definitely do not like some of the stuff under "her" media'.

And you'd both be right. One way to look at it is that he has 'his' media, but she can also share 'his' media—that she seems to have more choices than he does. Or you could say that he wouldn't be caught dead consuming her media, whereas the penalties when she crosses over into his media are far less severe.

And maybe some of the men reading this book are saying, 'Hey, come on! I love cooking blogs, and I always read *Chatelaine* when I'm at my sister's house—and I even buy *Canadian House and Home* sometimes'. And you're right too. 'He' might well be reading 'her' magazines—there are many men who read women's, cooking, and decorating magazines—but if he's your average straight man, he probably won't talk to his friends about them. It is not simply that the gendered world of media production and consumption is neatly divided into his and her realms. It is also useful to remember what Jessie Bernard said about marriage. Not only is there 'his' and 'hers', she wrote, but also 'his is better than hers'.

That's not just a reflection of difference: It's the production of inequality.

His and Hers TV

As the media are saturated with gender, we are saturated with the media. In 1949, Canada had only 3600 television sets. Today, there are more television sets in Canada than people. This is in line with US statistics, which are if anything more dramatic. The average American home today has 3 television sets, 1.8 VCRs, 3.1 radios, 2.6 tape players, 2.1 CD players, 1.4 video game players, and at least 1 computer. American kids between ages 8 and 18 spend seven hours a day interacting with some form of electronic media—which may explain why 40 per cent of 8- to 13-year-olds said they did not read any part of a book on the previous day, a figure that shoots up to 70 per cent of kids aged 14 to 18.[1]

Though 'the tube' is gradually being supplanted by the Internet, TV remains omnipresent: In the USA, 58 per cent of families with children have the TV on during dinner, and 42 per cent are 'constant television households'—that is, they have a TV on virtually all day, whether or not anyone is actually watching it.

Canadians watch slightly less TV than Americans, averaging about 21 hours per week (this number has declined since 1995 as a result of growing Internet and video-game use). Young men watch the least television, at about 12 hours a week, while women 60 and over watch the most, averaging almost 36 hours in front of the screen.[2] That's a lot of TV time. And whereas once restaurants and bars were a way to escape the isolation of being in front of the tube, now those restaurants and bars, and even dentist's offices, are likely to have TVs mounted on the walls so you don't have to miss a second.

Most of the television Canadians watch is American. There are exceptions, like *Corner Gas* and *Canadian Idol*. We like our CBC or CTV news, and we all love *Hockey Night in Canada* (more on that below). But when it comes to prime time, we like American programming. We watch American TV more than any non-American nation in the world, and many of us don't even think of it as 'foreign'.

As the above statistics on TV use suggest, different media appeal to different audiences who use them differently. These different ways of using 'his' and 'her' media are one of the primary ways in which we construct our gendered identities—and this, then, becomes one of the chief ways in which we naturalize gender inequality. However, the neat division between his and hers is blurring. The changing nature of television is a perfect illustration of these dynamics. For years, television neatly divided up its audience into its targeted demographic niches to better enable advertisers to reach the consumers they most wanted to reach.

At TV's dawn and for decades thereafter, all gender stereotypes were fully in place. Back then, male characters were more courageous and active, fighting crime and solving mysteries. Female characters were caring but befuddled housewives who occasionally ventured outside the home only to realize that they really loved baking cookies. These stereotypes are important, especially because increased exposure to images of inequality often can contribute to more stereotypical ideas; and the more television you watch, the more gender-stereotypic are your gender attitudes likely to be.[3]

The 1950s prototypical female character, Lucy, spent most of her time devising strategies to get out of the house and into the workplace—preferably acting, singing, or dancing in Ricky's nightclub revue. Lucy is the standard bearer of the genre, constantly coming up with hare-brained ideas to work outside the home and just as constantly screwing them up and returning to Ricky's admonishingly forgiving domestic embrace. Likewise, Alice Cramden of *The Honeymooners* found that by staying home she really was the authority figure.[4] (Though her husband might brandish his fist at her and threaten to send her 'to the moon', he never went through with it, unlike some husbands of the time).

By the late 1960s, the TV airwaves were stocked with cartoon-like people in evening programs that showed women as less visible and helpless, usually indoors, and constantly serving the needs of others; men, by contrast, were engaged in physical activities (like climbing trees) and depicted as the rescuers, leaders, actors, often outdoors.

But in 1970, a new female character appeared on *The Mary Tyler Moore Show*. Single and sexual, Mary Richards was also a go-getter on the job and quite unwilling to sacrifice career for family life. She wanted it all. It was the first time that a single 'career woman' had been the lead character in a TV show—and audiences loved it. Though Mary Richards may appear to modern viewers a kind of harmless Mary Poppins type, her character opened the door for a parade of women who were less subservient to men (*Rhoda* and *Cagney and Lacey*); more assertive in the workplace as well as at home (*Roseanne*); not even especially 'nice' (*Murphy Brown*); and, finally, gay (*Ellen*).

In fact, television in the 1970s and 1980s—in the wake of the civil rights and feminist movements—transformed itself pretty significantly, partly in response to feminist and minority media critics who began to point out just how separate and unequal the world of the small screen actually was. They highlighted how women and men watched (or were presumed to watch) different shows; how the scheduling of 'women's' programming during the day presumed that all women were 'housewives'; how news anchors were always white males, while women got stuck in social reporting and the role of 'weather girl'; how absent ethnic minorities were from representation, and how stereotypical their representation was when it occurred;

and how, in general, television characters fully reproduced gender and racial stereotypes. Networks' response? The 'ensemble' cast, including several female and minority characters, which became a new television norm by the mid-1980s. By the 1990s, ensembles could even be largely non-white; *North of Sixty* was a breakthrough program for Canada, offering the first substantial depiction of Aboriginal people on Canadian television.

The ensemble prime-time drama (like *LA Law* in the 1980s, *ER* and *NYPD Blue* in the 1990s, and *Grey's Anatomy, DaVinci's Inquest,* and *Lost* today) has far more racial and gender diversity than any other TV shows in our history. Today, women appear to be nearly as at home in the workplace as they are at home, and virtually all prime-time dramas include female doctors, lawyers, judges, and cops. Even standard formats like crime procedurals and detective stories have been refashioned with more diverse casts, as in the *CSI* and *Law and Order* franchises. Women have entered the formerly all-male workplace—the police station, court house, hospital operating theatre—in both real life and prime-time drama. (Even *Desperate Housewives* is a clever throwback that presumes a certain new equality of desire—and boredom—in domestic life!)

These changes in women's real and media-depicted lives have not been matched with parallel changes in the depiction (or the realities) of men's lives. Men still seem to troop off to work, as ambitious and motivated as ever, but maybe not as respected. Gone are the days when men found themselves depicted as devoted dads like Jim Anderson or Ward Cleaver, whose careers rarely tugged at their time. When men return home, they usually are the butt of humour—witness Homer Simpson's and Tim Allen's inability to rule the roost and Dan Conner's utter lack of interest in it. This isn't an entirely new phenomenon—the humour of fathers' incompetence, bluster, and loafing was a key feature of *The Honeymooners* and *Ozzie and Harriet* in the 1950s and 1960s. And, to be sure, there are exceptions, like Bill Cosby, who played a successful career man and loving father on *The Cosby Show* in the 1980s. But most men do most of their nurturing and caring (and demonstrate most competence) in the public sphere, in the workplace, the way Mark Greene did on *ER*.

Moreover, sexual diversity on television has been a longer time coming than a more accurate racial and gender representation of North American society. People often point to *Ellen,* but it's worth noting that Ellen was a closeted character until the end of the series. Really, not until the late 1990s with NBC's *Will & Grace* was there a program with openly gay main characters. The recent success of Showtime's Vancouver-filmed series *The L-Word* (2005–2009) may augur well for sexual diversity on TV.

In the representation of gender and sexuality, then, television images generally mirror North American ambivalence about change. Almost everybody is heterosexual, and ethnic stereotypes remain powerful. Women can leave the home but will encounter problems in sustaining a satisfying family life; men cannot find a way back into domestic life without being emasculated. Thus in our real lives and on TV, gender difference and gender inequality are mutually reinforcing ideologies.

At the same time, there are signs that the world of TV is changing. There are some encouraging fissures in the structure as well as moments of reform and resistance to traditional notions of gender difference. For one thing, American women have been abandoning the traditionally 'female' TV world of daytime soap opera, a decline of nearly 10 per cent in 2005 alone. Women cross over far more readily than men do, and they're leaving the all-female ghetto. 'I think women have broad tastes and are more likely to watch a show their husband or boyfriend wants to watch than the reverse', noted Susanne Daniels, president of entertainment at Lifetime Television. At the same time, in Canada, *Coronation Street* remains a franchise to be reckoned with. While American soap operas are in decline, the CBC has moved *CS* from its daytime slot to prime time to accommodate passionate viewers of *both* sexes. The popularity of *CS*, the UK's longest-running TV show, suggests that Canadians have an appetite for grittier, more realistic working-class representations than available on US soap operas. (Interestingly, this style of daytime drama was anticipated in the 1950s by Quebec's *La famille Plouffe*.)[5] And the CBC takes on multiculturalism in the current series *Little Mosque on the Prairie,* which deals with Muslim/non-Muslim interactions in a (fictional) small town on the Prairies.

While Canadian men and women both enjoy *Coronation Street*, the notion of women's programming is alive and well on American TV. Oprah—imitated by many—cocks her head to the side and nods empathically, really listening to your heartache. (Among the more notable exceptions are Dr Phil, who embodies tough love, empathic but stern, and Ann Coulter, who loves being tough.)

And while women watch Oprah, male viewers have been leaving network television in droves. Executives now worry about the 'feminization of prime time'. Late at night, though, it's a steady parade of men: Letterman, Leno, Kimmel (no relation!), Conan, and all the rest. This is the new male media, the 'den' of television, the garage, the barbecue pit—the 'man's zone'. At least here, in this virtual 'room of his own', a man can finally be alone—with other guys.

Networks want men because they are the consumers everyone wants to land, the supposed driving engine of North American consumerism. (This is, by the way, a myth, because women either influence or make about 85 per cent of all consumer purchases, including those of cars and stereo equipment. This shows how ideology—men buy stuff and women use it—trumps even the market research the networks pay so handsomely for.) Network executives are trying desperately to recapture these guys, who are bailing out for the Internet, cable, video games, and other media. Some networks are even gobbling up small video and Internet games to add content to lure the lads back.[6]

Fortunately for these desperate networks, there's sport: sports TV, sports radio, sports magazines and newspapers, and the sports section of the daily newspaper. There are dozens of sports on television every single day and dozens of shows about sports in between. And if you don't want to watch sports, talk about sports on sports radio, or read about sports in sports magazines or daily newspapers, perhaps you'll want to watch non-sports TV or listen to non-sports radio.

And if you're in Canada, there's *Hockey Night in Canada*, the greatest TV franchise in the nation and a cornerstone of national identity. Hockey was important across Canada before broadcasting, but *HNIC* made it into a *national* institution, first on radio (1931–1965) and most importantly on television (1952–present). This significantly predated any national sports programming in the USA.

When Canadian homes had only one television set and no Internet access, the rhythm of many families' Saturdays was dictated by *HNIC*. After an early dinner, while

Mom washed up, Dad and the kids settled around the television. (Notice the reproduction of gender part?)

Even today, on any given Saturday, millions of Canadians tune into the program. Canadians like *HNIC* so much that the cancellation of the 2004-05 season produced a significant, measurable drop in Canadian viewership of Canadian and sports programming. We might have tuned into other sports, but we didn't; instead, we turned on the American reality TV. *HNIC* is one of the few cultural institutions that unites us, as both anglophone and francophone viewers tune in to commune across the Two Solitudes. Along with key moments like the 1972 Summit Series—ask a man over 50 where he was when Paul Henderson scored—*HNIC*, not necessarily hockey itself, has shaped how we think of ourselves as Canadians. (The game is discussed further in Chapter 11.)

But the picture presented by *HNIC* is a curious one. On one hand, we have the beauty of the game; the intensity, the innocence and nostalgia of Everyman's connection between what he sees on the screen and his own experiences; and every winter, the Tim Hortons cup with the kids playing shinny on the pond. On the other hand, we have the corporate reality of a profit-driven league in partnership with sponsors and advertisers; 'a cultural ritual within a gendered social order', in Sandra Langley's phrase; a celebration of violence as spectacle; and a picture of Canada that is overwhelmingly male, white, heterosexual, able-bodied—in short, representative of hegemonic masculinity. No matter how much we pride ourselves on 'our game', the gender constructions *HNIC* produces may not be that different from those of the American programming that most of us enjoy. [7]

So far we've talked about gender on television only in terms of adults, and in Canada, adults indeed do watch more television than children or adolescents. But children remain staunch viewers of television, despite the fact that we are pretty sure it's not good for their waistlines or, in the youngest children, their development. According to a 2006 Angus Reid poll, 16 per cent of us put television in our children's rooms (a much lower percentage than in the USA, by the way). Canadian children watch an average of 14 hours of television per week; by the time a Canadian child graduates from high school, he/she may have spent more hours watching television than going to school. Children watch more television at different ages. According to one study, at age five, children watch about 2.5 hours per day; this rises to 4 hours at age 10, and then declines again in adolescence to 2–3 hours. Infant television watching is increasing. [8]

Television takes vast chunks of its time to deliver entertainment and commercial messages to younger children as well as to those in school. There are programs for preschoolers in the morning, for school children in the afternoon, and for all children every Saturday morning. For many children, this is one of their largest commitments of waking time; for parents, it often serves as a built-in baby sitter.

Television, films, and other media also habituate viewers, young and old, to a culture that accepts and expects violence. In the USA's most thorough investigation of violence on television, the National Television Violence Study, four teams of researchers systematically examined TV violence. They found that violence is ubiquitous (61 per cent of all shows contained some violence) and that typically it is perpetuated by a white male, who goes unpunished and shows little remorse. The violence is typically justified, although nearly one-half (43 per cent) of shows presented it in a humorous way. Consistently, 'the serious and long-lasting consequences of violence are frequently ignored'. Given that the context in which violence is shown is important to children's imitation of violence, this is disturbing.[9]

Canadian programming is often seen as less violent than that of the USA, which may be true. But this may not matter much to what kids see, given that much of our programming is of American origin. Disturbingly, violence on Canadian TV has been steadily increasing since 1993, despite public concern about the issue. And private networks' programming (much of it, of course, from the USA) contains three times the number of violent incidents seen on programs delivered by our public broadcaster.[10]

The presentation of gender roles on children's television shows has been, at least until recently, quite similar to that of children's readers, the playground, and the schools. Boys are the centrepiece of a story; they do things and occupy the valued roles. While iconic Canadian serials *The Friendly Giant* and *Mr Dressup* never presented harmful stereotypes, and offered gentler, slower fare to young viewers, it's difficult to imagine female characters becoming as successful or as beloved of both girls and boys.

In most American children's shows, girls serve as backdrop, are helpful and caring, and occupy the less-valued roles. Even *Sesame Street*, hailed as a breakthrough in enjoyable educational programming, presented far more male characters than female. The CRTC's 1990 study of television representations found that cartoons presented the most gender-imbalanced picture, with fewer than 25 per cent of depicted characters female. In children's live-action shows, slightly more than a third of all characters were female, in line with adult programming. If the number of female characters children see is a concern, the way those characters are depicted is highly stereotyped. According to the CRTC study, female characters are younger than males; more likely to be married; are often seen in a family setting; are shown with children and caring for children; and perform housework. Male characters have paid employment, and both commit and are victims of violence.[11]

Dora the Explorer presents a female character presented as both caring *and* competent, and a bicultural role model for both girls and boys. That's something to celebrate. But Nickelodeon could not resist introducing Diego, Dora's brother, who offers a more stereotypical action experience, in order to attract more boy viewers. Still, the presence of such an enormously successful show based on a competent female lead character suggests that things are changing.

But television isn't just about programming. The existence of advertising is what makes the programming possible, after all. Commercials for children on Saturday morning usually depict gender-stereotyped play (when was the last time you saw a boy on TV playing with a My Little Pony?). There has been some pressure to eliminate gender stereotyping in both commercials and show content, but television shows are linked to a gender-stereotyped system. Toy manufacturers sell gender-linked toys, parents buy them, and writers often take their stories from existing materials (including the toys that are for sale, such as GI Joe and the Ninja Turtles) for children.

Television commercials are especially powerful, perhaps even more powerful than the shows themselves, because they are expressly designed to persuade. Commercials also link gender roles to the significant adult roles that the young will be playing in the future. Similarly, gender stereotypes are attached to consumption, one of the most valued activities in North American society. By linking material benefits to gender roles, the commercials teach a powerful lesson—if you consume this product, this is the kind of man or woman you can be. Perhaps it's the commercials, and not the programming, that makes children who watch TV more likely to hold rigid ideas about gender.

Advertising for adults is no less stereotyped. (If you want an almost infinite catalogue of examples, see Scott Lukas's wonderful website, GenderAds.com.) One of the most popular ads of the 2009 SuperBowl used what Lukas calls a common advertising stereotype of women: The Nagger. In the ad, Mr Potato Head is driving a yellow convertible at high speeds on a winding mountain road. His tuberous female companion is sending up a litany of complaints, from the unsafe manner of his driving to the fact that the wind is messing her hair and he never listens to her. When he is forced to brake suddenly, her detachable mouth flies over a nearby embankment. She begins to berate him before realizing that she can no longer speak. She switches her bulging eyes for a glaring pair and they drive off, with Mr Potato Head displaying a delighted smirk at having finally shut her up.

Attention-getting and, to many male viewers, funny, this ad is an example of how advertising presumes and addresses itself to a male consumer, relying on a stereotyped idea of 'how women are' to build a bond between the advertiser and individual watchers. We can tell who's supposed to buy something by the nature of the commercials we see. According to CRTC research, though Canadian women drink alcohol as do men, most alcohol commercials feature men, and in the minority of ads where women do appear, they don't speak. You've seen those ads—they're the ones where women are there as decoration, not as people who might buy the alcohol being advertised.[12]

The role of women as decoration in commercials is almost too obvious to mention. Depictions of women's bodies are used to sell a panoply of products. Despite the fact that there are more men in commercials than women, women's bodies, often apparently nude or semi-nude, appear much more frequently than do men's. Men's voices, however, are most often heard in voice-overs, except in commercials for feminine hygiene. And older women, along with men and women of colour, are rarely seen at all unless a commercial specifically targets 'their demographic'. The Dove Real Beauty advertising campaign, which began in 2004, is an interesting counterpoint. Though the campaign has been criticized as opportunistic, Dove's Real Beauty ads have at least broadened the kinds of images we see on the screen: too much for the FCC, which banned Dove's recent 'Pro-aging' ad for showing 'too much' skin. (Maybe the fact that it was aging skin had something to do with it?)[13]

Thus advertising, like much of the programming on television, offers up a highly gendered vision of the world that, according to many commentators, is out of step with the realities of contemporary North America. Perhaps that's understandable. After all, people watch television primarily to be entertained, and not always to receive a crystal-clear reflection of the world they perceive around them. But the power of these representations to construct our desires and realities means that depictions of gender on television should be taken seriously. In the 1950s, for example, the *Father Knows Best* family was no more everyone's reality than it is now. But audiences responded to that representation and made it their own, modelling their own aspirations and realities upon what they saw on screen. Over time, the picture of 'family' represented in that show and others became what people saw as the 'traditional' family.

That doesn't mean that TV imprints itself on us as if we were blank slates. Although the media influence our ideas about gender, both children and adults negotiate a real world of people who do not fit these stereotypes. Nor do television representations have the dramatic and immediate effects that media critics often ascribe to them, because most human learning is a steady accumulation of information, attitudes, and ways of responding rather than a sudden revelation or recognition. TV simply provides another push toward accepting current arrangements as if they were natural, right, and preordained.

His and Hers Print Media

As TV is gendered, so too are those older, more established media, like books and magazines, particularly in their consumption. Women and men buy and read different sorts of books and magazines and read them differently. In the literary world, women outnumber men in the purchase of every single genre (except war and sports stories), and they also buy 80 per cent of all fiction sold in the United States and Europe. That's right—four out of every five novels are bought by women—and that includes 'guy-writers' like Tom Clancy, whose action- and intrigue-filled books are populated by 'evil villains who are often women, Communists, or both' and which 'vilify liberals, academics, homosexuals, the news media, and other putative challengers of the Cold War ethos'.[14]

So is the novel itself a 'feminine' form? Well, looking at Canada's bestseller list for 2008, you might think the novel was something particularly written for adolescent girls. The top-selling work of the year was the ostensibly gender-neutral New Age book *A New Earth*, by German-Canadian New Age mystic Eckhart Tolle. The remaining spots in the top five, however, were occupied by one or another volume of Stephanie Meyers' blockbuster *Twilight* series, representative of the power of gothic-light eroticism among today's female teens.

And think for a moment of the meteoric rise of 'chick lit'—the most successful new genre of fiction in the past quarter-century. **Chick lit**, like Helen Fielding's *Bridget Jones's Diary* in 1998, which sold two million copies, spawned two sequels, two films, and countless imitators, centres on affably befuddled modern urban women who struggle mightily to sustain careers that don't consume them and develop intimate relationships with men who do. It's the literary version of *Sex and the City*—or, according to some, it's what Jane Austen would have written were she alive today.

Now consider the sad fate of '**lad lit**'—the male riposte to chick lit. It was ostensibly heralded by Nick Hornby's *High Fidelity*, in which Rob, a 35-year-old London slacker, works at a record store and organizes his life by Top-5 lists; or *About a Boy*, in which the well-named Will Lightman drifts along on inherited family money (his father composed a truly horrific and massively successful Christmas jingle). Worldly wise and wisecracking, both men are temperamentally unable to commit to relationships or even to a sense of purpose in their own lives. But then something happens—and they actually do get a life, commit, and live, if not happily, then at least in a relationship, ever after.

But contemporary American purveyors of lad lit present a sort of anti-bildungsroman, in which a wry, clever, unapologetic slacker refuses to grow up, get a meaningful job, commit to relationships, or find some meaning in life. Works such as *Booty Nomad*, *Love Monkey*, and *Indecision* have tanked at the bookstore and failed miserably as TV adaptations. And they failed precisely because their protagonists refuse to be transformed in the course of the novel by their relationship with women. They failed because *women* won't read them unless there is some hope of redemption, and men won't read them because most men don't read fiction—at least not fiction about everyday guys going to bars. One waggish commentator has suggested that lad lit might have done better had it been given the name 'dick lit' to highlight the presence within it of so much sex![15]

While chick lit seems to have won out over lad lit, a quick browse through the list of Nobel Prize for Literature winners (about 90 per cent men), or any list of the top 100 novels of the twentieth century, should convince anyone that the genre is not feminine. Still, one of the most significant developments of the late twentieth century, particularly in Canada, was the emergence of internationally renowned female authors whose works were celebrated and read by both men and women. Think of Alice Munro, Margaret Atwood, or Miriam Toews. While bestseller lists may still look pretty gendered, Canadian readership is considerably more complex.

When we turn from novels to magazines, we turn from a medium that at least aims for longevity to one that is designed to be read and cast aside. Magazines are also unlike books in that they carry at least as much advertising as content. As a result of some analyses, it has become virtually axiomatic in feminist literature that women's magazines are a prime example of women's oppression—that the magazines construct unattainable ideals of femininity, lock women into never-ending struggles to be skinny enough, sexy enough, and gorgeous enough, and thus contribute to women's second-class status.

Actually, this critique is the well from which Betty Friedan poured the second wave of feminism itself with her incendiary call to women, *The Feminine Mystique* (1963). Friedan argued that women's magazines constructed 'a weak, passive, vacuous woman'.[16] 'This image', she wrote, 'created by the women's magazines, by advertisements, television, movies, novels, columns and books by experts on marriage and the family, child psychology, sexual adjustment and by the popularizers of sociology and psychoanalysis . . . is young and frivolous, fluffy and feminine; passive; gaily content in a world of bedroom and kitchen, sex, babies, and the home'.[17] (Never mind that Friedan's book was first serialized in *Mademoiselle* and later in *Ladies' Home Journal* and *McCall's*, where Friedan herself worked as an editor and writer—nor that *Chatelaine* had scooped Friedan by almost a decade!)

Ahead of Their Time? Doris Anderson and *Chatelaine* magazine

When Betty Friedan offered her critique of 'fluffy and feminine' women's magazines in the early 1960s, she clearly wasn't talking about *Chatelaine*. Indeed, as noted above, even the American magazines she criticized serialized her work. But not *Chatelaine*. Why not? Because *Chatelaine* was already 'ten years ahead of American feminism', and Friedan's critique was familiar to Canadian readers. The extraordinary character of the magazine is largely attributable to Doris Anderson, its editor from 1957 to 1977. During these years, the lives of Canadian women changed dramatically, and *Chatelaine* never shrank from examining the public issues most

Keith Beaty/GetStock.com

Doris Anderson

important to Canadian women: workforce equality, marriage and divorce law, discrimination under the Indian Act, pay equity, reproductive choice, prostitution, and political representation. These hard-hitting topics were covered in Anderson's editorials and in articles that coexisted with more traditional women's magazine fare: advice, fashion, family-related information, and recipes.

Chatelaine, now Canada's top-circulation magazine with millions of readers each issue, was founded in 1928. From the start, it cultivated a direct relationship with its readers; it was even named through a contest. And from the beginning, it combined seriousness with its more frivolous and conventional fare. The September 1929 issue, for example, contained an essay on the **Persons' Case**—accompanied by an ad that advised, 'Every man admires lovely, white hands'. *Chatelaine* was, then, a typically contradictory and multivocal women's magazine right from the start.

Under Anderson, however, the magazine became much more consistently identified with a second-wave feminist point of view. Increasingly, *Chatelaine*'s features were substantial and hard-hitting, and Anderson's editorials were the same, 'publicizing feminist issues, urging policy changes, and highlighting areas where Canadian society needed revision'. Readers didn't always like the magazine's editorial stance, but the magazine's circulation grew, and Anderson published reader opinion whether it favoured the magazine's articles or not. Readers remained faithful even when they were disgruntled, probably because Anderson always remembered that she was making the magazine for her 'aunt in Taber'—that is, that the magazine should represent the interests and values of a broad section of Canadian women, not just a regional, ethnic, or class elite.

In fact, the history of *Chatelaine* suggests that our ideas about the relationship between print media and their public need complicating. The magazine was not simply beaming out material to be absorbed by acquiescent readers; rather, it engaged in a long-term relationship with them. Sometimes the magazine seemed to readers to be too far in the political vanguard, and received vituperative letters from both women and men; but sometimes it was readers who accused the magazine of being behind the times.

Nowhere was this more clear than in the annual Mrs Chatelaine contest, which throughout the 1960s annually selected a 'Canadian homemaker' who would receive (in addition to the honour implied by the title) cash and other prizes. While thousands of women vied for the title, submitting lengthy application packages documenting their height and weight along with their housecleaning regimes and other required details, many readers submitted critical letters or mock entries that pointed out how conventional and narrow the Mrs Chatelaine contest was. In fact, one reader went so far as to suggest that instead they run a 'Mrs Slob' contest, which she and others like her might have a chance of winning. According to Valerie Korinek, while some readers enjoyed traditional women's magazine fare, others 'were resistant, critical, or dismissive and wrote to the magazine to challenge the sometimes narrow definitions of Canadian women'. They thus participated in a national conversation that redefined Canadian womanhood. Eventually, in 1969, a working mother won the contest for the first time.

Anderson's tenure as editor came to a close in 1977 when her hoped-for promotion to publisher failed to materialize. Thereafter, the magazine's circulation declined until the early 1990s, when the magazine (under Rona Maynard's stewardship) overhauled itself and sought a new generation of readers. Today, *Chatelaine* is the country's top-earning magazine, pulling in a remarkable $56 million in revenue in 2008. While some feel that 'something's missing from the mix', that the magazine has lost much of the impact it had in the Anderson years, *Chatelaine* remains a distinctive Canadian voice as well as the top-selling magazine in the country.[18]

Others have fully embraced this critique, from sociologist Gaye Tuchman in her 1977 co-edited volume, *The Symbolic Annihilation of Women by the Mass Media*, to media critic Jean Kilbourne in her trenchant critique of advertising images of women, *Killing Us Softly*, to, finally, Naomi Wolf in her debut work, *The Beauty Myth*.[19]

Recently, though, conservative commentators have assailed the American women's magazine for having exactly the opposite impact on women: rendering them dissatisfied by instilling ideals of careers, consumerism, and independence, and making them believe that they can 'have it all'. The Media Research Center, in Alexandria, Virginia, a conservative watchdog group, studied 13 popular women's magazines over a 12-month period and reported in late 1996 that all are 'left-wing political weapon[s]' that 'hammer home a pro-big government message and urge liberal activism'. Christina Hoff Sommers accused such magazines as *Redbook*, *Mademoiselle*, *Good Housekeeping*, and *Parenting* of advancing 'Ms.-information'.[20] So one side says women's magazines enslave women to household drudgery, and the other side says such magazines offer them liberal propaganda and false freedoms. Who's right?

Each polarized position focuses on only one element and is therefore wrong. Women's magazines do both. Pick up a copy of *Flare* or *Vogue* or *Jane* or *Marie Claire* sometime. Sure, there are several articles instructing readers on how to lose 10 pounds in a week or keep their boyfriends sexually delighted and photo spreads of the sexiest new bikinis and lipsticks. *And* there is also an article about how the right wing is trying to take away your right to choose and about how global warming might impact more than your shopping for next year's Uggs. In other words, women's magazines offer **polyvocality**—multiple voices, differing perspectives.

And it's always been that way. Since the first women's magazines appeared, Amy Aronson found, this polyvocality has been one of the hallmarks of women's magazines— which makes them, in a sense, so democratic. (The earliest women's magazines were largely composed of letters to the editor and articles cribbed from other magazines.) Women's magazines are so polyvocal because women cross over into men's arenas (like the workplace or sexual agency). Women are not duped into being household drudges or glamorous objects or liberal harpies because women are so diverse.[21]

Men's magazines in comparison are as monotonal as you can get. Pick up *Maxim* or *FHM*. On the front cover of virtually every issue are bikini-clad buxom babes, usually drenched in sweat or water. Inside, along with articles about muscles and sexual prowess, are nearly naked starlets, models, and other assorted hotties, all suggestively posed. 'All babes all the time' is, apparently, the only way to successfully launch a new magazine geared exclusively to this demographic segment. The two magazines boast 2.5 million and 1 million subscribers, respectively. According to its editors, *Maxim's* readers are overwhelmingly male (76 per cent), unmarried (71 per cent), and young (median age is 26).[22]

Maxim is but one of a spate of 'lad' magazines that began in Britain, in part as an anti-feminist backlash, a way to help men 'regain their self-esteem', having been 'diminished by the women's movement'. In North America, Madison Avenue advertisers have tried for years to figure out how to market cosmetics—shaving paraphernalia, colognes, skin-care products—to straight white men. But *Maxim* figured it out by being brazen enough to make every magazine cover a wet T-shirt contest. And it's been wildly successful.[23]

As has *Men's Health*, the most successful magazine launched in 1987. Once devoted to organic foods and herbal medicines for various men's illnesses, *Men's Health* reconfigured itself into a 'lifestyle' magazine with cover celebrities covers (including Barack Obama) and appearance-oriented articles. Next to pointers on how to have abs of steel, buns of iron, and other body parts turned into resilient metals flows a steady stream of articles about how to drive her wild in bed, how to be bigger, thicker, harder, and how to have more sexual endurance. *Men's Health* both reflects and creates sexual anxiety by suggesting one can never be potent enough or enough of a sexual athlete. There's more than a little of the lad in the man, apparently.

Recently, however, there have been signs that lad magazines may have had their run. In the first half of 2008, *Maxim's* circulation in the UK dropped by 59.6 per cent. Fellow 'lads' *FHM* and *Loaded* also dropped, while *Men's Health* and *GQ* saw increases in circulation. In spring 2009, the publishers pulled the plug on the UK print edition of *Maxim*. The end? Possibly, though *Maxim* still sells about 2.5 million issues in the USA, and remains the 'best-selling men's lifestyle magazine in the world'. No one has attempted to launch a Canadian lad mag, but there have been recent launches of fashion-oriented Canadian magazines in the *GQ* mode. So far, Canadian men seem to be rather unimpressed. *Toro*, a high-quality general interest magazine lunched in 2003, went belly-up in 2007. *Sharp*, launched in April 2008, may fare better, but doesn't appear regularly on the newsstands—in northern BC, anyway.[24]

And the best-selling single issues of men's magazines in America? The 'swimsuit' issue of *Sports Illustrated*, which depicts women who could not possibly swim in the skimpy bikinis they almost wear, and the 'Back to School' issue of *Playboy*,[25] which features a dozen or so 'co-eds' playfully disrobed. Everywhere, even on campus, the magazines tell us, men are entitled to look at naked women—and the women volunteer to do it. Even those brainy Yalies are, well, just girls who like to take their clothes off for men.

'What we discovered pretty quickly', UK lad magazine publisher Phil Hilton told a journalist, 'is that there is not an age any more when men suddenly grow up and start getting interested in IRAs and bathroom tiles. They are never interested in those things. For better or worse, most men stay interested in looking at girls and knowing about cars and talking about football'.[26]

Why are women's magazines so diverse and men's magazines so monochromatic? The only way to understand these dynamics, we've suggested, is to understand that the worlds of women and men may be separate, but they are not equal. She can enter his world—whether it's the military or science or business—and in both reality and media representation. Girls can play with boys' toys (sports equipment, action heroes, science games), but boys dare not play with girls' toys. Girls can play sports; boys dare not be uninterested in sports. Women can balance family and career; men must stay focused on their careers at all costs. Most of all, men must avoid the 'taint' of association with anything feminine.

Of course, she enters his world on somewhat unequal terms. Magazines that appear to be 'gender-neutral' illustrate this issue. For example, when *Forbes* or *Fortune* has an article about a female CEO, it's always the 'women's issue', and the female gender is played to attract female readers. That is, readers of these mainstream magazines about money and finance have two groups of consumers: 'female readers' (a specialized niche) and 'readers' (the general public, meaning, of course, *men*). *Bad Science*, by science-reporting gadfly Ben Goldacre, illustrates this perfectly when discussing the microscope. When you get a microscope, the author advises 'looking at your sperm; it's quite a soulful moment'. The presumption is obvious: if you're reading this book about science, you must have sperm.[27]

Thus far in our history, gender equality has come almost entirely from women entering 'male' spheres formerly closed to them. Everywhere, she crosses over, while he doesn't (or keeps it on the down-low if he does). This is particularly clear in the teen market. How many boys read *Twilight*? (Some do, but judging from the blogosphere, it's a real source of anxiety for them.) And while girls avidly read boy-oriented graphic novels and Japanese **manga**, it doesn't work in the other direction. *Shonen Jump*, a magazine that anthologizes manga series, premiered in 2003 and now sells hundreds of thousands of copies per issue to a readership that is at least one-third female. Meanwhile, its sister publication, *Shojo Beat*, which aimed at the female market, ceased publication in July 2009.[28]

As for adult men, many have retreated into smaller and smaller pristine preserves of 'pure' masculinity that become increasingly hyperbolic in their assertions of the one 'true' way to be a 'real man'. Though there are signs of change—who knew über-lad Phil Hilton was a Jane Austen fan?[29]—there are also signs of retrenchment, nowhere more than in certain genres of popular music.

Gender, Race, Rap, and Rock

So women and men are pretty much consuming 'his' media—at least a lot more than they are consuming 'her' media. Nowhere is that more the case than in the popular music world, dominated by rock and rap/hip-hop. While rock remains the top popular music genre in the USA, rap, since 2000, has been a solid second, selling more than the country and pop genres and numerous subgenres. Globally, hip-hop is even more successful than rock. Rap/hip-hop appeals most to younger audiences; thus, its continued popularity is predictable, even given recent declines in its US market share that have overeager pundits prematurely writing the genre's obituary.[30]

Rap is a 'loud scratchy, in-your-face aesthetic' that 'sprang off the uptown streets of New York City and has come to represent to the world the current generation of black male teenage life'. Rooted in both rhythm and rhyme, rap is a musical form now heard around the world. Its popularity transmits African-American culture and images around the world, and it has become entrenched in a variety of global contexts, including among Canadian Aboriginal youth, who are attracted to the gritty authenticity of the medium and its ability to tell their stories in unsanitized form; as a result, rap has become one of the most popular genres among youth both on and off reserves.[31]

Rap's rise to popularity has not been without controversy. The rap on rap music has long been its vile misogyny, its celebration of gangsta thuggery, predatory sexuality, and violence. In its defence, rap's promoters and fans argue that the genre's symbolic assertions of manhood are necessary for an inner-city black youth for whom racism and poverty have been experienced as so emasculating. And the more misogynist elements of rap, like the genre itself, seem to resonate with disaffected men in other parts of the world. This is evidenced by recent controversy over French rapper OrelSan's 'Sale Pute', (Dirty Slut), in which a character rages at his adulterous partner: 'I wonder how you'll play the princess with a broken leg/I wonder how you'll suck [cock] after I dislocate your jaw'.[32]

While some hip-hop artists and fans have denounced the misogyny of such representations, they fuel its commercial viability. Indeed, the broad-based success of rap was predicated upon its packaging of rappers as 'violent black criminals' and upon market research that found that consumers wanted harsh, explicit lyrics. Gangsta rap was just one form, rooted in the experience of 'the black underclass in the ghetto'. Yet it became *the* face of rap, in North America and around the world; while more socially conscious rap existed, gangsta *sold*. Rapper David Banner claims that his more positive songs had less impact than his hit 'Like a Pimp' because 'America is sick . . . America loves violence and sex'.[33]

And, of course, America has a non-black majority. According to US market researchers and music impresarios, between 70 per cent and 80 per cent of hip-hop consumers are white. Why? Part of the answer is that ghetto masculinity seems so much more 'authentic'. (Think of *Fight Club* and the search for some authentic feeling in a consumer world that leaves you numb.) 'We spend our entire days trying to fit into a perfect little bubble', said one such man to author Bakari Kitwana. 'The perfect $500,000 house. The perfect overscheduled kids . . . We love life, but we hate our lives. And so I think we identify more with hip-hop's passion, anger and frustration than we do this dream world'. Think of how some of these phrases—'you da man', 'keep it real', and 'pimp my ride'—have become standard in young people's lexicon throughout North America. As cultural critic Kevin Powell puts it, white fascination with hip-hop is 'just a cultural safari for white people'.[34]

Appropriation of inner-city presentations of self 'allows whites to contain their fears and animosities towards blacks through rituals not of ridicule, as in previous eras, but of adoration', writes communications professor Bill Yousman. The 'Afro-American-ization of White youth', as Cornell West puts it in his best-selling book, *Race Matters*, turns out to co-exist easily with discrimination. Cultural identification does not neces-sarily lead to political alliance.[35]

On the other hand, race is not the only measure of 'authenticity', as is proved by Eminem. Eminem burst onto the musical scene in 1999 with *The Slim Shady LP*. Emi-nem alternates among three different personae: Shady, his rapper persona, is his angry, vicious adolescent who imagines raping his male cousin and slashing his mother's throat; Marshall Mathers, the persona of his given name, reveals his 'real' emotions; and the Eminem persona allows him to become a show business spectacle. Though he's closing in on 40, he speaks to young white guys like few others. Like other rappers, he drew from a deep well of class-based, gendered rage—a murderous rage directed largely at his mother and girlfriend—as well as adolescent declarations of manhood that were part protest and part phallic fluff.

Eminem is not the first white rapper to make it big; the Beastie Boys beat him there by quite a few years. And he's struggled with claims that he was 'invented' to sell rap to a white audience, or that like Elvis Presley, he's a translator of black mu-sic for white people. Still, Eminem's got credibility. Anointed by hip-hop performer and impresario Dr Dre, Eminem is no fabricated product of white music promoters like Vanilla Ice. In his autobiographical film, *8 Mile*, his ultimate success comes as he defeats a middle-class black rapper (who goes to prep school), thus asserting class solidarity over racial divisiveness. Eminem taps into the desire and thrill of revenge that animate much adolescent masculinity. 'Eminem spoke of situations many of his fans shared', according to his biographer, 'broken homes, dead-end jobs, drug overindulgence—while exploring taboo emotions many couldn't face—parental hate, gender hate, self-loathing'.[36]

Like his black colleagues, Eminem has been criticized for misogyny and homopho-bia. Several songs are explicitly violent. Some offer soliloquies of murderous revenge, like 'Kim' from *The Slim Shady LP* (1999), in which he slits his ex-girlfriend's throat (and commits child murder) to punish her for infidelity. To most women he has only this to say: 'You ain't nothing but a slut to me'. And he boasts that he's been 'put here to put fear in faggots', then boasts of 'rapin' lesbians while they screamin': "let's just be friends!"' Indeed, according to Edward Armstrong's content analysis, Eminem's music contains significantly more violent misogynist content than gangsta rap; thus 'he authenticates his self-presentations by outdoing other gangsta rappers in terms of his violent misogyny.'[37]

Eminem's incessant homophobia and misogyny drew equally incessant criticism. Women's groups denounced his cavalier calls to murder the women who stand in your way; gay groups his obsession with 'faggots'. But he's been neither contrite nor apologetic. He's self-righteous, angrier at liberal critics. 'Now I'm catchin the flack from these activists, Why they raggin, Actin'like I'm the first rapper to smack a bitch and say faggot . . . '. In his recent autobiography, *The Way I Am* (2008), he remains unrepentant.

But is hip-hop (or rap) really that misogynist in comparison to other arenas of pop culture? Are rap's misogyny and homophobia all that different from the violence and macho swagger of heavy metal, hard rock, 80s 'cock rock', or hardcore punk? After all, the Beatles sang 'I'd rather see you dead, little girl than to be with another man' more than 40 years before OrelSan's 'Sale Pute' rant. And that's not the sole example of sexism and misogyny in rock. In 1971, the Rolling Stones released *Sticky Fingers,* an album notable for both its song and its cover art depicting the (masculine) crotch area of a pair of jeans—with a functional zipper! On the album was the rock classic 'Brown Sugar', which tells the story of (and eroticizes) the beating and sexual abuse of a young female slave. Later in the 1970s, the Stones promoted their *Black and Blue* album with an infamous billboard depicting a bruised and bound model and the caption 'I'm Black and Blue from the Rolling Stones . . . and I love it!' 'Some Girls' wasn't that far from rap with its claim that 'French girls they want Cartier/Italian girls want cars . . . Black girls just wanna get fucked all night/I just don't have that much jam'.

The term 'cock rock' arose precisely to describe the attitude toward women that became characteristic of the most popular rock music. The term comes from an essay by an anonymous feminist who went by the name of 'Susan Hiwatt'. She writes:

> [W]hen you get listening to male rock lyrics, the message to women is devastating . . . And all that sexual energy that seems to be in the essence of rock is really energy that climaxes in fucking over women—endless lyrics and a sound filled with feeling I thought I was relating to but couldn't relate to, attitudes about women like put-downs, domination, threats, pride, mockery, fucking around, and a million different levels of women-hating.[38]

Despite this critique, anthologized in 1971, little changed. Seventies glam rockers and the cock-rockers of the 80s had somewhat different representations of their own masculinities, but they agreed on women. Van Halen, Foreigner, Def Leppard, Motley Crüe, Bon Jovi and a host of other successful 80s bands built their image around macho swagger and its demand for 'Girls, Girls, Girls'. In their live performances, as in those of 70s bands like Led Zeppelin, the guitar functioned, in Steve Waksman's term, as an 'electrophallus' that highlighted 'the phallic dimensions of the performing male body'.[39] The body language might be different from that seen in rap videos, but the message is the same: I'm the Man.

And some critically acclaimed rock music goes beyond rampant sexuality to dark themes of violence: witness tortured geniuses Nick Cave and Trent Reznor. Cave's passion for brooding over murdering and murdered women is well known, while Reznor's 'Crushingly Close' has him respond to almost every abject declaration of feminine love with the blunt 'I wanna fuck you like an animal'.

So why, then, is all the talk about sexism and misogyny in rap music, rather than in rock? Part of the answer is race. Much of the debate about misogyny and violence in rap music has pretty much ignored the parallel themes in heavy metal or hard rock, letting white musicians off the same hook used to hang black artists. One UK journalist, while conceding that 'some rap lyrics are poisonously sexist', confesses to his irritation as seeing 'artists of the breadth and depth of [author John] Updike and [Nick] Cave reduced to nasty little sexists by the M-word'.[40] Apparently, a critique of lesser (black) men is all right, but a similar critique of great (white) men just won't do.

But part of the reason for hip-hop's bad rap is also that rock has been changed by the emergence of powerful female artists who contest their male colleagues' representations of women. Ever since Suzi Quattro's 1970s performances, female rockers have been proving that they can do cock rock with the best of the boys. Others crafted their own game; from Joni Mitchell, Patti Smith, and Kate Bush to **Riot Grrl** and Sarah McLachlan's Lilith Fair, there are copious—and successful—examples of powerful, feminist musicians who disprove the sexist cultural script that powered rock for so long. According to Charis Kubrin and Ronald Weitzer, it's not that all hip-hop is misogynist; their survey of 403 rap songs found that only about 20 per cent fell into this category. But, they also found, there's a general *absence* in rap music of 'lyrics that describe women as independent, educated, professional, caring, and trustworthy'. Feminist and non-sexist hip-hop artists have simply not been as influential or as commercially successful enough to impact the genre's message significantly.[41]

Kubrin and Weitzer also agree that 'rap stands out for the intensity and graphic nature of its lyrical objectification, exploitation, and victimization of women'. Hip-hop/rap do seem to delight in supplying stereotypical images of women that blur into frank misogyny. In the video for 'Tip Drill', which is pretty much soft-core porn, a young black male slides a credit card between a young black woman's buttocks. 'Tip drill' is, according to hip-hop scholar Mark Anthony Neal, a colloquialism for an 'ugly girl with a nice body' who is 'only good for one thing—and even then, only from the back'. In the world of hip-hop, Neal argues, women are motivated solely by gold lust, a desire for money that propels them to endure all sorts of degradations and sexually humiliating representations. (That would explain the constant brandishing of money throughout the video.) Rich rappers get all the booty they want, not because they are such swell guys, but rather because they're rich.

And women, whatever their colour, don't always reject the apparent misogyny of such representations; rappers never lack for female company. Ryan Heryford writes of his girlfriend's obsession with Eminem, whom she adores 'because he never backs down'. The appeal of macho posturing aside, it's always somewhat startling to see so many women singing along to lyrics like Dr Dre's 'Bitches ain't shit but hoes and tricks'. Meanwhile, men sing along with 50-Cent: 'If you fucking with me, you fucking with a P-I-M-P'. Male musicians and their listeners celebrate masculine promiscuity and an exaggerated sexuality that, when displayed by women, renders *them* 'freaks', 'chicken-heads', and 'hoes'. Jennifer McLune writes about this apparent contradiction:

> So when men rap about their big dicks, their money, and their power, they deserve to be respected and worshipped for possessing the very things they attack women for going after. Gotcha! Why does possession of those very attributes bring men status and simultaneously take it away from women? Because men are the possessors, that's why. The 'suckers' who don't have what men claim to have are socially, literally 'fucked'.[42]

Perhaps that's why the terms of abuse rappers use for one another echo the time-honoured terms of male degradation: bitch, pussy, faggot.

As for Mark Anthony Neal, he's had a change of heart since his first book defended hip-hop as an assertion of masculinity in the face of emasculating racism. Now, he says, 'taking seriously the world that my young daughters are charged with navigating, there was something disturbing and indeed frightening about the possibility of them being reduced to giant sexualized credit card machines'.[43]

Others, particularly in the African-American community, agree. Women at Spelman, a venerable African-American women's college in Atlanta, caused a stir in black collegiate circles in 2004 when they protested an appearance by Nelly on their campus. 'We can't continue to support artists and images that exploit our women and put us out there as over-sexed, non-intelligent human beings', Asha Jennings, the head of the college's Student Government Organization, told the *Atlanta Journal Constitution*. In 2005, *Essence* magazine launched its Take Back the Music Campaign to contest 'the "money, hoes, all a brotha knows" mentality' of current mass-market hip-hop. In the same year, a conference was held at the University of Chicago to discuss feminism and hop-hop. One attendee, African American Studies professor Dionne Bennett, said, 'When they're talking about chickenheads . . . they're talking about you'.[44]

Still, at the same time as we critique the misogyny so often present in rap and hip-hop, it's important to acknowledge the power of this musical form to provide a vehicle for change and cultural pride. From Sir Mix-A-Lot's celebration of feminine curves in 'Baby Got Back' to Salt 'N' Pepa's 'Let's Talk about Sex', there *are* contestations of misogyny and male sexual privilege to be found in hip-hop and rap. And from aboriginal Australia to our own nation (think Kinnie Starr and Red Power Squad), this musical genre is providing a lexicon for cultural resistance. In the words of Rex Smallboy (Cree), leader of the now-defunct but much celebrated band War Party from Hobbema, Alberta: 'It's all about social justice; we're not up there saying anything that isn't true'.[45] Speaking truth without entrenching sexist stereotypes is a worthy goal for the many people around the world now translating rap and hip-hop into their own cultures.

His Console or Hers? Gender and Gaming

During the war I did some bad things . . . bad things happened to us. I was very young. And very angry. Maybe that is no excuse. But I need money! This pays, and I'm good at it . . . A creature that could do this doesn't have a soul.

That's the theme, the set-up, or to use the gamers' language, the 'cinematic' for Grand Theft Auto IV, taken from the website of the manufacturer, Rockstar Games. The speaker is the main character of the game, Niko Bellic, an appealing Serb immigrant anti-hero whose job is crime, leading to the killing of an incredible number of police officers and apparently innocent bystanders. *GTA* is the most successful game series ever invented, but also a prime example of some of the stereotypical, misogynist, and violent representations that have become a concern as North Americans become more and more devoted to electronic media and, in particular, to **gaming**.[46]

As mentioned above, Canadians are starting to spend more time at their home computers than watching television; among younger Canadians, Internet use has already overtaken TV. Both in Canada and the USA, gaming is growing. In the US, 38 per cent of homes have at least one console. While the number of homes with consoles in Canada remains unclear, the fact that almost 2 million consoles were sold in 2008 alone suggests that numbers are high. And computer and on-line games account for many more passionate users. (Some games are played by one, two, or more players on a console hooked up to the TV. Others are played on a PC. And **MMORPG**s are played on-line, with thousands of people all over the world playing simultaneously.) Canada is a player in the world of video games, not just because of its millions of gamers, but because it houses two major production facilities, Electronic Arts Canada's Burnaby (BC) facility and UbiSoft, Montreal.[47]

Video games began innocently enough with a computer-generated ping-pong in 1972; *Centipede* was introduced later that same year. Who would have predicted then that video games would today be the fastest-growing segment of the entertainment industry? Worldwide, hundreds of millions of people play video games. Video games made about $34 billion in revenues in 2004, outselling box office receipts for movies ($21.4 billion), outselling books, CDs, and DVDs by a landslide. In the United States in 2007, video games earned about $9.5 billion on sales of over 267 million computer and console games every year. (Sales of hardware and game software topped $10 billion in 2003, 2004, and 2005.) Sixty-five per cent of US households play video games regularly—and 60 per cent of players are male.

Although the age range of gamers is wide—the average age is 35 and rising—games have in the past tended to appeal most to guys in their teens and 20s. But adults, and women, are a fast-growing segment of the game market. Women 18 and older now represent a much larger proportion of the game-playing population than do boys 17 and under. And in one survey, 36 per cent of household heads reported that they played games on their cell phones or PDAs. More than one-third of Americans rank computer and video games as 'the most fun family entertainment'.[48]

Fun for the family perhaps: but some of the top-selling games of recent years cannot be classified as appropriate family fare. As indicated above, *GTA* in its various incarnations is the best-selling console game of all time. **First-person shooter** games are also popular throughout North America. *Halo 2* sold $125 million—in the first 24 hours of its release, outselling the movie *Spider Man 2* as the year's top-grossing entertainment release. *Halo 3*, released in 2007, racked up 300 million in sales in its first week, but was outdone by *GTA IV*'s record $500 million in first-week sales.[49]

Of video games, sports games perennially command a large share of the market. Sports, racing, and flight games together accounted for about 24 per cent of games sold in the USA in 2007. NHL games have sold well in Canada, too. Still, violent, action-filled games like *GTA* and *Halo* are the most popular genre; adventure, fighting, shooter, and action games, taken together, accounted for over 43 per cent of units sold in the USA in 2007, while family, children, and arcade games covered only 19 per cent and strategy games 4.7 per cent. The latter, such as *Sims*, involve players in real-life decision-making and strategic thinking, not simply adventures in the land of blood and guts.

Gaming is gendered. Although the majority of gamers are apparently male, the percentages vary enormously when broken down by platform and genre. According to Mark Griffiths' 2003 study, console games (75 per cent male, 50 per cent over nineteen years old) are only slightly more gender-equal than on-line games (85 per cent male, 60 per cent over nineteen years old).[50] Sports and adventure games come close to 95 per cent male players; whereas strategy games, like *Sims* and *Second Life*, appeal to women. In *Sims*, the 'action', such as it is, has to do with real-life situations in the home. People get jobs, get married, have kids, and even clean the house. 'All the men in my class HATED that game', comments sociologist William Lugo, who studies video games and teaches a college course on them. 'It was a little too realistic for them'. A recent addition to the gaming world, so-called 'active games' or 'exergames', like Wii Fit, have tremendous appeal to women. Wii Fit offers the opportunity to plot your body's changes on your very own 'Mii' avatar (and to emulate hard-bodied virtual 'trainers'). Like Sims, then, Wii Fit offers a combination of fantasy with reality. Depressingly, however, Wii Fit may represent less an expansion of the video-game market than its colonization by the self-objectification discussed further in Chapter 11.[51]

Nina Huntmann, communications professor and avid gamer, is a keen observer who has researched games and created the documentary *Game Over* for the Media Education Foundation. 'The computer labs in college were completely dominated by guys', she says, 'and the fact that I liked games, and liked them for the same reasons that they did, made more than a few somewhat uncomfortable'. Jo Bryce and Jason Rutter argue that significant numbers of female gamers have been present since the early 1990s, but that male gaming communities, game manufacturers, and academic researchers have ignored their presence. Gareth Schott and Kirsty Horell found that even within individual homes where consoles are owned by girls, male family members may take control of the console and assume the role of 'expert'. Girl gamers are thereby encouraged to adopt the position of 'watcher', allowing male relatives to master games (even when the games and consoles belong to the girl!) before attempting to master them themselves. Within adult couples, women may be less able to use or complete games because of household responsibilities. As one female UK gamer put it, 'it's really important for my husband to know how *Spyro* works but it's more important for me to have the dinner cooked! I mean I want to be able to do it, but . . .'[52]

Given that video-game use may produce some benefits in computer literacy, entry into high-tech jobs, and comfort with technology, the gendering of gaming may be of some concern. Research recently conducted at the University of Toronto found that video-game players were much better at spatial rotation tasks than non-players. In fact, much of the observed gender difference in this task was actually a player vs. non-player difference! Playing action games for only 10 hours produced significant gains in mental rotation and spatial attention abilities (two areas generally perceived as gendered); the gains made by women were more significant than those made by men.[53] The gendering of gaming, then, has some implications for the world outside the screen.

Sex segregation of gaming itself is only one element of video games' obvious gendering. Within games, characters are almost always massively exaggerated gender and racial stereotypes. According to one California study, 64 per cent of game characters are male; that number rises to 73 per cent if only player-controlled characters are considered. Most male characters have biceps that would make GI Joe look puny; indeed, their upper torsos are so massive, their waists so small, and their thighs so powerfully bulging that there is no way that many could stand up. More than half of player-controlled characters are white males; of male characters, fewer than 40 per cent are black, and most of these are foils. Of 53 game heroes studied, 46 were white, with only 4 per cent African American and 2 per cent Latino. Aboriginal people of any gender account for fewer than 1 per cent of characters, and 80 per cent of African-American characters appear in one context: as competitors in sports games.[54]

Even if they resemble contemporary gay male stereotypes of pumped bodies, avatars in gameland are all straight. And so are the women, with bodies so exaggerated they make Barbie look realistic. (Lara Croft, for her part, has thighs bigger than her waist.) But women are a relative rarity in video games. According to one study, '[t]he most common portrayal of women was actually the complete absence of women at all'. Women account for only 17 per cent of characters (fewer characters than are non-human). As player-controlled characters, women are only 15 per cent of the total. Eighty per cent of female player-controlled characters are white; when African-American women appear, 90 per cent of them are victims of violence. Throughout, female characters are presented for the uses of male characters, often as 'eye candy'; 20 per cent of all female characters expose their breasts, which are almost always massive and pneumatic. (And of course, in mature-rated games like *GTA*, female characters often either start out or become unclothed and engage in sexual acts.)[55]

Women's appearance aside, they often appear as dependent, supporting, or as simple sex objects. They're eternally grateful to their hypermasculine muscle-bound rescuers. In one of the first shooter games, Duke Nukem, the 'Everyman American Hero' finds a landscape in which all the men have been killed, and only Duke can rescue a million 'babes' who have been captured by aliens. The women are, of course, grateful. Even Lara Croft is a hypersexualized 'babe'—she just happens to know how to handle a grenade launcher.[56]

Some games blur the boundaries between militarized urban war zones and pornographic revenge fantasies. Take *Panty Raider*. The object of this adventure is to lure super-models from their hiding places out into the open and shoot them, hit them with some cyber-goop to melt their clothes off, and snap a picture of them in their panties. The game is an enormous disappointment for the gamers who buy it, given the superior 3-D graphics and naked women available elsewhere. But for those who are looking for a misogynist dirty joke, Newgrounds in 2008 released a game called *Cunt*. It doesn't bear describing, frankly.[57]

For some players, the fantasy world of video games doesn't offer a sufficient real-time dose of reality. Millions of players—mainly male—around the world log on to MMORPGs. Games like *EverQuest* or *World of Warcraft* are elaborate fantasy worlds, often quite Tolkienesque, where players battle each other or battle against monsters, live, on-line, in real time. *World of Warcraft* reached 11.5 million subscribers in late 2008 (from 250,000 five years earlier). MMORPGs are so seductive because they are both virtual and real; the games utterly blur the boundaries between reality and fantasy, as commodities flow across the borders of cyberspace into the real marketplace. Edward Castronova worries that some players will experience a sort of 'toxic immersion', in which their virtual lives become more real, and more pressing, than their real-world lives.[58]

As more and more of us become gamers, spending more and more time at consoles or on-line, it's worth thinking about the implications of that activity. Though there is no clear causal relationship between playing *GTA IV* and, for example, murdering police officers, that doesn't mean that gaming has no effects; indeed, careful research suggests that playing violent video games may desensitize children to violence and diminish empathy. The gendered fantasy world of our games deserves our scrutiny. As David Leonard argues, 'Video games teach, inform, and control . . . we need to teach about games because games are teaching so much about us . . . and ' "them" '.[59]

Where His Does Hers: 'Mainstream' Pornography

Women's entry into a formerly all-male media environment is nowhere more evident than in the pornography industry. Women have always been present as performers, of course, in numbers roughly equal to men. The change is that women are *consuming* far more pornography than ever, and, some of them say, they are even liking it more than they ever did. By contrast, there are very few men who are renting movies from Femme Productions. Again, women can enter the men's space, but men dare not enter women's. And though pornography as a mechanism in the construction of our sexualities is dealt with in a later chapter, here we focus on pornography not only in its representation of sex, but also in its representation of gender.

Pornography is a massive industry in the United States, with gross sales of all pornographic media ranging somewhere around $15 billion annually for the whole industry—in media terms, revenues greater than ABC, NBC, and CBS combined. According to Internet Filter Review statistics from 2006, worldwide porn revenues approach $100 billion annually. Adult bookstores outnumber McDonald's restaurants in the United States—by a margin of at least three to one. On the Internet, pornography has increased 1,800 per cent, from 14 million web-pages in 1998 to 260 million in 2003. Canadian statistics are hard to come by, but according to one study, Canadians lead the world in the amount of time they spend downloading porn from the Internet.[60]

Back before the Internet, porn was available on the newsstand, in adult bookstores, or at special theatres. You had to seek it out, and it was not considered mainstream. Now, it seems, porn has become 'respectable'. 'The adult film industry in Southern California is not being run by a bunch of dirty old men in the back room of some sleazy warehouse', wrote *Hustler* founding editor Larry Flynt in an op-ed article in the *Los Angeles Times* in 2004. 'Today, in the state of California, XXX entertainment is a

$9 billion to $14 billion business run with the same kind of thought and attention to detail that you'd find at GE, Mattel, or Tribune Co'.[61]

As mainstream entertainment, pornography has mainstream consumers. A 2004 poll conducted by MSNBC.com and *Elle* magazine found that 75 per cent of American men said that they had downloaded or viewed erotic films and videos from the Internet. One in five had watched or sexually interacted with someone on a live web-cam. Another 2004 poll by the US Employment Law Alliance found that 25 per cent of workers say they or their co-workers visit pornographic websites or engage in other sexually oriented Internet activities on their work computers during office hours. And *Playboy* magazine boasted that two-thirds of human resources professionals 'said they had found porn on employees' computers'.[62]

But perhaps equally important is not simply the size of the pornographic market but its reach and its pervasiveness. It's everywhere, creeping into mainstream media as well as growing in the shadowlands to which it has historically been consigned. A large percentage of Americans use pornography 'as daily entertainment fare'. Our society has become, as journalist Pamela Paul titles her book, *Pornified*. As she puts it, pornography today 'is so seamlessly integrated into popular culture that embarrassment or surreptitiousness is no longer part of the equation'.[63]

The standard claim of pornography's defenders is that the women and men who participate in pornography are doing so out of free choice—they choose to do it—so it must be an accurate representation of *both* the women's and the men's sexual desires. Child pornography, as always, is depicted as somewhere beyond the pale. But according to Melinda Reist, 'mainstream' Australian pornographer and Eros Association secretary David Watt also imports titles depicting 'Pigtail Perverts' and 'Captive Virgins'. At the same time, Watt and the Eros Association promote porn use as the means to sexual liberation.[64] This is a familiar framing: pornography depicts an egalitarian erotic paradise, where people always want sex, get what they want, and have a great time getting it. On the surface, it appears to be equal—both women and men are constantly on the prowl, looking for opportunities for sexual gratification. More and more, this is the mainstream view of porn. If everyone consents, what's the problem?

This view of pornography is relatively recent. In the 1970s and 1980s, most people saw pornography as 'obscene'. While it might exist, it was a niche market kept largely out of sight. Even then, however, the porn market was growing, particularly after the popularization of VCRs in the 1970s. In response, second-wave feminists made pornography a political issue. Arguing that 'porn is the theory, rape is the practice', feminists like Robin Morgan, Andrea Dworkin, and Catherine McKinnon showed and described pornographic images (which many women had never seen) of women's degradation.

Bonnie Sherr Klein's 1981 NFB release *Not a Love Story* galvanized many Canadian women in opposition to the porn industry, fuelling debate and activism throughout the 1980s. In 1992, the Supreme Court of Canada enshrined the idea of pornography's harms in *Regina v. Butler*. In that case, Justice Sopinka decided that restrictions on pornography were a reasonable restriction where sex and violence were explicitly linked, where sex was linked with humiliating treatment, or where explicit sex involved children. Unfortunately, these restrictions were applied in a discriminatory fashion, targeting gay and lesbian pornography and, in particular, Little Sisters lesbian bookstore in Vancouver. The resulting outcry put feminists in a difficult position; on one hand, they opposed degrading pornography; on the other hand, the legislation they had considered a victory was used to discriminate against gay people. At the same time, the rise of the Internet and the greater availability of explicit material helped 'mainstream' the use of pornography. By the mid-1990s, debates over porn seemed almost as old-fashioned as the temperance movement. When the star of *Not a Love Story* claimed that she had been misrepresented in the film, that seemed to many to prove that feminists were wrong again.[65]

And, indeed, some of the claims made in the porn debates have proved difficult to confirm. Much has been made of the claim that pornography either makes men more prone to rape or gives men a cathartic release that makes them less prone to rape. Neither hypothesis turns out to be confirmable, nor does porn evidently make men dislike feminism or wish to limit women's rights. Still, the use of pornography by sexual offenders suggests that there is some connection between visual images and behaviours, even if it is not a simplistic causal link. And over focus on such causal connections also obscures more interesting questions about how casual pornography exposure affects children and how pornography shapes desire (discussed further in Chapter 10).[66]

Moreover, pornography is not a monolith. Gay and lesbian pornography differ significantly from one another and from heterosexual porn (with which we are here primarily concerned). There are porn performers, such as Annie Sprinkle, who have taken a critical and transformative approach to the medium. Still, as in the case of rap, the most commercially viable pornography is neither ethical nor particularly thoughtful, as a cursory web search or a trip to the back room of your local video store will show.

Most porn still follows a script in which the so-called equality of desire is a fiction. The typical porn scene finds a woman and a man immediately sexually aroused, penetration occurs immediately, and both are orgasmic within a matter of seconds. The penis, in mainstream heterosexual porn, is sufficient to accomplish all things. Women rapidly achieve orgasm not only from simple penile penetration, but also, apparently, from the act of fellatio itself. (That 'gag' was the premise of *Deep Throat* [1972], one of the first porn films to go 'mainstream'.) According to most pornography, the apotheosis of any sexual act is his orgasm, or what we can refer to euphemistically as the 'money shot'. Increasingly, that money shot is a 'facial', culminating in some versions in what Antonia Zerbiasias describes as 'waterboarding by ejaculate'.[67]

Even when the fantasy is not that explicitly degrading, the fantasy of mainstream porn is one in which women's sexuality dovetails neatly with men's desires. In the erotic paradise of pornography, both women and men want what men want, or what pornography thinks men want. No wonder anti-pornography activist John Stoltenberg writes that pornography 'tells lies about women' even though it 'tells the truth about men'.[68]

But does porn tell the truth about men? It certainly lies *to* men. And the major lie is that every woman really, secretly, deep down, wants to have sex with them. It is a lie that is a revenge fantasy more than an erotic fantasy, revenge for the fact that most men don't feel they get as much sex as they think they are supposed to get. Pornography also provides hassle-free vicarious sex. 'You don't have to buy them dinner, talk about what they like to talk about', says Seth, a 24-year-old computer programmer in New York. 'And even when you do, there's no guarantee that you're gonna get laid. I mean with pornography, no one ever says no'.

And if they do say no, well, they really mean yes. In a sexual marketplace that men feel is completely dominated by women—from women's having the power to decide if men are going to get sex in the first place to all those dispiriting reminders that 'no means no'—mainstream heterosexual pornography supplies a world in which no one takes no for an answer.

We need a conversation about pornography that looks at why porn's version of sex works for so many men (and an increasing number of women). As we transmit ever more depictions of explicit sexuality in what Robert Jensen calls 'one of the greatest social engineering experiments in history', we need to pay close attention. We need to listen to the voices of those who use pornography but articulate a critical and questioning stance toward its depiction and implications. We need egalitarian depictions of sexuality that exhibit, in Robert Jensen's words, 'the possibilities of becoming a human being'.[69] And if they don't do it for us—if only 'he does her' turns us on—we've got a problem.

Convergence and Equality

Despite all the ways in which women have begun to enter formerly all-male domains, and men have retreated in the face of this new media equality, the differences are shrinking. Despite all the efforts to keep women and men apart, so that men can stay men (even if women are changing), our media use is increasingly converging. And despite all the extraordinarily pervasive efforts of various media to convince us that we are Martians and Venutians, as different as night and day, we are increasingly Earthlings, using the same media, in roughly equal amounts, and for roughly the same reasons.

Nowhere is this more true than with newer media—like iPods, the Internet, and other digital technologies. Gender differences in the use of these media are actually far smaller than we assume they are. And on websites for younger people, like MySpace and Facebook, the percentages are about even.

On-line, for example, women and men are roughly equal users of the Internet. Judging from US data, it is true that, in general, men use the Internet more often than women— but it's only 68 per cent of adult men and 66 per cent of adult women. And the reason may not be what you might think. It has, in fact, to do with age. Among people over 65, men are far more likely to be on-line than women—34 per cent to 21 per cent. Women under 65 are more likely to use the Internet than men. Among the under-30 set, women outnumber men, 86 per cent to 80 per cent. The 'real' story is more about the interaction of age and gender.[70]

And it's also true that women and men use the Internet for somewhat different purposes. For example, although women and men equally use the Internet to buy products and do their banking on-line, men are more likely to pay bills, participate in auctions, trade stocks, and buy digital content (like Internet pornography). Men search for information more often than women; women use e-mail to maintain relationships and communicate with friends more than men do. According to Statistics Canada, women are more likely to use the Internet to locate information about health, while men are more likely to search for government-related data. Nonetheless, these behaviours are constantly changing, and research based on even two-year-old data is notoriously unreliable when it comes to the Internet.[71]

Even in some traditionally male bastions, like sports, the evidence of gender convergence is pretty hard to miss. Three-fourths of American adult men—and fully half of all adult women—say they are sports fans, according to a Gallup Poll.[72] The Super Bowl still dwarfs all other single-event shows for sheer numbers of viewers, and weekend football games continue to attract huge audiences. But whereas some sports—like the spectacle of professional wrestling—skew almost entirely toward men, the other really popular sports—including NASCAR and golf—are approaching gender parity. Women currently make up 40 per cent of NASCAR's 75 million viewers—as well as a full 50 per cent of the Super Bowl's 86 million viewers. Not content with a single 'super' event, women also constitute 38 per cent of the NFL's 120 million total annual viewers. Quick—how many men watch Oprah—let alone the WNBA?[73]

One of the best titles for any book in recent years is Mariah Burton Nelson's *The Stronger Women Get, the More Men Love Football*. In her book, she showed how women's increasing equality on the sports field had led men to increasingly proclaim the superiority of football over all other sports—it's the one sport exempt from Title IX, it's the one sport women don't play. Nelson's title perfectly illustrates the increasing anxiety men feel from women's equality. The more and more equal women get in the real world, the more men are retreating into mediated fantasy worlds of video games, pornography, on-line poker, and sports talk. Only there do they feel that they are still the masters of the universe, sexually omnipotent, kings of the world.

Gender equality in the virtual world of the media, just like the real world, will come not when gender difference disappears, but rather when gender *inequality* disappears, when his media are no longer 'better' than hers, when Nelson's book could be titled, *The Stronger Women Get, the More Men Like It*.

Summary

The media are now considered a primary institution of socialization. This wasn't always true; sociologists used to believe that there were only three such institutions: family, school, and church (religion). The recognition that the media play a major role in shaping us came as the media's influence grew in our lives. But the media are both like and unlike other social institutions. The media are, obviously, mediated communication, and their effect has often been seen as uni-directional. But we are not simply sponges absorbing the media's messages. To effectively analyze how the media socialize us, we need to consider our active negotiation of media, the multiplicity and complexity of media, and how a particular medium (rather than merely its content) affects us. We need to treat the media as a deeply gendered but complex institution saturated with depictions of gender that influence us in complex, powerful ways.

One of the first things to note about the gendered media is that there are 'his' and 'hers'. Though some of the barriers are breaking down, genres still remain gendered. Where crossover occurs, it's much more likely that 'she' will cross over into 'his' media than the other way around.

Television has changed a great deal since its beginnings, and it no longer holds the sway it once did over our leisure hours; it is being overtaken by the Internet. Even so, television remains popular. Character depictions were once highly stereotyped, but from the 1970s on stereotyping has been breaking down. The emergence of the ensemble cast in the 1980s provided a means for networks to depict both gender and ethnic diversity. Sexual diversity had to wait for the late 90s, when the first gay main characters appeared on network television. Still, there's a way to go. *Hockey Night in Canada*, as a depiction of national culture, enshrines ideals of hegemonic masculinity. And though children's programming may be changing with the emergence of strong female characters like Dora, here too continued gender stereotyping and increasingly violent depictions are cause for concern. Finally, advertising remains one of the most gender-stereotyped areas of television programming, though in this area too there are signs of change.

Print media have also been highly gender-segregated. Women's magazines, however, are quite different from men's magazines in their contradictory and multivocal messages. *Chatelaine*, uniquely, is a magazine that promoted second-wave feminism while remaining the 'mainstream' magazine for Canadian homemakers through the 1960s and 1970s. Men's magazines are more monovocal in nature, particularly when they're the 'lad' magazines that poured onto the market in the 1990s. As in the media in general, gender divisions are breaking down, but that breakdown is coming largely from women's consumption of formerly men's genres. Many men, at the same time, show signs of retreating into hypermasculine media rather than embracing less overtly gendered genres.

The popular music world is dominated by two genres that can be fairly called 'his': rock and rap/hip-hop. Rap has been the biggest new story within pop music for over a decade. Today, it is the second-biggest genre in the music market and globally, is probably number one. Gangsta rap is only one form of the genre, but it's by far the most successful, and is noted for its misogyny. Rock too has had its share of machismo and misogyny; but since the 1970s women have contested rock's stereotypical representations of women. Though race undoubtedly and unfairly plays a role in the demonization of rappers as misogynists, many within the African-American community have become increasingly concerned about the portrayals of women within the genre. As rap becomes 'the world's music', translated into cultures around the world, its misogyny should be questioned even as its ability to speak for so many is celebrated.

Gaming is one of the fastest-growing media in the world, now overtaking more conventional entertainment media in revenues. Gaming too remains gendered. A majority of gamers are male, and though this is changing, women and girls remain marginalized within the world of gaming. Women and men also remain attracted to different genres. Within games, gender and ethnic stereotypes are alive and well; women remain a minority of those depicted, and are often hypersexualized. Men, at the same time, are represented as hypermasculine heroes, most of whom are white. Non-white men play restricted and stereotyped roles within most games. On-line games are one of the fastest-growing sectors within gaming, offering a level of complexity and ongoing engagement console games can't supply. As more of us enter into the fantasy worlds of gaming for hours each week, considering the gender implications of that fantasy realm seems particularly important.

Another fantasy world is that offered by pornography, which also remains highly gendered. The growth of the Internet has made porn a massive business that is a key part of the Internet and entertainment economies. While pornography was previously viewed as obscene, and seen as degrading to women by second-wave feminists, it has become increasingly 'mainstreamed' within North American society, even while the growth of marginal areas such as overtly violent and child pornography remains 'beyond the pale'. While mainstream heterosexual porn is not harmful in the clear ways that those kinds of porn are, it nonetheless presents a problematic view of sexuality. It portrays women's desires and pleasures as dovetailing neatly with men's (perceived) needs. Porn also focuses on the penis and male orgasm as the centre of sexual action. Many previous claims about pornography's harms have been disproved or at least criticized, but that doesn't mean that there are no questions to be asked about porn. Porn, no matter how 'mainstream', is still 'his'.

Women and men are more than ever converging. The boundaries between his and hers are becoming more porous. But as this happens, there are also signs in a variety of media that men are responding with a retrenchment and a retreat into the ideals of hyper- or hegemonic masculinity, whether that be in lad magazines, porn use, or RAW and MMA. As the media become more complex in their representations of gender on one hand, they become more simplistic on the other. True gender equality within the media will exist when 'his' no longer needs to assert its difference and superiority so aggressively, and when he can appreciate 'hers' in addition to permitting her access to 'his'.

Questions for Critical Thinking

1. Can you think of three examples of how we 'negotiate' our relationship with media? How are we 'active' rather than 'passive' consumers of media products?
2. This chapter did not discuss movies in detail. Are there 'his' and 'hers' movies? Do movies depict a more or less gender-stereotyped world than does television?
3. Think about one of your favourite television shows. Does it contain clear messages about gender, or are the messages it contains contradictory? What does this tell you about the nature of gendered messages within the media?
4. Why do so many men read Alice Munro, but few boys read *Twilight*?
5. Thinking about gaming and pornography, what relationship do these areas of entertainment have with reality? How, if at all, do they influence our views of the world and our behaviour?

Key Terms

chick lit

first-person shooter

gaming

lad lit

manga

MMORPGs (massively multiplayer on-line role-playing games)

Persons' Case

polyvocality

Riot Grrrl

Part 3

Gendered Interactions

Chapter 10

Gendered Intimacies

Communication, Friendship, Love, and Sex

Two are better than one . . . For if they fall, the one will lift up his fellow; but woe
to him that is alone when he falleth, for he hath not another to help him up. Again,
if two lie together, then they have heat; but how can one be warm alone?
— ECCLESIASTES 5

The need for intimacy is fundamentally human; and yet we express it in gendered
ways. 'Man's love is of man's life a thing apart', wrote the legendary British romantic
poet George Gordon, Lord Byron, ''Tis woman's whole existence'. A century and a half
later, novelist Doris Lessing commented that she'd never met a man who would destroy
his work for a love affair—and she'd never met a woman who wouldn't.

However dated they now appear, such sentiments underscore how unconsciously
our intimacies have been shaped by gender. Indeed, even today, women and men have
different experiences and expectations in friendships, in love, and in sex. Part of the
'interplanetary theory' of gender emphasizes these differences between women and
men. We hear that it is our celestial or biological natures that decree that women be
emotionally adept communications experts and that men be clumsy unemotional
clods.

And yet the gender differences in intimate relationships often don't turn out to be
the ones we expected; nor are the differences as great as commonsense assumptions
predict. Likewise, although it is true that men and women often have different ways of
talking, liking, loving, and lusting, these differences are neither as great as predicted,
nor do they always go in the directions that common sense would lead us to expect.

Moreover, the differences we observe in contemporary North America did not always exist and are affected by other differences such as ethnicity, sexual orientation,
and class. Nor are these differences present in other cultures. In this chapter, we explore
the gender of **intimacy** by examining communication, friendship, love, and sexuality.
(Love, in this chapter, refers only to the form we emphasize most, romantic love, and
not to parental love or other forms.) What we'll see is that the gendering of intimate life
is the result of historical and social developments—and the site of continuing change.

The Historical 'Gendering' of Intimate Life

Today, women are often considered 'emotional experts' relative to men. This was not always the case. From Greek and Roman myths to Renaissance balladry, men's friendships were celebrated as the highest expression of the noblest virtues—bravery, loyalty, heroism, duty—which only men were thought to possess.[1] Many women agreed. For example, the great eighteenth-century British feminist and writer Mary Wollstonecraft believed that although 'the most holy bond of society is friendship', it is men, not women, who are most adept at it. And Simone de Beauvoir, whose book *The Second Sex* is one of modern feminism's groundbreaking works, commented that 'women's feelings rarely rise to genuine friendship'. That is, women might gather to gossip and quilt, but their emotions were simply not as profound as those of men. This, it was thought, also affected women's ability to love as truly as did men. Women were diffident friends and fickle lovers.[2]

Much of this historical view of gendered intimacies rested on sexist views of women's capacities for 'higher' mental and emotional processes. But some modern scholars have also viewed men as more gifted friends. Anthropologist Lionel Tiger, the theorist of male bonding (remember him from Chapter 2?), argued that the gender division of labour in hunting-and-gathering societies led to deeper and more durable friendships among men. Hunting and warfare, the domains of male activity, required deep and enduring bonds among men for survival, and thus close male friendships became a biologically based human adaptation.[3]

Whatever the virtue of Tiger's theories for explanation of early hominid societies, contemporary North Americans have reversed the historical notion of intimacy since the early 1970s, fuelled in part by two related developments. On one hand, feminism began to celebrate solidarity among women. Historians like Carroll Smith-Rosenberg found such solidarity in the past, reversing the traditional notion that women could not be friends and uncovering the richness and profundity of Victorian women's lifelong friendship ties.[4] Increasingly, women's emphasis on intimacy and emotional expressiveness were seen not as a liability but rather as an asset. On the other hand, a new generation of male psychologists and advocates of 'men's liberation' were critical of the traditional male sex role as a debilitating barrier to emotional intimacy.

Reversing centuries of tradition, *women's* experiences in friendships and women's virtues—emotional expressiveness, dependency, the ability to nurture, intimacy—were now desirable. Psychologist Robert Lewis concurred, identifying four 'barriers' to emotional intimacy among men: (1) competition; (2) the need to be 'in control', which forbids self-disclosure and openness; (3) homophobia; and (4) lack of skills and positive role models for male intimacy. In a widely cited study, psychologist Daniel Levinson concluded that for men, friendship is noticeable largely by its absence, 'rarely experienced by American men'. And Joseph Pleck, critic of traditional masculinity, lamented the 'weak and often absent' nature of men's emotional relationships.[5]

So if men are no longer seen as 'better' at friendship and love than women, and are in fact seen as emotionally limited in these areas, what explains this gender difference? Some writers offer psychoanalytic answers. For example, scholars like Lillian Rubin and Nancy Chodorow, who are both sociologists and psychologists, argue, as Rubin puts it, that 'the traditional structure of parenting comes together with the developmental tasks of childhood and the cultural mandates about masculinity and femininity to create differences in the psychological structures of women and men'. The young boy must separate from his mother—the source of love, nurturance, and connection—and establish his independence. For girls, by contrast, continued connection with their mothers ensures a continuity of emotionality, love, and nurturance: In fact, it becomes the foundation for women's experience of sexual intimacy, rather than its negation. As a result, separation and individuation are more difficult for women; connection and intimacy more difficult for men. This constellation permits women 'to be more closely in touch with both their attachment and dependency needs than men are'.[6]

Although such explanations 'feel' right to many of us, they are not universal explanations or evidence of some essential difference. In some societies, for example, boys must still undergo rigorous ritual separation from their mothers; and yet they, and not women, are still seen as having the deeper interior emotional lives and the more intimate and expressive friendships. For example, anthropologist Robert Brain documents several societies in Africa, South America, and Oceania in which men develop very close male friendships, ritually binding themselves together as 'lifetime comrades, blood brothers, or even symbolic "spouses"'.[7]

Psychoanalytic explanations take us part of the way, but even they must be inserted into the larger-scale historical transformation of which they are a part. The notion that boys and girls have such dramatically different developmental tasks is, itself, a product of the social, economic, and cultural transformation of Europe and America in the nineteenth and twentieth centuries. That transformation had several components that transformed the meaning and experience of friendship, love, and sexuality. Both Rubin and Chodorow recognize this. 'Society and personality live in a continuing reciprocal relationship with each other', Rubin writes. 'The search for personal change without efforts to change the institutions within which we live and grow will, therefore, be met with only limited reward'.[8]

The nineteenth and twentieth centuries witnessed a dramatic transformation in the gendered division of emotional labour. This change began among the upper and middle classes, but eventually affected all groups within Western society. As the separation between the private and public spheres grew (see Chapter 6), masculine norms changed to emphasize the home as refuge from the competition of the hurly-burly of the working world. Men were encouraged to reorient themselves toward a spouse whose 'job description' now included meeting her husband's emotional needs. By the late nineteenth century, the spectre of homosexuality also hung over male friendships, barring the kind of intimacies (for example, hugging or sharing a bed) that now seem to many North Americans to indicate homosexuality.[9]

These changes did not eliminate either the existence or the presumed superiority of male-male friendships, however. Now, as men left their homes and went to work in factories or offices, they socialized in male groups and cultivated new forms of sociability. Yet finding friends in the workplace was tricky, given that expressions of vulnerability or openness might give a potential competitor an economic advantage. Men 'learned' to be **instrumental**—focusing on tasks or shared activities rather than self-disclosure—in their relationships with other men. In their friendships, men have come to 'seek not intimacy but companionship, not disclosure but commitment'. The passionate male friendship, so celebrated in myths and legend, became a historical artifact.[10]

Simultaneously, the separation of spheres also positioned women as the domestic experts: Women became increasingly **expressive**—adept at emotional communication— as men were abandoning that style. The doctrine of separate spheres implied more than the spatial separation of home and workplace; it divided the mental and social world into two complementary halves. Men were to express the traits and emotions associated with the workplace—competitiveness, individual achievement, instrumental rationality— whereas women were to cultivate the softer domestic virtues of love, nurturance, and compassion. Love itself changed meanings, coming to mean tenderness, powerlessness, and emotional expression. Women, said to possess 'all the milder virtues of humanity', became the ministers of love.[11]

The cultural equation of femininity with emotional intimacy exaggerated gender differences in friendships, love, and sexuality. These differences, then, were the *result* of the broad social and economic changes, not their cause; the exclusion of women from the workplace was the single most important differentiating experience. Once again, gender inequality produced the very differences that then legitimated the inequalities.

At the same time, the idea of **companionate marriage** became the norm in Western society, replacing earlier, more pragmatic views of the institution. Increasingly, from the eighteenth century on, we viewed 'love' as the primary purpose of marriage. It wasn't always this way. Troubadours of the eleventh to thirteenth centuries described undying passion as a hallmark of love for both women and men. But the **romantic love** they described was generally experienced outside marriage; in fact, the most typical form of courtly love emphasized a young man's service to and love for a married lady. Thus this romantic love, though celebrated, was also seen as socially disruptive, a threat to the power of the church, the state, and the family.

'Passionate attachments between young people can and do happen in any society', writes historian Lawrence Stone, 'but the social acceptability of the emotion has varied enormously over time and class and space, determined primarily by cultural norms and property arrangements'. For example, in many European cultures, parents provided a **dowry** for their daughters (a custom that persists in many places, as does the different but related system of **bride price**). Parents provided goods and wealth to ensure a 'good match', and also carefully considered candidates. Indeed, though good parents attempted to consider their children's feelings, fathers and mothers, not children, were the primary makers of marriage; courtship was generally limited. Thus in the sixteenth and seventeenth centuries, 'every advice book, every medical treatise, every sermon and religious homily . . . firmly rejected both romantic passion and lust as suitable bases for marriage'. By the eighteenth century, attitudes had softened, and individuals were advised to make marital choices based on love and affection—provided, of course, that the two families approved and the individuals' social and economic statuses were roughly equal.[12]

It wasn't until the nineteenth century that love became the ordinary experience for couples, that it was 'normal and indeed praiseworthy for young men and women to fall passionately in love, and that there must be something wrong with those who fail to have such an overwhelming experience sometime in late adolescence or early adulthood'. But in the nineteenth-century marriage manuals, love is rarely mentioned as a reason to get married. In fact, love 'is presented more as a product of marriage than its prerequisite'. By the end of the century, though, 'love had won its battle along the whole line in the upper sections of the middle class. Dating developed to allow young people to 'fall in love' and thus select mates, becoming by 1950 the principal mode of courtship. Romantic love 'has since been regarded as the most important prerequisite to marriage', though vestiges of the older family-directed model of marriage persist in some Canadian ethnic groups and among the very wealthy.[13]

So romantic love as we know it—as the basis for marriage, sexuality, and family—is relatively recent. Nor is it the foundation of marriage and/or sexual expression every-where else in the world or among every group. As the basis for sexual activity, love turns out to be relatively rare. Even in our society, love may or may not accompany sexual activity or family life, and it may wax and wane in its intensity. In a classic article, sociologist William J. Goode noted that there was little evidence that the ideology of romantic love was widely or deeply believed by all strata of the American population.[14] Still, most North Americans are repelled by the idea of arranged marriage, seeing it as the antithesis of free choice and individualism. This can blind us to the novelty, in hu-man history, of our distinctive view of love and marriage. When we began to marry for love and to distrust all other reasons for marrying, we made the fusion of sexual pas-sion and deep friendship the standard basis of married life.

The emergence of women as 'emotional specialists' and the development of com-panionate marriage had dramatic effects on the gendering of intimacy. So too did new ideas about homosexuality as a fixed sexual orientation. French philosopher Michel Foucault argued that 'the disappearance of friendship as a social institution, and the declaration of homosexuality as a social/political/medical problem, are the same pro-cess'. Prior to the end of the nineteenth century, concern about same-sex acts focused on behaviours (such as **sodomy**), not identity. Late in the 1800s, however, a new word— homosexual—was coined to describe those with a persistent sexual orientation toward the same sex. As sexologists and psychologists developed a picture of 'the homosexual', **homophobia** became increasingly significant in men's lives. Homophobia increases the gender differences between women and men, because 'the possible imputation of ho-mosexual interest to any bonds between men ensured that men had constantly to be aware of and assert their difference from both women and homosexuals', writes soci-ologist Lynne Segal.[15]

Industrialization, cultural ideals of companionate marriage and the separation of spheres, and the emergence of 'the modern homosexual'—these simultaneous forces created the arena in which we have experienced emotional life. Intimacy's division into two complementary gendered domains is part of the story of our gendered society.

Gendered Communications

The first of these gendered domains lies where intimacy begins: with communication, whether it be verbal or non-verbal. Unsurprisingly, studies have found that language and communication are heavily gendered.

Perhaps the most celebrated of studies of gendered communication was by Deborah Tannen, who presented evidence that men and women use language differently and for different *goals*. Indeed, she argues that talk between men and women is 'cross-cultural communication'. Men, she argues, use language to establish their position in a hierarchy. To men, conversations 'are negotiations in which people try and achieve and maintain the upper hand if they can, and protect themselves from some others' attempts to put them down and push them around'. Women, by contrast, use conversations as 'negotiations for closeness in which people try and seek and give confirmation and support, and to reach consensus'. No matter the good intentions of both parties 'to relate to each other with attention and respect', their different communication styles will get in the way. So for Tannen, men and women simply do intimacy differently.[16]

In addition to the apparently different goals of gendered communication, the *content* of speech often varies by sex. Men disclose less personal information, use fewer intensifiers, and make direct and declarative statements. Women negotiate in private, ask more questions to maintain the flow of conversation, and use more personal pronouns.

Finally, *styles* of speech are gendered. Style, first of all, can include pitch. Obviously, pitch or speech register is partly determined by biology; men's voices are simply deeper as a result of size and structural differences. But these differences may be exaggerated well beyond what is 'natural' to men and women. Many cultures have different ideals for male and female speech, and these ideals can vary and change. For example, there is some evidence that Japanese women's speech is significantly higher than that of European and American women, but that lower pitch is becoming increasingly common in Japan.[17] Intonation also reflects gender. When women speak, they sometimes end a declarative sentence with a slight rise in tone, as if ending it with a question mark. (This seems to be changing, at least among the current generation of university students!)

Other style differences are informative. Women tend to 'hedge'—to express tentativeness—and to 'backchannel'—using words or making sounds that confirm listening and encourage the speaker to continue speaking. Men, in conversation with women, tend to do more 'topic rejection'—deciding what's going to be talked about. And as we saw in Chapter 1, men interrupt women far more than women interrupt men. But crucially, all of these differences are differences in *cross-sex* talk. In same-sex conversations, they tend to either disappear, or even more critically, to be replicated on the basis of power differences between the same-sex speakers (for example, employer and employee). This finding led researchers to conclude that it's not the gender of the speaker, but rather the gender of the person to whom one is speaking that makes the difference. So gender matters, but not in the way that interplanetary stereotypes would have it.

The question of *amount* of talk is also an important feature of gendered communication. According to Jennifer Coates and other linguists, in most cultures cultural beliefs about language, or 'folklinguistics', devalue women's speech and elevate that of men. Many people believe that women talk more, incessantly 'chattering' and 'gossiping'. While gossip is important to both male and female cultures, data suggest that in fact men talk more than women, particularly in public. In mixed-sex groups, men dominate, and according to a recent metastudy, 'contrary to prediction, men were significantly more talkative than were women'.[18]

But what about the stereotype of the silent, uncommunicative man? Men, it seems, mainly grow silent within intimate relationships. The same man, silent and uncommunicative at home, may be quite talkative at work, where he uses conversation to make sure everyone feels all right. Men's silence, therefore, is not an immutable gender trait, but a response to a particular situation. And silence, as psychologist Carol Tavris writes, is power:

> The person who is silent may neither wish to be powerful nor feel powerful, but silence is power nonetheless. The silent partner feels no obligation to speak, no duty to change; he is mysterious, his wishes and feelings unknown. His silence causes those around him either to walk on tiptoe, to avoid the moods they imagine he feels, or to pursue him for connection, communication, and affection. The silent man has a resource that others want: information about what he is thinking, what he desires, how he is reacting, whether he approves of them.[19]

Thus, what we are seeing, when we observe gendered conversation, may be how 'observed sex differences in language mirror the overall difference in power between men and women'. In fact, according to one influential study from the 1980s, power differences can *by themselves* produce 'the conversational division of labour parallel to the one ordinarily associated with sexual differentiation', while more egalitarian sexual arrangements can overturn conventional gendered communication patterns.[20]

So typical 'man-talk', as opposed to 'woman-talk', is in large part 'power-talk'. Some of the classic differences we attribute to gendered style reflect the fact that women have traditionally been less *powerful* than men. This may explain why women's communications are often marked by more 'politeness strategies' than those of men. Women tend to compliment, apologize, and express sympathy with others more than do men. However, similar social location (status and power) may eliminate these differences. In fact, according to Melanie Ayres and Campbell Leaper, 'gender differences appear and disappear, depending on the interaction context'. They are not simply the reflection of some fixed gender *difference*, but are the result of cultural preference and gender inequality. This explains why communication patterns are increasingly converging, and reminds us that gendered communication is a reflection of a gendered society.[21]

Gender Differences in Friendship: Real and Imagined

Friends are important to North Americans. In fact, for North American youth, friends are arguably more important than family. One recent study compared Belgian, Canadian, and Italian youth and found dramatic differences in the importance of family interactions to adolescents. Canadian youths who participated in the study spent more time each day with friends than with their families, in contrast to Italian youths who spent twice as much time with family as with friends. Clearly, we are a friend-oriented culture. And yet friendship is very different from our other important relationships with spouses or family. There we have clear legal ties and obligations. Friendship, in contrast, seems voluntary and somewhat ephemeral. 'Being friends' with someone else is a delicate and nuanced matter. There is no clear marker for what constitutes a friend, and yet each of us has a clear idea of 'what friends do'.[22]

Not surprisingly, such ideas are influenced by gender. Most of the research on gender differences in friendship turns out to reinforce existing stereotypes of women as emotionally expressive and men as inexpressive and either incapable or uninterested in nurturing. There's even some evidence that brain differences account for friendship differences. A recent study found that whereas men respond to stress with the now-famous 'fight-or-flight' response, women look to friends or allies as a source of emotional sustenance in a response labelled 'tend and befriend'. The researchers believe that this is because men respond to stress by releasing testosterone, which causes the fight-or-flight response, whereas women release oxytocin, which produces a calming effect and a desire for closeness.[23]

Some psychologists have found both differences and similarities in how women and men experience friendship. Mayta Caldwell and Letitia Peplau, for example, studied college students' friendships and found that although both women and men desire intimacy and closeness, have roughly the same number of close and casual friends, and spend about the same amount of time with their friends, they often have different ways of expressing and achieving intimacy with them. Men were almost twice as likely to say they preferred 'doing some activity' with their best friend and looked for friends who liked 'to do the same things' as they did. Women, by contrast, were more likely to choose someone 'who feels the same way about things' as a friend and to favour 'just talking' as their preferred mode of interaction. Sociologist Beth Hess found that women were twice as likely to talk about personal issues with their friends. Still, women and men are far more similar than different in both providing and responding to supportive communication from a friend during 'trouble talk'—that is, when they are feeling some relationship distress.[24]

Other studies have found what appear striking differences. In a revealing portrait of the role of friendship in our lives, Lillian Rubin interviewed over 300 women and men and found startling differences in both the number and the depth of friendships. 'At every life stage between 25 and 55, women have more friendships, as distinct from collegial relationships or workmates, than men', she writes, 'and the differences in the content and quality of their friendships are marked and unmistakable'. Three-fourths of the women Rubin interviewed could identify a best friend, whereas over two-thirds of the men could not. While many married men identified their wives as their best friends, wives almost never identified their husbands in this way. Even when a man could identify a best friend, Rubin found that 'the two usually shared little about the interior of their lives and feelings'. If we understand intimacy to be based on both verbal and non-verbal sharing of thoughts and feelings so that the intimate understands the inner life of the other, then men's friendships are, Rubin concludes, 'emotionally impoverished'.[25]

Other research corroborates some of her findings. Women seem far more likely to share their feelings with their friends than were men; to engage in face-to-face interactions instead of men's preferred side-to-side style; and to discuss a wider array of issues than men do. Women's friendships seem to be more person-oriented; men's, more activity-oriented. Women's friendships appear to be more 'holistic', and men's more 'segmented'. And even when women seem to have fewer friends, as some studies have found, those they have are more intimate.[26]

In general, gender differences in friendships tend to be exactly what common-sense observation and talk-show pseudo revelations would suggest. Men are more reserved in their emotional patterns and less likely to disclose personal feelings, lest they risk being vulnerable to other men; women tend to be comparatively more open and disclosing. Of course, at the same time, we should be careful not to overstate the case. In fact, it turns out that there is 'much more similarity than dissimilarity in the manner in which women and men conduct their friendships', writes psychologist Paul Wright in a review of the existing literature of gender differences. Although it is true, he notes, that women are 'somewhat more likely to emphasize personalism, self-disclosure, and supportiveness' and that men are 'somewhat more likely to emphasize external interest and mutually involving activities', these differences 'are not great, and in many cases, they are so obscure that they are hard to demonstrate'. What's more, what differences there are tend to diminish markedly and virtually disappear 'as the strength and duration of the friendship increases'.[27]

For example, when women and men choose a best friend, they look for the same virtues—communication, intimacy, and trust. And the majority of us—75 per cent of women and 65 per cent of men—choose someone of the same sex as our best friend. What's more, both women and men select the same indicators of intimacy. In fact, Wall and her colleagues' study of 58 middle-class men revealed a pattern—stressing confidentiality and trust over simply the pleasure of one's company—that was more consistent with middle-class British women than middle-class British men.[28]

Differences in self-disclosure, so often identified as a significant difference between the sexes, turn out to be very small. Men's friendships seem to be based on 'continuity, perceived support and dependability, shared understandings, and perceived compatibility'. Men's friendships also centre on 'self-revelation and self-discovery, having fun together, intermingled lives, and assumed significance'—as do women's.[29]

In sum, most studies that measure interpersonal skills, friendship styles, or self-disclosure find few significant differences between women and men when it comes to friendship. Barbara Bank reports that men are just as likely to defend their friends, to ask for help when needed, and to go out of their way to help their friends as are the women she studied. What's more, women are just as capable of developing friendships that incorporate traditionally 'masculine' friendship virtues—trust, loyalty, obligation—as are men, and it is these qualities that often lead women to value friendship highly in their social worlds.[30]

Perhaps it's the combination of gender with other factors that best predicts our friendship patterns. For example, some of the studies that found gender differences compared working men with housewife women. But surely whether one works outside the home or not dramatically affects both the quality and the quantity of one's friendships.

Sociologists who explore the impact of race, ethnicity, age, class, or sexuality on social life suggest that factors other than gender may complicate the convenient gendering of friendship. Men and women may be more alike in their emotional lives, but there may be big differences among, say, working-class white women and men, on the one hand, and middle-class immigrant men and women on the other.

Ethnicity, for example, directly affects both men's and women's experiences of friendships, not only because we tend to choose friends of our own ethnic group, but because racialized groups may develop their own modes of friendship against the backdrop of a racist society. 'For Black men in [US] society', writes journalist Martin Simmons 'the world is a hostile, dangerous place—a jungle'. Friendship is a survival strategy: 'Me and him against the world'.[31]

Class also shapes emotional experiences. In the USA, for example, working-class black male friendships are often self-disclosing and close. Yet middle-class black men have fewer friends, and those they have are less intimate, than do their working-class counterparts. Moreover, some forms of class- and race-based intimacy may be a double-edged sword. Shanette Harris suggests that the very strategies embraced by black men to 'promote African American male empowerment and survival' may also lead to such maladaptive behaviours as gang membership.[32]

Age and marital status also affect friendship patterns. Unmarried men are more likely to maintain close and intimate friendships with both women and other men than are married men, for example.[33]

When we sift through the conflicting evidence, three gender differences in friendships do assert themselves with a certain insistence. The first is sexual tension— whether avoiding it with same-sex friends or confronting it with cross-sex friends. Sex does show up in cross-sex friendship among heterosexual women and men. Inevitably. But men and women *can* still be friends. It's just more work. Virtually all the men and women Rubin interviewed described sexual tension in their cross-sex friendships, which made stability and trust in the relationship more fragile.[34]

Because emotional disclosure equals vulnerability and dependency, most men reported that they were less comfortable disclosing their true feelings to a close male friend than to a woman friend. To be emotionally open and vulnerable with another man raises the second significant gender difference in friendship—the impact of homophobia. Homophobia is one of the central organizing principles of same-sex friendships for men but virtually non-existent for women. Homophobia is more than simply the irrational fear and hatred of gay people; it is also the fear that one might be misperceived as gay by others.

For men, friendship itself may be seen as a problem to be explained. Needing, caring about, being emotionally vulnerable and open to another man are acts of nonconformity to traditional notions of masculinity. Thus to even raise the question of male friendships is to raise the 'spectre' of homosexuality. In the opening pages of his book on male friendships, Stuart Miller writes that the first person he sought to interview, a philosophy professor, said to him 'Male friendship. You mean you're going to write about homosexuality?' 'Everywhere I have gone', Miller reports, 'there has been the same misconception. The bizarre necessity to explain, at the beginning, that my subject is not homosexuality'. And Lillian Rubin found association of friendship with homosexuality 'so common among men'.[35]

Homophobia inhibits men's and women's experience of physical closeness. In one famous experiment from the early 1970s, high school girls behaved as close friends had behaved in the nineteenth century. They held hands, they hugged each other, sat with their arms around the other, and kissed on the cheek when they parted. They were instructed to make sure that they did not give any impression that such behaviour was sexual. And yet, despite this, their peers interpreted their behaviour as an indication that they were lesbian, and their friends ostracized them. For North American men, even more than for women, homophobia restricts expressions of intimacy. One man explained why he would feel weird if he hugged his best friend:

> The guys are more rugged and things, and it wouldn't be rugged to hug another man. That's not a masculine act, where it could be, you know, there's nothing unmasculine about it. But somebody might not see it as masculine and you don't want somebody else to think that you're not, you know—masculine or . . . but you still don't want to be outcast. Nobody I think wants to be outcast.[36]

For lesbians and gay men, cross-sex and same-sex friendships often have different styles. In a 1994 survey, Peter Nardi and Drury Sherrod found significant similarities in the same-sex friendship patterns of gay men and lesbians. Both value close, intimate friendships, define intimacy in similar ways, and behave similarly with their friends. Two differences stood out to the researchers—how gay men and lesbians dealt with conflict and the role of sexuality within their friendships. Gay men, for example, are far more likely to sexualize their same-sex friendships than are lesbians. Like straight men, then, they experience more sexual tension in friendships with people to whom they might conceivably be attracted. On the other hand, '[l]ike their straight sisters, lesbians can have intensely intimate and satisfying relationships with each other without any sexual involvement', writes Lillian Rubin. Although it may overstate the case to claim, as Rubin does, that asexual gay male friendships are 'rare', such gender differences between lesbians and gay men underscore that gender, not sexual orientation, is often the key determinant of our intimate experiences.[37]

Gay men, after all, also report far more cross-sex friendships than do lesbians, who report few, if any, male friends. Yet lesbians have far more friendships with heterosexual women than gay men have with heterosexual men. Lesbians' friendships tend to be entirely among women—straight or gay. Gay men, by contrast, find their friends among straight women and other gay men. 'Lesbians apparently feel they have more in common with straight women than with either gay or straight men', writes one commentator.[38]

Of course, they do. Gender is one of the key determinants in their social lives. And yet gay men and lesbians also share one important theme in the construction of their friendships. Whereas heterosexuals clearly distinguish between friends and family, many gay men and lesbians have fused the two, both out of necessity (being exiled from their families when they come out) and choice. 'A person has so many close friends', comments a gay male character in Wendy Wasserstein's Pulitzer Prize-winning play *The Heidi Chronicles*. 'And in our lives, our friends are our families'. As more and more gay people build legally and socially recognized families, this situation will of course alter, but 'the chosen family' remains an institution within gay culture.[39]

As families become smaller, as more of us live alone, and as peers have increasingly become more important, friends are an ever-more-significant part of our lives. All of us want the same things in friends, it seems, but differences affect whom and how we befriend. It's not as simple as 'his' friendship and 'hers'; indeed, age, marital status, ethnicity, and class play important roles in our friendships. But there remain a few significant differences in our friendships and friendship styles; these are not the result of innate differences, but the product of the gendered society.

Gendered (Romantic) Love

It seems absurd to need to define something that our culture spends so much time talking about, but when we discuss romantic love, what exactly do we mean? Most scholars would agree that romantic love is characterized by a strong attachment to, physical attraction to, and idealization of another person; in the grips of romantic love, we may feel exhilarated, obsessed with, and absolutely focused on uniting with our love object. As neuroscientists are fond of pointing out, these feelings are accompanied and facilitated by chemical changes including the elevation of **dopamine** levels.[40]

The nature of such processes across cultures, historically, and in North American gay and non-gender-conforming teens may vary somewhat; but the existence and experience of romantic love is seen as nearly universal. What modern North American culture does with the experience of romantic love, however, is not. Commonly beginning in adolescence, our **culturally scripted** experience of romantic love is supposed—perhaps after one or two 'heartbreaks' along the way—to lead to marriage, after which we will settle down into a less passionate but still, ideally, deep romantic attachment.[41]

The power of this cultural script has been steadily growing in North American society; traditionally, however, men were more likely than women to agree that 'love and marriage go together like a horse and carriage'. This was demonstrated by a series of experiments conducted by William Kephart in the late 1960s. Kephart asked more than one thousand American college students, 'If a boy (girl) had all the other qualities you desired, would you marry this person if you were not in love with him (her)?' In the 1960s, Kephart found dramatic differences between men, who thought that marriage without love was out of the question, and women, who were more likely to admit that the absence of love wouldn't necessarily deter them from marriage. He connected this to women's relative economic dependency.[42]

Since the 1960s, sociologists have continued to ask this question, and each year fewer women and men say they are willing to marry for any reason but love. By the mid-1980s, 85 per cent of both women and men considered such a marriage out of the question; and by 1991, 86 per cent of the men and 91 per cent of the women responded with an emphatic no. The more dramatic shift among women indicates how much the women's movement has transformed women's lives: Women's economic independence now affords women, too, the luxury of marrying for love alone.[43]

But such studies yield very different results in different countries, suggesting that our definitions of love may have more to do with cultural (and economic!) differences than they do with gender. When students in Japan and Russia were asked the same question in 1992, their answers differed dramatically from those of Americans. More Russian women (41 per cent) and men (30 per cent) answered yes than did either Japanese (20 per cent of the men and 19 per cent of the women) or the Americans (13 per cent of the men and 9 per cent of the women).[44]

Another study compared American men and women with Chinese men and women. The differences between women and men were small—as were the differences between the Chinese and American samples. Culture, not gender, was a far more salient variable in understanding these differences. In both cases, men were more likely to hold romantic and idealized notions about love but were slightly more likely to be willing to marry without love. Note that the difference here is not in the existence of romantic love, as scholars have not yet found a society in which it does not exist; the difference is in the connection between love and marriage.[45]

The experience of falling in love is governed by rules of attraction that (for heterosexuals at least) draw deeply on gender stereotype. For example, most women and girls are attracted 'up': that is, to men and boys who are in some way 'above' them, whether that be in terms of wealth, worldly power, age, achievement, or simply body size; men, traditionally, have been attracted 'down', to women of lesser achievement, size, and age. (Think about it: How many women are willing to date a man smaller than they are? Until very recently, how many men were willing to date a woman who earned more than they did?)

French theorist Pierre Bourdieu calls this our culture's (and women's) 'spontaneous' acceptance of male domination; it's spontaneous because no one has to force us. In fact, for most of us, this kind of attraction just 'feels natural'. Before we start blaming ourselves—or as Bourdieu seems to do, blame women for complicity with male domination—let's remember that every fairy tale, from *Cinderella* to *Pretty Woman*, relies on inequality between the partners for its narrative power. But it's certainly worth considering the implications of our attraction to partners either 'above' or 'below' us in these ways.[46]

As our attraction to 'appropriate' mates is gendered, so too is the experience of falling in love. For example, there is evidence that men are more likely to respond to ephemeral qualities such as physical appearance when they fall in love and are far more likely to say they are easily attracted to members of the opposite sex. Yet most studies have found *men* to be stronger believers in romantic love ideologies than are women. (On the other hand, men also tend to be more cynical about love at the same time.) Men, it seems, are more likely to believe myths about love at first sight, tend to fall in love more quickly than women, and are more likely to enter relationships out of a desire to fall in love. Romantic love, to men, is an irrational, spontaneous, and compelling emotion that demands action.[47]

Women, on the other hand, show a more 'pragmatic orientation' toward falling in and out of love and are more likely to also like the men they love. Once in love, women tend to experience the state more intensely. One experiment found that after only four dates, men were almost twice as likely as women to define the relationship as love (27 per cent to 15 per cent). But by the twenty-first date, 43 per cent of the women said that they were in love, whereas only 30 per cent of the men did. The researchers write:

> If by 'more romantic' we refer to the speed of involvement and commitment, then the male appears to be more deserving of that label. If, on the other hand, we mean the experiencing of the emotional dimension of romantic love, then the female qualifies as candidate for 'more romantic' behaviour in a somewhat more judicious and

rational fashion. She chooses and commits herself more slowly than the male but, once in love, she engages more extravagantly in the euphoric and idealizational dimensions of loving.[48]

Despite the fact that men report falling out of love more quickly, it's women who initiate the majority of break-ups. And women, it seems, also have an easier time accepting their former romantic partners as friends than men do. After a break-up, men—supposedly the less emotional gender—report more loneliness, depression, and sleeplessness than women do. This is equally true after divorce: Married men live longer and emotionally healthier lives than divorced or single men; unmarried women live longer and are happier than married women.[49] So are men the 'romantic' sex, women the 'pragmatic' one? It's probably not that simple.

The separation of spheres 'feminized' romantic love so that today love implies 'an overemphasis on talking and feeling, a mystification of the material basis of attachment, and a tendency to ignore physical love and the practical aspects of nurturance and mutual assistance'. . As with friendship, women have come to be seen as the love experts—notice how all the advice columns on love and relationships are written for and by women? 'Part of the reason that men seem so much less loving than women', argues sociologist Francesca Cancian, 'is that men's behaviour is measured with a feminine ruler'.[50]

Men's more 'instrumental' style of loving, focusing on 'practical help, shared physical activities, spending time together, and sex', has been demoted to 'less than' the feminine style. These different styles of loving are the products of the large-scale transformations that created the modern system of gender relations. Men's and women's styles of romantic love are the result of gender inequality; these differences, as psychologist Carol Tavris tells us, emerged 'because women are expected, allowed, and required to reveal certain emotions, and men are expected and required to deny or suppress them'. They are the source of so much miscommunication between women and men that it often feels as though we are from different planets, or at least, in Lillian Rubin's phrase, 'intimate strangers'.[51]

Consider, for example, the classic 'he said/she said' tussle about whether we really love our partner. Here's what one husband said to Lillian Rubin:

> What does she want? Proof? She's got it, hasn't she? Would I be knocking myself out to get things for her—like to keep up this house—if I didn't love her? Why does a man do things like that if not because he loves his wife and kids? I swear, I can't figure out what she wants.

His wife said something very different. 'It is not enough that he supports us and takes care of us. I appreciate that, but I want him to share things with me. I need for him to tell me his feelings'.

These two statements aptly illustrate the differences between 'his' and 'her' ways of loving. Or do they? The empirical research on the gender of romantic love reveals fewer differences, and of less significance, than we might otherwise expect. One recent review of the literature, for example, found that women's and men's experiences and attitudes are statistically similar on 49 of the 60 correlates of love. And a recent study found that generally women and men are pretty much equally emotionally expressive—although women are more likely to express those emotions associated with inequality (smoothing things over, unruffling feathers, and the like).[52]

And it may be that other factors enhance or diminish women's and men's ways of loving. The statements of the man and woman above seem to speak loudly about intractable gender differences, but may actually say more about the transformation of love in a marriage than they do about deep-seated personality differences between women and men. Some startling research was undertaken by sociologist Cathy Greenblat on this issue. Greenblat asked 30 women and 30 men two questions just before they were to get married: 'How do you know you love this person?' 'How do you know you are loved by this person?'[53]

Prior to marriage, the answers revealed significant gender differences that meshed in a happy symmetry. The men 'knew' that they loved their future wives because they were willing to do so much for them, willing to sacrifice for them, eager to go out of their way to buy them flowers or demonstrate their love in some other visible way— willing, as one might say, to drop everything in the middle of the night and drive three hours in a blinding snowstorm because the women were upset. Happily, conveniently, their future wives 'knew' that they were loved precisely because the men were willing to go to such extraordinary lengths to demonstrate it. The women 'knew' that they loved their future husbands because they wanted to take care of them, to nurture and support them, to express their emotions of caring and tenderness. And, happily, the men 'knew' they were loved because the women took care of them, nurtured them, and were emotionally caring.

So far, so good—and perfectly symmetrical. Greenblat then interviewed 25 couples who had been married at least 10 years. She added a question, asking whether the men and women questioned whether they loved their spouse or whether their spouse loved them. Overwhelmingly, women had no doubts that they still loved their husbands but had significant doubts whether they were still loved by their husbands. By contrast, the husbands had no doubts that they were loved by their wives but had serious doubts about whether they loved their wives any longer.

It would be easy to interpret such data as revealing an essential gender difference: Men fall in love sooner but also fall out of love sooner than women. But such research may tell us more about how the structure of marriage transforms our ability to love and to be loved. After all, when you are married, you no longer have many opportunities to go well out of your way to do extraordinary things in order to demonstrate your love. You live together, come home from work to each other every day, and raise children together. Although that may be heroic enough in itself, it does not lead men to feel that they are expressing their love in the way they 'know' they love someone. Hence, they may begin to doubt whether they truly love their wives. By contrast, the nuclear family in the suburban single-family home enhances women's expression of loving as domestic, nurturing, and care giving. Thus the wives were certain that they still loved their husbands but were unsure that their husbands still loved them.

To 'read' such differences as revealing something *essential* about women and men would be to miss the structural impact of the modern family arrangement and the way that structural arrangements enhance some relational styles and inhibit others. Our current feminization of love, psychologist Carol Tavris argues, has detrimental effects on women's lives:

> The feminization of love in America, the glorification of women's ways of loving, is not about the love between autonomous individuals. It celebrates a romantic, emotional love that promotes the myth of basic, essential differences between women and men. It supports the opposition of women's love and men's work. In so doing, it derails women from thinking about their own talents and aspirations, rewarding instead a narrowed focus on finding and keeping Mr. Right.[54]

Fortunately, love need not be feminized, as Francesca Cancian argues. Men's way of loving—'the practical help and physical activities'—is, she notes, 'as much a part of love as the expression of feelings'. And the feminization of love as the expression of feelings, nurturing, and intimacy also obscures women's capacity for instrumental, activity-centred forms of love and thus, in effect, freezes men and women into patterns that mask some of their traits, as if right-handedness meant one could never even use one's left hand. Cancian poses an important question: 'Who is more loving', she asks, 'a couple who confide most of their experiences to each other but rarely cooperate or give each other practical help, or a couple who help each other through many crises and cooperate in running a household but rarely discuss their personal experiences?' Perhaps, Cancian suggests, what we need is a more embracingly *universal* definition of love that has as its purpose individual development, mutual support, and intimacy—and that women and men are equally capable of experiencing.[55]

Gendered Desires: Sexuality

Nowhere in our intimate lives is there greater expression of gender difference than in our sexual relationships. Yet even here, as we shall see, there are signs of change and convergence. As friendship and love have become 'feminized'—that is, as the model of appropriate behaviour has come to resemble what we labelled as traditionally 'feminine' models of intimacy—sexuality has become increasingly 'masculinized'. The 'masculinization of sex'—including the pursuit of pleasure for its own sake, the increased attention to orgasm, the multiplication of sexual partners, the universal interest in sexual experimentation, and the separation of sexual behaviour from love—is partly a result of the technological transformation of sexuality (from birth control to the Internet) and partly a result of the sexual revolution's promise of greater sexual freedom with fewer emotional and physical consequences.

Much of that sexual revolution was a rejection of the Victorian **double standard**, which was, after all, merely the nineteenth-century version of the interplanetary theory of gender. According to the double standard, women were essentially uninterested in sex and were held to a high standard of sexual behaviour, while men experienced powerful sex drives that found 'natural' outlets for which men were not to be blamed. 'The majority of women (happily for them) are not much troubled with sexual feelings of any kind', wrote one physician (obviously male) in the 1890s.[56]

Though few physicians would write or say the same thing today, the double standard persists, as do widespread gender differences in sexual attitudes and behaviours. To be sure, gender is not the only meaningful variable. Ethnicity is related to sexual attitudes and behaviours, at least according to studies that found less masturbation among Asian-Canadians and African-Americans and more adultery among African-American men.[57] Yet gender remains a meaningful influence on what we believe about sex and what we do sexually.

Men still stand to gain status and women to lose status from sexual experience: He's a stud who 'scores'; she's a slut who 'gives it up'. 'The whole game was to get a girl to give out', one man told sociologist Lillian Rubin. 'You expected her to resist; she had to if she wasn't going to ruin her reputation. But you kept pushing. Part of it was the thrill of touching and being touched, but I've got to admit, part of it was the conquest, too, and what you'd tell the guys at school the next day'. 'I felt as if I should want to get it as often as possible', recalled another. 'I guess that's because if you're a guy, you're supposed to want it'. The double standard makes sex something men 'get' from and do to women, as is recognized by the crude expression, 'he *did* her'.[58]

The sexual double standard is itself a product of gender inequality, of sexism—the unequal distribution of power in our society based on gender. With such a view, sex becomes a contest, not a means of connection; when sexual pleasure happens, it's often seen as his victory over her resistance. Sexuality becomes, in the words of feminist lawyer Catharine MacKinnon, 'the linchpin of gender inequality'. Not surprisingly, heterosexual women tend, on average, to be more sexually selective than are men. In one survey, women were about 20 per cent more likely to agree that one-night stands are degrading (47 per cent of the men agreed, 68 per cent of the women agreed).

Heterosexual men report many more partners than do women. 'Women need a reason to have sex', commented comedian Billy Crystal. 'Men just need a place'. In the 2007–2008 global Durex survey, Canadian men claimed to have had an average of 23 sexual partners compared to women's 10. (Interestingly, Canadians' numbers were significantly higher than those of most Europeans and Americans. Only the Swiss and Austrians reported higher numbers of lovers, which suggests something, perhaps, about the relationship between sex and winter!) This may reflect dishonesty, men's 'enhancement' motivations, or estimation error on the part of men or women, or perhaps that more heterosexual men have sex with fewer (but even more prolific) heterosexual women (including, of course, prostitutes). Whatever the explanation, the gender differential here reflects the double standard.[59]

Gender differences also appear in infidelity, which is relatively common. (In the USA, between 1.5 and 3.6 per cent of survey participants report having had sex outside their primary relationships in the past year.) Though the gender gap in infidelity has closed considerably in the past two decades, North American men are still more likely to stray than women, as are gay men, people in cohabiting relationships, people with permissive sexual attitudes, and members of some ethnic groups. Interestingly, studies have found that male-female differences in infidelity are amplified among homosexuals, with gay men dramatically more likely than lesbians (82 per cent versus 28 per cent, in one study) to have sex outside their primary relationships.[60]

Along with double standards come deeper differences in the understanding of sexual expression. Intercourse and orgasm seem to be more important forms of sexual expression for men than they are for women. Men's orgasmic focus leads to a greater emphasis on the genitals as men's single most important erogenous zone. If men's sexuality is often '**phallocentric**'—revolving around the glorification and gratification of the penis—then it is not surprising that men often develop elaborate relationships with their genitals. Some men name their penises or give them cute nicknames taken from mass-produced goods like 'Whopper' and 'Big Mac'. If men do not personify the penis, they objectify it; if it is not a little person, then it is supposed to act like a machine, an instrument, a 'tool'. A man projects 'the coldness and hardness of metal' onto his flesh, writes the French philosopher Emmanuel Reynaud.[61]

Few women name their genitals; fewer still think of their genitals as machines. In fact, women rarely refer to their genitals by their proper names at all. Most generally describe their external genitalia with the inaccurate 'vagina'. (We might ask why the term for the part of the female genitalia that envelops the penis has become synonymous with the whole package.) Some even resort to the more euphemistic 'down there' or 'private parts'. And it would be rare indeed for a woman to have a conversation with her vulva.[62]

Because North American cultures (post-colonization), like most cultures in the world, have been male-dominant, our view and language of sexuality reflect a male perspective. Most heterosexual men and women, if asked whether they had 'had sex' with someone, would immediately reply on the basis of whether or not penile-vaginal intercourse had taken place. This is 'real sex', while activities such as cunnilingus (which for most women results in more reliable orgasms than vaginal intercourse) are seen as 'foreplay'. Calling such activities foreplay means that they are inevitably seen as the prelude to the 'real thing'—once again, sex cannot occur without his orgasm, preferably through vaginal penetration. This view affects not only heterosexual sexuality, but also the sexuality of non-heterosexuals, whose sexual acts may be seen as 'not the real thing' or 'abnormal' as a result.

The definition of vaginal intercourse as real sex often results in complex rules about what constitutes a '**technical virgin**', and permits the fudging of questions about sexual activity. The impeachment trial of US President Bill Clinton in the late 1990s bears this out. Because he and intern Monica Lewinsky did not have vaginal intercourse, Clinton argued that he did not lie when he denied having sex with Lewinsky.[63]

So when they think about sex, heterosexual men and women are often thinking about different things. Actually, thinking about sex at all seems to be a gendered activity, with men reporting far more sexual thoughts than women. Over 54 per cent of the men surveyed in the most recent large-scale sex survey conducted by the National Opinion Research Center (NORC) at the University of Chicago reported that they think about sex 'very frequently', compared with 19 per cent of the women. And 14 per cent of the women said they rarely or never think about sex, compared with only 4 per cent of the men. In a recent study of Canadian adults, almost half of the men (47.1 per cent) reported 'having sexual thoughts several times a day', compared to only 10 per cent of the female respondents.[64]

Men, straight and gay, seem to want more sex than do women. At virtually every age and relationship stage, heterosexual men tend to want more sex, while women tend to report either satisfaction with the amount of sex they are having or a desire for less frequent sex. Heterosexual men are ready to begin sex earlier in a relationship than are women. In short, 'within heterosexual relationships, men want sex more than women at the start of a relationship, in the middle of it, and after many years of it'.[65]

There is also a significant difference in the number and nature of sexual fantasies reported by men and women. Women fantasize less frequently and about fewer partners. One study of university students asked whether participants had fantasized about one thousand or more sexual partners. Men were four times more likely than women to report having achieved such a staggering total of fantasy partners! The gendered content of sexual fantasies also differs dramatically. Michael and a research assistant collected over one thousand sexual fantasies from students during the 1990s. In those fantasies, definite gender patterns emerged. Men tend to fantasize about strangers, often more than one at a time, doing a variety of well-scripted sexual acts; women tend to fantasize about setting the right mood for lovemaking with their boyfriend or husband but rarely visualize specific behaviors.[66]

Not surprisingly, given their reported greater frequency of sexual fantasy, men also report more interest in masturbation. Indeed, masturbation produces some of the largest gender differences found in the study of sexuality. On average, most men masturbate, men begin masturbation earlier than women, and men masturbate much more frequently than do women.[67]

Men are also more sexually adventurous than are women, expressing interest in a much wider range of sexual practices. While this holds true for practices now (but not always!) considered 'normal', such as fellatio, it is also true that men are much more represented among those attracted to abnormal sexual practices, or **paraphilias**.[68]

Where does this sexual gender gap come from? It is quite possible that some of the gender differences we have discussed are the result of differential biology or evolution—that men do, in fact, have a biologically stronger sex drive than women.[69] But even if that were true—and we cannot yet prove that—a stronger sex drive would not account for all of the sexual differences we have enumerated. Fundamentally, our sexual differences are the result of differential socialization.

One source of this socialization is pornography. Men are significantly more likely than women to use pornography to stimulate sexual fantasy and as a masturbatory aid.[70] Indeed, porn occupies a special place in the development of men's sexuality. Nearly all men have had some exposure to pornography, at least as adolescents; indeed, for many men the first naked women they see are in pornographic magazines. (This is increasingly true for young people of both sexes, with implications discussed below.)

As discussed in the previous chapter, the 1980s feminist critique of pornography transformed the political debate, arguing that pornography expressed a culture-wide hatred and contempt for women. In contemplating pornography's role in shaping desire, we would be unwise to discount this theory out of hand. Here is one pornographic director and actor, commenting on his 'craft':

> My whole reason for being in the [pornography] Industry is to satisfy the desire of the men in the world who basically don't much care for women and want to see the men in my Industry getting even with the women they couldn't have when they were growing up . . . So when we come on a woman's face or somewhat brutalize her

sexually, we're getting even for their lost dreams. I believe this. I've heard audiences cheer me when I do something foul on screen. When I've strangled a person or sodomized a person or brutalized a person, the audience is cheering my action, and then when I've fulfilled my warped desire, the audience applauds.[71]

As we saw in the previous chapter, causal connections between pornography and violent or aberrant sexual behaviour are hard to establish. Yet whether or not there is *any* empirical evidence that pornography alone causes rape or violence, there remains the shocking difference between the genders: On any given day in North America, there are men masturbating to images of women and children enduring torture, genital mutilation, rape, and violence. Violence is rarely sexualized for women; that such images can be such a routine and casual turn-on for many men should at least give us pause. The increasing availability, in every North American home, of the most shocking images of sexual violence has implications that we are only beginning to contemplate.[72]

But pornography shapes desire in more mundane ways. First, pornography exaggerates the masculinization of sex. In typical heterosexual porn video scenes, both women and men want sex, full stop—even when women don't want it, when they are forced or raped, it turns out that they wanted it after all. Both women and men are always looking for opportunities to have sex, both are immediately aroused and ready for penetration, and both have orgasms within 15 seconds of penetration. For some commentators, like Marty Klein, this reflects a 'discourse of abundance' that porn viewers recognize as the fantasy it is. What porn offers them, then, is 'a narrative of validation—of the viewer's eroticism, of deliberately focusing on (and even enhancing) desire, of the possibility of mutual male-female satisfaction, of the viewer's vision of a world of erotic abundance, playfulness, and self-acceptance'.[73]

While some pornography may indeed offer such laudable visions, the most cursory tour of the Internet offers a more accurate and less transformative perspective. *Mainstream* hard-core pornography displays women with surgically enhanced breasts and shaved (and, increasingly, surgically 'trimmed' genitals). (However, as Klein suggests, the body images of women in pornography may well be less restrictive than those of women's magazines.) In porn women engage willingly and enthusiastically in anal sex, double and triple penetration, and the bathing in and ingestion of semen in the act euphemistically described as a 'facial'. To attract viewers to websites, women are described as 'bitches', 'whores', and 'sluts' who 'gag', 'swallow', and get 'pounded', 'hammered', 'face fucked', and 'split open'.

Where interracial sexual contact is depicted, whether that be in straight or gay pornography, racist stereotypes are often invoked; black men have 'huge schlongs' and 'gang-bang', black women are insatiable 'ghetto skanks', Asian women servile objects of sex tourism—and Aboriginal people virtually absent. This may indeed be a world of abundance, where women and ethnic minorities embrace servitude to phallocentric desire, but it is not the utopian playground Klein describes. As Daniel Bernardi writes,

> This is not intimacy or affection, or mutual desire or sexual expression. It is not, dare I say, love. This is semiotic hate, the history of mediated whiteness, and the opposite of love. This is not truly open sex. This is sex open to white eyes. This is not multiculturalism. This is colourized hate.[74]

As a result, as anti-pornography activist John Stoltenberg writes, pornography 'tells lies about women' (and, one would add, racialized subjects) but it 'tells the truth about men'. Perhaps more troublingly, pornography *changes* the truth about men (and women), shaping their desire for sexual practices, body characteristics, and sexual partners. For example, the popularity of **bukkake** pornography and so-called 'facials' has almost certainly affected the attitudes, desires, and practices of youth.[75]

But sexual socialization occurs even in the absence of pornography, of course, and begins before adulthood. The first element in the sexual socialization of children is the social institution of **compulsory heterosexuality**, first theorized by feminist Adrienne Rich in an article published in 1980. Focusing on female sexuality, Rich described how heterosexuality is made 'compulsory' through a variety of social mechanisms, of which the most important is the cultural assumption—'the lie'—that heterosexuality is 'natural' or 'innate':

> The lie is many-layered. In Western tradition, one layer—the romantic—asserts that women are inevitably, even if rashly and tragically, drawn to men; that even when that attraction is suicidal (e.g., *Tristan und Isolde*, Kate Chopin's *The Awakening*) it is still an organic imperative. In the tradition of the social sciences it asserts that primary love between the sexes is 'normal', that women need men as social and economic protectors, for adult sexuality and for psychological completion; that the heterosexually constituted family is the basic social unit; that women who do not attach their primary intensity to men must be, in functional terms, condemned to an even more devastating outsiderhood than their outsiderhood as women.[76]

Rich's theory of compulsory heterosexuality has been enormously influential, fuelling studies in a wide variety of disciplines. As an instrument of socialization, this institution works through promoting heterosexuality—for example, through stories and films that emphasize heterosexual attraction, courtship, and marriage—while rendering invisible other forms of sexual and intimate partnership. When not strictly invisible, non-heterosexuality becomes abhorrent and unnatural. This form of socialization exists from children's books and movies—think of Disney and fairy tales—all the way through the adult life course.

Compulsory heterosexuality is slowly breaking down, largely as a result of feminist theory and LGBTQ activism. But its power as an institution remains strong.

Socialization and Sexuality: The Heterosexual Questionnaire

The Heterosexual Questionnaire (of which there are several editions) was developed in the 1970s by Dr Martin Rochlin, an American psychologist. Its intent was to reverse the questions conventionally asked of homosexuals. It remains a potent and humorous reminder of the power of compulsory heterosexuality.

Heterosexual Questionaire

This questionnaire is for self-avowed heterosexuals only. If you are not openly heterosexual, pass it on to a friend who is. Please try to answer the questions as candidly as possible. Your responses will be held in strict confidence and your anonymity fully protected.

1. What do you think caused your heterosexuality?

2. When and how did you first decide you were a heterosexual?

3. Is it possible your heterosexuality is just a phase you may grow out of?

4. Could it be that your heterosexuality stems from a neurotic fear of others of the same sex?

5. If you've never slept with a person of the same sex, how can you be sure you wouldn't prefer that?

6. To whom have you disclosed your heterosexual tendencies? How did they react?

7. Why do heterosexuals feel compelled to seduce others into their lifestyle?

8. Why do you insist on flaunting your heterosexuality? Can't you just be what you are and keep it quiet?

9. Would you want your children to be heterosexual, knowing the problems they'd face?

10. A disproportionate majority of child molesters are heterosexual men. Do you consider it safe to expose children to heterosexual male teachers, pediatricians, priests, or scoutmasters?

11. With all the societal support for marriage, the divorce rate is spiraling. Why are there so few stable relationships among heterosexuals?

12. Why do heterosexuals place so much emphasis on sex?

13. Considering the menace of overpopulation, how could the human race survive if everyone were heterosexual?

14. Could you trust a heterosexual therapist to be objective? Don't you fear s/he might be inclined to influence you in the direction of her/his own leanings?

15. Heterosexuals are notorious for assigning themselves and one another rigid, stereotyped sex roles. Why must you cling to such unhealthy role-playing?

16. With the sexually segregated living conditions of military life, isn't heterosexuality incompatible with military service?

17. How can you enjoy an emotionally fulfilling experience with a person of the other sex when there are such vast differences between you? How can a man know what pleases a woman sexually or vice-versa?

18. Shouldn't you ask your far-out straight cohorts, like skinheads and born-agains, to keep quiet? Wouldn't that improve your image?

19. Why are heterosexuals so promiscuous?

20. Why do you attribute heterosexuality to so many famous lesbian and gay people? Is it to justify your own heterosexuality?

21. How can you hope to actualize your God-given homosexual potential if you limit yourself to exclusive, compulsive heterosexuality?

22. There seem to be very few happy heterosexuals. Techniques have been developed that might enable you to change if you really want to. After all, you never deliberately chose to be a heterosexual, did you? Have you considered aversion therapy or Heterosexuals Anonymous?[77]

For children, sexual socialization can range from the normal—'nice girls don't play doctor'—to the abhorrent, but unfortunately frequent, experience of sexual abuse at the hands of an adult or older child. For most children, adolescence is the time of the most intense socialization, and peers are the most important 'teachers'. As one feminist researcher put it, '[a]lthough their sexual interest is focused on the opposite sex, it is primarily to their same-sex peers that adolescents will look for validation of their sexual attitudes and accomplishments'.[78]

Consider the contortions of two adolescents trying to negotiate, usually without words, the extent of their sexual contact. It's tremendously complicated for LGBTQ youth, of course; in fact, though almost all non-heterosexual youth report romantic relationships in adolescence, openly courting or dating a same-sex partner is difficult and 'faking' heterosexuality is common.[79] Heterosexual relationships, though protected by privilege, are still not simple; both the boy and the girl have goals, though the goals may be very different. 'His' goal, of course, is to score—and toward that end he has a variety of manoeuvres, arguments, and other strategies his friends have taught him. 'Her' goal may be pleasure, but it is also to preserve and protect her reputation as a 'good girl', which requires that she be seen as alluring but not 'easy'. 'Young men come to sex with quite different expectations and desires than do young women', the NORC sex survey declared. 'Young women often go along with intercourse the first time, finding little physical pleasure in it, and a substantial number report being forced to have intercourse'.[80]

That is, significant numbers of young women are raped the first time they have intercourse. Until the 1980s, no one would have called such incidents rape. Rape was something done by strangers in dark alleys. But in the 1980s, US psychologist Mary Koss conducted a series of surveys of young women that led to her coining the term '**date rape**' (now often called acquaintance sexual assault). What she found was that coercion and lack of consent were prevalent in sexual encounters between acquaintances. While her results were controversial at the time, they are generally accepted by academics and have led to many studies of the complexity of sexual consent.[81]

In fact, for women, the whole idea of consent, or 'wanting it', is fraught with difficulties. Because of the double standard, girls and women have traditionally not been permitted to express sexual desire. To do so would be to risk social disapproval and even, up until very recently, rape. Until the 1980s, a standard defence against rape prosecution involved the assertion that 'she wanted it', which could be 'proved' through evidence of a victim's 'wanton' dress, previous sexual activity, or imprudent behaviour—for example, being alone with a boy or man. Racialized or otherwise marginal women were (and remain) particularly vulnerable to such 'presumed consent'. Small wonder, then, that girls and women have been cautious about overt statements of sexual desire.

That girls (and boys) have sexual experiences for reasons other than intimacy and pleasure has been a truism in sex research. While coercion or force play a strong role in girls' experiences of unwanted intercourse, other factors influence boys. Psychologist Charlene Muehlenhard, for example, found that more men (57.4 per cent) than women (38.7 per cent) reported that they had engaged in unwanted sexual intercourse due to being enticed—that is, the other person made an advance that the person had difficulty refusing. More men (33.5 per cent) than women (11.9 per cent) had unwanted sexual intercourse because they wanted to get sexual experience, wanted something to talk about, or wanted to build up their confidence. And more men (18.4 per cent) than women (4.5 per cent) said they engaged in sexual intercourse because they did not want to appear to be homosexual, shy, afraid, or unmasculine or unfeminine. Peer pressure was a factor for 10.9 per cent of the men but only 0.6 per cent of the women.[82]

Peers provide sexual socialization to adolescents, but so too do the media. Beginning at an increasingly young age, children learn from the media how to perform their appropriate sexual roles. For boys, this means learning heterosexual assertiveness; for girls, it means cultivating self-objectification. While children and teenagers are increasingly finding this information through on-line pornography (as a 2007 University of Alberta study found), 'pornification' of mainstream society makes sexual messages readily available in mainstream media—magazines, video games, and even children's toys such as the infamous Bratz.[83]

Peers and the media also shape adult sexuality. For example, when men seek therapeutic evaluation for sexual problems, they rarely describe not experiencing enough pleasure. How do they know how much pleasure is enough? Because at least since the launch of *Playboy* in the 1950s, men have been able to access and share information on their sexual experiences, and they have been schooled by media and advertisers on 'normal' male sexuality. Thus they are now perfectly capable of assessing 'how they measure up'. One man who experienced premature ejaculation reported that he felt like he 'isn't a real man' because he 'can't satisfy a woman'. Another, with erectile problems, told a therapist that 'a real man never has to ask his wife for anything sexually' and that he 'should be able to please her whenever he wants'. Each of these men thus expressed a sexual problem in gender terms; each feared that his sexual problem damaged his masculinity, made him less of a real man. Men with sexual problems are rarely gender nonconformists, unable or unwilling to follow the rules of masculine sexual adequacy. If anything, they are overconformists to norms that define sexual adequacy by the ability to function like a well-oiled machine (or a porn star).[84]

In this gendered context, we can better understand the enormous popularity of sildenafil citrate (Viagra) and other drugs that minister to men's 'sexual problems'. (Viagra and similar drugs enable men to achieve and sustain erections.) The drug company Pfizer marketed Viagra not merely as a product that would assist men with diabetes and spinal cord damage to lead 'normal' sexual lives, but as a 'lifestyle' drug that would enable middle-aged (and older) men to 'perform'. This entailed 'educating' North American men about the prevalence of erectile dysfunction through questionable statements such as 'more than half of all men over 40 have difficulties getting or maintaining an erection'. Viagra was the most successful new drug ever launched in the United States; over 35 thousand prescriptions were filled within the drug's first two weeks on the market (in late 1998). Many men crowed that they had found the 'magic bullet', the fountain of sexual youth. 'You just keep going all night', gushed one man. 'The performance is unbelievable'. The fastest-growing use group for the drug, between 1998 and 2002, was men between the ages of 18 and 45. The Viagra story demonstrates the power of the media—and the fear of judgment—in the sexual socialization of men of all ages.[85]

Closing the Sexual Gender Gap

Despite the persistence of gender differences in sexual attitudes and behaviours, the sexual gender gap has been closing in recent years, as women's and men's sexual experiences come to more closely resemble one another's. Or, rather, women's have come to resemble men's. As argued earlier, our experience of love has been feminized, and our sexuality has been increasingly 'masculinized'. Whereas men's sexual behaviour has hardly changed, women's sexual behaviour has changed dramatically, moving increasingly closer to the behaviour of men.

Part of this transformation has been the result of the technological breakthroughs and ideological shifts that have come to be known as the 'sexual revolution'. Since the 1960s, adequate and relatively safe birth control and legal abortion have made it possible to separate sexual activity from reproduction. (Men, of course, always were able to pursue sexual pleasure for its own sake; thus, in this sense, women's sexuality has come to more closely resemble men's.) 'I guess sex was originally to produce another body; then I guess it was for love; nowadays it's just for feeling good', was the way one 15-year-old boy summed up the shift. In addition, widespread sex education has made people more sexually aware—but not necessarily more sexually active. In one recent review of 53 studies that examined the effects of sex education and HIV education on sexual activity, 27 found no changes in rates of sexual activity, 22 observed marked decreases, delayed onset of activity, and reduced number of sexual partners. Only three studies found any increase in sexual activity associated with sex education. It would appear that sex education enables people to make *better* sexual decisions and encourages more responsibility, not less.[86]

Ideologically, feminism made the pursuit of sexual pleasure, the expression of women's sexual autonomy, a political goal. No longer would women believe that they were sexually disinterested, passive, and virtuous asexual angels. Women were as entitled to pleasure as men were. And, practically, they knew how to get it. After feminists exposed 'the myth of the vaginal orgasm', women no longer had reason to feel ashamed of desiring clitoral stimulation. Feminism was thus, in part, a political resistance to what we might call the 'socialized asexuality' of feminine sexuality.[87]

In the past three decades, then, women's sexuality that has been transformed, as women have sought to express their own sexual agency. Consider, for example, the transformation of the idea of sexual experience in the first place. Whereas it used to be that men were expected to have some sexual experience prior to marriage, many women and men placed a premium on women's virginity. Not any more. As Lillian Rubin writes, 'in the brief span of one generation—from the 1940s to the 1960s—we went from mothers who believed their virginity was their most prized possession to daughters for whom it was a burden'. Virginity was no longer 'a treasure to be safeguarded'; now, it was 'a problem to be solved'. North Americans, male and female, heterosexual and non-heterosexual, now come to the marriage bed with at least some sexual experience.[88]

Rates of and motivations for masturbation have also begun to converge. What, after all, is masturbation but self-pleasuring—surely an expression of sexual agency. The most recent large-scale national sex survey found that men's and women's motivations for masturbation are roughly similar. As are sexual attitudes. In the NORC sex survey, 36 per cent of men and 53 per cent of women born between 1933 and 1942 believed that pre-marital sex is almost always wrong. These numbers declined for both groups but de-clined far more sharply for women, so that for those born between 1963 and 1974, only 16 per cent of men and 22 per cent of women believed that premarital sex is almost al-ways wrong.[89]

Sexual behaviours, too, have grown increasingly similar. Among teenage boys, sexual experience has remained virtually the same since the mid-1940s, with about 70 per cent of all high school–aged American boys having had sexual intercourse (the rates were about 50 per cent for those who went to high school in the late 1920s). But the rates for high school girls have increased dramatically, up from 5 per cent in the 1920s to 20 per cent in the late 1940s, to 55 per cent in 1982 and 60 per cent in 1991. About one in five US teenagers has had sex before age 15.[90]

One place where one can observe the political ramifications of the gender conver-gence in sexual behaviour is the university campus, where a culture of **hooking up** has virtually erased the older pattern of 'rating-dating-mating' observed by sociologist Willard Waller decades ago. Waller saw a competitive marketplace, in which students evaluated their marketability in reference to both the opposite sex and the evaluations of their same-sex friends and sought to date appropriately—slightly up, but not too much.[91] No longer do students meet and mate with the intention of marrying. On campus, 'hooking up' is common.

'Hooking up' is a deliberately vague blanket term; one set of researchers defines it as 'a sexual encounter which may nor may not include sexual intercourse, usually occurring on only one occasion between two people who are strangers or brief acquaintances'.[92] Although that seems to cover most cases, it fails to include those peo-ple who hook up more than once or twice or 'sex buddies' (acquaintances who meet regularly for sex but rarely, if ever, associate otherwise) or 'friends with benefits' (friends who do not care to become romantic partners but may include sex among the activities they enjoy together).

On many campuses, the heterosexual marketplace is organized around groups of same-sex peers who go out together and meet an opposite-sex peer group in a casual setting like a bar or a party. Almost all hooking up involves more alcohol than sex. It would appear that Willard Waller's 1937 observation of 'rating-dating-mating' has been, in some ways, reversed. Today, it is less about dating to find an appropriate mate and more, one might say, about mating to find an appropriate date!

Unfortunately, as Melanie Beres's research in Jasper, Alberta demonstrates, youth hookup culture conveys multiple and conflicting meanings. If on the surface hooking up is understood as casual sex for its own sake, Beres found that many young women saw it as a potential means to begin relationships. As a result, they might avoid inter-course at a first encounter to signal that they were 'relationship material', but such efforts were not always successful.[93]

For adults, rates of premarital sex and the number of sex partners also seem to be moving closer. In one US survey, 99 per cent of male college graduates and 90 per cent of female college graduates said that they had had sex before marriage. And this is a long-term trend. Researchers in one survey of sexual behaviour from the 1970s found far greater sexual activity and greater variety among married women in the 1970s than Kinsey had found in the late 1940s.[94]

What turns us on sexually is also growing more similar. In the 1970s, psychologist Julia Heiman developed a way to measure women's sexual arousal. Samples of college women listened to two sorts of tapes—romantic and explicitly sexual—while wearing a intravaginal device that measured blood flow to the vagina. Like men, women were far more sexually aroused by explicit sex talk than they were by romance. And interest in sexual variety also appears to be converging. Experiences of oral sex have increased dramatically for both women and men.[95]

Conservative groups fret about women's lost modesty, chastity, or even their capitulation to male standards of sexual conduct. Women, they counsel, must remember the message that their grandmothers might once have told them: 'Men want only one thing'. And so women, if they yearn for commitment and marriage, have to relearn how to just say 'no'. Such strategies, though, ignore the pleasure-seeking behaviours and intentions of both women *and* men. Such an image is probably insulting to women, who have shown themselves capable of sexual entitlement and agency themselves; and it is certainly insulting to men, because it assumes that men are, equally inevitably, violent, rapacious predators.

Perhaps the problem is not the sex, but rather the gender—that is, not the consensual sexual activity between two consenting near-adults, but rather the gender inequality that accompanies it. Mutually negotiated sexual contact—mutually and *soberly* negotiated—with care for the integrity of the partner, can be a pleasurable moment or form the basis of a longer-lasting connection. The question is who gets to decide.

The evidence of gender convergence does not mean that there are no differences between women and men in their sexual expression. It still means different things to be sexual, but the rules are not enforced with the ferocity and consistency that they were in the past. 'It's different from what it used to be when women were supposed to hold out until they got married. There's pressure now on both men and women to lose their virginity', is how one 29-year-old man put it. 'But for a man it's a sign of manhood, and for a woman there's still some loss of value'.[96]

The recent popular panic over the dramatic increases of oral sex among teenagers is a good indication of both gender convergence (the 'masculinization of sex') and gender inequality. It's possible that parents' concern is fuelled by the different meaning of oral sex to their generation—as a sexual behaviour that was even more intimate than intercourse. Today, oral sex is viewed far more casually, just a 'kind of recreational activity that is separate from a close personal relationship'. But a closer look at the sex research data indicates that a concern over 'oral sex' among teenagers misses the real story. Whereas there has been a small increase in cunnilingus among teens, there has been an epic rise in fellatio. The oral sex craze is not about mutual pleasuring, but rather about girls servicing boys. Teenage girls are often faced with a cruel dilemma: Because 'guys rule' in teenland, guys get to set the rules for sexual engagement. If girls 'hold out' on intercourse, they have to service the guys if they are going to be able to hang out with them, get invited to the right parties, and the like. Such a demand may lead to the undervaluing of oral sex as sexual intimacy, because it's a way for teenaged girls to accommodate these new social demands. One teenager described this conversation at a party: 'I was talking to this guy for like, I dunno, 10 minutes, and he asked if I wanted to have sex, and I said no. So he said, "OK, but could you, like, come into the bathroom and go down on me" and I was like, "Huh?" '

In several other interviews, teenage girls described the 'pressure' to perform oral sex on the popular boys. 'They told me, like, it was like a ticket for admission or something, like they wouldn't invite me to parties and stuff if I didn't do it. So I told myself, it's no big deal anyway, and it's not like I'm gonna get pregnant, so, like, whatever'. Although today, both women and men feel entitled to pleasure, this is hardly a discourse of mutual pleasuring; rather it is a discourse of gender inequality. This extends to other forms of entitlement and coercion. 'I paid for a wonderful evening', commented one college man, 'and I was entitled to sex for my effort'. As a result of attitudes like these, cases of date rape and acquaintance rape continue on our campuses.[97]

About 15 per cent of college women report having been sexually assaulted; more than half of these assaults were by a person the woman was dating. Some studies have estimated the rates to be significantly higher, nearly double (27 per cent) that of the studies undertaken by Mary Koss and her colleagues. Men continue to be the principal sexual predators. Several studies estimate the likelihood that a woman will be the victim of a completed rape to be about one in five. The figure for an attempted rape is nearly double that.[98]

Women's increase in sexual agency, revolutionary as it is, has not been accompanied by a decrease in male sexual entitlement, nor by a sharp increase in men's capacity for intimacy and emotional connectedness. Some have suggested that men's 'non-relational' sexuality is the problem; psychologists like Ronald Levant seek to replace 'irresponsible, detached, compulsive, and alienated sexuality with a type of sexuality that is ethically responsible, compassionate for the well-being of participants, and sexually empowering of men'.[99]

The notion of non-relational sex means that sex is, to men, central to their lives; isolated from other aspects of life and relationships; often coupled with aggression; conceptualized socially within a framework of success and achievement; and pursued despite possible negative emotional and moral consequences. Sexual inexperience is viewed as stigmatizing.[100]

Although it may be true that non-relational sexuality may be a problem for some men, especially for those for whom it is the only form of sexual expression, it is not necessarily the only way men express themselves sexually. Many men are capable of both relational and non-relational sexuality. Some men don't ever practice non-relational sexuality because they live in a subculture in which it is not normative; other men develop values that oppose it.[101] One possibly worthy goal might be to enlarge our sexual repertoires to enable both women and men to experience a wide variety of permutations and combinations of love and lust, without entirely reducing one to the other—as long as all these experiences are mutually negotiated, safe, and equal.

Homosexuality, Bisexuality, and Gender

Thus far, we have been emphasizing the ways in which heterosexual men and women are socialized toward 'his' and 'her' sexualities. In some cases, this gendering of sexuality is as applicable to homosexuals as it is to heterosexuals. In fact, it may be even *more* obvious among gay men and lesbians, because in homosexual encounters there are two gendered men or two gendered women. Gender differences may even be exaggerated by sexual orientation.

This is, of course, contrary to our 'commonsense' understandings of homosexuality, as well as those biological studies that suggest that gay men have some biological affinity with women, as opposed to with heterosexual men. This research on the origins of sexual *orientation* is related to research on the basis of sex differences between women and men because, culturally, we tend to understand sexuality in terms of gender. Gender stereotypes dominate the discussion of sexual orientation; we may assume, for example, that gay men are not 'real' men, i.e., are not sufficiently masculine, identify with women, and even adopt feminine affectations and traits. Similarly, we may assume that lesbians are insufficiently feminine, identify with and imitate men's behaviours, etc. Homosexuality, our stereotypes tell us, is a *gender* 'disorder'.[102]

We have a century-long legacy upon which we draw such stereotypic ideas. Homosexuality emerged as a distinct identity in the late nineteenth century, when it was regarded as an 'inborn, and therefore irrepressible drive', according to one Hungarian physician. Earlier, there were homosexual *behaviours*, of course, but identity did not emerge from nor inhere in those behaviours. By the turn of the twentieth century, though, 'the homosexual' was characterized by a form of 'interior androgyny, a hermaphroditism of the soul', writes Foucault. 'The sodomite had been a temporary aberration; the homosexual was now a species'. Since Freud's era, we have assumed that male homosexuality, manifested by effeminacy, and lesbianism, manifested by masculine affectations, might not be innate but are, nonetheless, intractable products of early childhood socialization and that differences between gays and straights, once established, prove the most telling in their lives' trajectories.[103]

Indeed, our commonsense assumption is that gay men and lesbians are gender *non*conformists—lesbians are 'masculine' women; gay men are 'feminine' men. But such commonsense thinking has one deep logical flaw— it assumes that the gender of your partner is more important, and more decisive in your life, than your own gender. But our own gender—the collections of behaviours, attitudes, attributes, and assumptions about what it means to be a man or a woman—is far more important than the gender of the people with whom we interact, sexually or otherwise. Sexual behaviour, gay or straight, confirms gender identity.

That doesn't mean that these commonsense assumptions haven't completely saturated popular discussions of homosexuality, especially in those advice books designed to help parents make sure that their children do not turn out 'wrong'. For example, — Peter and Barbara Wyden's book *Growing Up Straight: What Every Thoughtful Parent Should Know About Homosexuality*, argued that 'pre-homosexual' boys were identifiable by their lack of early childhood masculinity, which could be thwarted by an overly 'masculine' mother, i.e., one who had a job outside the home and paid attention to feminist ideas![104]

A few empirical studies have also made such claims. For example, psychiatrist Richard Green tracked a small group of boys (about 55) from preschool to young adulthood. All the boys were chosen for patterns of frequent cross-dressing at home. They liked to play with girls at school, enjoyed playing with dolls, and followed their mothers around the house doing housework. Their parents were supportive of this behaviour. These 'sissy boys', as Green called them, were four times more likely to have homosexual experiences than non-feminine boys. But this research has also been widely criticized: Such gender nonconformity is extremely rare (there was great difficulty in finding even 55 boys) and thus cannot be the source of the great majority of homosexual behaviour. Extreme patterns of nonconformity are not equivalent to milder patterns, such as not liking sports, preferring music or reading, and being indifferent to rough-and-tumble play. The homosexual experience may be a result of the social reactions to their conduct (persecution by other boys or the therapy to which they were often exposed), which thwarted their ability to establish conventional heterosocial patterns of behaviour. It may have been the ostracism itself, and not the offending behaviour, that led to the sexual experiences. When milder forms of gender nonconformity are examined, most boys who report such behaviour turn out to be heterosexual. Finally, when studies by Green and his colleagues were extended to 'tomboys', it was found that there was no difference in eventual sexual preference between girls who reported tomboy behaviour and those who did not. (What Green and his colleagues seem to have found is that being a sissy is a far more serious offence to the gender order than is being a tomboy.)[105]

The evidence points overwhelmingly the other way: that homosexuality is deeply gendered and that gay men and lesbians are, when it comes to sexuality, gender conformists. To accept such a proposition leads to some unlikely alliances, with gay-affirmative writers and feminists lining up on the same side as an ultraconservative writer like George Gilder, who writes that lesbianism 'has nothing whatever to do with male homosexuality. Just as male homosexuals, with their compulsive lust and promiscuous impulses, offer a kind of caricature of typical male sexuality, lesbians closely resemble other women in their desire for intimate and monogamous coupling'.[106]

Since the birth of the gay liberation movement in the Stonewall riots of 1969—when gay men fought back against the police who were raiding a New York City gay bar—a gay culture has emerged that militates against the idea of gay men as 'feminine'. In fact, many gay men are extremely successful as 'real' men, enacting a hypermasculine code of anonymous sex, masculine clothing, and physical appearance, including body-building.

By contrast, the sexual lives of lesbians were quite different. For many lesbians, gay liberation did not mean sexual liberation. In the lesbian community, there was more discussion of 'the tyranny of the relationship' than of various sexual practices; lesbian couples in therapy complained of 'lesbian bed death', the virtual cessation of sexual activity for the couple after a few years. One woman told an interviewer:

> As women we have not been socialized to be initiators in the sexual act. Another factor is that we don't have to make excuses if we don't want to do it. We don't say we have a headache. We just say no. We also do a lot more cuddling and touching than heterosexuals, and we get fulfilled by that rather than just the act of intercourse . . . Another thing is that such a sisterly bond develops that the relationship almost seems incestuous after a while. The intimacy is so great. We know each other so well.[107]

Feminism also played a large role in the social organization of lesbian life in the 1970s. During the early waves of the women's movement, lesbianism was seen as a political alternative, a decision not to give aid and comfort to the enemy (men). How could a woman be truly feminist, some people asked, if she shares her life and bed with a man? The 'political lesbian' represented a particular fusion of sexual and gender politics, an active choice that matched one's political commitment. 'For a woman to be a lesbian in a male-supremacist, capitalist, misogynist, racist, homophobic, imperialist culture', wrote one woman, 'is an act of resistance'.[108]

The debate over 'political' versus 'intrinsic' forms of lesbianism obscures another gendered difference between male and female sexuality that is now the focus of research: bisexuality and 'female **sexual fluidity**'. Alfred Kinsey, in his pioneering research on male sexuality, discovered that many men had had same-sex sexual encounters. This discovery was key to his development of the **Kinsey scale**, which could be used to rate sexual subjects from 0 (exclusively heterosexual) to 6 (exclusively homosexual). A 3, on the Kinsey Scale, was someone attracted equally to either men or women. Nonetheless, the existence of these '**bisexuals**' has always been hotly disputed. For many people, bisexuals are simply people who can't 'make up their minds'.

More recently, researchers have found intriguing evidence that for women at least, same-sex attraction may be a relatively common phenomenon unassociated with lesbianism or even with bisexual identification. According to one random-sample study, the vast majority of women who report same-sex behaviour or desires identify as heterosexual despite their experience with same-sex attraction. Researchers posit that such women represent a characteristically female sexual fluidity, defined as the 'capacity for situation dependence in some women's erotic response'. One of the key situations capable of eliciting erotic response, for such women, is an intense, passionate relationship, so that women may report experiencing same-sex desire only within the context of one deep friendship. What this reveals about women's overall sexuality is unclear; recent suggestions that women are 'naturally bisexual' are probably premature. But it is noteworthy that women's stories of same-sex attraction—whether transitory or a fixed orientation—often emphasize an exclusively emotional (rather than explicitly sexual) basis, unlike similar stories told by men. Sexual fluidity confirms the idea that sexual behaviours and desires remain heavily gendered.[109]

The weight of evidence from research on homosexuality bears out this argument. Remember that men report more sexual partners than women. This gender difference is amplified among gay men and lesbians. In one study, sex researchers found that most lesbians reported having had fewer than 10 sexual partners, and almost half said they had never had a one-night stand. A 1982 survey of unmarried women between the ages of 20 and 29 found an average of 4.5 sexual partners over the course of their lives. But the average gay male in the same study had had hundreds of partners and many one-night stands, and more than a quarter of the men reported 1000 or more partners. HOW Masters and Johnson found that 84 per cent of males and 7 per cent of females claimed between 50 and 1000 or more sexual partners in their lifetimes and that 97 per cent of men and 33 per cent of women had had 7 or more relationships that had lasted four months or less. Whereas 11 per cent of straight husbands and 9 per cent of straight wives in another study described themselves as promiscuous, 79 per cent of gay men and 19 per cent of lesbians made such a claim. (Among heterosexual cohabitors, though, 25 per cent of the men and 22 per cent of the women described themselves as promiscuous.) Gay men have the lowest rates of long-term committed relationships, whereas lesbians have the highest. Thus it appears that men—gay (or) straight—place sexuality at the centre of their lives and that women—straight or lesbian—are more interested in affection and caring in the context of a love relationship.[110]

Research on frequency of sexual activity bears this out. In one study, among heterosexual married couples, 45 per cent reported having sex three or more times per week during the first two years of their marriage, and 27 per cent of those married between 2 and 10 years reported such rates. By contrast, 67 per cent of gay men together up to two years and 32 per cent of those together 2 to 10 years had sex three or more times per week. One-third of lesbians had sex three or more times per week in the first two years of their relationship, but only 7 per cent did after two years. After ten years, the percentages of people reporting sex more than three times per week were 18 for married couples, 11 for gay men, and 1 for lesbians. Nearly half the lesbians (47 per cent) reported having sex less than once a month after 10 years together. One interviewer described a lesbian couple:

> She and her roommate were obviously very much in love. Like most people who have a good, stable, five year relationship, they seemed comfortable together, sort of part of one another, able to joke, obviously fulfilled in their relationship. They work together, have the same times off from work, do most of their leisure activities together. They sent me off with a plate of cookies, a good symbolic gesture of the kind of welcome and warmth I felt in their home.[111]

If heterosexuality and homosexuality are so similar, in that men and women express and confirm their gendered identities through sexual behaviour, what then, are the big differences between heterosexuals and homosexuals—aside, of course, from the gender of the partner? One major difference is that gay relationships are more egalitarian, both sexually and otherwise. Thus we can say that in some ways, homosexual relationships model a possible future for heterosexual ones.

Gay men and lesbians have also been more sexually experimental, especially with non-penetrative sex. As one sex therapist writes, 'gay men have more ways of sexually relating than do heterosexual men'. And Masters and Johnson found that gay couples have longer lovemaking sessions than heterosexual couples. Among lesbians, the emergence of the 'stone butch', who focuses on pleasuring her/his partner but prefers not to be touched her/himself, is evidence of another kind of sexual experimentalism: the idea that pleasure need not be orgasmically reciprocal to be intensely, mutually rewarding.[112]

If homosexuality pushes the sexual envelope to some extent, homosexuality and heterosexuality are alike in being affected by homophobia. Institutionalized heterosexuality, the systematic devaluation of homosexuality, the stigma attached to being homosexual, become crucial elements in one's identity.

Whereas it is clear that homophobia constructs gay experience, we are less aware of the power of homophobia to structure the experiences and identities of heterosexuals. Although there is evidence that social attitudes toward homosexuality have become increasingly accepting in recent decades, homophobia is more than the lack of 'acceptance', or the fear or hatred of homosexuals; it is also, for men, the fear of being perceived as unmanly, effeminate, or, worst of all, gay. This fear seems less keen among heterosexual women, though many (at least in the USA) worry about the dangers of homosexuals (nearly always men) to their children.[113]

Male heterosexuals often spend a significant amount of time and energy in masculine display so that no one could possibly get the 'wrong' impression about them. In one study, many heterosexual men said they had sex in order to prove they weren't gay. Because our popular misperceptions about homosexuality usually centre on gender inversion, compensatory behaviours by heterosexuals often involve exaggerated versions of gender stereotypic behaviours. In this way, homophobia reinforces the gender of sex, keeping men acting hypermasculine and women acting ultrafeminine. 'Heterosexuality as currently construed and enacted (the erotic preference for the other gender) requires homophobia', write sex researchers John Gagnon and Stuart Michaels.[114]

Cultural Variations in Desire

Although gender remains one of the organizing principles of sexuality, other aspects of our lives also profoundly influence our sexual behaviours and expectations. For one thing, sexual behaviour, as we've seen, varies widely among different cultures. Margaret Mead found that in some cultures, the idea of spontaneous sex is not encouraged for either women or men. Among the Arapesh, she writes, the exceptions are believed to occur in women. 'Parents warn their sons even more than they warn their daughters against permitting themselves to get into situations in which someone can make love to them'. Another anthropologist reported that in one southwest Pacific society, sexual intercourse is seen as highly pleasurable and deprivation as harmful to both sexes. And Bronislaw Malinowski saw significant convergence between women and men in the Trobriand Islands, where women initiate sex as often as men and where couples avoid the 'missionary' position because the woman's movements are hampered by the weight of the man so that she cannot be fully active.

In contemporary North America, several variables other than gender affect sexuality, such as class, age, education, marital status, religion, race, and ethnicity. Take class, for example. Kinsey found that, contrary to the American ideology that holds that working-class people are more sensual because they are closer to their 'animal natures', lower class position does not mean hotter sex. In fact, he found that upper- and middle-class people were more sophisticated in the 'arts of love', demonstrating wider variety of activities and greater emphasis on foreplay, whereas lower-class people dispensed with preliminaries and did not even kiss very much.

There is evidence that race and ethnicity also produce some variations in sexual behaviour. For example, in the USA, some studies suggest that blacks hold somewhat more sexually liberal attitudes than whites and have slightly more sex partners, but they also masturbate less frequently, have less oral sex, and are slightly more likely to have same-sex contacts. Hispanics are also more sexually liberal than whites and masturbate more frequently than blacks or whites, but they also have less oral sex than whites (yet more than blacks) and have fewer sex partners, either of the same or opposite sex, than do whites or blacks.[115]

Age also affects sexuality. What turns us on at 50 will probably not be what turned us on at 15. Our attitudes toward sexuality may also change. Sexual attraction, activity, and orientation may be a less important part of our identities. Most intriguingly, we may even find our sexual orientation changing through the life cycle. Ideas of a fixed sexual orientation, cemented in adolescence and with us throughout our lives, are somewhat confounded by research that suggests that for women at least, same-sex desire may ebb and flow, leading some researchers to propose that 'variability in the emergence and expression of female same-sex desire during the life course is normative rather than exceptional'.[116]

Where sexual orientation remains constant, other changes occur. Age and other life-course changes may produce a decline in sexual energy and interest, but also change in marital status and family obligations. As Lillian Rubin writes,

> On the most mundane level, the constant negotiation about everyday tasks leaves people harassed, weary, irritated, and feeling more like traffic cops than lovers. Who's going to do the shopping, pay the bills, take care of the laundry, wash the dishes, take out the garbage, clean the bathroom, get the washing machine fixed, decide what to eat for dinner, return the phone calls from friends and parents? When there are children, the demands, complications, and exhaustion increase exponentially.[117]

Yet despite this, the longer-range historical trend over the past several centuries has been to sexualize marriage, to link the emotions of love and nurturing to erotic pleasure within the reproductive relationship. Thus sexual compatibility and expression have become increasingly important in our married lives, as the increased amount of time before marriage (prolonged adolescence), the availability of birth control and divorce, and an ethic of individual self-fulfillment have combined to increase the importance of sexual expression throughout the course of our lives.

It turns out that the more equal are women and men, the more satisfied women and men are with their sex lives. In a recent survey of 29 countries, sociologists found that people in countries with higher levels of gender equality—Spain, Canada, Belgium, and Austria—reported being much happier with their sex lives than those people in countries with lower levels of gender equality, like Japan. 'Male-centred cultures where sexual behaviour is more oriented toward procreation tend to discount the importance of sexual pleasure for women', said Ed Laumann of the University of Chicago, lead author of the study.[118]

What's more, within each country, the greater the level of equality between women and men, the happier women and men are with their sex lives. It turns out that those married couples who report the highest rates of marital satisfaction—and the highest rates of sexual activity in the first place—are those in which men do the highest amounts of housework and child care.[119] This led an article in *Men's Health* magazine to proclaim, 'Housework Makes Her Horny'—but only when *he* does it. The series of books and products called *Porn for Women* resonate with women; open one of these little spoof volumes and you'll find 'her' porn—photos of attractive, semi-clothed men vacuuming, doing dishes, and saying things like, 'As soon as I finish the laundry, I'll do the grocery shopping and take the kids with me so you can relax'.[120] It's silly, but it makes intuitive sense: the more housework and child care he does, the more time and energy she has, and the more loving she feels. Whether we compare countries or couples, gender equality turns out to be sexier than gender inequality.[121]

Conclusion

Love, friendship, and sexuality are perhaps the major avenues of self-exploration and the chief routes we take in our society to know ourselves. 'Love provides us with identities, virtues, roles through which we define ourselves, as well as partners to share our happiness, reinforce our values, support our best opinions of ourselves, and compensate for the anonymity, impersonality or possibly frustration of public life', writes Robert Solomon. Our friends, Lillian Rubin writes, 'are those who seem to us to call up the best parts of ourselves, even while they also accept our darker side'.[122]

Yet friendship is so precarious. 'Unlike a marriage', Rubin writes, friendship 'is secured by an emotional bond alone. With no social compact, no ritual moment, no pledge of loyalty and constancy to hold a friendship in place, it becomes not only the most neglected social relationship of our time, but, all too often, our most fragile one as well'. So, too, are love relationships, which require much care and nurturing in a world that seems to present an infinite number of distractions and subterfuges. Sexual encounters are more fragile still, holding at any particular moment only the most fleeting promise of sustained emotional connection.

To sustain our lives, to enable us to experience the full range of our pleasures, to achieve the deep emotional connections with lovers and friends, we must remember the ways that gender does *and does not* construct our emotional lives. Love, sex, and friendship are deeply *human* experiences—ones that should unite rather than divide us. As the great British novelist E. M. Forster once wrote of passionate human connection, 'men and women are capable of sustained relations, not mere opportunities for an electrical discharge'.

Summary

Though we often hear of 'interplanetary' differences between the sexes in intimate life, these differences are not as great as we sometimes believe. Moreover, these differences are not inevitable, but are the result of historical and social changes, which continue.

Women are now considered the 'relationship experts', but this was not always the case. Men's friendships and ways of loving have often been considered superior. However, the nineteenth-century development of industrialization and the so-called separate spheres ideology positioned women as the ministers of love, men as competitors in the strife-filled public arena. As a result, men's and women's styles of intimacy diverged, with men adopting more instrumental styles and women increasingly specializing in the expressive.

The nineteenth century also elevated the idea of companionate marriage and romantic love, making love for the first time the most important basis for marriage. At the same time, homosexuality (as a fixed sexual orientation) was 'discovered', leading to new homophobic scrutiny of male friendships. Thus intimacy was divided into two gendered domains, with effects that are still with us.

Communications are one of the most-studied areas of gender difference in intimacy, particularly since the groundbreaking research conducted by Deborah Tannen and others. Indeed, it seems that content, styles, and amount of talk are heavily gendered. Many of these differences are seen across cultures, with 'men's talk' generally valued more than characteristically female speech. However, research has found that most differences emerge in cross-sex talk, and that men adopt characteristically 'female' modes of talk in situations where they are required to be deferent; the language of gender, therefore, may be less about gender than about power.

Friendship continues to grow in importance in our lives, and scholars have found both similarities and differences in gendered friendship styles. Pioneering research found that women seem to have more and closer friends, and to engage in more expressive kinds of friendship. More recent research has failed to reliably identify significant differences in these areas, particularly when other factors—such as employment, ethnicity, class, age, and marital status—are considered. Still, there are key areas where gender differences can be seen. Homophobia affects male friendships more than female ones; moreover, men (straight and gay) experience more sexual tension in friendships than do women.

Romantic love exists across cultures; in the modern Western world, however, it is seen as the ideal basis for marriage. Indeed, though women have historically been more pragmatic about marriage, fewer and fewer people of either sex are willing to entertain the idea of marrying without being 'in love'. Falling in love for most heterosexuals is still governed by rules of attraction that depend heavily on gender stereotypes, particularly the stereotype that a man should be attracted 'down', a woman 'up'. Once attracted to a partner, heterosexual men and women experience falling in love in gendered ways. Women remain somewhat more pragmatic about love, tending to fall into love (and out of it) more slowly, and accepting the end of relationships with less loneliness and depression than men experience. Women also accept divorce more readily. When marriages remain intact, as most do, gender differences emerge, particularly in instrumental versus expressive relationship styles. These differences may reflect not men's incompetence in love, but the feminization of what we think of as appropriate intimacy. Francisca Cancian suggests that we need a universal model of love that brings both expressive and instrumental styles together and that focuses, most importantly, upon more meaningful measures such as individual development and mutual support.

Sexual relationships seem to express the greatest degree of gendered difference, but there are signs of change and convergence in this area too. Here, models of sexual interaction seem to be becoming masculinized, in part as a rejection of the Victorian double standard. Nonetheless, while women may appear to be free to pursue pleasure for its own sake, the double standard persists. Men and women are judged differently as sexual actors, and their attitudes and behaviours, not surprisingly, remain distinct.

Men are less sexually selective than women, and have more partners during their lives. Men are also more likely to be unfaithful than women (as are people in a number of other groups). Male-female differences in this area are amplified among homosexuals. Men think about sex more than women, want sex more than women, experience more sexual fantasies, masturbate more and at an earlier age, and are more sexually adventurous than women. Male sexuality also tends to be phallocentric, focused on the penis and male pleasure. (Indeed, our culture often defines sex on the basis of penile-vaginal contact.)

Where do these gender differences come from? Some researchers suggest that an evolutionary or biological difference in sex drive produces these distinctions. However, a stronger sex drive would not in itself account for all of the differences. Fundamentally, differential sexual socialization must play the largest role. For example, pornography plays a strong role in male sexual socialization (and increasingly the sexual socialization of youth of both sexes).

Another potent source of sexual socialization is the social institution of compulsory heterosexuality, which operates in two ways. First, it promotes heterosexuality as 'normal' and natural, and second, it renders invisible or represents as abnormal all other forms of sexuality. While compulsory heterosexuality is breaking down, its power (particularly in media representation) remains strong.

Sexual socialization of children can include not just the usual operations of compulsory heterosexuality, but the experience of sexual abuse at the hands of adults or peers. Indeed, peers are the most significant sexual socializers of youth. Sexual socialization continues in adulthood, both as the result of peer interactions and, especially, through interactions with the media.

Gay men and lesbians tend to express gendered socialization in some ways replicating or exaggerating masculine and feminine modes of sexuality in their sexual interactions. Still, gays and lesbians are more sexually experimental than heterosexuals. Both homosexuals and non-homosexuals are affected by homophobia, however, so socialization remains a powerful force in the construction of both homosexual and heterosexual desire and behaviour

The gender gap in sexuality appears to be closing, but given the persistence of gender ideologies and stereotypes, we remain far from a degendered sexuality based on mutual attraction, consent, and pleasure. In friendship, communications, and love, and particularly in sexuality, our society remains gendered.

Questions for Critical Thinking

1. What are the criteria you use to assess whether someone is a 'true friend'? Do you think that these criteria are influenced by your gender?
2. Why do you think women have a more 'pragmatic' approach to falling in love?
3. Why are men and women attracted 'down' and 'up' respectively? Do you think there are implications for the relationships we enter on this basis?
4. What are the most powerful influences on sexual desires and behaviours, in your opinion?

Key Terms

bisexual
bride price
bukkake
companionate marriage
compulsory heterosexuality
culturally scripted
date rape
dopamine
double standard
dowry
expressive
homophobia

hooking up
instrumental
intimacy
Kinsey scale
paraphilias
phallocentric
romantic love
sexual fluidity
sodomy
stone butch
technical virgin

Chapter 11

The Gendered Body

Prescriptions and Inscriptions

The body is an instrument which only gives off music when it is used as a body.
—ANAIS NIN

We think of our bodies either as our own private possessions, over which we exercise complete control, or as collections of biological impulses over which we have virtually no control at all. For centuries, the body has been shrouded in myth, taboo, and ignorance.

Yet nothing could be more gendered than this most individual, private organism. First, the attributes of our bodies become, whether we like it or not, key elements of our identities. Our skin colour, features, visible sex characteristics, height, weight, visible ability or disability—all become who we are in the eyes of the world. Second, we negotiate our bodily identities with the world. We inscribe—dress, pose, style, tattoo, pierce, shape—our bodies with a wide range of cultural signs and symbols. Our bodies become social texts that we construct to be 'read' by others. And significant changes in the past few decades—new surgical procedures, birth control, the Internet—have transformed this system of gendered signifying, making us more aware of our bodies than ever before and enabling new groups to claim their own embodied agency, a kind of embodied democracy that has also been met, characteristically, with increased backlash.[1] Our bodies are, then, neither private property nor simple biological entities. They are shaped, made meaningful, and scrutinized by our relations with the gendered society.

Gender and Dis/ability

One of the ways in which our bodies are constructed by society relates to ability. If in modern societies the 'universal' idea of a person has often been constructed as a male, it has also been constructed as able-bodied. Quick: picture a human being. In all likelihood, you pictured someone standing, perhaps nude, probably quite young. (We'll leave aside, for now, any racial and gender attributes of your imagined human.) Did you picture someone with a cane? In a wheelchair? With a developmental disability? If not, you are not alone. In our culture, **disability** is often ignored or rendered invisible, seen only when the specific topic of disability is addressed.

This study is not immune to the problem of failing to 'see' disability when we talk about gender. In fact, as Helen Meekosha writes, 'Nowhere is the problem more acute than in feminist discourses on the body, their claim to universality corrupted by their unselfconscious exclusion of disability from their worldviews'.[2] Both within broader culture and in the field of gender studies, then, disability often goes unseen. To the categories of privilege we have thus far enumerated (class, race, gender, sexual orientation), we must therefore add the privilege of ability. And to the familiar phenomena of sexism, racism, classism, and homophobia, we need to add **ablism**, which can be defined both as active discrimination against disabled people and as attitudes that diminish disabled people's competence and focus on disability as their defining characteristic.

Like other forms of discrimination, ablism rests to some extent upon fear. Robert Murphy writes,

> The kind of culture the handicapped American must face is just as much a part of the environs of his disability as his wheelchair. It hardly needs saying that the disabled, individually and as a group, contravene all the values of youth, virility, activity, and physical beauty that Americans cherish, however little most individuals may embody them. Most handicapped people, myself included, sense that others resent them for this reason; we are subverters of an American Ideal, just as the poor betray the American Dream . . . The disabled serve as constant, visible reminders to the able-bodied that the society they live in is shot through with inequity and suffering, that they live in a counterfeit paradise, and that they too are vulnerable. We represent a fearsome possibility.[3]

While the experience of invisibility that Murphy describes is probably familiar to almost every disabled person, 'not being seen' is not the only thing disabled people share. Disabled people are often infantilized or seen as childlike. Murphy describes how many adults with disabilities recount the same experience of going to a shop or public office and being ignored while their companions are asked what the disabled person wants—as though the adults with disabilities cannot explain it themselves.

Up to 16.5 per cent of the Canadian population experiences some form of disability (visible or invisible); the risk of disability increases with age. These Canadians are at much greater risk of poverty than the non-disabled. (And of course, the risk is even higher for the 80 per cent of disabled people worldwide who live in low-income countries.) According to Statistics Canada data, the 2006 overall rate of poverty for Canadian adults was 10.5 per cent (9.7 per cent for non-disabled adults). For disabled adults, the rate is 14.4 per cent—despite the higher cost of living with a disability! Those with cognitive or psychological disabilities face an ever higher rate of poverty (22.3 per cent). Adults with disabilities face significant barriers to employment, particularly discrimination, lack of accommodation, and underestimation of their abilities. When these adults are immigrants, Aboriginal, or from racialized groups, the barriers can be even greater.[4]

If disabled men and women share many aspects of the experience of disability, gender nonetheless interacts with ability in important ways. Women are 'overrepresented' among Canadian adults with disabilities. Fifty-five per cent of adults with disabilities are female, and these women have an even higher rate of poverty than do their male counterparts. Given women's greater representation among lone parents, women also face a double whammy with regard to poverty, since lone parents with disabilities are even more likely to live in poverty than able-bodied lone parents (themselves, as we saw in Chapter 6, a vulnerable group). Because employers' ideas of the 'ideal worker' may be both sexist and ableist, women with disabilities also face additional barriers to employment.[5]

Women living both with disabilities and in poverty are tremendously vulnerable to violence and sexual abuse, even while their sexual agency has often been denied. According to Helen Meekosha, women with disabilities are (and have been) more likely than men to be institutionalized. Eugenics-driven sterilization (see Chapter 6) has also been directed primarily at disabled women (and in North America disproportionately at indigenous and African-American women). For all of these reasons, disabled women may face greater body threat and body scrutiny than do disabled men. Still, some women may feel 'liberated' from social expectations as a result of disability—the experience is neither uniform nor monotone, and highlighting the problems disabled women face may end up stereotyping them as victims.[6]

For men, disability may strike at the heart of both physical and sexual performance, which are key elements in hegemonic masculine ideologies. In fact, because masculinity (unlike femininity) is constructed on the basis of strength, damage to self-esteem and a sense of 'invalidated masculinity' may be the experience of men with disabilities. As Tom Shakespeare notes, many war films hinge on a veteran's grappling with this issue. Some disabled men may be able to 'recover' their masculinity through participation in sport, but for many men this is impossible. However, at least for heterosexual men, damaged masculinity may be more an issue to them than to their female partners; men with disabilities are significantly less likely than disabled women to experience marital breakup. For all men, however, disability is a complex experience, influenced by issues of sexual orientation, ethnicity, personality, and all of the other attributes that make us unique individuals.[7]

Gender and Sport

Bodily play and sport provide some of our most enjoyable experiences—and can be enjoyed throughout the life cycle. Sport and physical activity produce enormous benefits that we are only beginning to understand: not just enhanced bodily health, but also improved mood, cognition, and self-esteem. Yet our relationship with play can vary dramatically with sex, race, class, ability, and sexuality. From our earliest days, play is one of the most heavily gendered aspects of our existence. This gendering carries on into adulthood, and is perhaps most powerfully expressed in sports, particularly at the highest levels.

As discussed in Chapter 6, children learn quite early on to play in gender-specific ways. In early childhood, boys are encouraged to participate in more physical, rough-and-tumble play than are girls, and boys' mastery of sports-related skills is considered important to their development as gendered beings. With the decline, in modern societies, of fighting as a key component of masculine identity, sport has emerged as perhaps the key area in which masculinity is proved and defined. Indeed, it is in sport that a boy may be first exposed to slurs against his masculinity, such as 'sissy' or the dreaded 'you throw like a girl'. The latter comment, unfortunately still heard today, is not just about the way a boy throws; instead, it serves as a damning indictment of his total gender identity.

In fact, throwing is one of the areas of greatest gender difference. According to a recent metastudy by Janet Hyde, the differences between men's and women's throwing speeds are significantly greater than any measured cognitive, communication, or even sexual differences—all of which pale in comparison. Throwing is an interesting phenomenon to study, and it sheds light on the gendering of sport. Predictably, many have traced female and male throwing styles (and competence) to biological differences. Such explanations, however, are confounded first by the existence of women who throw baseballs competently enough to strike out major league players, and second, by the fact that many *men* outside of North America also 'throw like girls'.[8]

So if biology doesn't completely explain this robust difference, what does? The philosopher Iris Young wondered the same thing, given the dramatic differences she saw not just in throwing, but in a variety of other motor skills essential to sport:

> The relatively untrained man . . . engages in sport generally with more free motion and open reach than does his female counterpart. Not only is there a typical style of throwing like a girl, but there is a more or less typical style of running like a girl, climbing like a girl, swinging like a girl, hitting like a girl. They have in common, first, that the whole body is not put into fluid and directed motion, but rather, in swinging and hitting, for example, the motion is concentrated in one body part; and second, that the woman's motion tends not to reach, extend, lean, stretch, and follow through in the direction of her intention.

In various versions of her essay 'Throwing like a Girl', Young suggested that girls in modern industrialized societies throw (and use their bodies) awkwardly not because of their anatomy, but because of 'basic modalities of feminine body comportment, manner of moving, and relation in space'. That is, girls learn to use their bodies in a fundamentally different way than do boys. They learn to hold their bodies modestly, in a 'closed' fashion; they become tentative about using their bodies; and they greatly underestimate their physical capabilities. Whether throwing a ball or hitting a tennis backhand, one must 'put the body into it', opening the stance and chest and abandoning concerns about modesty. Feminine body comportment is thus the enemy of sporting competence.[9]

So too is the **self-objectification** that girls learn as inhabitants of female bodies in a gendered society. When we objectify ourselves, we adopt the perspective of an outsider on our bodies and selves. This undermines ability to be comfortable in one's skin, to move the body unselfconsciously in space, and most importantly, to focus completely—another critical skill for sports success. A recent study looked at the relationship of self-objectification and motor performance in girls 10 to 17. Researchers found that 'girls who exhibited greater self-objectification also showed poorer throwing performance', regardless of ethnic group. The older girls in the study were more likely to self-objectify (and throw poorly) than were younger girls; this is in line with research that has found the gap between male and female performance widening between the age of three and puberty. If self-objectification can lead to poor sports performance, a more positive influence can flow in the other direction. According to research conducted in Manitoba, Grade 11 girls who participated in non-competitive sports reported increased self-esteem.[10]

That is, the gap between girls and boys widens before and during their time in the school system. School is also the occasion for most children's first exposure to orga-nized sports (though many children begin sports lessons and some even join sports teams before entering school). School experiences thus have a profound effect on life-long attitudes toward and experiences of sport. The development of school sports (and organized sport in general) can be traced to the nineteenth-century ideals of 'imperial manhood' and 'muscular Christianity' (discussed in Chapter 7). Sport was conceived of as an inherently masculine pursuit aimed at training boys' bodies and minds to fit them for their roles as men.

Not until the twentieth century was sport seen as a desirable pursuit for North American girls, despite the existence of some sporting women and the long-standing participation of women in physical games in both European and Aboriginal societies. In schools, sport entered the girls' curriculum at various Canadian schools in the early twentieth century, but 'athleticism never acquired anything like the same hold it had over the equivalent boys' schools'. Sport remained associated with masculinity, and was extended to girls only to fit them for greater health 'and ultimately motherhood'.[11]

This changed gradually through the twentieth century, particularly after the growth of the second-wave feminist movement in the 1960s and 1970s. Abby Hoffman, one of Canada's greatest track athletes of the day, became a fervent spokesperson for the expansion of sports opportunities to girls and women. In 1975, she told *Maclean's* magazine that 'most girls leave school in a physically autistic [sic] state and haven't the faintest idea how to get any pleasure out of sport'. Hoffman, who won many medals for Canada as a middle-distance runner, was familiar with both achievement and exclusion. As a girl, she had disguised her sex in order to play on an Ontario boys' hockey team.[12]

Meanwhile, in the USA, the same debates resulted in the 1972 passage of **Title IX**, an amendment to the Education Act that abolished all forms of sex discrimination in public schools. Title IX has been interpreted as meaning that women's and girls' sports must be funded at the same levels as those played by men and boys. Since then, girls' participation in interscholastic sports has soared from 300,000 to over two million, and the involvement of college-age women has expanded by more than 600 per cent. Canada has no equivalent to Title IX, though such an amendment has been suggested by the Canadian Association for the Advancement of Women and Sport and Physical Activity. Nonetheless, Canadian human rights cases have established the rights of girls and women to full and equal participation in sports. Since 1996, Canada's Olympic teams have been gender-balanced. Indeed, in the past three Winter Olympics (not including Vancouver 2010), women have won most of Canada's medals. This was also true of Canada's Paralympic Team at the Athens summer games, when women (though less than half of athletes) won almost two-thirds of Canada's medals.[13]

But girls' and women's relationships with sport continue to be dogged by more subtle forms of discrimination. For example, women who excel in sport are still likely to be perceived as unfeminine or suspected of homosexuality. This is one area in which women are at least as influenced as men by homophobia. Since the traits required for success in sport (e.g., competition and physical mastery) are still usually seen as masculine, successful sporting women are 'masculinized' by society. And because gender nonconformity and sexual orientation are still powerfully linked in the minds of many, this leads to a 'slippage': female athlete=lesbian. This stereotypes (and stigmatizes, given the persistence of homophobia) female athletes and serves as a limiter on female behaviour. Sadly, it sometimes limits athletes' solidarity as heterosexual athletes struggle to distance themselves from lesbianism and establish their 'feminine' credentials. Thus for lesbian athletes, homophobia remains a powerful reality.[14]

Discrimination also remains, as can be seen in two events reported widely in the media in 2009. The first concerned Victoria's Beacon Hill Little League major girls' softball team, which won its divisional championship on July 25, 2005, thus qualifying for the national championship. Little League organizers told the girls that they would have to fund their own travel, even though Victoria's winning divisional boys' team had been provided with travel funding to enable them to attend the nationals. Fortunately, a private donor stepped up to the plate, permitting the girls to travel to the nationals (where they won!) and, from there, to represent Canada at the world championship. Little League Canada denied that the funding decisions had anything to do with sex, but the team's coach disagreed. He filed a complaint with BC's Human Rights Tribunal, which awarded the girls $1,000 each in damages and ordered Little League to refrain from any such discrimination in future.[15]

A less successful attempt to use the courts to force sport to be more sporting was a BC Supreme Court challenge launched by 15 former and current female ski jumpers, who argued that the International Olympic Committee's decision to exclude women's ski jumping from the 2010 games violated Canada's Charter of Rights. Like Little League, the IOC denied that the decision had anything to do with gender, arguing instead that the decision was based 'purely on technical merit'; that is, women ski jumpers are neither plentiful nor skilful enough to ensure that their presence in the game would not 'dilute' the medals of other athletes. This time, while Justice Lauri Ann Fenlon agreed that there was discrimination, she said she had no authority to compel the IOC to comply with Canada's Charter. In December 2009, women ski jumpers' last hope was dashed when the Supreme Court of Canada declined to hear their case. In some areas of sport, gender equality is yet to be attained.[16]

More subtle discrimination exists at the level of compensation. While there is still an income gap between men and women (see Chapter 8) in the world of work generally, in sport the gap is dramatically wider. In 2009, the highest paid male athlete in the world was Tiger Williams, who has held that spot for years (though the beating his image took in 2009 may affect his future earnings somewhat). The highest paid female athlete in the world was tennis star Maria Sharapova, who earned approximately one quarter of what Woods earned and only just over half of what the lowest-earning of the top eleven male athletes earned. (Interestingly, while most of the highest-earning male athletes are top-ranked, Sharapova out earns higher-ranked athletes seemingly on the basis of attractiveness.) Average salaries are also informative; despite growing fan interest, women's salaries in the WNBA remain a paltry fraction of what male NBA players earn.[17]

Caster Semenya and the Gender of Sport

Jeffrey Barbee/Guardian News & Media Ltd 2009

Caster Semenya poses for a portrait at her training facility in fall 2009.

One of the areas in which the gendering of sport becomes clearest is at its boundaries, when an athlete's very ability to participate in sport may be denied. In summer 2009, after South African runner Caster Semenya won a medal at the world championships in Berlin, she found herself at the centre of a sex/gender controversy that now threatens her ability to compete in the sport she loves. Her personal best time in the 800 m final earned her not only the gold medal (and the record time for a woman in 2009) but an unfortunate comment from an Italian runner: 'she is a man'. Semenya's time is even more impressive when one considers that she was running under a cloud. The day before the final, the International Association of Athletics Federations (IAAF) had revealed that Caster had been subjected to 'gender verification tests'. In the days and months that followed, Semenya became a global newsmaker and celebrity. She was the subject of innumerable media reports—a Google search of her name generates more than 7.5 million hits—and unprecedented speculation. Was she a victim of racism? Intersexed? A 'hermaphrodite'? And did it matter?

It is generally agreed that in most sports, biological males enjoy some advantages. This is the rationale for separate competitions for the sexes (though there are at least a few sports in which such separate competition seems to lack reason). In order to prevent men from disguising themselves as women and unfairly winning competitions, female athletes were subjected to tests to ensure their biological sex. While this may seem an odd rationale, there was at least one case in which a putatively male (though perhaps intersex) high jumper competed (for Germany) in female disguise. (He placed fourth at the Berlin Olympics in 1936.) Also in the Berlin Games, two female sprinters accused each other of being male.

As a result of such concerns, **sex testing** (generally called **gender verification** today) gradually became part of amateur sport. Prior to 1968, for example, female Olympic athletes had to appear nude in front of an examining board who scrutinized their bodies for signs of masculinity. Because of the degrading nature of this exercise, chromosomal tests were substituted, generally relying on a cheek-swab sample of the athlete's cells. After the controversy generated by the sex-testing decision involving Spanish hurdler Maria Patiño (see Chapter 2), the IOC revisited sex testing, discontinuing the practice in 1999. Nonetheless, sex testing remains common in amateur sport.

One problem with 'gender verification' is that biological sex is not merely a matter of having an XX or XY chromosome. For example, XY people with Androgen Insensitivity Syndrome (see Chapter 2) look female-typical (and even 'more feminine' than many XX women), and have less testosterone in their bodies than average women. Yet chromosomally speaking, AIS people are male. Should they therefore be disqualified from women's sporting events? If the issue is the amount of testosterone in a woman's body and the 'advantage' it confers, where do we draw the line? Do we test all women and disqualify those with naturally higher levels of androgens? Success at the highest level of sport relies to a large degree on natural advantages (for example, swimmer Michael Phelps's unusually long arms, or a pro basketball player's unusual height); should we therefore consider higher levels of androgens, or a woman's structurally 'masculine' body, as another form of natural advantage? Given the difficulty of the issue, we cannot expect clear guidelines any time soon.

If controversy dogs many female athletes, transgendered athletes are particularly susceptible. The first well-known case involving a transgendered athlete's right to compete was that of tennis player Renee Richards. Richards was a prominent player as a junior and young man, making it to the final of the US nationals. At the age of about 40, the 6'2" Richards became a woman and entered professional tennis. Though she had to fight for the right to compete, she triumphed and enjoyed a relatively successful pro career (particularly given her age). But the advantages gained from her years as a man by no means resulted in her dominating women's tennis.

More recently, BC mountain bike racer Michelle Demaresq faced similar barriers. A mountain biker since her boyhood, Demaresq was open about being a transsexual and was welcomed by other women racers. This changed, however, as she began to do better in competition. In July 2006, Demaresq beat a fellow racer by one second to win the national downhill mountain bike championships. On the podium, the second-place winner removed her jersey to reveal a T-shirt that read '100% pure woman'. Her racing licence was suspended for three months, and Demaresq's right to compete has been accepted. But the incident nonetheless reveals persistent issues.

And what about Caster Semenya, who was born female and raised as a woman? Rumours continue to suggest that she has some kind of intersex condition. But if she does, it didn't make her an instant star performer. In fact, before she began working with her current coach, she showed natural talent but regularly posted 'very slow' times. Training made the difference.

Semenya's story shows both the gendered difficulties within sport and the power of sport to enact liberating independence. In a fall 2009 interview, Caster made this clear when she said of her track group, 'I am myself here . . . Everyone just accepts me. They know who I am. I am just Caster to these guys. I feel good with them'. While Caster may be accepted by her fellow athletes, her right to run remains in question. The IAAF has not decisively ruled on her eligibility as this book goes to press.[18]

Much of the discussion so far has centred on women and girls—and how they have been excluded from sport and discriminated against within it. But we began by stating that sport is wrapped up in notions of manliness. If sport is a ground upon which women often feel like aliens, it is for many boys and men a testing ground and a central site of gender socialization. Sports participation, sports competence, and even sports fandom are the opportunity not only for profound enjoyment and benefit, but for the demonstration and loss of masculinity.

The proof of masculinity in sport has been, at least since the nineteenth century, tied to the proof of the power and 'manliness' (as was then said) of nations. This provides a male athlete an opportunity to become a nation's hero (while female athletes are more likely to become, say, 'Canada's darling'). For racialized men, this is an opportunity found in few other areas of endeavour. But it comes at a risk, as the case of Ben Johnson suggests. Johnson was Canada's most successful track athlete in history in the late 1980s; with an astonishing world-record time, he won gold for Canada at the Seoul Olympics in 1988. Unfortunately, he tested positive for anabolic steroids and was stripped of his medal. He was also, as Gamal Abdel-Shehid writes, symbolically stripped of his citizenship, transformed in the media from Canadian athlete-hero to disgraced Caribbean immigrant. (Johnson was born in Jamaica.)[19]

If masculine sport is important to nations, it is even more important in individual lives. In earliest childhood, sports serve as an avenue for 'disciplining' boys into appropriate gender norms. Boys learn to be tough, to endure pain, and to compete. Boys also learn that aggression is necessary and rewarded. In hockey, Canada's most cherished game, boys from about the age of six participate in a game that tolerates aggression and rule violation.

> From an early age, players are taught that competence (a player's ability to contribute to team success) includes certain penalties that are considered good such as hooking (placing the stick around another player's legs or waist and taking them down to the ice) and tripping that prevent goals. Certain penalties are considered bad such as slashing (using one's stick to chop at another player) or elbowing that show a lack of discipline but may not contribute to team success. Bad penalties are those benefitting the opposition. Rule infractions which are expected in certain situations (e.g., to prevent scoring chances) are supplemented by the use of aggressive tactics which are defined as essential for team success.[20]

Willingness to make sacrifices for the team are valorized in hockey, perhaps even more than in other team sports. Sacrificing one's body and safety are also considered characteristic of good (and masculine) players. (This is also true of major-league football, in which players 'spend' their bodies so generously that many end up with dementia in their 50s and 60s.) In the 1990s, as skilled European players like Pavel Bure flooded into the National Hockey League, CBC commentator Don Cherry reserved his special contempt for visor-wearing Russians and 'Chicken Swedes' who protected themselves and shied away from fights. And he's still at it; in 2009 he referred to Cal Clutterbuck as 'Buttercup' for failing to remove his visor during a fight.[21]

Indeed, hockey may be one of the only games in which fighting, though not formally part of the game, is expected and evaluated as if it were. Fighting is seen as 'an essential element of the tradition and culture of hockey', and as something that distinguishes the Canadian game from its effete European counterparts. The team 'enforcer', while he may lack the skill and finesse of his teammates, plays a critical role in the game, and is often beloved of hometown fans (though threatened at away games!). And fans love a fight. Anyone who has ever attended an NHL game at which two well-known team enforcers played will remember the palpable excitement as fans waited to see whether they would 'go'. Players experience that excitement as both stimulation and pressure:

> [I]t was enough for me to see that they wanted to see that violence thing, and it does promote it—I mean, when the crowd is behind you and cheer when you knock people into the boards—I'm not going to lie, it gets you fired up and wants to make you do [sic] more banging of guys into the boards, and lots of times, if it takes that to get the team fired up, then that's what you're going to do.
>
> [F]ans would come up to you and say, that's a great fight you were in . . . and basically, you're getting rewarded for . . . fighting with someone, and people remembered that.[22]

While some spontaneous violence may be an unavoidable consequence of the intense nature of hockey (line) play, the ritualized and important place of fighting in hockey is evidence of its connection with constructs of hegemonic masculinity such as domination and violence.

Not surprisingly, that violence sometimes spills off the rink, whether into arena parking-lot team fights or more diffused violent behaviour. The combination of violence, what Don Szabo calls 'the myth of the sexual athlete', and sexist sport culture also leads to a great overrepresentation of athletes in sexual assaults.[23]

Sport, then, is a gendered arena in which the most troubling aspects of the relationship between gender and the body can be seen. But sport is also where we can establish the healthiest, most transformative relationships with our bodies, and where we find some of the most exhilarating role models for gender-role transformation.

Gender and the Beauty Myth

The relationship of beauty with the gendered body has so far provided less food for transformation. Our ideals of beauty and attractiveness themselves remain deeply gendered and, for many of us, the source of personal pain.

And that pain is unequally distributed between the genders (though this is an area of rapid change). For one thing, we know a lot more about standards of female beauty in other cultures than we know about standards of male beauty—in part because it's men who were creating those standards in the first place, and their valuation derived from other things, like wealth and power. Specifically sexual standards of beauty often vary. In many tropical cultures, women do not cover their breasts, but this doesn't mean that the men there are in a constant state of sexual frenzy. The breasts are simply not considered a sexual stimulus in those cultures, and attention may be focused elsewhere. Yet in some Islamic cultures, women are believed to be so sexually alluring (and men so unable to control themselves when confronted with temptation) that women practice **purdah**, which requires varying degrees of female seclusion and body covering.

Sexual standards of beauty often change and are subject to societal influence. This is true in the West, as is well known, but also in other cultures. The bound foot, once erotically attractive to Chinese men, would be repellent to almost all today. So too the whaleboned 'wasp waist' of nineteenth-century Europe. In Japan, prior to the Second World War, breasts 'had a subsidiary role in sexual fantasy and practice', and women's clothing flattened rather than accentuated the breasts. The primary 'visible' breast was associated with breastfeeding rather than sexuality. More recently, Japan has been over-taken by 'mammary mania' (as any casual viewer of manga or anime can attest). This is an example of how a culture's preference for certain characteristics can alter in a rela-tively short time. There do appear to be some consistent and 'universal' features of feminine beauty among men, such as a preference for symmetry and hips significantly larger than the waist. (Both of these features may reflect a biological tendency to seek mates who are fecund and healthy.) But aside from these characteristics, what consti-tutes 'beauty' varies widely.[24]

The importance placed on beauty also varies. In the United States (and Canada is not so different), women's beauty is placed at such a high premium and the standards of beauty are so narrow that many women feel trapped by what Naomi Wolf calls the **'beauty myth'**—a nearly unreachable cultural ideal of feminine beauty that 'uses im-ages of female beauty as a political weapon against women's advancement'. Just as Max Weber decried the 'iron cage' of consumption in modern society, so too, does Wolf decry the 'Iron Maiden' created by this beauty myth, which entraps women in an end-less cycle of cosmetics, beauty aids, diets, and exercise fanaticism and makes women's bodies into 'prisons their homes no longer were'. As Fatima Mernissi writes of her first encounter with North American beauty norms, 'Being frozen into the passive position of an object whose very existence depends on the eye of its beholder turns the educated modern Western woman into a harem slave'.[25]

And who is the beholder to whom the modern woman is so beholden? It would be too simplistic to say 'men', but that's part of the answer. More accurately, the beauty myth constantly subjects women not so much to the scrutiny of men as to the **male gaze**. The male gaze is a concept first articulated by Laura Mulvey in the context of film studies, where she noted how, when watching movies, we are often encouraged to take the perspective of a desiring heterosexual male subject. One example of this would be the frequent panning of a woman's body from the ground up when she is first intro-duced as a character. The camera 'forces' us to look at the woman the way a desiring man might. This device is frequently used in slasher films, where the camera not only lingers on women's bodies (often just before they become victims), but also sometimes forces us to view the victims from the perspective of the killer.

The idea of the male gaze has been expanded far beyond film studies to explain how people—regardless of their gender and sexual orientation—look at women in a way that assesses their sexual desirability and positions them as sexual objects. Women even look at themselves in this way; in fact, they must learn to look at themselves in this way if they are to succeed in improving their beauty. As Sandra Bartky writes, 'subject to the evaluating eye of the male connoisseur, women learn to evaluate themselves first and best'. This is to say, women learn self-objectification in the name of self-improvement (understood as the enhancement of beauty).[26]

Is this emphasis on working to achieve beauty an ironic outcome of women's increased independence—a kind of backlash attempt to keep women in their place just as they are breaking free? It's unlikely that it is any more than a coincidence, but it is worth noting that the first Miss America pageant was held in 1920—the same year women obtained the right to vote.

white

North American women are particularly concerned with weight and breast size. Breasts are 'the most visible signs of a woman's femininity', writes Iris Young, 'the sign of her sexuality'. Women are often trapped in what we might call the 'Goldilocks dilemma' after the young girl of the fairy tale. As Goldilocks found the porridge 'too hot' or 'too cold' but never 'just right', so too do women believe their breasts are either too large or too small—but never just right. In 2008, US cosmetic surgeons performed over 350,000 breast augmentations. Though the economic downturn caused the first decline in the number of surgeries in recent memory, 350,000 is still greatly above the 2001 figures (closer to 200,000). Indeed, women are the keenest consumers of all forms of cosmetic surgery. In 2007, 91 per cent of all cosmetic surgery procedures in North America were carried out on women; and 76 per cent were conducted on 'Caucasian' consumers. While men and non-white patients are a growing segment of the market for cosmetic surgery, it remains dominated, in North America, by white women.[27]

This is despite the fact that North American standards of beauty have been based on celebration of a particular ethnic form of whiteness that we might call Northern European. This has led to a number of trends among white women themselves, most notably the tendency to lighten hair (and, increasingly, to alter eye colour using contact lenses). Among non-white women, most notably women of Asian heritage, a common operation has been eyelid surgery aimed at producing a rounder-looking eye. Such surgeries obviously reflect, in the words of Eugenia Kaw, 'persisting racial prejudice', but it is interesting that white women's attempts to look 'whiter' are rarely viewed in such racial terms.[28]

The beauty myth rests, then, not only on the pursuit of beauty, but on the avoidance of 'ugliness'. Despite the popularity of *Ugly Betty* (who isn't at all ugly) and *Shrek,* ugly is by no means 'the new pretty'. Attractiveness still rules. It confers social benefits such as higher earning power, greater attractiveness to potential marriage partners, and even imputations of intelligence and moral superiority.[29] For women, whose attractiveness has been seen as more important to their identities than it is for men, being called 'ugly' can be devastating.

Because North American standards of beauty celebrate a particular kind of able-bodied fantasy of whiteness, racialized and disabled women are at greater risk of the 'ugly' slur (and self-perception). In North America, the racist stereotype of the 'ugly squaw' (as opposed to the 'Indian princess') has had a negative effect on generations of indigenous women. African-American women have also often been slandered as 'ugly', an attribution that rests not only on racism but on **colourism**. Light skin, among African-American women, may operate as a form of 'social capital' that enhances their earning power, attractiveness to potential partners, educational attainment, and

OITNB lots of conventional body types but also non-typical
- Taystee
- Black Cindy
- Big Boo
- Daya
non-typical beauty
- Pennsatucky
- Leanne
- Flaca

rep of varying colour + race

self-esteem. This remains true despite the 1960s 'Black is Beautiful' campaign and subsequent attempts to contest racist ideas of beauty. Today, ironically, 'Black is Beautiful' can be one more way of sexualizing women of colour, perpetuating, in bell hooks's phrase, 'the pornographic fantasy of the black female as wild sexual savage'.[30]

The beauty myth and its corollary, the 'ugliness myth', also interact with notions of ability. On one hand, the feminine 'beauty myth' may render women with disabilities invisible. On the other hand, as Meekosha writes, disabled women are subject to pressure to 'normalize the less than perfect body'. While the able female body 'is identified as an object for desire', writes Per Solvang, the disabled body is constructed 'as an object of disgust', adding to the pressure to disguise or redress 'abnormal' characteristics. And even when the disabled female body is seen as sexually desirable, as among devotees of amputation, all other characteristics of the 'standard' beauty myth remain in place, suggesting that disabled women are being **fetishized** rather than valued in their own right.[31]

For North American women of all ethnic groups, and particularly perhaps for white women, the fear of fat often forces submission to the tyranny of slenderness. Though average North American women are heavier than they were a generation ago, images of women are not. The average weight of Miss America and *Playboy* pinups has decreased steadily since 1978, even though their average height and breast size have increased. In 1954, Miss America was 5'8"(173 cm) and weighed 132 pounds (60 kg). Today, the average Miss America contestant still stands 5'8" but now weighs just 117 pounds (53 kg). (An article in *Harper's Bazaar* in 1908 declared the normal weight for a healthy woman of 5'8" to be 155 pounds (70 kg); 133 (60 kg) would have been normal for a woman of 5'3" (160 cm), and 117 less than the prescribed weight of 120 pounds (54 kg) for a woman who stood 5'1" (155 cm).) In 1975, the average fashion model weighed about 8 per cent less than the average American woman; by 1990, that difference had grown to 23 per cent. Marilyn Monroe, perhaps the twentieth century's most recognizable sex symbol, wore a size 12 dress; contemporary sex symbols are more likely to wear a size 4.

If women are concerned about weight, girls are too. 'Girls are terrified of being fat', writes Mary Pipher. 'Being fat means being left out, scorned, and vilified . . . Almost all adolescent girls feel fat, worry about their weight, diet and feel guilty when they eat'. Perhaps most telling is that 42 per cent of girls in first through third grades say they want to be thinner, and 81 per cent of 10-year-olds are afraid of being fat. Forty-six per cent of 9 to 11-year-olds are on diets; by college the percentage has nearly doubled. And at the same time, childhood obesity has become a major concern, with approximately 18 per cent of Canadian children overweight according to Statistics Canada. Given the 'fatphobia' of North American culture, it seems odd that North Americans are becoming heavier and heavier. But it certainly seems understandable, as research suggests, that overweight is associated with a decline in self-esteem both for children and for adults.[32]

Current standards of beauty for women combine two images—dramatic thinness and muscularity and buxomness—that are virtually impossible to accomplish. Research on adolescents suggests that a large majority consciously trade off health concerns in their efforts to lose weight. As a result, increasing numbers of young women are diagnosed with either anorexia nervosa or bulimia every year. Anorexia involves chronic and dangerous starvation dieting and obsessive exercise; bulimia typically involves 'binging and purging' (eating large quantities of food and then either vomiting or taking enemas to excrete the food). Although anorexia and bulimia are extreme and very serious problems that can, if untreated, threaten a girl's life, they represent only the furthest reaches of a continuum of preoccupation with the body that begins with such 'normal' behaviours as compulsive exercise or dieting.

It is important to remember that rates of anorexia and bulimia are higher in the United States than in any other country—by far. Though estimates ranges widely, as many as 5 and 10 per cent of all post-pubescent girls and women in the USA struggle with eating disorders—that means about 5 million to 10 million girls and women. According to the National Eating Disorder Institute of Canada, 1.5 per cent of women aged 15 to 24 have an eating disorder. Across Europe only 14.5 of every 10,000 women suffer from bulimia or anorexia, according to the European Medical Association. That's just over one-tenth of 1 per cent—about 50 times less than in the United States.[33]

By contrast, many non-Western societies value plumpness, and there is a correlation between body weight and social class; throughout Europe and the United States, non-white girls are far less likely to exhibit eating disorders than are white and middle-class girls. (Ironically, in societies where food is plentiful, ideals of thinness are imposed constantly, whereas in societies where the food supply is erratic, plumpness is more often the feminine ideal.) Recent dramatic increases have, however, been observed among young middle- and upper-class Japanese women.[34]

Although some stereotypic understandings would have it that such dramatic emphasis on thinness afflicts only middle-and upper-class white girls and women, the evidence suggests that this emphasis also defines working-class and black ideals of the feminine body. Largeness 'was once accepted—even revered—among black folks', lamented an article in *Essence* magazine in 1994, but it 'now carries the same unmistakable stigma as it does among whites'. And a study the following year found that black adolescent girls demonstrated a significantly higher drive for thinness than did white adolescent girls. The media coverage of Oprah's dramatic weight loss and the depiction of ultra thin African-American models and actresses may have increased black women's anxieties about their weight; indeed, it may be a perverse signal of assimilation and acceptance by the dominant culture that 'their' ideal body type is now embraced by the formerly marginalized.[35]

It is also true that men have become increasingly concerned with their bodies, especially in fitness and weight. Although men have long been concerned about appearing strong and fit—witness the enormous success of Charles Atlas body building apparatus since the turn of the twentieth century—the building of strong muscles seems to increase as a preoccupation and obsession during periods when men are least likely to actually have to use their muscles in their work.[36] Muscles, it seems, are appealing only when they don't suggest that one might be a member of the working classes. So men want to look stronger during periods when they actually don't need it, recreating in their appearances what they no longer require in actuality! Today, successful new men's magazines like *Men's Health* encourage men to see their bodies as women have been taught to see theirs—as ongoing projects to be worked on. (As described in Chapter 9, the magazine's circulation grew from 250,000 to over 1.5 million in its first seven years—the most successful magazine launch in history.) In part, this coincides with general concerns about health and fitness, and in part it is about looking young in a society that does not value aging. But more than that, it also seems to be about gender.

Men's bodily anxieties mirror those of women. Whereas women are concerned with breast size and weight, men are concerned with muscularity—that is, both are preoccupied with those aspects of the male and female body that suggest and exaggerate innate biological differences between the sexes. It would appear that the more equal women and men become in the public sphere, the more standards of beauty would emphasize those aspects that are biologically different. On the other hand, both men and women now grapple with the imperative to remove virtually all of their body hair, which would suggest conversion rather than the emphasis of difference.)[37]

Standards of male muscularity have also increased dramatically. Many men experience what some researchers have labelled 'muscle dysmorphia', a belief that one is too small, insufficiently muscular. Harrison Pope and his colleagues call it the 'Adonis Complex'—the belief that men must look like Greek gods, with perfect chins, thick hair, rippling muscles, and washboard abdominals. The increasing packaging of men's bodies in the media—it is now common to see men's bodies displayed in advertising in ways that were conceivable only for women's bodies a generation ago—coupled with increased economic anxiety (which leads us to focus on the things we *can* control, like how we look) has led to a dramatic shift in men's ideas about their bodies.[38]

In 1999, Pope and his colleagues took GI Joe's proportions and translated them into real-life proportions (parallel to the descriptions of Barbie's changes). In 1974, GI Joe was 5'10" (178 cm) tall, and had a 31-inch (79 cm) waist, a 44-inch (112 cm) chest, and 12-inch (30 cm) biceps. Strong and muscular, it's true, but at least within the realm of the possible. GI Joe in 2002 was a little bit different. He was still 5'10" tall, but his waist had shrunk to 28 inches (71 cm), his chest had expanded to 50 inches (127 cm), and his biceps were now 22 inches (56 cm)—almost the size of his waist. Such proportions would make one a circus freak, not a role model.[39]

These models make many men feel utterly inadequate. Nearly half of all men in one survey reported significant body image disturbance. A study reported in *Psychology Today* found that 43 per cent of the men were dissatisfied with their appearance, compared with only 15 per cent 25 years earlier. As one college student told a journalist:

> When I look in the mirror, I see two things: what I want to be and what I'm not. I hate my abs. My chest will never be huge. My legs are too thin. My nose is an odd shape. I want what *Men's Health* pushes. I want to be the guy in the Gillette commercials.[40]

And increasing numbers of men are also exhibiting eating disorders. Pope believes that over one million men suffer from some form of eating disorder; 10 per cent of those people seeking treatment for eating disorders are male. (According to one study, men are far less likely to seek treatment for eating disorders because they believe such disorders to be a woman's illness.) Although these problems may be more prevalent among gay men, increases among heterosexual men are also pronounced. A recent survey of Australian college men found that one in five had used restrained eating, vomiting, laxative abuse, or cigarette smoking for weight control. About one in five also reported binge eating and weight control problems. In 2008, 'manorexia' got its first public face when actor Dennis Quaid went public with his struggle with disordered eating. Though no one is quite sure how many men are struggling with eating disorders, they now account for 10 per cent of those treated in some clinics.[41]

And just as women have resorted to increasingly dangerous surgical and prosthetic procedures—such as having silicone-filled bags placed in their breasts or being given mild localized doses of botulism to paralyze facial muscles and thereby 'remove' wrinkles—so, too, are men resorting to increasingly dramatic efforts to get large. The use of anabolic steroids has mushroomed, especially among college-aged men. Steroids enable men to increase muscle mass quickly and dramatically, so that one looks incredibly big. Prolonged use also leads to dramatic mood changes, increased uncontrolled rage, and a significant shrinkage in the testicles.[42]

Eating disorders among women and muscular dysmorphia among men are parallel processes, extreme points on a continuum that begins with almost everyone. There are, for example, very few women who do not have a problematic relationship with food—many, if not most, women see food as something other than simple taste or nourishment but instead mentally count the calories, determine whether this indulgence is worth it, and calculate how much extra time they can spend in the gym to compensate and how much they weigh. Men, at the same time, have a problematic relationship with physical power. 'Looking strong' is their version of women's 'looking slim'. If a measure of successful femininity is being thin, and if a measure of masculinity is appearing strong and powerful, then anorexics and obsessive body builders are not psychological misfits or deviants: They are over conformists to gender norms to which all of us, to some degree, are subject.[43]

Just as there has been an increase in the gap between rich and poor, so too, has there been an increased bifurcation between the embodied 'haves' and 'have-nots'. North Americans are both increasingly thin and increasingly overweight, obsessive exercisers or sedentary couch potatoes, eating tofu and organic raw vegetables or Big Macs and supersized fried foods. This growing divide reflects different class and racial cultures, but it also is deeply gendered.

Changing the Body

Virtually all of us spend some time and energy in some forms of bodily beautification, by wearing fashionable clothes and jewellery, for example. But until recently, only a few marginalized 'out-groups', like motorcycle gangs, practised any forms of permanent bodily transformation—running the gamut beyond simply piercing ears to piercing other body parts, getting tattoos, having cosmetic surgery, and even undergoing sex-change operations. Today, body piercing involves far more than the earlobes and can include the tongue, eyebrows, navel, nose, lips, nipples, and even the genitals. Increasing numbers of young people are also getting tattoos. Given their vaguely transgressive character in North American society, tattoos and piercing denote a slight sexualized undertone—if only because they indicate that the bearer is aware of his or her body as an object of pleasure or desire.

Eighteen per cent of Canadians have at least one tattoo, described by one psychiatrist as a 'bumper sticker of the soul'. Among young people, 31 per cent are inked. Men are most likely to have 'tats' on their arms, women on their backs. Design and placement are also highly sexually charged; we believe they say something about our selves and our sexuality. Witness the popularity of the 'tramp stamp' among young women. (The new popularity of tattooing in general has also spawned a new industry—tattoo removal.)[44]

One of the fastest-growing methods of bodily transformation is cosmetic surgery. According to one study by the American Society of Plastic and Reconstructive Surgeons (ASPRS), the total number of cosmetic procedures increased from 413,208 in 1992 to 1.62 million in 2001. And the most common procedures increased by almost 500 per cent. In addition to breast augmentation and reduction, these procedures included 275,463 liposuctions (compared with 47,212 in 1992), 238,213 eyelid surgeries (59,461 in 1992), and 124,531 facelifts (40,077 in 1992).[45]

Though, as discussed above, women continue to be the primary consumers of such cosmetic surgery, male patients have increased their numbers. 'More men are viewing cosmetic surgery as a viable way of looking and feeling younger', observed ASPRS President Dennis Lynch, MD, 'especially to compete in the workplace'. This comment raises what may be most interesting from our gender perspective: not which gender is *having* the surgery, but rather which gender is the one *for whom* the surgery is being performed. It may be that, as one writer explains, 'the traditional image of women as sexual objects has simply expanded: everyone has become an object to be seen'. The question remains: seen by whom? Whom do we imagine seeing us in our newly reconstructed state? For women, the answer is usually men.[46]

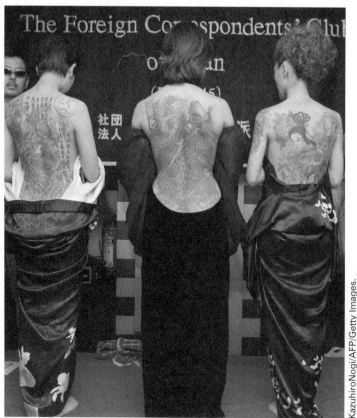

KazuhiroNogi/AFP/Getty Images.

Models show off their tattoos.

For men, though, the answer is also men. Men too are the object of the 'male gaze' and feel a need to look big, strong, and virile in front of other men. Among gay men, this can produce levels of body dissatisfaction more often associated with women. Though men experience more satisfaction with their bodies than do women, many men are still insecure enough about their bodies to take drastic steps to alter them. Take one extreme example of this—penile enlargement surgery. This is a dramatic (and expensive) procedure—every year about 15 thousand men in the USA pay about $6,000 to have it done—by which the penis can be lengthened by about two inches. (The average flaccid penis is about 3.5 inches long; erect it's about 5.1 inches long.) In one of the few studies that relies on data and not anecdotal evidence and thrilled testimonials, psychologist Randy Klein found that, of men seeking surgery, the average penile length before surgery was 2.6 inches (flaccid) and 5.4 inches (erect); after surgery, penile length was 3.8 inches (flaccid) and 5.7 inches (erect). That is, the only significant difference in length was when the penis was flaccid.[47]

One would think that men engage in this painful procedure to be 'better' lovers or to please women more, and indeed many men say that is part of their motivation. But in many cases it has far less to do with women's potential pleasure than men's visual perception. Men who have this procedure more often experience what one physician called 'locker room syndrome'—the fear of being judged as inadequately masculine *by other men*. Take, for example, the testimonial letter from a satisfied customer:

> I was always afraid to get into situations where I would have to shower with other men or be seen by anyone. I can remember avoiding many of the sports and activities I loved dearly, all because I was afraid that I would be seen and made fun of . . . I even avoided wearing shorts and tight clothes because of my fear that others would notice me.

'The thing I missed most was the changing room camaraderie and male bonding associated with these sports which was always something I enjoyed', writes another. 'I felt ashamed to even go to the urinals in a public place and have made sure I never use these whilst other men are there too'.[48]

Women, too, undergo genital 'reconstruction' surgery. According to the Toronto Cosmetic Clinic, 'within weeks of undergoing the procedure, you and your partner will be able to see, and feel, the results. Both of you will experience a renewal of sexual pleasure and dramatic increase in sensation from intercourse, achieving a level of sexual gratification that was missing before'. The increased availability and acceptability of pornography also have some women requesting 'designer vaginas' comparable to the vulvas on display in porn, which are often much 'smaller' than those of the average woman. Women increasingly request the trimming of their labia to conform to ideals of beauty on these new frontiers. Finally, hymenoplasty—the surgical reconstruction of the hymen, which is usually broken during first intercourse—was once used by panic-stricken parents of 'deflowered' Muslim, Asian, or Latina girls whose value in the marriage market had suddenly plummeted. Now available at some North American clinics, it's increasingly popular among heterosexual women who want to keep their earlier sexual experience a secret, who want their partners to have the 'thrill' of being their 'first', or who have violated their Christian abstinence pledges.[49]

Nowhere is gender inequality better observed than in the motivations of both women and men in changing their bodies. It is the male gaze—whether of a potential sexual partner, a potential sexual rival, or a competitor in the marketplace or athletic field—that motivates such drastic measures, among both women and men.

Sexual Bodily Transformation: Transgenderism

Though there are significant penalties for boys who are effeminate ('sissies') and some, but fewer, penalties for girls who are 'tomboys', many adult men and women continue to bend, if not break, gender norms in their bodily presentation. **Transvestites** dress in the clothing of the opposite sex, disrupting the equation of biological sex and social gender by playing with gender (the socially and culturally prescribed adornments and dress). Again, this runs along a continuum. Up until the twentieth century, a woman who wore trousers (in North America and Europe) was 'cross-dressing', which was illegal during much of European history. Today, women readily wear masculine (and even men's) clothing without incurring much disapproval or the label of 'cross-dresser'. A man who wears a skirt, on the other hand, will find himself the object of much more attention. So the continuum is gendered. At one end of our gender-bending continuum we might have women who wear man-tailored clothing and power suits to work, because such clothing gives them the air of confidence as they downplay femininity and exude competence (which are often seen as antithetical); at the other end are those who wear full cross-gender regalia as a means of self-expression.

For some people, though, the bending of gendered norms is insufficient, because their biological sex doesn't match their internal sense of gender identity. **Transgendered** people feel **gender dysphoria**, a 'persistent discomfort and sense of inappropriateness about one's assigned sex (feeling trapped in the wrong body)', as the diagnosis in the American Psychiatric Association's *Diagnostic and Statistical Manual* (DSM-III) put it. Historically, transgenderism was quite rare, if only because most societies had strict rules regarding appropriate gender norms for the sexes. Third genders, discussed in Chapter 4, are an exception. But because most third-gender individuals came to their gender status through channels other than free choice, it's difficult to view them as proof of historical transgender identity in the modern sense.[50]

Transgendered people offer living proof that the social construction of gender and sexuality is more than simply metaphoric. Typically, transgenderism is experienced as a general discomfort that becomes increasingly intense during puberty, that is, with the emergence of secondary sex characteristics. As one female-to-male transgendered person told an interviewer:

> I hated the changes in my body . . . I couldn't stand it . . . It affected my identity. I became very upset and depressed. As a matter of fact, by this time in my life, I spent most of my time in my room . . . I thought about suicide . . . [51]

Although transgenderism remains relatively uncommon, its implications are enormous. Once, a discrepancy between one's biological sex and what one experienced internally as one's gender would privilege the body, as if the body contained some essential truth about the person. If therapeutic interventions were to resolve such conflicts, they would 'help' the person accept his or her body's 'truth' and try to adjust feelings about gender. Transgenderism enables us to dissolve what is experienced as an arbitrary privileging of the body-at-birth and to give more weight to who we feel we are, bringing us close to a world in which we can freely choose our gender.

And in changing gender, some choose to change (permanently) their biological sex to match their felt gender identity. The term **transsexual** came into use in the 1950s, when surgery and endocrinology had made it possible to change not only one's clothing but one's body. One of the first well-known transsexuals was Christine Jorgenson, a young American who travelled to a Scandinavian clinic for surgery and hormonal treatment, returning to the USA to become, for some years, a media darling. Others followed Jorgenson's example, all of them submitting to a variety of tests in order to prove that they were legitimate candidates for what came to be known as **SRS**, or sexual reassignment surgery. In 1966, Harry Benjamin published *The Transsexual Phenomenon,* a text that distinguished three categories of transsexuals on the basis of their degree of discomfort with their biological sex. These changes combined to make it possible to change one's sex, particularly after legal challenges established (at least in some cases) the right to be considered as a member of the sex to which one was reassigned.[52]

By 1980, about 4000 people in the USA had undergone these surgical interventions, and almost all of them were males seeking to become females. Though numbers are difficult to come by, it is clear that tens of thousands of North Americans, and over one hundred thousand individuals worldwide, have undergone some form of sex reassignment. Though the majority of transsexuals today are biological males, the number of biological women seeking surgery is increasing. For both sexes, the transition from one sex to the other requires two years of radical hormone therapies to mute or reverse secondary sex characteristics (like body hair, voice, breasts); thereafter, some of these people undergo full SRS, by which the original genitalia are surgically excised and new realistic medical constructions of vulvas (vaginoplasty) or penises (phalloplasty) are created.

New medical and surgical procedures have continued to facilitate both male-to-female and female-to-male transsexual operations. Moreover, the listing of transsexualism as a disorder in *DSM-III* in 1980 allowed for some insurance coverage for SRS. (Transsexualism now appears as a subset of gender identity disorder.) In the USA, the recognition of sex-change operations by Medicare (1978) has meant funded treatment, while in Canada, the province of Ontario funded operations at the Clarke Institute of Psychiatry from 1969 until 1998. Currently, BC, Ontario, and Quebec cover at least some of the costs associated with hormonal and surgical sex reassignment, but other provinces offer less, and policy can change from one year to the next.[53]

Because Medicare funding for sex reassignment hinges on the idea that transsexuals are suffering from a mental disorder for which SRS is the 'cure', many have been reluctant to challenge the idea that they are mentally ill. Others, though, particularly in the USA, have agitated for the removal of gender identity disorder from the DSM, most recently at the April 2009 meeting of the American Psychiatric Association.[54]

Transgenderism and transsexualism are often difficult to understand: How, people might ask, could one locate the source of one's unhappiness in having the wrong anatomy? Or, more sociologically, people wonder if transsexual surgery doesn't reinstate the body as the source of gendered knowledge and underscore the biological—indeed, anatomically genital—foundations of gender. Who more vigorously subscribes to biological essentialism than people who change their biological sex to match their internal perceptions of the gender? This has made for some tensions between transsexuals and the feminist movement, which critiques biological essentialism and is more likely to call for a breaking down of gender than its realignment with a resexed body. The famous second-wave feminist Gloria Steinem famously commented, 'If the shoe doesn't fit, why change the whole foot?' Since then, feminism has become more receptive to transsexualism, particularly as transwomen have entered the feminist movement. Nonetheless, tensions remain, as is proved by the conflict that erupted in the 1990s when transwoman Kimberly Nixon sought to work for Vancouver Rape Relief. She was expelled from training session on the basis of her biological origins as a man. Vancouver Rape Relief held that as someone who had lived much of her life as a man, Nixon could not serve in a position reserved for women. Nixon's contention that she had the right to work as a woman in a woman's shelter was first upheld by the BC Human Rights Tribunal, but ultimately overturned by higher courts.[55]

While some transwomen (and many transmen) engage with feminist critiques of gender, evidence based largely on studies of transwomen suggests that many are gender conservatives. That is, on measures of conservatism, researchers have found transwomen score as more conservative than either non-transsexual men or non-transsexual women. Transwomen are also more conventionally feminine than non-transsexual women. This has led to the claim that transpeople are, in some ways, the ultimate gender conformists.[56]

On the other hand, transgendered people may be the consummate social constructionists. Who better than they understand the performance of gender, the routine ways we present our bodies and our biological sex to others to ensure a successful social presentation? Transgendered individuals, by uprooting gender from its biological foundations and reversing the relationship between gender and sex, make their biological sex emanate from their gender identity, whereas conventional wisdom says gender identity must emanate from biological sex. Who says? And if anatomical sex is as malleable as gender identity, then the possibilities of self-expression multiply exponentially—and the fears of such free-floating freedom expand just as rapidly.

Gender and Health

If transsexualism highlights the ways in which we gender bodies, health and illness tend to obscure gendering. After all, we all experience health, illness, aging, and eventually death, regardless of our gender. The strongest exemplar of hegemonic masculinity must too deal with the body's changes, as has been amply proved by widely circulated images of Arnold Schwarzenegger that make news out of his aging body.

Because health and illness are in some ways 'levellers', we have often ignored their gendered nature or seen male bodies as stand-ins for 'universal' health studies. For example, studies of heart health long based symptomologies, treatment protocols, and prognoses upon male patients; it is now known that heart disease, heart attacks, and prognoses for recovery vary according to gender. The conflation of masculine bodies with human ones has also meant that 'women's diseases' have either received minimal attention or been cloaked in shame. Breast cancer is a stellar example of this. Forty years ago, women diagnosed with breast cancer faced a great deal of shame and stigmatization along with uncertain outcomes. Today, as a result of women's health activism, breast cancer research is much better funded. Despite what some have criticized as the corporatization of the breast cancer movement, it cannot be denied that survivors are profoundly involved in advocacy, research, and policy-making. Embracing pink as its symbol, the breast cancer movement has foregrounded gender and its relationship to health.[57]

Indeed, careful researchers have long understood gender to be a primary factor in health, particularly as regards health-related social behaviour. As men's health researcher and advocate Will H. Courtenay puts it:

> A man who does gender correctly would be relatively unconcerned about his health and well-being in general. He would see himself as stronger, both physically and emotionally, than most women. He would think of himself as independent, not needing to be nurtured by others. He would be unlikely to ask others for help. He would spend much time out in the world and away from home . . . He would face danger fearlessly, take risks frequently, and have little concern for his own safety.

And Courtenay is quite right. Men take more health-related risks, both by engaging in behaviours like drinking and taking drugs, and by considering it unmasculine to seek health-care treatment. Ignoring health issues, 'playing through pain', has been, in fact, a symbol of masculinity. Women, meanwhile, take fewer risks, take better care of their health, take vitamins, exercise, and see doctors more regularly. An old adage among those who study gender and health is that 'women get sicker, but men die quicker'. That means that men, in general, report less illness, but women outlive men. Recent data confirm the latter sex difference. Canadian life expectancy is now over 80 years, but a 4.7-year gap remains between the sexes.[58]

Class and ethnicity complicate the picture. In Canada, Aboriginal people in general experience tuberculosis, HIV/AIDS, heart disease, and diabetes at much higher rates than are characteristic of the general population, Aboriginal life expectancy is significantly lower than the Canadian average, and Aboriginal infant mortality and youth suicide rates are much higher. Throughout the life cycle, Aboriginal people face greater health risks than non-Aboriginals. Clearly, then, gender is only one of many determinants of health. But gender interacts with those determinants in important ways.[59] Middle-aged black men in the US, for example, have much lower longevity (up to seven years less) and much higher rates of stress and lifestyle-related diseases (heart attack, stroke, diabetes) than their white counterparts. Although some part of this is attributable to age (young black males have astronomically higher health risks than do whites) and to class (working-class men of all races also have lower longevity and higher morbidity than middle-class men); this holds true even for middle-aged black men at every level of the class hierarchy.

Racialization provides the rest of the answer. The stresses of living in a context of racial discrimination lead to a distinct ethic of masculinity. Whereas men, 'overall, have a particular set of pressures to show strength and not reveal weakness', writes columnist Ellis Cose, 'this feeling is intensified in black men'. There is, he continues, 'an ethic of toughness among black men, built up to protect yourself against racial slights and from the likelihood that society is going to challenge you or humiliate you in some way. This makes it hard to admit that you are in pain or need help'. In the USA, African-American and Latino men are significantly less likely to see a doctor—even when they are in poor health.[60]

Masculinity also affects one of the most important areas of gender divergence, sexual health. Nowhere is the gendering of health more clear than in the gendering of HIV/AIDS. The onset of the HIV/AIDS epidemic in North America defined the disease as a disease of men—gay men in particular. As a result, major changes occurred in the sexual patterns of gay men, including fewer partners, less anonymous sex, and increases in the practice of safe sex and the number of gay male couples. However important in containing the disease, the emphasis on 'safe sex' was seen by many as an effort to 'feminize' sexuality, to return it to the context of emotional and monogamous relationships, thus abandoning the earlier gay liberationist ethic of sexual freedom. To many men, the very phrase 'safe sex' was experienced as an oxymoron: What's sexy—heat, passion, excitement, spontaneity—was the exact opposite of what's safe—soft, warm, cuddly. Many men feared that practising safe sex would mean no longer having sex like men and that programs encouraging such gender nonconformity would be doomed to failure. (This is not simply an issue for gay men, of course. Heterosexual women have been trying to get heterosexual men to practice a form of safe sex for decades, finding that their own sexual expressivity is less encumbered when both partners take responsibility for birth control. Fear of pregnancy and fear of HIV transmission both require that one fuse sexual pleasure with sexual responsibility.)[61]

Of course, the epicentre of the HIV epidemic has shifted dramatically since the disease was first diagnosed in 1984. Globally, more than 21 million men, women, and children have died from AIDS, and another 42 million are living with it—that's 1 out of every 162 people on Earth. The global epicentre of AIDS has shifted dramatically since it was first diagnosed in the United States. Seven out of every 10 people infected live in sub-Saharan Africa; adding South and Southeast Asia and Latin America brings the total up to 88 per cent.[62]

It is noteworthy that in the developing world, and particularly in Sub-Saharan Africa, AIDS is emphatically not a masculine disease. According to United Nations statistics, of the roughly 33 million people living with AIDS in 2008, 22.4 million were resident in Sub-Saharan Africa. Of these, roughly 60 per cent were female, and in some hard-hit areas girls and women experience an infection rate more than twice that of men. These statistics cannot be separated from social factors. In many regions, women's significantly lower status often renders them powerless to resist sexual advances or refuse sex to their husbands, to insist on safe sex practices, or to have much access to health care; and women's economic vulnerability leads many into sex-trade work where they may face even greater risk of infection. Empowering women, affording women equal rights, will prove the major mechanism to reduce HIV. Dr Pascoal Mocumbi, former prime minister of Mozambique, challenged Africans to 'break the silence regarding the sexual behaviour and gender inequalities that drive the epidemic'.[63]

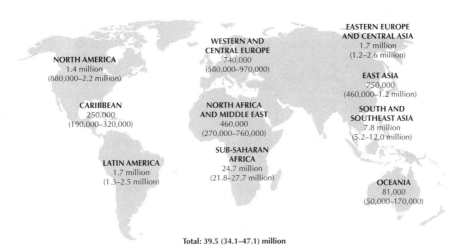

NORTH AMERICA
1.4 million
(880,000–2.2 million)

WESTERN AND
CENTRAL EUROPE
740,000
(580,000–970,000)

EASTERN EUROPE
AND CENTRAL ASIA
1.7 million
(1.2–2.6 million)

EAST ASIA
750,000
(460,000–1.2 million)

CARIBBEAN
250,000
(190,000–320,000)

NORTH AFRICA
AND MIDDLE EAST
460,000
(270,000–760,000)

SOUTH AND
SOUTHEAST ASIA
7.8 million
(5.2–12.0 million)

SUB-SAHARAN
AFRICA
24.7 million
(21.8–27.7 million)

LATIN AMERICA
1.7 million
(1.3–2.5 million)

OCEANIA
81,000
(50,000–170,000)

Total: 39.5 (34.1–47.1) million

Map 11.1

Adults and children estimated to be living with HIV in 2006. World Health Organization.

In North America and western Europe, the percentage of HIV-positive women is less than 25 per cent; in Australia and New Zealand only 7 per cent.[64] In these places, AIDS remains a highly 'masculine' disease. Although women and men are both able to contract the virus that causes AIDS—and, in fact, women are actually more likely to contract the disease from unprotected heterosexual intercourse than are men—and despite the fact that rates of new infection among women are increasing faster than among men, the majority of all AIDS patients in North America are men. Of the approximately 58,000 Canadians living with AIDS, about 80 per cent are male. Class and racialization continue to be important features of the epidemic. In the USA, rates of new infections are far higher among young black men than white men; and in Canada, the rates of infection among Aboriginal people are more than three times the rate of non-Aboriginals, and black Canadians are also particularly vulnerable.[65]

Seen in this way, AIDS is the most highly gendered disease in American history—a disease that both women and men could get but one that overwhelmingly disproportionately affects one gender and not the other. It would be useful to understand masculinity—risk taking, avoidance of responsibility, pursuit of sex above all other ends—as a risk factor in the spread of the disease, in the same way as we understand masculinity to be a risk factor in drunk driving accidents.[66]

Yet even in areas like drunk driving, there are signs of gender convergence. First, more women are disregarding traditional strictures of femininity and taking increased risks—in their sexual behaviours and elsewhere. Take drinking, for example. Of course, far more men drink to excess than women do; in the USA, drinking is heaviest among young, white, male students attending four-year institutions and often revolves around fraternities and sports events. But an increasing number of women are binge drinking as well. 'To be able to drink like a guy is kind of a badge of honour', commented one female student. 'For me, it's a feminism thing'. Although few feminists would actually suggest that binge drinking is an index of women's liberation, many young women have come to feel that drinking, fighting, smoking, and other typically 'masculine' behaviours are a sign of power—and therefore cool. Barbara Ehrenreich disagrees, suggesting that, 'Gender equality wouldn't be worth fighting for if all it meant was the opportunity to be as stupid and self-destructive as men can be'.[67]

And there are signs that more men are seeking health professionals, taking better care of their health—a domain that had been traditionally reserved to women. Efforts to develop men's health awareness have been especially successful in the developing world, where campaigns for reproductive health and family planning for women have branched out to include men in health planning. In such campaigns, it is clear that the health interests of women and men are hardly the conflicting interests of Martians and Venutians. There is no zero-sum game; rather, our interests are complementary. Both women's and men's health needs confront dominant ideas about gender that inhibit men's health-seeking behaviour and often prohibit women's. Gender inequality is bad for both women's and men's health.[68]

There are also signs of convergence in lifespan, one of the most enduring sites of gender difference. While Canadian women outlived men by 4.7 years in 2005, this is a reduction from 1991, when the gap was more like 6 years. And this gap is not found in the global South, where men typically outlive women by the same six years—or more. Gender inequality—unequal access to health care, unequal nutrition, and men's control of reproduction—led the Nobel laureate economist Amartya Sen to estimate that worldwide there are 100 million 'missing women'—women whose deaths are directly attributable to unequal access to health care, poor prenatal, maternity, and postnatal care, sex-selective abortion, infanticide, and other aspects of gender inequality. The lowest lifespan in the world, in 2006, belonged to Zimbabwean women, with an average life expectancy of just 34 years.[69]

Gender differences persist in our sexual expression and our sexual experiences, in our health experiences and our health seeking, but they (in the global North at least) are far less significant than they used to be, and the signs point to continued convergence.

Summary

Our bodies are not merely 'biological realities', but are key elements of our identities. They are shaped, made meaningful, and scrutinized by the gendered society.

First, our bodies are constructed on the basis of a 'universal' ideal that is able-bodied. Disability often goes unseen, and ablism affects those who live with disabilities. Canadians with disabilities experience a greater risk of poverty than non-disabled Canadians, and face significant barriers to employment. There are various ways in which disability is gendered. Women are overrepresented among the disabled, and are even more vulnerable to poverty, violence, and sexual abuse than are disabled men. For men, however, disability may be experienced differently, striking at sexual and physical performance and thus at the heart of masculine identity. For both men and women, however, disability is experienced in complex ways that interact with other elements of gender and identity.

Sport is also a gendered arena. In early childhood, children are encouraged to adopt different forms of play. As childhood progresses, sport becomes a training (and testing) ground for boys' masculinity. 'Throwing like a girl' reveals the need for boys to prove themselves against a denigrated model of femininity; but the way that girls tend to throw and participate in sport also reveals how ideals of feminine bodily comportment can limit women's and girls' achievement. Self-objectification, characteristic of 'normal' female development, inhibits athletic performance.

During the course of the twentieth century, girls and women slowly gained access to sporting opportunities that were once reserved for boys. This led, eventually, to second-wave activism that opened greater opportunities, including enforced equality in girls' and boy's sport as exemplified by the USA's Title IX legislation. Male and female athletes now have relatively equal opportunities to participate in sport, despite some continuing discrimination.

More subtle forms of discrimination include the ways we see athletes. Female athletes continue to be seen as unfeminine or suspected of homosexuality. In addition, female athletes continue to be compensated less favourably than male athletes. Finally, the sex testing of female athletes and controversies over transgendered athletes continue the debate over the gendering of sport.

Sport is also gendered, of course, in that it embodies masculinity. For boys, sport is the premier testing ground for masculinity, and also serves as the terrain on which boys are taught to be men. In sport, boys and men learn masculine ideals of stoicism, aggression, self-sacrifice, and disregard of pain. In hockey, hegemonic masculinity is upheld through these ideals and through the valorization of violence in the service of the team. Nonetheless, for males and females alike, sport provides not only confirmation of the more negative aspects of gender ideology but also models for gender transformation.

If sport is about physical mastery, our bodies are also valued for their beauty. The cultivation of beauty is a heavily gendered aspect of our relationship with our bodies. Around the world, women are more likely to be valued for physical beauty than are men, though standards of beauty vary and are subject to change. In North America, women are particularly vulnerable to the 'beauty myth', which emphasizes an unreachable cultural ideal of beauty as the pinnacle of female achievement. This cultural construct makes many women overly concerned with their appearances, enhancing self-objectification under the scrutiny not of men per se, but of the so-called male gaze. Both men and women utilize the male gaze, assessing women's attractiveness and adopting the stance of a desiring heterosexual male subject.

Weight and breast size are particular North American obsessions, fuelling the diet and cosmetic surgery industries. White women continue to be the premier clients for cosmetic surgery, though such surgery valorizes Northern European ethnic models of beauty. Because of this implied ethnic model, racialized women are much more vulnerable to cultural slurs of 'ugliness'. Light skin, 'good' hair, and other attributes based on the value of the dominant ethnic beauty model may operate as 'social capital' for racialized women. Disabled women may also be constructed as 'ugly', or may face social pressure to 'perfect' the disabled body where possible.

Fear of fat unites many North American women, and this increasingly affects all groups. Men have become increasingly concerned about their weight, and body anxieties among men seem to be increasing. If this is an area of gender convergence, the disproportionate concern of women for their appearance remains a key feature of the gendering of bodies. Not surprisingly, then, women remain by far the most willing consumers of cosmetic surgery, even if thousands of men do subject themselves to dubious procedures such as penis enlargements. The male gaze remains critical to both sexes, with disproportionate power over women.

One case in which men are more likely than women to seek radical bodily transformation is that of transgenderism. While both men and women experience gender dysphoria, men are far more likely to seek sexual reassignment. Since about 1950, sexual reassignment has become ever more possible and successful, and there are now over 100,000 people worldwide who have had such treatment and changed sex. Controversy has ensued over whether transsexuals are gender conformists or gender rebels. On one hand, research among transwomen has shown them to be more conservative and gender-conformist than non-transsexual women. On the other hand, transsexuals point out the distinction between sex and gender and the malleability of these categories.

Health provides both gender similarities and radical gender difference. Health and illness are in some ways levellers, but differences persist. Masculinity and femininity interact with health-related behaviours, and these gender differences interact with class, ethnicity, and sexual orientation. The gendering of the HIV/AIDS epidemic is an excellent example of how gender differences can emerge in strikingly different ways in different contexts.

In health, as in other areas in the gendered society, there are increasing signs of gender convergence. Young women's risk-taking behaviours are starting to replicate those of young men. Men appear to be seeking health care more consistently. And for unknown reasons, there are signs of convergence in lifespan in North America, though in some nations the challenges of gendered health continue to result in a lifespan gap favouring men. We are still, therefore, parsing the many complexities of embodiment in a gendered society.

Questions for Critical Thinking

1. How would foregrounding disability change your view of the themes dealt with in the previous chapters of this book?
2. Do you believe that sex testing should be eliminated from sport? Should transgendered/transsexual athletes be able to compete with those of their sex?
3. Do you see the 'Beauty Myth' as important in Canadian society?
4. Is transsexualism a form of gender rebellion, or gender conformity?
5. What is the role of *sex* difference and *gender* difference in determining health?

Key Terms

ablism

beauty myth

colourism

disability

fetishization

gender dysphoria

gender verification see sex testing.

male gaze

purdah

self-objectification

sex testing

transgendered

transsexual

transvestites

Title IX

SRS

Chapter 12

The Gender of Violence

Domination's Endgame

> All violence consists in some people forcing others, under threat of suffering or death, to do what they do not want to do.
>
> —LEO TOLSTOY

Nightly, we watch news reports of Somali pirates, brutal sex crimes in a variety of countries, racist attacks against ethnic minorities in Russia, school shootings, suicide bombers, homophobic gay-bashing murders, murderous family violence, or Mexican drug lords and their legions of gun-toting thugs. We are warned by pundits that the recent global economic downturn may engender 'a global epidemic of violent crime', 'as people worldwide grow desperate to make ends meet'.[1] Seldom do the news reports note that most of the crime, and virtually all of the violent crime, in the world is committed by men—despite the fact that women are more likely to be represented among the poorest and most downtrodden citizens of the globe. Imagine, though, if the violence were perpetrated largely by women. Would that not be *the* story, the only issue to be explained? Would not a gender analysis occupy the centre of every single story? The fact that violent criminals are generally men seems so natural as to raise no questions, generate no media analysis.

You would think the numbers alone would tell the story: All over the world, men constitute 98 per cent of all persons arrested for rape; and the vast majority of those arrested for murder, robbery, assault, family violence, and disorderly conduct. Men are overwhelmingly more violent than women.[2]

From early childhood to old age, violence is the most obdurate, intractable behavioural gender difference; and though age is an important predictor of violence and criminality, gender by far outstrips it in significance. Gender *alone* is a highly significant predictor of violent behaviour. The US National Academy of Sciences puts the case starkly: 'The most consistent pattern with respect to gender is the extent to which male criminal participation in serious crimes at any age greatly exceeds that of females, regardless of source of data, crime type, level of involvement, or measure of participation.'[3] Yet how do we understand this obvious and nearly universal association between masculinity and violence? Is it a product of biology, a fact of nature, caused by something inherent in male anatomy? Or is it yet another result of a gendered society?

Masculinity and Violence

In assessing the relationship between masculinity and violence, we begin by noting that men dominate the field of criminality in general. This is true wherever one looks. In part, male propensity toward violence is related to men's greater tendency toward risk-taking behaviours and rule-breaking in general.[4]

These male tendencies may also affect the police. Although fewer than 5 per cent of high-speed chases involve suspects wanted for violent felonies—most of the suspects are suspected of traffic violations—20 per cent of all high-speed chases end in serious injury or death, most often of innocent bystanders. Why? Because it is almost always younger male police officers who do the chasing. In one study in southern Florida, 'winning a race' was cited by officers as the objective in a pursuit. This links young male police officers to the young men predominant in risky driving in general and street racing in particular. But here again, both scholars and media often overlook the operations of gender. Though 90 to 95 per cent of participants in street racing are male, a major US Department of Justice report describes the typical street racer as '18 to 24 years of age, generally living at home and typically having little income' without mentioning gender. Elsewhere, the same report recommends analyzing the 'age, ethnicity, [and] group affiliation' of racers—again, gender disappears.[5]

invisibility of gender in association to crime

However invisible gender may become in some analyses, men *are* overrepresented among risk-takers and criminals, and this overrepresentation remains particularly acute in the area of violent crime. Criminologist Marvin Wolfgang notes that violent crime rises any time there is an unusually high proportion of the population of young men between the ages of 15 and 24. Psychiatrist James Gilligan observes that the only two innate biological variables that are predictors of violence are youth and maleness.[6] The relationship is immediately apparent if you look at a chart, as in Figure 12.1 for mid-nineteenth-century Britain. And things aren't so different today, as you can see from a similar chart for Chicago between 1965 and 1990 (see Figure 12.2).

Thus gender and age are the two most powerful predictors of violence. Men are far more violent than women, and the likelihood of violence by either gender decreases as one ages.

There has been no shortage of explanations for male violence. Some researchers suggest that 'the durability, universality, and generality of the relative aggressiveness of males' points definitively toward a biological difference. So, for example, scholars argue that androgens (male hormones), especially testosterone, drive male aggression. Other scholars have looked to more evolutionary explanations such as homosocial competition, in which male violence is the result of the evolutionary competition for sexual access to females. Men fight with each other to create dominance hierarchies; the winners of those fights have their choice of females. The fact that violence is such a significant gender difference suggests at least some validity for these arguments.[7]

But as discussed earlier, by itself the biological evidence is unconvincing. Testosterone *is* highly correlated with aggressive behaviour; still, it seems that the hormone does not *cause* the aggression but rather facilitates an aggressiveness that is already present. (It does nothing for non-aggressive males, for example.) Nor does the causal arrow always point from hormone to behaviour. Winners in athletic competition experience

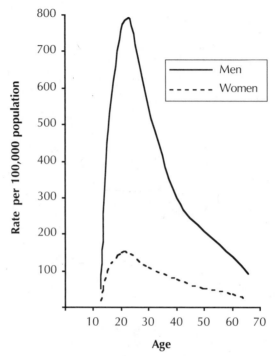

Figure 12.1 Criminal offenders by age and gender, England and Wales, 1842–1844.

Source: Copyright © 1983, University of Chicago Press. Travis Hirschi and Michael Gottfredson, 'Age and the Explanation of Crime,' based on data from F.G.P. Nelson, Contributions to Vital Statistics . . . , 3d ed. (London, 1857), 303–4.

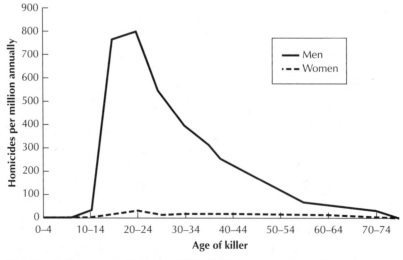

Figure 12.2 Homicide rates in Chicago, 1965–1990, by age and gender.

Source: Homicide rates in Chicago, 1965–1990, by age and gender. Illustrated by Laurie Grace. From 'Darwinism and the Roots of Machismo,' *Scientific American*. Reprinted by permission of the artist.

increased testosterone levels *after* they win, just as prisoners' testosterone levels rise in response to the hierarchical, competitive, and violent nature of prison life. (Interestingly, androgens seem not to promote violence against those who are significantly higher on the dominance ladder. As we saw in Chapter 2, increased testosterone will cause a mid-level male baboon, for example, to increase his aggression against the male just below him, but it will not embolden him to challenge the hierarchical order.) So, in sum, violence causes increased testosterone levels, and hormonal increases enable violence. Androgens, and biological factors in general, thus provide a partial but insufficient explanation for male violence.[8]

Following Freud, some psychoanalysts have looked for the roots of masculine violence in the Oedipal drama: The frustration of the young boy's sexual desires is translated into aggression (the frustration-aggression hypothesis). Stated more neutrally, the young boy must constantly and publicly demonstrate that he has successfully separated from his mother and transferred his identity to his father—that is, that he has become masculine. Male violence is a way to prove successful masculinity. Sex role theorist Talcott Parsons (discussed earlier in this text), concurred, viewing delinquency and violence as a way for boys to dissociate themselves from their mothers. Some theorists posited violence as a particularly male response to role strain; both men and women experience strain within their roles, but women are socialized to blame themselves, while men blame (and attack) others in self-righteous anger.[9]

Others see male violence as rooted in evolutionary psychology. Sociobiologists and evolutionary psychologists see violence as the result of men's competition for reproductive success—or as an adaptive strategy that enables males to avoid becoming prey themselves. In a fascinating study, Barbara Ehrenreich argues that the origins of war lie less in an innate propensity for aggression than in the fear of becoming someone else's dinner entrée. Thus, she says, the origins of society lie in defence—we became social not because we had some deep need for sociability, but rather because only together could we defend ourselves successfully. The near-universal association of masculinity and war, says Ehrenreich, is compensatory and defensive, a 'substitute occupation for underemployed male hunter-defenders'.[10]

Whether one accepts psychological and evolutionary arguments or not, violence *has* long been understood as the best way to ensure that others publicly recognize one's manhood. Fighting was once culturally prescribed for boys. In one of the best-selling American advice manuals of the first part of the twentieth century, parents learned that:

> There are times when every boy must defend his own rights if he is not to become a coward and lose the road to independence and true manhood . . . The strong willed boy needs no inspiration to combat, but often a good deal of guidance and restraint. If he fights more than, let us say, a half dozen times a week—except, of course, during his first week at a new school—he is probably over-quarrelsome and needs to curb. The sensitive, retiring boy, on the other hand, needs encouragement to stand his ground and fight.

In this bestseller, boys were encouraged to fight once a day, except during the first week at a new school, when, presumably, they would fight more often![11]

Lurking beneath such advice was the fear that boys who were not violent would not grow up to be real men. The spectre of the 'sissy'—encompassing the fears of emasculation, humiliation, and effeminacy that North American men carry with them—is responsible for a significant amount of masculine violence. Violence is proof of masculinity; one is a 'real' man, because one is not afraid to be violent. James Gilligan speaks of 'the patriarchal code of honour and shame which generates and obligates male violence'—a code that sees violence as the chief demarcating line between women and men.[12]

fear of effeminity

Listen to one New York gang member describing the reasons that his gang requires random knife slashings as initiation rituals. 'Society claims we are notorious thugs and killers but we are not', he says. 'We're a family of survivors . . . proud young black men living in the American ghetto. Harlem princes trying to rise up and refusing to be beaten down'. Another man recalls his days in a juvenile detention facility where 'you fought almost every day because everybody trying to be tougher than the next person'. In Canada, where at least 22 per cent of gang members are Aboriginal, hypermasculine violence may also offer a way of compensating for 'the elimination of traditional means of achieving masculinities (such as supporting families through hunting and trapping)'; being 'jumped in' or 'doing minutes' (being beaten by other gang members) may also be familiar experiences for youth who have come from abusive, violent backgrounds.[13]

But even for those who are not gang-involved, the defence of masculinity through violence is a familiar trope. Sociologist Vic Seidler writes that 'as boys, we have to be constantly on the alert to either confront or avoid physical violence. We have to be alert to defend ourselves . . . Masculinity is never something we can feel at ease with. It's always something we have to be ready to prove and defend'. And criminologist Hans Toch adds that 'in cultures of masculinity, the demonstrated willingness to fight and the capacity for combat are measures of worth and self-worth'. As criminologist James Messerschmidt suggests, this element of masculinity may appeal to girls, too, and some adopt masculine violence and masculine identities in part as a response to gender inequality and gendered violence. Masculinity and violence, then, are not synonymous with *maleness* and violence.[14]

From the locker room to the chat room, men and boys of all ages learn that violence is a socially sanctioned form of expression. Male socialization is in part a socialization to the legitimacy of violence—from infant circumcision to violence from parents and siblings to routine fights with other boys to the socially approved forms of violence in the military, sports, and prison, to epigrams that remind us that we should get even, not mad, and that the working world is the Hobbesian war of each against all, a jungle where dogs eat dogs.

Although not necessarily describing a cultural universal, the psychological models described above do help explain the particular association of masculinity with violence, especially among younger males. Still, psychological explanations often assume universal generalizability. They take little account of either cross-cultural variation or the historical shifts in any culture over time. But such cultural and historical shifts are important if we are adequately to explain violence in the first place.

In the 1980s, social anthropologists Signe Howell and Roy Willis tackled this problem by asking: What can we learn from those societies in which there is very little violence? They found that *the definition of masculinity had a significant impact on the propensity toward violence.* In societies in which men were permitted to acknowledge fear, levels of violence were low. But in societies in which masculine bravado—the posture of strength and the repression and denial of fear—was a defining feature of masculinity, violence was likely to be high. It turns out that those societies in which bravado is prescribed for men are also those in which the definitions of masculinity and femininity are very highly differentiated. For example, Joanna Overing studied two groups living in the Amazon jungle. The extremely violent Shavante define manhood as 'sexual bellicosity', a state both superior to and opposed to femininity, whereas their peaceful neighbouring Piaroas define manhood *and womanhood* as the ability to co-operate tranquilly with others in daily life. Overing's findings confirm Howell and Willis's contention that more violent societies are those where masculinity and femininity are seen to be polar opposites.[15]

In sum, these are a few of the themes that anthropologists have isolated as leading toward both interpersonal violence and intersocietal violence:

1. the ideal for manhood is the fierce and handsome warrior;
2. public leadership is associated with male dominance, both of men over other men and of men over women; ——→ Sexual violence as power.
3. women are prohibited from public and political participation;
4. most public interaction is between men, not between men and women or among women;
5. boys and girls are systematically separated from an early age;
6. initiation of boys is focused on lengthy constraint of boys, during which time the boys are separated from women, taught male solidarity, bellicosity, and endurance, and trained to accept the dominance of older groups of men;
7. emotional displays of male virility, ferocity, and sexuality are highly elaborated;
8. the ritual celebration of fertility focuses on male generative ability, not female ability;
9. male economic activities and the products of male labour are prized over female.[16]

One of the most significant 'causes' of male violence, then, is gender inequality. And the victims of this are not only women, but also men. Taken together, these works provide some insight into what might reduce the amount of gendered violence in society. It seems clear that the less gender differentiation between women and men, the less likely gendered violence will be. This means that the more men can be 'like women'—nurturing, caring, frightened—and the more women can be 'like men'—capable, rational, competent in the public sphere—the more likely a decline in gendered violence.[17]

So what is the relationship between masculinity and violence? Men's violence against women is the result of entitlement thwarted; men's violence against other men often derives from the same thwarted sense of entitlement and moral outrage. To find peaceful societies, we might want to look at societies in which entitlement to power is not present, gender polarity is not entrenched, and bravado is not celebrated as the hallmark of masculinity.

Female Criminality and Violence

The association of masculinity and violence, as we have seen, is so well known as to be virtually invisible to us. While the media often overlook the gendered nature of crime, we have reviewed some of the ways in which scholars acknowledge and engage with the relationship between violence and masculinity. Yet we should not pretend that males' overwhelmingly greater tendency to commit an act of violence or a crime means that women never do so.

Still, women are a small minority of offenders. In 2005, only about 20 per cent of those accused of committing Criminal Code offences in Canada were female; the rate of crime among females, based on these statistics, is about a quarter of the male rate. So women commit crimes, but they have a much lower rate of criminality than do men. What's more, the crimes women commit and their reasons for committing them are sometimes very different from those of men. In Canada, women tend to commit theft (especially shoplifting), common assault, fraud, and bail violations. The only area of crime in which females and males are accused at an equal rate is prostitution. (There are more female prostitutes, but men are frequently charged as pimps and customers.)[18]

The female tendency to cluster in more minor areas of criminality means that women are even less represented among prison populations than among those charged with crimes in general. In Canada, there are now more than 900 federal women prisoners in five federal prisons for women (replacing Kingston's infamous Prison for Women, which closed its doors in 2000). While this number may sound large, it still represents only about 6 per cent of admissions to federal institutions (which generally house those convicted of the most serious crimes). Even if provincial and remand custody are taken into consideration, women are still only about 10 per cent of inmates. Women's lower rate of imprisonment also reflects their lesser tendency to reoffend and to 'escalate' their criminal involvement. Nonetheless, if women diverge from men in some ways, the female inmate population tends to mirror the male inmate population demographically, including a disproportionate number of non-white, poor, and undereducated and unemployed women—and Aboriginal women are even more overrepresented among federal prisoners than are Aboriginal men.[19]

Thus, despite dramatic changes in women's lives in the past 40 years, they have remained a minority among offenders—particularly those accused of violent crime. In the mid-1970s, though, crime rates for women appeared to be increasing significantly precisely as women gained new rights and roles outside their 'traditional' spheres. Sociologists Freda Adler and Rita Simon argued that feminism explained women's increasing criminality. 'Is it any wonder', asked Adler, 'that once women were armed with male opportunities they should strive for status, criminal as well as civil, through established male hierarchical channels?' Simon nuanced her claims a bit more, arguing that feminism actually decreased the rates of female violent crime but increased female property crimes. Others have argued, through curious misreading of data, that female criminality and violence are as significant as men's but are somehow ignored because women commit violent crimes without being charged, or because media ignore supposedly burgeoning rates of female police involvement.[20]

Although both claims may be politically useful to those who want to return women to their 'natural' place in the home, they are not supported by empirical evidence. First, the most interesting long-term historical evidence suggests that women's criminality has actually *decreased* since the eighteenth century. Court records reveal a steady decline in women's arrests and prosecutions since that time, brought about in part by changes in the definition of femininity and the 'cult of domesticity' that made women angels of their households.[21]

Despite increases in some crime rates for women over the past few decades, the base numbers were so small to begin with that *any* modest increase would appear to be a larger percentage increase than that among men. Moreover, reported increases reflected property crime, especially fraud, forgery, and embezzlement, and most of those increases have been in petty crimes— i.e., shoplifting, credit card fraud, passing bad cheques. More recently, particularly in the last decade, female criminality has declined within Canada. And even in the USA, the sex differential in crime has remained roughly the same when seen as a number per 100,000 of population. Thus it becomes clear that, as one criminologist put it simply, 'relative to males, the profile of the female offender has not changed'.[22]

Women and girls who engage in crime are less likely to engage in violent crime than their male counterparts. Females are accused of crimes 'against the person' at a rate about one-fifth of the male rate. As the severity of violence increases, female representation appears to decrease: In 2006, according to Canadian government statistics, '[f]emale rates for homicide, attempted murder, and sexual assault were negligible'. Still, when girls and women *do* commit violent crimes, they are as likely as male offenders to inflict injury and to use weapons; women are fully capable of violence even if they deploy it with much less frequency.[23]

Furthermore, we have some evidence that the gender gap in violence is decreasing. Evidence of this is still spotty. However, in the United States, while women constitute only 6.3 per cent of the prison population (about 75,000 inmates), that number represents a 9.1 per cent increase since 1995, indicating a growing female tendency to commit serious crimes. In Canada, while the overall rate at which female youth and adults are charged with crime has been declining steadily since 1992, this is not true for 'serious violent crimes'. Charge rates for those crimes continued to climb dramatically until 2001. Rates of serious violent crime among female adults nearly doubled between 1986 and 2005, while the corresponding rate for men declined. This has brought men's and women's rates of serious violent crime closer together. In 1986, nine men were charged for every woman charged with a serious violent crime. By 2005, this ratio had shifted to five to one. Will this trend eventually lead to a levelling of gender distinctions within violent crime? Such a conclusion would be premature to say the least, but the increase in this one area of criminality suggests significant changes in at least some women's relationship to serious criminality and, by implication, to violence.[24]

When it comes to the most serious violence, however, we see less evidence of gender convergence. Canada's **homicide** rate is relatively low—significantly less than half the US rate, for example—and has been declining since the 1970s. In Canada in 2005, only 10 per cent of the 643 people accused of homicide were female. So women kill much less frequently; and they also kill differently. Between 1996 and 2005, they were *self defence?*

most likely to murder their spouses (30 per cent of victims) or their children (28 per cent of victims). (In the USA, there has been a precipitous decline in women's spousal homicide rates, at least in part because of the expansion of services for battered women; now women abused by intimate partners have alternatives that support leaving abusive relationships.) Women remain much less likely to kill strangers or casual acquaintances than are men, and are much less likely to engage in multiple homicide or **familicide**. Women are also much less likely than men to kill with guns.[25]

Although women convicted of murder receive, on average, shorter sentences than do men convicted of murder, this sentencing differential seems to have less to do with the gender of the murderer and more to do with the circumstances of the murder, the past criminal history of the murderer, and the murderer's relationship to the murdered. Men who murder an intimate partner tend to receive sentences roughly equal in length to those of women who commit the same crime.[26]

Overall, women and girls represent a minor force in the pattern of criminality. They commit much less crime, are less represented in prison, and tend to cluster in 'minor' areas of offending. They are even less represented among perpetrators of violent crime than among offenders in general. Despite somewhat troubling growth in female participation in serious crime, violence remains perhaps the most gendered behaviour in our culture.[27]

School Violence: Shooters and 'Mean Girls'

We have considered gendered patterns of violent criminality among men and women. The gendered patterns of violence among children are also revealing, demonstrating the greater tendency of males to commit violence against both other males and females. Among three-year-olds, for example, the most frequent acts of violence are boy-to-boy; girl-to-girl violence, by contrast, is the least frequent. Boy-to-girl violence is far more frequent than girl-to-boy. In one study, two Finnish psychologists contrasted physical, verbal, and 'indirect' forms of aggression. They found that girls at all ages (except the youngest) were more likely to engage in indirect aggression (telling lies behind a person's back, trying to be someone's friend as revenge to another, saying to others, 'let's not be friends with him or her'). Boys at all ages were more likely to engage in direct aggression (kicking, hitting, tripping, shoving, arguing, swearing, and abusing) and verbal aggression. Does this mean that the sexes were essentially equal in their aggression, but favoured different modes of expression? Not really. Indeed, girls at all ages were also more likely to use peaceful conflict resolution (talking to clarify things, forgetting about it, telling a teacher or parent)—or to withdraw.[28]

As children grow older, peer aggression becomes more threatening; for some, school becomes a dangerous place indeed. Consider the data from a survey of US high school seniors in 1994. Nearly one-fifth of high-school boys reported that they hurt someone so badly that he or she needed to be bandaged or to see a doctor. (Only one-twentieth of girls reported that level of violence.) A 2007 US survey of youth in grades 9 to 12 found little change. Sixteen per cent of male students and 8.5 per cent of female students reported being in a physical fight on school property within the previous year, and many more reported crimes against their property. In 2006, about 10 per cent of Canadian youth crimes reported to the police took place on school property; about 27 per cent of those crimes were assaults. So young people face a high risk of violence—even from those they consider friends; Canadian youth who reported physical assaults to police in 2003 were most likely to be assaulted by a close friend, acquaintance, or associate.[29]

So youth, it seems, is a violent time. Yet we continue to talk about 'teen violence', 'youth violence', 'gang violence', 'suburban violence', and 'violence in the schools' without considering the role of gender in such violence. We ignore gender even when discussing the rare but hyperviolent school shootings that leave us speechless and sick at heart. When we think about these wrenching events, do we ever consider that, whether white or black, inner city or suburban, bands of marauding 'youths' or troubled teen-aged shooters are virtually all male? A recent synthesis of school shootings suggests the minimal importance placed on gender as a category of analysis. While the author devotes several pages to discussing the distinctions between types (terrorist, mass murder, etc.) of school shootings, masculinity merits only a mention within a laundry list of causes identified by scholars. According to Patricia Leavy and Kathryn Mahoney, coverage of Columbine (1999) and other school shootings as 'kids killing kids' obscured 'one of the main issues to flow from these events—the social construction of masculinity in the USA'. Instead of looking at gender, a Columbine-obsessed media focused on the alleged bullying of the boys (since called into question) and the deleterious effects of vaguely labelled 'goth culture'.[30]

Let it be stated clearly, then: virtually every recorded school shooting was carried out by a boy or man, almost all of them white. (According to Leavy and Mahoney, class and ethnicity are analysed in relation to shootings only in those rare cases involving a non-white shooter.) And while the gender of the shooters has received little attention, even less attention has been paid to the victims, who have been disproportionately female. In a systematic analysis of hundreds of media reports of 12 school shootings between 1997 and 2002, Jessie Klein found that reports mentioned peer abuse (bullying) as a precipitating factor, but tend to focus on parents, media, and access to guns as more significant causes. This is despite the facts that girls are targeted as victims in a significant number of cases; and shooters often have exhibited failed relationships with, hostility toward, and abuse of girls. Even when adult men enter schools expressly to sexually assault and murder girls—as happened in Pennsylvania and Colorado in 2007—media reports gloss over the relationship between these murders and the larger issues of gendered violence. School violence, then, cannot be divorced from gender and from the kind of gendered entitlement that we saw when discussing male violence in general.[31]

From this perspective, the targeting of girls in school shootings starts to look much more like the extreme end of a spectrum that includes a ubiquitous and tolerated level of gender harassment and violence within schools. As discussed in Chapter 7, North American schools fail to protect girls from sexual harassment and sexual assault, and homophobic slurs and violence are similarly widespread. School shootings and youth violence cannot be divorced from the broader social context of gender inequality.

So what about the 'mean girls' whom we read about in media reports, and the violent girls we see on widely publicized YouTube videos of 'girl fights'? Indeed, mean girls' existence has some basis in fact. First, girls are more likely than women to engage in criminality. Female offending peaks at age 15, and female youth are 3.5 times more likely to be accused of Criminal Code offences than are female adults. Still, though females are more highly represented in the criminal justice system during youth, the vast majority (77 per cent) of Canadian youth charged with a crime in 2006 were male. As in adulthood, female youth offenders tend to cluster in less serious areas of criminality. The introduction of the Youth Criminal Justice Act, which seeks to divert non-violent youth away from the criminal justice system, has led to an even greater decline in charges laid against girls than in charges laid against boys. This is in large part because girls' crimes tend to be 'minor' relative to those of boys. (Nonetheless, in Canada, girls are as likely as boys to be convicted if charged.) Troublingly, despite the decline in youth criminal charges overall, violent crimes now make up a larger proportion of crimes. The violent crime rate among youth has risen more than 30 per cent in the past two decades, and the rate of increase for girls has far outstripped that for boys.[32]

So despite the fact that girls remain much less likely to engage in crime than boys, and despite the fact that they are less likely to be violent, there is some cause for concern. During the 1990s, a number of incidents galvanized public panic about the 'rising tide' of girl violence. One of the most brutal and tragic of these events was the 1997 murder of Reena Virk, a 14-year-old Indo-Canadian girl from Victoria, BC. In an attack rooted both in 'competitive heterosexuality' and racism, Reena endured brutal violence at the hands of a large group of schoolmates before being abandoned to find her way home. Before she could make her way to safety, she was set upon by a girl and a boy from the initial group, who returned and eventually drowned Reena. In the aftermath of the attack, *Maclean's* magazine sounded a nationwide 'alarm about rising violence among teenage girls', and numerous media outlets followed the same trend. Despite the fact that ethnicity was a 'key factor' in the attack, it was ignored in media coverage in favour of panic over girl violence as a logical outcome of family and social changes including the rise of feminism.[33]

The relationship between feminism and girl violence is difficult to puzzle out. One study from Finland found that girls in the 1980s were much less violent than in the 1990s, both from self-reports and from reports of their peers. The study also found greater acceptance of violence among the girls. But in the late 1990s, the study found, violence had a more positive connotation for girls, 'something that makes the girl feel powerful, strong, and makes her popular'—in short, doing for girls what violence and aggression have historically done for boys. As James Messerschmidt suggests, this may even lead some girls to adopt masculine identities in the context of gang involvement, thus gaining the benefit of being 'one of the guys'. However, such gender-bending seems to be less common among violent girls than is something much more akin to emphasized femininity. According to Sibylle Artz, a University of Victoria researcher who has studied girl violence extensively, violent girls tend to be disconnected from meaningful relationships with their mothers, see women as second-class citizens, and focus intensely on heterosexual relationships at the cost of relationships with other girls.[34]

Whether or not their aggression results in violence, girls do experience and suffer from girl-on-girl hostility, whether that takes direct or subtle forms. A spate of recent books about girls' aggression throws new light on these issues.[35] Some writers, like Rachel Simmons, argue that indirect aggression may have devastating effects on girls' development, self-esteem, and aspirations:

> Unlike boys, who tend to bully acquaintances or strangers, girls frequently attack within tightly knit friendship networks, making aggression harder to identify and intensifying the damage to the victims. Within the hidden culture of aggression, girls fight with body language and relationships instead of fists and knives. In this world, friendship is a weapon, and the sting of a shout pales in comparison to a day of someone's silence. There is no gesture more devastating than the back turning away.

Girls' indirect forms of aggression are not the expression of some innately devious feminine wiles, but rather the consequences of gender inequality. Similarly, when girls act violently, they are acting on gendered scripts that may either celebrate emphasized femininity or seek to escape it through strategic alliances with masculinity. In neither case does their violence reflect feminism.[36]

Youth violence continues to be a serious issue with which Canadians must grapple. It remains profoundly gendered, both in the representation of the sexes within it (males far outnumbering females) and in the nature of violence it involves. The dominant early childhood pattern is one in which boys aggress both other boys and girls; this pattern holds in youth violence, but is complicated by the emergence, in adolescence, of heterosexual abuse that in many ways mirrors that found in adult life. However, rates of victimization, harassment, and abuse among youth far outstrip those found among adults, suggesting that the gendered society serves its youngest members poorly indeed.

Gendered Violence: An Institutional Problem

After he had successfully tested a nuclear bomb in November 1952, creating a fusion explosion about 1000 times more powerful than the fission bomb that destroyed Hiroshima seven years earlier, Edward Teller, the Nobel Prize-winning nuclear physicist, wrote the following three-word telegram, to his colleagues: 'It's a boy'. No one had to point out to Teller the equation of military might—the capacity for untold violence—with masculinity. Such a tragic connection remains fixed for both the military heroes of our masculine fantasies and the bespectacled scientists who create the technology that enables those Rambo-wannabes to conquer the world.

It would be easy to catalogue all the phallic images and rhetoric in that vast historic parade of military heroes in decorated uniforms and scientists in white lab coats, suggesting that proving masculinity is a common currency for both warrior and wonk, gladiator and geek. Pop psychologists have yet to run out of sexually tinged phrases to describe this; one feminist calls masculine militarism a case of 'missile envy'; another writes about how men 'created civilization in the image of a perpetual erection: a pregnant phallus'. But these images turn gender into a screen against which individuals project their psychological fears and problems, reducing war and the state's use of institutional violence to a simple aggregation of insecure men desperate to prove their masculinity. Although this argument is not entirely without merit, as we shall see, it leaves us without an understanding of the institutional violence that is implicit in the construction of the modern bureaucratic state. For that understanding we need to explore the link between the two realms, how 'militarism perpetuates the equation between masculinity and violence' and how war 'encodes violence into the notion of masculinity generation after generation'.[37]

Though masculinity may be associated historically with war, the way we fight today would leave many men without the ability to test and prove their manhood in a conventional military way. After all, most soldiers today are not combatants. Most are in support services—transport, administration, technical support, maintenance. The increasingly technological sophistication of war has only sped up this process—nuclear weapons, 'smart bombs', automatic weaponry, self-propelled military vehicles, and long-distance weapons all reduce the need for Rambo-type primitive warriors and increase the need for cool, rational button-pushers.[38]

Yet there is something powerful in the ways that our political leaders seek to prove an aggressive and assertive masculinity in the political arena. War and its technology confer upon men a 'virile prestige', as French philosopher Simone de Beauvoir put it. Military prowess and the willingness to go to war have been tests of manhood. Explaining why US President Lyndon Johnson continued to escalate the war in Vietnam, a biographer writes

> He wanted the respect of men who were tough, real men, and they would turn out to be hawks. He had unconsciously divided people around him between men and boys. Men were activists, doers, who conquered business empires, who acted instead of talked, who made it in the world of other men, and had the respect of other men. Boys were the talkers and the writers and the intellectuals, who sat around thinking and criticizing and doubting instead of doing.

When opponents criticized the war effort, Johnson attacked their masculinity. When informed that one member of his administration was becoming a 'dove' on Vietnam, Johnson scoffed, 'Hell, he has to squat to piss!' And, as Johnson celebrated the bombings of North Vietnam, he declared proudly that he 'didn't just screw Ho Chi Minh. I cut his pecker off'.[39]

Carol Cohn conducted an ethnographic analysis of defence intellectuals in the last days of the Cold War. She recalls that 'lectures were filled with discussion of vertical erector launchers, thrust-to-weight ratios, soft lay-downs, deep penetration, and the comparative advantage of protracted versus spasm attacks—or what one military advisor to the National Security Council has called 'releasing 70 to 80 per cent of our mega tonnage in one orgasmic whump'. There was serious concern about the need to harden our missiles, and the need to 'face it, the Russians are a little harder than we are'. Disbelieving glances would occasionally pass between me and my ally—another woman—but no one else seemed to notice'.[40]

It would be simplistic to reduce the complexities of military and political decisions to psychological 'pissing contests', but it is equally important to include a discussion of gender in our investigations. From the top political leaders to military strategists and technological experts, issues of gender play themselves out in the formulation of military policy. And public opinion also plays an important role in these demonstrations of sexual potency.

Recall, for example, how during the Gulf War, US enemy Saddam Hussein was constantly sexualized on American bumper stickers that read, 'Saddam, Bend Over' and 'USA—Up Saddam's Ass', insults that equated military conflict with homosexual rape. One widely reprinted cartoon showed Saddam Hussein bending over as if in Muslim prayer, with a huge US missile approaching, about to penetrate him from behind. Thus was the sexual nature of military adventurism played out in paraphernalia.

The relationship of militarism to sexual conquest often becomes painfully clear. While not every conflict is marked by sexual violence, many produce sexual violence, sometimes used systematically. This is true in Darfur (Sudan), where rape of women and children has formed part of the strategy of armed militias; in the infamous 'rape camps' that emerged during ethnic war in the former Yugoslavia; in the 'rape of Nanking' in 1937, in which Japanese soldiers systematically raped and murdered thousands of girls and women; in the Japanese use of 'comfort women' (sexual slaves, most of them girls) and German concentration-camp brothels during the Second World War; and in any number of horrific incidents of military sexual violence. The rapes and murders of women and children by the Red Army in the aftermath of the Second World War have only recently been discussed; in 2010, an 80-year-old woman became the first German to speak publicly about the experience. Such violence has been part and parcel of the domination of the 'enemy'; but more recently, as women have joined combat forces, sexual violence has also been a major problem *within* military units. In the fiscal year ending in September 2008, the US army dealt with 2908 reported cases of sexual abuse involving its members; 10 per cent of victims were men, revealing that women are not alone in their vulnerability to gendered domination.[41]

Family Violence

For too many people—children and parents alike—the family bears only a passing resemblance to the 'haven in a heartless world' of nostalgic myth. For some people, far from shielding their members from the cold and violent world outside its doors, the family *is* that cold and violent world. Family violence is remarkably gendered, reproducing and reinforcing gender inequality. Though women are sometimes violent, most family violence is perpetrated by males—husbands beating wives, fathers hitting children, sons hitting their parents, boys hitting their brothers or their sisters. 'The actual or implicit threat of physical coercion is one of many factors underlying male dominance in the family', writes sociologist Murray Straus. For this reason, feminist theorist bell hooks does not write of 'domestic' violence, which she sees as a 'soft' term that avoids gender; instead, she describes abuse within the family as '**patriarchal violence**', which is 'based on the belief that is acceptable for a more powerful individual to control others through various forms of coercive violence'. This belief is associated with male domination, but can be used to describe not just men's violence against women, but also same-sex violence and adult violence against children.[42]

For most people, however, the term 'domestic violence' conjures images of what used to be called 'wife-battering'. For much of our history and until quite recently, a husband enjoyed the right to 'discipline' his wife. Only 30-odd years ago, discussion of violence against women could evoke laughter in the House of Commons. Through concerted efforts at consciousness-raising and legal changes, violence against women is a high-profile issue, not just in Canada but around the world.

Though police-reported spousal or **intimate-partner violence** has declined in Canada since the late 1990s, it still accounts for more than half of incidents of family violence reported to police in Canada (2006 data). Female victims of family violence are more likely to suffer spousal violence, while males are more likely to be victimized by some other member of the family. And men, while they are more likely in general to face violence, tend to face it at the hands of other men. Twenty per cent of all female victims of violent crimes were victimized by their spouses, compared to only 4 per cent of male victims of violent crimes. This gender imbalance is significant everywhere. Of the victims of violence in the US who were injured by spouses or ex-spouses, women outnumber men by about nine to one. In Canada, female victims account for 83 per cent of cases of spousal violence reported to police. Criminal harassment, or '**stalking**', is also heavily gendered. Women, especially young and Aboriginal women, are at much higher risk of being stalked than are men; of stalking incidents reported to police in 2006, 76 per cent involved female victims, and many male victims were stalked not by women but by other men. When stalking involved spouses or former partners, women were 90 per cent of victims.[43]

Despite the overwhelming evidence of the problems of domestic violence against women, we often hear a chorus of voices shouting about 'husband abuse'. When one sociologist claims that the abuse of husbands by wives is the most underreported form of domestic violence, suddenly legions of anti-feminists trot out such arguments in policy discussions. Some of the studies of '**gender symmetry**' in domestic violence—a presumption that rates of domestic violence are roughly equal by gender—suggest that women are 'as likely' to hit men as men are to hit women. And indeed, data from Canada's General Social Survey support the notion of symmetry. In contrast to police data, the survey elicits roughly equal numbers of men and women (6 per cent and 7 per cent, respectively) who report experiencing spousal violence in the previous five years. So are women 'just as violent' as men? [44]

If these data were true, you might ask, why are there no shelters for battered men, no epidemics of male victims turning up in hospital emergency rooms, no legions of battered men coming forward to demand protection? Partly, pundits tell us, men who are victims of domestic violence are so ashamed of the humiliation, of the denial of manhood, they are unlikely to come forward and are more likely to suffer in silence the violent ministrations of their wives—a psychological problem that one researcher calls 'the battered husband syndrome'. Because men have been taught to 'take it like a man' and are ridiculed when they feel that they have been battered by women, women are nine times more likely to report their abusers to the authorities', observe two writers. And partly, the pundits tell us, because the power of the 'feminist lobby' is so pervasive, there has been a national cover-up of this demonstrably politically incorrect finding. As one polemicist puts it,

> While repeated studies consistently show that men are victims of domestic violence at least as often as are women, both the lay public and many professionals regard a finding of no sex difference in rates of physical aggression among intimates as surprising, if not unreliable, the stereotype being that men are aggressive and women are exclusively victims.[45]

Such assertions are not supported by empirical research at all, and the inferences drawn from them are even more unwarranted. For example, in the original study of 'the battered husband syndrome', sociologist Susan Steinmetz surveyed 57 couples. Four of the wives, but not one husband, reported having been seriously beaten. From this finding, Steinmetz concluded that men simply don't report abuse, that there must be a serious problem of husband abuse, that some 250,000 men were hit every year—this, remember, from a finding that no husbands were abused. By the time the media hoopla over these bogus data subsided, the figure had ballooned to twelve million battered husbands every year! [46]

One problem is the questions asked in the research. Those studies that found that women hit men as much as men hit women asked men and women if they had ever, during the course of their relationship, hit their partner. An equal number of women and men answered yes. The number changed dramatically, though, when men and women were asked who initiated the violence (was it offensive or defensive?), how severe it was (did she push him before or after he'd broken her jaw?), and how often the violence occurred. When these three questions were posed, the results looked like what we knew all along: The amount, frequency, severity, and consistency of violence against women are far greater than anything done by women to men. Similarly, in Canada's General Social Survey, women were much more likely to reported having been choked, beaten, or attacked with a weapon than were men. While 44 per cent of women who experienced violence reported being injured, 19 per cent of men did. And while 34 per cent of women reported fearing for their lives, 10 per cent of men did. The fact that in one year (2007–2008) 101,000 women and children were admitted to women's shelters in Canada is testament to the gender imbalance in violence. Clearly, even on the basis of self-reporting, gender has a powerful effect on spousal violence.[47]

Another problem results from *when* the informants were asked about domestic violence. The studies that found comparability asked about incidents that occurred in a single year, thus equating a single slap with a reign of domestic terror that may have lasted decades. And, although the research is clear and unequivocal that violence against women increases dramatically during and after divorce or separation, the research that found comparable results *excluded* incidents that occurred after separation or divorce. In the USA, about 76 per cent of all assaults take place at that time, though—with a male perpetrator more than 93 per cent of the time.[48]

Finally, the research that suggests comparability is all based on the Conflict Tactics Scale (CTS), a scale that does not distinguish between offensive and defensive violence, equating a vicious assault with a woman's wrestling or hitting her husband while he is, for instance, assaulting their children. Nor does it take into account the physical differences between women and men, which lead to women's being six times more likely to require medical care for injuries sustained in family violence. Nor does it include the non-physical means by which women are compelled to remain in abusive relationships (income disparities, fears about their children, economic dependency) or the greater prevalence of men among emotional abusers. Nor does it include marital rape or sexual aggression. As one violence researcher asks, 'Can you call two people equally aggressive when a woman punches her husband's chest with no physical harm resulting and a man punches his wife's face and her nose is bloodied and broken? These get the same scores on the CTS'.[49]

The point is not to suggest that women's violence is 'okay' while men's is 'bad'. No amount of violence is defensible. The point is, rather, to demonstrate that allegations of 'symmetry' are inherently flawed. To be sure, some research suggests that women are fully capable of using violence in intimate relationships, but at nowhere near the same rates or severity. According to the US Department of Justice, females experience over ten times as many incidents of intimate violence as do men. On average, according to one report, women experienced about 575,000 such violent victimizations, compared with about 49,000 for men.

Again, though, women are fully capable of deploying 'patriarchal violence'. Perhaps as much as 3 to 4 per cent of all spousal violence is committed by women, according to criminologist Martin Schwartz. And when women are violent, they tend to use the least violent tactics and the most violent ones. Women shove, slap, and kick, Straus and his colleagues found. But they also use guns, and sometimes rely more on weapons while male assailants rely on physical force. That may explain why, though male victims of spousal assault are fewer, they report major assault at twice the rate reported by female victims.[50]

Domestic violence varies with the balance of power in a relationship. When all the decisions are made by one spouse, rates of spouse abuse—whether committed by the woman or the man—are at their highest levels. Violence against women is thus most common in those households in which power is concentrated in the hands of the husband. Interestingly, violence against husbands is *also* more common (though much less likely) in homes in which the power is concentrated in the hands of the husband or, in extremely rare cases, in the hands of the wife. Concentration of power leads to higher rates of violence, period—whether against women or against men. Rates of wife abuse and husband abuse both plummet when relationships are equal, and there are virtually no cases of wives hitting their husbands when all decisions are shared equally, i.e., when the relationships are fully equal.[51]

So women and men do not commit acts of violence at the same rate—nor do they use them for the same reasons. Family violence researcher Kersti Yllo argues that men tend to use domestic violence instrumentally, for the specific purpose of striking fear and terror in their wives' hearts, to ensure compliance, obedience, and passive acceptance of the men's rule in the home. Women, by contrast, tend to use violence expressively, to express frustration or immediate anger—or, of course, defensively, to prevent further injury. Using violence to express frustration and anger is, of course, inappropriate. But rarely is women's violence systematic, purposive, and routine. As two psychologists recently put it:

> in heterosexual relationships, battering is primarily something that men do to women, rather than the reverse . . . [T]here are many battered women who are violent, mostly, but not always, in self-defense. Battered women are living in a culture of violence, and they are part of that culture. Some battered women defend themselves: they hit back, and might even hit or push as often as their husbands do. But they are the ones who are beaten up.[52]

In the results of a survey that simply adds up all violent acts, women and men might appear to be equally violent. But hospital emergency rooms, women's shelters, and morgues suggest that such appearances are often deadly deceptive.

At the extreme end of spousal violence, its gendering becomes clear. Women, particularly young women, are much more likely than men to be killed by their opposite-sex partners. Between 1977 and 2006, Canadian women were three to five times more likely than men to be killed by a spouse. And both Canadian and US data suggest that women are much more likely to be killed by common-law partners than by husbands. For example, despite the fact that married couples vastly outnumber common-law ones, between 1997 and 2006, 39 per cent of partner homicides involved common-law partners (compared to 36 per cent involving married ones). Age difference between partners is also associated with a greater risk of homicide for women. Interestingly, the risk of victimization by family homicide diminishes significantly with age, but gender continues to be important. So while seniors in Canada are very unlikely to be murdered by a family member, senior *female* victims are generally murdered by spouses or adult sons, while senior male victims are more likely to be murdered by their adult sons or stepsons.[53]

The rates for spousal murder are significantly different for women and men; so too are the events leading up to such murders. R. Emerson and Russell Dobash and their colleagues argue that,

> men often kill wives after lengthy periods of prolonged physical violence accompanied by other forms of abuse and coercion; the roles in such cases are seldom if ever reversed. Men perpetrate familial massacres, killing spouse and children together; women do not. Men commonly hunt down and kill wives who have left them; women hardly ever behave similarly. Men kill wives as part of planned murder-suicides; analogous acts by women are almost unheard of. Men kill in response to revelations of wifely infidelity; women almost never respond similarly, though their mates are more often adulterous.[54]

It is also worth noting that these disparate rates of spousal homicide in Western societies are relatively modest compared with the rates in developing societies, where the ratio is even greater. Where patriarchal control is relatively unchallenged, assault, rape, and even murder may be seen less as a crime and more as a prerogative.[55]

Intimate-partner violence knows no class, racial, or ethnic bounds. Yet there are some differences. For example, one of the best predictors of the onset of domestic violence is unemployment. In the USA, a few studies have found rates of domestic violence to be higher in African-American families than in white families. One study found that black men hit their wives four times as often as white men did and that black women hit their husbands twice as often as white women did. Although subsequent studies have indicated a decrease in violence among black families, the rates are still somewhat higher than for white families. Among Latinos the evidence is contradictory. In Canada, immigrant women may face a greater risk of spousal violence, though data are inconclusive. What is clear is that 'immigrant-specific factors' such as immigration status, isolation, economic dependency, and language barriers make immigrant women much more vulnerable than other Canadians. For example, many women immigrate as **family-class immigrants**, and may fear having to leave Canada if they separate from abusive partners.[56]

In Canada, the most significant differences emerge when Aboriginal and non-Aboriginal Canadians are compared; as already mentioned, Aboriginal women face a risk of spousal violence three times higher than do non-Aboriginal women; and Aboriginal women are eight times more likely to fall victim to spousal homicide. According to the 2004 General Social Survey, 21 per cent of Aboriginal people had experienced spousal violence (physical, sexual, or both) in the five years previous to the study. (This compares with 6 per cent for the non-Aboriginal population.) Clearly, domestic violence is significantly more likely within Aboriginal communities, interacting with substance abuse and other legacies of colonization. According to Health Canada, 75 per cent of Aboriginal women have experienced domestic violence, and Aboriginal women are at least three times more likely than non-Aboriginal women to die as the result of such abuse. Poverty and other conditions associated with Aboriginal life in Canada—such as overcrowded on-reserve housing—exacerbate the problem and make it more difficult for women and children to escape abusers.[57]

Because intimate-partner violence is not simply an attribute of sex, gay men and lesbians are also at risk. A recent informal survey of gay victims of violence in six major cities found that gay men and lesbians were more likely to be victims of domestic violence than of anti-gay hate crimes. One study presented to the Fourth International Family Violence Research Conference found that abusive gay men had profiles similar to those of heterosexual batterers, including low self-esteem and an inability to sustain intimate relationships. While prevalence of partner abuse among lesbians remains poorly understood, lesbians report being violently abused by their female partners in forms quite similar to those of heterosexual spousal abuse.[58]

Domestic violence is not simply spousal. Children are often exposed to domestic violence, either as victims or as witnesses. The negative effects of this are well documented. When children who witness intimate-partner violence grow up, they are at greater risk to use violence in domestic situations (especially if they are male) and may suffer from low self-esteem (especially if female) and various emotional problems. Girls who grow up in homes where their mothers are abused are much more likely than other girls to suffer from abuse in their adult relationships. Moreover, children who witness violence within the home are much more likely to exhibit aggressive behaviour toward other children. Though boys are much more likely than girls to exhibit aggressive behaviour, both sexes show significantly more aggression if they have witnessed violence.[59]

Violence against children by parents is perhaps the most widespread type of family violence all over the world. Broad support exists for **corporal punishment**—over three-fourths of Americans and most Canadians believe that it is all right for a parent to 'spank' a child. Most Americans have hit their children, and most children have been hit by their parents, often starting in infancy. Most North American toddlers and pre-schoolers are physically punished. In a recent survey of almost 2,500 Quebec mothers, over half said they used corporal punishment, and almost half of their children aged zero to two years had already experienced it. Parents approve of corporal punishment, but its costs may outweigh the benefit of immediate compliance from the child. Spanking is associated with several negative behaviours in children, including aggression, anti-social behaviour, and mental-health problems. The American Academy of Pediatrics has taken an official stand against spanking. And as of 2004, the Canadian Paediatrics Society's position is that 'Physicians should actively counsel parents about discipline and should strongly discourage the use of spanking'.[60]

The most evident consequence of parental violence against children is observed in the behaviours of children. Children see that violence is a legitimate way to resolve disputes and learn to use it themselves. Violence against siblings is ubiquitous in American families. As Straus writes:

> Violence between siblings often reflects what children see their parents doing to each other, as well as what the child experiences in the form of discipline. Children of non-violent parents also tend to use non-violent methods to deal with their siblings and later with their spouses and children. If violence, like charity, begins at home, so does non-violence.[61]

Parents wondering how to discourage violence *among* their children might begin by ending violence *against* them—and by settling marital problems without resorting to violence. In ending sibling violence, no message can be more powerful than 'in this home, *no one* hits'.

The long-term consequences of parental violence against children are also clear. The greater the corporal punishment experienced by the child, the greater the probability that the child will hit a spouse as an adult. And the likelihood is also higher that children hit by their parents will strike back. (However, it should be noted that this is a relatively minor risk, even when parents are seniors. Seniors' rates of victimization by adult children are only about an eighth of the rate at which children are physically and sexually assaulted by parents.)[62]

North Americans' support for corporal punishment disappears when such violent behaviour by parents against children becomes systematic or extreme, and most who 'spank' see themselves as fundamentally different from those who abuse their children physically. Although the most common forms of parental violence against children are spanking or slapping, 20 per cent of American parents have hit their child with an object, almost 10 per cent have kicked, bit, or hit their child with their fist, and almost 5 per cent of families have experienced a parent beating up a child. While spanking does not indicate that one is a child abuser, the most severe psychological and physical abuse is associated with corporal punishment, and some researchers have found correlation between corporal punishment and other societal indicators, such as child and overall homicide rates. And although mothers as well as fathers commit violence against children, this is another area where gender symmetry does not exist. In one study, Bergman and his colleagues found that men are over 10 times more likely to inflict serious harm on their children and that every perpetrator of the death of a child in this limited sample was either a father or a father surrogate.[63]

Of physical assaults against children under age six reported to Canadian police in 2003, 60 per cent were perpetrated by a family member. Forty-four per cent of accused in family-perpetrated physical assaults of children were fathers, with mothers and brothers accounting for 21 and 15 per cent respectively. Similarly, children under the age of 10 are most likely to be murdered by a family member, and infants under one year of age are the most vulnerable to murder. Baby boys are murdered at a slightly higher rate than girls. Of family-perpetrated homicides against children and youth in 2003, 60 per cent were perpetrated by fathers, 32 per cent by mothers, and the remainder by other family members.[64]

Both women and girls are vulnerable to yet another form of extreme familial violence, the so-called '**honour killing**'. This kind of murder seeks to 'cleanse' a family's honour through the murder of a non-conforming female family member who has 'stained' the family in some way. According to the UN Population Fund, at least 5,000 women are killed (globally) each year in such murders. In recent years, similar killings have occurred in Canada. In 2009, for example, 23-year-old Hasibullah Sadiqi of Ottawa shot his sister and her fiancé after she moved in with him before the wedding and refused to have her estranged abusive father involved in wedding plans.[65]

Such murders have become controversial within North America and Europe because they tend to be associated with particular immigrant communities. Some feel that categorizing these killings as domestic violence obscures their nature and rootedness in religion and culture. Phyllis Chesler notes that 'honour' murders are carefully planned, involve multiple perpetrators and the most extreme forms of violence, and suffer little social stigma from extended family and community. Despite these differences from the more common forms of domestic violence, 'honour killings' appear here as a subset of domestic violence, however, because they share with domestic violence the desire to control and dominate. Indeed, in many 'honour' murders, most victims of such murders had also survived family violence and abuse. Like the other forms of family violence we have examined, these murders reflect the deadly logic of patriarchal violence.[66]

Sexual Assault

That logic is also reflected in **sexual assault**. In Canada, sexual assault has been defined, since 1983, not as penile penetration but more holistically as any non-consensual sexual act. The degree of sexual assault is determined not by penetration, but by level of injury, use of weapon, and danger to life. Our understandings of sexual assault, then, are relatively new and evolving. Indeed, historically it has often been difficult—or irrelevant—to try to understand the difference between consensual and non-consensual sex.

Many disciplines have grappled with understanding sexual assault, primarily by focusing on **rape**. Sociobiologist David Barash explains rape as a reproductive adaptation by men who otherwise couldn't get a date. Following their study of scorpion flies and mallard ducks, Barash, Thornhill, and other evolutionists argue that men who rape are fulfilling their genetic drive to reproduce in the only way they know how. 'Perhaps human rapists, in their own criminally misguided way, are doing the best they can to maximize their fitness', writes Barash. Rape, for men, is simply an 'adaptive' reproductive strategy of the less successful male—sex by other means. If you can't pass on your genetic material by seduction, then pass it on by rape.[67]

In their book *A Natural History of Rape*, Randy Thornhill and Craig Palmer amplify these arguments and make wildly unfounded assertions in the process. Rape, they write, is 'a natural, biological phenomenon that is a product of human evolutionary heritage'. Males' biological predisposition is to reproduce, and their reproductive success comes from spreading their seed as far and wide as possible; women are actually the ones with the power because they get to choose which males will be successful. 'But getting chosen is not the only way to gain sexual access to females', they write. 'In rape, the male circumvents the females' choice'.[68] Rape is the evolutionary mating strategy of losers, males who cannot otherwise get a date. Rape is an alternative to romance; if you can't always have what you want, you take what you need.

Such arguments ignore the fact that most rapists are not interested in reproduction but rather in humiliation and violence, motivated more by rage than by lust. Most rapists have regular sex partners; quite a few are married. Many children, and women well past reproductive age, are raped. And why would some rapists hurt and even murder their victims, thus preventing the survival of the very genetic material that they are supposed to be raping in order to pass on? And why would some rapists be homosexual rapists, passing on their genetic material to those who could not possibly reproduce? And what about rape in prison? Using theories of selfish genes or evolutionary imperatives to explain human behaviour cannot take us very far.

Other scholars analyze sexual assault cross-culturally. The research of Peggy Reeves Sanday and others suggests that rape is not the evolutionary reproductive strategy of the less-successful males. Rather, rape is a *cultural* phenomenon. Sexual assault may be a strategy to ensure continued male domination or a vehicle by which men can hope to conceal maternal dependence, according to ethnographers, but it is surely not an alternative dating strategy.

Think, for example, of the way that sexual assault is used in warfare (discussed above). The mass rape of Bosnian or Sudanese women and children is not some convoluted evolutionary mating strategy, but rather a direct and systematic effort on the part of one militarized group of males to express and sustain the subordination of a conquered group. Mass rape in warfare is about the final humiliating appropriation of the conquered group.

And what about rape not as a crime to be punished but as the *restitution* for a crime that has been committed? In June 2002, a Pakistani woman, Mukhtar Mai, was gang-raped in a small village in southern Punjab. She was ordered to be raped by a local judicial council as punishment for non-marital sex. Except she didn't actually have non-marital sex—her brother did. Or so they believed. Mukhtar was ordered raped because of a crime her brother was said to have committed. (It was later revealed that her brother, age 12, had himself been abducted and sodomized by three elder tribesmen, who fabricated the sex story as a cover-up.) Were these elder tribesmen tried and convicted of the rape of the 12-year-old boy? No. Were the men who sentenced Mukhtar Mai to be gang-raped brought to justice? Eventually, after a world outcry against such obvious injustice. Although neither of these rapes could even be remotely tied to some evolutionary strategy for reproductive success, together they reveal the way that rape serves to reproduce male domination. Both the dominance hierarchies among men and the hierarchies that place men over women were revealed in this horrific moment.[69]

In her ethnographic study of a gang rape at the University of Pennsylvania, Peggy Reeves Sanday underscores how a campus gang rape looks surprisingly like this Pakistani judicial council. She suggests that gang rape has its origins in both the gender inequality that allows men to see women as pieces of meat and in men's needs to demonstrate their masculinity to one another. Gang rape cements the relations among men. But more than that, gang rape permits a certain homoerotic contact between men. When one participant reported his pleasure at feeling the semen of his friends inside the woman as he raped her, Sanday sensed a distinct erotic component. The woman was the receptacle, the vehicle by which these men could have sex with one another and still claim heterosexuality. Only in a culture that degrades and devalues women could such behaviours take place. Rape, then, is hardly an evolutionary strategy by which less-successful males get to pass on their reproductive inheritance. It is an act that occurs only in those societies where there is gender inequality and by men who may be quite 'successful' in other forms of mating but believe themselves entitled to violate women. It is about *gender*, not about *sex*, and it is a way in which gender inequality produces gender difference.[70]

Psychologists enable us to differentiate between rapists and non-rapists by understanding the psychodynamic processes that lead an individual man to such aberrant behaviour. Whether because of childhood trauma, unresolved anger at their mothers, or a sense of inadequate gender identity, rapists are characterized by their deviance from the norm. 'Rape is always a symptom of some psychological dysfunction, either temporary and transient, or chronic and repetitive'. In the popular view, and in many psychological studies, rapists are 'sick individuals'.[71]

A sociological perspective builds upon these other perspectives. But it also offers a radical departure from them. Sexual assault in general, and rape in particular, are particularly illustrative because they are something that is performed almost exclusively by one gender—men—although it is done to women, children, and even other men. Thus it is particularly useful for teasing out the dynamics of both difference (because only men do it) and dominance. Instead of seeing a collection of sick individuals, sociologists look at how ordinary, how normal, rapists can be—and then at the culture that legitimates their behaviours. A sociological perspective also assesses the processes and dynamics that force all women to confront the possibility of sexual victimization—a process that reproduces both gender division and gender inequality.

Studies of rapists have found that many are married or have steady, regular partners. Studies of gang rape reveal an even more 'typical' guy who sees himself simply as going along with his friends. Rapists see their actions in terms that express power differentials between women and men. They see what they do to women as their 'right', a sense of entitlement to women's bodies.

Although rape is an act of aggression by an individual man, or a group of men, it is also a social problem that women, as a group, face. Women may deal with rape as individuals—by changing their outfits, their patterns of walking and talking, their willingness to go to certain places at certain times—but rape affects all women. Rape is a form of 'sexual terrorism', writes legal theorist Carol Sheffield, a 'system of constant reminders to women that we are vulnerable and targets solely by virtue of our gender. The knowledge that such things can and do happen serves to keep all women in the psychological condition of being aware that they are potential victims'.[72]

To the sociologist, then, rape expresses both a structure of relations and an individual event. At the individual level, it is the action of a man (or group of men) against a woman. It is sustained by a cultural apparatus that interprets it as legitimate and justified. It keeps women in a position of vulnerability as potential targets. In this way, rape reproduces both gender difference (women as vulnerable and dependent upon men for protection, women afraid to dare to enter male spaces such as the street for fear of victimization) and gender inequality.[73]

It doesn't have to be this way, of course. As we saw earlier, societies may be located on a continuum from rape-free to rape-prone. Peggy Reeves Sanday found that the best predictors of rape-proneness were levels of militarism, interpersonal violence in general, ideologies of male toughness, and distant father-child relationships. Those societies in which rape was relatively rare valued women's autonomy (women continued to own property in their own name after marriage) and valued children (men were involved in child rearing). Stated most simply, 'the lower the status of women relative to men, the higher the rape rate'.[74]

North American rates of sexual assault are high relative to those of other industrialized countries. Between 12 and 25 per cent of all American women have experienced rape, and another 12 to 20 per cent have experienced attempted rape. That means that between one-quarter and nearly one-half of all women have been sexually assaulted and that between two-thirds and four-fifths of these rapes involved acquaintances. One calculation estimates that between 20 per cent and 30 per cent of all girls now 12 years old will suffer a violent sexual attack during their lives. According to Statistics Canada data, 51 per cent of adult women have experienced sexual or physical assault at least once. In police-reported sexual assaults, 80 per cent of assailants were known to the victim; 28 per cent of victims were assaulted by family members. However, victimization surveys suggest that only 1 in 10 women who experiences a sexual assault reports it to the police.[75]

What is perhaps more frightening is that many sexual assault victims are children. According to the US Department of Justice, half of those victimized by rape in 1992 (a typical year) were juveniles under 18 years old, and 16 per cent were younger than 12. Another study found that 96 per cent of female rape victims under 12 knew their attackers. In one of five cases, a victim's rapist was also her father.[76]

In fact, though we tend to think of sexual assault as a crime most commonly perpetrated against women, sexual assault is in large part a crime against children and youth. According to 2003 statistics, children and youth were the victims of 61 per cent of sexual assaults reported to Canadian police. (Given that children and youth are even less likely than adults to report such assaults, this number may even be too low.) Assaults of children and youth are gendered, though boy children are much more vulnerable to such assaults than are men. Eighty per cent of assaulted children and youth in 2003 were female, and the peak age for their victimization was 13. Half of sexual assault victims were assaulted by people within their families; female children and youth were more likely to be sexually assaulted within the family, male children and youth by someone from outside it. Girls are four times more likely than boys to be sexually assaulted by their family members. Of family-related sexual assaults, 98 per cent were perpetrated by male relatives. Over one-third of assaults were perpetrated by fathers. Aboriginal children are at particularly high risk.[77]

Children are also at risk from exploitation for child pornography, which is itself a form of sexual assault. Between 1998 and 2003, the number of charges laid by Canadian police for child pornography has increased by a factor of eight. Roman Catholic bishop Raymond Lahey resigned in late 2009 after charges of child pornography were laid against him. Bill Surkis, a prominent member of Toronto's Jewish community, faced similar charges in May 2009. In February 2010, seven Canadian children were rescued after police received a tip regarding the production and distribution of child pornography by a 36-year-old Surrey (BC) man. Revelations of pervasive child sexual abuse by Catholic priests (and the Church's subsequent efforts to cover up these crimes) remind us of how vulnerable boys are as well.[78]

As we saw earlier, different theoretical schools offer different explanations for sexual assault. Arguments that rape is simply the reproductive strategy for losers in the sexual arena are unconvincing. Equally unconvincing are arguments that sexual assault is an isolated, individual act, committed by sick individuals who experience uncontrollable sexual impulses. Arguments that sexual assaulters are those who were themselves sexually abused are suggestive—many sexual abusers, particularly pedophiliac ones, have been abused—but are obviously quite limited. As a recent metastudy concludes, 'A leading candidate for a vulnerability factor is being male: the large majority of sex offenders are male, yet the majority of child victims of sexual abuse are female'. If histories of sexual abuse turned one into a victimizer, we would expect to see more *female* than male perpetrators. Maleness, rather than a history of sexual abuse, remains the most potent predictor of a tendency to abuse; males may abuse at various ages, including in adolescence. Though Internet pundits are fond of muttering about the 'hidden epidemic' of female-perpetrated sexual abuse, women remain a tiny minority of abusers; in most cases, women offenders are charged with helping their male partners sexually assault rather than with perpetrating the assault themselves. This is, of course, abhorrent and fully culpable behaviour. However, it suggests that women, for whatever reason, are much less likely to sexually assault than are men (and certainly much less likely to sexually assault than to physically assault).[79]

An adequate explanation of sexual assault has to recognize that it is almost entirely perpetrated by men. We must also ask the more frightening question: Why do so many 'otherwise' typical, normal men commit sexual assault? As sociologist Allan Johnson puts it, how can such a pervasive event be the work of a few lunatics? 'It is difficult to believe that such widespread violence is the responsibility of a small lunatic fringe of psychopathic men', he writes. 'That sexual violence is so pervasive supports the view that the focus of violence against women rests squarely in the middle of what our culture defines as 'normal' interaction between men and women'. The reality is that much rape is committed by 'regular guys'. And 'women are at greater risk of being raped or aggressed against by the men they know and date than they are by lunatics in the bushes'.[80]

Surveys of young women reveal the prevalence of rape; and surveys of young men indicate how casually rape can be viewed. Mary Koss's research on acquaintance rape (discussed in Chapter 10), became the subject of vicious backlash attacks. Nonetheless, her work remains the most impressive and thorough research we have on rape's frequency and scope. She found that nearly half (44 per cent) of all women surveyed experienced some forms of sexual activity when they didn't want to, 15 per cent experienced attempted rape, 12 per cent were coerced by drugs and alcohol, a full 25 per cent had sexual intercourse when they didn't want to because they were 'overwhelmed' by a man's unyielding arguments and pressure, and 9 per cent were forcibly raped.[81]

No wonder feminist writer Susan Griffin called rape 'the all-American crime', engaged in by normal, all-American guys. And even at the fringes of the phenomenon, where sexual assaults are brutal and even murderous, men may view rape relatively casually. Diana Scully and Joseph Marolla interviewed 114 convicted rapists of adult women in the early 1980s. These rapists, and their crimes, varied widely, though most were violent and some had resulted in deaths. Nonetheless, a significant number of the rapists denied that the 'sex' they had engaged in was non-consensual. These men described their motivations for rape in terms that Scully and Marolla grouped under several themes: revenge and punishment; an 'added bonus' (i.e., part of another crime such as burglary); sexual access to women who would otherwise not be available; impersonal sex and power; recreation and adventure; and feeling good. One of the interviewees described the feeling of having raped as 'like I had just ridden the bull at Gilley's'; sexual assault provided a sense of achievement and conquest. Scully and Marolla conclude that rape is not merely the act of a twisted, psychotic mind, but an extreme reflection of everyday objectification of women, or 'the end point in a continuum of sexually aggressive behaviours that reward men and victimize women'.[82]

But can these violent rapists be in any way normal? Scully developed these themes further, finding that rapists have higher levels of consensual sexual activity than other men, are as likely to have significant relationships with women, and are as likely to be fathers as are other men. This finding should effectively demolish the evolutionary arguments that men who rape do so out of sexual frustration, desire for relationships with women, or their status as 'losers' in the sexual marketplace. Rape was used by Scully's interviewees 'to put women in their place', she writes. 'Rape is a man's right', one convicted rapist told her. 'If a woman doesn't want to give it, a man should take it. Women have no right to say no. Women are made to have sex. It's all they are good for. Some women would rather take a beating, but they always give in; it's what they are for'. Men rape, Scully concludes, 'not because they are idiosyncratic or irrational, but because they have learned that in this culture sexual violence is rewarding' and because 'they never thought they would be punished for what they did'.[83]

Yet if Scully and Marolla's work suggested that rapists were in many ways 'normal', it is also equally true that most men do not commit rape. Understanding why may be the most critical way to understand rape. Troublingly, in several surveys, many men indicated that they *would* consider rape—provided the conditions were 'right' and they knew that they would not get caught. In a survey of American college men (most of these studies have used such samples), 28 per cent indicated that they would be likely to commit rape and use force to get sex; 6 per cent said they would commit rape but not use force, and 30 per cent said they might use force but would not commit rape. Forty per cent indicated that they would neither use force nor commit rape—less than half!

In another survey, 37 per cent indicated some likelihood of committing rape if they were certain they would not be caught.[84]

In a sense, what we see is that rapists are *not* nonconformists—psychologically unbalanced perverts who couldn't otherwise get sex—but rather *over* conformists, exceptionally committed to a set of norms about masculinity that makes every encounter with every woman potentially, even inevitably, about sexual conquest, that turns every date into a contest, and that turns a deaf ear to what a woman might want because, after all, women aren't men's equals to begin with. 'The most striking characteristic of sex offenders', writes one researcher, 'is their apparent normality'. Bernard Lefkowitz, author of a chillingly detailed portrait of a gang-rape of a developmentally disabled girl by several high-status high school athletes in Glen Ridge, New Jersey, argues that '[f]or a lot of boys, acting abusively toward women is regarded as a rite of passage. It's woven into our culture'.[85]

Listen to the voice of 'Jay', a 23-year-old stock boy in a San Francisco corporation, who was asked by author Tim Beneke to think about under what circumstances he might commit rape. Jay has never committed rape. He's simply an average guy, trying to imagine the circumstances under which he would commit an act of violence against a woman. Here's what Jay says:

> Let's say I see a woman and she looks really pretty and really clean and sexy and she's giving off very feminine, sexy vibes. I think, wow I would love to make love to her, but I know she's not interested. It's a tease. A lot of times a woman knows that she's looking really good and she'll use that and flaunt it and it makes me feel like she's laughing at me and I feel degraded . . . If I were actually desperate enough to rape somebody it would be from wanting that person, but also it would be a very spiteful thing, just being able to say 'I have power over you and I can do anything I want with you' because really I feel that they have power over me just by their presence. Just the fact that they can come up to me and just melt me makes me feel like a dummy, makes me want revenge. They have power over me so I want power over them.[86]

Jay speaks not from a feeling of power, but rather from a feeling of powerlessness. 'They have power over me so I want power over them'. In his mind, rape is not the initiation of aggression against a woman, but rather a form of revenge, a retaliation after an injury done to him. But by whom?

Beneke explores this apparent paradox by looking at language. Think of the terms we use in this culture to describe women's beauty and sexuality. We use a language of violence, of aggression. A woman is a 'bombshell', a 'knockout', a 'femme fatale'. She's 'stunning', 'ravishing', 'dressed to kill'. We're 'blown away', 'done in'. Women's beauty is experienced by men as an act of aggression: It invades men's thoughts, elicits unwelcome feelings of desire and longing, makes men feel helpless, powerless, vulnerable. Then, having committed this invasive act of aggression, women reject men, say no to sex, turn them down. Rape is a way to get even, to exact revenge for rejection, to retaliate. These feelings of powerlessness, coupled with the sense of entitlement to women's bodies expressed by the rapists Diana

Scully interviewed, combine in a potent mix—powerlessness and entitlement, impotence and a right to feel in control.

Thus rape is less a problem of a small number of sick individuals and more a problem of social expectations of male behaviour, expectations that stem from gender inequality (disrespect and contempt for women) and may push men toward sexual predation. A completed rape is only the end point on a continuum that includes sexual coercion as well as the premeditated use of alcohol or drugs to dissolve a woman's resistance. In the most famous study of college men's behaviours, Mary Koss and her colleagues found that 1 in 13 men admitted to forcing (or attempting to force) a woman to have sex against her will, but 10 per cent had engaged in unwanted sexual contact, and another 7.2 per cent had been sexually coercive. In another study, Scott Boeringer found that more than 55 per cent had engaged in sexual coercion, 8.6 per cent had attempted rape, and 23.7 per cent had provided drugs or alcohol to a woman in order to have sex with her when she became too intoxicated to consent or resist (which is legally considered rape in most jurisdictions). Such numbers belie arguments that rape is simply the crime of sick individuals.[87]

And just as children face the threat of sexual assault from family members, marriage fails to protect women from rape. In one study of 644 married American women, 12 per cent reported having been raped by their husbands. One researcher estimates that between 14 per cent and 25 per cent of women are forced by their husbands to have sexual intercourse against their will during the course of their marriage, whereas another claims that about one-third of women report having 'unwanted sex' with their partner. In yet another study of 393 randomly selected women, a date or a spouse was more than three times more likely to rape a woman than was a stranger, a friend, or an acquaintance. Fully 50 per cent of the sample reported more than 20 incidents of marital rape, and 48 per cent indicated that rape was part of the common physical abuse by their husbands. In that study, David Finklehor and Kirsti Yllo also found that nearly 75 per cent of the women who had been raped by their husbands had successfully resisted at least once, and that 88 per cent reported that they never enjoyed being forced (in case there was any doubt).[88]

One of the more dramatic changes in rape laws has been the removal of exemptions of husbands from prosecution for rape. Before the 1983 reforms of Canada's rape law contained in Bill C-127, for example, there was no way to prosecute a husband for raping his wife. Indeed, before 1983 many Canadians believed that rape was a crime one could not commit against one's wife. The case was similar in the USA, where as recently as 1985, more than half of states still expressly prohibited prosecution for marital rape, on the grounds that women had no legal right to say no to sex with their husbands. When a woman said 'I do', it apparently also meant 'I will . . . whenever *he* wants to'.

Marital rape is a significant problem in other countries as well, where husbands remain excluded from prosecution. Sexual assault within marriage often goes hand in hand with other forms of intimate violence; in Hong Kong and Quito, Ecuador, for example, as many as 50 per cent of all married women are estimated to be regularly beaten by their husbands. In one study, 80 per cent of rural Egyptian women described beatings as common, particularly when women refused their husbands sex.[89]

Stolen Sisters, the Highway of Tears, and Missing/Murdered Aboriginal Women in Canada

In 1971, Cree high-school student Helen Betty Osborne was abducted by four men on the streets of The Pas, Manitoba. She was taken outside town, beaten, sexually assaulted, and stabbed 64 times before being left in the woods by her murderers. Despite the fact that police received information regarding the perpetrators in 1972, and despite physical evidence found in the car of one of the accused, no charges were laid. Not until 1983 was the case reopened, even though rumours circulated in The Pas about the case—and the perpetrators themselves spoke of it. Finally, in 1986, murder charges were laid against two suspects. One man, Dwayne Archie Johnston, was convicted of the crime and sentenced to life in prison with no chance of parole for ten years.

In the aftermath of the Johnston trial, Aboriginal and non-Aboriginal groups called for inquiry into the causes of the long delay in justice. In the summer of 1989, the Public Inquiry into the Administration of Justice and Aboriginal People heard testimony on 'the murder, the investigation, the attitudes prevailing in the community, the situation of Aboriginal students in The Pas, and the relationship between the police and the Aboriginal community'. The inquiry also examined the conduct of two lawyers and the Manitoba Attorney General's department. Among other findings of the inquiry, one stands out:

> It is clear that Betty Osborne would not have been killed if she had not been Aboriginal. The four men who took her to her death from the streets of The Pas that night had gone looking for an Aboriginal girl with whom to 'party'. They found Betty Osborne. When she refused to party she was driven out of town and murdered. Those who abducted her showed a total lack of regard for her person or her rights as an individual. Those who stood by while the physical assault took place, while sexual advances were made and while she was being beaten to death showed their own racism, sexism, and indifference. Those who knew the story and remained silent must share their guilt.

The Osborne inquiry told Canadians what they might not have wanted to admit, but what most of us who grew up in small towns knew: In The Pas, as in cities and towns across the country, non-Aboriginal men harassed Aboriginal women with impunity; they cruised the streets and bars specifically seeking easy sexual access to Aboriginal girls and women. Among many other elements of racism uncovered by the inquiry was the indifference of the RCMP to complaints of Aboriginal girls and women about sexual harassment.

It is now more than 20 years since the inquiry. Unfortunately, the problem endures. In 2004, Amnesty International released *Stolen Sisters: A Human Rights Response to Discrimination and Violence against Indigenous Women in Canada,* a report that documented the extreme risk of violence faced by Aboriginal women and the frequent indifference of authorities to even the most egregious cases of violence. In March of that same year, the Native Women's Association of Canada (NWAC) launched its Sisters in Spirit campaign to publicize the unsolved murders and disappearances of over 500 Aboriginal women, and to demand change. In 2005, the Sisters in Spirit campaign became a five-year initiative involving NWAC, other Aboriginal groups, and the Canadian government.

British Columbia provides ample evidence of the tragic costs of ignoring this issue. For more than 10 years, women disappeared from Vancouver's Downtown Eastside. Aboriginal women were overrepresented among such disappearances. Because many missing women were Aboriginal, drug-involved, and engaged in sex work, police were often reluctant to treat them as missing persons, despite persistent rumours that a serial killer was on the loose. Only in 2001 did the RCMP and Vancouver Police form the Missing Women Task Force to investigate the disappearances of more than 50 women. In 2002, Robert Pickton, a suburban pig farmer, was charged with the first of what would be over 20 murder charges relating to the disappearances. Trial related to many of the charges is still pending.

In Northern British Columbia, disappearances of women and girls are also well documented, and Aboriginal women and girls are even more overrepresented among the disappeared. Many of these women and girls disappeared along the Yellowhead route (Highway 16) between Prince Rupert and Prince George, a 724-kilometre stretch of lonely highway now known to many as the Highway of Tears. For years, the cases were neglected; for example, teenaged girls who disappeared were seen as runaways who had simply drifted elsewhere, despite family insistence that this was not the case. Not until a young non-Aboriginal tree planter disappeared while hitchhiking outside Prince George in summer 2002 was the issue given a high profile in the province. In 2005, BC's Unsolved Homicide Unit reviewed the files of three murders of teenaged girls, all of whom disappeared between June and December 1994, and whose bodies were found along the highway. Project E-Pana (named after an Inuit goddess who cares for the souls of the deceased in transit) began in fall of that year. Echoing the Downtown Eastside Vancouver experience, the project now has a staff of about 60 people and involves collaboration among police forces. The task force is now investigating at least 18 disappearances and murders of girls and women on BC highways, 10 of which are from the Highway of Tears. Federal Liberals have called for a national inquiry into the disappearances and the treatment of such cases by police.

The unexplained murders and disappearances of so many Aboriginal women and girls across the country highlight the deadly legacies of colonialism and the intertwining of racism with sexual violence. Meanwhile, families of the missing and murdered girls and women, deeply traumatized by these murders and disappearances, have shown tremendous courage and resolve as continuing advocates for their loved ones and the cause of justice.[90]

Gendered Hate Crimes

The murders and disappearances of women in British Columbia link Canada to the phenomenon of **femicide**. Femicide is a term developed by Diana Russell in the 1970s to describe woman-killing as a gendered hate crime. Though there is much debate about what constitutes femicide and what does not, the term has been widely used to describe serial killings of the type found in Ciudad Juárez, Mexico. There, since 1993, at least 400 girls and women have been abducted, horribly tortured and sexually assaulted—sometimes for days—and murdered. Though numerous suspects have been identified and arrested, the Mexican state has been derelict in ending the killings, and some have even suggested police complicity. In Guatemala, meanwhile, the end of decades of civil conflict has not created a peaceful society. Thousands of women have been murdered in that country since 2001. In 2007 alone, more than 700 women and girls were killed, many of them abducted, tortured, and sexually assaulted before their murders. As in Mexico, the Guatemalan state has permitted a climate of impunity for the perpetrators of such crimes, and families have had to endure not only inaction but open allegations by police that their loved ones were prostitutes who 'deserved' to be victimized. Nonetheless, family members have joined together to advocate for their murdered mothers, sisters, and daughters. The concept of femicide allows us to identify in these killings what may be too obvious—they target women and girls precisely because they are women and girls. Femicide is the most common of gendered hate crimes—so common, in fact, that it remains uncommon to view misogynist sexual attacks as hate crimes.[91]

Occasionally, murders happen that defy any other interpretation. Such a case is the infamous 1989 Montreal Massacre at the Ecole Polytechnique, in which 14 female engineering students were murdered by a gunman who identified 'feminists' as his target. Though in the aftermath of the incident many commentators denied that the massacre was anything but the work of a 'sick gunman', the killings are now seen as a gendered hate crime precisely because the murderer explicitly identified the victims' sex as the reason for his activities.

While femicide targets individuals because of their sex, other gendered hate crimes target what Ki Namaste calls 'a perceived transgression of normative sex-gender relations'. Such crimes tend to victimize **sexual-minority** men, women, and youth (or those perceived as such). Like femicide, such crimes have only recently come to be seen as hate crimes. Men charged with assaulting or murdering a gay man could, until quite recently, defend themselves by recourse to '**homosexual panic**', a supposed enraged, out-of-control state brought on by being solicited for sex by a homosexual. In fact, until the 1998 'gay-bashing' murder of Wyoming's Matthew Shepard, attacks on gay, lesbian, and trans people were often ignored, minimized, or even applauded. (The infamous Westboro Baptist Church picketed Shepard's funeral carrying signs that said 'rot in hell'.)

In late 2009, US President Barack Obama signed into law the Matthew Shepard law, which adds sexual orientation, gender identity, and disability as protected categories for the purposes of hate-crime prosecution (gender was added to the list in 1994). The hate provisions in the Canadian Criminal Code, sections 318 and 319, have included sexual orientation since 2004; while gender and gender identity are not explicitly protected categories, they can be considered by judges. Such protection is clearly necessary, given the frequent victimization of sexual-minority North Americans. According to a 2005 US study of 719 self-identified lesbian, gay, and bisexual individuals, 13.1 per cent of the sample had experienced violence based on sexual orientation at least once during adult life. Gay men were the group most likely to have experienced this kind of violence, with 24.9 per cent reporting having experienced anti-gay violence. Reports of threatened violence and other forms of aggression and discrimination were also frequent, and about half of respondents indicated harassment on the basis of sexual orientation. In sum, according to the authors, 'data indicate that approximately 20 per cent of the US sexual minority population has experienced a crime against their person or property since age 18 based on their sexual orientation'. The number of hate crimes against sexual-minority North Americans, serious as it is, is dwarfed by the many such crimes perpetrated against sexual minorities throughout the world. [92]

Perhaps the most vulnerable sexual-minority group globally is the transgendered. Though statistical data on hate crimes against trans people are rare (in part because of constantly evolving definitions of transgender), it is clear that they are frequently victimized both globally and in North America. Transgendered people report incredibly high rates of sexual violence, ranging from 10 to 59 per cent in various studies. Youth are particularly at risk, as exemplified in a US case from summer 2008. Allen Andrade, 32, met 18-year-old Angie Zapata on line. The couple met and spent three days together at Zapata's apartment before Andrade viciously attacked and murdered her. The 'panic' defence was deployed at Andrade's trial—lawyers argued that 'he acted in the heat of passion after discovering that Zapata was biologically male'. The jury in the trial was having none of it, however, and Andrade was convicted of first-degree murder and a bias-motivated (hate) crime—the first time in the USA that such a conviction was obtained in the murder of a transgender person. While the conviction cannot return Angie to her family, the decision sends a clear signal that attacks on the transgendered will no longer enjoy impunity.[93]

Conclusion

Violence takes an enormous social toll not just on its victims but on the very notion of a cohesive and healthy society. It also takes an economic toll, in the massive costs of maintaining legal systems, prisons, and police forces, and in providing care for those harmed by violence. And it takes an incalculable psychological toll.

Violence has many causes, but we cannot understand it without understanding the role of gender within it. 'To curb crime we do not need to expand repressive state measures, but we do need to reduce gender inequalities', writes criminologist James Messerschmidt. Currently, women and children bear a differential burden with regard to fear of crime. And assuaging that fear, as criminologist Elizabeth Stanko puts it, 'will take more than better outdoor lighting'.[94]

Of course, better lighting is a start. And we have to protect women and girls from a culture of violence that so often targets them. But we also have to protect boys 'from a culture of violence that exploits their worst tendencies by reinforcing and amplifying the atavistic values of the masculine mystique'. After all, men are victims of violence—just as men are overwhelmingly its perpetrators.

Often, biological explanations are invoked as evasive strategies. 'Boys will be boys', we say, throwing up our hands in helpless resignation. But even if all violence were biologically programmed by testosterone or the evolutionary demands of reproductive success, we still would have to ask: Are we going to organize our society so as to maximize this propensity for violence or to minimize it? These are political questions, and they demand political answers. 'All violent feelings', wrote the great nineteenth-century British social critic John Ruskin, 'produce in us a falseness in all our impressions of external things'. Until we transform the meaning of gender, we will continue to produce that falseness—with continued tragic consequences.

Summary

Violence remains a key problem in Canada and globally. Violence is also one of the most intractable gender differences. Maleness is a significant predictor of criminal involvement and violence. While the greater male tendency toward violence may be at least partially biologically determined, biological evidence is not a sufficient explanation. Similarly, psychoanalytic and sex role analyses offer some insight, but they are not universalizable. Anthropological explanations suggest that gender inequality and an emphasis on stark gender difference produce societies in which violence and male bravado are celebrated. Thus masculinity's association with violence is a gender difference associated not with biology but with gender inequality.

Nonetheless, women can and do commit violent acts and engage in criminality. About 20 per cent those accused in criminal offences in 2005 were female. This much lower rate of criminality is matched by an even lower rate of *violent* crime; in fact, women tend to cluster in areas of minor crimes, tend to reoffend less, and tend not to escalate their criminal involvement. Still, there is evidence of increasing female violence. While women remain a minority among offenders, increasing female violence is a worrying trend.

In youth, the general patterns of adult violence are replicated. Boys tend to be more violent both toward girls and toward other boys. Peer aggression has become a significant problem for youth, even within schools. School shootings, though rare, have attracted much media and scholarly attention; yet little attention has been paid to gender dynamics within them. Virtually every shooter has been male, and females are over-represented among their victims (and sometimes explicitly targeted). Rising rates of 'girl violence', meanwhile, have attracted great media scrutiny. While much of the panic is overblown, it is true that violent crimes make up a larger proportion of youth crimes than was previously the case; and it is also true that the increase in girls' violent criminality has outstripped the corresponding rate for boys. The degree of violence among youth is cause for concern and demands a gendered analysis.

The gendering of violence also occurs at the institutional and government levels. This is demonstrated by foreign policy and wartime theorizing that uses the terms of hegemonic masculinity to describe (and criticize) national actions. Sexualization in discussions of military policy is well documented. Equally well known is the tragic tendency, in a variety of conflict situations, toward the sexual assault (and, sometimes, murder) of 'enemy' women and children. More recently, this tendency has affected newly sex-integrated armed forces, as suggested by the enormous number of sexual assault complaints laid by US soldiers in Iraq.

The family has been seen as a refuge from such violent tendencies. But for too many people, the family is also a site of violence. Though women are fully capable of family violence, most family violence is perpetrated by males (husbands, fathers, sons, brothers). Regardless of the sex of their perpetrators, such acts rest on the logic of patriarchal violence.

Intimate-partner violence still accounts for over half of all incidents of family violence reported to police. Women far outnumber men in numbers of injuries, and their likelihood of being victimized by their spouses is greater. The idea of gender symmetry recognizes that women use spousal violence too; however, it grossly distorts the nature of spousal violence, and ideas of gender symmetry rest on CTS data that 'levels' all forms of violence. Nature, severity, and context of spousal violence are gendered. This becomes clear when spousal homicide is considered; women are significantly more likely to be killed by their spouses than are men. Intimate-partner violence also interacts with ethnic and class issues. In addition, immigrant women may face a greater risk of spousal abuse, and are certainly made vulnerable by immigrant-specific factors. The most significant differences in levels of intimate-partner violence emerge between Aboriginal and non-Aboriginal Canadians.

Violence against children is widespread all over the world and is licit (legal) in most countries. Though most North American parents favour corporal punishment, its negative effects on children have been well documented, and pediatricians warn against the practice. While most parents do not physically abuse their children, most physical abuse is associated with corporal punishment. Men are overrepresented among assaulters of children (relative to other family member). Nonetheless, mothers' presence as 21 per cent of those accused in family-related assaults against children suggests that women are capable of using patriarchal violence against children. An ultimate form of such violence is the 'honour killing', which differs from family violence in several significant ways but shares its logic of domination and control.

Domination and control are also hallmarks of sexual assault. Sexual assault has often been seen as synonymous with rape, and as such has been analyzed by sociobiologists and evolutionary psychologists, who argue that it reflects a male evolutionary strategy. Cross-cultural studies of rape, however, suggest that it is a cultural phenomenon, varying widely from place to place but associated with male domination. While psychologists tend to look at the processes that lead someone to become a rapist, sociologists emphasize the general 'normalcy' of rapists and rape.

Sexual assault is widely reported in North America relative to other industrialized regions. Most victims of Canadian police-reported sexual assaults in 2003 were children and youth. Girls are much more likely to be victimized than boys, and virtually all perpetrators are men and male youth. Many children and youth are assaulted by male family members. Similarly, many married women report being sexually assaulted by their male partners; though such assaults have been illegal in Canada and much of the USA since the 1980s, marital rape remains legal in much of the world. Marital, familial, and acquaintance sexual assault are much more common than assault by strangers. And sexual assault itself is far from strange; it is a problem not of a few sick individuals, but of society.

Sexual assault interacts with racialization and other class and ethnic issues. This can be seen in the murders and disappearances of Aboriginal women and girls in Canada, which has exposed patterns of sexual victimization and, sometimes, official indifference. Recent events suggest that such indifference may be changing, thanks to efforts of families and advocates.

Indifference toward other forms of gendered violence is also changing. Horrific woman-killings are increasingly understood as femicide, a kind of killing that targets women because they are women. Other forms of violence target those perceived as gender nonconformists. Gay, lesbian, bisexual, and trans people report high levels of victimization by targeted violence. Canadian and (recently changed) US laws recognize these as hate crimes.

A society without violence may be a utopian dream, but minimizing violence should be a high priority for all of us, both within Canada and globally. A good way to start is through analysis of the ways in which violence is produced and reproduced in a gendered society.

Questions for Critical Thinking

1.   What accounts for boys' and men's greater tendency to commit violent acts?
2.   Do you believe that girls and women are becoming 'more violent'? What factors limit and/or encourage female violence?
3.   Are 'honour killings' a form of domestic violence, in your opinion?
4.   Is rape a crime of sex or a crime of violence?
5.   What kind of killings of women and girls would you consider gendered hate crimes?

Key Terms

corporal punishment

familicide

family-class immigrants

femicide

gender symmetry

homicide

homosexual panic

'honour' killing

intimate-partner violence (IPV)

patriarchal violence

rape

sexual assault

sexual-minority

stalking

Epilogue: The Future of Gender in a Globalizing World

'A Degendered Society'?

> The principle which regulates the existing social relations between the two sexes—the legal subordination of one sex to the other—is wrong in itself, and now one of the chief hindrances to human improvement; and . . . it ought to be replaced by a principle of perfect equality, admitting no power or privilege on the one side, nor disability on the other.
>
> —John Stuart Mill, The Subjection of Women (1869)

Early in the twenty-first century, we live in a world that would have astonished John Stuart Mill and his contemporaries; and we have transformed gender relations in ways that Mill cannot have even imagined. We now stand upon the brink of pure possibility, looking into an uncharted expanse of the future. Among the many urgent questions we confront as human beings—some of which concern our very future as a species—we now must consider: What kind of society do we want to live in? What will be the gender arrangements of that society?

To see gender differences as intransigent leads also to a political resignation about the possibilities of social change and increased gender equality. Those who proclaim that men and women come from different planets would have us believe that the best we can hope for is a sort of interplanetary détente, an uneasy truce in which we exasperatedly accept the inherent and intractable foibles of the other sex.

This book, in contrast, has argued that women and men are more alike than we are different, that we're not at all from different planets. We've argued that it is gender inequality that produces the differences we do observe and that that inequality also produces the cultural impulse to search for such differences, even when there is little or no basis for them in reality. We've also argued that gender is not a property of individuals, which is accomplished by socialization, but rather a set of relationships produced in our social interactions with one another and within gendered institutions. As gender inequality has been reduced, so too have the gendered differences observable in individuals and institutions.

Indeed, this book has presented evidence of a significant gender convergence within North America over the past half-century. Whether we look at sexual behaviour, friendship dynamics, efforts to balance work and family life, or women's and men's experiences and aspirations in education or the workplace, we find the gender gap growing ever smaller. (One exception to this process, as we saw in the last chapter, is violence.)

Many of our ideas about gender have rested on ideas about biology and the body. As we have seen, much of the research on biologically rooted sex difference is problematic to say the least. Moreover, the body has arguably become less significant and more malleable than ever before in human history. Our ability to change biological sex is one clear example of this. But so is the widespread use, in North America and much of the global north, of birth control. And what about the growth of Internet-mediated communication, which permits the adoption of completely new identities without links to our embodiment? These are all examples of how the relationship between sex and gender is being broken down.

A recent book by Judith Lorber makes a case for degendering. She argues that, as one reviewer put it, 'degendering reduces gender inequality by eliminating gender difference as a meaningful consequential component of institutions and identities'. Such an argument, however utopian, still puts the cart before the horse, claiming that eliminating difference will lead to eliminating inequality. It is just as important to start by eliminating inequality, allowing difference to recede until the variations among us—by race, age, ethnicity, sexuality, and, yes, biological sex—prove largely epiphenomenal.[1]

This may seem a rarefied debate given the persistent gender issues in Canadian society. Globally speaking, it is even more absurd to speak of a severing of the relationship between sex and gender, or of processes of degendering. Globally, gender inequality remains a massive problem. Poverty, maternal and infant mortality, domestic and sexual violence, abuse and neglect of girl children, differential education rates, exploitation in employment, and an absence of reproductive choices characterize much of the world.

Within Canada, the importance of gender convergence is overshadowed by persistent inequalities between Aboriginal and non-Aboriginal Canadians (and between visible minorities and others); poverty; discrimination; precarious employment of many women (particularly immigrants); and a plethora of other gendered issues.

In some cases, gendered transformations in the global North have brought ambivalent changes to the global South. For example, as North American women have entered the workforce, many have delegated responsibility for daily child care to women from lower socio-economic groups and to immigrant women (many admitted as immigrants for precisely this purpose). While many North American families struggle with poverty, many others have experienced a growth in disposable income because of women's earning power. This disposable income has in part fuelled the growth in consumption that brings employment to a new 'flexible' global workforce made up, disproportionately, of young women who work in product assembly in countries around the world. Finally, the tremendous growth of tourism in the late twentieth century has not only brought economic growth to many regions, but has fuelled the mobility of sexual exploitation, from trafficking to sex tourism. We can, therefore, no longer divorce our countries from the gendered realities of the rest of the world. While we highlight gender convergence and the many dramatic changes in gender, therefore, we must also acknowledge that the gendered society, with its many inequalities, is alive and well in Canada and abroad—and that globalization has in fact produced new constellations of gender inequality.[2]

Yet there are signs of change, growth, and convergence everywhere. Throughout the world, the dawn of the twenty-first century has seen increasing demands for women's rights, which have officially become a global priority. Domestic and sexual violence laws have been reformed in many nations, and civil-society groups are demanding not only legal reforms but social ones. For example, India enacted a Protection of Women from Domestic Violence Act in 2006, largely in response to feminist campaigns, replacing a 1980s law on marital 'cruelty'. Though enforcement of the law is not yet uniform, advocates note that '[h]aving a law on domestic violence has the merit of putting in place a norm that violence against women is unacceptable.'[3]

Indian women have not only agitated for new laws, but are pushing for cultural and social change outside the legal arena. This was amply demonstrated by a humorous but powerful campaign launched by Indian women in early 2009 in response to extremist attacks on 'loose' young women who went to pubs in the city of Mangalore. Instead of being intimidated by the attacks, women formed a Facebook support group. When extremists insisted they would target women who went on dates for Valentine's Day, women organized a protest that involved sending 40,000 pairs of pink 'chaddis' (panties) to the fundamentalists' head office. Though social tensions over women's changing roles are far from resolved, the 'pink chaddi' campaign halted the violence and led to the arrest of the extremists' 'chief mentor'.[4]

Extremists lament changes to gendered rules as 'defeminizing' women. If submission is, as we have seen, one of the traits most associated with femininity globally, then critics are right; women *are* being defeminized. The elimination of gender inequality *will* eliminate many of the differences we observe (or think we see) between the sexes. But is this such a bad thing? Many of the gender differences we identify amount to an arbitrary dividing of human potentialities. Love, tenderness, nurturance, dependence; competence, ambition, assertion, autonomy—these are *human* qualities, and all human beings—both women and men—should have equal access to them. What a strange notion, indeed, that such emotions should be labelled as masculine or feminine, when they are so deeply human and when both women and men are so easily capable of a so much fuller range of feelings.

Strange, and also a little sad. 'Perhaps nothing is so depressing an index of the inhumanity of the male supremacist mentality as the fact that the more genial human traits are assigned to the underclass: affection, response to sympathy, kindness, cheerfulness', was the way feminist writer Kate Millett put it in her landmark book, *Sexual Politics*, first published in 1969.[5]

So much has changed since then. And these enormous changes will only accelerate in the next few decades, both in North America and around the world. The society of the third millennium will increasingly degender traits and behaviours.

Such a process may sound naively optimistic, but the signs of change are everywhere around us. In fact, the historical evidence points exactly in that direction. In Canada and elsewhere, the twentieth century witnessed an amazing transformation in the lives, roles, and rights of women—possibly the most significant transformation in gender relations in world history. From the rights to vote and work, asserted early in the century, to the rights to enter every conceivable workplace, educational institution, and the military in the latter half, women shook the foundations of the gendered society. And at the end of the twentieth century, Canadian women had accomplished half a revolution—a transformation of their opportunities to be workers and mothers.

The second half of the transformation of gender is just beginning and may be far more difficult to accomplish than the first. That's because the transformation of the twenty-first century involves the transformation of men's lives.

Men are just beginning to realize that the 'traditional' definition of masculinity leaves them unfulfilled and dissatisfied. The nineteenth-century ideology of separate spheres justified gender inequality based on putative natural differences between the sexes. What was normative—enforced by sanction—was asserted to be normal, a part of the nature of things. Women have spent the better part of a century making clear that such an ideology did violence to their experiences, effacing the work outside the home that women actually performed and enforcing a definition of femininity that allowed only partial expression of their humanity.

It did the same for men, of course—valorizing some emotions and experiences, discrediting others. As with women, it left men with only partially fulfilled lives. Only recently, though, have men begun to chafe at the restrictions that such an ideology placed on their humanity.

Some men (and a few women) express their frustration and confusion by hoping and praying for a return to the old gender regime, the very separation of spheres that made both women *and* men unhappy.

But the direction of the gendered society in the new century and the new millennium is for women and men to become more *equal,* for those traits and behaviours heretofore labelled as masculine and feminine—competence and compassion, ambition and affection—to be labelled as distinctly human qualities, accessible to both women and men who are grown-up enough to claim them. This suggests a form of gender proteanism—a temperamental and psychological flexibility, the ability to adapt to one's environment with a full range of emotions and abilities. The protean self, articulated by psychiatrist Robert Jay Lifton, is a self that can embrace difference, contradiction, and complexity, a self that is mutable and flexible in a rapidly changing world.[6] Such a transformation is urgently needed if men, women, and children all over the world are to embrace the challenges and opportunities of our century. Our top priority can no longer be to uphold the systems of gendered domination that have persisted for so long. Rather, we must focus on our lives and potential as human beings with responsibilities to the earth and one another, and with full rights and dignity; we must focus on building a fully human society, not a gendered one.

Glossary

ablism prejudice on the basis of ability, with two main features: first, ignoring or rendering invisible of people with disabilities, and second, viewing people with disabilities as fundamentally defined and limited by disabilities. Ablism has obvious links to overt discrimination against the disabled, but this is not its only form. (Chapter 11)

Aboriginal a member of one of three indigenous groups (Inuit, First Nations, and Métis) recognized by the Canadian Constitution (Chapter 6)

alliance theorists those who study the constitution of society from the perspective of family formation, in particular emphasizing how women 'circulate' as marriage partners in a given society, and how acceptable marriage partners are defined as 'not-kin' in varying ways (Chapter 4)

alyha among the Mojave people, a boy who underwent a transformation to the social role of a female (Chapter 4)

androgen insensitivity syndrome a defect on the A chromosome that impairs androgen reception, preventing the XY fetus from responding to testosterone. Chromosomally male, AIS children are born resembling girls, and are generally raised as girls. In many cases they are 'diagnosed' as intersexed only when they fail to menstruate. (Chapter 2)

androgenital syndrome (AGS) the previously used name for **congenital adrenal hyperplasia** (see below) (Chapter 2)

androgyny for Sandra Bem, 'the combined presence of the socially valued, stereotypic, feminine and masculine characteristics'. Bem originally argued that the most androgynous individuals were psychologically healthiest. (Chapter 3)

beauty myth according to Naomi Wolf, the beauty myth is a system of social control that encourages women to focus on their appearances to the detriment of full development of their humanity. Wolf identifies the development of this myth as a retrenchment of male domination in the face of women's increasing equality in the twentieth century. (Chapter 11)

berdache the term used by anthropologists to describe third-gender individuals of male sex. The term 'female berdache' is also sometimes used in anthropological literature. This term is regarded as offensive by First Nations and other Aboriginal people. (See **two-spirited**.) (Chapter 4)

biological determinism the view that the behaviour and character of an organism, group, or system are determined by biological factors. Most careful scientists shun true determinism, but determinist tendencies can be found both among scientists and in popular culture. (Chapters 1, 2)

biological essentialism closely related to the idea of biological determinism; an argument that rests on the naturalness of social relations and their rootedness in biology. This stance is generally taken by social conservatives, but recently, both feminist and gay activists have adopted essentialist positions. (Chapter 2)

bisexual sexually attracted to either men or women. Debates still rage over the existence of the phenomenon and its definition, for example, whether one needs to be equally attracted to both sexes in order to be judged bisexual. (Chapter 10)

bona fide occupational requirement (BFOR) a BFOR is a true requirement of a job that merits a possibly discriminatory effect. For example, to work in a warehouse, one might have to meet height and strength requirements that have the effect of discriminating against many women and all disabled people. Because the requirement is a BFOR, the discrimination is legal. (Chapter 8)

breadwinner an individual whose earnings support dependants. This term arose in the nineteenth century, when most families relied upon multiple sources of income. It has always been gendered; even when women supported families, they have been rarely seen as breadwinners. (Chapter 6)

bride price common in various Asian and African societies, the bride price is a sum of money paid by a groom to his wife's family, generally thought to exist in order to compensate the bride's family for the loss of the daughter's productive labour and for her social value (Chapter 10)

bukkake a form of pornography that emphasizes the use of a woman by many men, with its most important feature being communal ejaculation onto the woman's face. A December 2009 Google search of this term generated more than 7 million hits. (Chapter 10)

castration anxiety for Freud, a deep-seated fear of castration arising when boys see female genitalia and conclude that girls and women have been castrated. Hence, 'if it happened to Mom, it can happen to me!' Castration anxiety is most important during the Oedipal crisis. (Chapter 3)

chick lit a literary genre that came to prominence in the 1990s. Chick lit features the adventures (romantic and otherwise) of young, single working women. (Chapter 9)

child poverty the phenomenon whereby those under the age of 18 live below the poverty line as established by the LICO (Chapter 6)

chilly climate the phenomenon whereby one is 'frozen out' in a particular environment. One may be tolerated, but one feels excluded and is not welcomed as members of other groups apparently are. (Chapter 7)

circumcision the excision of the foreskin of the penis to permanently expose the glans. The term 'female circumcision' is sometimes used to describe procedures more analogous to the removal of the penis than to what we call 'circumcision' in males. (See FGM/FGC.) Though circumcision exists in many societies, its routine use on infants in North America is being abandoned. (Chapter 4)

clan a group of people united by kinship, whether actual or symbolic. In First Nations societies before European contact, clans were the basic social unit and often connoted not only kinship, but particular social roles and responsibilities. (Chapter 6)

clitoridectomy the excision of the clitoris, sometimes performed on girls with masculinized genitalia (Chapter 2)

cognitive development theory Jean Piaget originally defined cognitive development theory, arguing that mental development takes place in a set of relatively orderly and discrete stages involving greater complexity at each level. Lawrence Kohlberg applied this to gender acquisition, arguing that children 'learn' gender cognitively, according to their level of reasoning at different stages. (Chapter 3)

colourism within racialized communities, 'colourism' refers to a system that privileges and values lighter skin and rewards lighter-skinned people. It may also privilege certain other features, e.g., 'good' (straighter, non-kinky) hair in African-descent communities. It should be noted, however, that within 'white' culture, there is also 'good' (blond) hair. (Chapter 11)

common-law marriage a system of customary marriage by which people who present themselves as spouses and fulfill certain criteria (established provincially) are entitled to legal recognition, though not necessarily all of the rights and responsibilities of legally wedded spouses (Chapter 6)

companionate marriage an ideal of marriage as a loving partnership, which became more common after the late eighteenth century and eventually implied free choice and 'marriage for love'. Not to be confused with current practices of egalitarian, childless, dissoluble partnerships sometimes described under the same name. (Chapter 10)

compulsory heterosexuality a theory first articulated by Adrienne Rich, who described heterosexuality as a social institution based on the assumption that heterosexuality was innate and all other forms of sexual expression either deviant or simply invisible (Chapter 10)

confirmation bias the phenomenon whereby a few cases of the expected behaviour confirm the belief, especially when the behaviour is attention-getting or widely reported (Chapter 5)

congenital adrenal hyperplasia (CAH) one of a number of conditions producing intersexed children. In CAH, chromosomally female fetuses undergo abnormal hormonal development in utero and are born with masculinized genitalia, though they have the potential to bear children. Genetically male fetuses are also affected, though not in ways that create ambiguity of sex. (Chapter 2)

consciousness-raising a technique of analysis, pioneered by North American feminists and Latin American political activists, that emphasized raising awareness of social and political issues through small-group discussion of everyday issues and experiences (Chapter 5)

corporal punishment physical punishment inflicted upon the body of someone. Historically, corporal punishment was licit, and widely used against a variety of groups, including wives, slaves, employees, soldiers, and servants. Corporal punishment of children remains legal in North America (though not in some European countries). (Chapter 12)

couvade the term used by anthropologists to describe a variety of rituals observed by men whose wives are pregnant in order to 'mimic' pregnancy. Men perform the same acts and adhere to the same restrictions as their pregnant wives, and may even feign morning sickness or childbirth itself. (Chapter 4)

cult of compulsive masculinity Talcott Parsons' theorized result of the long period of contact with femininity characteristic of boys in modern nuclear families. Because boys must rebel against femininity, being a 'bad boy' becomes a way of establishing a masculine identity. For Parsons, this 'cult' is associated with hypermasculine and/or violent behaviour. (Chapter 3)

cultural determinism the belief that the cultures in which we are raised determine our character, personalities, emotional lives, and behaviours. (Compare with **biological determinism**.) (Chapter 4)

cultural relativism the belief, developed and named by anthropologists, that any individual's beliefs and behaviours should be understood in the context of his or her own culture rather than as the product of innate or universal tendencies and values (Chapter 4)

culturally scripted based on a pattern of speech and interaction that is normative within a particular group or culture (Chapter 10)

date rape non-consensual intercourse forced on someone by someone s/he knows, either through physical force or through coercion. (Chapter 10)

deceptive distinctions differences between men and women that appear to be gender differences, but may be the result of different positions within society (Chapter 1)

descent theorists in anthropology, those who study kinship; in particular, they examine the ways in which cultures think about and structure consanguineal ('blood') relationships (Chapter 4)

deviance neutralization rationalization strategies engaged in to minimize the extent to which one deviates from a real or perceived norm. For example, a woman who worries about how her higher income affects her husband's self-esteem might claim that his work pays less, but is higher-level than hers, or might actually minimize her earnings. (Chapter 8)

difference feminism in contrast to **liberal feminism**, which emphasizes the equality or sameness of men and women, this tendency within feminism focuses on the differences between men and women, calling for a valuation of women's distinct traits and abilities and, in some cases, focusing on separation from the world and values of men (Chapter 5)

differential socialization associated with the 'nurture' side of the nature-nurture debate, this perspective asserts that men and women are different because they are socialized differently from birth, thus acquiring 'masculine' or 'feminine' traits, behaviours, and attitudes (Chapter 1)

disability as defined by the World Health Organization, disability is 'an umbrella term, covering impairments, activity limitations, and participation restrictions. An impairment is a problem in body function or structure; an activity limitation is a difficulty encountered by an individual in executing a task or action; while a participation restriction is a problem experienced by an individual in involvement in life situations. Thus disability is a complex phenomenon, reflecting an interaction between features of a person's body and features of the society in which he or she lives'. (Chapter 11)

Divorce Act federal legislation introduced in 1968, and revised in 1985, governing the provision of divorce in Canada (Chapter 6)

dopamine a brain chemical or neurotransmitter associated with pleasure (Chapter 10)

double standard a moral code that prescribes different things for different groups; most commonly associated with differential (and conflicting) sexual standards prescribed to men and women (Chapter 10)

dowry a sum of money settled upon a bride by her family, or transferred to her groom, at marriage (Chapter 10)

educational premium the monetary return one receives by pursuing further education. This can be calculated statistically based on average earnings for people with varying degrees of education. (Chapter 7)

ego a component of Freud's concept of the psyche. It is the rational, problem-solving portion of our personality that translates **id** impulses into effective strategies for gratification. (Chapter 3)

Electra complex Carl Jung's name for what Freud called the 'feminine Oedipus attitude'. The term describes a girl's situation during the Oedipal crisis, when she, like the boy, discovers the anatomical distinction between the sexes and believes that she and her mother have been castrated. Experiencing 'penis envy' as a result, she first transfers her desire to her father, competing with her mother, and eventually to the desire for a baby of her own. (See **penis envy**.) (Chapter 3)

emphasized femininity R.W. Connell's model of female gender ideology, which asserts that femininity is displayed as compliance with gender inequality and is 'oriented to accommodating the interests and desires of men' (Chapter 1)

employment equity a term coined in the 1980s by Justice Rosalie Abella to describe a process of planning for full workplace integration of Canada's four equity groups (women, Aboriginal people, people with disabilities, and visible minorities). Employment Equity distinguishes itself from USA-style affirmative action. (Chapter 8)

estrus in most female mammals, the reproductive cycle that produces periods of sexual receptivity (often described as 'heat') that coincide with ovulation; generally these periods of estrus are accompanied by external signals (visual, olfactory, etc.) (Chapter 2)

ethic of care Carol Gilligan's term for the mode of moral reasoning she found more prevalent in women than in men. This 'different voice' makes moral judgments on the basis of the interdependence of human beings and the effects of actions on them. (See **ethic of justice**.) (Chapter 3)

ethic of justice Gilligan's term for the mode of reasoning she sees as more characteristic of men and of institutions in Western society; ethic of justice describes moral reasoning based on principle and abstract concepts of justice (See **ethic of care**.) (Chapter 3)

eugenics the theory that natural selection can be assisted through conscious efforts to improve human populations, either by preventing the production of the 'unfit' or by increasing the health and fitness of reproductive populations (Chapter 2)

evolutionary psychology the field of study that studies and explains human psychology and mind as the result of evolutionary adaptation. Like sociobiology, evolutionary psychology uses studies of animal behaviour to understand human psychology. (Chapter 2)

expressive roles according to Talcott Parsons, these roles exist to perpetuate the kinship system;

they demand tenderness and nurturing (See **instrumental roles**.) (Chapter 3)

expressive traits associated with co-operation, warmth, sensitivity, and communication (Chapter 10)

extended family a term used to refer to kin beyond the nuclear family, whether they share the same household or not (Chapter 6)

external world the fourth component of Freud's notion of the psyche; the external world is experienced as frequently thwarting the **id**'s desire (Chapter 3)

familicide the murder of one's spouse and at least one of one's children (Chapter 12)

family-class immigrants according to Canadian immigration law, family-class immigrants are those who come to Canada through sponsorship by a spouse, common-law partner, conjugal partner, parent, or other eligible relative (Chapter 12)

family-friendly workplace policies policies and workplace cultural changes that reduce conflict between workers' employment and their family responsibilities. Examples include child care, support for breastfeeding mothers, provisions for eldercare, flexible working arrangements such as job sharing or teleworking, leave provisions, and employee assistance programs. (Chapter 8)

female genital mutilation/female genital cutting (**FGM/FGC**) a number of practices that involve the alteration of the female genitalia in forms ranging from the removal of the hood of the clitoris (analogous to male circumcision) to infibulation. The term female genital mutilation is preferred by some scholars, while others argue that it places a stigma on women who have undergone the procedure and on cultures that practise it. People of this opinion prefer the term female genital cutting. (Chapter 4)

femicide literally, this means the murder of a woman. Scholars generally use it to refer to a killing that targets someone because she is female, though those who use the term vary in the breadth of their definitions. (Chapter 12)

fetishized in this context, to be made into an object of habitual erotic fixation (Chapter 11)

first-person shooter a video-game genre focused on shooting in which one plays 'through the eyes' or from the visual perspective of an avatar (Chapter 9)

first-wave feminism a social movement that lasted from approximately 1850 to the end of the First World War. While first-wave feminism emphasized women's legal status and, eventually, suffrage, first-wave activists took on many social issues. (Chapter 5)

functionalism a school of thought that maintains that the sex-based division of labour arose because it was necessary for the survival of early human societies. Some functionalists also argue that the preservation of the division of labour might be an evolutionary imperative. (Chapter 4)

gaming the playing of video games on consoles, on PCs, or on-line. (In Canada, the term 'gaming' as used by governments refers to legal gambling, which is not discussed in this text.) (Chapter 9)

gender the meanings attached to the anatomical differences between men and women, or, according to feminist theorist Joan Scott, 'a way of referring to the social construction of the relationship between the sexes' (Chapter 1)

gender complementarity the idea that men and women have distinct talents, characters, roles, and spheres of influence that are not ranked hierarchically (that is, in a system of male dominance) (Chapter 6)

gender constancy Lawrence Kohlberg's concept to explain children's realization, at approximately age six, that gender is permanent and fixed (Chapter 3)

gender divisions according to Joan Acker, these are the ways in which 'ordinary organizational practices produce the gender patterning of jobs, wages, and hierarchies, power and subordination' (Chapter 5)

gender dysphoria a psychiatric category describing persistent discomfort with one's biological sex (Chapter 11)

gender intensification this term refers to two linked phenomena of adolescence: (a) increased pressure to conform to gendered expectations; and (b) an increased rigidity regarding gender norms (Chapter 7)

gender schema an understanding regarding gender and gender roles, allowing traits, behaviours, personalities, and occupations to be assessed as 'for males' or 'for females'. This idea is important to both Kohlberg's **cognitive development theory** and Bem's **gender schema theory**. (Chapter 3)

gender schema theory in one important version, developed by Sandra Bem through her use of the Bem Sex Role Inventory (BSRI), gender schema theory argues that though children do develop ideas of gender through gender schemas, adults vary in

the rigidity of their schemas. The healthiest individuals, Bem argued, were those with less polarized views of gender. (Chapter 3)

gender symmetry in studies of intimate-partner violence, gender symmetry refers to the concept of relative 'balance' in woman-to-man and man-to-woman violence. This theory has been powerfully debunked by Russell Dobash and others. (Chapter 12)

gender verification see **sex testing** (Chapter 11)

gendered society any society in which social institutions reproduce and reinforce dominant definitions of gender and 'discipline' those who deviate from these definitions (Chapter 1)

glass ceiling barriers (often informal, unconscious, or invisible) to the advancement of a qualified person within a given organization, solely on the basis of that person's sex or minority status (Chapter 8)

glass cellar Warren Farrell's term for the clustering of male workers within hazardous occupations (Chapter 8)

glass escalator the phenomenon whereby men in female-dominated occupations experience preferential hiring and promotion (Chapter 8)

grrrl power a cultural phenomenon that emerged in the 1990s, emphasizing (in its adult form) female assertiveness, individualism, and the power of sexuality (Chapter 6)

hegemonic in this book, something that is upheld as the model; hegemonic ideals may be contested, but cannot be ignored because of their cultural power and ubiquity (Chapter 1)

hegemonic masculinity a theory developed in the 1980s, most notably by R.W. Connell, to explain male gender ideology. There may be many versions of masculinity operating in a culture, but only one is 'culturally honoured' or hegemonic, and other masculinities are organized under it in a hierarchical fashion. This theory emphasizes competition among men for power and dominance within systems of gender inequality or patriarchy. (Chapter 1)

hidden curriculum the lessons and rules learned in school that are not part of what is formally transmitted by the teachers and the official curriculum (Chapter 7)

hijras in India, biological males or intersexed people who adopt female social identities. *Hijras* once formed a distinct caste and now constitute a socially marginalized community that nonetheless has sacred and religious significance (and, as of 2009, legal recognition in India and Pakistan). (Chapter 4)

homicide the killing of a human being by another; both murder and manslaughter are forms of homicide (Chapter 12)

homophobia an exaggerated fear and/or hatred of homosexuals and homosexuality (Chapters 3, 10)

homosexual panic a purported state of psychotic rage brought on by receiving unwanted homosexual advances. Homosexual panic has been successfully used as a defence against criminal charges (including murder) in a variety of nations. (Chapter 12)

'honour' killing family murder, often involving multi-party collusion or multiple perpetrators. These murders target someone, almost always a girl or woman, perceived to have brought shame upon the family. (Chapter 12)

hooking up a sexual encounter between two people who may or may not know one another as friends or acquaintances, and who may or may not engage in sex more than once; whatever its other variations, hooking up implies a casual sexual encounter without commitment to a relationship (Chapter 10)

horizontal segregation segregation within occupations in different fields that are roughly similar in terms of education and skill, for example secretarial work and truck driving (Chapter 8)

hostile environment originally an American legal category that describes a workplace where workers are subjected to sexual harassment and thus fear the workplace. The concept is easily transferred to schools. (Chapter 7)

hostile environment sexual harassment the creation of a threatening and hostile atmosphere aimed at making women (or others) feel unwelcome, unsafe, and compromised (Chapter 8)

hwame among the Mojave people, a girl who underwent transformation to a male social role (Chapter 4)

hypermasculinity the exaggerated display of or adherence to behaviours, traits, and beliefs seen as masculine (Chapter 4)

id a component of Freud's concept of the psyche. It represents basic animal needs, and 'knows' only that it wants gratification. It lacks both morality and the means to get what it wants. (Chapter 3)

imperial manhood a concept that linked 'manliness' to one's duty to the British Empire and to the success and superiority of British culture; this idea had strong effects on education in the nineteenth century (Chapter 7)

Indian Act federal legislation of 1876, revised periodically since then, that governs and defines registered Indians (First Nations) and their reserves (Chapter 6)

infibulation generally performed on girls, this is a practice that involves the removal of the clitoris and much of the tissue of the external genitalia, after which the vaginal opening is either stitched or held together with thorns until it heals into a closed structure with only a small opening to permit urination and menstruation (Chapter 4)

institution a structure governing the behaviour of individuals and ensuring the society's smooth functioning. Though institutions are ever-changing, they nonetheless have a permanence or longevity that exceeds that of the individual. The study and theorizing of institutions is central to the social sciences, and particularly to sociology. Sociologists identify five primary institutions (family, religion, school, media, and peers) and innumerable social ('secondary') institutions. These might be formal—clearly locatable and often governmental or legally constituted (e.g., law or banking). Other institutions are informal—customary and based in behaviour (e.g., politeness or civility). An institution might partake of both of these characteristics, as when we discuss the 'institution of marriage'. (Chapter 5)

institutional gender neutrality the idea that while people have gender, institutions are gender-neutral (rather than being the product of historical and social constructions in which gender played a great role). The assumption that institutions are gender-neutral can obscure the importance of gender within them. (Chapter 1)

instrumental traits associated with competition, assertiveness, and action (Chapter 10)

instrumental roles for Talcott Parsons, these roles exist to perpetuate the occupational system. They demand rationality, autonomy, and competitiveness. (See **expressive roles**.) (Chapter 3)

'interplanetary theory' of gender difference the idea that men are from Mars and women are from Venus, or that men and women are 'opposites' who exhibit complete and universal gender difference (Chapter 1)

intersexed/intersexuals people affected by hormonal and chromosomal disorders leading to some degree of ambiguity in biological sex. In the last third of the twentieth century, at least some of the intersexed were subjected to radical and aggressive interventions to 'recreate' them as 'properly' sexed individuals. They were also studied for evidence of the biological basis of gendered behaviour. (Chapter 2)

intimacy the feeling of closeness, warmth, and relationship with another (Chapter 10)

intimate-partner violence (IPV) physical, sexual, and emotional abuse and/or threats directed against an intimate partner, whether in a marital or non-marital relationship. IPV may occur within heterosexual or non-heterosexual relationships. (Chapter 12)

invisibility of privilege the idea that those who are dominant in a society may not be aware of their dominance or special status, but can see themselves as 'universal' human beings or citizens. Because of the invisibility of privilege, people may not be aware of the extent of discrimination and may become angry when confronted with evidence or assertions of racism or sexism. (See **privilege**.) (Chapter 1)

Kinsey scale a seven-point scale measuring sexual orientation on which research subjects can be placed by way of a questionnaire. The scale was first published by Alfred Kinsey in his 1948 study of male sexual behaviour. (Chapter 10)

lad lit a literary genre sometimes seen as the less successful 'little brother' of **chick lit**. Lad lit highlights the coming to adulthood of young men who are often grappling with self-doubt or confusion about the meaning of manhood. (Chapter 9)

lateralized brain lateralization can refer to the relative domination of one hemisphere over another or, more commonly, to the location of a function (for example, language) in one hemisphere of the brain. In popular culture, this is often grossly oversimplified to describe individuals as 'left-brain' or 'right-brain' people. (Chapter 2)

LGBTQ Lesbian, Gay, Bi, Trans, Queer, Questioning. This is, today, the most commonly used term to encompass all non-heterosexuals. (Chapter 7)

lesbian feminism a social movement within 1970s feminism that contributed a critique of heterosexuality as an institution and, in some cases, advocated lesbianism or separatism as a political option (Chapter 5)

liberal feminism a form of feminism that focuses on legal remedies for inequality between men and women and creating the most gender-neutral society possible (Chapter 5)

LICO the Low-Income Cut-Off, a boundary established by Statistics Canada that serves as Canada's unofficial measure of poverty. Statistics Canada establishes a number of LICOs based on family size and size of community of residence. (Chapter 6)

male breadwinner/female housewife model a theoretical construct, once supported by legislation and policy, that saw the family as constituted by an earner whose wages supported a dependent non-earner. In this model, 'his' role was to provide, 'hers' to care. (Chapter 8)

male dominance a system that grants greater power, value, authority, and access to resources to men. Most often, in systems of male dominance, men's authority is reinforced throughout society and its social, political, religious, cultural, and economic institutions. Male dominance is sometimes referred to as 'patriarchy', though this term is controversial when used as a synonym for male dominance. (Chapter 1)

male gaze the dominant cultural way of seeing, which adopts the perspective of a desiring heterosexual male subject. Originally theorized by Laura Mulvey.

male sex role identity (MSRI) Joseph Pleck's model of the often-contradictory propositions associated with masculine roles (Chapter 3)

male sex role strain (MSRS) Joseph Pleck's theory that, given the contradictory and damaging nature of the MSRI (see above), male 'problems' were the result not of men's failures to acquire masculine gender identities, but of the sex role itself (Chapter 3)

manga comic books, generally printed in black and white. **Manga** are a major literary genre (with numerous subgenres) in Japan and are read by all ages. Since the 1990s, **manga** (and anime, Japanese animation) have become globally popular. (Chapter 9)

Marxist and socialist feminisms these forms of feminism are united by their emphasis on material conditions as a critical component of gender oppression. Marxist feminisms, however, tend to view the eradication of capitalism as the way to create gender equality, while socialist feminisms have criticized Marxists for their too-rigid focus on economic oppression. Socialist feminism views cultural and economic realities as equally important to the status of women. (Chapter 5)

matriarchy a woman-centred form of social organization in which women, particularly mothers, are at the centre of prestige and power (Chapter 4)

matrilineality the practice of reckoning kinship, naming, inheritance, and descent through the mother, rather than the father (Chapter 4)

matrilocal determining residence by female kinship rather than by male. Thus a married couple would reside with the woman's family rather than the man's (Chapter 6)

mean differences differences in the *average* scores of men and women (or boys and girls) on standardized tests, which may be taken as representative of *absolute* differences between the sexes (See Figure 1.1.) (Chapter 1)

Meiorin test a stringent and multi-part test that employers can apply to ascertain whether a potentially discriminatory requirement is a BFOR (see above) (Chapter 8)

M-F Test a multi-component test designed by Lewis Terman and Catherine Miles and used for over 30 years to assess 'successful' acquisition of masculine or feminine gender identity (Chapter 3)

mid-life crisis in middle-aged men (and some women), a developmental 'crisis' characterized by a pressure to make wholesale changes in their work, relationships, and leisure (Chapter 5)

MMORPGs (massively multiplayer on-line role-playing games) role-playing video games distinguished from others by the number of players who participate and by the 'persistent worlds' in which the games take place (Chapter 9)

mommy track the phenomenon whereby mothers might retain paid employment while giving up the possibility of career advancement they might have enjoyed had they not had children and remained on the 'fast track' (Chapter 8)

moral panic a popular idea about societal decline; often, moral panics link a real or imagined social problem (e.g., crime) to a particular group of people (e.g., single mothers/fatherlessness) (Chapter 7)

multiracial/ethnic feminisms Multiracial and ethnically based feminisms emerged in the 1970s as part of a critique of racism and Eurocentrism within the second-wave feminist movement. By the 1980s, important black and Chicana feminist movements

had emerged, to be joined later by Asian-American, African, Aboriginal, and other ethnically-based feminist movements. Multiracial feminisms have contributed not only a critique of mainstream feminism but insights on racism, social location, and identity as contributors to the status of women. (Chapter 5)

muxes in Zapotec communities in Mexico, males who take on feminine modes of dress and social roles (Chapter 4)

nadle among the Navajo, a third gender assigned to either individuals of ambiguous sex or biological males. Individuals might also choose this role (Chapter 4)

narrative coherence In the simplest terms, narrative coherence is 'a story that hangs together'. Its application to human life-story telling comes from narrative theory, which argues that the making of stories is fundamental to human cognitive processes. (Chapter 5)

New Woman a feminine ideal that emerged at the end of the nineteenth century along with feminist activism and theory. The New Woman would be independent, educated, and assertive. By the early twentieth century, commentators were concerned about the New Woman as a symbol of societal decline. (Chapter 6)

nuclear families a twentieth-century term describing a family structure or household composed of a couple and their children. While it is a common historical form, particularly in Western Europe, it has never been universal. (Chapter 6)

object-relations theory a body of theory identified with Melanie Klein that emphasizes the role of the external world or 'others' (both other people and imagined others such as 'The Breast') in the development of the personality. (Chapter 3)

Oedipal crisis in Freudian theory, the critical part of the genital stage during which a boy learns to desire sex with women, repudiate femininity, and identify as a man. The boy initially desires his mother, whom he sees as being castrated, and seeks to replace his father. His fear of castration by his father leads him to instead identify with his father and defer his desire for his mother until adulthood, when it is transferred to other women. (Chapter 3)

organizational gender neutrality the vehicle by which the gender order is reproduced. According to Joan Acker, this 'covers up, obscures, the underlying gender structure, allowing practices that perpetuate it to continue even as efforts to reduce gender inequality are also underway'. (Chapter 5)

palliative system justification motive a psychological theory that explains why individuals who are disadvantaged by a system justify it. The theory argues that individuals use system justifications to lessen (palliate) their anxiety, guilt, and discomfort, despite the fact that such a justification may be against their own interests. (Chapter 2)

paraphilias abnormal or deviant sexual desires and behaviours; familiar examples include exhibitionism, fetishism, pedophilia, sexual masochism, sexual sadism, and voyeurism (Chapter 10)

parental investment in evolutionary theory, the investment of time, energy, etc., made by a parenting organism that might otherwise be directed toward the fitness of the organism itself. The often-heavier investment by female organisms (particularly mammals) in parenting is thought to lead to greater mating selectivity. (Chapter 2)

patriarchal violence bell hooks's term for family violence 'based on the belief that it is acceptable for a more powerful individual to control others through various forms of coercive violence'. Hooks links this idea to male domination, but notes that women can and do enact patriarchal violence, particularly against children. (Chapter 12)

patrilineality the practice of reckoning kinship, naming, inheritance, and descent through the father (Chapter 4)

pay equity a theory and body of legislation and policy comprising two main concepts: the notion of equal pay for the same work and the idea of equal pay for work of equal value. Increasingly, pay equity means simply the latter. (Chapter 8)

penis envy in Freudian theory, a critical part of girls' psychosexual development. The term describes the girl's assumed reaction to her discovery of anatomical sex difference, which she, like the boy, views as the 'castration' of the female. (See **Electra complex**.) (Chapter 3)

Persons' Case the October 1929 legal decision (in response to a petition from five women now known as the 'Famous Five') that redefined 'persons' under the British North America Act to include women, thus dramatically expanding the legal rights available to them (Chapter 9)

phallocentric focused on male power and privilege, particularly as expressed by the phallus (the erect penis). Phallocentric sexuality centres on the penis and, more broadly, male sexual gratification. (Chapter 10)

pin money dating back to the seventeenth century, the term 'pin money' is still used to describe small amounts of money that can be used for discretionary or frivolous spending (Chapter 8)

polygamy in anthropology and sociology, marriage to more than one partner at the same time. Generally, this takes the form of **polygyny** (see below). (Chapter 4)

polygyny a man's marriage to more than one woman at one time. (Chapter 4)

polyvocality literally, many-voicedness. Within any text, the presence of **polyvocality** means that multiple meanings and readings are possible. (Chapter 9)

post-colonial feminism a form of feminism, closely associated with women of the so-called 'Third World', that offers a critique of Western feminism's universalizing tendencies and that analyses colonialism, racism, and global capitalism in relation to the status of women (Chapter 5)

post-modern feminism Sometimes referred to as post-structural feminism, post-modern feminism draws upon literary and linguistic theory to argue that reality is constructed, primarily through language, and that sex itself has no stable character. Post-modern feminisms have been influential in scholarship, less so in activism. (Chapter 5)

precarious employment Sometimes called 'contingent' or 'non-standard' employment, precarious employment is work that does not conform with the typical understanding of a stable, full-time job in which one works full-time on the employer's premises with some degree of job security. (Chapter 8)

primary feminine phase for Klein and other psychoanalysts, the phase in which a child (of either sex) comes to identify with the mother and her desire for the father. (Chapter 3)

primary sex characteristics sex characteristics present at birth (Chapter 5)

privilege the advantages that come from being a member of a dominant group (based on gender, race, class, ability, or sexuality), the principal of which may be the presumption of normalcy and universality (Chapter 1)

psychoanalysis an umbrella term for a diverse body of theory and practice based upon the theories of mind and personality developed by Sigmund Freud. Psychoanalysis extends beyond the study and treatment of individual personality to theories of social organization. (Chapter 3)

purdah the (primarily Islamic) practice of the social seclusion of women; a system of segregation aimed at keeping women (particularly married and marriageable ones) completely separated from the world of men (Chapters 4, 11)

quid pro quo sexual harassment a form of sexual harassment legally recognized in the USA; the offer of benefit in exchange for sexual favours, or the threat of retribution if sexual favours are not received (Chapter 8)

race suicide a late nineteenth-century/early twentieth-century concept that argued, on the basis of evolutionary theory, that the 'white race' was in decline; a particular cause, proponents argued, was the declining birth rate among middle- and upper-class white women and the 'rampant' fertility of poor whites and racial 'others' (Chapter 6)

racialized seen in terms of and subjected to the application of meaning on the basis of race. Racialization, as a concept, recognizes that the attribution of 'race', and the consequences of that attribution, are a process rather than the outcome of an immutable and obvious characteristic; and that race is a *cultural* category and idea rather than a *biological* one. Racialization also recognizes that in terms of experience and identity, one may be made aware of one's 'race' in certain contexts or locations but not in others. (Chapter 1)

radical feminism a form of feminism that sees women's unequal status as rooted in patriarchy, and particularly in its control over the bodies and sexuality of women (Chapter 5)

rape penile penetration without consent (Chapter 12)

residential schools in the Canadian context, boarding schools first founded in the nineteenth century to help 'assimilate' Aboriginal children (Chapter 6)

Riot Grrrl a cultural movement of the 1990s based on punk/alternative music and consciously feminist politics. Ani diFranco, Bikini Kill, and Sleater-Kinney are names sometimes associated with the movement. (Chapter 9)

ritual segregation the segregation of the sexes through rituals that provide a sense of identity and group membership (Chapter 4)

romantic love a strong attachment to, physical attraction to, and idealization of another human

being. While romantic love seems to be universal, it is not always seen as desirable or as the appropriate basis for marriage. (Chapter 10)

second shift housework performed after putting in a workday, or more broadly, the responsibility for the 'job' of housework in addition to paid employment (Chapter 6)

secondary sex characteristics sex characteristics that develop at puberty, and are less decisive than primary sex characteristics (Chapter 5)

second-wave feminism a social movement and body of theory that developed after the Second World War, particularly in Western industrialized societies during the 1960s. The movement's greatest impact and vitality can be traced to the 1970s, when many varieties of second-wave feminism emerged. (Chapter 5)

self-esteem a person's sense of his or her worth. It can be measured either by particular indicators, which assess how well one feels about particular aspects of oneself (e.g., 'I like my body') or 'globally', in overall terms. (Chapter 7)

self-objectification the process of internalizing an outsider's perspective on one's own body, leading to a preoccupation with one's appearance and comportment as perceived by others (Chapter 11)

separation of spheres a nineteenth-century ideology that distinguished between private and public in a new way, separating the world of family and love from the world of employment, politics, and competition. Women were to be protected from the latter by their confinement in the private realm, while men could find respite there from the hurly-burly of their activities in the public realm. (Chapter 6)

sex the chromosomal, chemical, and anatomical organization of human bodies that determines biological maleness or femaleness (Chapter 1)

sex difference chromosomal, anatomical, and hormonal differences between females and males; to be considered sex differences, these distinctions must be biologically rather than culturally derived (Chapter 1)

sex role theory a broad body of theory, drawing from both psychology and sociology, that studies individuals' socialization into gender roles and acquisition of gender identities (Chapter 3)

sex segregation the concentration of men and women in gender-specific roles and locations within a society. It has been argued that sex segregation is associated with lower status for women. Within employment, the term refers to the concentration of men and women within different occupations, industries, jobs, and fields. This form of sex segregation may be either **vertical** or **horizontal**. (Chapters 4, 8)

sex testing Now called **gender verification**, sex testing has involved a variety of tests conducted on female athletes to be sure that they are biological females. (Chapter 11)

sexual assault any form of sexual touching without consent. Canada's Criminal Code distinguishes among categories of sexual assault based on degrees parallel to the degrees of common assault (Chapter 12)

sexual fluidity the ability for one's erotic response to be influenced by situational factors; according to some scholars, particularly prevalent among women (Chapter 10)

sexual harassment a broad concept that encompasses many behaviours: unwelcomed sexual attention, the offering of benefits for sexual favours, coercion into sexual activity, or bullying and harassment on the ground of one's gender. The standard definition in Canada is 'unwelcome conduct of a sexual nature that detrimentally affects the work environment or leads to adverse job-related consequences for the victim of the harassment'. In the USA, two subtypes are distinguished, **quid pro quo** and **hostile environment**. (Chapters 7, 8)

sexual-minority a descriptor for anyone whose sexual orientation, gender identity, or sexual identity differs from that of the majority culture (Chapter 12)

social constructionism in this book, the theoretical orientation that sees the expression and organization of gender not as the outcome of biology, but as the result of historical and cultural change, the socialization of individuals, and the continuous interplay between gendered individuals and gendered institutions. Social constructionists view human nature as much more malleable and variable than do biological determinists. (Chapters 1, 5)

social Darwinism only thinly associated with the theories and work of Charles Darwin, this philosophy applies the theory of natural selection to differences, competition, and inequality among 'races', nations, and families, and between men and women (Chapter 2)

social psychologists either sociologists or psychologists, scholars in the field of social psychology study individual psychology as the result of interactions between individuals and their environments, whether defined as 'other people' or as institutions and social structures (Chapter 3)

socio-biology the study of the biological basis of behaviour in all organisms, including human beings (Chapter 2)

sociology a discipline within the social sciences that studies social structures and relations, described by C. Wright Mills as 'the intersection of biography and history' (Chapter 5)

sodomy strictly speaking, anal sexual intercourse; historically and in modern 'sodomy laws', more broadly applied to any 'unnatural' sexuality, particularly if between members of the same sex (Chapter 10)

stalking under Canadian law (Section 264), a form of criminal harassment involving some combination of repeatedly following a person, watching a person, communicating with a person when such communication is not desired, and threatening a person either directly or by proxy (Chapter 12)

sticky floor the phenomenon, linked to the glass ceiling, that traps women and minorities at the lower levels of organizations regardless of their qualification for advancement (Chapter 8)

stone butch a masculine or 'butch' lesbian who prefers not to be sexually touched and whose sexuality is focused on pleasing her partner (Chapter 10)

super-ego a component of Freud's concept of the psyche, the super-ego is an outgrowth of **ego**'s efforts to seek acceptable outlets for **id**'s gratification. Freud saw super-ego as the seat of morality, accepting of the legitimacy of social limitations on gratification. (Chapter 3)

sworn virgin in Albanian society, a daughter who swore perpetual chastity and took on the social role of a man in order to serve as her family's head of household (Chapter 4)

technical virgin a term used to describe young women who, in a desire to preserve their virginity, engage in 'everything but' vaginal intercourse. This seems to have been less a cultural phenomenon than a media one. (Chapter 10)

tenure in universities, a form of permanent labour contract that prohibits termination without just cause and ensures the academic freedom of a professor (Chapter 7)

third-wave feminism a form of feminist theory and activism that emerged c. 1990. Third-wave feminism critiques what it sees as the universalizing tendencies of second-wave feminism and incorporates the insights of post-modern, post-colonial, and multiracial feminisms. It also insists on a 'positive' view of sexuality. (Chapter 5)

Title IX a US law, enacted in 1972, that states, 'No person in the United States shall, on the basis of sex, be excluded from participation in, be denied the benefits of, or be subjected to discrimination under any education program or activity receiving Federal financial assistance' (Chapter 7)

tokenism the phenomenon that makes women and minorities highly visible within previously unintegrated organizations. Because they are always regarded as representing a group, tokens experience a variety of difficulties and frustrations, and their hiring and promotion may not change the workplace significantly for others. (Chapter 8)

transgendered feeling a strong sense of gender identity consonant with inhabiting an opposite-sex body (Chapter 11)

transsexual an individual who seeks sex reassignment and thus changes sex (Chapter 11)

transvestites those who dress in the clothing of the opposite sex, for reasons including matters of identity, disruption of social norms, or sexual fetishism (Chapter 11)

two-spirited a term, in use since the 1990s, to describe transgendered or gender-variant people in North American indigenous cultures. The term is sometimes applied to both historical people (e.g., 'berdaches') and to contemporary indigenous people. (Chapter 4)

vertical segregation segregation associated with differences of education, experience, and skill within the same field, for example, legal secretarial work and judging, both subsumed within the field of 'law' (Chapter 8)

wage gap the difference between the average earnings of male and female full-time workers, either broadly or within a particular field (Chapter 8)

womb envy a concept, first articulated by Karen Horney, that argues that males envy women's potential to give birth and therefore both disparage and seek to dominate women (Chapter 3)

xanith Omani biological male whose social and sexual role is female. **Xanith**s can retain this role throughout life or adopt masculine identities. (Chapter 4)

Notes

Chapter 1

1. John Gray, *Men Are from Mars, Women Are from Venus* (New York: HarperCollins, 1992), p. 5.
2. Barbara Risman, *Gender Vertigo* (New Haven: Yale University Press, 1998), p. 25. See also Judith Lorber, *Paradoxes of Gender* (New Haven: Yale University Press, 1994).
3. Catharine Stimpson, *Where the Meanings Are* (New York: Methuen, 1988).
4. See Michael Kimmel, *Manhood in America: A Cultural History* (New York: The Free Press, 1996).
5. Simmel is cited in Lewis Coser, 'Georg Simmel's Neglected Contributions to the Sociology of Women' in *Signs*, 2(4), 1977, p. 872.
6. Cited in Coser, 'Georg Simmel's Neglected Contributions . . ', p. 872.
7. Cited in James Brooke, 'Men Held in Beatings Lived on the Fringes' in *New York Times*, October 16, 1998, p. A16. Valerie Jenness, the sociologist who was quoted in the story, told Michael that she was misquoted and that, of course, she had mentioned gender as well as age—which suggests that the media's myopia matches that of the larger society.
8. Robert McElvaine, *Eve's Seed: Biology, the Sexes, and the Course of History* (New York/Toronto: McGraw-Hill, 2001), pp. 76–79.
9. R.W. Connell, *Gender and Power* (Stanford: Stanford University Press, 1987), p. 183.
10. Erving Goffman, *Stigma* (Englewood Cliffs, NJ: Prentice-Hall, 1963), p. 128.
11. Connell, *Gender and Power*, pp. 183, 188, 187.
12. Cited in Risman, *Gender Vertigo*, p. 141.
13. Carol Tavris, 'The Mismeasure of Woman' in *Feminism and Psychology* 3 (No. 2), 1993, p. 153.
14. Cynthia Fuchs Epstein, *Deceptive Distinctions* (New Haven: Yale University Press, 1988).
15. Deborah Tannen, *You Just Don't Understand* (New York: William Morrow, 1991).
16. William O'Barr and Jean F. O'Barr, *Linguistic Evidence: Language, Power and Strategy—The Courtroom* (San Diego: Academic Press, 1995); See also Alfie Kohn, 'Girl Talk, Guy Talk' in *Psychology Today*, February 1988, p. 66.
17. Alex Witchel, 'Our Finances, Ourselves' in *New York Times*, June 4, 1998, p. 13.
18. Ibid.
19. Rosabeth M. Kanter, *Men and Women of the Corporation* (New York: Harper and Row, 1977).
20. Kathleen Gerson, *Hard Choices* (Berkeley: University of California Press, 1985); *No Man's Land* (New York: Basic Books, 1993).
21. Risman, *Gender Vertigo*, p. 70.
22. David Almeida and Ronald Kessler, 'Everyday Stressors and Gender Differences in Daily Distress' in *Journal of Personality and Social Psychology*, 75(3), 1998. See also Nancy Stedman, 'In a Bad Mood—for a Good Reason' in *New York Times*, October 24, 1998.
23. Risman, *Gender Vertigo*, p. 21.
24. Gayle Rubin, 'The Traffic in Women' in *Toward an Anthropology of Women*, R.R. Reiter, ed. (New York: Monthly Review Press, 1975), pp. 179–180.
25. Catharine MacKinnon, *Towards a Feminist Theory of the State* (Cambridge: Harvard University Press, 1989), pp. 218–219.

Chapter 2

1. Jerre Levy, cited in Jo Durden-Smith and Diane deSimone, *Sex and the Brain* (New York: Warner Books, 1983), p. 61.
2. Rev. John Todd, *Woman's Rights* (Boston: Lee and Shepard, 1867), p. 26.
3. Londa Schiebinger, 'Skeletons in the Closet: The First Illustrations of the Female Skeleton in Eighteenth-Century Anatomy', in *Sexuality and Society in the Nineteenth Century*, Catherine Gallagher and Thomas Laqueur, eds. (Berkeley: University of California Press, 1987).
4. Cited in Carl Degler, *In Search of Human Nature: The Decline and Revival of Darwinism in American Social Thought* (New York: Oxford University Press, 1991), p. 107.
5. Todd, *Woman's Rights*, p. 25.

6. California State Historical Society Library, San Francisco, ms. #2334. For a summary of the way biological arguments were used to exclude women from public participation, see Michael Kimmel, 'Introduction', *Against the Tide: Pro-Feminist Men in the United States, 1776–1990, a Documentary History*, M. Kimmel and T. Mosmiller, eds. (Boston: Beacon, 1992).

7. Cited in Stephen Jay Gould, *The Mismeasure of Man* (New York: W. W. Norton, 1981), pp. 104–105.

8. Edward C. Clarke, *Sex in Education; or, A Fair Chance for the Girls* (Boston: Osgood and Co., 1873), p. 152.

9. See Cynthia Eagle Russet, *Sexual Science: The Victorian Construction of Womanhood* (Cambridge: Harvard University Press, 1989).

10. Jennifer Henderson, *Settler Feminism and Race Making in Canada* (Toronto: University of Toronto Press, 2003), p. 173.

11. See Angus Maclaren, *Our Own Master Race: Eugenics in Canada, 1885–1945* (Toronto: University of Toronto Press, 1990); Jana Grekul, Harvey Krahn, and Dave Odynak, 'Sterilizing the "Feeble-Minded": Eugenics in Alberta, Canada, 1929–1972', *Journal of Historical Sociology* 17 (4), 2004, pp. 358–384.

12. There are several important texts that provide good ripostes to the biological arguments. Among them are Ruth Bleir, ed., *Feminist Approaches to Science* (New York: Pergamon, 1986); Lynda Birke, *Women, Feminism and Biology: The Feminist Challenge* (New York: Methuen, 1986). Anne Fausto-Sterling's *Myths of Gender: Biological Theories About Women and Men* (New York: Basic Books, 1985) is indispensable. Deborah Blum, *Sex on the Brain: The Biological Differences between Men and Women* (New York: Viking, 1997), provides a good summary. Robert Nadeau, *S/He Brain: Science, Sexual Politics and the Myths of Feminism* (New York: Praeger, 1996), illustrates the conservative and antifeminist uses to which this research can so effortlessly be put.

13. E.O. Wilson, *Sociobiology: The New Synthesis* (Cambridge: Harvard University Press, 1977).

14. Richard Dawkins, *The Selfish Gene* (New York: Oxford University Press, 1976), p. 152; Edward O. Wilson, *On Human Nature* (Cambridge: Harvard University Press, 1978), p. 167.

15. Anthony Layng, 'Why Don't We Act Like the Opposite Sex?' in *USA Today* magazine, January 1993; Donald Symons, 'Darwinism and Contemporary Marriage' in *Contemporary Marriage: Comparative Perspectives on a Changing Institution*, K. Davis, ed. (New York: Russell Sage Foundation, 1985), cited in Carl Degler, 'Darwinians Confront Gender; or, There Is More to It Than History' in *Theoretical Perspectives on Sexual Difference*, D. Rhode, ed. (New Haven: Yale University Press, 1990), p. 39.

16. Lionel Tiger, 'Male Dominance?' in *New York Times Magazine*, October 25, 1970.

17. Wilson, *Sociobiology: The New Synthesis*.

18. See, for example, Judy Stamps 'Sociobiology: Its Evolution and Intellectual Descendants' in *Politics and Life Science* 14 (2), 1995.

19. David Buss, *The Evolution of Desire: Strategies of Human Mating* (New York: Basic Books, 1994), but see also Robert Sapolsky, *Monkeyluv* (New York: Scribner, 2006), p. 175.

20. Margo Wilson and Martin Daly, 'The Man Who Mistook His Wife for a Chattel', in *The Adapted Mind: Evolutionary Psychology and the Generation of Culture*, ed. Jerome Barkow, Leda Cosmides, and John Tooby (Oxford: Oxford University Press, 1995), pp. 289–324.

21. Elisabeth Pillsworth, Martie Hasleton, and David Buss, 'Ovulatory Shifts in Female Sexual Desire', in *Journal of Sex Research,* 41 (1), February 2004, pp. 55–65: 56. Pillsworth and her co-authors do point out, however, methodological flaws within these inconsistent studies, such as their reliance on women's self-reporting of stage of menstrual cycle.

22. N. Burley, 'The Evolution of Concealed Ovulation' in *The American Naturalist* 114, 1979; Mary McDonald Pavelka, 'Sexual Nature . . .', p. 19. See also Sarah Blaffer Hrdy, *The Woman That Never Evolved* (Cambridge: Harvard University Press, 1981).

23. Elisabeth Lloyd, *The Case of the Female Orgasm: Bias in the Science of Evolution* (Cambridge: Cambridge University Press, 2005).

24. Steven Gangestad, Randy Thornhill, and Christine Garver, 'Changes in Women's Sexual Interests and Their Partners' Mate-Retention Tactics across the Menstrual Cycle: Evidence for Shifting Conflicts of Interest' in *Proceedings of the Royal Society*, 2002. Not surprisingly, Gangestad repudiated the journalist's interpretation, because it's pretty much the mirror image of his

argument that it is more in males' interest to be promiscuous and in females' interest to be monogamous. Personal communication (with M. Kimmel), December 16, 2002.

25. See Evelyn Fox Keller, *A Feeling for the Organism: The Life and Work of Barbara McClintock* (San Francisco: W. H. Freeman, 1983).

26. See Natalie Angier, 'Men, Women, Sex, and Darwin' in *New York Times*, February 21, 1999; see also her *Woman: An Intimate Geography* (Boston: Houghton, Mifflin, 1999).

27. Fausto-Sterling, *Myths of Gender,* pp. 160–163.

28. Sapolsky, *Monkeyluv,* p. 30.

29. Carol Tavris and Carole Wade, *The Longest War: Sex Differences in Perspective* (New York: Houghton-Mifflin, 1984).

30. See Frans de Waal, *Our Inner Ape: A Leading Primatologist Explains Why We Are Who We Are* (New York: Riverhead Books, 2005); see also Mary McDonald Pavelka, 'Sexual Nature: What Can We Learn from a Cross-Species Perspective?' in *Sexual Nature, Sexual Culture,* P. Abrahamson and S. Pinkerton, eds. (Chicago: University of Chicago Press, 1995), p. 22.

31. See Jonah Lehrer, 'The Effeminate Sheep—and Other Problems with Darwinian Sexual Selection', in *Seed*, June 2006; Simon Le Vay, 'Survival of the Sluttiest', at Nerve.com, 2000, available at www.nerve.com.

32. Richard Bribiescas, *Men: Evolutionary and Life History* (Cambridge, MA: Harvard University Press, 2006), p. 12.

33. Turner is cited in *South Side Observer*, April 29, 1896; C.A. Dwyer, 'The Role of Tests and Their Construction in Producing Apparent Sex-related Differences' in *Sex-Related Differences in Cognitive Functioning*, M. Wittig and A. Peterson, eds. (New York: Academic Press, 1979), p. 342.

34. Christina Hoff Sommers, 'Why Can't a Woman Be More Like a Man?' in *The American* online, March/April 2008, available at http://www.american.com/archive/2008/march-april-magazine-contents/why-can2019t-a-woman-be-more-like-a-man. Accessed December 3, 2008.

35. Canadian Council of Learning, *Why Boys Don't Like to Read: Gender Differences in Reading Achievement*, available at http://www.ccl-cca.ca/CCL/Reports/LessonsInLearning/LinL-20090218Whyboysdontliketoread.htm February 18, 2009. Accessed April 2, 2009.

36. Diane Halpern et al., 'The Science of Sex Differences in Science and Mathematics', in *Psychological Science in the Public Interest*, 8(1), 2007, pp. 1–51. Jacqueline is grateful to Cheyenne Murray for bringing this recent article to her attention.

37. Janet Hyde, 'How Large Are Cognitive Differences? A Metaanalysis' in *American Psychologist*, 26, 1981; Janet Hyde, Elizabeth Fennema, and S. J. Laman, 'Gender Differences in Mathematics Performance: A Meta-Analysis' in *Psychological Bulletin*, 107, 1990.

38. Darren Lauzon, 'Gender Differences in Large-Scale, Quantitative Assessments of Mathematics and Science Achievement'. Unpublished conference paper, available at http://qed.econ.queensu.ca/pub/jdi/deutsch/edu_conf/Lauzon2_paper.pdf. Accessed 2 April 2009.

39. Halpern et al., 'The Science of Sex Differences', p. 13.

40. Emile Durkheim, *The Division of Labor in Society* [1893] (New York: The Free Press, 1984), p. 21; see also Ehrenreich and English, *For Her Own Good*, p. 117.

41. James C. Dobson, *Straight Talk to Men and Their Wives* (Dallas: Word Publishing Co., 1991), p. 177; Adam Begley, 'Why Men and Women Think Differently' in *Newsweek*, 1995, p. 51.

42. See Elizabeth Fee, 'Nineteenth Century Craniology: The Study of the Female Skull' in *Bulletin of the History of Medicine*, 53, 1979.

43. Doreen Kimura's summary of these brain differences, *Sex and Cognition* (Cambridge, MA: MIT Press, 1999), catalogues a large variety of brain differences in spatial, verbal, and other forms of reasoning. Because she never tells the reader about the shape of the distribution of these traits, we have no idea whether such differences actually mean anything at all, if they are categorical, or if the distribution is larger among women and among men than it is between women and men—which is the case in virtually every one of these studies. Such is typically the case when authors argue from ideology rather than evidence. A better source is Lesley Rogers, *Sexing the Brain* (New York: Columbia University Press, 2001), which is at least intellectually honest and does not conceal or obscure conflicting information.

44. Norman Geschwind, cited in Jo Durden-Smith and Diane deSimone, *Sex and the Brain*, p. 171.

Other influential studies on hormone research include G.W. Harris, 'Sex Hormones, Brain Development and Brain Function' in *Endocrinology*, 75, 1965.

45. Ruth Bleier, *Science and Gender: A Critique of Biology and Its Theory on Women* (New York: Pantheon, 1984).

46. A.W.H. Buffery and J. Gray, 'Sex Differences in the Development of Spatial and Linguistic Skills' in *Gender Differences: Their Ontogeny and Significance*, C. Ounsted and D.C. Taylor, eds. (London: Churchill Livingston, 1972); Jerre Levy, 'Lateral Specialization of the Human Brain: Behavioral Manifestation and Possible Evolutionary Basis' in *The Biology of Behavior*, J.A. Kiger, ed. (Corvallis, Eugene: University of Oregon Press, 1972); see also Anne Fausto-Sterling, *Myths of Gender*, p. 40.

47. Jean Christophe Labarthe, 'Are Boys Better Than Girls at Building a Tower or a Bridge at 2 Years of Age?' in *Archives of Disease in Childhood*, 77, 1997, pp. 140–144.

48. Joseph Lurito cited in Robert Lee Hotz, 'Women Use More of Brain When Listening, Study Says' in *Los Angeles Times*, November 29, 2000.

49. Levy, 'Lateral Specialization'.

50. Durden-Smith and deSimone, *Sex and the Brain*, p. 60.

51. Michael Peters, 'The Size of the Corpus Callosum in Males and Females: Implications of a Lack of Allometry' in *Canadian Journal of Psychology*, 42(3), 1988; Christine de Lacoste-Utamsing and Ralph Holloway, 'Sexual Dimorphism in the Human Corpus Callosum' in *Science*, June 25, 1982; but also see William Byne, Ruth Bleier, and Lanning Houston, 'Variations in Human Corpus Callosum Do Not Predict Gender: A Study Using Magnetic Resonance Imaging' in *Behavioral Neuroscience*, 102(2), 1988.

52. Cited in Anne Fausto-Sterling, *Sexing the Body: Gender Politics and the Construction of Sexuality* (New York: Basic Books, 2000), p. 116. See Michael Gurian, *The Wonder of Girls* (New York: Pocket Books, 2002); see also Caryl Rivers, 'Pop Science Book Claims Girls Hardwired for Love' in *Women's E-News*, June 29, 2002.

53. Fausto-Sterling, *Sexing the Body*, p. 140.

54. Cordelia Fine, 'Will Working Mothers' Brains Explode? The Popular New Genre of Neurosexism', in *Neuroethics*, 1 (2008): pp. 69–72.

55. Cited in Le Anne Schreiber, 'The Search for His and Her Brains' in *Glamour*, April, 1993; Kimura, cited in Rivers, 'Pop Science Book . . .'.

56. Fine, 'Will Working Mothers' Brains Explode?'

57. Steven Goldberg, *The Inevitability of Patriarchy* (New York: Simon & Schuster, 1973), p. 93.

58. Kate Melville, 'Male Scientists Not So Manly', in *ScienceAGogo*, October 22, 2004, available at http://www.scienceagogo.com/news/20040922054756data_trunc_sys.shtml, accessed April 22, 2009.

59. See James McBride Dabbs (with Mary Godwin Dabbs), *Heroes, Rogues and Lovers: Testosterone and Behavior* (New York: McGraw-Hill, 2000), p. 8; Andrew Sullivan, 'The He Hormone' in *New York Times Magazine*, April 2, 2000, p. 48. There is some evidence that AndroGel is dangerous and should not be taken without significant testing. See Jerome Groopman, 'Hormones for Men' in *The New Yorker*, July 29, 2002, pp. 34–38.

60. Robert Sapolsky, *The Trouble with Testosterone* (New York: Simon & Schuster, 1997), p. 155.

61. Theodore Kemper, *Testosterone and Social Structure* (New Brunswick: Rutgers University Press, 1990); Arthur Kling, 'Testosterone and Aggressive Behavior in Man and Non-Human Primates' in *Hormonal Correlates of Behavior*, B. Eleftheriou and R. Sprott, eds. (New York: Plenum, 1975); See also E. Gonzalez-Bono, A. Salvador, J. Ricarte, M.A. Serrano, and M. Arendo, 'Testosterone and Attribution of Successful Competition' in *Aggressive Behavior* 26(3), 2000, pp. 235–240.

62. Anu Aromaki, Ralf Lindman, and C.J. Peter Eriksson, 'Testosterone, Aggressiveness and Antisocial Personality' in *Aggressive Behavior* 25, 1999, pp. 113–123; Sapolsky cited in Richard Lacayo, 'Are You Man Enough?' in *Time*, April, 24, 2000.

63. Peter B. Gray, Sonya Kahlenberg, Emily Barrett, Susan Lipson, and Peter T. Ellison, 'Marriage and Fatherhood Are Associated with Lower Testosterone in Males' in *Evolution and Human Behavior*, 23, 2002, pp. 193–201; see also the coverage of this study, William Cromie, 'Marriage Lowers Testosterone' in *The Harvard Gazette*, September 19, 2002; Ellen Barry, 'The Ups and Downs of Manhood' in *Boston Globe*, July 9, 2002.

64. See, for example, Jed Diamond, *Male Menopause* (Napierville, IL: Sourcebooks, 1998); and

Jerome Groopman, 'Hormones for Men'. For discussion, see Bribiescas, *Men*, pp. 175–191; 'Androgel™ Approved in Canada', in *Doctors' Guide: Global Edition*. Available at http://www.pslgroup.com/dg/215536.htm. Accessed April 22, 2009.

65. See Anne Fausto-Sterling's summary of William Young's classic 1940s experiments in *Sexing the Body*, pp. 212–216; see Bribiescas, *Men*, p. 187, for a summary of studies on the association of testosterone and libido.

66. Winifred Gallagher, 'Some Differences between Men and Women II: Sex and Hormones', in *The Atlantic Monthly*, March 1998, pp. 77–82; Jane Brody, 'Personal Health: A Tad of Testosterone Adds Zest to Menopause', *New York Times*, February 24, 1998, available at http://www.nytimes.com/specials/women/warchive/980224_1133.html. Accessed April 22, 2009.

67. Angier, *Woman: An Intimate Geography*, p. 207.

68. Health Canada, 'Benefits and Risks of Hormone Replacement Therapy' (January 2003/March 2004), available at http://www.hc-sc.gc.ca/hl-vs/iyh-vsv/med/estrogen-eng.php. Accessed April 23, 2009.

69. Gloria Steinem, 'If Men Could Menstruate' in *Outrageous Acts and Everyday Rebellions* (New York: Holt, Rinehart and Winston, 1983).

70. Shari Roan, 'The Basis of Sexual Identity', in *Los Angeles Times*, March 14, 1997, p. E1.

71. See John Colapinto, As *Nature Made Him: The Boy Who Was Raised as a Girl* (NewYork: HarperCollins, 2000), and John Colapinto, 'Gender Gap: What Were the Real Reasons Behind David Reimer's Suicide?' in *Slate*, June 3, 2004, available at www.slate.com /id/2101678. Scholarly papers include M. Diamond, 'Sexual Identity, Monozygotic Twins Reared in Discordant Sex Roles and a BBC Follow-Up', in *Archives of Sexual Behavior*, 11(2), 1982, pp. 181–185; M. Diamond and H.K. Sigmundson, 'Sex Reassignment at Birth: Long Term Review and Clinical Implications' in *Archives of Pediatrics and Adolescent Medicine*, 151, March, 1997, pp. 298–304.

72. Gunter Dorner, W. Rohde, F. Stahl, L. Krell, and W. Masius, 'A Neuroendocrine Predisposition for Homosexuality in Men' in *Archives of Sexual Behavior*, 4(1), 1975, p. 6. Several books offer useful summaries of 'gay biology' research, including Dean Hamer and Peter Copeland,

The Science of Desire (New York: Simon & Schuster, 1994); Simon LeVay, *Queer Science: The Use and Abuse of Research into Homosexuality* (Cambridge: MIT Press, 1996); Lee Ellis and Linda Ebertz, eds., *Sexual Orientation: Toward Biological Understanding* (New York: Praeger, 1997). Several other works provide valuable rejoinders to the scientific research; see, for example, Vernon Rosario, ed., *Science and Homosexualities* (New York: Routledge, 1997); Timothy Murphy, *Gay Science: The Ethics of Sexual Orientation Research* (New York: Columbia University Press, 1997); John Corvino, ed., *Same Sex: Debating the Ethics, Science and Culture of Homosexuality* (Lanham: Rowman and Littlefield, 1997). A double issue of *Journal of Homosexuality* 28(1–2), 1995, was devoted to this theme. For a strong dissenting opinion, see William Byne, 'Why We Cannot Conclude That Sexual Orientation Is Primarily a Biological Phenomenon' in *Journal of Homosexuality* 34(1), 1997; William Byne, 'Science and Belief: Psychobiological Research on Sexual Orientation' in *Journal of Homosexuality*, 28(2), 1995.

73. Simon LeVay, 'The "Gay Brain" Revisited' at Nerve.com, 2000; LeVay, 'A Difference in Hypothalamic Structure Between Homosexual and Heterosexual Men' in *Science*, 253, August 30, 1991; Simon LeVay, *The Sexual Brain* (Cambridge: MIT Press, 1994); Simon LeVay and Dean Hamer, 'Evidence for a Biological Influence in Male Homosexuality' in *Scientific American*, 270, 1994. See also 'Born or Bred?' in *Newsweek*, February 24, 1992.

74. P. Yahr, 'Sexually Dimorphic Hypothalamic Cell Groups and a Related Pathway That Are Essential for Masculine Copulatory Behavior' in *The Development of Sex Differences and Similarities in Behavior*, M. Haug, R. Whalen, C. Aron, and K. Olsen, eds. (Dordrecht, Netherlands: Kluwer Academic Publishers, 1993), p. 416.

75. See *Chronicle of Higher Education*, November 10, 1995.

76. Ivanka Savic, Hans Berglund, and Per Lindstrom, 'Brain Response to Putative Pheromones in Homosexual Men' in *Proceedings of the National Academy of Sciences*, 102(20), May 17, 2005, pp. 7356–7361.

77. Savic cited in Nicholas Wade, 'For Gay Men, an Attraction to a Different Kind of Scent' in *New*

York Times, May 10, 2005, available at http://www.nytimes.com/2005/05/10/ science/10smell.html, accessed May 10, 2005.

78. 'PET and MRI Show Differences in Cerebral Asymmetry and Functional Connectivity between Homo- and Heterosexual Subjects', in *Proceedings of the National Academy of Sciences,* 105 (27), pp. 9403–9408; 'What the Gay Brain Looks Like', in *Time,* June 17, 2008, available at http://www.time.com/time/health/article/0,8599,1815538,00.html, accessed 22 April 2009.

79. See, for example, Dennis McFadden and Edward G. Pasanen, 'Comparison of the Auditory Systems of Heterosexuals and Homosexuals: Click-Evoked Otoacoustic Emissions' in *Proceedings of the National Academy of Sciences,* 95, March 1998, pp. 2709–2713; and McFadden and Pasanen, 'Spontaneous Otoacoustic Emissions in Heterosexuals, Homosexuals, and Bisexuals' in *Journal of the Acoustical Society of America,* 105(4), April 1999, pp. 2403–2413; and Dennis McFadden and Craig Champlin, 'Comparison of Auditory Evoked Potentials in Heterosexual, Homosexual and Bisexual Males and Females' in *Journal of the Association for Research in Otolaryngology,* 1, 2000, pp. 89–99.

80. Marc Breedlove in Pat McBroom, 'Sexual Experience May Affect Brain Structure' at http://www.berkeley.edu/news/berkeleyan/1997/1119/sexexp.html; see also Jim McKnight, 'Editorial: The Origins of Male Homosexuality' in *Psychology, Evolution and Gender,* 2(3), December, 2000, p. 226.

81. See F. Kallmann, 'Comparative Twin Study on the Genetic Aspects of Male Homosexuality' in *Journal of Nervous Mental Disorders,* 115, 1952, pp. 283–298. Kallmann's findings may have been an artifact of his sample, which was drawn entirely from institutionalized mentally ill patients—some of whom had been institutionalized because they were gay. See also Richard Lewontin, Steven Rose, and Leon Kamin, *Not in Our Genes: Biology, Ideology and Human Nature* (New York: Pantheon), 1984.

82. E.D. Eckert et al., 'Homosexuality in Monozygotic Twins Reared Apart', *The British Jounral of Psychiatry* 148, 1986, pp. 421–425. J. Michael Bailey and Richard Pillard, 'A Genetic Study of Male Sexual Orientation' in *Archives of General Psychiatry,* 48, December, 1991; J. Michael Bailey and Richard Pillard, 'Heritable Factors In-

fluence Sexual Orientation in Women' in *Archives of General Psychiatry,* 50, March, 1993.

83. This is equally a problem in Frederick Whitam, Milton Diamond, and James Martin, 'Homosexual Orientation in Twins: A Report on 61 Pairs and Three Triplet Sets' in *Archives of Sexual Behavior,* 22(3), 1993.

84. Richard Pillard and James Weinrich, 'Evidence of a Familial Nature of Male Homosexuality' in *Archives of General Psychiatry,* 43, 1986.

85. See Peter Bearman and Hannah Bruckner, 'Opposite Sex Twins and Adolescent Same-Sex Attraction' in *American Journal of Sociology,* March, 2002.

86. Durden-Smith and deSimone, *Sex and the Brain,* p. 92.

87. Gunter Dorner, B. Schenk, B. Schmiedel, and L. Ahrens, 'Stressful Events in Prenatal Life of Bisexual and Homosexual Men', in *Explorations in Clinical Endocrinology,* 81, 1983, p. 87. See also Dorner et al., 'Prenatal Stress as a Possible Paetiogenic Factor of Homosexuality in Human Males' in *Endokrinologie,* 75, 1983; and G. Dorner, F. Gotz, T. Ohkawa, W. Rohde, F. Stahl, and R. Tonjes, 'Prenatal Stress and Sexual Brain Differentiation in Animal and Human Beings', Abstracts, International Academy of Sex Research, Thirteenth Annual Meeting, Tutzing, June 21–25, 1987. The other side is presented in a clever article by Gunter Schmidt and Ulrich Clement, 'Does Peace Prevent Homosexuality?' in *Journal of Homosexuality,* 28(1–2), 1995.

88. Terrance Williams, Michelle Pepitone, Scott Christensen, Bradley Cooke, Andrew Huberman, Nicolas Breedlove, Tess Breedlove, Cynthia Jordan, and S. Marc Breedlove, 'Finger Length Ratios and Sexual Orientation' in *Nature,* 404, March 30, 2000, p. 455; see also S.J. Robinson, 'The Ratio of 2nd to 4th Digit Length and Male Homosexuality' in *Evolution and Human Behavior,* 21, 2000, pp. 333–345. Also see Tim Beneke, 'Sex on the Brain' in *East Bay Express,* September 22, 2000, for a superb profile of Breedlove and his research; and Susan Rubinowitz, 'Report: Index Finger Size May Indicate Homosexuality' in *New York Post,* March 30, 2000.

89. Marc Breedlove, personal communication with M. Kimmel, February 13, 2001; see also David Puts, Cynthia Jordan, and S. Marc Breedlove, 'O Brother, Where Are Thou? The Fraternal Birth-Order Effect on Male Sexual Orientation'

in *Proceedings of the National Academy of Science*, 103(28), July 11, 2006, pp. 10531–10532. For penis size, see Anthony Bogaert and Scott Hershberger, 'The Relation between Sexual Orientation and Penile Size,' in *Archives of Sexual Behavior*, 28 (3), 1999: pp. 213–221.

90. Anthony Bogaert, 'Biological Versus Nonbiological Older Brothers and Men's Sexual Orientation' in *Proceedings of the National Academy of Science*, 103(28), July 11, 2006, pp. 10771–10774.

91. See Alice Domurat Dreger, *Hermaphrodites and the Medical Invention of Sex* (Cambridge: Harvard University Press, 1998); Gert Hekma, ' "A Female Soul in a Male Body": Sexual Inversion as Gender Inversion in Nineteenth Century Sexology' in *Third Sex, Third Gender*, Gilbert Herdt, ed. (Cambridge: MIT Press, 1993). The term 'intersexed' was preferred by the Intersex Society of North America, an advocacy group active from 1993 to 2008. Largely as a result of the success of its advocacy work, it has been replaced by the Accord Alliance, which works on behalf of people with 'disorders of sex development', including but not limited to intersexuality. See http://www.accordalliance.org/. The 1.7% figure (higher than the generally accepted, though unclearly derived, estimate of 1%) is from Anne Fausto-Sterling's research. See *Sexing the Body*, p. 51.

92. John Money and Anke Ehrhardt, *Man and Woman, Boy and Girl* (Baltimore: Johns Hopkins University Press, 1972).

93. Fausto-Sterling, *Myths of Gender*, pp. 136–137.

94. Ibid.

95. John Stossel, 'Just Too Taboo to Talk About', in *Orange County Register,* January 30, 2005.

96. See Meyer-Behlberg et al., 'Prenatal Androgenization Affects Gender-Related Behavior But Not Gender Identity in 5–12-Year-Old Girls with Congenital Adrenal Hyperplasia', in *Archives of Sexual Behavior*, 33 (2), 2004, pp. 97–104.

97. Irvin Yalom, Richard Green, and N. Fisk, 'Prenatal Exposure to Female Hormones—Effect on Psychosexual Development in Boys' in *Archives of General Psychiatry* 28. 1973.

98. María José Martínez-Patiño, 'A Woman Tried and Tested', in *The Lancet,* 366 (2005).

99. See Julianne Imperato-McGinley et al., 'Steroid 5-Alpha Reductase Deficiency in Man: An Inherited Form of Pseudohermaphroditism' in *Science*, 186, 1974; Julianne Imperato-McGinley et al., 'Androgens and the Evolution of Male-Gender Identity Among Male Pseudohermaphrodites with 5-Alpha Reductase Deficiency' in *New England Journal of Medicine*, 300, 1979, p. 1235. For an excellent summary of the research, see Gilbert Herdt, 'Mistaken Sex: Culture, Biology and the Third Sex in New Guinea' in Herdt, *Third Sex, Third Gender*.

100. Herdt, 'Mistaken Sex'.

101. Cited in Carol Tavris and Carole Wade, *The Longest War*, pp. 208–209.

102. Goldberg, *The Inevitability of Patriarchy*, pp. 233–234; see also Fausto-Sterling, *Myths of Gender*, p. 124.

103. A recent effort to use hormone research and evolutionary imperatives is J. Richard Udry, 'Biological Limits of Gender Construction' in *American Sociological Review*, 65, June, 2000, pp. 443–457. Udry's thesis is elegantly demolished by Eleanor Miller and Carrie Yang Costello, 'Comment on Udry' in *American Sociological Review*, 65, June, 2000, pp. 592–598.

104. Lewontin et al., *Not in Our Genes*, p. 147.

105. Alice Rossi, *Gender and the Life Course* (Chicago: Aldine, 1982).

106. Darrell Yates Rist, 'Are Homosexuals Born That Way?' in *The Nation*, October 19, 1992, p. 427; 'Born or Bred?' in *Newsweek*, February 24, 1992.

107. Karen De Witt, 'Quayle Contends Homosexuality Is a Matter of Choice, Not Biology' in *New York Times*, September 14, 1992; Ashcroft cited in Eric Alterman, 'Sorry, Wrong President' in *The Nation*, February 26, 2001, p. 10. See John Leland and Mark Miller, 'Can Gays Convert?' in *Newsweek*, August 17, 1998. Although it is certain that some therapeutic interventions can lead people to change their sexual behaviour and sexual object choice, the evidence that people's orientations change is less than convincing.

108. Simon LeVay, *The Sexual Brain* (Cambridge: MIT Press, 1994), p. 6.

109. Ruth Hubbard, 'The Political Nature of Human Nature' in *Theoretical Perspectives on Sexual Difference*, Deborah Rhode ed. (New Haven: Yale University Press, 1990), p. 69.

110. Robert A. Padgug, 'On Conceptualizing Sexuality in History' in *Radical History Review*, 20, 1979, p. 9.

111. Adam Begley, 'Why Men and Women Think Differently' in *Newsweek*, 1995.

112. Fausto-Sterling, *Sexing the Body*, pp. 253–254.

Chapter 3

1. Carol Gilligan, affidavit in Johnson v. Jones (D Ct, S.C., filed January 7, 1993), p. 3; affidavit on file with M. Kimmel.

2. Sigmund Freud, 'The Dissection of the Psychical Personality' in *New Introductory Lectures on Psychoanalysis* [1933] (New York: W.W. Norton, 1965), p. 74.

3. Sigmund Freud, 'The Dissolution of the Oedipus Complex' [1924] in The Standard Edition of the *Complete Psychological Works*, Vol. 19, p. 179.

4. Sigmund Freud, *Letters of Sigmund Freud, 1873-1939*, Ernst Freud, ed. (London: Hogarth Press, 1961), pp. 419–420.

5. See, for example, Jeffrey Masson, *The Assault on Truth* (New York: Farrar, Straus and Giroux, 1984); and Alice Miller, *Thou Shalt Not Be Aware: Society's Betrayal of the Child* (New York: Farrar, Straus and Giroux, 1984), *For Your Own Good* (New York: Farrar, Straus and Giroux, 1983).

6. See Carol Glover, 'Her Body, Himself: Gender in the Slasher Film', in Barry Keith Grant, ed., *The Dread of Difference: Gender and the Horror Film* (Austin: University of Texas Press, 1996), pp. 66–114; Barbara Creed, 'Dark Desires: Male Masochism in the Horror Film', in Steven Cohan and Ina Rae Hark, *Screening the Male: Exploring Masculinities in Hollywood Cinema* (Routledge, 1992), pp. 118–133; Joelle Ruby Ryan, 'Reel Gender: Examining the Politics of Trans Images in Media and Film', (Ph.D. diss, Bowling Green State University, 2009), pp. 178–192; 8.

7. Lewis Terman and Catherine Cox Miles, *Sex and Personality* (New York: McGraw-Hill, 1936); see also Henry Minton, 'Femininity in Men and Masculinity in Women: American Psychiatry and Psychology Portray Homosexuality in the 1930s' in *Journal of Homosexuality*, 13(1), 1986.

8. Ronald LaTorre and William Piper, 'The Terman-Miles M-F Test: An Examination of Exercises 1, 2, and 3 Forty Years Later', in *Sex Roles*, 4 (1), 1978: pp. 141–154.

9. George Henry, 'Psychogenic Factors in Overt Homosexuality' in *American Journal of Psychiatry*, 93, 1937; cited in Minton, 'Femininity in Men . . .', p. 2. Note, however, that Henry's secondary claim is not that these tendencies will simply emerge, but rather that the social response to these traits will exaggerate and sustain them; i.e., that overt responses of homophobia will actually encourage the tendency toward homosexuality.

10. Joseph Pleck offered a superb summary of these studies in 'The Theory of Male Sex Role Identity: Its Rise and Fall, 1936 to the Present' in *In the Shadow of the Past: Psychology Views the Sexes*, M. Lewin, ed. (New York: Columbia University Press, 1984). Much of this summary draws from his essay.

11. Teodor Adorno et al., *The Authoritarian Personality* (New York: Harper and Row, 1950).

12. See Robb Willer, 'Overdoing Gender', unpublished manuscript, Department of Sociology, Cornell University, 2005. Available at http://willer.berkeley.edu/WillerOverdoingGender.pdf. The study was widely reported. See Mary Beckman, 'How to Sell Humvees to Men', *Science*, August 4, 2005, available at http://sciencenow.sciencemag.org/cgi/content/full/2005/804/1; accessed August 20, 2009; one recent confirming study is Peter Glick, Candice Gangl, Samantha Gibb, Susan Klumpner, and Emily Weinberg, 'Defensive Reactions to Masculinity Threat: More Negative Affect toward Effemininate (but Not Masculine) Gay Men', *Sex Roles* 57, 2007, pp. 55–59.

13. Walter Miller and E. Guy Swanson, *Inner Conflict and Defense* (New York: Holt, 1960).

14. Talcott Parsons, 'Certain Primary Sources and Patterns of Aggression in the Social Structure of the Western World', *Psychiatry*, 10 (1947):309.

15. Sandra Bem, 'The Measurement of Psychological Androgyny' in *Journal of Consulting and Clinical Psychology*, 42, 1974; Sandra Bem, 'Androgyny vs. the Tight Little Lives of Fluffy Women and Chesty Men' in *Psychology Today*, September, 1975; Sandra Bem, 'Beyond Androgyny: Some Presumptuous Prescriptions for a Liberated Sexual Identity' in *The Future of Women: Issues in Psychology*, J. Sherman and F. Denmark, eds. (New York: Psychological Dimensions, 1978). See also Alexandra Kaplan and Mary Anne Sedney, *Psychology and Sex Roles: An Androgynous Perspective* (Boston: Little Brown, 1980), quote is on p. 6; Janet Spence, Robert Helmreich, and Joy Stapp, 'The

Personal Attributes Questionnaire: A Measure of Sex-Role Stereotypes and Masculinity-Femininity' in *JSAS Catalog of Selected Documents in Psychology*, 4, 1974; Sandra Bem, *Lenses of Gender* (New Haven: Yale University Press, 1993), p. 124.

16. Joseph Pleck, *The Myth of Masculinity* (Cambridge: MIT Press, 1981).

17. See, for example, James M. O'Neil, 'Assessing Men's Gender Role Conflict' in *Problem Solving Strategies and Interventions for Men in Conflict*, D. Moorer and F. Leafgren, eds. (Alexandria, VA: American Association for Counseling and Development, 1990); J.M. O'Neil, B. Helms, R. Gable, L. David, and L. Wrightsman, 'Gender Role Conflict Scale: College Men's Fear of Femininity' in *Sex Roles*, 14, 1986, pp. 335–350; Joseph Pleck, 'The Gender Role Strain Paradigm: An Update' in *A New Psychology of Men*, R. Levant and W. Pollack, eds. (New York: Basic Books, 1995); James Mihalik, Benjamin Locke, Harry Theodore, Robert Cournoyer, and Brendan Lloyd, 'A Cross-National and Cross-Sectional Comparison of Men's Gender Role Conflict and Its Relationship to Social Intimacy and Self-Esteem' in *Sex Roles*, 45(1/2), 2001, pp. 1–14.

18. Warren Farrell, *The Myth of Male Power* (New York: Simon & Schuster, 1993), p. 40.

19. That's not to say that Pleck doesn't try valiantly to do so. His 'Men's Power over Women, Other Men and in Society' in *Women and Men: The Consequences of Power*, D. Hiller and R. Sheets, eds. (Cincinnati: University of Cincinnati Women's Studies, 1977), takes the theory as far as it will go. But the theory is still unable to theorize both difference and institutionalized gender relations adequately.

20. Jean-Paul Sartre, *Anti-Semite and Jew* (New York: Schocken Press, 1965), p. 60.

21. See Jean Piaget, *Plays, Dreams and Imitation in Children* (New York: Norton, 1951), *The Language and Thought of the Child* (London: Routledge, 1952), and *The Moral Judgment of the Child* (New York: Free Press, 1965).

22. Lawrence Kohlberg, 'A Cognitive-Developmental Analysis of Children's Sex Role Concepts and Attitudes' in *The Development of Sex Differences*, E. Maccoby, ed. (Stanford: Stanford University Press, 1966), and Lawrence Kohlberg and Edward Zigler, 'The Impact of Cognitive Maturity on the Development of Sex Role

Attitudes in the Years 4 to 8' in *Genetic Psychology Monographs*, 75, 1967.

23. Albert Bandura and Althea Huston, 'Identification as a Process of Incidental Learning' in *Journal of Abnormal and Social Psychology*, 63, 1961; Albert Bandura, Dorothea Ross, and Sheila Ross, 'A Comparative Test of the Status Envy, Social Power, and Secondary Reinforcement Theories of Identificatory Learning' in *Journal of Abnormal and Social Psychology*, 67, 1963; Walter Mischel, 'A Social-Learning View of Sex Differences' in *The Development of Sex Differences*, E. Maccoby, ed.

24. Julia Kristeva, *Melanie Klein*, trans. Ross Guberman (New York: Columbia University Press, 2001), 118; Karen Horney, 'On the Genesis of the Castration Complex in Women' in *Psychoanalysis and Women*, J.B. Miller, ed. (New York: Bruner/Mazel, 1973); Melanie Klein, *A Study of Envy and Gratitude* (New York/London: Routledge, 2003 [1957]).

25. Bruno Bettelheim, *Symbolic Wounds* (New York: Collier, 1962); Wolfgang Lederer, *The Fear of Women* (New York: Harcourt Brace Jovanovich, 1968).

26. Nancy Chodorow, *The Reproduction of Mothering* (Berkeley: University of California Press, 1978); Jessica Benjamin, *The Bonds of Love* (New York: Pantheon, 1984); Dorothy Dinnerstein, *The Mermaid and the Minotaur* (New York: Harper and Row, 1977); Lillian Rubin, *Intimate Strangers* (New York: Harper and Row, 1983).

27. Chodorow, *The Reproduction of Mothering*; see also Chodorow, 'Family Structure and Feminine Personality' in *Women, Culture and Society*, M. Rosaldo and L. Lamphere, eds. (Stanford: Stanford University Press, 1974).

28. Chodorow, 'Family Structure . . .', p.50.

29. Carol Gilligan, *In a Different Voice* (Cambridge: Harvard University Press, 1982), p. 173.

30. Belenky et al., *Women's Ways of Knowing* (New York: Basic Books, 1987); Deborah Tannen, *You Just Don't Understand*; Robert Bly, *Iron John* (Reading: Addison-Wesley, 1991).

31. See H. Crothers, *Meditations on Votes for Women* (Boston: Houghton, Mifflin, 1914), p. 74.

32. Carol Gilligan, 'Reply' in 'On In a Different Voice: An Interdisciplinary Forum' in *Signs*, 11(2), 1986, p. 327; affidavit of Carol Gilligan in Johnson v Jones, D Ct, S.C., filed January 7, 1993, p. 3.

33. See Madam Justice Bertha Wilson, 'Will Women Judges Really Make a Difference? The Fourth Annual Barbara Betcherman Memorial Lecture', in *Family and Conciliation Courts Review*, 30 (1), January, 1992, pp. 13–25: 24.

34. Carol Tavris, 'The Mismeasure of Woman' in *Feminism and Psychology*, 3(2), 1993, p. 153.

35. Eleanor Maccoby and Carol Jacklin, *The Psychology of Sex Differences* (Stanford: Stanford University Press, 1974), p. 355.

36. Janet Hyde, 'The Gender Similarities Hypothesis', *The American Psychologist*, 60, 2005, pp. 581–592.

Chapter 4

1. Margaret Mead, *Sex and Temperament in Three Primitive Societies* (New York: William Morrow, 1935).

2. For an example of how broadly Mead's theories were applied, see Doris Chang, 'Reading *Sex and Temperament* in Taiwan: Margaret Mead and Postwar Taiwanese Feminism', in *NWSA Journal*, 21 (1), Spring 2009, pp. 51–75.

3. Mead, *Sex and Temperament*, pp. 29, 35, 57–58, 84, 101, 128.

4. Margaret Mead, *Male and Female* (New York: William Morrow, 1949), p. 69; Mead, *Sex and Temperament*, p. 171.

5. Mead, *Sex and Temperament*, pp. 189, 190, 197; Mead, *Male and Female*, p. 98.

6. See, among many other sources, Derek Freeman, *Margaret Mead and Samoa: The Making and Unmaking of an Anthropological Myth* (Cambridge, MA/London: Harvard University Press, 1983) and *The Fateful Hoaxing of Margaret Mead: A Historical Analysis of Her Samoan Research* (New York: Basic Books, 1999); Paul Roscoe, 'Margaret Mead, Reo Fortune, and Mountain Arapesh Warfare', in *American Anthropologist*, 105 (3), January 2008, pp. 581–591; Micaela di Leonardo, 'Margaret Mead and the Culture of Forgetting in Anthropology: A Response to Paul Roscoe', in *American Anthropologist,* 105 (3), 2003, pp. 592–595; and David Lipset, 'Rereading *Sex and Temperament*: Margaret Mead's Sepik Triptych and Its Ethnographic Critics', *Anthropological Quarterly*, 76 (4), Fall 2003, pp. 693-713.

7. Mead, *Sex and Temperament*, p. 228.

8. Adrienne Zihlman, 'Woman the Gatherer: The Role of Women in Early Hominid Evolution' in *Gender and Anthropology*, S. Morgen, ed. (Washington: American Anthropological Association, 1989), p. 31.

9. Friedrich Engels, *On the Origin of the Family, Private Property and the State* (New York: International Publishers, 1970).

10. Eleanor Leacock, 'Women's Status in Egalitarian Society: Implications for Social Evolution' in *Current Anthropology*, 19(2), 1978, p. 252; see also Eleanor Leacock, 'Montagnais Women and the Jesuit Program for Colonization' in *Women and Colonization*, M. Etienne and E. Leacock, eds. (New York: Praeger, 1980).

11. Karen Sacks, 'Engels Revisited: Women, Organization of Production, and Private Property', in *Women, Culture, and Society*, M. Rosaldo and L. Lamphere, eds. (Stanford: Stanford University Press, 1974).

12. Marvin Harris, *Cows, Pigs, Wars and Witches: The Riddle of Culture* (New York: Random House, 1974); and *Cannibals and Kings* (New York: Random House, 1977).

13. Lionel Tiger and Robin Fox, *The Imperial Animal* (New York: Holt, 1971).

14. Claude Levi-Strauss, *The Elementary Structures of Kinship* (London: Tavistock, 1969); see also Collier and Rosaldo, 'Politics and Gender in Simple Societies' in *Sexual Meanings: The Cultural Construction of Gender and Sexuality*, S.B. Ortner and H. Whitehead, eds. (Cambridge: Cambridge University Press, 1981).

15. H. Barry, M. Bacon, and A. Child, 'A Cross-cultural Survey of Some Sex Differences in Socialization', *Journal of Abnormal and Social Psychology*, 55, 1957, pp. 327–332.

16. Judith Brown, 'A Note on the Division of Labor by Sex', in *American Anthropologist*, 72(5), 1970.

17. Scott Coltrane; *Family Man: Fatherhood, Housework, and Gender Equity* (Oxford: Oxford University Press, 1996), p. 191 passim; Margaret Mead, *Male and Female*, pp. 189, 190.

18. Daphne Spain, *Gendered Spaces* (Chapel Hill: University of North Carolina Press, 1992); 'The Spatial Foundations of Men's Friendships and Men's Power' in *Men's Friendships*, Peter Nardi, ed. (Newbury Park, CA: Sage Publications, 1992), p. 76.

19. Thomas Gregor, *Mehinaku: The Drama of Daily Life in a Brazilian Indian Village* (Chicago:

University of Chicago Press, 1977), p. 255; see also pp. 305–306; In another passage, Gregor recounts a child's game in which a girl pretends to invade the men's house, and the boys pretend to gang rape her (p.114). See also Thomas Gregor, 'No Girls Allowed', *Science*, 82, December, 1982.

20. Peggy Reeves Sanday, *Female Power and Male Dominance* (New York: Cambridge University Press, 1981), pp. 75, 128. See also Maria Lepowsky, 'Gender in an Egalitarian Society: A Case Study from the Coral Sea' in *Beyond the Second Sex: New Directions in the Anthropology of Gender*, P. R. Sanday and R. G. Goodenough, eds. (Philadelphia: University of Pennsylvania Press, 1990); See Carol Tavris and Carole Wade, *The Longest War* (New York: Harcourt, Brace, 1984), pp. 330–331.

21. Tavris and Wade, *The Longest War,* pp. 330–331.

22. John W. Whiting, Richard Kluckhohn, and Albert Anthony, 'The Function of Male Initiation Ceremonies at Puberty' in *Readings in Social Psychology*, E. Maccoby, T. M. Newcomb, and E. L. Hatley, eds. (New York: Henry Holt, 1958); Edgar Gregersen, *Sexual Practices* (New York: Franklin Watts, 1983), p. 104.

23. Marc Lacey, 'African Activists Urge End to Female Mutilation' in *International Herald Tribune*, February 7, 2003, p. 10.

24. Cited in 'Unmasking Tradition' by Rogaia Mustafa Abusharaf in *The Sciences*, March/April, 1998, p. 23.

25. 'Canada Circumcision Statistics'. Circumcision Reference Library. Available at http://www.cirp.org/library/statistics/Canada/. Accessed April 28, 2009.

26. Karen Paige and Jeffrey Paige, *The Politics of Reproductive Ritual* (Berkeley: University of California Press, 1981).

27. Tavris and Wade, *The Longest War*, p. 314; see also Paige and Paige, *The Politics of Reproductive Ritual*; Fatima Mernissi, *Beyond the Veil: Male-Female Dynamics in a Modern Muslim Society* (New York: Wiley, 1975).

28. Frederick Nzwili, 'New Ritual Replaces Female Genital Mutilation' in *Women's ENews*, April 10, 2003 available at www.womensenews.org/article.cfm/dyn/ aid/1284.

29. L. Amede Obiora, 'Bridges and Barricades: Rethinking Polemics and Intransigence in the Campaign against Female Circumcision', in

A.K. Wing, eds., *Global Critical Race Feminism: An International Reader* (New York: New York University Press, 2000).

30. See, for example, Joseph Zoske, 'Male Circumcision: A Gender Perspective' in *Journal of Men's Studies*, 6(2), Winter, 1998; see also Michael Kimmel, 'The Kindest Uncut' in *Tikkun*, 16(3), May, 2001.

31. See 'Tostan (Senegal), Laureate of the 2007 UNESCO King Sejong Literacy Prize', UNESCO Education Literacy Portal, available at http://portal.unesco.org/education/en/ev.php-URL_ID=53774&URL_DO=DO_TOPIC&URL_SECTION=201.html, accessed May 6, 2009. Also see 'Abandoning Female Genital Cutting'. Available at http://www.tostan.org/web/page/586/sectionid/547/pagelevel/3/interior.asp, accessed May 6, 2009.

32. Michael Olien, *The Human Myth* (New York: Harper and Row, 1978); M.K. Martin and B. Voorhies, *Female of the Species* (New York: Columbia University Press, 1975).

33. Walter Williams, *The Spirit and the Flesh* (Boston: Beacon Press, 1986).

34. Sabine Lang, *Men as Women, Women as Men* (Austin: University of Texas Press, 1998).

35. For discussion, see Will Roscoe, 'How to Become a Berdache', in Gilbert Herdt, ed., *Third Sex, Third Gender: Beyond Sexual Dimorphism in Culture and History* (New York: Zone Books, 1996), pp. 329–72; 339.

36. Edgar Gregersen, *Sexual Practices*, p. 270.

37. Antonia Young, *Women Who Become Men: Albanian Sworn Virgins* (Palgrave MacMillan, 2001); Rene Gremaux, 'Woman Becomes Man in the Balkans', in Gilbert Herdt, *Third Sex, Third Gender*, pp. 241–81; Mike Lanchin, 'Last of Albania's "Sworn Virgins" ', BBC News, October 22, 2008, available at http://news.bbc.co.uk/2/hi/europe/7682240.stm, accessed May 5, 2009; Nicola Smith, 'Sworn Virgins Dying out as Albanian Girls Reject Manly Role', Times Online, January 6, 2008, available at http://www.timesonline.co.uk/tol/news/world/europe/article3137518.ece, accessed May 5, 2009.

38. Martin and Voorhies, *Female of the Species*, p. 97.

39. Marc Lacey, 'A Lifestyle Distinct: The Muxe of Mexico', *New York Times*, December 6, 2008, available at http://www.nytimes.com/2008/12/07/weekinreview/07lacey.html; accessed May 10, 2009.

40. Serena Nanda, 'Hijras: An Alternative Sex and Gender Role in India', in Herdt, ed., *Third Sex, Third Gender*, pp. 373–417; RIA Misra, 'Pakistan Recognizes Third Gender', *Politics Daily*, December 25, 2009, available at http://www.politicsdaily.com/2009/12/25/pakistan-recognizes-third-gender/; accessed January 1, 2010.

41. Cited in Clyde Kluckholn, *Mirror for Man* (Greenwich, CT: Greenword, 1970).

42. Gilbert Herdt, *Guardians of the Flutes* (Chicago: University of Chicago Press, 1981), pp. 1, 165, 282.

43. F.E. Williams, *Papuans of the Trans-Fly* (Oxford: Oxford University Press, 1936), p. 159; see also E. L. Schiefflin, *The Sorrow of the Lonely and the Burning of the Dancers* (New York: St. Martin's Press, 1976); R. Kelly, *Etero Social Structure* (Ann Arbor: University of Michigan Press, 1977); J. Carrier, 'Sex Role Preference as an Explanatory Variable in Homosexual Behavior' in *Archives of Sexual Behavior*, 6, 1977; Stephen O. Murray, *Homosexualities* (Chicago: University of Chicago Press, 2000).

44. William Davenport, 'Sex in Cross-Cultural Perspective' in *Human Sexuality in Four Perspectives*, F. Beach and M. Diamond, eds. (Baltimore: Johns Hopkins University Press, 1977); see also Gilbert Herdt, ed., *Ritualized Homosexuality in Melanesia* (Berkeley: University of California Press, 1984), p. 66.

45. Gregersen, *Sexual Practices*, p. 257.

46. Ibid.

47. Davenport, 'Sex in Cross-Cultural Perspective'.

48. Ernestine Friedel, *Women and Men: An Anthropologist's View* (New York: Holt, Rinehart, 1975).

49. Gregersen, *Sexual Practices*.

50. Kluckholn, 1948; see also Gregersen, *Sexual Practices*.

51. Gregersen, *Sexual Practices*.

52. Nancy Tanner and Adrienne Zihlman, 'Women in Evolution' in *Signs*, 1(3), Spring, 1976. Nancy Tanner, *Becoming Human* (New York: Cambridge University Press, 1981); Adrienne Zihlman, 'Motherhood in Transition: From Ape to Human', in *The First Child and Family Formation*, W. Miller and L. Newman, eds. (Chapel Hill: Carolina Population Center, 1978).

53. Helen Fischer, *The Anatomy of Love* (New York: Norton, 1992), p. 57.

54. Michelle Rosaldo, 'The Use and Abuse of Anthroplogy: Reflections on Feminism and Cross-Cultural Understanding' in *Signs*, 5(3), Spring, 1980, p. 393; Bonnie Nardi, review of Peggy Reeves Sanday's *Female Power and Male Dominance* in *Sex Roles*, 8(11), 1982, p. 1159.

55. Marija Gimbutas, *The Goddesses and Gods of Old Europe, 7000–3500 B.C.* (Berkeley: University of California Press, 1982), and Marija Gimbutas, *The Living Goddesses* (Berkeley: University of California Press, 1999). See also Riane Eisler, *The Chalice and the Blade* (New York: HarperCollins, 1987).

56. Eisler, *The Chalice and the Blade*, pp. 45, 58.

57. Frances Fukuyama, 'Women and the Evolution of World Politics' in *Foreign Affairs*, September, 1998, p. 27; see also Lawrence Keely, *War Before Civilization*.

58. Maria Lepowsky, *Fruit of the Motherland: Gender in an Egalitarian Society* (New York: Columbia University Press, 1993), p. 219.

59. Peggy Reeves Sanday, *Women Center: Life in a Modern Matriarchy* (Boston: Beacon, 2002), p. 116.

60. Eleanor Leacock, 'Montagnais Women . . .', p. 200.

Chapter 5

1. M. Pines, 'Civilizing of Genes' in *Psychology Today*, September, 1981.

2. Helen Z. Lopata and Barrie Thorne, 'On the Term "Sex Roles" ' in *Signs*, 3, 1978, p. 719.

3. Tim Carrigan, Bob Connell, and John Lee, 'Toward a New Sociology of Masculinity' in *Theory and Society*, 14, 1985. See also R.W. Connell, *Gender and Power* (Stanford: Stanford University Press, 1987); R.W. Connell, *Masculinities* (Berkeley: University of California Press, 1995); Judith Stacey and Barrie Thorne, 'The Missing Feminist Revolution in Sociology' in *Social Problems*, 32(4), 1985, for elaboration and summaries of the sociological critique of sex role theory.

4. Deborah Rhode, *Speaking of Sex* (Cambridge: Harvard University Press, 1997), p. 42.

5. Stacey and Thorne, 'The Missing Feminist Revolution . . .', p. 307.

6. Carrigan, Connell, and Lee, 'Toward a New Sociology . . .', p. 587; see also Connell, *Gender and Power*.

7. David Tresemer, 'Assumptions Made About Gender Roles' in *Another Voice: Feminist Perspectives on Social Life and Social Science*, M. Millman and R.M. Kanter, eds., (New York:

Anchor Books, 1975), p. 323; R. Stephen Warner, David Wellman, and Leonore Weitzman, 'The Hero, the Sambo and the Operator: Three Characterizations of the Oppressed' in *Urban Life and Culture*, 2, 1973.

8. Hannah Arendt, *On Revolution* (New York: Viking, 1976).

9. David P. Schmitt et al., 'Is There an Early-30s Peak in Female Sexual Desire? Cross-Sectional Evidence from the United States and Canada', in *The Canadian Journal of Human Sexuality*, 11 (1), Spring 2002, pp. 1–18: p. 3.

10. Ibid.

11. P.T. Costa and R.R. McCrae, 'Age Difference in Personality Structure: A Cluster Analytic Approach' in *Journal of Gerontology*, 31 (1978): 564–570; See also G.E. Valliant, *Adaptations to Life* (Boston: Little Brown, 1978).

12. Elaine Wethington, 'Multiple Roles, Social Integration, and Health' in K. Pillemer, P. Moen, E. Wethington, and N. Glasgow, eds., *Social Integration in the Second Half of Life* (Baltimore, MD: Johns Hopkins University Press, 2000).

13. See Stanley Rosenberg, Harriet Rosenberg, and Michael Farrell, 'The Midlife Crisis Revisited', in Sherry Willis and James Reid, eds., *Life in the Middle: Psychological and Social Development in Middle Age* (Toronto: Academic Press, 1998), pp. 47–76.

14. David Blanchflower and Andrew Oswald, 'Is Well-Being U-Shaped over the Life Cycle?' *Social Science & Medicine*, 11 (8), April 2008, pp. 1733–49.

15. 'Gender Gap in Life Expectancy Narrows to 5.2 Years', *Canadian Medical Association Journal* 168 (11), May 27, 2003; 'Canadian Babies Can Expect to See Their 80s: StatsCan', CBC News.ca, December 20, 2006. Available athttp://www.cbc.ca/health/story/2006/12/20/life-span.html?ref=rss; accessed 15 January 2009.

16. Such predictions are difficult, of course. For discussion, see Jim Oeppen and James W. Vaupel, 'Broken Limits to Life Expectancy', *Science*, 296, May 10, 2002, pp. 1029–1031.

17. Ahifa Kassam, 'Turf War: Bullying of Belinda Stronach Tells Women "Stay Out" ', in *Herizons: Women's News and Feminist Views*, 21 (2), Fall 2007, pp. 16–19.

18. Janet Saltzman Chafetz, 'Toward a Macro-Level Theory of Sexual Stratification' in *Current Perspectives in Social Theory*, 1, 1980.

19. Erving Goffman, 'The Arrangement Between the Sexes' in *Theory and Society*, 4, 1977, p. 316.

20. Rosabeth Moss Kanter, *Men and Women of the Corporation* (New York: Basic Books, 1977). See also Rosabeth Moss Kanter, 'Women and the Structure of Organizations: Explorations in Theory and Behavior' in *Another Voice: Feminist Perspectives on Social Life and Social Science*, M. Millman and R.M. Kanter, eds. (New York: Anchor Books, 1975).

21. Joan Acker, 'Hierarchies, Jobs, Bodies: A Theory of Gendered Organizations' in *Gender & Society*, 4(2), 1990, p. 146; see also Joan Acker, 'Sex Bias in Job Evaluation: A Comparable Worth Issue' in *Ingredients for Women's Employment Policy*, C. Bose and G. Spitze, eds. (Albany: SUNY Press,1987); 'Class, Gender and the Relations of Distribution' in *Signs: Journal of Women in Culture and Society*, 13, 1988; *Doing Comparable Worth: Gender, Class and Pay Equity* (Philadelphia: Temple University Press, 1989), and Joan Acker and Donald R. Van Houten, 'Differential Recruitment and Control: The Sex Structuring of Organizations' in *Administrative Science Quarterly*, 19(2), 1974.

22. Cathy Gulli and Kate Lunau, 'Adding Fuel to the Doctor Crisis', *Maclean's*, January 2, 2008. Available at http://www.macleans.ca/science/health/article.jsp?content=20080102_122329_6200, accessed on November 18, 2009; Cathy Gulli, 'Where Have All the Men Gone?' *Maclean's*, September 17, 2007. Available at http://www.macleans.ca/education/postsecondary/article.jsp?content1120070924_109282_1, accessed November 14, 2009.

23. Wendy Robbins, 'Tenure Track and Reproductive Track on Collision Course', Canadian Association of University Teachers, available at http://www.academicwork.ca/en_career_articles_details.asp?cID=7. Accessed 6 May 2009.

24. Judith Gerson and Kathy Peiss, 'Boundaries, Negotiation, Consciousness: Reconceptualizing Gender Relations' in *Social Problems*, 32(4), 1985, p. 320.

25. Acker, 'Hierarchies, Jobs, Bodies . . .', p. 258.

26. Candace West and Don Zimmerman, 'Doing Gender' in *Gender & Society*, 1(2), 1987, pp. 140.

27. Claudia Dreifus, 'Declaring with Clarity When Gender Is Ambiguous' in *New York Times*, May

31, 2005, p. F2; see also Suzanne J. Kessler, 'The Medical Construction of Gender: Case Management of Intersexed Infants' in *Signs* 16(1), 1990, p. 12, 13.

28. The phrase comes from R.W. Connell; we take it from the title of Barbara Risman, *Gender Vertigo* (New Haven: Yale University Press, 1998).

29. Cited in West and Zimmerman, 'Doing Gender' pp. 133–134.

30. Carey Goldberg, 'Shunning 'He' and 'She,' They Fight for Respect' in *New York Times*, September 8, 1996, p. 24.

31. Ibid.

32. Harold Garfinkel, *Studies in Ethnomethodology* (Englewood Cliffs: Prentice-Hall, 1967), pp. 128, 132.

33. Suzanne Kessler, 'The Medical Construction of Gender . . .', p. 25.

34. Simone de Beauvoir, *The Second Sex*, trans. H. M. Parshley (New York: Vintage Books, 1989 [1952]), 267.

35. Mary Wollstonecraft, *A Vindication of the Rights of Woman* (New York: The Modern Library, 2001).

36. Susan Oliver, *Betty Friedan: The Personal is Political* (New York/Toronto: Pearson Longman, 2008), 71.

37. Leslie McCall, 'The Complexity of Intersectionality', *Signs*, 30(3), 2005, pp. 1771–1800.

38. West and Zimmerman, 'Doing Gender', p. 140; Barrie Thorne, 1980, p. 11; E.P. Thompson, *The Making of the English Working Class* (New York: Pantheon, 1963), p. 11.

39. James Messerschmidt, *Masculinities and Crime* (Lanham, MD: Rowman and Littlefield, 1993), p. 121.

40. Carrigan, Connell, and Lee, 'Toward a New Sociology of Masculinity', p. 589; Karen D. Pyke, 'Class-Based Masculinities: The Interdependence of Gender, Class and Interpersonal Power' in *Gender & Society*, 10(5), 1996, p. 530.

Chapter 6

1. REAL Women of Canada, 'Ongoing Discrimination by the Status of Women', *REALity* XXV, No. 3 (May/June 2006). Available at http://www.realwomenca.com/page/newslmj0607; accessed June 2, 2009.

2. The American debate over family values is too extensive to be summarized here. See, for a few examples, Barbara Dafoe Whitehead, 'Dan Quayle Was Right' in *The Atlantic*, April, 1993, which became the touchstone for her book, *The Divorce Culture* (New York: Random House, 1996); David Popenoe, *Life Without Father: Compelling New Evidence That Fatherhood and Marriage Are Indispensable for the Good of Children and Society* (New York: The Free Press, 1996), and his 'Modern Marriage: Revising the Cultural Script' in *Promises to Keep: Decline and Renewal of Marriage in America*, D. Popenoe, J.B. Elshtain, and D. Blankenhorn, eds. (Lanham, MD: Rowman and Littlefield, 1996). On the other side, see Judith Stacey, *Brave New Families* (New York: Basic Books, 1990), and *In the Name of the Family: Rethinking Family Values in a Postmodern Age* (Boston: Beacon 1997), as well as Stephanie Coontz, *The Way We Never Were: American Families and the Nostalgia Trap* (New York: Basic Books, 1995), and *The Way We Really Are: Coming to Terms with America's Changing Families* (New York: Basic Books, 1998).

3. For a discussion of kinship (and the effects of colonialism upon it) in one group, see Laura Peers and Jennifer Brown, '"There Is No End to Relationship among the Indians": Ojibwa Kinship and Family in Historical Perspective', *The History of the Family*, 4, No. 4 (1999), pp. 529–555.

4. See, for example, Mary-Ellen Turpel-Lafond, 'Patriarchy and Paternalism: The Legacy of the Canadian State for First Nations Women', in Caroline Andrew and Sanda Rodgers, eds., *Women and the Canadian State/Les femmmes et l'état Canadien* (Montreal: McGill-Queen's press, 1997), pp. 64–79.

5. For discussion of this process among the Huron and Montagnais, see Karen Anderson, *Chain Her by One Foot: The Subjugation of Native Women in Seventeenth-Century New France* (London/New York: Routledge, 1993). For insight into marriage norms within New France's settler society, see Sylvie Savoie, 'Women's Marital Difficulties: Requests of Separation in New France', *The History of the Family*, 4, No. 4 (1999), pp. 473–485.

6. This is Nancy Shoemaker's argument in 'Kateri Tekakwitha's Tortuous Path to Sainthood', in Mona Gleason and Adele Perry, eds., *Rethinking Canada: The Promise of Women's History* (Toronto: Oxford, 2006), pp. 10–25.

7. The classic treatments of fur-trade families, though in a later period than discussed here,

are Jennifer Brown, *Strangers in Blood: Fur Trade Families in Indian Country* (Vancouver: University of British Columbia Press, 1980); and Sylvia Van Kirk, *Many Tender Ties: Women in Fur-Trade Society, 1670—1870* (Norman: University of Oklahoma Press, 1983).

8. Quoted in Margaret Conrad, ' "Sundays Always Make Me Think of Home": Time & Place in Canadian Women's History', in Barbara K. Latham and Roberta J. Pazdro, eds., *Not Just Pin Money: Selected Essays on the History of Women's Work in British Columbia* (Victoria, BC: Camosun College, 1984), pp. 1–16: p. 7.

9. Laurel Thatcher Ulrich, *A Midwife's Tale: The Life of Martha Ballard, Based on Her Diary, 1785–1812* (New York: VintageBooks, 1991), p. 76.

10. John Demos, *Past, Present, and Personal: The Family and Life Course in American History* (New York: Oxford University Press, 1986), p. 32; see also Tamara Hareven, *Family Time and Industrial Time* (New York: Cambridge University Press, 1982). Tennyson, 'The Princess', is cited in Skolnick, *Embattled Paradise*, p.35.

11. Cited in David Popenoe, *Life Without Father*, p. 95.

12. Gerda Lerner, 'The Lady and the Mill Girl: Changes in the Status of Women in the Age of Jackson' in *American Studies Journal*, 10(1), Spring, 1969, pp. 7, 9. Theodore Dwight, *The Father's Book* (Springfield, MA: G. and C. Merriam, 1834). See, generally, Michael Kimmel, *Manhood in America: A Cultural History* (New York: The Free Press, 1996), chapters 1 and 2.

13. Christopher Lasch, *Women and the Common Life: Love, Marriage, and Feminism* (New York: Norton, 1997), p. 162.

14. Bonnie Thornton Dill, 'Our Mothers' Grief: Racial-Ethnic Women and the Maintenance of Families' in *Journal of Family History*, 13(4), 1988, p. 428.

15. For statistics on Canadian alcohol consumption in the nineteenth century, see 'Alcohol, Consumption of, Per Capita (Canada)' in Jack Blocker, David Fahey, and Ian Tyrrell, *Alcohol and Temperance in Modern History: A Global Encyclopedia* (Oxford: ABC-Clio, 2003), pp. 20–21.

16. John Gillis, 'Making Time for Family: The Invention of Family Time(s) and the Reinvention of Family History' in *Journal of Family History*, 21, 1996; John Gillis, *A World of Their Own*

Making: Myth, Ritual, and the Quest for Family Values (New York: Basic Books, 1996).

17. Skolnick, *Embattled Paradise*, p. 41; Steven Mintz and Susan Kellogg, *Domestic Revolutions: A Social History of the American Family* (New York: The Free Press, 1991), p. 110.

18. See Lynne Marks, ' "A Fragment of Heaven on Earth?" Religion, Gender, and Family in Turn of the Century Canadian Church Periodicals', in Gleason and Perry, *Rethinking Canada*, pp. 124–143.

19. Quoted in Celia Haig-Brown, *Resistance and Renewal: Surviving the Indian Residential School* (Vancouver: Arsenal Pulp Press, 1988), p. 31. The literature on the residential school experience is vast. For a powerful recent publication, see Gregory Younging, Jonathan Dewar, and Mike De Gagne, eds., *Response, Responsibility, and Renewal: Canada's Truth and Reconciliation Journey* (Ottawa: Aboriginal Healing Foundation, 2009).

20. Katrina Srigley, ' "In Case You Hadn't Noticed": Race. Ethnicity, and Women's Wage-Earning in a Depression-Era City', *Labour/Le Travail*, 55, Spring 2005, pp. 69–105. See also Joy Parr's classic study *The Gender of Breadwinners: Women, Men, and Change in Two Industrial Towns, 1880-1950* (Toronto: University of Toronto Press, 1998).

21. E.D. Nelson and Barrie Robinson, *Gender in Canada* (Scarborough: Prentice-Hall, 1998), 88.

22. See Ralph LaRossa, *The Modernization of Fatherhood: A Social and Political History* (Chicago: University of Chicago Press, 1997).

23. Mintz and Kellogg, *Domestic Revolutions*, p. 179, 237; Coontz, *The Way We Really Are*, p. 30.

24. Statistics Canada, *Canada E-book*. Available at http://www43.statcan.ca/02/02d_001a_e.htm; accessed June 2, 2009. For the nineteenth-century data and comparisons between Canada and the USA, see Lisa Dillon, 'Women and the Dynamics of Marriage, Household Status, and Aging in Victorian Canada and the United States', *The History of the Family*, 4(4), pp. 447–483.

25. Mintz and Kellogg, *Domestic Revolutions*, p. 179, 237; Coontz, *The Way We Really Are*, p. 30.

26. William Chafe, *The Unfinished Journey: America Since World War II* (New York: Oxford University Press, 1986), p. 125; Morris Zelditch, 'Role Differentiation in the Nuclear Family: A Comparative Study' in *Family, Socialization and Interaction Process*, T. Parsons and R.F. Bales, eds. (New York: The Free Press, 1955), p. 339.

27. Robert Griswold, *Fatherhood in America: A History* (New York: Basic Books, 1993), p. 204; Lasch, *Women and the Common Life*, p. 94; Ruth Schwartz Cowan, *More Work for Mother: The Ironies of Household Technology from the Open Hearth to the Microwave* (New York: Basic Books, 1983), p. 216; Lerner, cited in Skolnick, *Embattled Paradise*, p. 115.

28. Doris Anderson, 'We've Been Emerging Long Enough', reprinted in Mary Eberts, ' "Write It for the Women": Doris Anderson, the Changemaker', *Canadian Woman Studies/Les cahiers de la femme* 26(2), Summer/Fall 2007, pp. 6–13.

29. See, for example, Barbara Ehrenreich, *The Hearts of Men* (New York: Doubleday, 1983), on the 'male revolt' against breadwinner responsibilities. Also see Michael Kimmel, *Manhood in America*, especially chapter 7.

30. Nancy A. Crowell and Ethel M. Leeper, eds., *America's Fathers and Public Policy* (Washington, DC: National Academy Press, 1994), p. 1.

31. Campaign 2000, '2008 Report Card on Child and Family Poverty in Canada' (Toronto: Campaign 2000, 2008). Available at www.campaign2000.ca; accessed July 5, 2009; Community Foundations of Canada, *Canada's Vital Signs 2008*; summary available at http://www.vitalsignscanada.ca/pdf/2008-national-news-release-and-backgrounder.pdf; accessed July 12, 2009. The Fraser Institute, using its basic-needs calculation, argues that only about 5 percent of Canada's children live in poverty. See Chris Sarlo, 'Poverty in Canada: 2006 Update', *FraserAlert* November 2006. Available at http://www.fraserinstitute.org/Commerce.Web/product_files/PovertyinCanada2006.pdf; accessed July 13, 2009.

32. UNICEF/NCCAH, *Aboriginal Children's Health: Leaving No Child Behind* (Toronto: UNICEF Canada, 2009); Human Resources and Skills Development Canada, 'Canadians in Context—Households and Families'. Available at http://www4.hrsdc.gc.ca/.3ndic.1t.4r@eng.jsp?iid=37; accessed June 24, 2009.

33. There is an ample literature on the topic of the Aboriginal family and its relations with Canadian governments and society. See, inter alia, Ernie Crey and Suzanne Fournier, *Stolen from Our Embrace: The Abduction of First Nations Children and the Restoration of Aboriginal Communities* (Vancouver: Douglas & McIntyre,

1997); Marlee Kline, 'Complicating the Ideology of Motherhood: Child Welfare Law and First Nations Women', in Martha Fineman and Isabel Karpin, eds., *Mothers in Law: Feminist Theory and the Legal Regulation of Motherhood* (New York: Columbia University Press, 1995), pp. 118–141; Cindy Blackstock. Nico Trocme, and Marlyn Bennett, 'Child Maltreatment Investigations among Aboriginal and Non-Aboriginal Families in Canada', *Violence against Women* 10(8), August 2004, pp. 901–916; Marlene Brant Castellano, *Aboriginal Family Trends: Extended Families, Nuclear Families, Families of the Heart* (Toronto: Vanier Institute of the Family, 2002).

34. Statistics Canada, *Canada E-book*. Available at http://www43.statcan.ca/02/02d_001a_e.htm; accessed June 6, 2009; Statistics Canada, *The Daily*, Wednesday, January 17, 2007. Available at http://www.statcan.gc.ca/daily-quotidien/070117/dq070117a-eng.htm; accessed June 6, 2009.

35. Statistics Canada, *The Daily*, Wednesday, March 9, 2005. Available at http://www.statcan.gc.ca/daily-quotidien/050309/dq050309b-eng.htm; accessed June 6, 2009.

36. REAL Women of Canada, 'Families in the Western World Enduring Perilous Times', Newsletter July/August 2008. Available at http://www.realwomenca.com/index.cfm?page=149&string=families%20in%20the%20western%20world; accessed June 8, 2009.

37. James Snell, *In the Shadow of the Law: Divorce in Canada 1900–1939* (Toronto: University of Toronto Press, 1991), p. 9.

38. J.K. Footlick, 'What Happened to the Family?' in 'The 21st Century Family', special edition, *Newsweek*, Winter-Spring, 1990, p. 14; for Canada, see Anne-Marie Lambert, *Divorce: Facts, Causes, and Consequences* (Ottawa: Vanier Institute for the Family, 2005). Available at http://www.vifamily.ca/library/cft/divorce_05.pdf; accessed July 8, 2009.

39. Scott Coltrane, *Family Man*, p. 203; Andrew Cherlin, 'By the Numbers', in *New York Times Magazine*, April 5, 1998, p. 39; Lianne George, 'Maclean's Poll 2006: What We Believe', *Maclean's*, July 4, 2006. Available at http://www.macleans.ca/article.jsp?content=20060701_130104_130104&source=srch; accessed July 4, 2009.

40. Jessie Bernard, *The Future of Marriage* (New York: World, 1972); Walter R. Gove, 'The Relationship Between Sex Roles, Marital Status and Mental Illness' in *Social Forces*, 51, 1972; Walter Gove and M. Hughes, 'Possible Causes of the Apparent Sex Differences in Physical Health: An Empirical Investigation' in *American Sociological Review*, 44, 1979; Walter Gove and Jeanette Tudor, 'Adult Sex Roles and Mental Illness' in *American Journal of Sociology*, 73, 1973; 'The Decline of Marriage' in *Scientific American*, December, 1999.

41. Natalie Angier, 'Men. Are Women Better Off with Them or without Them?' *New York Times*, June 21, 1998, p. 10.

42. See Linda J. Waite and Maggie Gallagher, *The Case for Marriage: Why Married People Are Happier, Healthier and Better Off Financially* (New York: Doubleday, 2000). See also, for example, Hynubae Chun and Injae Lee, 'Why Do Married Men Earn More: Productivity or Marriage Selection?' in *Economic Inquiry*, 39(2), April, 2001, pp. 307–319; and Leslie Stratton, 'Examining the Wage Differential for Married and Cohabiting Men' in *Economic Inquiry*, 40(2), April, 2002, pp. 199–212. See also Paula England's review of *The Case for Marriage* in *Contemporary Sociology*, 30(6), 2001.

43. Jamie Brownlee, 'Satisfaction', in Lance Roberts, Rodney Clifton, and Barry Ferguson, eds., *Recent Social Trends in Canada, 1960–2000* (Montreal: McGill-Queen's, 2005), pp. 627–633.

44. 'Wedding Trends in Canada', *Wedding Bells*. Available at www.weddingbells.ca; accessed July 7, 2009. For the 2006 survey, see http://www.weddingbells.ca/articles/article/weddingtrends/. Accessed July 7. 2009. For the most complete study of the wedding phenomenon, see Chrys Ingraham, *White Weddings: Romancing Heterosexuality in Popular Culture*, now in a 2nd edition (New York: Routledge, 2008).

45. Bebin and statistics cited in Elaine Carey, 'Kids Put a Damper on Marital Bliss: Study' in *Toronto Star*, August 15, 1997, pp. A1, A14; Lee Chalmers and Anne Milan, 'Marital Satisfaction during the Retirement Years', *Canadian Social Trends* Spring 2005 (StatsCan Catalogue 11-008), pp. 14–17.

46. J. Condry and S. Condry, 'Sex Differences: A Study in the Eye of the Beholder' in *Child Development*, 47, 1976.

47. For the quote, and a succinct discussion of various studies' findings, see Richard Lippa, *Gender, Nature, and Nurture* (Hillsdale, NJ: Lawrence Erlbaum Associates, 2001), pp. 132–137.

48. B. Lott, *Women's Lives: Themes and Variations in Gender Learning* (Monterey: Brooks/Cole, 1987). See also L.A. Schwartz and W.T. Markham, 'Sex Stereotyping in Children's Toy Advertisements' in *Sex Roles*, 12, 1985; and S.B. Ungar, 'The Sex Typing of Adult and Child Behavior in Toy Sales' in *Sex Roles*, 8, 1982.

49. See Carol Jacklin, 'Female and Male: Issues of Gender' in *American Psychologist*, 44, 1989, for a report on this and related research.

50. See 'Bratz Beat Barbie in Q4', *Playthings*, February 6, 2007. Available at http://www.playthings.com/article/CA6413828.html; accessed July 6, 2009; Margaret Talbot, 'Little Hotties', *The New Yorker*, December 4, 2006; Abby West, 'Bratz Dolls: Worse than Barbie?' *Sirens Magazine*, August 22, 2007, available at http://www.alternet.org/story/60387/; accessed July 6, 2009; 'Barbie Beats Bratz in US Court', CBC News, December 4, 2008. Available at http://www.cbc.ca/consumer/story/2008/12/04/bratz-mga.html; accessed July 6, 2009.

51. See, for example, Barrie Thorne, 'Boys and Girls Together . . . But Mostly Apart: Gender Arrangements in Elementary Schools' in *Relationships and Development*, W. Hartup and Z. Rubin, eds. (Hillsdale, NJ: Lawrence Erlbaum, 1986).

52. See, for example, Barrie Thorne and Zella Luria, 'Sexuality and Gender in Children's Daily Worlds' in *Social Problems*, 33, 1986; Barrie Thorne, *Gender Play* (New Brunswick: Rutgers University Press, 1993), p. 3.

53. Arlie Hochschild, *The Second Shift* (New York: Viking, 1989); Paul Amato and Alan Booth, 'Changes in Gender Role Attitudes and Perceived Marital Quality' in *American Sociological Review*, 60, 1995.

54. For example, see 'Stress: Relevations sur un mal francais' in *le Figaro*, April 15, 2006, p. 46.

55. Pat Mainardi, 'The Politics of Housework' in *Sisterhood Is Powerful*, R. Morgan, ed. (New York: Vintage, 1970).

56. Ballard and Foote are cited in Ruth Schwartz Cowan, *More Work for Mother*, p. 43; Campbell is cited in Susan Strasser, *Never Done: A History of American Housework* (New York: Pantheon, 1982), p. 62.

57. Dirk Johnson, 'More and More, the Single Parent Is Dad', p.A15; Amy Kroska, 'Exploring the Consequences of Gender Ideology–Work Discrepancies', *Sex Roles* 60, 2009, pp. 313–328; Lisa Belkin, 'When Mom and Dad Share It All', *The New York Times*, June 15, 2008. Available at http://www.nytimes.com/2008/06/15/15parenting-t.html; accessed October 12, 2009.

58. Scott Coltrane, *Family Man*, p. 46; Dana Vannoy-Hiller and William W. Philliber, *Equal Partners: Successful Women in Marriage* (Newbury Park: Sage Publications, 1989), p. 115; Phyllis Moen and Patricia Roehling, *Career Mystique: Cracks in the American Dream* (Lanham, MD: Rowman and Littlefield, 2004); Arlie Hochschild, *The Second Shift*.

59. See John Conway, *The Canadian Family in Crisis*, Fifth Edition (Halifax; Lorimer, 2003), pp. 213–215; Statistics Canada, 'General Social Survey: Paid and Unpaid Work', *The Daily*, Wednesday, July 19, 2006. Available at http://www.statcan.gc.ca/daily-quotidien/060719/dq060719b-eng.htm; accessed July 6, 2009.

60. Sheryl Ubelacker, 'Men Inch Forward in Housework, Childcare' (Canadian Press). Thestar.com, March 4, 2008. Available at http://www.thestar.com; accessed July 9, 2009. For a discussion of emotion work, see Daphne Stevens, Gary Kiger, and Pamela Riley, 'Working Hard and Hardly Working: Domestic Labor and Marital Satisfaction among Dual-Earner Couples', *Journal of Marriage and the Family* 63(2), May 2001, pp. 514–526.

61. See Meg Luxton, 'Two Hands for the Clock: Changing Patterns in the Gendered Division of Labour in the Home', in Meg Luxton, Harriet Rosenberg, and Sedef Arat-Koc, eds., *Through the Kitchen Window: The Politics of Home and Family* (Toronto: Garamond Press, 1990), pp. 39–55. For multitasking, see Joel Hektner, Jennifer Schmidt, and Mihály Csikszentmihályi, *Experience Sampling Method: Measuring the Quality of Everyday Life* (Thousand Oaks, CA: Sage Publications, 2007), p. 151.

62. Anna Quindlen, cited in Deborah Rhode, *Speaking of Sex* (Cambridge: Harvard University Press, 1997), p. 8; Moen and Roehling, *Career Mystique*.

63. Julie Press and Eleanor Townsley, 'Wives' and Husbands' Housework Reporting: Gender, Class and Social Desirability' in *Gender & Society*, 12(2), 1998, p. 214; On men's involvement in family work, see Joseph Pleck, 'Men's Family Work: Three Perspectives and Some New Data' in *The Family Coordinator*, 28, 1979; 'American Fathering in Historical Perspective' in *Changing Men: New Directions in Research on Men and Masculinity*, M.S. Kimmel, ed. (Beverly Hills, CA: Sage Publications, 1987); *Working Wives/Working Husbands* (Newbury Park: Sage Publications, 1985); 'Families and Work: Small Changes with Big Implications' in *Qualitative Sociology*, 15, 1992; 'Father Involvement: Levels, Origins and Consequences' in *The Father's Role* (3rd ed.), M. Lamb, ed. (New York: John Wiley, 1997).

64. Hiromi Ono, 'Husbands' and Wives' Resources and Marital Dissolution in the United States', *Journal of Marriage and the Family* 60, (1998): pp. 674–89.

65. Ono; see also Dirk Johnson, 'Until Dust Do Us Part' in *Newsweek*, March 25, 2002, p. 41; see also Sanjiv Gupta, 'The Effects of Transitions in Marital Status on Men's Performance of Housework' in *Journal of Marriage and the Family*, August, 1999.

66. *Ladies Home Journal*, September, 1997; John Gray, 'Domesticity, Diapers and Dad' in *The Globe and Mail*, June 15, 1996.

67. See Bart Landry, *Black Working Wives: Pioneers of the American Family Revolution* (Berkeley: University of California Press, 2001); Margaret Usdansky, 'White Men Don't Jump into Chores' in *USA Today*, August 20, 1994; Julia Lawlor, 'Blue Collar Dads Leading Trend in Caring for Kids, Author Says' in *New York Times*, April 15, 1998.

68. Barbara Vobejda, 'Children Help Less at Home, Dads Do More' in *Washington Post*, November 24, 1991, p. A1.

69. Jerry Adler, 'Building a Better Dad' in *Newsweek*, June 17, 1996; Tamar Lewin, 'Workers of Both Sexes Make Trade-Offs for Family, Study Shows' in *New York Times*, October 29, 1995, p. 25.

70. Benjamin Spock and Steven J. Parker, *Dr. Spock's Baby and Child Care* (7th ed.) (New York: Pocket Books, 1998), p. 10.

71. United Nations, *The World's Women, 1970–1990: Trends and Statistics* (New York: United Nations, 1991); Katherine Marshall, 'Fathers' Use of Paid Parental Leave', in *Perspectives*, June 2008 (Statistics Canada Catalogue Number

75–001-X), 5–14; Pat Schroeder, cited in Deborah Rhode, *Speaking of Sex*, p. 7.

72. 'Working Parents—Who Puts Family First When a Child Gets Sick?' *Science Daily*, August 15, 2007. Available at http://www.sciencedaily.com/releases/2007/08/070813162452.htm; accessed July 6, 2009.

73. 'Sex, Death, and Football' in *The Economist*, June 13, 1998, p. 18; Robert D. Mintz and James Mahalik, 'Gender Role Orientation and Conflict as Predictors of Family Roles for Men' in *Sex Roles*, 34(1–2), 1996, pp. 805–821; Barbara Risman, 'Can Men "Mother"? Life as a Single Father' in *Family Relations*, 35, 1986; see also Caryl Rivers and Rosalind Barnett, 'Fathers Do Best' in *Washington Post*, June 20, 1993, p. C5.

74. Cherlin, 'By the Numbers', p. 41.

75. Jane R. Eisner, 'Leaving the Office for Family Life' in *Des Moines Register*, March 27, 1998, p. 7A.

76. 'Daycare: The Debate over Space', CBC News, February 11, 2009. Available at http://www.cbc.ca/consumer/story/2009/02/06/f-daycare.html; accessed January 12, 2010; Rianne Mahon, 'Child Care in Canada and Sweden: Policy and Politics', *Social Politics* 4(3), 1997, pp. 382–418.

77. Statistics Canada, 'Child Care: An Eight-Year Profile', *The Daily*, April 5, 2006. Available at http://www.statcan.gc.ca/daily-quotidien/060405/dq060405a-eng.htm; accessed July 6, 2009; Susan Chira, 'Can You Work and Have Good Happy Kids?' in *Glamour*, April, 1998.

78. Jay Belsky, 'A Reassessment of Infant Day Care', and Thomas Gamble and Edward Zigler, 'Effects of Infant Day Care: Another Look at the Evidence', both in *The Parental Leave Crisis: Toward a National Policy*, E. Zigler and M. Frank, eds. (New Haven: Yale University Press, 1988); J. Douglas Willms and Elizabeth A. Sloat, 'Literacy for Life', Atlantic Centre for Policy Research *Policy Brief*, No. 4 (December 1998); see also Susan Chira, 'Study Says Babies in Child Care Keep Secure Bonds to Mother' in *New York Times*, April 21, 1996. For a handy summary of these data, see 'Child Care in the United States, 1972 vs. 1999', a flyer from the National Council of Jewish Women at www.ncjw.org.

79. 'Child Care Linked to Assertive, Noncompliant, and Aggressive Behaviors: Vast Majority of Children within Normal Range'. NIH News Release, July 16, 2003. Available at http://www.nichd.nih.gov/news/releases/child_care.cfm; accessed July 5, 2009; Michael Baker, Jonathan Gruber, and Kevin Milligan, 'What Can We Learn from Quebec's Universal Childcare Program?' C.D. Howe Institute E-brief, February 1, 2006; Canadian Research Institute for Social Policy, 'Daycare Attendance, Stress, and Mental Health', *CRISPfacts* July 2007.

80. For a theoretical/historical analysis, see Shelley Gavigan and Dorothy Chunn, 'From Mothers' Allowance to Mothers Need Not Apply: Canadian Welfare Law and Liberal and Neo-Liberal Reforms', *Osgoode Hall Law Journal* 45(4), 2007, pp. 733–771; for a discussion of short-term and long-term effects, see Matthew Brzozowski, 'Welfare Reforms and Consumption among Single Mother Households: Evidence from Canadian Provinces', Working Paper #2005-10 (RBC Financial Group Economic Policy Institute EPRI Working Paper Series), December 2005; Andrew Cherlin, 'By the Numbers', p. 40.

81. See S. M. Bianchi and Daphne Spain, *American Women in Transition* (New York: Russell Sage Foundation, 1986); E.G.Menaghan and Toby Parcel, 'Parental Employment and Family Life: Research in the 1980s' in *Journal of Marriage and the Family*, 52, 1990; Glenna Spitze, 'Women's Employment and Family Relations: A Review' in *Journal of Marriage and the Family*, 50, 1988.

82. Campaign 2000, '2008 Report Card on Child and Family Poverty in Canada', (Toronto: Campaign 2000, 2008); Joan K. Peters, *When Mothers Work: Loving Our Children Without Sacrificing Our Selves* (Reading, MA: Addison-Wesley, 1997).

83. Anita Shaw, 'Media Representations of Adolescent Pregnancy', *Atlantis: A Women's Studies Journal*, 34(2), 2010, pp. 55–65; Gail Collins, 'Bristol Palin's New Gig', *New York Times*, May 7, 2009. Available at http:///www.nytimes.com/2009/05/07/opinion/07collins.html; accessed May 7, 2009; Heather Dryburgh, 'Teenage Pregnancy', *Health Reports* 12(1), October 2000, pp. 9–19; Nicholas Bakalar, 'Trends Shift, with Births on the Rise', *New York Times*, January 20, 2009. Available at http://www.nytimes.com/2009/01/20/health/research/20stat.html; accessed May 7, 2009; Vanessa Richmond,

'Why Canada's on Top in Teen Pregnancy', *The Huffington Post,* April 26, 2009. Available at http://www.huffingtonpost.com/vanessa-richmond/why-canadas-on-top-in-tee_b_178734.html; accessed July 11, 2009.

84. M.A. Males, *The Scapegoat Generation: America's War on Adolescents* (Monroe, ME: Common Courage Press, 1996) and 'Adult Liaison in the "Epidemic" of "Teenage" Birth, Pregnancy, and Venereal Disease', *The Journal of Sex Research* 29(4), pp. 525–545. Thanks to Anita Shaw for these references.

85. Alexander McKay, 'Trends in Teen Pregnancy in Canada with Comparisons to U.S.A. and England/Wales', *The Canadian Journal of Human Sexuality* 15(3/4), 2006, pp. 157–161.

86. 'The Many Fatherless Boys in Black Families', *The Globe and* Mail, November 26, 2005. Available at http://www.theglobeandmail.com/news/national/the-many-fatherless-boys-in-black-families/article921794/; accessed July 11, 2009; Pittman, cited in Olga Silverstein, 'Is a Bad Dad Better Than No Dad?' in *On the Issues,* Winter, 1997, p. 15; David Blankenhorn, *Fatherless America: Confronting Our Most Urgent Social Problem* (New York: Basic Books, 1993), p. 30; Robert Bly, *Iron John* (Reading, MA: Addison-Wesley, 1990), p. 96; David Popenoe, *Life Without Father,* p. 12.

87. Gertrude Schaffner Goldberg, 'Canada: Bordering on the Feminization of Poverty', in Gertrude Schaffner Goldberg and Eleanor Kremen, eds., *The Feminization of Poverty: Only in America?* (Westport, CT; Praeger Publishers, 1990), pp. 59–90; Statistics Canada, 'Families, Households, and Housing', *Canada Yearbook Overview 2008.* Available at http://www41.statcan.ca/2008/40000/ceb40000_000-eng.htm; accessed July 10, 2009. Carey Goldberg, 'Single Dads Wage Revolution One Bedtime Story at a Time' in *New York Times,* June 17, 2001, pp. A1, 16.

88. Goldberg, 'Canada Bordering . . .'; Cherlin, 'By the Numbers', p. 40; Kristin Luker, 'Dubious Conceptions: The Controversy over Teen Pregnancy' in *The American Prospect,* 5, 1991; Paul Amato and Alan Booth, *A Generation at Risk: Growing Up in an Era of Family Upheaval* (Cambridge: Harvard University Press, 1997), p. 229; P. Amato and J. Gilbreth, 'Nonresident Fathers and Children's Well-Being: A Meta-

Analysis' in *Journal of Marriage and the Family,* 61, 1999, pp. 557–573.

89. Martin Sanchez-Jankowski, *Islands in the Street: Gangs and American Urban Society* (Berkeley: University of California Press, 1991), p. 39.

90. David Popenoe, 'Evolution of Marriage and Stepfamily Problems' in *Stepfamilies: Who Benefits? Who Does Not?* A. Booth and J. Dunn, eds. (Hillsdale, NJ: Lawrence Erlbaum, 1994), p. 528.

91. Blankenhorn, *Fatherless America,* pp. 96, 102, 122.

92. Kate Fraher, 'Wanted: Canada's Missing Divorce Debate', *IMFC Review,* Spring/Summer 2007, pp. 17–19.

93. Lawrence Stone, 'A Short History of Love' in *Harper's Magazine,* February, 1988, p. 32.

94. Constance Ahrons, *The Good Divorce* (New York: HarperCollins, 1994); Pascal Beaupre, 'I Do . . . Take Two? Changes in Intentions to Marry among Divorced Canadians during the Past Twenty Years', *Matter of Fact,* July 2008. Available at http://www.statcan.gc.ca/pub/89-630-x/2008001/article/10659-eng.pdf; accessed on July 13, 2009; Lambert, 'Divorce'.

95. Demie Kurz, *For Richer, For Poorer: Mothers Confront Divorce* (New York: Routledge, 1995); Leonore Weitzman, *The Divorce Revolution: The Unexpected Social and Economic Consequences for Women and Children in America* (New York: The Free Press, 1985); Patricia A. McManus and Thomas A. DiPrete, 'Losers and Winners: The Financial Consequences of Separation and Divorce for Men' in *American Sociological Review,* 66, April, 2001, pp. 246–268; Paul Amato, 'The Impact of Divorce on Men and Women in India and the United States' in *Journal of Comparative Family Studies,* 25(2), 1994; Tahany Ladalla, 'Impact of Marital Dissolution on Men's and Women's Incomes: A Longitudinal Study', *Journal of Divorce and Remarriage* 50(1), 2009, pp. 55–65; Dorien Manting and Anne Marthe Bouman, 'Short- and Long-Term Economic Consequences of the Dissolution of Marital and Consensual Unions: The Example of the Netherlands', *European Sociological Review* 22(4), 2006, pp. 413–429.

96. Andrew Schepard, *Children, Courts, and Custody: Interdisciplinary Models for Divorcing Families* (Cambridge: Cambridge University Press, 2004), pp. 15–22; Susan Boyd, 'Investi-

gating Gender Bias in Canadian Child Custody Law: Reflections on Questions and Methods', in Joan Brockman and Dorothy Chunn, eds., *Investigating Gender Bias in Law: Socio-Legal Perspectives* (Toronto: Thompson, 1993), pp. 169–190; Mary Jane Mossman, *Families and the Law in Canada: Cases and Commentary* (Toronto: Emond Montgomery, 2004), pp 635–638, 645.

97. For a critical ethnographic view of the fathers' rights movement, see the article by University of Windsor researchers Carl Bertoia and Janice Drakich, 'The Fathers' Rights Movement: Contradictions in Rhetoric and Practice', *Journal of Family Issues* 14(4), December 2003, pp. 592–615.

98. See, for example, Joan Kelly, 'Longer-Term Adjustments of Children of Divorce', *Journal of Family Psychology*, 2(2), 1988, p. 131; D. Leupnitz, *Child Custody: A Study of Families After Divorce* (Lexington: Lexington Books, 1982); D. Leupnitz, 'A Comparison of Maternal, Paternal and Joint Custody: Understanding the Varieties of Post-Divorce Family Life' in *Journal of Divorce*, 9, 1986; V. Shiller, 'Loyalty Conflicts and Family Relationships in Latency Age Boys: A Comparison of Joint and Maternal Custody' in *Journal of Divorce*, 9, 1986.

99. Joan Kelly, 'Longer-Term Adjustments . . .', p. 136; Nancy Crowell and Ethel Leeper, eds, *America's Fathers and Public Policy*, p. 27.

100. For more about the U.S. fatherhood movement, see Anna Gavanas, *Fatherhood Politics in The United States* (Urbana: University of Illinois Press, 2004).

101. Maccoby, quoted in Dirk Johnson, 'More and More, the Single Parent is Dad', p. A15; Furstenberg and Cherlin, *Divided Families*; Frank Furstenberg, 'Good Dads–Bad Dads: Two Faces of Fatherhood' in *The Changing American Family and Public Policy*, A.Cherlin, ed. (Lanham, MD: Urban Institute Press,1988); William J. Goode, 'Why Men Resist' in *Rethinking the Family: Some Feminist Questions*, B. Thorne and M. Yalom, eds. (New York: Longman, 1982).

102. Debra Umberson and Christine Williams, 'Divorced Fathers: Parental Role Strain and Psychological Distress' in *Journal of Family Issues*, 14(3), 1993; Popenoe, *Life Without Father*, p. 27; Frank Furstenberg and Andrew Cherlin, *Divided Families: What Happens to Children When Parents Part?* (Cambridge: Harvard University Press, 1991).

103. Valerie King, 'Nonresident Father Involvement and Child Well-Being' in *Journal of Family Issues*, 15(1), 1994; Edward Kruk, 'The Disengaged Noncustodial Father: Implications for Social Work Practice with the Divorced Family' in *Social Work*, 39(1), 1994.

104. Paul Amato and Alan Booth, *A Generation at Risk*, p. 74.

105. Judith Wallerstein and J. Kelly, *Surviving the Breakup: How Children and Parents Cope with Divorce* (New York: Basic Books, 1980); Judith Wallerstein and Susan Blakeslee. *Second Chances: Men, Women, and Children a Decade After Divorce* (New York: Ticknor and Fields, 1989), p. 11; Judith Wallerstein, Julia Lewis, and Sandra Blakeslee, *The Unexpected Legacy of Divorce: A 25 Year Landmark Study* (New York: Hyperion, 2000).

106. For criticism of Wallerstein's study, see, for example, Andrew Cherlin, 'Generation Ex-' in *The Nation*, December 11, 2000; Katha Pollitt, 'Social Pseudoscience' in *The Nation*, October 23, 2000, p. 10 (and subsequent exchange, December 4, 2000); Thomas Davey, 'Considering Divorce' in *The American Prospect*, January 1–15, 2001; Walter Kirn, 'Should You Stay Together for the Kids?' in *Time*, September 25, 2000; and Elisabeth Lasch-Quinn, 'Loving and Leaving' in *The New Republic*, May 6, 2002.

107. Andrew Cherlin, 'Going to Extremes: Family Structure, Children's Well-Being and Social Science' in *Demography*, 36(4), November, 1999, p. 425; Lisa Strohschein, 'Parental Divorce and Child Mental Health Trajectories', *Journal of Marriage and the Family* 67, December, 2005, pp. 1286–1300; For the British study, see Jane Brody, 'Problems of Children: A New Look at Divorce' in *New York Times*, June 7, 1991; Jeanne Block, J. Block, and P.F. Gjerde, 'The Personality of Children . . . '; president of council cited in Stephanie Coontz, *The Way We Really Are*, p. 108.

108. Joan B. Kelly, 'Mediated and Adversarial Divorce: Respondents' Perceptions of Their Processes and Outcomes' in *Mediation Quarterly*, 24, Summer, 1989, p. 125. See also J. Block, J. Block, and P.F. Gjerde, 'The Personality of Children Prior to Divorce: A Prospective Study' in *Child Development*, 57, 1986; Arlene Skolnick, *Embattled Paradise*, p. 212; 98–99; B.

Berg and R. Kelly, 'The Measured Self-Esteem of Children from Broken, Rejected and Accepted Families' in *Journal of Divorce*, 2, 1979; R.E. Emery, 'Interparental Conflict and Children of Discord and Divorce' in *Psychological Bulletin*, 92, 1982; 100; H.J. Raschke and V.J. Raschke, 'Family Conflict and the Children's Self-Concepts' in *Journal of Marriage and the Family*, 41, 1979; J.M. Gottman and L.F. Katz, 'Effects of Marital Discord on Young Children's Peer Interaction and Health' in *Developmental Psychology*, 25, 1989; D. Mechanic and S. Hansell, 'Divorce, Family Conflict and Adolescents' Well-Being' in *Journal of Health and Social Behavior*, 30, 1989; Paul Amato and Juliana Sobolewski, 'The Effects of Divorce and Marital Discord on Adult Children's Psychological Well-Being' in *American Sociological Review*, 66, December, 2001, pp. 900–921.

109. Amato and Booth, *A Generation at Risk*, pp. 201, 230, 234; Paul Amato and Alan Booth, 'The Legacy of Parents' Marital Discord: Consequences for Children's Marital Quality' in *Journal of Personality and Social Psychology*, 81(4), 2001, pp. 627–638; see also Paul Amato, 'The Impact of Divorce . . . '; 'The Implications of Research Findings on Children in Stepfamilies' in *Stepfamilies: Who Benefits? Who Does Not?;*'Single-Parent Households as Settings for Children's Development, Well-Being and Attainment: A Social Networks/Resources Perspective' in *Sociological Studies of Children*, 7, 1995; Paul Amato and Alan Booth, 'Changes in Gender Role Attitudes and Perceived Marital Quality' in *American Sociological Review*, 60, 1995; Paul Amato, Laura Spencer Loomis, and Alan Booth, 'Parental Divorce, Marital Conflict, and Offspring Well-Being During Early Adulthood' in *Social Forces*, 73(3), 1995. 'Low conflict', by the way, is unhappy but not physically violent.

110. Quoted in Leah McLaren, 'The Kids (of Divorce) Are All Right', *The Globe and Mail*, September 11, 1999; Stephanie Coontz, *The Way We Really Are*, p. 83.

111. Paul Amato and Alan Booth, *A Generation at Risk*, p. 207; see also Susan Jekielek, 'The Relative and Interactive Impacts of Parental Conflict and Marital Disruption on Children's Emotional Well-Being', paper presented at the annual meeting of the American Sociological Association, New York, 1996; Carl Degler, *At Odds: Women and the Family in America from the Revolution to the Present* (New York: Oxford University Press,1980); Terry Arendell, 'Divorce American Style' in *Contemporary Sociology*, 27(3), 1998, p. 226. See also Terry Arendall, *Mothers and Divorce: Legal, Economic and Social Dilemmas* (Berkeley: University of California Press, 1986); 'After Divorce: Investigations into Father Absence' in *Gender & Society*, December, 1992; *Fathers and Divorce* (Newbury Park: Sage Publications, 1995).

112. 'Canadians Would Keep Same-Sex Marriage Legal', *Angus Reid Global Monitor,* December 6, 2006; available at http://www.angus-reid.com/polls/view/14013; accessed July 11, 2009.

113. For the Defense of Marriage Act, see Anne Marie Smith, 'The Politicization of Marriage in Contemporary American Public Policy: The Defense of Marriage Act and the Personal Responsibility Act', *Citizenship Studies* 5 (3), 2001, pp. 303–320; Barry D. Adam, 'The Defense of Marriage Act and American Exceptionalism: The 'Gay Marriage' Panic in the United States', *Journal of the History of Sexuality* 12(2), April 2003, pp. 259–276; Michael J. Kanotz, 'For Better or for Worse: A Critical Analysis of Florida's Defense of Marriage Act' in *Florida State University Law Review*, 25(2), 1998; Guy Adams, 'State of the Union: 18000 California Gay Couples Are Married in a State Which Outlaws It', *The Independent,* July 11, 2009, available at http://www.independent.co.uk/news/world/americas/state-of-the-union-18000-californian-gay-couples-are-legally-married-in-a-state-which-outlaws-it-1739835.html; accessed 11 July 2009; 'Bill Clinton Apparently Supports Gay Marriage', CBS News, July 15, 2009. Available at http://cbs4.com/national/bill.clinton.gay.2.1087129.html; accessed July 15, 2009; Jeffrey M. Jones, 'Majority of Americans Continue to Oppose Same-Sex Marriage: No Change in Support from Last Year', available at http://www.gallup.com/poll/118378/Majority-Americans-Continue-Oppose-Gay-Marriage.aspx; accessed July 13, 2009.

114. See Jenni Millbank, 'Lesbians, Child Custody, and the Long Lingering Gaze of the Law', in Susan Boyd, ed., *Challenging the Public/Private Divide: Feminism, Law, and Public Policy* (Toronto: University of Toronto Press, 1997), pp. 280–303; see also Phyllis Chesler, *Mothers*

on Trial: The Battle for Children and Custody (Toronto/NY: McGraw-Hill, 1986), pp. 48–49 passim.

115. John Gagnon and William Simon, *Sexual Conduct* (Chicago: Aldine, 1973), p. 213.

116. J. Schulenberg, *Gay Parenting* (New York: Doubleday, 1985); F. W. Bozett, ed. *Gay and Lesbian Parents* (New York: Praeger, 1987); Katherine Allen and David H. Demo, 'The Families of Lesbians and Gay Men: A New Frontier in Family Research' in *Journal of Marriage and the Family*, 57, 1995; Ann Sullivan, ed., *Issues in Gay and Lesbian Adoption: Proceedings of the Fourth Annual Peirce-Warwick Adoption Symposium* (Washington, DC: Child Welfare League of America, 1995), p. 5; John J. Goldman, 'N.J. Gays Win Adoption Rights' in *Los Angeles Times*, December 18, 1997.

117. REAL Women of Canada, 'Same-Sex Parenting is Harmful to Children', *REALity* 23(2), March/April 2004; Mary Ann Mason, Arlene Skolnick, and Stephen D. Sugarman, *All Our Families: New Policies for a New Century* (New York: Oxford University Press, 1998), p. 8; 'Study: Same-Sex Couples Just as Good, If Not Better, at Parenting', *The Ottawa Citizen,* May 6, 2007. Available at http://www.canada.com/theprovince/news/story.html?id=38cc20ce-7f14-44ea-b4d9-d4cd16d7a269&k=9378; accessed July 9, 2009; William Beezon and Jonathan Rauch, 'Gay Marriage, Same-Sex Parenting, and America's Children', *The Future of Children* 15(2), 2005, pp. 97–113; Bozett, *Gay and Lesbian Parents.*

118. Judith Stacey, 'Gay and Lesbian Families: Queer Like Us' in *All Our Families: New Policies for a New Century*, M. Mason, A. Skolnick, and S. Sugarman, eds. (New York: Oxford University Press, 1998), p. 135.

119. Judith Stacey and Timothy J. Biblarz, '(How) Does the Sexual Orientation of Parents Matter?' in *American Sociological Review*, 66, April, 2001, pp. 159–183; see also Michael Bronski, 'Queer as Your Folks' in *Boston Phoenix*, August 3, 2001, and Erica Goode, 'A Rainbow of Differences in Gays' Children' in *New York Times*, July 17, 2001; Lisa Belkin, 'When Mom and Dad Share It All'.

120. Skolnick, *The Intimate Environment,* p. 426.

121. *Harvard Men's Health Watch*, 2(11), June, 1998.

122. Lasch, *Women and the Common Life*, p. 119.

123. Coltrane, *Family Man*, pp. 223–225.

Chapter 7

1. M.G. Lord, *Forever Barbie: The Unauthorized Biography of a Real Doll* (New York: William Morrow, 1994).

2. Deborah Rhode, *Speaking of Sex* (Cambridge: Harvard University Press, 1997), p. 56.

3. Alvin Finkel, *Social Policy and Practice in Canada: A History* (Waterloo: Wilfrid Laurier University Press, 2006), pp. 55, 59, 133; Buller quoted in Bruce Curtis, 'The State of Tutelage in Lower Canada, 1835–1851', *History of Education Quarterly* 37(1), Spring 1997, pp. 25–43: 26; Neil Guppy, Doug Balson, and Susan Vellutini, 'Women and Higher Education in Canadian Society', in Jane Gaskell and Arlene McLaren, eds., *Women and Education: A Canadian Perspective* (Calgary: Detselig Enterprises, 1987), pp. 171–192; Kristin McLaren, ' "We Had No Desire to Be Set Apart": Forced Segregation of Black Students in Canada West Public Schools and Myths of British Egalitarianism', in Barrington Walker, *The History of Immigration and Racism in Canada* (Toronto: Canadian Scholars Press, 2008), pp. 69–80.

4. There is a vast and accessible literature on imperial manhood, sport, and the colonial educative mission that carried British notions of manhood around the world. For the purposes of the argument made here, see, inter alia, Myra Rutherdale, *Women and the White Man's God: Gender and Race in the Canadian Mission Field* (Vancouver: University of British Columbia Press, 2002); Rhonda Semple, 'Missionary Manhood: Professionalism, Belief, and Masculinity in the Nineteenth-Century British Imperial Field', *The Journal of Imperial and Commonwealth History* 36(3), September 2008, pp. 397–415; Satadru Sen, *Migrant Races: Empire, Identity, and K.S. Ranjitsinhji* (Manchester: Manchester United Press, 2004); Patrick McDevitt, *'May the Best Man Win': Sport, Masculinity, and Nationalism in Great Britain and the Empire, 1880–1935* (New York/Houndmills UK; Palgrave Macmillan, 2004); Axel Bundgaard, *Muscle and Manliness: The Rise of Sport in American Boarding Schools* (Syracuse, NY: Syracuse University Press, 2005); Clifford Putney, *Muscular Christianity: Manhood and Sports in Protestant America, 1880—1920*

(Cambridge, MA: Harvard University Press, 2001).

5. Edward C. Clarke, *Sex in Education; or, A Fair Chance for the Girls* (Boston: Osgood, 1873), pp. 128, 137. W.W. Ferrier, *Origin and Development of the University of California* (Berkeley: University of California Press, 1930); see also Myra Sadker and David Sadker, *Failing at Fairness: How Schools Shortchange Girls* (New York: Simon & Schuster, 1994), p. 22; Carlotta Hacker, *The Indomitable Lady Doctors* (Halifax: Formac, 2001), p. 22.

6. Johanna Maria Selles, *Methodists and Women's Education in Ontario, 1851–1925* (Montreal: McGill-Queens University Press, 2003); Henry Fowle Durant, 'The Spirit of the College' [1977], reprinted in Michael S. Kimmel and Thomas Mosmiller, *Against the Tide: Pro-Feminist Men in the United States, 1776–1990, a Documentary History* (Boston: Beacon Press, 1992), p. 132.

7. Guppy et al., 'Women and Higher Education', pp. 173–175.

8. Council of Ministers of Education, Canada, 'Education in Canada', July 2005.

9. Myra Sadker and David Sadker, *Failing at Fairness*, p. 14. These stereotypes are complicated by other, racially based stereotypes; for example, Asian-American girls are expected to like math and science more than are white girls. For an update, see David Sadker and Karen Zittleman, *Still Failing at Fairness: How Gender Bias Cheats Girls and Boys in School and What We Can Do about It* (New York: Scribner, 2009).

10. David Karp and William C. Yoels, 'The College Classroom: Some Observations on the Meanings of Student Participation' in *Sociology and Social Research*, 60(4), 1976: American Association of University Women, *How Schools Shortchange Girls: A Study of Major Findings on Girls and Education* (Washington, DC: American Association of University Women, 1992), p 68; Myra Sadker and David Sadker, *Failing at Fairness*, p. 5; Michael Younger, Molly Warrington, and Jacquetta Williams, 'The Gender Gap and Classroom Interactions: Reality and Rhetoric?' *British Journal of Sociology of Education* 20 (3), September 1999, pp. 325–341.

11. Peggy Orenstein, *Schoolgirls* (New York: Doubleday, 1994), pp. 11, 12; Leanne Dalley-Trim, 'The Call to Critique "Common-Sense" Understandings about Boys and Masculinity(Ies), *Australian Journal of Teacher Education* 34(1), February 2009, pp. 54–67; Diane Reay, ' "Spice Girls", "Nice Girls", "Girlies", and "Tomboys": Gender Discourses, Girls' Cultures, and Femininities in the Primary Classroom', in Nancy Cook, ed., *Gender Relations in Global Perspective: Essential Readings* (Toronto: Canadian Scholar's Press, 2007), pp. 213–22.

12. See Leonore Weitzman and Diane Russo, *The Biased Textbook: A Research Perspective* (Washington, DC: Research Center on Sex Roles and Education, 1974); Leonore Weitzman et al., 'Sex Role Socialization in Picture Books for Preschool Children' in *American Journal of Sociology*, 77(6), 1972; Deborah Rhode, *Speaking of Sex*, p. 56; Angela M. Gooden and Mark A. Gooden, 'Gender Representation in Notable Children's Picture Books: 1995–1999' in *Sex Roles*, 45(1/2), July, 2001, pp. 89–101; Rae Lesser Blumberg, 'The Invisible Obstacle to Educational Equality: Gender Bias in Textbooks', *Prospects: Quarterly Review of Comparative Education* online, April 7, 2009. Available at http://www.springerlink.com/content/8372103568644370/fulltext.pdf; accessed July 17, 2009; For the Alberta study, see Joyce Bainbridge, Dianne Oberg, and Mike Carbonaro, ' "No Text Is Innocent": Canadian Children's Books in the Classroom', *Journal of Teaching and Learning* 3(2), 2005, pp. 1–14; As of 2002, the Surrey School Board was ordered to desist from banning books involving same-sex couples as parents. 'Supreme Court Says B.C. School Board Wrong to Ban Same-Sex Books', CBC News, December 20,2002; available at http://www.cbc.ca/canada/story/2002/12/20/sex_books021220.html; accessed July 17, 2009.

13. On gender intensification, see J. Hill and M. Lynch, 'The Intensification of Gender-Related Role Expectations during Early Adolescence', in J. Brooks-Gunn and A. Peterson, eds., *Girls at Puberty; Biological and Psychological Perspectives* (New York: Plenum Books, 1982); Lisa Pettit, 'Gender Intensification of Peer Socialization during Puberty', *New Directions for Chikld and Adolescent Development*, Number 106, Winter 2004, pp. 23–34; Jacqueline Granleese and Stephen Joseph, 'Self-Perception of Adolescent Girls at a Single-Sex and a Mixed-Sex School', *Journal of Genetic Psychology* 154(4), December 1993, pp. 525–561.

14. On girls' being valued for appearance and not achievement, see Myra Sadker and David Sadker, *Failing at Fairness*, pp. 55, 134. On girls' downplaying their talents, see American Association of University Women, *Shortchanging Girls, Shortchanging America* (Washington, DC: American Association of University Women, 1991), p. 48; Carolyn Heilbrun, cited in Peggy Orenstein, *Schoolgirls*, p. 37.

15. K.M. Brown et al., 'Changes in Self-Esteem in Black and White Girls between the Ages of 9 and 14 Years: The NHLBI Growth and Health Study', *Journal of Adolescent Health* 23(1), July 1998, pp. 7–19; Anne Bowker, Shannon Gadbois, and Becki Cornock, 'Sports Participation and Self-Esteem; Variations as a Function of Gender and Gender Role Orientation', *Sex Roles* 49(1/2), July 2003, pp. 47–58.

16. American Association of University Women, *Hostile Hallways: The AAUW Survey on Sexual Harassment in America's Schools* (Washington, DC: American Association of University Women, 1993); Sandler cited in Myra Sadker and David Sadker, *Failing at Fairness*, p. 111; Jason Winters, Robert Clift, and Anne Maloney, 'Adult-Student Sexual Harassment in British Columbia High Schools', in Robert Geffner, Mark Braverman, Joseph Galasso, and Janessa Marsh, eds., *Aggression in Organizations: Violence, Abuse, and Harassment at Work and in Schools* (Routledge, 2005), pp. 177–196.

17. Pat Staton and June Larkin, *Sexual Harassment: The Intimidation Factor,* A Report to the Ontario Ministry of Education (Toronto: Green Dragon Press, 1992); June Larkin, 'Walking through Walls: The Sexual Harassment of High School Girls', *Gender & Education* 6(3), 1994, pp. 263–280; Rosalyn Shute, Larry Owens, and Phillip Slee, 'Everyday Victimization of Adolescent Girls by Boys: Sexual Harassment, Bullying, or Aggression?' *Sex Roles* 58, 2008, pp. 477–489; 'Girls Accepting Sexual Assault at School as Fact of Life: Reports', CityNews.ca, available at http://www.citynews.ca/news/news_19880.aspx; accessed July 20, 2009; Christopher Bagley et al., 'Sexual Assault in School, Mental Health, and Suicidal Behaviors in Adolescent Women in Canada', *Adolescence* 32(126), Summer 1997, pp. 361–366; Pat Staton and June A. Larkin, ' "If We Can't Get Equal, We'll Get Even": A Transformative Model of Gender Equity', *Canadian Woman Studies* 17 (4), 1998, pp. 16–22.

18. Jill Smolowe, 'Sex with a Scorecard' in *Time*, April 5, 1993, p. 41; Jane Gross, 'Where "Boys Will Be Boys" and Adults Are Bewildered' in *New York Times*, March 29, 1993, p. A1.

19. Anthea Lipsett, 'Huge Gender Gap in Young Children's Abilities Revealed in Government Figures', *The Guardian*, July 30, 2009, available at http://www.guardian.co.uk/education/2009/jul/29/early-learning-gender-gap; accessed July 30, 2009; also see William Pollack, *Real Boys: Rescuing Our Sons from the Myths of Boyhood* (New York: Random House, 1998).

20. Christina Hoff Sommers, *The War Against Boys* (New York: Scribner's, 1999). Sommers, cited in Debra Viadero, 'Behind the "Mask of Masculinity" ' in *Education Week*, May 13, 1998; Thompson, cited in Margaret Combs, 'What About the Boys?' in *Boston Globe*, June 26, 1998. For more of this backlash argument, see Michael Gurian, *The Wonder of Boys* (New York: Jeremy Tarcher/Putnam, 1997), and Judith Kleinfeld, 'Student Performance: Male Versus Female' in *The Public Interest*, Winter, 1999. For dissenting opinions, see Michael's review of Gurian, 'Boys to Men . . .', in *San Francisco Chronicle*, January 12, 1997; Martin Mills, 'What About the Boys?' and R.W. Connell, 'Teaching the Boys' in *Teachers College Record.*

21. *Boys Adrift: The Five Factors Driving the Growing Epidemic of Unmotivated Boys and Underachieving Young Men* (New York: Basic Books, 2007).

22. Sax, *Boys Adrift*, pp. 51–2; Kate Fillion, 'How to Fix Boys: Let Them Start School Later and, Yes, Let Them Fight and Play with Toy Guns' (interview with Leonard Sax), *Macleans,* January 9, 2008. Available at http:///www.macleans.ca/article.jsp?content=20080109_70985_70985&source=srch; accessed July 19, 2009.

23. On harassment and homophobia in high schools, see Dalley-Trim, 'Call to Critique', pp. 60–1; C.J. Pascoe, *Dude, You're a Fag: Masculinity and Sexuality in High School* (Berkeley/Los Angeles: University of California Press, 2007); Tommi Avicolli, 'He Defies You Still: The Memoirs of a Sissy', in Estelle Disch, ed., *Reconstructing Gender: A Multicultural Anthology* (McGraw-Hill, 2006), pp. 108–154; Egale Canada, *Youth Speak up about Homophobia and Transphobia: The*

First National Climate Survey on Homophobia in Canadian Schools, Phase One Report March 2009; available at http://www.egale.ca/index. asp?lang=&menu=1&item=1401; accessed July 20, 2009.

24. Richard Kim, 'Eminem—Bad Rap?' in *The Nation*, March 13, 2001, p. 4. In his film, *8 Mile*, and in subsequent albums, Eminem attempts to repudiate his earlier homophobia.

25. T.R. Nansel, M. Overpeck, R.S. Pilla, W.J. Ruan, B. Simons-Moore, and P. Scheidt, 'Bullying Behaviors Among U.S. Youth: Prevalence and Association with Psychosocial Adjustment' in *Journal of the American Medical Association*, 285(16), 2001, pp. 2094–2100; S.P. Limber, P. Cunningham, V. Florx, J. Ivey, M. Nation, S. Chai, and G. Melton, 'Bullying Among School Children: Preliminary Findings from a School-Based Intervention Program', paper presented at the Fifth International Family Violence Research Conference, Durham, NH, June 1997; Juvonen Jaana, Sandra Graham, and Mark Schuster, 'Bullying Among Young Adolescents: The Strong, the Weak and the Troubled' in *Pediatrics*, 112(6), December, 2003, pp. 1231–1237.

26. 'Fear of Classmates' in *USA Today*, April 22, 1999, p. A1; 'Half of Teens Have Heard of a Gun Threat at School' in *USA Today*, November 27, 2001, p. 6D. Also see Michael Kimmel and Matthew Mahler, 'Adolescent Masculinity, Homophobia, and Violence: Random School Shootings, 1982–2001' in *American Behavioral Scientist*, 46(10), June, 2003.

27. Pollack, cited in Debra Viadero, 'Behind the Mask . . .'; see also William Pollack, *Real Boys*.

28. Shelley Correll, 'Gender and the Career Choice Process: The Role of Biased Self-Assessments' in *American Journal of Sociology*, 106(6), pp. 1691–1730.

29. Ibid.

30. Wayne Martino, 'Masculinity and Learning: Exploring Boys' Underachievement and Under-Representation in Subject English' in *Interpretation*, 27(2), 1994; 'Boys and Literacy: Exploring the Construction of Hegemonic Masculinities and the Formation of Literate Capacities for Boys in the English Classroom' in *English in Australia*, 112, 1995; 'Gendered Learning Experiences: Exploring the Costs of Hegemonic Masculinity for Girls and Boys in Schools' in *Gender Equity: A Framework for Australian Schools* (Canberra: Publications and Public Communications, Department of Urban Services, ACT Government, 1997). Catharine Stimpson, quoted in Tamar Lewin, 'American Colleges Begin to Ask, Where Have All the Men Gone?' in *New York Times*, December 6, 1998.

31. Wayne Martino, 'Gendered Learning Experiences', pp. 133, 134. Martain Mac an Ghaill, *The Making of Men: Masculinities, Sexualities and Schooling* (Buckingham: Open University Press, 1994), p. 59; David Gillborne, *Race, Ethnicity and Education* (London: Unwin Hyman, 1990), p. 63; James Coleman, *The Adolescent Society* (New York: Harper and Row, 1961).

32. Dalley-Trim, 'Call to Critique', p. 59.

33. 'Boys will be boys' are, not so incidentally, the last four words of Hoff Sommers's antifeminist screed.

34. See, for example, the essays in Rodney Clifton, Lance Roberts, and Raymond Perrys, eds., *Gender Equity in Canadian Postsecondary Educational Institutions* (Winnipeg: Centre for Educational Research and Development, University of Manitoba, 1998); see also Joanne Cooper and Pamela Eddy et al., 'Improving Gender Equity in Post Secondary Education', in Susan Klein, ed., *Achieving Gender Equity through Education,* Second Edition (New Jersey: Lawrence Erlbaum Associates, 2007), pp. 631–654.

35. Kirsteen Burton and Ian Wong, 'A Force to Contend with: The Gender Gap Closes in Canadian Medical Schools', *CMA Journal* 170(9), April 27, 2004. Available at http://www.cmaj. ca/cgi/content/full/170/9/1385; accessed July 21, 2009; Brendan Koerner, 'Where the Boys Aren't' in *U.S. News & World Report*, February 8, 1999; Levin, 'Where Have All the Men Gone?'; Michael Fletcher, 'Degrees of Separation' in *Washington Post*, June 25, 2002; Jamilah Evelyn, 'Community Colleges Start to Ask, Where Are the Men?' in *The Chronicle of Higher Education*, June 28, 2002; Ridger Doyle, 'Men, Women and College' in *Scientific American*, October, 1999.

36. Daniel Drolet, 'Minding the Gender Gap', *University Affairs*, September 10, 2007. Available at http://www.universityaffairs.ca/minding-the-gender-gap.aspx; accessed July 17, 2009; for the importance of class-related expectations in BC youths' postsecondary education decisions, see

Lesley Andres et al., 'Educational Expectations, Parental Social Class, Gender, and Postsecondary Attainment: A 10-Year Perspective', *Youth & Society* 39(2), December 2007, pp. 135–163.

37. Cited in Michael S. Kimmel, 'The Struggle for Gender Equality: How Men Respond' in *Thought and Action: The NEA Higher Education Journal*, 8(2), 1993.

38. Finkel, *Social Policy and Practice in Canada*, 56; for a US comparison, and excellent examples of relative nineteenth-century salaries for male and female teachers, see David Tyack and Elizabeth Hansot, *Learning Together: A History of Coeducation in American Public Schools* (Russell Sage Foundation, 1992), pp. 83–89.

39. Sheila Cavanaugh, 'Female-Teacher Gender and Sexuality in Twentieth-Century Ontario, Canada', *History of Education Quarterly* 45(2), Summer 2005, pp. 247–273.

40. Catell, cited in William O'Neil, *Divorce in the Progressive Era* (New Haven: Yale University Press, 1967), p. 81; Admiral F.E. Chadwick, 'The Woman Peril' in *Educational Review*, February, 1914, p. 47; last cited in Myra Sadker and David Sadker, *Failing at Fairness*, p. 214.

41. United States Department of Education, 1996; Patrick Harrigan, 'The Schooling of Girls and Boys in Canada', *Journal of Social History* 23(4), June 1990; Laverne Smith, 'The Gender Composition of the Pool of Prospective School Principals', *Canadian Journal of Education* 16(2), 1991, pp. 198–205; Cooper and Eddy et al., 'Improving Gender Equity', 636; 'Ontario Urged to Counter Drop in Male Teachers', CBC News, November 13, 2004. Available at http://www.cbc.ca/canada/story/2004/11/12/male_teacher_041112.html; accessed July 12, 2009; Niall Murray, 'Decline in Male Teachers "Robbing Young Boys of Role Models" ', *Irish Examiner*, Thursday, April 1, 2004. Available at http://archives.tcm.ie/irishexaminer/2004/04/01/story715017167.asp; accessed July 6, 2009; Wayne Martino and Michael Kehler, 'Male Teachers and the "Boy Problem": An Issue of Recuperative Masculinity Politics', *McGill Journal of Education* 41(2), Spring 2006, pp. 113–131.

42. Valerie Lee and Julia Smith, 'Gender Equity in Teachers' Salaries: A Multilevel Approach', *Educational Evaluation and Policy Analysis* 12(1), 1990, pp. 57–81; Cooper and Eddy et al., 'Improving Gender Equity', 636; David

Levinson, Peter Cookson, and Alan Sadnovik, *Education and Sociology: An Encyclopedia* (Routledge, 2001), 671; 'Study: Rising Education of Women and the Gender Earnings Gap', *The Daily*, June 12, 2007. Available at http://www.statcan.gc.ca/daily-quotidien/070612/dq070612b-eng.htm

43. See Ayers, 'A Teacher Ain't Nothin' But a Hero: Teachers and Teaching in Film', in Pamela Joseph and Gail Burneford, eds., *Images of Schoolteachers in America* (Mahwah, NJ: Lawrence Erlbaum Associates, 2001), pp. 201–210. See also Robert Lowe's essay in the same volume, 'Teachers as Saviors, Teachers Who Care'.

44. Martino and Kehler, 'Male Teachers', 118; Alanah May Erickson and Martha McKenzie Minifie, 'Primary Principals Seek More Real Men', *New Zealand Herald*, February 5, 2008. Available at http://www.nzherald.co.nz/nz/news/article.cfm?c_id=1&objectid=10490687; accessed July 21, 2009; Alanah May Erickson, 'Knitting Trend Used to Attract Male Teachers', *New Zealand Herald*, January 31, 2009; Available at http://www.nzherald.co.nz/alanah-may-eriksen/news/article.cfm?a_id=344&objectid=10554414; accessed July 21, 2009.

45. National Science Foundation, 'Characteristics of Doctoral Students', cited in Londa Schiebinger, *Has Feminism Changed Science?* (Cambridge: Harvard University Press, 1999), p. 34.

46. Jane Lin, 'The Teaching Profession: Trends from 1999 to 2005', available at http://www.statcan.gc.ca/pub/81-004-x/2006004/9540-eng.htm#a; accessed July 10, 2009.

47. See 'Disparate Burden' at www.insidehighered.com/news/2005/03/21/care, accessed March 31, 2005.

48. Peggy Orenstein, *Schoolgirls*, p. 27.

49. See Kim Gandy, 'Segregation Won't Help' in *USA Today*, May 10, 2002. 'Harlem Girls School vs. the Three Stooges' in *New York Observer*, March 30, 1998, p. 4; Mike Bowler, 'All-Male, All-Black, All Learning' in *Baltimore Sun*, October 15, 1995; Susan Estrich, 'For Girls' Schools and Women's College, Separate Is Better' in *New York Times*, May 22, 1994.

50. Jabali Sawicki, quoted in Elizabeth Weil's lengthy and well-researched 'Teaching Boys and Girls Separately', *The New York Times Magazine*, March 2, 2008. Available at http://www.

nytimes.com/2008/03/02/magazine/02sex3-t. html; accessed July 17, 2009.

51. The claims of benefits were challenged empirically by a study by the American Association of University Women (AAUW), which found that although many girls report that they feel single-sex classrooms are more conducive to learning, they also show no significant gains in achievement in math and science. Another researcher found some significant differences between coeducational and single-sex classes—but only in Catholic schools, not in private single-sex schools, and only for girls. A third researcher found no advantages of one or the other type of school for middle-class and otherwise advantaged students but found some positive outcomes for black or Hispanic girls from low socioeconomic homes. See Pamela Haag, 'Single-Sex Education in Grades K–12: What Does the Research Tell Us?' in *Separated by Sex: A Critical Look at Single-Sex Education for Girls* (Washington, DC: American Association of University Women Educational Foundation, 1998), p. 34; Valerie Lee, 'Is Single-Sex Secondary Schooling a Solution to the Problem of Gender Inequity?' in *Separated by Sex: A Critical Look at Single-Sex Education for Girls*, p. 43; Cornelius Riordan, 'The Future of Single-Sex Schools', p. 53; Connie Leslie, 'Separate and Unequal?' in *Newsweek*, March 23,1998, p. 55; Clark, cited in Charles Whitaker, 'Do Black Males Need Special Schools?' in *Ebony*, March 1991, p. 18.

52. Maria Jimenez, 'All Girls—Better Grades', *Globe and Mail*, April 21, 2009. Available at http:www. theglobeandmail.com/servlet/story/RT-GAM.20090421.wlsamesex21art1831/E; accessed April 24, 2009; Pamela Haag, 'What Does the Research Say?' *Eric Digest* September 2000, EDO-PS-00-9; Linda Sax et al., *Women Graduates of Single-Sex and Coeducational High Schools; Differences in Their Characteristics and the Transition to College* (Los Angeles: The Sudikoff Family Institute for Education and New Media/UCLA Graduate School of Education and Information Studies, 2009); Jacqueline Granleese and Stephen Joseph, 'Self-Perception of Adolescent Girls at a Single-Sex and a Mixed-Sex School'; Heather Blair and Kathy Sanford, 'Single-Sex Classrooms: A Place for Transformation of Policy and Practice', Conference paper presented at the Annual Meeting of

the American Educational Research Association, Montreal, April 1999.

53. Sax, quoted in Jimenez, 'All Girls'.

54. All examples are from Weil, 'Teaching Boys and Girls Separately'.

55. Amanda Datnow, Lea Hubbard, and Elisabeth Woody, 'Is Single Gender Schooling Viable in the Public Sector? Lessons from California's Pilot Program' (Toronto: Ontario Institute for Studies in Education, 2001).

56. Gambell is quoted in Jimenez, 'All Girls'.

57. John Dewey, 'Is Coeducation Injurious to Girls?' in *Ladies Home Journal*, June 11, 1911, p. 60.

Chapter 8

1. Parks Canada, *Canadian Workers in History: An Interpretation*, available at http://www.pc. gc.ca/eng/culture/proj/tch-cwh/index.aspx; accessed July 29, 2009; Lance Roberts, Robert Clifton, and Barry Ferguson, *Recent Social Trends in Canada, 1960—2000* (Montreal: McGill-Queen's University Press, 2005), pp. 158–159; Irene Padavic and Barbara Reskin, *Women and Men at Work* (2nd ed.) (Thousand Oaks, CA: Pine Forge, 2002), pp. 26–27.

2. Jerry Jacobs, 1993, see GS2, FN3, p. 318; also see Felice Schwartz, 'Management Women and the New Facts of Life' in *Harvard Business Review*, January–February, 1989.

3. Taylor, cited in Ashley Montagu, *The Natural Superiority of Women* (New York: Anchor, 1952), p. 28.

4. Michael Kimmel, *Manhood in America: A Cultural History* (New York: The Free Press, 1996); Willard Gaylin, *The Male Ego* (New York: Viking, 1992), cited also in Michael Kimmel, 'What Do Men Want?' in *Harvard Business Review*, November–December, 1993.

5. Willard Gaylin, *The Male Ego*, p. 64.

6. Amy Kroska, 'Examining Husband-Wife Differences in the Meaning of Family Financial Support', *Sociological Perspectives* 51(1), 2008, pp. 63–90; Belkin, 'When Mom and Dad Share It All'.

7. Peg Tyre and Daniel McGinn, 'She Works, He Doesn't' in *Newsweek*, May 12, 2003, pp. 45–53.

8. Marc Feigen-Fasteau, *The Male Machine* (New York: Dell, 1974), p. 120.

9. See Patricia Yancey Martin, '"Mobilizing Masculinities": Women's Experiences of Men at Work' in *Organization*, 8(4), 2001, pp. 587–618.

10. See Arlie Hochschild, *The Managed Heart* (Berkeley: University of California Press, 1982).

11. Reginald Bibby, 'Childcare Aspirations' (Press Release), Vanier Institute for the Family, February 10, 2005, available at http://www.vifamily. ca/newsroom/press_feb_10_05_c.html; accessed August 3, 2009; Katha Pollitt, 'Killer Moms, Working Nannies' in *The Nation*, November 24, 1997.

12. For a description of the rationale for and contents of the PARE, see RCMP Recruiting, 'PARE', available at http://www.rcmp-grc.gc.ca/ recruiting-recrutement/resources-ressources/ pare-tape-eng.htm; accessed August 13, 2009.

13. 'British Columbia (Public Service Employee Relations Commission) *v.* BCGSEU, [1999] 3 S.C.R', *Judgments of the Supreme Court of Canada*, available at http://scc.lexum.umontreal. ca/en/1999/1999rcs3-3/1999rcs3-3.html; accessed August 13, 2009; see also Coriaan de Villiers, 'Addressing Systemic Sex Discrimination: Employer Defences to Discrimination in Canada and South Africa', *Acta Juridica* (2001), p. 175; The Honourable Claire L'Heureux-Dube, 'A Conversation about Equality', *Denver Journal of International Law and Policy* 29, 2000, p. 65; Dianne Pothier, 'Connecting Grounds of Discrimination to Real People's Real Experiences', *Canadian Journal of Women and the Law* 13, 2001, p. 37; Rachel Cox and Karen Messing, 'Legal and Biological Perspectives on Employment Testing for Physical Abilities: A Post-Meiorin Review', *Windsor Yearbook of Access to Justice* 24, 2006, p. 23.

14. John Baden, 'Perverse Consequences (P.C.) of the Nanny State' in *Seattle Times*, January 17, 1996; Del Jones, 'Hooters to Pay $3.75 Million in Sex Suit' in *USA Today*, October 1, 1997, p. 1A.

15. Barbara Reskin, 'Sex Segregation in the Workplace' in *Women and Work: A Handbook*, P. Dubeck and K. Borman, eds. (New York: Garland, 1996), p. 94; see also Barbara Reskin, ed., *Sex-Segregation in the Workplace: Trends, Explanations, Remedies* (Washington, DC: National Academy Press, 1984); Barbara Reskin, 'Bringing the Men Back In: Sex Differentiation and the Devaluation of Women's Work' in *Gender and Society*, 2(1), 1988, and Barbara Reskin and Patricia Roos, eds., *Job Queues, Gender Queues: Explaining Women's Inroads into Male Occupa-*tions (Philadelphia: Temple University Press, 1990).

16. Padavic and Reskin, Women and Men at Work, pp. 65, 67; see also Andrea Beller and Kee-Ok Kim Han, 'Occupational Sex Segregation: Prospects for the 1980s' in *Sex-Segregation in the Workplace: Trends, Explanations, Remedies,* B. Reskin, ed., p. 91; Mary Cornish and Fay Faraday, 'Redressing Gender Discrimination in Employment: The Canadian Experience', paper presented to Seminar on Workplace Discrimination and the Law in North America, Washington, DC, November 18–19, 2004.' Roberts et al., *Recent Social Trends in Canada*, p. 161; Christine Alksnis, Serge Desmarais, and James Curtis, 'Workforce Segregation and the Gender Wage Gap: Is "Women's" Work Valued as Highly as "Men's"?' *Journal of Applied Social Psychology* 38(6), 2008), pp. 1416–1441.

17. Dana Dunn, 'Gender-Segregated Occupations' in *Women and Work*, P. Dubeck and K. Borman, eds., p. 92; StatsCan data cited and analyzed in 'Men/Women and the 10 Highest/ Lowest Paid Occupations in Canada', Women and the Economy: A Project of UNPAC. Available at http://www.unpac.ca/economy/ wagegap3.html' accessed April 9, 2009.

18. Margaret Mooney Marini and Mary C. Brinton, 'Sex Typing in Occupational Socialization' in *Sex-Segregation in the Workplace*, B. Reskin, ed., p. 224; Jerry A. Jacobs, *Revolving Doors: Sex Segregation and Women's Careers* (Stanford: Stanford University Press, 1989), p. 48.

19. Samuel Cohn, *The Process of Occupational Sex-Typing: The Feminization of Clerical Labor in Great Britain* (Philadelphia: Temple University Press, 1985).

20. Yilu Zhao, 'Women Soon to Be Majority of Veterinarians' in *New York Times*, June 9, 2002, p. 24; Jeanne Lofstedt, 'Gender and Veterinary Medicine', *The Canadian Veterinary Journal* 44(7), 2003, pp. 533–535.

21. Katharine Donato, 'Programming for Change? The Growing Demand among Computer Specialists' in *Job Queues, Gender Queues: Explaining Women's Inroads into Male Occupations*, B. Reskin and P. Roos, eds. (Philadelphia: Temple University Press, 1990), p. 170.

22. William Bielby and James Baron, 'Undoing Discrimination: Job Integration and Comparable Worth' in *Ingredients for Women's Employment Policy*, C. Bose and G. Spitze, eds. (Albany:

SUNY Press, 1987), p. 226; Barbara Reskin, 'Bringing the Men Back In . . ', p. 64.

23. Reed Abelson, '6 Women Sue Wal-Mart, Charging Job and Promotion Bias' in *New York Times*, June 20, 2001, pp. C1, 17; 'Court: Wal-Mart Gender Pay Lawsuit Can Go to Trial', CNN, May 2, 2010, available at http://www.wibw.com/nationalnews/headlines/92640459; accessed May 3, 2010.

24. EEOC v Sears, Roebuck and Co., 628 F Supp 1264 (N.D. Ill 1986); 839 F 2d 302 (7th. Cic. 1988).

25. Cynthia Cranford, Leah Vosko, and Nancy Lukewich, 'The Gender of Precarious Employment in Canada', *Relations industrielles / Industrial Relations* 58(3), 2003, pp. 454-482.

26. Leah Vosko, Nancy Zukewich, and Cynthia Cranford, 'Precarious Jobs: A New Typology of Employment', *Perspectives on Labour and Income* 4(10), 2003; also see Ontario Federation of Labour, 'Contingent Work Fact Sheet: Global Action against Precarious Work', *Metal World* No. 1, 2007, pp. 18–21.

27. Deena Ladd and Len Lewenza, 'The Precarious Economy', *The Mark*, October 6, 2009. Available at http://www.themarknews.com/articles/542-the-precarious-economy; accessed January 10, 2010.

28. See Abigail Bess Dakan and Daiva Stasiulas, *Not One of the Family: Foreign Domestic Workers in Canada* (Toronto: University of Toronto Press, 1997).

29. Statistics Canada, *Earnings and Income of Canadians over the Past Quarter Century, 2006 Census* (Ottawa: Ministry of Industry, 2008), pp. 18–19; Statistics Canada, *Earnings and Income of Canadians over the Past Quarter Century, 2006*; M. Drolet, 'The Male-Female Wage Gap', *Perspectives on Labour and Income* 2, No. 12 (2001), pp. 5–13; A.D. Bernhardt, M. Morris, and M.S. Handcock, 'Women's Gains or Men's Losses? A Closer Look at the Shrinking Gender Gap in Earnings' in *American Journal of Sociology*, 101, 1995, pp. 302–328; see also Rhode, *Speaking of Sex*, p. 175; Tamar Lewin, 'Women Losing Ground to Men in Widening Income Difference' in *New York Times*, September 15, 1997, pp. 1, 12. See also David Cay Johnston, 'As Salary Grows, So Does a Gender Gap' in *New York Times*, May 12, 2002.

30. Nicole Fortin and Michael Huberman, 'Occupational Gender Segregation and Women's

Wages in Canada: An Historical Perspective' (report), CIRANO Scientific Series 2002s-22 (Montreal: CIRANO, 2002); Bradley Brooks, Jennifer Jarman, and Robert Blackburn, 'Occupational Gender Segregation in Canada 1981–1996: Overall, Vertical, and Horizontal Segregation', *Canadian Review of Sociology and Anthropology* 40(2), 2003, pp. 197–213.

31. Alksnis, Desmarais, and Curtis, 'Workforce Segregation and the Gender Wage Gap', p. 1435; [US] Census 2000, http://www.census.gov/Press-Release/www/2002/demoprofiles.html; see also Ronnie Steinberg, 'How Sex Gets into Your Paycheck' in *Women's VU*, 20(2), 1997, p. 1.

32. Elizabeth Becker, 'Study Finds a Growing Gap Between Managerial Salaries for Men and Women' in *New York Times*, January 24, 2002, p. 18; Shannon Henry, 'Wage Gap Widens' in *Washington Post*, January 23, 2002; Statistics Canada, 'Occupational Skill Groups by Sex, Canada, 1991, 1996, and 2001', available at http://www12.statca.ca/english/census01/Products/Analtyic/companion/paid/tables; accessed August 14, 2009; Judith Lorber, 'Women and Medical Sociology: Invisible Professionals and Ubiquitous Patients' in *Another Voice*, M. Millman and R. M. Kanter, eds. (Garden City, NY: Anchor, 1975), p. 82.

33. Alksnis, Desmarais, and Curtis, 'Workforce Segregation and the Gender Wage Gap', p. 1435.

34. Cited in Julie Mathaei, *An Economic History of Women in America* (New York: Schocken, 1982), p. 192.

35. Lynn Martin, *A Report on the Glass Ceiling Initiative* (Washington, DC: U.S. Department of Labor, 1991), p. 1.

36. 'The Conundrum of the Glass Ceiling' in *The Economist*, July 21, 2005.

37. *Good for Business: Making Full Use of the Nation's Human Capital* (Washington, DC: U.S. Government Printing Office, 1995); Ruth Simpson, 'Does an MBA Help Women?—Career Benefits of the MBA' in *Gender, Work and Organization*, 3(2), April, 1996, p. 119.

38. Tonda MacCharles, 'Ex-Bell Execs Allege Sexism', The Star.com, January 14, 2008. Available at http://www.thestar.com/293750; accessed October 12, 2009. Moya Greene, 'Remarks for the HSBC Women of Influence Luncheon

Series', 28 September 2007. Available at http://www.canadapost.ca/cpo/mc/about us/corporate/management/moyagreene/women.isf; accessed 10 September, 2009; 'Study: Women Create "Their Own Glass Ceiling": Female Managers More likely to Underestimate How Their Work is Valued', Associated Press, August 10, 2009; available at http://www.msnbc.msn.com/id/32364451/ns/business-careers; accessed August 24, 2009.

39. Warren Farrell, *The Myth of Male Power* (New York: Simon & Schuster, 1993), pp. 105–106.

40. Rosabeth Moss Kanter, *Men and Women of the Corporation* (New York: Basic Books, 1977), p. 209.

41. Ibid., pp. 216, 221, 230.

42. Lynn Zimmer, 'Tokenism and Women in the Workplace: The Limits of Gender-Neutral Theory' in *Social Problems*, 35(1), 1988, p. 64; Nina Toren and Vered Kraus, 'The Effects of Minority Size on Women's Position in Academia' in *Social Forces*, 65, 1987, p. 1092.

43. Christine Williams, 'The Glass Escalator: Hidden Advantages for Men in the 'Female' Professions' in *Social Problems*, 39(3), 1992; *Still a Man's World: Men Who Do 'Women's Work'* (Berkeley: University of California Press, 1995); see also Marie Nordberg, 'Constructing Masculinity in Women's Worlds: Men Working as Pre-School Teachers and Hairdressers' in *NORA: Nordic Journal of Women's Studies*, 10(1), 2002, pp. 26–37.

44. Christine Williams, 'The Glass Escalator', p. 296.

45. Ibid.; Alfred Kadushin, 'Men in a Woman's Profession' in *Social Work*, 21, 1976, p. 441.

46. Constance Backhouse, '*Bell v. The Flaming Steer Steak House Tavern*: Canada's First Sexual Harassment Decision', *University of Western Ontario Law Review* 19(1), 1981, pp. 141–151; Margaret Crouch, *Thinking about Sexual Harassment: A Guide for the Perplexed* (Oxford: Oxford University Press, 2000), pp. 92–93.

47. See Catharine MacKinnon, *Sexual Harassment of Working Women* (Cambridge: Harvard University Press, 1977).

48. Canadian Advisory Council on the Status of Women, *CACSW Fact Sheet: Sexual Harassment* (Ottawa: CASCW, n.d.).

49. Susan Crawford, 'Sexual Harassment at Work Cuts Profits, Poisons Morale' in *Wall Street Journal*, April 19, 1993, p. 11F; Elizabeth Stanko, *Intimate Intrusions* (London: Routledge,1985); E.Couric, 'An NJL/West Survey, Women in the Law: Awaiting Their Turn' in *National Law Journal*, December 11, 1989; 1997 study by Klein Associates; Ellen Neuborne, 'Complaints High from Women in Blue Collar Jobs' in *USA Today*, May 3–6, 1996.

50. 'Harassment Scandal Grows in BC Fire Department', CBC News, March 30, 2006. Available at http://www.cbc.ca/canada/story/2006/03/30/richmond-firefighters.html; accessed October 12, 2009; 'Female Firefighters All off the Job', *Vancouver Province*, March 22, 2006; 'Fire Department's Sexual Harassment Slammed by Mediator', CBC News, September 22, 2006. Available at http://www.cbc.ca/canada/british-columbia/story/2006/09/22/bc-firefighters-ready.html; accessed October 12, 2009.

51. Deborah Rhode, *Speaking of Sex*, p. 28.

52. W. Ann Maggiore, 'Sexual Harassment: It's Not about Women', *EMS Insider* 34, No. 12 (2007).

53. *USA Today* 'Snapshot', April 5, 2006; Dave McGinn, 'The New Harassment? Same-sex Abuse', *Globe and Mail*, October 5, 2009.

54. Eve Tahmincioglu, 'Your Career: Female Bosses and Harassment', MSNBC.com, August 24, 2009. Available at http://www.msnbc.com/id/32476564/business-careers; accessed August 24, 2009; 'Female Supervisors More Susceptible to Workplace Sexual Harassment' (American Sociological Association media release). Available at http://www.eurekalert.org/pub_releases/2009-08/asa-fsm073009.php; accessed October 12, 2009.

55. Wallace Immen, 'The Plague that Haunts Us Still', *Globe and Mail*, September 8, 2004. Susan Crawford, 'Sexual Harassment at Work Cuts Profits . . . ' p. 11F.

56. The text of ILO Convention 100 is available at http://www.ilocarib.org.tt/projects/cariblex/pdfs/ILO_Convention_100.pdf.; Mary Cornish, 'Closing the Global Gender Pay Gap: Securing Justice for Women's Work', *Comparative Labor Law & Policy Journal* 28(2), Winter 2007, pp. 219–250.

57. Fortin and Huberman, 'Occupational Gender Segregation and Women's Wages in Canada', 21; 'Bell Canada Settles Pay Equity Case for $178 Million', CBC News, September 4, 2002. Available at http://www.cbc.ca/money/story/2002/09/04/bell020904.html; accessed August 12, 2009.

58. Ronnie Steinberg, 'How Sex Gets Into Your Paycheck', p. 2; Aaron Wherry, 'Is This the Quiet End to Pay Equity?' *Macleans.ca,* February 21, 2009. Available at http://www2.macleans.ca/2009/02/21/is-this-the-quiet-end-to-pay-equity; accessed October 2, 2009.

59. Cited in Rhode, *Speaking of Sex,* pp. 165, 169.

60. Kate Harding, 'Lactate on Your Own Time, Lady', *Salon.com,* August 28, 2009. Available at http://www.salon.com/mwt/broadsheet/feature/2009/08/28/fired_for_pumping/print.html; accessed September 1, 2009.

61. See, for example, Felice Schwartz and Gigi Anders, 'The Mami Track' in *Hispanic,* July, 1993.

62. 'Stay the Course on Creating a Family-friendly Workplace, Says Ernst & Young' (media release), June 8, 2009. Available at http://www.ey.com/CA/en/Newsroom/News-releases/2009-Progressive-Employer; accessed October 10, 2009.

63. See *The Week,* p. 36.

64. Ronnie Steinberg and Alice Cook, 'Policies Affecting Women's Employment in Industrial Countries' in *Women Working,* A. Stromberg and S. Harkess, eds. (Mountain View, CA: Mayfield, 1988), p. 326.

65. Karen Oppenheim Mason, 'Commentary: Strober's Theory of Occupational Sex Segregation' in *Sex-Segregation in the Workplace,* B. Reskin, ed. p. 169.

66. Catherine Rampell, 'As Layoffs Surge, Women May Pass Men in Job Force', *The New York Times,* February 6, 2009. Available at http://www.nytimes.com/2009/02/06/business/06women.html; accessed February 6, 2009; Raveena Aulakh, 'In Shrinking Workforce, Women May Surpass Men', *thestar.com,* February 7, 2009. Available at http://www.thestar.com/583904; accessed August 14, 2009.

67. Coontz, *The Way We Never Were,* p. 52.

Chapter 9

1. Bart Beaty and Rebecca Sullivan, *Canadian Television Today* (Calgary: University of Calgary Press, 2006), p. 113; Donald Roberts, Ulla Foehr, Victoria Rideout, and Mollyann Brodie, *Kids and Media @ the New Millennium: A Comprehensive Analysis of Children's Media Use* (Menlo Park: Henry J. Kaiser Foundation, 1999).

2. Roberts et al., *Kids and Media;* 'Television Viewing: Fall 2004', *The Daily,* March 31, 2006. Available at http://www.statcan.gc.ca/daily-quotidien/060331/dq060331b-eng.htm; accessed July 20, 2009.

3. P. McGhee and T. Frueh, 'Television Viewing and the Learning of Sex-Role Stereotypes', *Sex Roles* 6, 1980, pp. 179–188.

4. See, for example, Kay Bussey and Albert Bandura, 'Social Cognitive Theory of Gender Development and Differentiation', *Psychological Review* 106, pp. 676–713.

5. John Consoli, 'What Women Don't Want? Soap Operas' in *Adweek,* November 1, 2004; Betty Goodwin, 'Cable Channels Take Aim at Women' in *Television Week,* November 5, 2005. Richard Collins, 'Reflections across the Atlantic: Contrasts and Complementarities in Broadcasting Policy in Canada and the European Community in the 1990s', *Canadian Journal of Communication,* 20(4), 1995.

6. See Stuart Elliott, 'NBC Looks Beyond TV for a Prime Time Revival' in *New York Times,* May 16, 2006, p. C10; Alec Foge, 'Searching for the Elusive Male' in *Mediaweek,* September 5, 2005; Betty Goodwin, 'Programmers Cast a Wide Net' in *Television Week,* November 7, 2005; Zondra Hughes, 'Prime-Time 2005: More Stars, More Soul, More Sensation' in *Ebony,* October, 2005.

7. Richard Gruneau and David Whitson, *Hockey Night in Canada: Sport, Identities, and Cultural Politics* (Toronto: Garamond Press, 1993); David Whitson, 'Circuits of Promotion: Media, Marketing, and the Globalization of Sport', in Lawrence Wenner, ed., *Mediasport* (Routledge, 1998), pp. 57–73; Neil Earle, 'Hockey as Canadian Popular Culture: Team Canada 1972, Television, and the Canadian Identity', in Jeanette Sloniowski and Joan Nicks, *Slippery Pastimes: Reading the Popular in Canadian Culture* (Waterloo: Wilfrid Laurier University Press, 2002), pp. 321–344; J.C.H. Jones, D.G. Ferguson, and K.G. Stewart, 'Blood Sports and Cherry Pie: Some Economics of Violence in the National Hockey League', *American Journal of Economics and Sociology* 52(1), January 1993, pp. 63–78; Sandra Langley, 'Gender, Talk, TV, Hockey, and "Canadian Identity": Feminist Takes on "Television Rejection"', *Canadian Journal of Communication* 28(4), 2003.

8. See the results of a study done at the University of Guelph, which found links between television use and physical inactivity that were not found when other sedentary activities (video game use, computer use, reading) were examined. 'TV Watching Linked to Increased Physical Inactivity' (news release, December 11, 2006). Available at http://www.uoguelph.ca/news/2006/12/post_25.html; accessed May 12, 2009; for the Angus Reid poll, see 'Not Tonight, Dear, I'm Watching the News', *Backbone Magazine*, December 10, 2007. Available at http://www.backbonemag.com/Press_Release/Items/press_release_12100704.asp; accessed July 11, 2009; Rachel Naud, 'Caution Needed When Allowing Children to Watch TV', Canada.com. Available at http://www.canada.com/entertainment/Caution+needed+when+allowing+kids+watch/1331738/story.html; accessed July 23, 2009; Jane Ledingham, C. Anne Ledingham, and John Richardson, 'The Effects of Media Violence on Children' (report) (Ottawa: Health Canada, n.d.). Available at http://www.phac-aspc.gc.ca/ncfv-cnivf/publications/nfntseffemediarech-eng.php; accessed July 21, 2009.

9. National Television Violence Study (2 vols.) (Thousand Oaks, CA: Sage Publication, 1998), Vol. 2, p. 97; Wendy Josephson, 'Television Violence: A Review of the Effects on Children of Different Ages' (report) (Ottawa: Health Canada, n.d.).

10. Guy Paquette, 'Violence on Canadian Television Networks', *Journal of the Canadian Academy of Child and Adolescent Psychiatry* 13(1), February 2004, pp. 13–15.

11. George Spears and Casia Seydegart, 'Gender and Violence in the Mass Media' (report prepared for the Family Violence Prevention Unit, Health Canada) (Ottawa: Health Canada, 1993). Available at http://www.phac-aspc.gc.ca/ncfv-cnivf/publications/femviomedia-eng.php#Children's; accessed July 19, 2009.

12. Ibid.

13. Ibid.; http://www.campaignforrealbeauty.com/; Rebecca Traister, ' "Real Beauty"–or Really Smart Marketing?' *Salon.com*, July 22, 2005. Available at http://dir.salon.com/story/mwt/feature/2005/07/22/dove/index1.html; Rikki Arundel, 'Is America's FCC Stupid? Or Is Dove Just Very Clever?' *The Gendershift Blog*.

Available at http://gendershift.blogspot.com/2007/04/is-americas-fcc-stupid-or-is-dove-just.html; accessed July 21, 2009.

14. Walter Hixson, ' "Red Storm Rising": Tom Clancy Novels and the Cult of National Security', *Diplomatic History* 17(4), 1993, pp. 599–614; 607.

15. See, for example, Scott Mebus, *Booty Nomad* (New York: Hyperion, 2004); Benjamin Kunkel, *Indecision* (New York: Random House, 2005); Kyle Smith, *Love Monkey* (New York: HarperCollins, 2005); Nancy Pearl, 'Dick Lit', in *Book Lust: 1000 New Reading Recommendations for Every Mood, Moment, and Reason* (Seattle: Sasquatch Books, 2005), p. 78; for a gendered comparison of chick lit and lad lit, and some pointed commentary on the amount of masturbation in lad lit, see Susan Jeffris and Brandon Robshaw, 'Shaking Hands across the Great Divide', *The Independent*, June 17, 2000. Available at http://www.independent.co.uk/arts-entertainment/books/reviews/shaking-hands-across-the-great-divide-625595.html; accessed July 21, 2009.

16. See Amy Beth Aronson, *Taking Liberties: Early American Women's Magazines and Their Readers* (Westport, CT: Praeger, 2002), p. 3; Betty Friedan, *The Feminine Mystique* (New York: Dell Publishing, 1983), pp. 15–79.

17. Friedan, *The Feminine Mystique*, p. 36.

18. Wendy Robbins, 'The Celebration of Her Life', *Canadian Woman Studies* 26(2), December 2007, pp. 126–128; 'We're Celebrating Eighty Years', Chatelaine.com. Available at http://en.chatelaine.com/english/celebration/article.jsp?content=20080225_154938_6272; accessed July 23, 2009; Valerie Korinek, 'The *Chatelaine* Legacy', *Canadian Woman Studies* 26(2), December 2007, pp. 14–21; 21; Katherine Govier, 'Rebel Daughter', *Canadian Woman Studies* 26(2), December 2007, pp. 114–116; Mary Eberts, ' "Write It for the Women": Doris Anderson, Changemaker', *Canadian Woman Studies* 26(2), December 2007, pp. 6–13; Valerie Korinek, ' "Mrs Chatelaine" vs. "Mrs Slob": Contestants, Correspondents and the Chatelaine Community in Action, 1961–1969', *Journal of the Canadian Historical Association* 7(1) 1996, pp. 251–285; Marco Ursi, 'The Top 50', *Masthead Special Report*, June 25, 2009; Lisa Rundle, 'What Women Want', *This Magazine*, January-February 2005. Available at http://

www.thismagazine.ca/issues/2005/01/what-womenwant.php; accessed July 23, 2009.

19. Aronson, *Taking Liberties*, p. 3; see also, for example, Tanya Modeski's characterization of women soap opera fans as 'egoless receptacles'. See Tanya Modeski, 'The Search for Tomorrow in Today's Soap Operas' in *Loving with a Vengeance: Mass-Produced Fantasies for Women* (Hamden, CT: Shoestring Press, 1982). Marjorie Ferguson, *Forever Feminine: Women's Magazines and the Cult of Femininity* (London: Gower, 1983), p. 3. Gaye Tuchman, Arlene Daniels, and James Benit, eds., *Hearth and Home: Images of Women in the Mass Media* (New York: Oxford University Press, 1978); Jean Kilbourne, 'Killing Us Softly', available from the Media Education Foundation (www.mef.org); Naomi Wolf, *The Beauty Myth* (New York: William Morrow, 1991).

20. Media Research Center, *Landmark Study Reveals Women's Magazines Are Left-Wing Political Weapon* (Alexandria, VA). Christina Hoff Sommers, 'The Democrats' Secret Woman Weapon: In the Pages of Glossy Women's Magazines, the Party's Line Is in Fashion' in *Washington Post*, January 13, 1997, p. 22. See also Danielle Crittenden, *What Our Mothers Didn't Tell Us: Why Happiness Eludes the Modern Woman* (New York: Simon & Schuster, 1999), pp. 20–21.

21. Aronson, *Taking Liberties*.

22. Laramie Taylor, 'All for Him: Articles About Sex in American Lad Magazines' in *Sex Roles*, 52(3/4), 2005, p. 155.

23. Tim Adams, 'New Kid on the Newsstand' in *Observer*, January 23, 2005.

24. Rachel Gallagher, 'Magazine ABCs: Maxim Circulation in 60 Percent Crash', Press Gazette: Journalism Today August 14, 2008. Available at http://www.pressgazette.co.uk/story.asp?storycode=41925; accessed July 22, 2009; Stephen Brook, 'Maxim Closes UK Print Edition', The Guardian Online, April 2, 2009. Available at http://www.guardian.co.uk/media/2009/apr/02/maxim-magazine-closes-uk-print-edition; accessed July 22, 2009; 'Canadian Men's Magazine Toro Axed', CBC News, February 12, 2007; available at http://www.cbc.ca/arts/media/story/2007/02/12/toro-magazine-ax.html; accessed July 23, 2009; 'Canada's Only National Men's Lifestyle Magazine Launches This April', CNW Group. Available at http://

www.newswire.ca/en/releases/archive/February 2008/08/c8335.html; accessed July 23, 2009.

25. Circulation figures cited in David Brooks, 'The Return of the Pig' in *Atlantic Monthly*, April, 2003.

26. Tim Adams, 'New Kid on the Newsstand'; in fact, however, Hilton left *Nuts* in 2007 to focus on developing a new magazine that would appeal to men who found lad magazines 'smutty and adolescent'. See 'Launch Diary: Former "Nuts" editor Phil Hilton Reveals How a New Magazine All Comes Together', *The Independent*, September 17, 2007. Available at http://www.independent.co.uk/news/media/launch-diary-former-nuts-editor-phil-hilton-reveals-how-a-new-magazine-all-comes-together-402561.html; accessed July 20, 2009.

27. Ben Goldacre, *Bad Science* (Fourth Estate Ltd, 2008); see also Carrie Dunn, 'Bad Science? Bad Gender Politics?' on *The FWord: UK Feminism*, Blog, 3 February 2009. Available http://www.thefword.org.uk/blog/2009/02/bad_science_bad; accessed July 21, 2009.

28. 'Shonen Jump Media Kit' (VIZ Media), available at http://www.shonenjump.net/mediakit/images/SJ_MEDIAKIT_Web.pdf; accessed July 20, 2009; 'VIZ Confirms Shojo Beat Manga Magazine's End in June', Anime News Network, May 19, 2009, available at http://www.animenewsnetwork.com/news/2009-05-19/viz-confirms-shojo-beat-manga-magazine-end-in-june; accessed July 21, 2009.

29. Denise Winterman, 'Jane Austen—Why the Fuss?' *BBC Newsmagazine*, March 9, 2007. Available at http://news.bbc.co.uk/2/hi/uk_news/magazine/6426195.stm; accessed July 12, 2009.

30. Matt Benz, 'Rock Still the Top-Selling Genre', *Billboard*, March 31, 2001, available at http://www.allbusiness.com/retail-trade/miscellaneous-retail-retail-stores-not/4643869-1.html; accessed July 30, 2009; 'Sales of Rap Albums Take Stunning Nosedive', FoxNews.com, March 1, 2007; Ta-Nehisi Coates, 'Hip-Hop's Down Beat', *Time*, August 12, 2007, available at http://www.time.com/time/magazine/article/0,9171,1653639,00.; accessed July 30, 2009. Jacqueline thanks Jeff Slack for his useful comments on this section.

31. Nelson George, *Hip Hop America* (New York: Penguin, 1998), p. xi; This is also the argument

Byron Hurt makes in his film *Beyond Beats and Rhymes*; see also Patricia Hill Collins, *From Black Power to Hip-Hop: Racism, Feminism, and Nationalism* (Philadephia: Temple University Press, 2006), pp. 3–5; for urban Aboriginal youth and rap, see Brett Lashua and Karen Fox, 'Rec Needs a New Rhythm Cuz Rap Is Where We're Livin', *Leisure Sciences* 28, No. 3 (2006), pp. 267–283; for one example of rap on a (Mohawk) reserve, see Robert Hollands, 'Rappin' on the Reservation: Canadian Mohawk Youth's Hybrid Cultural Identities', *Sociological Research Online* 9, No, 3 (2004). Available at http://www.socresonline.org.uk/cgi-bin/perlfect/search/search.pl?q=multiculturalism&showurl=%2F9%2F3%2Fhollands.html; accessed July 22, 2009.

32. Jennifer McClune, ' "You Told Harpo to Beat Me?" How Hip-Hop Music Defines and Divides Black Women', 2008, available at http://hiphopnews.yuku.com/topic/997; accessed July 30, 2009. Deborah Finding, 'Why Do We Tolerate Misogyny in Music?' *The Guardian,* March 31, 2009, available at http://www.guardian.co.uk/comment isfree/2009/mar/31/music-orelsan-rap-misogyny; accessed July 30, 2009; OrelSan lyrics at ParolesMusiques.com, available at http://www.paroles-musique.com/paroles-Orelsan-Sale_Pte-lyrics,p59677; accessed on 30 July 2009, translated by Jacqueline Holler.

33. Edward Armstrong, 'Eminem's Construction of Authenticity', *Popular Music and Society* 27(3), 2004, pp. 335–355; 343–344; Charis Kubrin, 'Gangstas, Thugs, and Hustlas: Identity and the Code of the Street in Rap Music', *Social Problems* 52(3), 2005, pp. 36–378; Banner quoted in 'Sales of Rap Take Stunning Nosedive'.

34. Julie Watson, 'Rapper's Delight: A Billion Dollar Industry' in *Forbes*, February 18, 2004; available at: www.forbes.com/2004/02/18/cx_jw_0218hiphop.html, accessed December 24, 2005; see also figures cited in Bill Yousman, 'Blackophilia and Blackophobia: White Youth, the Consumption of Rap Music, and White Supremacy' in *Communication Theory*, 13(4), November, 2003, p. 367. See also Mary Bucholtz, 'You da Man: Narrating the Racial Other in the Production of White Masculinity' in *Journal of Sociolinguistics*, 3/4, 1999, pp. 443–460; Cecelia Cutler, ' "Keeping It Real": White Hip Hoppers' Discourses of Language, Race and Authenticity' in *Journal of Linguistic Anthropology* 13(2),

2003, pp. 1–23; Cecelia Cutler, 'Yorkville Crossing: White Teens, Hip Hop and African American English' in *Journal of Sociolinguistics* 3/4, 1999, pp. 428–442; Mary Bucholtz, 'Borrowed Blackness: African American Vernacular English and European American Youth Identities', Ph.D. dissertation, University of California at Berkeley, 1997. The white suburban youth and Powell are cited in Bakari Kitwana, *Wankstas, Wiggers, Wannabes and the New Reality of Race in America* (New York: Basic Books, 2005), p. 41, p. 53. Kitwana argues that white suburban consumption of hip-hop heralds the arrival of new racial politics in America, a new inclusiveness and opposition to racism on the part of white music consumers.

35. Bill Yousman, 'Blackophilia and Blackophobia'; Melvin Donaldson, cited in Kitwana, *Why White Kids Love Hip Hop*, p. 148.

36. Anthony Bozza, *Whatever You Say I Am: The Life and Times of Eminem* (New York: Crown, 2004), p. 31. This interpretation of Eminem's meaning and importance has been greatly influenced by Michael's conversations with Steven Zyck and his 'Undressing Eminem: Intersection and Abjection in the Formation of a Cultural Icon', B.A. honors thesis, Dartmouth College, June 2004.

37. Armstrong, 'Eminem's Construction of Authenticity', p. 344.

38. Susan Hiwatt, 'Cock Rock: Men Always Seem to End up on Top', in Theo Calefono, ed., *The Rock History Reader* (Routledge, 2006), pp. 125–130; p. 126.

39. Steve Waksman, *Instruments of Desire: The Electric Guitar and the Shaping of Musical Experience* (Harvard University Press, 2001), pp. 237–276; p. 244.

40. Adam Wolstenholme, 'The Misogyny Police Get the Wrong Men', *Batley & Birstall News*, April 17, 2009, available at http://www.batleynews.co.uk/adam-wolstenholme/The-misogyny-police-get-the.5181247.jp; accessed July 30, 2009.

41. See Philip Auslander, 'I Wanna Be Your Man: Suzi Quatro's Musical Androgyny', *Popular Music* 23(1), 2004, pp. 1–16; Ronald Weitzer and Charis Kubrin, 'Misogyny in Rap Music: A Content Analysis of Prevalence and Meanings', *Men and Masculinities Online First,* February 19, 2009, pp. 1–27; 23, available at http://jmm.sagepub.com/cgi/rapidpdf/

1097184X08327696v1.pdf; accessed July 20, 2009.

42. Jennifer McLune, 'Hip-Hop's Betrayal of Black Women', April 26, 2006, *Davey D's Hip-Hop Corner,* available at http://hiphopandpolitics. wordpress.com/2006/04/26/hip-hops-betrayal-of-black-women-by-jennifer-mclune/, accessed July 28, 2009.

43. Mark Anthony Neal, 'Spelman Women Take a Stand', at http://archive. blackvoices.com/articles/daily/mu20040414tipdrill.asp, accessed on March 2, 2005.

44. Ibid; Camille Jackson, 'Misogyny and Rap: "Chickenhead" Means You', *Teaching Tolerance,* April 11, 2005, available at http://www. tolerance.org/news/article_print.jsp?id=1196; accessed July 30, 2009.

45. Thomas DeFrantz, 'Wait . . . Hip-Hop Sexualities', in Steven Seidman, Nancy Fischer, and Chet Meeks, eds., *Introducing the New Sexuality Studies: Original Essays and Interviews* (London/NY: Routledge, 2006), pp. 303–308; Tom Murray, 'Facing the Music', AlbertaVenture. com, April 1, 2005. Available at http://www. albertaventure.com/?p=2339; accessed July 21, 2005.

46. While *GTA* has been the focus of lawsuits and much media controversy, some scholars see it as a sophisticated cultural critique or satire that has both worth and cultural influence. See the essays in Nate Garrelts, ed., *The Meaning and Culture of "Grand Theft Auto": Critical Essays* (Jefferson, NC: McFarland & Co., 2006).

47. 'Internet Use Threatens to Overtake TV in Canada', CTV.ca, August 10, 2005. Available at http:///www.ctv.ca/servlet/ArticleNews/print/ CTV News/20050810/internet_overtakes_tv_0; accessed July 23, 2009; 'Canadian Teens Choosing TV Less Often', *CBC News,* March 31, 2006. Available at http://www.cbc.ca/canada/story/ 2006/03/31/teens-tv060331.html; accessed July 23, 2009; 'Banner Year for Canadian Video-Game Sales', *CBC News,* January 16, 2009, available at http://www.cbc.ca/technology/ story/ 2009/01/16/video-games.html; accessed July 27, 2009; Leonard J. Paul, 'Canadian Content in Video Games', in *Changing Views-World in Play* (Proceedings of the 2005 DiGRA Conference).

48. Video game data are drawn from Michel Marriott, 'The Color of Mayhem' in New York Times, August 12, 2004, p. G3; www.idsa.com; www.digiplay.org.uk; *Essential Facts about the Computer and Video Game Industry; 2008 Sales, Demographic and Usage Data.*

49. http://www.rockstargames.com; Paul Goldsmith, 'The New Players' in *Southwest Airlines Spirit,* December, 2004, p. 170; Rasanth Sridharan, 'GTA IV: The Biggest Video Game Of All Time Is A Mediocre Movie (TTWO)', BusinessInsider.com, May 5, 2008. Available at http://www.businessinsider.com/2008/5/gta-iv-vs-movies-movies-win; accessed July 21, 2009; Barbara Prtutay, 'Take-Two's "Grand Theft Auto IV" tops $500M in week 1 sales', Boston.com, May 7, 2008. Available at http://www.boston.com/business/ articles/2008/05/07/take_twos_grand_theft_ auto_iv_tops_500m_in_1st_week_sales/; accessed July 21, 2009; *Essential Facts about the Computer and Video Game Industry; 2008 Sales, Demographic and Usage Data* (report) (n.p: Entertainment Software Association, 2008).

50. See, for example, M.D. Griffiths, Mark N.O. Davies, and Darren Chappell, 'Online Computer Gaming: A Comparison of Adolescent and Adult Gamers' in *Journal of Adolescence,* 10, 2003; James D. Ivory, 'Still a Man's Game: Gender Representations in Online Reviews of Video Games', *Mass Communication and Society,* 2006; Mark Griffiths, Mark N.O. Davies, and Darren Chappell, 'Breaking the Stereotype: The Case of Online Gaming', manuscript, Nottingham Trent University, 2005.

51. William Lugo, interview, February 2, 2005. The one game in which relationships exist is Sims, because the game makes it possible for same-sex characters to live together, share a bed, kiss, have a baby, etc. (Nina Huntemann, personal communication, December 19, 2005). And, of course, Sims is the one game that 'real guys' can't stand!; for the Wii Fit, see Brad Millington, 'Wii Has Never Been Modern: "Active" Video Games and the "Conduct of Conduct" ', *New Media & Society* 11(4), 2009, pp. 621–640.

52. Interview with Nina Huntemann, November 1, 2005. *Game Over* is available from the Media Education Foundation; Jo Bryce and Jason Rutter, 'Killing Like a Girl: Gendered Gaming and Girl Gamers' Invisibility', *CGDC Proceedings* (Tampere: University of Tampere Press, 2002), pp. 243–255; Gareth Scott and Kirsty Horrel, 'Girl Gamers and Their Relationship with the Gaming Culture', *Convergence: The Interna-*

tional Journal of Research into New Media Technologies 6(4), 2000, pp. 36–53; see also Kristen Lucas and John Sherry, 'Sex Differences in Video Game Play: A Communication-Based Explanation', *Communication Research* 31(5), November 2004, pp. 499–523.

53. Jing Feng, Ian Spence, and Jay Pratt, 'Playing an Action Video Game Reduces Gender Differences in Spatial Cognition', *Psychological Science* 18(10), 2007, pp. 850–855.

54. See Derek Burrill, 'Watch Your Ass: The Structure of Masculinity in Video Games', unpublished manuscript, University of California at Riverside, 2005; David Leonard, 'Not a Hater, Just Keepin' It Real: The Importance of Race and Gender-Based Game Studies', *Games and Culture* 1(1), January 2006, pp. 83–88.

55. Tracy Dietz, 'An Examination of Violence and Gender Role Portrayals in Video Games: Implications for Gender Socialization and Aggressive Behavior', *Sex Roles* 38(5/6), 1998, pp., 425–442; Leonard, 'Not a Hater', pp. 85–86.

56. Helen Kennedy, 'Lara Croft: Feminist Icon or Cyberbimbo?' in *Game Studies*, 2(2), December, 2002.

57. Those interested in the game, or the controversy that followed its release, can see Mighty Ponygirl's post on the Feminist Gamers blog, September 1, 2008. Available at http://www.feministgamers.com/?p=493; accessed July 23, 2009.

58. Seth Schiesel, 'The Year in Gaming: Readers Report' in *New York Times*, December 31, 2005, p. B21; Henry Wilson, 'World of Warcraft Subscribers Now 11.5 million (Timeline Included)', *International Business Times*, December 23, 2008, available at http://www.ibtimes.com/articles/20081223/world-warcraft.htm; accessed July 23, 2009; Edward Castronova, *Synthetic Worlds* (Chicago: University of Chicago Press, 2005).

59. Jeanne Funk, Heidi Bechtoldt Baldacci, Tracie Pasold, and Jennifer Baumgardner, 'Violence Exposure in Real-Life, Video Games, Television, Movies, and the Internet: Is There Desensitization?' *Journal of Adoelscence* 27, 2004, pp. 23–39; Leonard, 'Not a Hater', p. 88.

60. Jessica Williams, 'Facts That Should Change the World: America Spends $10bn Each Year on Porn' in *New Statesman*, June 7, 2004; Melinda Tankard Reist, 'Incensed about Censorship', *Online Opinion: Australia's E-Journal of Social and Political Debate,* December 5, 2008, available at http://www.onlineopinion.com.au/print.asp?article=8176; Ian Gillespie, 'Nowadays It's Brutal, Accessible: Pornography', *London Free Press,* June 11, 2008, p. A3; Chris Gudgeon, *The Naked Truth: The Untold Story of Sex in Canada* (Vancouver: Douglas & McIntrye, 2003), p. 184.

61. Larry Flynt, 'Porn World's Sky Isn't Falling—It Doesn't Need a Condom Rule' in *Los Angeles Times*, April 23, 2004.

62. Cited in Pamela Paul, *Pornified: How Pornography Is Transforming Our Lives, Our Relationships and Our Families* (New York: Times Books, 2005), pp. 15, 30, 69.

63. Stacy L. Smith and Ed Donnerstein, 'The Problem of Exposure: Violence, Sex, Drugs and Alcohol' in *Kid Stuff: Marketing Sex and Violence to America's Children*, Diane Ravitch and Joseph Viteritti, eds. (Baltimore: Johns Hopkins University Press, 2003), p. 83; Pamela Paul, *Pornified*, p.4.

64. Reist, 'Incensed about Censorship'.

65. Alexandra Bennett, 'From Theory to Practice: Catharine MacKinnon, Pornography, and Canadian Law', *Modern Language Studies* 27(3/4), 1997, pp. 213–230; Susan R. Taylor, 'Gay and Lesbian Pornography and the Obscenity Laws in Canada', *Dalhousie Journal of Legal Studies* 8, 1994, pp. 94–129; Susan Barrowclough, 'Not a Love Story', *Screen* 23(5), 1982, pp. 26–36; Catherine Dunphy, 'Lindalee Tracey, 49: Filmmaker Eyed Naked Truth', The Star.com, Nov. 3, 2006, available at http://www.thestar.com/article/127032; accessed July 30, 2009.

66. Kimberly Davies, 'Voluntary Exposure to Pornography and Men's Attitudes toward Feminism and Rape', *The Journal of Sex Research* 34(2), 1997, pp. 131–137; Feona Attwood, 'What Do People Do with Porn? Qualitative Research into the Consumption, Use, and Experience of Pornography and Other Sexually Explicit Media', *Sexuality & Culture* 9(2), Spring 2005, pp. 65–86.

67. Antonia Zerbisias, 'Packaging Abuse of Women as Entertainment for Adults', *The Star.Com*, January 26, 2008, available at http://pqasb.pqarchiver.com/thestar/access/1418827751.html?dids=1418827751:1418827751&FMT=ABS&FMTS=ABS:FT&type=current&date=Jan+26%2C+2008&author=Antonia+Zerbisias&pub=Toronto+Star&edition=&startpage=L.4&desc

=Packaging+abuse+of+women+as+entertain
ment+for+adults%3B+Cruel%2C+degrading
+scenes+%27normalized%27+for+generati
on+brought+up+in+dot-com+world;   accessed July 28, 2009.

68. John Stoltenberg, 'Pornography and Freedom'
in *Men Confront Pornography*, M. Kimmel, ed.
(New York: Crown, 1990), p. 64.

69. Jensen quoted in Ian Gillespie, 'Now It's Brutal,
Accessible: Pornography'; Robert Jensen, 'Just a
John? Pornography and Men's Choices', in Shira
Tarrant, ed., *Men Speak Out: Views on Gender,
Sex, and Power* (Routledge, 2008), pp. 64–69.

70. Deborah Fallows, *How Women and Men Use
the Internet* (Washington, DC: Pew Internet
and American Life Project, 2005).

71. Fallows, Ibid; Statistics Canada, 'Canadian Internet Use Survey', *The Daily*, August 15, 2006,
available at http://www.statcan.gc.ca/daily-
quotidien/060815/dq060815b-eng.htm; accessed
July 30, 2009.

72. Jeffrey Jones, 'Six in 10 Americans Are Pro
Football Fans' The Gallup Poll, February 4,
2005.

73. *Brandweek*, September 29, 2003; 'World Wrestling Entertainment's Monday Night RAW De-
livers Best Ratings Since April 2002' in *Business
Wire, Inc.*, March 23, 2004.

Chapter 10

1. Cited in Drury Sherrod, 'The Bonds of Men:
Problems and Possibilities in Close Male Relationships' in *The Making of Masculinities: The
New Men's Studies*, H. Brod, ed. (Boston: Allen
and Unwin, 1987), p. 230; cited in Lillian Rubin,
Intimate Strangers (New York: Harper and Row,
1983), p. 59.

2. Wollstonecraft, *A Vindication of the Rights of
Women*, p. 56; de Beauvoir, *The Second Sex*,
p. 142.

3. Lionel Tiger, *Men in Groups* (New York: Vintage,
1969).

4. Carroll Smith-Rosenberg, 'The Female World
of Love and Ritual: Relations between Women
in Nineteenth-Century America', *Signs* 1(1),
Autumn, 1975, pp. 1–29; also see a special
journal volume dedicated to the article and its
impact, *Women's History in the New Millennium: Carroll Smith-Rosenberg's "The Female
World of Love and Ritual" after Twenty-Five
Years, Journal of Women's History* 12(3),
Autumn, 2000.

5. Joseph Pleck, 'The Male Sex Role: Definitions,
Problems and Sources of Change' in *Journal of
Social Issues*, 32(3), 1976, p. 273; Jack Balswick,
'The Inexpressive Male: A Tragedy of American
Society' in *The Forty-Nine Percent Majority*, D.
David and R. Brannon, eds. (Reading, MA:
Addison-Wesley, 1976); Mirra Komorovsky,
Blue Collar Marriage (New York: Vintage,
1964); Robert Lewis, 'Emotional Intimacy
Among Men' in *Journal of Social Issues*, 34,
1978.

6. Lillian Rubin, *Intimate Strangers*, pp. 58, 159,
205.

7. Drury Sherrod, 'The Bonds of Men', p.231.

8. Lillian Rubin, *Intimate Strangers*, p. 206.

9. See the recent furor over claims that Abraham
Lincoln was gay. Richard Brookhiser, 'Was Lincoln Gay?' *The New York Times*, January 9,
2005.

10. Drury Sherrod, 'The Bonds of Men', p. 221; E.
Anthony Rotundo, 'Romantic Friendships:
Male Intimacy and Middle-Class Youth in the
Northern United States, 1800–1900' in *Journal
of Social History*, 23(1), 1989, p. 21. http://
query.nytimes.com/gst/fullpage.html?res=9f05
e5d61439f93aa35752c0a9639c8b63; accessed
October 11, 2009.

11. Francesca Cancian, *Love in America*, pp. 19, 21,
23; see also Mary Ryan, *The Cradle of the Middle Class: The Family in Oneida County, N.Y.,
1790–1865* (New York: Cambridge University
Press, 1981).

12. Lawrence Stone, 'Passionate Attachments in
the West in Historical Perspective' in *Passionate
Attachments: Thinking About Love*, W. Gaylin
and E. Person, eds. (New York: The Free Press,
1988), p. 33; Francesca Cancian, *Love in America*, p. 70.

13. Lawrence Stone, 'Passionate Attachments', p. 32;
Michael Gordon and M.Charles Bernstein,
'Mate Choice and Domestic Life in the Nine-
teenth Century Marriage Manual' in *Journal of
Marriage and the Family*, November, 1970,
pp. 668, 669.

14. William J. Goode, 'The Theoretical Importance
of Love' in *American Sociological Review*, 24(1),
1959.

15. Foucault cited in Peter Nardi, *Men's Friendships*, p. 184; Lynne Segal, *Slow Motion:
Changing Masculinities, Changing Men* (New
Brunswick, NJ: Rutgers University Press,
1990), p. 139.

16. Tannen, *You Just Don't Understand*, pp. 42, 181, passim; see also Tannen, *Gender and Discourse* (New York: Oxford University Press, 1994).

17. Nicholas Kristof, 'Japan's Feminine Falsetto Falls Right out of Favor', *New York Times*, December 13, 1995; Laura Miller, 'You Are Doing *Burikko*! Censoring/Scrutinising Artificers of Cute Femininity in Japanese', in Shikego Okamoto and Janet Shibamoto Smith, eds., *Japanese Language, Gender, and Ideology: Cultural Models and Real People* (Oxford/New York: Oxford University Press, 2004), pp. 148–165, 151–153.

18. Jennifer Coates, ed., *Language and Gender: A Reader* (Oxford: Blackwell, 1998), pp. 2–3; Campbell Leaper and Melanie Ayres, 'A Meta-Analytic Review of Gender Variations in Adults' Language Use: Talkativeness, Affiliative Speech, and Assertive Speech', *Personality and Social Psychology Review* 11, 2007, pp. 328–363.

19. Carol Tavris, *The Mismeasure of Woman* (New York: Simon & Schuster, 1992), pp. 271–272.

20. Peter Kollock, Philip Blumstein, and Pepper Schwartz, 'Sex and Power in Interaction: Conversational Privileges and Duties', *American Sociological Review* 50, February 1985, pp. 34–46.

21. See Pamela Hobbs, 'The Medium is the Message: Politeness Strategies in Men's and Women's Voice Mail Messages', *Journal of Pragmatics* 35, 2003, pp. 243–262; Penelope Brown, 'How and Why Women Are More Polite: Some Evidence from a Mayan Community', and Janet Holmes, 'Complimenting: A Positive Politeness Strategy', in Coates, ed., *Language and Gender*, pp. 81–120.

22. Michael Claes, 'Adolescents' Closeness with Parents, Siblings, and Friends in Three Countries: Canada, Belgium, and Italy', *Journal of Youth and Adolescence* 27(2), 1998, pp. 165–184.

23. See S. E Taylor, L.C. Klein, B.P. Lewis, T.L. Gruenwald, R.A.R. Gurung, and J.A. Updegraff, 'Biobehavioral Female Responses to Stress: Tend and Befriend, Not Fight or Flight' in *Psychological Review*, 107(3), 2000, pp. 411–429.

24. Mayta Caldwell and Letita Peplau, 'Sex Differences in Same-Sex Friendships' in *Sex Roles*, 8(7), 1982; Beth Hess, 'Friendship' in *Aging and Society*, M. Riley, M. Johnson, and A. Foner, eds. (New York: Russell Sage, 1972); Erina MacGeorge,

Angela Graves, Bo Feng, Seth Gillihan, and Brant Burleson, 'The Myth of Gender Cultures: Similarities Outweigh Differences in Men's and Women's Provision of and Responses to Supportive Communication' in *Sex Roles*, 50(3/4), February 2004, pp. 143–175.

25. Lillian Rubin, *Just Friends* (New York: Harper and Row, 1985), pp. 60–61, 62–63; Lillian Rubin, *Intimate Strangers*, pp. 130, 135.

26. Sandra Brehm, *Intimate Relationships* (New York: Random House, 1985), p. 346. Lynne Davidson and Lucille Duberman, 'Friendship: Communication and Interactional Patterns in Same-Sex Dyads' in *Sex Roles*, 8(8), 1982, p. 817.

27. Paul Wright, 'Men's Friendships, Women's Friendships and the Alleged Inferiority of the Latter' in *Sex Roles*, 8(1), 1982, p. 19; Daniel Levinson, *The Seasons of a Man's Life* (New York: William Morrow, 1978), p. 335.

28. N.L. Ashton, 'Exploratory Investigation of Perceptions of Influences on Best-Friend Relationships' in *Perception and Motor Skills*, 50, 1980; Shavaun Wall, Sarah M. Pickert, and Louis V. Paradise, 'American Men's Friendships: Self-Reports on Meaning and Changes' in *The Journal of Psychology*, 116, 1984.

29. Helen Hacker, 'Blabbermouths and Clams: Sex Differences in Self-Disclosure in Same-Sex and Cross-Sex Friendship Dyads' in *Psychology of Women Quarterly*, 5(3), Spring, 1981.

30. Barbara Bank, 'Friendships in Australia and the United States: From Feminization to a More Heroic Image' in *Gender & Society*, 9(1), 1995, p. 96.

31. Shanette Harris, 'Black Male Masculinity and Same Sex Friendships' in The Western *Journal of Black Studies*, 16(2), 1992, p 77.

32. Shanette Harris, 'Black Male Masculinity . . .', pp. 78, 81; see also Clyde W. Franklin II, ' "Hey Home"—"Yo, Bro": Friendship Among Black Men' in *Men's Friendships*, P. Nardi, ed. (Newbury Park: Sage Publications, 1992).

33. Helen M. Reid and Gary Alan Fine, 'Self-Disclosure in Men's Friendships: Variations Associated with Intimate Relations' in *Men's Friendships*; Jeanne Tschann, 'Self-Disclosure in Adult Friendship: Gender and Marital Status Differences' in *Journal of Social and Personal Relationships*, 5, 1988; Paul Wright, 'Men's Friendships', pp. 16–17.

34. Lillian Rubin, *Intimate Strangers*, pp. 154, 150.

35. Stuart Miller, *Men and Friendship* (Boston: Houghton, Mifflin, 1983), pp. 2–3; Lillian Rubin, *Intimate Strangers*, p. 103.

36. On experiment, see Lillian Faderman, *Surpassing the Love of Men* (New York: Columbia University Press,1981); quote from Scott Swain, 'Covert Intimacy', pp. 83–84.

37. Peter Nardi and Drury Sherrod, 'Friendship in the Lives of Gay Men and Lesbians' in *Journal of Social and Personal Relationships*, 11, 1994; Lillian Rubin, *Intimate Strangers*, p. 105.

38. Cited in Lillian Rubin, *Intimate Strangers*, p. 130.

39. Peter Nardi, 'The Politics of Gay Men's Friendships' in *Men's Lives* (4th ed.), M. Kimmel and M. Messner, eds. (Boston: Allyn and Bacon, 1998), p. 250.

40. See, inter alia, Helen E. Fisher et al., 'Defining the Brain Systems of Lust, Romantic Attraction, and Attachment', *Archives of Sexual Behavior* 31(5), October 2002, pp. 413–419.

41. Brent Miller and Brad Benson, 'Romantic and Sexual Relationship Development during Adolescence', in Wyndol Furman, Benson Brown, and Candace Feiring, eds., *The Development of Romantic Relationships in Adolescence* (Cambridge: Cambridge University Press, 1999), pp. 99–121; pp. 100–101.

42. William Kephart, 'Some Correlates of Romantic Love' in *Journal of Marriage and the Family*, 29, 1967.

43. Jeffry Simpson, Bruce Campbell, and Ellen Berscheid, 'The Association between Romantic Love and Marriage', *Personality and Social Psychology Bulletin*, 42(3), 1986, pp. 363–372.

44. Susan Sprecher, E. Aron, E. Hatfield, A. Cortese, E. Potapava, and A. Levitskaya, 'Love: American Style, Russian Style, and Japanese Style', paper presented at the Sixth Annual Conference on Personal Relationships, Orono, Maine, 1992.

45. Susan Sprecher and Maura Toro-Morn, 'A Study of Men and Women from Different Sides of Earth to Determine If Men Are from Mars and Women Are from Venus in Their Beliefs About Love and Romantic Relationships' in *Sex Roles*, 46(5/6), March, 2002, pp. 131–147.

46. Pierre Bourdieu, *Masculine Domination*, trans. Richard Nice (Stanford: Stanford University Press, 2001).

47. William Kephart, 'Some Correlates of Romantic Love'; Kenneth Dion and Karen Dion, 'Correlates of Romantic Love' in *Journal of Consulting and Clinical Psychology*, 41, 1973; Charles Hill, Zick Rubin, and Letitia Anne Peplau, 'Breakups Before Marriage: The End of 103 Affairs' in *Divorce and Separation: Context, Causes and Consequences*, G. Levinger and O. C. Moles, eds. (New York: Basic Books, 1979); Charles Hobart, 'Disillusionment in Marriage and Romanticism' in *Marriage and Family Living*, 20, 1958; Charles Hobart, 'The Incidence of Romanticism During Courtship' in *Social Forces*, 36, 1958; David Knox and John Spoakowski, 'Attitudes of College Students Toward Love' in *Journal of Marriage and the Family*, 30, 1968; George Theodorson, 'Romanticism and Motivation to Marry in the United States, Singapore, Burma and India' in *Social Forces*, 44, 1965.

48. Kenneth Dion and Karen Dion, 'Correlates of Romantic Love'; Zick Rubin, 'Measurement of Romantic Love' in *Journal of Personality and Social Psychology*, 16(2), 1970; Arlie Hochschild, 'Attending to, Codifying and Managing Feelings: Sex Differences in Love', paper presented at the annual meeting of the American Sociological Association, August 1975; Eugene Kanin, Karen Davidson, and Sonia Scheck, 'A Research Note on Male-Female Differentials in the Experience of Heterosexual Love' in *Journal of Sex Research*, 6, 1970, p. 70.

49. Charles Hill, Zick Rubin, and Letitia Ann Peplau, 'Breakups Before Marriage'.

50. Cancian, *Love in America*, p. 70.

51. Cancian, *Love in America*, p. 121; Carol Tavris, *The Mismeasure of Woman*, p. 263; Lillian Rubin, *Intimate Strangers*.

52. Robin Simon and Leda Nath, 'Gender and Emotion in the United States: Do Men and Women Differ in Self-Reports of Feelings and Expressive Behavior?' in *American Journal of Sociology*, 109(5), pp. 1137–1176.

53. Cathy Greenblat, personal communication with M. Kimmel. This research has not yet been published.

54. Carol Tavris, *The Mismeasure of Woman*, p. 284.

55. Cancian, 'The Feminization of Love', pp. 705, 709.

56. Cited in Barbara Ehrenreich and Deirdre English, *For Her Own Good: 150 Years of Medical Advice to Women* (New York: Anchor, 1974).

57. Cited in Brian Zamboni and Isaiah Crawford, 'Using Masturbation in Sex Therapy', in *Masturbation as a Means of Achieving Sexual Health*, ed. Walter Bockling and Eli Coleman (New York: The Haworth Press, 2002), p. 127; Judith Treas and Deirdre Giesen, 'Sexual Infidelity among Married and Cohabiting Americans', *Journal of Marriage and the Family* 62, No. 1 (February 2000), pp. 48–60. Pauline Bart, 'Male Views of Female Sexuality: From Freud's Phallacies to Fisher's Inexact Test', paper presented at the Second National Meeting of the Special Section of Psychosomatic Obstetrics and Gynecology, Key Biscayne, FL, 1974, pp. 6–7.

58. Lillian Rubin, *Erotic Wars* (New York: Farrar, Straus and Giroux, 1991), pp. 28, 42.

59. Catharine MacKinnon, *Only Words* (Cambridge: Harvard University Press, 1996); Kate Lunau, 'Are We Blushing Yet?' *Macleans,* June 29, 2009; available at http://www.macleans.ca/2009/06/29/are-we-blushing-yet; accessed July 9, 2009; Billy Crystal, quoted in *The Week*, May 10, 2002, p. 17.

60. Alan Bell and Martin Weinberg, *Homosexualities* (New York: Simon & Schuster, 1978); William Masters and Virginia Johnson and Richard Kolodny, *Human Sexuality* (New York: Harper and Row, 1978); Philip Blumstein and Pepper Schwartz, *American Couples,* (New York: William Morrow, 1983), p. 317.

61. Emmanuel Reynaud, *Holy Virility*, R. Schwartz, trans. (London: Pluto Press, 1983), p. 41.

62. See, for example, Tavris, *The Mismeasure of Woman*; Harriet Lerner, *Women in Therapy* (New York: Harper and Row, 1989), chapter 2.

63. Stephanie Sanders and June Machover Reinisch, 'Would you say 'Had Sex' If . . . ' in *JAMA*, 281, January 20, 1999.

64. Dayna Fischstein, Edward Herold, and Serge Desmarais, 'How Much Does Gender Explain in Sexual Attitudes and Behaviors? A Survey of Canadian Adults', *Archives of Sexual Behavior,* 36, 2007, pp. 451–461.

65. On rates of masturbation, see Edward Laumann, John Gagnon, Robert Michael, and Stuart Michaels, *The Social Organization of Sexuality* (Chicago: University of Chicago Press, 1994), p. 86; Pepper Schwartz and Virginia Rutter,

The Gender of Sexuality, (Thousand Oaks: Pine Forge Press, 1998), p. 39. Also Roy F. Baumeister, Kathleen R. Catanese, and Kathleen D. Vohs, 'Is There a Gender Difference in Strength of Sex Drive? Theoretical Views, Conceptual Distinctions, and a Review of Relevant Evidence', *Personality and Social Psychology* Review 5(3), 2001, pp. 242–273; 251.

66. Michael Kimmel and Rebecca Plante, 'Sexual Fantasies and Gender Scripts: Heterosexual Men and Women Construct Their Ideal Sexual Encounters' in *Gendered Sexualities*, vol. 6 of *Advances in Gender Research*, ed. Patricia Gagné and Richard Tewksbury, pp. 55–78 (Amsterdam: JAI Press, 2002). See also E. Barbara Hariton and Jerome Singer, 'Women's Fantasies During Sexual Intercourse: Normative and Theoretical Implications' in *Journal of Consulting and Clinical Psychology,* 42(3), 1974; Daniel Goleman, 'Sexual Fantasies: What Are Their Hidden Meanings?' in *New York Times*, February 28, 1983; Daniel Goleman, 'New View of Fantasy: Much Is Found Perverse?' in *New York Times*, May 7, 1991; Robert May, *Sex and Fantasy: Patterns of Male and Female Development* (New York: W. W. Norton, 1980); David Chick and Steven Gold, 'A Review of Influences on Sexual Fantasy: Attitudes, Experience, Guilt and Gender' in *Imagination, Cognition and Personality*, 7(1), 1987–1988; Robert A. Mednick, 'Gender Specific Variances in Sexual Fantasy' in *Journal of Personality Assessment*, 41(3), 1977; Diane Follingstad and C. Dawne Kimbrell, 'Sexual Fantasies Revisited: An Expansion and Further Clarification of Variables Affecting Sex Fantasy Production' in *Archives of Sexual Behavior*, 15(6), 1986; Danielle Knafo and Yoram Jaffe, 'Sexual Fantasizing in Males and Females' in *Journal of Research in Personality*, 18, 1984.

67. Baumeister, Catanese, and Vohs, 'Is There a Gender Difference in Strength of Sex Drive?'

68. Ibid.

69. Ibid.

70. Laumann et al., *The Social Organization of Sexuality*, p. 347.

71. Robert Stoller, *Porn* (New Haven: Yale University Press, 1991), p. 31.

72. Eric Spitznagel, 'How Internet Porn is Changing Teen Sex', *Details*, September 2009, available at http://www.details.com/sex-relationships/porn-and-perversions/200907/how-internet-porn-is-changing-teen-sex; accessed August 18,

2009. See also Tracy Clark-Fiory, 'Generation XXX: Having Sex like Porn Stars', *Salon.com*, August 18, 2009, available at http://www,salon.com/mwt/broadsheet/feature/2009/08/18/gen_porn.html; accessed August 18, 2009. For a review of the empirical literature on pornography, see Michael Kimmel and Annulla Linders, 'Does Censorship Make a Difference? An Aggregate Empirical Analysis of Pornography and Rape' in *Journal of Psychology and Human Sexuality*, 8(3), 1996.

73. John Stoltenberg, 'Pornography and Freedom' in *Men Confront Pornography*, M. Kimmel, ed. (New York: Crown, 1990). Marty Klein, 'Pornography: What Men See When They Watch', in Peter Lehman, ed., *Pornography: Film and Culture* (New Brunswick, NJ: Rutgers University Press, 2006), pp. 244–257; pp. 248–249.

74. Daniel Bernardi, 'Interracial Joysticks: Pornography's Web of Racist Attractions', in Lehman, *Pornography*, pp. 220–243.

75. Spitznagel, 'How Internet Porn is Changing Teen Sex', Clark-Fiory, 'Generation XXX: Having Sex like Porn Stars'; Jessica Bennett, 'The Pornification of a Generation', *Newsweek*, October 7, 2008; available at http://www.newsweek.com/id/162792; accessed December 3, 2009.

76. Adrienne Rich, 'Compulsory Heterosexuality and Lesbian Existence', *Signs*, 5(4), Summer, 1980, pp. 631–660; p. 657.

77. The heterosexual questionnaire is widely available in many versions.

78. Stevi Jackson, 'The Social Construction of Female Sexuality', in *Feminism and Sexuality: A Reader*, S. Jackson and S. Scott, eds. (New York: Columbia University Press, 1996), p. 71.

79. See Ritch Savin-Williams, 'Dating and Romantic Relationships among Gay, Lesbian, and Bisexual Youths', in Michael Kimmel, Amy Aronson, and Amy Kaler, eds., *The Gendered Society Reader: Canadian Edition* (Toronto: Oxford University Press, 2008), pp. 347–357.

80. Edward Laumann et al., *The Social Organization of Sexuality*, p. 347.

81. Mary Koss has published prolifically and been widely cited. See, inter alia, 'Sexual Experiences Survey: A Research Instrument Investigating Sexual Aggression and Victimization', *Journal of Consulting and Clinical Psychology* 50(3), 1982, pp. 455–457; 'Hidden Rape: Sexual Aggression and Victimization in a National Sample of Students in Higher Education', in *Rape and Sexual Assault II*, ed. Ann Wolbert Burgess (New York, Garland Publishing, 1988), pp. 3–25.

82. Charlene Muehlenhard, ' "Nice Women" Don't Say Yes and "Real Men" Don't Say No: How Miscommunication and the Double Standard Can Cause Sexual Problems' in *Women and Therapy*, 7, 1988, pp. 100–101.

83. Bennett, 'The Pornification of a Generation'.

84. See Jeffrey Fracher and Michael Kimmel, 'Hard Issues and Soft Spots: Counseling Men About Sexuality' in *Handbook of Counseling and Psychotherapy with Men*, M.Scher, M. Stevens, G. Good, and G. Eichenfeld, eds. (Newbury Park: Sage Publications, 1987).

85. Joel Lexchin, 'Bigger and Better: How Pfizer Redefined Erectile Dysfunction', *PLoS Medicine* 3(4), April, 2006, pp. 429–432. Available at www.plosmedicine.org. See also Bruce Handy, 'The Viagra Craze' in *Time*, May 4, 1998, pp. 50–57; Christopher Hitchens, 'Viagra Falls' in *The Nation*, May 25, 1998, p. 8.

86. Lillian Rubin, *Erotic Wars*, p. 13; A.C. Grunseit, S. Kippax, M. Baldo, P.A. Aggleton, and G. Slutkin, 'Sexuality, Education and Young People's Sexual Behavior: A Review of Studies' manuscript from UNAID, 1997.

87. Amber Hollibaugh, 'Desire for the Future: Radical Hope in Passion and Pleasure' in *Feminism and Sexuality: A Reader*; Lillian Rubin, *Erotic Wars*, pp. 5, 46.

88. On rates of masturbation, see Laumann et al., *The Social Organization of Sexuality*, p. 86; on attitudes, see Schwartz and Rutter, *The Gender of Sexuality*, p. 39.

89. Lillian Rubin, *Erotic Wars*, p. 13; on rates of change in sexual activity, see Grunseit et al., 'Sexuality, Education and Young People's Sexual Behavior'.

90. Tamar Lewin, 'One in Five Teenagers Has Sex Before 15, Study Finds' in *New York Times*, May 20, 2003.

91. Willard Waller, 'The Rating and Dating Complex' in *American Sociological Review*, 2, October, 1937, pp. 727–734.

92. ' "Hookups": Characteristics and Correlates of College Students' Spontaneous and Anonymous Sexual Experiences' in *Journal of Sex Research*, 37(1), February, 2000, pp. 76–88.

93. Melanie Beres, ' "It Just Happens": Negotiating Casual Heterosexual Sex', in Kimmel et al., *The*

Gendered Society Reader: Canadian Edition, pp. 370–380.

94 Alfred Kinsey, Wendall Pomeroy, and Charles Martin, *Sexual Behavior in the Human Female* (Philadelphia: W.B. Saunders, 1953); Laumann et al., *The Social Organization of Sexuality*; see also Schwartz and Rutter, *The Gender of Sexuality*, pp. 102–103; Sam Janus, *The Janus Report on Sexual Behavior* (New York: John Wiley, 1993), pp. 315–316; Blumstein and Schwartz, *American Couples*; see also *New Sexual Agendas*, Lynne Segal, ed. (New York: New York University Press, 1997), p. 67.

95. Gina Kolata, 'Women and Sex: On This Topic, Science Blushes' in *New York Times*, June 21, 1998, p. 3; young woman cited in Lillian Rubin, *Erotic Wars*, p.14.

96. Laura Sessions Stepp, 'Study: Half of All Teens Have Had Oral Sex' in *Washington Post*, September 15, 2005; Sharon Jayson, 'Teens Define Sex in New Ways' in *USA Today*, October 18, 2005.

97. Cited in Lillian Rubin, *Erotic Wars*, p. 58; Mary Koss, L.A. Goodman, A. Browne, L.F. Fitzgerald, G.P. Keita, and N.F. Russo, *No Safe Haven: Male Violence Against Women at Home, at Work, and in the Community* (Washington, DC: American Psychological Association, 1994).

98. Mary Koss, P.T. Dinero, C.A. Seibel, and S.L. Cox, 'Stranger and Acquaintance Rape: Are There Differences in the Victim's Experience?' in *Psychology of Women Quarterly*, 12(1), 1988; Edward Laumann et al., *The Social Organization of Sexuality*, p. 336; see also Mary Koss et al., *No Safe Haven*.

99. Ronald F. Levant, 'Nonrelational Sexuality in Men' in *Men and Sex: New Psychological Perspectives*, R. Levant and G. Brooks, eds. (New York: John Wiley, 1997), 26.

100. See, for example, J.O. Billy, G.K. Tanfer, W.R. Grady, and D.H. Klepinger, 'The Sexual Behavior of Men in the United States' in *Family Planning Perspectives*, 25(2), 1993; Edward Laumann et al., *The Social Organization of Sexuality*.

101. Gary Brooks, *The Centerfold Syndrome* (San Francisco: Jossey-Bass, 1995), and Gary Brooks, 'The Centerfold Syndrome' in *Men and Sex: New Psychological Perspectives*, R. Levant and G. Brooks, eds. (New York: John Wiley, 1997). See also Ron Levant, 'Nonrelational Sexuality', p. 19; Joni Johnston, 'Appearance Obsession: Women's Reactions to Men's Objectification of

Their Bodies' in *Men and Sex*, pp. 79, 101; Glenn Good and Nancy B.Sherrod, 'Men's Resolution of Nonrelational Sex Across the Lifespan' in *Men and Sex*, pp. 186, 189, 190.

102. See, for example, Peter Wyden and Barbara Wyden, *Growing Up Straight: What Every Thoughtful Parent Should Know About Homosexuality* (New York: Trident Press, 1968); Richard Green has provided a more thoughtful discussion of gender and homosexuality in, *The "Sissy Boy" Syndrome* (New Haven: Yale University Press, 1986).

103. Michel Foucault, *The History of Sexuality* (New York: Pantheon, 1978). See also Jonathan Ned Katz, *The Invention of Heterosexuality* (New York: E.P. Dutton, 1993).

104. Wyden and Wyden, *Growing Up Straight*.

105. Green, *The "Sissy Boy" Syndrome*.

106. George Gilder, *Men and Marriage* (Gretna, LA: Pelican Publishers, 1985).

107. Cited in Steve Chapple and David Talbot, *Burning Desires: Sex in America* (New York: Doubleday, 1989), p. 356.

108. See the work of Victoria Clarke, including Victoria Clarke and Celia Kitzinger, 'Lesbian and Gay Parents on Talk Shows: Resistance or Collusion in Heterosexism?' *Qualitative Research in Psychology*, No. 1, 2004, pp. 195–217.

109. Lisa Diamond, *Sexual Fluidity: Understanding Women's Love and Desire* (Boston: Harvard University Press, 2008).

110. Bell and Weinberg, *Homosexualities*; Masters, Johnson and Kolodny, *Human Sexuality*; Blumstein and Schwartz, *American Couples,* p. 317.

111. Data from Blumstein and Schwartz, *American Couples*; woman is quoted in Bell and Weinberg, *Homosexualities*, p. 220.

112. Leslie Feinberg, *Stone Butch Blues* (Firebrand Books, 1993).

113. See Jeni Loftus, 'America's Liberalization in Attitudes Toward Homosexuality, 1973–1998' in *American Sociological Review*, 66, October, 2001, pp. 762–782.

114. Charlene Muelenhard, 'Nice Women Don't Say Yes . . .'; John Gagnon and Stuart Michaels, 'Answer No Questions: The Theory and Practice of Resistance to Deviant Categorization', unpublished manuscript, 1989, p. 2. On the impact of homophobia on heterosexual men's lives, see also Richard Goldstein, 'The Hate That Makes Men Straight' in *The Village Voice*, December 22, 1998.

115. Laumann et al., *The Social Organization of Sexuality*, pp. 82–84, 98, 177, 192, 302–309, 518–529.

116. Lisa Diamond and Ritch Savin-Williams, 'Explaining Diversity in the Development of Same-Sex Sexuality Among Young Women', *Journal of Social Issues* 56(2),pp. 297–313; p. 298.

117. Rubin, *Erotic Wars*, p. 165. For the significance of sexual orientation to identity, see Robert Kertzner, 'The Adult Life Course and Homosexual Identity in Midlife Gay Men', *Annual Review of Sex Research* 12, 2001, pp. 75–92; Diamond and Savin-Williams, 'Explaining Diversity'.

118. Does Equality Produce a Better Sex Life?' in *Newsday*, April 19, 2006; see Edward O. Laumann, Anthony Paik, Dale Glasser, Jeong-Han Kang, Tianfu Wang, Bernard Levinson, Edson Moreira,Anfredo Nocolosi, and Clive Gingell, 'A Cross-National Study of Subjective Sexual Well-Being Among Older Women and Men: Findings from the Global Study of Sexual Attitudes and Behaviors' in *Archives of Sexual Behavior*, 35(2), April, 2006, pp. 145–161.

119. See John Gottman, *Why Marriages Succeed or Fail* (New York: Simon & Schuster, 1995).

120. Cambridge Women's Pornography Collective, *Porn for Women* (Chronicle Books, 2007).

121. But see Laura Agustin's dissenting opinion on this, 'The Other Swedish Model: Gender, Sex, and Culture', at http://www.thelocal.se/blogs/theotherswedishmodel/2010/01/11/good-sex-equal-sex-who-has-the-best-sex/, accessed January 10, 2010.

122. Lillian Rubin, *Just Friends*, p. 41.

Chapter 11

1. It is ironic, perhaps, that some of these developments that have made us more aware of our bodies have also enabled us to change (surgery) or conceal (Internet) them.

2. Helen Meekosha, 'Body Battles: Bodies, Gender, and Disability', in Tom Shakespeare, ed., *The Disability Reader: Social Science Perspectives* (London/New York: Continuum Books, 1998), p. 164.

3. Robert Murphy, 'Encounters: The Body Silent in America', in Benedicte Ingstad and Susan Reynolds Whyte, eds., *Disability and Culture* (Berkeley/Los Angeles: University of California Press, 1995), p. 143.

4. Council of Canadians with Disabilities, 'As a Matter of Fact: Poverty and Disability in Canada', available at http//www.ccdonline.ca/em/socialpolicy/poverty-citizenship/poverty-disability-canada; Cara Williams, 'Disability in the Workplace', *Perspectives* 7(2), February, 2006.

5. Fiona Sampson, 'Globalization and the Inequality of Women with Disabilities', in Nancy Cook, ed., *Gender Relations in Global Perspective: Essential Readings* (Toronto: Canadian Scholars' Press, 2007), pp. 153–163.

6. Tom Shakespeare, 'The Sexual Politics of Disabled Masculinity', *Sexuality and Disability* 17, No. 1 (1999), 53–64.

7. Slawomir Rapala and Lenore Manderson, 'Recovering In-validated Adulthood, Masculinity, and Sexuality', *Sexuality and Disability* 23(3), Fall, 2005, pp. 161–180; Adrienne Asch and Michelle Fine, 'Beyond Pedestals: Revisiting the Lives of Women with Disabilities', in Michelle Fine, ed., *Disruptive Voices: The Possibilities of Feminist Research* (Ann Arbor: University of Michigan Press, 1992), pp. 139–170; Shakespeare, 'The Sexual Politics of Disabled Masculinity'.

8. Janet Shibley Hyde, 'New Directions in the Study of Gender Similarities and Differences', *Current Directions in Psychological Science* 16(5), 2007, pp. 259–263; for a discussion of competent throwing in some women and less-competent throwing in many non-North American men, see Greg Downey's post (based on a forthcoming book chapter), 'Throwing like a Girl ('s Brain)', February 1, 2009, Neuroanthropology.net, available at http://neuroanthropology.net/2009/02/01/throwing-like-a-girls-brain. Accessed December 21, 2009.

9. Iris Marion Young, 'Throwing like a Girl: A Phenomenology of Feminine Body Comportment Motility and Spatiality', *Human Studies* 3, 1980, pp. 137–156.

10. Barbara Fredrickson and Kristen Harrison, 'Throwing like a Girl: Self-Objectification Predicts Adolescent Girls' Motor Performance', *Journal of Sport and Social Issues* 29(1), 2005, pp. 79–101; Thomas and French's 1985 study of motor performance, which demonstrated the widening gap over time, is referenced in Downey's post (see above); Anne Bowker, Shannon Gadbois, and Becki Cornock, 'Sports Participation and Self-Esteem: Variations as a Function of Gender and Gender Role Orientation', *Sex*

Roles 49(1/2), July, 2003, pp. 47-58; Don Sabo, Kathleen Miller, Merrill Melnick, Michael Farrell, and Grace Barnes, 'High School Athletic Participation and Adolescent Suicide: A Nationwide Study' in *International Review for the Sociology of Sport*, 40(1), 2005, pp. 5–23; Don Sabo, Kathleen Miller, Merrill Melnick, and Leslie Haywood, *Her Life Depends on It: Sport, Physical Activity and the Health and Well-Being of American Girls* (East Meadow, NY: Women's Sports Foundation, 2004); Don Sabo, Kathleen Miller, Merrill Melnick, Michael Farrell, and Grace Barnes, 'High School Athletic Participation, Sexual Behavior and Adolescent Pregnancy: A Regional Study' in *Journal of Adolescent Health*, 25(3), 1999, pp. 207–216.

11. Margaret Ann Hall, *The Girl and the Game: A History of Women's Sport in Canada* (Toronto: University of Toronto Press, 2002), p. 29.

12. Hoffman quoted in Hall, *The Girl and the Game*, p. 161; see Abby Hoffman's profile at the Canada's Sports Hall of Fame, available at http://www.sportshall.ca/hm_profile.php?i=461; accessed January 3, 2010.

13. Myra Sadker and David Sadker, *Failing at Fairness*, pp. 125–126; 'The Attack on Women's Sports' in *New York Times*, February 17, 2003, p. A22; Christine Stolba, 'We've Come the Wrong Way Baby' in *The Women's Quarterly*, Spring, 2002. On the other side, see the 'Title IX FAQ Packet', published by the Women's Equity Resource Center at www.edc.org/womensequity; 'CAAWS Tells Committee to Add Gender Clause', *The Ottawa Citizen*, May 22, 2002, available at http://www.caaws.ca/e/about/article.cfm?id=195; accessed January 11, 2010; Sport Canada, *Actively Engaged: A Policy on Sport for Women and Girls,* January 1, 2009, available at http://www.pch.gc.ca/pgm/sc/pol/fewom/101-eng.cfm; accessed January 1, 2010.

14. Nancy Theberge and Susan Birrell, 'Structural Constraints Facing Women in Sport', in Jean O'Reilly and Susan Cahn, eds., *Women and Sports in the United States: A Documentary Reader* (Lebanon, NH: Northeastern University Press, 2007), pp. 173–174.

15. 'Girls Win Big Victory in Softball Team's Discrimination Battle', CBC News, January 13, 2009, available at http://www.cbc.ca/canada/british-columbia/story/2009/01/12/bc-softball-team-victory.html#ixzz0ePrHZXVY; accessed January 13, 2009.

16. 'Female Ski Jumpers Lose Olympic Battle', CBC News, July 10, 2009, available at http://cbc.ca/canada/british-columbia/story/2009/07/10/bc-olympic-women-ski-jumpers; accessed July 13, 2009; 'Women Ski Jumpers Lose Final Canadian Court Bid', Reuters Canada, December 22, 2009. Available at http://ca.reuters.com/article/domesticNews/idCATRE5BL2SQ20091222; accessed January 18, 2010.

17. Kurt Badenhausen, 'The World's Highest Paid Athletes', *Forbes,* June 17, 2009, available at http://www.forbes.com/2009/06/17/top-earning-athletes-business-sports-top-earning-athletes.html; accessed January 30, 2010; Ann Travers, 'The Sports Nexus and Gender Injustice', *Studies in Social Justice* 2(1), 2008, pp. 79–101.

18. Donald McRae, 'Caster Semenya', *The Guardian*, November 14, 2009, available at http://www.guardian.co.uk/sport/2009/nov/14/caster-semenya-donald-mcrae-training-camp; accessed January 21, 2010; Fausto-Sterling, *Sexing the Body*, pp. 1–5; Alice Dreger, 'Where's the Rulebook for Sex Verification?' *The New York Times,* August 22, 2009; available at http://www.nytimes.com/2009/08/22/sports/22runner.html; accessed September 21, 2009; Robert Ritchie, John Reynard, and Tom Lewis, 'Intersex and the Olympic Games', *Journal of the Royal Society of Medicine* 101, 2008, pp. 395–399; Ross Tucker and Malcolm Collins, 'The Science and Management of Sex Verification in Sport', *South African Journal of Sports Medicine* 21(4), 2009; Jon Billman, 'Michelle Raises Hell', *Outside*, April 2004, available at Outside online, accessed January 21, 2010; 'Banned for Mocking Transgender Winner', *The Vancouver Sun*, August 3, 2006, available at http://www.canada.com/vancouversun/news/story.html?id=b49de62b-e7dc-4699-83ab-ada11000f500; accessed January 21, 2010; 'Doubts Raised over Semenya's return', BBC Sport, January 15, 2010, available at http://newsvote.bbc.co.uk; accessed January 21, 2010.

19. Gamal Abdel-Shahid, *Who Da Man? Black Masculinities and Sporting Cultures* (Toronto: Canadian Scholars' Press, 2005), p. 73.

20. Marc Weinstein, Michael Smith, and David Wiesenthal, 'Masculinity and Hockey Violence', *Sex Roles* 33(11/12), 1995, pp. 831–847.

21. Alan Schwarz, 'Wives United by Husbands' Post-NFL Trauma', *New York Times,* March 14, 2007; Michael Russo, 'Clutterbuck Rejects Cherry's Critique of His Fighting Stance', *Star Tribune,* February 2, 2009, available at http://www.startribune.com/sports/wild/38783922.html, accessed January 21, 2010.

22. Nick Pappas, Patrick McKenry, and Beth Skilken Catlett, 'Athlete Aggression on the Rink and off the Ice: Athlete Violence and Aggression in Hockey and Interpersonal Relationships', *Men and Masculinities* 6(3), 2004, pp. 291–312.

23. Don Sabo, 'The Myth of the Sexual Athlete', in Estelle Disch, ed., *Reconstructing Gender,* pp. 274–278.

24. Laura Miller, 'Mammary Mania in Japan', *Positions* 11(2), 2003, pp. 271–300; for a recent example of the fertile literature on cross-culture preferences for a certain hip-waist ratio, see Frank Marlowe, Coren Apicella, and Dorian Reed, 'Men's Preferences for Women's Profile Waist-to-Hip Ratios in Two Societies', *Evolution and Human Behavior* 26, 2005, pp. 458–468.

25. Naomi Wolf, *The Beauty Myth* (New York: William Morrow, 1991), pp. 10, 184; Fatima Mernissi, 'Size 6: The Western Woman's Harem', in Cook, ed., *Gender Relations in Global Perspective,* pp. 147–151; p. 151.

26. Sandra Bartky, *Femininity and Domination: Studies in the Phenomenology of Oppression* (New York/London: Routledge, 1990), p. 28.

27. See Cressida Hayes and Meredith Jones, 'Cosmetic Surgery in the Age of Gender', in Cressida Heyes and Meredith Jones, eds,. *Cosmetic Surgery: A Feminist Primer* (Farnham, UK: Ashgate, 2009).

28. See Eugenia Kaw, 'Medicalization of Racial Features: Asian-American Women and Cosmetic Surgery', *Medical Anthropological Quarterly* 7(1), 1993; see also Cressida Heyes, 'All Cosmetic Surgery is 'Ethnic': Asian Eyelids, Feminist Indignation, and the Politics of Whiteness', in Heyes and Jones, eds. *Cosmetic Surgery.*

29. Sarah Kershaw, 'Move Over, My Pretty, Ugly Is Here', *New York Times,* October 30, 2008, available at http://www.nytimes.com/2008/10/30/fashion/30ugly.html; accessed October 30, 2008; Anthony Synnott, 'What Is Ugly? Part 2', *Psychology Today* blogs, July 7, 2009, available at http://www.psychologytoday.com/blog/rethinking-men/200907/what-is-ugly-part-2

30. For a recent look at the stereotype and the term, see Nancy J. Parezo and Angelina R. Jones, 'What's in a Name: The 1940s–1950s Squaw Dress', *The American Indian* Quarterly 33(3), 2009, pp. 373–379; Margaret L. Hunter, ' "If You're Light You're Alright": Light Skin Color as Social Capital for Women of Color', *Gender & Society* 16(2), April, 2002, pp. 175–193; Kathy Davis, 'Black is Beautiful' in European Perspective', *European Journal of Women's Studies* 16(2), 2009, pp. 99–101; bell hooks, 'Selling Hot Pussy: Representations of Black Female Sexuality in the Cultural Marketplace', in Rose Weitz, ed., *The Politics of Women's Bodies: Sexuality, Appearance, and Behavior* (Oxford: Oxford University Press, 2003), pp. 122–134.

31. Meekosha, 'Body Battles'; Per Solvang, 'The Amputee Body Desired: Beauty Destabilized? Disability Re-Valued?' *Sexuality and Disability* 25(2), June, 2007, pp. 51–64.

32. See Debra Gimlin, *Body Work: Beauty and Self-Image in American Culture* (Berkeley: University of California Press, 2002), p. 5; 'How to Get Plump' in *Harper's Bazaar,* August, 1908, p. 787; Mary Pipher, *Reviving Ophelia* (New York: Ballantine, 1996); Sharon Kirkey, 'Childhood Obesity Underpins Low Self-Esteem: Study', *The Gazette,* June 17, 2009, available at http://www.montrealgazette.com/health/family-child/Childhood+obesity+underpins+self-+esteem+Study/1706007/story.html; accessed July 21, 2009.; M.E. Collins, 'Body Figure Perceptions and Preferences Among Preadolescent Children' in *International Journal of Eating Disorders,* 10, 1991, pp. 199–208; A. Gustafson-Larson and R. Terry, 'Weight-Related Behaviors and Concerns of Fourth Grade Children' in *Journal of the American Dietetic Association,* 92(7), 1992, pp. 818–822; see also www.healthywithin.com/STATS.htm.

33. See L. Smolak and R. Striegel-Moore, 'The Implications of Developmental Research for Eating Disorders' in *The Developmental Psychopathology of Eating Disorders: Implications for Research, Prevention and Treatment,* M. Smolak, P. Levine, and R. Striegel-Moore, eds. (Mahwah, NJ: Erlbaum, 1996), pp. 235–257. For statistics on eating disorders in Canada, see http://www.nedic.ca/knowthefacts/statistics.shtml; for the UK, Europe, and the USA, see

http://www.disordered-eating.co.uk; 'Europe Targets Eating Disorders' at http://news.bbc.uk/1/hi/health/197334.stm and 'Eating Disorders Factfile' at http://news.bbc.co.uk/1/hi/health/medical_notes/ 187517.stm.

34. See A. Furnham and N. Alibhai, 'Cross-Cultural Differences in the Perception of Female Body Shapes' in *Psychological Medicine*, 13(4), 1983, pp. 829–837; D. B. Mumford, 'Eating Disorders in Different Cultures' in *International Review of Psychiatry*, 5(1), 1993, pp. 109–113; N. Shuriquie, 'Eating Disorders: A Transcultural Perspective' in *Eastern Mediterranean Health Journal*, 5(2), 1999, pp. 354–360, also at http://www.emro.who.int/Publications/EMHJ/0502/20.htm; Sonni Efron, 'Eating Disorders on the Increase in Asia' at http://www. dimensionsmagazine.com/news/asia/html.

35. Deborah Gregory, 'Heavy Judgment' in *Essence*, August 1994, pp. 57–58; G.B. Schreiber, K.M. Pike, D.E. Wilfley, and J. Rodin, 'Drive for Thinness in Black and White Preadolescent Girls' in *International Journal of Eating Disorders*, 18(1), 1995, pp. 59–69.

36. For discussion of the growth of white men's obsession with body image, see John Kasson, *Houdini, Tarzan, and the Perfect Man: The White Male Body and the Challenge of Modernity in America* (New York: Hill and Wang, 2001).

37. For discussion, see Matthew Immergut, 'Manscaping: The Tangle of Nature, Culture, and Male Bodily Hair', in Lisa Moore and Mary Kosut, eds., *The Body Reader: Essential Social and Cultural Readings* (New York: New York University Press, 2010).

38. See Susan Bordo, *The Male Body* (New York: Farrar, Straus and Giroux, 2000).

39. Harrison Pope, Katharine Phillips, and Roberto Olivardia, *The Adonis Complex: The Secret Crisis of Male Body Obsession* (New York: The Free Press, 2000).

40. Cited in Richard Morgan, 'The Men in the Mirror' in *Chronicle of Higher Education*, September 27, 2002, p. A53.

41. Woodside, 2001; Dotson, 1999; McNulty, 1997; Pope et al., *The Adonis Complex*; 'Anorexic Men Begin to Share Their Hellish Secrets', *The Edmonton Journal,* April 18, 2008, available at http://www.canada.com/topics/bodyandhealth/story.html?id=a49a2706-ae4c-4573-8882-7cc0ca5471f7; accessed January 19, 2010.

42. Gina Kolata, 'With No Answers on Risks, Steroid Users Still Say "Yes" ' in *New York Times*, December 2, 2002, pp. A1, 19.

43. See, for example, Christine Webber, 'Eating Disorders' at http://netdoctor.co.uk/ diseases/facts/eatingdisorders.htm. But note that thinness is making inroads among men, as can be seen in the changing shape of male fashion models.

44. Canadian Press/Leger Marketing, 'How Canadians Feel about Tattoos and Body Piercing' (Montreal: Leger Marketing, n.d.); See 'Motivation for Tattoo Removal' in *Archives of Dermatology*, December, 1996; See also the website of the American Society of Plastic Surgeons at http:///www. plasticsurgery.org/mediactr/92sexdis.html.

45. See Lynne Luciano, *Looking Good: Male Body Image in Modern America* (New York: Hill and Wang, 2001).

46. Gimlin, *Body Work*, p. 102.

47. For a study that reviews the effects of homosexuality on body satisfaction among a group of gym-active men, see Jac Brown and Doug Graham, 'Body Satisfaction in Gym-Active Males: An Exploration of Sexuality, Gender, and Narcissism', *Sex Roles* 59, 2008; Sam Fields, 'Penis Enlargement Surgery', at www.4-men.org/penisenlargementsurgery.html, and Randy Klein, 'Penile Augmentation Surgery', in *Electronic Journal of Human Sexuality*, 2, March, 1999, chapter 2, p. 1; chapter 5, pp. 8–9.

48. Letters testimonial to Dr. E. Douglas Whitehead at www.penile-enlargementsurgeon.com/diary.html.

49. http://www.tcclinic.com/vaginal-tightening-surgery.php#ixzz0eQ86YVEm; Lisa Rapaport and Elizabeth Lopatko, ' "Designer Vagina" Surgery Growing Because of Porn', Bloomberg.com, May 25, 2007, available at http://www.bloomberg.com/apps/news?pid=20601102&sid=abrbOGFfldl0&refer=ukl; accessed December 12, 2009; also see David L. Matlock, MD, *Sex by Design* (Los Angeles: Demiurgus Press, 2004); and www.drmatlock.com, accessed June 2, 2006.

50. See Vern Bullough, 'Transsexualism in History', *Archives of Sexual Behavior* 4(5), 1975, pp. 561–571.

51. Cited in Aaron Devor, *FTM: Female-to-Male Transsexuals in Society* (Bloomington, IN: Indiana University Press, 1997).

52. See Joanne Mayerowitz, *How Sex Changed: A History of Transsexuality in the United States* (Cambridge, MA: Harvard University Press, 2002), pp. 1–9.

53. Egale Canada, 'Sex Reassignment Surgery Backgrounder', October 1, 2004, available at http://www.egale.ca/index.asp?lang=E&item=1086; accessed February 2, 2010; Kaj Hasselriis, 'Manitoba Rejects Funding for Trans Surgeries', Xtra.ca, May 8, 2009, available at http://www.xtra.ca/public/National/Manitoba_rejects_funding_for_trans_surgeries-6745.aspx; accessed February 2, 2010; Noreen Fagan, 'Sex Reassignment Surgery in Canada: What's Covered and Where', Xtra.ca, October 26, 2009, available at http://www.xtra.ca/public/Montreal/Sex_reassignment_surgery_in_Canada_whats_covered_and_where-7706.aspx; accessed February 2, 2010.

54. L. Wingerson, 'Gender Identity Disorder: Has Accepted Practice Caused Harm?' *Psychiatric Times,* May 19, 2009. Available at http://www.psychiatrictimes.com/display/article/10168/1415037?verify=0; accessed August 18, 2009.

55. Lori Chambers, 'Unprincipled Exclusions: Feminist Theory, Transgender Jurisprudence, and Kimberly Nixon', *Canadian Journal of Women and Law* 19(2), 2009, pp. 305–333.

56. Judith Shapiro, 'Transsexualism: Reflections on the Persistence of Gender and the Mutability of Sex', in Jennifer Ellen Robertson, ed., *Same-Sex Cultures and Sexualities: An Anthropological Reader* (Malden, MA/Oxford: Blackwell Publishing, 2005), pp. 141–146. See also Douglas Schrock, Lori Reid, and Emily Boyd, 'Transsexuals' Embodiment of Womanhood' in *Gender & Society*, 19(3), June, 2005, pp. 317–335.

57. Samantha King, 'Pink Ribbons, Inc.: The Emergence of Cause-Related Marketing and the Corporatization of the Breast Cancer Movement', in Lori Reed and Paula Saukko, eds., *Governing the Female Body: Gender, Health, and Networks of Power* (Albany, NY: SUNY Press, 2010), pp. 85–111.

58. See Will Courtenay, 'Engendering Health:A Social Constructionist Examination of Men's Health Beliefs and Behaviors' in *Psychology of Men and Masculinity*, 1(1), 2000, pp. 4–15; 'Men's Health', editorial in *British Medical Journal*, January 13, 1996, pp. 69–70. For more about men's health specifically, see *Men's Health on the Internet*, M. Sandra Wood and Janet M. Coggan, eds. (Binghamton, NY: Haworth Information Press, 2002); Will H. Courtenay, 'College Men's Health: An Overview and a Call to Action', *Journal of American College Health*, 46(6), 1998; see also Lesley Doyal, 'Sex, Gender and Health: The Need for a New Approach' in *British Medical Journal*, November 3, 2001, pp. 1061–1063; CBC News, 'Life Expectancy Hits 80.4 Years: Statistics Canada', available at http://www.cbc.ca/canada/story/2008/01/14/death-stats.html; accessed February 10, 2010.

59. J. Reading, *The Crisis of Chronic Disease among Aboriginal Peoples: A Challenge for Public Health, Population Health and Social Policy* (Victoria: University of Victoria Centre for Aboriginal Health Research, n.d.).

60. Linda Villarosa, 'As Black Men Move into Middle Age, Dangers Rise' in *New York Times*, September 23, 2002, pp. F1, 8.

61. On these changes generally, see Martin Levine, *Gay Macho: The Life and Death of the Homosexual Clone*, M.S. Kimmel, ed. (New York: New York University Press, 1998).

62. World Health Organization, http://www.who/int/hiv/facts/plwha_m.jpg

63. Michele Landsberg, 'UN Recognizes Women Double Victims of AIDS', Toronto Star, July 1, 2001.See also Judith Lorber, *Gender and the Social Construction of Illness* (Newbury Park, CA: Pine Forge Press, 1997); Amartya Sen, 'The Many Faces of Gender Inequality' in *The New Republic*, September 17, 2001, pp. 35–40.

64. CBC News, 'AIDS: The Global Epidemic', November 24, 2009, available at http://www.cbc.ca/health/story/2009/11/24/f-aids-hiv-global-epidemic.html; accessed February 1, 2010; Barbara Clow, 'An Invisible Epidemic: The Implications of Gender Neutrality for Managing HIV/AIDS in Low-incidence Countries', Canadian Women's Health Network, available at http://www.thefreelibrary.com/An+invisible+epidemic:+the+implications+of+gender+neutrality+for+ . . . -a0162990550; accessed February 1, 2010.

65. CBC News, 'AIDS'; Clow, 'An Invisible Epidemic'.

66. See, for example, 'Whatever Happened to Men's Health?' published by Men's Health America, www.egroups.com/group/menshealth.

67. See Diana Jean Schemo, 'Study Calculates the Effects of College Drinking in the U.S.' in *New York Times*, April 10, 2002, p. A21; Jodie Morse, 'Women on a Binge' in *Time*, April 1, 2002, pp. 57–61; Barbara Ehrenreich, 'Libation as Liberation?' in *Time*, April 1, 2002, p. 62.

68. Lorber, *Gender and the Social Construction of Illness*.

69. Sen, 'The Many Faces of Gender Inequality'; Sen, ' More Than 100 Million Women Are Missing', *The New York Review of Books*, 37(20), December 20, 1990; Elizabeth Croll, 'Amartya Sen's 100 Million Missing Women', *Oxford Development Studies* 29(3), October 2001, pp. 225-244; Bob Herbert, 'Zimbabwe is Dying', *New York Times*, January 16, 2009, available at http://www.nytimes.com/2009/01/17/opinion/17herbert.html; accessed January 3, 2010.

Chapter 12

1. Michael Klare, 'A Global Epidemic of Violent Crime', *Salon.com*, April 7, 2009, available at http://www.salon.com/news/feature/2009/04/07/crime_wave/html; accessed January 20, 2010.

2. United States Department of Justice, Uniform Crime Reports, 1991, p. 17; Diane Craven, *Sex Differences in Violent Victimization*, 1994 (NCJ-164508) (Washington, DC: U.S. Department of Justice, 1994); see also Martin Daly and Margo Wilson, *Homicide* (Chicago: Aldine, 1988).

3. Cited in Michael Gottfredson and Travis Hirchi, *A General Theory of Crime* (Stanford: Stanford University Press, 1990), p. 145. See also Steven Barkan, 'Why Do Men Commit Almost All Homicides and Assault?' in *Criminology: A Sociological Understanding* (Englewood Cliffs, NJ: Prentice-Hall, 1997); *Masculinities and Violence*, Lee Bowker, ed. (Thousand Oaks: Sage Publications, 1998); Fox Butterfield, *All God's Children: The Bosket Family and the American Tradition of Violence* (New York: Avon, 1995), p.325; Wray Herbert, 'Behind Bars' in *US News & World Report*, March 23, 1998, p. 33; Jay Livingston, 'Crime and Sex: It's a Man's World' in *Crime and Criminology* (2nd ed.) (Englewood Cliffs, NJ: Prentice-Hall, 1996).

4. See James Q. Wilson and Richard Herrnstein, *Crime and Human Nature* (New York: Simon & Schuster, 1985), p. 121.

5. Joe Sharkey, 'Slamming the Brakes on Hot Pursuit', *New York Times*, December 14, 1997, p. 3; Kenneth J. Peak and Ronald W. Glensor, 'Street Racing', Problem Oriented Guides for Police No. 28. US Department of Justice, 2004, p. 13. The 90 to 95 percent figure comes from Andrew Leigh, 'Youth and Street Racing', *Current Issues in Criminal Justice* 388, 1995–1996.

6. Marvin Wolfgang, *Youth and Violence* (Washington, DC: US Dept of Health, Education, and Welfare, 1970); James Gilligan, *Violence: Our Deadly Epidemic and Its Causes* (New York: G.P. Putnam's Sons, 1996).

7. Wilson and Herrnstein, *Crime and Human Nature*.

8. See the discussion of androgens in Chapter Two.

9. James Messerschmidt, 'Masculinities and Crime: Beyond a Dualist Criminology', in C. Renzetti, L. Goodstein, and S. Miller, eds,. *Gender, Crime, and Criminal Justice: Original Feminist Readings* (Los Angeles: Roxbury, 2006), pp. 29–43.

10. Barbara Ehrenreich, *Blood Rites: Origins and History of the Passions of War* (New York: Metropolitan Books, 1997), pp. 45, 127. On the sociology of men's violence, see, especially, Michael Kaufman, *Cracking the Armour: Power, Pain and the Lives of Men* (Toronto: Viking, 1993), and Michael Kaufman, 'The Construction of Masculinity and the Triad of Men's Violence' in Men's Lives (4th ed.), M. Kimmel and M. Messner, eds. (Boston: Allyn and Bacon, 1997); see also Jackson Toby, 'Violence and the Masculine Ideal: Some Qualitative Data' in *The Annals of the American Academy of Political and Social Science*, 364, March, 1966.

11. J. Adams Puffer, *The Boy and His Gang* (Boston: Houghton, Mifflin, 1912), p. 91.

12. Gilligan, *Violence*.

13. Fox Butterfield, *All God's Children*, pp. 206–207; Kit Roane, 'New York Gangs Mimic California Original' in *New York Times*, September 14, 1997, p. A37; others cited in Jack Katz, *Seductions of Crime*, pp. 88, 107; Vic Seidler, 'Raging Bull' in *Achilles Heel*, 5, 1980, p. 9; Hans Toch, 'Hypermasculinity and Prison Violence' in *Masculinities and Violence*, L. Bowker, ed. (Newbury Park: Sage Publications, 1998), p. 170; Mark Totten, 'Preventing Aboriginal Youth Gang Violence in Canada: A Gendered

Approach', paper prepared for Aboriginal Policy Research Conference, March 2009.

14. James Messerschmidt, *Masculinities and Crime: Critique and Reconceptualization of Theory* (Lanham, Maryland: Rowman and Littlefield, 1993); Messerschmidt, 'Masculinities and Crime: Beyond a Dualist Criminology'.

15. Signe Howell and Roy Willis, eds., *Societies at Peace* (New York: Routledge, 1983); Joanna Overing, 'Styles of Manhood: An Amazonian Contrast in Tranquility and Violence', in Howell and Willis, eds., *Societies at Peace*, pp 79-99.

16. Howell and Willis, *Societies at Peace*, p. 38.

17. See, for example, D. Stanistreet,C. Bambra,and A. Scott-Samuel, 'Is Patriarchy the Source of Men's Higher Mortality?' in *Journal of Epidemiology and Community Health*, 59, 2005, pp. 873–876; Elizabeth Stanko, *Everyday Violence* (London: Pandora, 1990), p. 71.

18. Rebecca Kong and Kathy AuCoin, 'Female Offenders in Canada', *Juristat* 28, No. 1 (2008). Statistics Canada Catalogue No. 85-002-XIE.

19. Kong and AuCoin, 'Female Offenders'.

20. Freda Adler, *Sisters in Crime* (New York: McGraw-Hill, 1975), p. 10; Rita Simon, *Women and Crime* (Washington, DC: U.S. Government Printing Office, 1975), p. 40. Also see Patricia Pearson, *When She Was Bad: Violent Women and the Myth of Innocence* (New York: Viking, 1998); see also Larissa MacFarquhar, 'Femmes Fatales' in *The New Yorker*, March 9, 1998, pp. 88–91.

21. Malcolm Feely and Deborah L. Little, 'The Vanishing Female: The Decline of Women in the Criminal Process' in *Law and Society Review*, 25(4), 1991, p. 739.

22. Darrell J. Steffensmeier, 'Trends in Female Crime: It's Still a Man's World' in *The Criminal Justice System and Women*, B.R. Price and N.J. Sokoloff, eds. (New York: Clark, Boardman, 1982), p. 121.

23. Kong and AuCoin, 'Female Offenders in Canada', p. 4.

24. Ibid.

25. See Laura Dugan, Daniel Nagin, and Richard Rosenfeld, 'Explaining the Decline in Intimate Partner Homicide: The Effects of Changing Domesticity, Women's Status and Domestic Violence Resources' in *Homicide Studies* 3(3), 1999, pp. 187–214, and Richard Rosenfeld, 'Changing Relationships Between Men and Women: A Note on the Decline in Intimate Partner Homicide' in *Homicide Studies*, 1(1), 1997, pp. 72–83; Chris Huffine, personal communication.

26. Erich Goode, personal communication, December 5, 2002; Jerome Skolnick, personal communication, December 5, 2002; see also Erich Goode, *Deviant Behavior* (5th ed.) (Englewood Cliffs, NJ: Prentice-Hall), p. 127, and Kathleen Daly, *Gender Crime and Punishment* (New Haven: Yale University Press, 1994).

27. See, for example, Ann Donahue, 'Population of Female Inmates Reaches Record' in *USA Today*, July 21, 1997; Darrell Steefensmeier and Ellie Allen, 'Criminal Behavior . . .', p. 85; Correctional Service Canada, *Ten-Year Status Report on Women's Corrections 1996—2006* (Ottawa: Correctional Service of Canada, 2006).

28. Adam Fraczek, 'Patterns of Aggressive-Hostile Behavior Orientation Among Adolescent Boys and Girls' in *Of Mice and Women: Aspects of Female Aggression*, K. Bjorkvist and P. Niemela, eds. (San Diego: Academic Press, 1992); Kirsti M.J. Lagerspetz and Kaj Bjorqvist, 'Indirect Aggression in Boys and Girls' in *Aggressive Behavior: Current Perspectives*, L. R. Huesmann, ed. (New York: Plenum, 1994).

29. Centers for Disease Control, 'Youth Violence: Facts at a Glance' available at www.cdc.gov/violenceprevention; Andrea Taylor-Butts and Angela Bressan, 'Youth Crime in Canada, 2006', *Juristat* 28, No. 3. Statistics Canada Catalogue No. 85-002-XIE; Kathy AuCoin, 'Children and Youth as Victims of Violent Crime', *Juristat* 25, No. 1. Statistics Canada Catalogue No. 85-002-XIE.

30. Glenn W. Muschert, 'Research in School Shootings', *Sociology Compass*, 1(1), 2007, 60–80; Patricia Leavy and Kathryn Mahoney, 'American Reporting of School Violence and "People Like Us": A Comparison of Newspaper Coverage of the Columbine and Red Lake School Shootings', *Critical Sociology* 35(2), 2002, pp. 273–292; see also Dave Cullen, *Columbine* (New York: Twelve Publishers, 2009), which debunks long-held media-fuelled understandings of the massacre and its causes.

31. See Jessie Klein, 'Teaching Her a Lesson: Media Misses Boys' Rage Relating to Girls in School Shootings', *Crime, Media, Culture* 1(1), 2005, pp. 90–97; Kim Gandy, 'School Shooters Target Girls, Point to Larger Problem of Violence

against Women', *National NOW Times,* Winter, 2007.

32. 'Teen-on-teen Girl Fights Sweeping Internet', CBS News, February 3, 2010, available at http://wcbstv.com/national/girl.fights. youtube.2.146559.html; accessed February 3, 2010; Taylor-Butts and Bressan, 'Youth Crime in Canada, 2006'.

33. Sheila Batacharya, 'Racism, "Girl Violence," and the Murder of Reena Virk', in *Girls' Violence: Myths and Realities,* ed. Christine Alder and Anne Worrall (Albany, NY: SUNY Press, 2004), pp. 61–80; Margaret Jackson, 'Race, Gender, and Aggression: The Perceptions of Girls about the Violence in Their Lives', *Humanitas* [Simon Fraser University], Spring 2003.

34. Vappu Viemero, 'Changes in Female Aggression over a Decade' in Bjorkvist and Niemela, *Of Mice and Women,* p. 105; Messerschmidt, 'Masculinities and Crime: Beyond a Dualist Criminology'; Sibylle Artz, *Sex, Power, and the Violent Schoolgirl* (New York: Teachers' College Press, 1992); Sibylle Artz and Diana Nicholson, 'Aggressive Girls: Female Violence' (report). Ottawa: National Clearinghouse on Family Violence, 2002.

35. See, for example, Rachel Simmons, *Odd Girl Out: The Hidden Culture of Aggression in Girls* (New York: Harcourt, 2002); Rosalind Wiseman, *Queen Bees and Wannabes: A Parents' Guide to Helping Your Daughter Survive Cliques, Gossip, Boyfriends, and Other Realities of Adolescence* (New York: Crown, 2002); Sharon Lamb, *The Secret Lives of Girls: Sex, Play, Aggression and Their Guilt* (New York: The Free Press, 2002). See also Margaret Talbot, 'Mean Girls' in *New York Times Magazine,* February 24, 2002, pp. 24–29, 40, 58, 64–65; and Carol Tavris, 'Are Girls Really as Mean as Books Say They Are?' in *Chronicle of Higher Education,* July 5, 2002, pp. B7–9.

36. Simmons, *Odd Girl Out.*

37. Helen Caldicott, *Missile Envy* (New York: William Morrow, 1984); Barbara Ehrenreich, 'The Violence Debate Since Adam and Eve' in *Test the West: Gender Democracy and Violence* (Vienna: Federal Minister of Women's Affairs, 1994), p. 34.

38. R.W. Connell, 'Masculinity, Violence and War' in *Men's Lives* (3rd ed.), M. Kimmel and M. Messner, eds. (Boston: Allyn and Bacon, 1995), p. 129.

39. David Halberstam, *The Best and the Brightest* (New York: Random House, 1972), p. 531. See also Brian Easlea, *Fathering the Unthinkable: Masculinity, Scientists and the Nuclear Arms Race* (London: Pluto Press, 1983), p. 117; see also his 'Patriarchy, Scientists and Nuclear Warriors' in *Beyond Patriarchy: Essays by Men on Pleasure, Power and Change,* M. Kaufman, ed. (Toronto: Oxford University Press, 1987). I.F. Stone, 'Machismo in Washington' in *Men and Masculinity,* J. Pleck and J. Sawyer, eds. (Englewood Cliffs: Prentice-Hall, 1974).

40. Carol Cohn, ' "Clean Bombs" and Clean Language' in *Women, Militarism and War: Essays in History, Politics and Social Theory,* J. B. Elshtain, ed. (Savage, MD: Rowman and Littlefield, 1990), p. 137.

41. Elisabeth Jean Wood, 'Variation in Sexual Violence during War', *Politics & Society* 34(3), 2006, pp. 307–341; Steven Lee Myers, 'A Peril in War Zones: Sexual Abuse by Fellow G.I.'s', *New York Times,* December 28, 2009; Allan Hall, 'German Victim is First to Break Silence on Red Army Rapists after 65 Years', *Mail Online,* March 1, 2010. Available at http://www.dailymail. co.uk/news/article-1254521; accessed March 1, 2010.

42. Cited in Richard Gelles, *The Violent Home* (Beverly Hills, CA: Sage Publications, 1972), p. 14; bell hooks, *Feminism is for Everybody: Passionate Politics* (Cambridge, MA: South End Press, 2000), p. 61.

43. Data from *New York Times,* August 25, 1997; United States Department of Justice, Family Violence, 1997; Reva Siegel, 'The 'Rule of Love': Wife Beating as Prerogative and Privacy' in *Yale Law Journal,* 105(8), June, 1996; Deborah Rhode, *Speaking of Sex: The Denial of Gender Inequality* (Cambridge: Harvard University Press, 1997), p. 108; June Stephenson, *Men Are Not Cost Effective,* p. 285; see also Neil Websdale and Meda Chesney-Lind, 'Doing Violence to Women: Research Synthesis on the Victimization of Women' in *Masculinities and Violence,* L. Bowker, ed.

44. Armin Brott, 'The Battered Statistic Syndrome'in *Washington Post,* July, 1994; Jodi-Anne Brzozowski and Robyn Brazeau, 'What Are the Trend in Self-Reported Spousal Violence in Canada?' *Matter of Fact* No. 6, 2008, Statistics Canada Catalogue No. 89-630-X.

45. R. L. McNeely and G. Robinson-Simpson, 'The Truth About Domestic Violence: A Falsely Framed Issue' in *Social Work*, 32(6), 1987.

46. Susan Steinmetz, 'The Battered Husband Syndrome' in *Victimology*, 2, 1978;

47. M.D. Pagelow, 'The 'Battered Husband Syndrome': Social Problem or Much Ado About Little?' in *Marital Violence*, N. Johnson, ed. (London: Routledge and Kegan Paul, 1985); Elizabeth Pleck, Joseph Pleck, M. Grossman, and Pauline Bart, 'The Battered Data Syndrome: A Comment on Steinmetz's Article' in *Victimology*, 2, 1978; G. Storch, 'Claim of 12 Million Battered Husbands Takes a Beating' in *Miami Herald*, August 7, 1978; Jack C. Straton, 'The Myth of the "Battered Husband Syndrome" ' in *Masculinities*, 2(4), 1994; Kerrie James, 'Truth or Fiction:Men as Victims of Domestic Violence?' in *The Australian and New Zealand Journal of Family Therapy*,17(3), 1996; Betsy Lucal, 'The Problem with ' "Battered Husbands" ' in *Deviant Behavior*, 16, 1995, pp. 95–112. After the first edition of this book was published, Michael became increasingly distressed that social science research was being so badly misused for political ends and undertook an attempt to thoroughly investigate the case of 'gender symmetry'. See Michael Kimmel, 'Gender Symmetry in Domestic Violence: A Substantive and Methodological Research Review' in *Violence Against Women*, 8(11), November, 2002, pp. 1332–1363. Useful data can be found in Callie Marie Rennison, 'Intimate Partner Violence and Age of Victim, 1993–1999', US Department of Justice, Bureau of Justice Statistics, October 2001; Kerrie James, 'Truth or Fiction . . .', who found the same results in a sample of Australian and New Zealand couples; J.E. Stets and Murray Straus, 'The Marriage License as a Hitting License: A Comparison of Assaults in Dating, Cohabiting and Married Couples' in *Journal of Family Violence*, 4(2), 1989; J.E. Stets and Murray Straus, 'Gender Differences in Reporting Marital Violence and Its Medical and Psychological Consequences' in *Physical Violence in American Families*, M. Straus and R. Gelles, eds. (New Brunswick, NJ: Transaction Publishers, 1990); Julie Sauvé and Mike Burns, 'Residents of Canada's Shelters for Abused Women, 2008', *Juristat* 29(2), May 2009, Statistics Canada Catalogue No. 85-002-X.

48. United States Department of Justice, Bureau of Justice Statistics, *Family Violence*, 1984.

49. Glanda Kaufman Kantor, Jana Janinski, and E. Aldorondo, 'Sociocultural Status and Incidence of Marital Violence in Hispanic Families' in *Violence and Victims*, 9(3), 1994; and Jana Janinski, 'Dynamics of Partner Violence and Types of Abuse and Abusers', available at http://www.nnfr.org/nnfr/research/pv_ch1.html; Kersti Yllo, personal communication.

50. R. Bachman and L.E. Saltzman, 'Violence Against Women . . .', p. 6; Murray Straus and Richard Gelles, *Physical Violence in American Families*; Canadian Centre for Justice Statistics, 'Family Violence in Canada', p. 13.

51. See, for example, Kersti Yllo, 'Through a Feminist Lens: Gender, Power, and Violence' in *Current Controversies on Family Violence*, R.J. Gelles and D. Loseke, eds. (Thousand Oaks, CA: Sage Publications, 1993).

52. Neil Jacobson and John Gottman, *When Men Batter Women* (New York: Simon & Schuster, 1998), p. 36.

53. Todd K. Shackelford, 'Cohabitation, Marriage, and Murder: Woman-Killing by Male Romantic Partners', *Aggressive Behavior* 27, 2001, pp. 284–291; Noelia Breitman, Todd K. Shackelford, and Carolyn Rebecca Black, 'Is Age Discrepancy a Risk Factor for Intimate Partner Homicide?' *Illinois Criminal Justice Information Authority Research Bulletin* 1(3), 2003.

54. R. Emerson Dobash, Russell Dobash, Margo Wilson, and Martin Daly, 'The Myth of Sexual Symmetry in Marital Violence' in *Social Problems*, 39, 1992, p. 81; see also R. Emerson Dobash, and Russell Dobash, *Violence Against Wives* (New York: The Free Press, 1979); 'The Case of Wife Beating' in *Journal of Family Issues*, 2, 1981.

55. Barbara Ehrenreich, 'The Violence Debate'. Also see note 89 below.

56. 'Immigrant Women and Domestic Violence', CLEO Immigration and Refugee Factsheet; for US data and perspectives, see Noel Cazenave and Murray Straus, 'Race, Class, Network Embeddedness and Family Violence: A Search for Potent Support Systems' in *Physical Violence in American Families*, M. Straus and R. Gelles, eds. (New Brunswick, NJ: Transaction, 1990); Pam Belluck, 'Women's Killers and Very Often Their Partners' in *New York Times*, March 31, 1997, p. B1; C. Saline, 'Bleeding in the Suburbs'

in *Philadelphia Magazine*, March, 1984, p. 82; Murray Straus et al., *Behind Closed Doors*; R.L. Hampton, 'Family Violence and Homicides in the Black Community: Are They Linked?' in *Violence in the Black Family: Correlates and Consequences* (Lexington, MA; Lexington Books, 1987); R. L. Hampton and Richard Gelles, 'Violence Towards Black Women in a Nationally Representative Sample of Black Families', in *Journal of Comparative Family Studies*, 25(1), 1994.

57. Native Women's Association of Canada, 'Aboriginal Women's Health' (Background paper). NWAC, 2004; Jodi-Anne Brzozowski, Andrea Taylor-Butts, and Sarah Johnson, 'Victimization and Offending among the Aboriginal Population in Canada', *Juristat* 26, No. 3 (June 2006).

58. Vicki Haddock, 'Survey Tracks Gay Domestic Violence' in *San Francisco Examiner*, October 22, 1996; Janice Ristock, *No More Secrets: Violence in Lesbian Relationships* (New York/London: Routledge, 2002).

59. Tina Hotton, 'Childhood and Exposure to Violence in the Home' (research paper). Ottawa: Statistics Canada/Ministry of Industry, 2003; Richard Gelles, *Family Violence* (Newbury Park: Sage Publications, 1987), p. 165; Canadian Centre for Justice Statistics, *Family Violence in Canada: A Statistical Profile, 2008* (Ottawa: Minstry of Industry/Statistics Canada, 2008), 6–7.

60. Elizabeth Thompson Gershoff, 'Corporal Punishment by Parents and Associated Child Behaviors and Experiences: A Meta-Analytic and Theoretical Review' in *Psychological Bulletin*, 128(4), 2002, pp. 539–579. Gershoff's critics suggest that the negative effects are the result of 'inept harsh parenting' and not specifically 'spanking'. See Diana Baumrind, Robert Larzelere, and Philip A. Cowan, 'Ordinary Physical Punishment: Is It Harmful?' in *Psychological Bulletin*, 128(4), 2002, pp. 580–589; Marie-Hélène Gagné, Marc Tourigny, Jacques Joly, and Joëlle Pouliot-Lapointe, 'Predictors of Adult Attitudes toward Corporal Punishment of Children', *Journal of Interpersonal Violence*, 22(10), 2007, pp. 1285–1304. Canadian Paediatric Society, 'Effective Discipline for Children', *Paediatric Child Health*, 9(1), 2004, pp. 37–41.

61. Murray Straus, Richard Gelles, and Suzanne Steinmetz, *Behind Closed Doors: Violence in the American Family* (New York: Anchor, 1981), p. 94; see also Murray Straus, *Beating the Devil out of Them* (New York: Jossey-Bass, 1994).

62. Gelles, *Family Violence*, p. 165.

63. Abraham Bergman, Roseanne Larsen, and Beth Mueller, 'Changing Spectrum of Child Abuse' in *Pediatrics*, 77, 1986; Joan Durrant, Nico Trocme, Barbara Fallon, Cheryl Milne, Tara Black, and Della Knoke, 'Puntive Violence against Children in Canada', CECW Information Sheet No. 41E (Toronto: University of Toronto Faculty of Social Work, 2006).

64. Kathy AuCoin, 'Children and Youth as Victims of Violent Crime', *Juristat* 25(1), 2005, Statistics Canada Catalogue No. 85-002-XIE.

65. Chris Cobb, 'Brother Gets Life in Honour Killing', *The Ottawa Citizen*, May 31, 2009, available at http://www.ottawacitizen.com/news/Brother+gets+life+honour+killing/1647215/story.html, accessed February 20, 2010

66. Phyllis Chesler, 'Are Honor Killings Simply Domestic Violence?' *Middle East Quarterly* 16, No. 2 (Spring 2009), 61–69; Amber Hildebrandt, 'Honour Killings: Domestic Abuse by Another Name?' CBC News, July 24, 2009; Regina Leader-Post, 'Cultural "Honour Killing" Brought to Canada', Canada.com, June 11, 2007, available at Chttp://www.canada.com/vancouversun/story.html?id=d05e437f-4661-4965-9455-ff30c6b9d4a5&k=20265; accessed February 2, 2010; Jill Colvin, 'Family Members Charged with Murder in Submerged Car Case', *The Globe and Mail*, July 23, 2009.

67. David Barash, *The Whisperings Within* (New York: Harper and Row, 1979), p. 54; see also W.M.Shields and L. M. Shields, 'Forcible Rape: An Evolutionary Perspective' in *Ethology and Sociobiology*, 4, 1983, p. 119.

68. Randy Thornhill and Craig T. Palmer, 'Why Men Rape' in *The Sciences*, January, 2000, p. 30; Randy Thornhill and Craig T. Palmer, *A Natural History of Rape* (Cambridge: MIT Press, 2000), p. 53. See also Richard Alexander and K.M. Noonan, 'Concealment of Ovulation, Parental Care and Human Social Evolution' in *Evolutionary Biology and Human Social Behavior*, N. Chagnon and W. Irons, eds. (North Scituate, MA: Duxbury, 1979), p. 449.

69. See Salman Masood, 'Pakistan's High Court Reviewing Officially Ordered Gang Rape', in *New York Times*, June 28, 2005, p. 3.

70. See Peggy Reeves Sanday, *Fraternity Gang Rape* (New York: NYU Press, 1996).

71. See Robb Willer, Nicholas Groth, Ann Burgess, and Suzanne Sgroi, *Sexual Assault of Children and Adolescents* (San Francisco: Jossey-Bass, 1978).

72. Carol Sheffield, *Feminist Jursiprudence* (New York: Routledge, 1997), p. 203.

73. In this way, rape may itself be understandable as a social institution.

74. Peggy Reeves Sanday, *Female Power and Male Dominance* (New York: Cambridge University Press, 1981); quote from Larry Baron and Murray Straus, 'Four Theories of Rape: A Macrosociological Analysis' in *Social Problems*, 34(5), 1987, p. 481.

75. See, for example, Diana Scully, *Understanding Sexual Violence: A Study of Convicted Rapists* (New York: HarperCollins, 1990); Diana Russell, *Rape in Marriage* (New York: Macmillan, 1982), and *Sexual Exploitation* (Beverly Hills, CA: Sage Publications, 1984); Deborah Rhode, *Speaking of Sex*, pp. 119–120; Allan Johnson, 'On the Prevalence of Rape in the United States' in *Signs*, 6(1), 1980, p. 145. For more on this, see also Diana Scully and J. Marolla, ' "Riding the Bull at Gilley's": Convicted Rapists Describe the Rewards of Rape' in *Social Problems*, 32, 1985.

76. United States Department of Justice, 'Child Rape Victims, 1992' (NCJ-147001), June, 1994; Eugene Kanin, 'False Rape Allegations', *Archives of Sexual Behavior*, 23(1), 1994.

77. AuCoin, 'Children and Youth as Victims of Violent Crime'.

78. AuCoin, 'Children and Youth as Victims of Violent Crime'; 'Bishop Surrenders on Child Porn Charges', *Toronto Sun*, October 1, 2009, available at http://www.torontosun.com/news/canada/2009/10/01/11230971.html; accessed October 10, 2009; 'Former Jewish Community Activist Facing Child-Porn Charges', May 29, 2009. CTV.ca, available at http://montreal.ctv.ca/servlet/an/local/CTVNews/20090529/mtl_surkis_child_porn_charges_090529?hub=MontrealHome; accessed January 20, 2010; 'Seven Children "Rescued" as Surrey Child Porn Charges Laid', *Vancouver Sun*, February 5, 2010, available at http://www.vancouversun.com/life/relationships/Seven+children+rescued+Surrey+child+porn+charges+laid/2527908/story.html

79. Ashley Jespersen, Martin Lalumiere, and Michael Seto, 'Sexual Abuse History among Adult Sex Offenders and Non-Sex Offenders: A Meta-Analysis'. *Child Abuse and Neglect*, 33(3), 2009, pp. 179–182; David Finkelhor, 'The Prevention of Childhood Sexual Abuse', *The Future of Children*, 19(2), 2009, pp. 170–194.

80. Johnson, 'On the Prevalence of Rape . . .', p. 145; Scully, *Understanding Sexual Violence*, p. 53.

81. Mary Koss, Christine A. Gidycz, and Nadine Misniewski, 'The Scope of Rape: Incidence and Prevalence of Sexual Aggression and Victimization in a National Sample of Higher Education Students' in *Journal of Consulting and Clinical Psychology*, 55(2), 1987.

82. Scully and Marolla, ' "Riding the Bull at Gilley's" . . . '; also Scully, 'Convicted Rapists' Perceptions of Self and Victim: Role Taking and Emotions', *Gender and Society*, 2(2), June, 1988, pp. 200–213.

83. Scully, *Understanding Sexual Violence*, pp. 74, 140, 159, 166.

84. John Briere and Neil Malamuth, 'Self-Reported Likelihood of Sexually Aggressive Behavior: Attitudinal Versus Sexual Explanations' in *Journal of Research in Personality*, 17, 1983; Todd Tieger, 'Self-Rated Likelihood of Raping and Social Perception of Rape' in *Journal of Research in Personality*, 15, 1991.

85. J.L. Herman, 'Considering Sex Offenders: A Model of Addiction' in *Signs*, 13, 1988; Bernard Lefkowitz, *Our Guys* (Berkeley: University of California Press, 1997); Don Terry, 'Gang Rape of Three Girls Leaves Fresno Shaken and Questioning' in *New York Times*, April 28, 1998; see also Jane Hood, ' "Let's Get a Girl": Male Bonding Rituals in America' in *Men's Lives* (4th ed.), M. Kimmel and M. Messner, eds. (Boston: Allyn and Bacon, 1997).

86. Tim Beneke, *Men on Rape* (New York: St. Martin's Press, 1982), p. 81.

87. See Mary P. Koss, Christine Gidycz, and Nadine Misniewski, 'The Scope of Rape', and Scot Boeringer, 'Pornography and Sexual Aggression: Associations of Violence and Nonviolent Depictions with Rape and Rape Proclivity' in *Deviant Behavior*, 15, 1994, pp. 289–304.

88. Diana Russell, *Rape in Marriage* (New York: Macmillan, 1982); David Finklehor and Kirsti

Yllo, *License to Rape: Sexual Abuse of Wives* (Newbury Park: Sage Publications, 1985), pp. 217, 208. On marital rape generally, see also Raquel Kennedy Bergen, 'Surviving Wife Rape: How Women Define and Cope with the Violence' in *Violence Against Women*, 1(2), 1995, pp. 117–138 and the special issue *Violence Against Women*, 5(9), September, 1999, she edited; Raquel Kennedy Bergen, *Wife Rape: Understanding the Response of Survivors and Service Providers* (Thousand Oaks: Sage Publications, 1996); Anne L. Buckborough, 'Family Law: Recent Developments in the Law of Marital Rape' in *Annual Survey of American Law*, 1989; 'To Have and to Hold: The Marital Rape Exemption and the Fourteenth Amendment' in *Harvard Law Review*, 99, 1986.

89. See, inter alia, John Simister and Parnika S. Mehta, 'Gender-Based Violence in India: Long-term Trends', *Journal of Interpersonal Violence*, 20(10), pp. 1–18; Faridah Ali, Syed Israr, Badar Ali, and Naveed Janjua, 'Association of Various Reproductive Rights, Domestic Violence, and Marital Rape with Depression among Pakistani Women', *BMC Psychiatry* 9(77), 2009; David Frank, Tara Hardinge, and Kassia Woswick-Correa, 'The Global Dimensions of Rape-Law Reform: A Cross-national Study of Policy Outcomes', *American Sociological Review* 74, April, 2009, pp. 272–290; Kwong-Leung Tang, 'Rape Law Reform in Canada: The Success and Limits of Legislation', *International Journal of Offender Therapy and Comparative Criminology* 42(23), 1998, pp. 258–270; Indira Jaising, 'Bringing Rights Home: Review of the Campaign for a Law on Domestic Violence', *Economic and Political Weekly,* 44(44), October 31, 2009, pp. 50–57.

90. *The Death of Helen Betty Osborne,* Volume II of the Report of the Aboriginal Justice Inquiry of Manitoba (Aboriginal Justice Implementation Commission, 1999), available at http://ajic.mb.ca/volume.html, accessed December 19, 2009; Amnesty International, *Stolen Sisters: A Human Rights Response to Discrimination and Violence against Indigenous Women in Canada* (report) (Ottawa: Amnesty International, 2004); Native Women's Association of Canada, 'Sisters in Spirit—Background', available at http://www.nwac.hq.org/en/background.html; Shelagh Day, Dani Bryant, and Christian Morey, 'Nothing to Report' (submission of the BC CEDAW Group to the United Nations Committee on the Elimination of All Forms of Discrimination against Women), 2009. Yasmin Jiwani and Mary Lynn Young, 'Missing and Murdered Women: Reproducing Marginality in News Discourse', *Canadian Journal of Communication* 31, 2006, pp. 895–917; 'Federal Liberals Call for Highway of Tears National Investigation', *Vanderhoof Omineca Express,* February 9, 2010, available at http://www.bclocalnews.com/bc_north/ominecaexpress/community/83847667.html; accessed February 9, 2010; 'List of Women on 'Highway of Tears' Doubles', CTV.ca, October 12, 2007, available at http://www.ctv.ca; Lori Cuthbert and Neal Hall, 'Highway of Tears Probe Points to 2,000 'Persons of Interest'', Canwest News Service, December 13, 2009, available at http://www.calgaryherald.com; 'Police Reveal Details of E-Pana Investigation into 18 female unsolved Cases in Northern BC', Canwest News Service, December 12, 2009, available at http://www.kelowna.com.

91. 'What Is a Hate Crime?' CBC News online, June 2004, available at http://www.cbc.ca/news/background/hatecrimes; Nadera Shalhoub-Kevorkian, 'Reexamining Femicide: Breaking the Silence and Crossing 'Scientific' Borders', *Signs* 28(2), 2003, pp. 581–608; Mark Ensalaco, 'Murder in Ciudad Juarez: A Parable of Women's Struggle for Human Rights', *Violence against Women* 12(5), 2006, pp. 417–440; Teresa Bo, 'Guatemala's Femicide Crisis', Al-Jazeera.net, August 5, 2009. Available at http://english.aljazeera.net/focus/2009/08/200984134334229388.html; accessed January 9, 2010; Roselyn Costantino, 'Femicide, Impunity, and Citizenship: The Old and New in the Struggle for Justice in Guatemala', *Chicana/Latina Studies* 6(1), Fall 2006, pp. 108–121.

92. Ki Namaste, 'Genderbashing: Sexuality, Gender, and the Regulation of Public Space', *Environment and Planning D: Society and Space* 14(2), 1996, pp. 221–240; 'Obama Signs Hate Crimes Bill into Law', CNN, October 28, 2009. Available at http://www.cnn.com/2009/POLITICS/10/28/hate.crimes/index.html; Gregory M. Herek, 'Hate Crimes and Stigma-Related Experiences among Sexual Minority Adults in the United States: Prevalence Estimates from a National Probability Sample',

Journal of Interpersonal Violence, 24 (1), January, 2009, pp. 54–74.

93. Ontario Human Rights Commission, 'Toward a Commission Policy on Gender Identity' (report) (Ontario Human Rights Commission, October 1999), 21–23; Rebecca L. Stotzer, 'Violence against Transgender People: A Review of United States Data', *Aggression and Violent Behavior 14, 2009,* pp. 170–179; Jim Spellman, 'Transgender Murder, Hate Crime Conviction a First', CNN, 2008, available at http://www.cnn.com.

94. James Messerschmidt, *Masculinities and Crime,* p. 185; Elizabeth Stanko, 'The Image of Violence' in *Criminal Justice Matters,* 8, 1992, p. 3.

Epilogue

1. See Judith Lorber, *Breaking the Bowls: Degendering and Feminist Change* (New York: W. W. Norton, 2005), and Lisa Brush, review of Lorber in *Contemporary Sociology,* 35(3), 2006, p. 246.

2. For an overview of some of these issues, see Barbara Ehrenreich and Arlie Russell Hochschild, eds., *Global Woman: Nannies, Maids, and Sex Workers in the New Economy* (New York: Metropolitan Books, 2003).

3. Indira Jaising, 'Bringing Rights Home: Review of the Campaign for a Law on Domestic Violence', *Economic and Political Weekly,* 44(44), October 31, 2009, pp. 50–57; p. 57.

4. Randeep Ramesh, 'Indian Pub Attacks Prompt Pink Knickers Protest', *Guardian.co.uk,* February 20, 2009; available at http://www.guardian.co.uk/world/2009/feb/20/india-knickers-protest.htm; accessed February 21, 2009.

5. Kate Millett, *Sexual Politics* (New York: Random House, 1969).

6. Robert Jay Lifton, *The Protean Self* (New York: Basic Books, 1994). See also Cynthia Fuchs Epstein, 'The Multiple Realities of Sameness and Difference: Ideology and Practice' in *Journal of Social Issues,* 53(2), 1997; and Floyd Dell, 'Feminism for Men' in *The Masses,* February, 1917, reprinted in *Against the Tide: Profeminist Men in the United States, 1776–1990* (A Documentary History), M. S. Kimmel and T. Mosmiller, eds. (Boston: Beacon Press, 1992).

Index